Jo

Associate Professor of Computer Science
Park University
Parkville, Missouri

# WEB PROGRAMMING

## with HTML5, CSS, and JavaScript

JONES & BARTLETT
LEARNING

*World Headquarters*
Jones & Bartlett Learning
5 Wall Street
Burlington, MA 01803
978-443-5000
info@jblearning.com
www.jblearning.com

Jones & Bartlett Learning books and products are available through most bookstores and online booksellers. To contact Jones & Bartlett Learning directly, call 800-832-0034, fax 978-443-8000, or visit our website, www.jblearning.com.

09369-8

**Production Credits**
VP, Product Management: David D. Cella
Director of Product Management: Matthew Kane
Product Manager: Laura Pagluica
Product Assistant: Mary Menzemer
Production Editor: Vanessa Richards
Director of Marketing: Andrea DeFronzo
Product Fulfillment Manager: Wendy Kilborn
Composition: codeMantra U.S. LLC
Cover Design: Kristin E. Parker
Rights & Media Specialist: Thais Miller
Media Development Editor: Shannon Sheehan
Cover Image (Title Page, Chapter Opener): Blue abstract:
© StationaryTraveller/Getty Images; Web: © Supanat Chantra/EyeEm/
Getty Images
Printing and Binding: LSC Communications
Cover Printing: LSC Communications

**Library of Congress Cataloging-in-Publication Data**
Names: Dean, John, 1962- author.
Title: Web programming with HTML5, CSS, and JavaScript / John Dean, PhD,
    associate professor of computer science, Park University-Parkville Campus,
    Department of Computer Science and Information Systems,
Description: Burlington, Massachusetts: Jones & Bartlett Learning, 2017. |
    Includes bibliographical references and index.
Identifiers: LCCN 2017023256 | ISBN 9781284091793 (pbk.)
Subjects: LCSH: Internet programming. | HTML (Document markup language) |
    Cascading style sheets. | JavaScript (Computer program language)
Classification: LCC QA76.625 .D43 2017 | DDC 006.7/4—dc23
LC record available at https://lccn.loc.gov/2017023256

6048

Printed in the United States of America
22 21 20 19 18   10 9 8 7 6 5 4 3 2 1

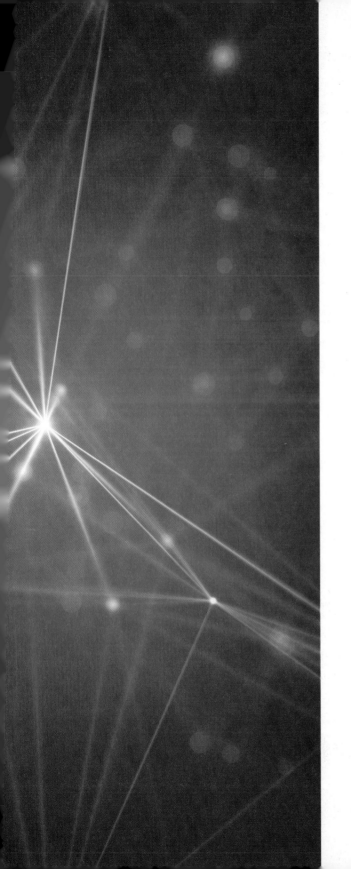

# DEDICATION

To my father, Ray Dean.

# BRIEF TABLE OF CONTENTS

# TABLE OF CONTENTS

## 8   Introduction to JavaScript: Functions, DOM, Forms, and Event Handlers     311

## 9   Additional JavaScript Basics: `window` Object, `if` Statement, Strings, Numbers, and Input Validation     351

## 10 Loops, Additional Controls, Manipulating CSS with JavaScript                     425

## 11 Object-Oriented Programming and Arrays                     499

## 12 Canvas                                                                        569

Since HTML's introduction in 1993, web-programming technologies have been in flux, with web programmers using different versions of HTML for different browsers. The constant change made it difficult for authors to write quality textbooks about the subject. Consequently, most of the books were trade books, not textbooks. With HTML5's approval as a "stable recommendation" in 2014, web programmers and browsers appear to have embraced it fully. With the huge demand for web programmers in the workforce, there has been a significant demand for web-programming courses for quite a while. Now that web programming has coalesced around HTML5, there is a need for better textbooks about web programming.

Web programming is a large field, with different types of web programming implemented by different tools. All the tools work with the core language, HTML, so almost all the web-programming books describe HTML to some extent. This textbook covers HTML5, CSS, and JavaScript, all in depth. Those three technologies are known to be the pillars of client-side web programming. With client-side web programming, all web page calculations are performed on end users' computers (the client computers). There's also server-side web programming, which uses technologies such as ASP.NET, JSP, and PHP. With server-side web programming, most of the web page calculations are performed on the computers that host the web pages permanently (the server computers). Many books attempt to cover one of the server-side technologies; in doing so, they necessarily have to cover some HTML and CSS as well, because all web pages need those technologies to display results on the client computer. Typically, such books try to cram in too much for beginning web programmers to digest. Many books go to the opposite extreme and cover only HTML and CSS, leaving out JavaScript, which is essential for calculations. This book hits a sweet spot—covering all three client-side technologies in depth (HTML, CSS, and JavaScript), with no dependence on server-side technologies. After finishing this book, you should be prepared to write nicely format-ted, interactive web pages that are able to perform calculations and show the results. And down the road if you decide that you want to write server-side web pages, your solid client-side foundation should properly prepare you to go forth and learn a server-side technology(ies).

## Target Audience

Unlike many client-side web programming books, this book presents not only HTML and CSS, but also JavaScript, the document object model (DOM), and canvas. With that programming depth, the book works well for sophomore and junior Computer Science majors who have pro-gramming experience. With the first seven chapters devoted to HTML and CSS and a gentle intro-duction to programming concepts in the JavaScript chapters, the textbook can also work well for non-Computer Science majors with no prerequisite programming knowledge.

In addition to targeting students in a college setting, this textbook targets high school students with or without programming experience. Most likely, in a high school setting, this book's content would be covered in a year-long course. Finally, this book targets industry practitioners who want to learn client-side web programming. Industry practitioners should read the entire textbook at a pace determined on a case-by-case basis.

## Approach

Some web-programming books try to present exhaustive content without trying to explain it fully. That can lead to readers with poor understanding and weak retention of the content. In this book, we carefully consider the proper amount of content to present in each chapter, so that there is ample opportunity for explanations and learning. We try to engage readers by using a fun, conversational tone. Readers who are engaged are more likely to retain what they're reading. Readers who are having fun are more likely to dig deep and yearn to learn more.

Although we take the time to carefully explain HTML, CSS, and JavaScript syntax, we realize how important it is to develop the creativity and problem-solving skills necessary to become adept at web programming. With that in mind, we present the content in a manner that supports such development. Several of the leading web-programming textbooks embed much of their content within tutorials. Each tutorial provides step-by-step instructions that explain how to paste together code fragments to form a web page. That technique helps readers feel good about producing results, but when that's all there is, not much actual learning takes place. Because there's not much of a framework for organizing the content, that presentation strategy makes it difficult for readers to integrate new material into what they already know and to remember what they've learned. On the other hand, this book presents content with an optimal organization for learning. Within each chapter, we explain concepts, present problems, and solve those problems with short code fragments and also complete web pages.

At the end of each chapter, we present optional case study sections that build upon each other to create an increasingly sophisticated website. In the case studies, we provide guidance and a discussion of design decisions, rather than step-by-step instructions. This forces readers to apply what they've learned earlier in the chapter, and it gives readers a feel for the real-world design process. Perhaps most importantly, the case studies provide practice for readers in fostering their creativity and problem-solving skills.

## Proper Flow

In conjunction with our careful consideration of what's covered in each chapter, we carefully consider the flow between content topics. We make sure that the order in which we present content and the transitions between concepts follow a natural progression that is conducive to learning and retention. For example, in the first three chapters, we present basic HTML concepts and then a thorough, but not exhaustive, explanation of CSS. This gives the reader an opportunity to appreciate the richness of HTML and CSS without feeling overwhelmed by details.

Other web programming textbooks present form controls (e.g., text boxes, pull-down menus, and buttons) without showing how to process the controls' input data. Without processing, the forms are impractical and readers are left to wonder, "What's the point?" The reason they don't show how to process the controls' input data is because such processing requires JavaScript, and they don't cover JavaScript until later or don't cover it at all. The solution is a no-brainer—cover JavaScript before form controls. That's what we do in this book, so when we introduce form controls, we're able to use JavaScript to process the input data. Processing the input data means we can calculate and display results, and that leads to more satisfied readers.

# Real-World Context

More often than not, today's classroom students and industry practitioners prefer to learn with a hands-on, real-world approach. The following subsections illustrate that approach.

## Complete Web Page Examples

Different books have different strategies for using code to illustrate new concepts. Most books provide short code fragments to illustrate new concepts, and that can be very helpful. But when books rely almost exclusively on code fragments and provide few complete web pages, readers tend to complain about their inability to run the code and their inability to get a feel for the big picture. In this book, we strike an appropriate balance between short code fragments and complete web pages so readers are able to grasp new concepts quickly (with short code fragments) and apply those concepts in the context of complete web pages.

## Industry-Standard Web-Programming Software

The term "HTML5 standard" is a loose term in that it can refer to any of the different HTML5 versions. At the time of this book's writing, HTML 5.1 was the latest official "recommendation," so we present syntax and semantics from HTML 5.1.[1] For CSS and JavaScript, we present syntax and semantics for their latest versions as well.

In choosing to describe the latest versions of client-side web-programming software, we are cognizant of the risk of presenting content that industry hasn't caught up with yet. Thus, we present constructs only if they are supported by at least two of the three most popular web browsers—Google Chrome, Mozilla Firefox, and Microsoft Edge. But even more importantly, we present constructs only if they are part of the standards put forth by the World Wide Web Consortium (W3C), the Web Hypertext Application Technology Working Group (WHATWG), and Ecma International. The W3C and the WHATWG are the standards organizations for HTML5, CSS, and the DOM. Ecma International is the standards organization for JavaScript.

---

[1] At the time of this book's writing, HTML 5.2 was a "working draft." It's a superset of HTML 5.1, and it doesn't appear to add all that many new constructs.

## Industry-Standard Coding-Style Conventions

We follow Google's recommended coding-style conventions consistently throughout the book. In the book's appendices, we provide complete references for the book's HTML, CSS, and JavaScript coding-style conventions, which are based on Google's coding conventions. To supplement those references and to emphasize how important good style is, we include coding-style tips whenever we use new coding conventions for code that we're explaining.

## Tutorials for Software Tools

We do not tie the textbook to any particular software tools. To develop and publish web pages, readers are free to use any tools they like. But to make learning easier, on the book's website, we provide tutorials for several popular tools: Visual Studio integrated development environment (IDE) for entering and testing web page code, WinSCP for uploading web pages to a web server, and Chrome's debugger for JavaScript debugging. Please visit go.jblearning.com/webprogramming to access these tutorials.

# Homework Problems

At the end of each chapter, we provide three types of homework problems—review questions, exercises, and projects. Review questions serve as a review of what was covered earlier in the chapter. Most review questions use a short-answer format, but there are multiple-choice, true/false, and fill-in-the-blank questions as well. You can find solutions for the review questions at the end of the book.

Exercises are a bit more challenging than the review questions. They require readers to do more than just recall what they've read; they require readers to apply what they've learned. The exercises use short-answer, debugging, and write-a-code-fragment formats. Qualified instructors can access the exercise solutions by visiting go.jblearning.com/webprogramming.

Projects consist of problem descriptions whose solutions are complete web pages. Like the exercises, the projects require students to apply what they've learned in the chapter. But additionally, they require readers to employ design, creativity, and problem-solving skills in order to go from a description to a complete web page. Qualified instructors can access the project solutions by visiting go.jblearning.com/webprogramming.

# Organization

There are three conceptual components of a web page: content, presentation, and behavior. We introduce content code, in the form of HTML elements, throughout the book, but the majority of such content code appears in the first 60% of the book. We introduce most of the presentation code, in the form of CSS, near the beginning of the book, but we sprinkle in additional CSS code as necessary later on. We introduce the behavior code, in the form of JavaScript, in the last 40% of the book. Throughout the entire book, while describing content, presentation, and behavior details, we put those details into practice by building web pages that nurture the development of problem-solving skills and web-design skills.

We start with two chapters that are introductory in nature. They discuss general concepts involving the Web and basic HTML elements that enable readers to get a taste of what's possible. The book then devotes a whole chapter to CSS. Although the chapter describes CSS extensively, it does not attempt to cover CSS exhaustively. Later chapters introduce additional CSS details when appropriate. After the CSS chapter, the next four chapters present HTML element details and web-programming design principles. The last five chapters describe JavaScript basics, plus some advanced JavaScript constructs that unleash the power of dynamic HTML.

## Chapters 1 and 2

In Chapters 1 and 2, we first explain basic concepts needed for building a website. For example, we describe text editors, web-hosting services, and browsers. We then narrow the focus and describe the basic components of a web page: HTML elements, tags, and attributes. We put those components into practice by examining a simple, but complete, web page. Chapter 1 concludes with a brief history of HTML.

Chapter 2 continues the theme of introducing material that is somewhat general in nature. For example, we describe the W3C, coding conventions, and comments. After that, the chapter provides details on quite a few HTML elements: block elements, editing elements, phrasing elements, and so on. The chapter concludes with a discussion of character references.

## Chapter 3

In Chapter 3, we first present an overview of CSS concepts such as syntax, the different types of CSS rules, the different places where CSS rules can be applied, and how cascading determines the rules' priorities. The rest of the chapter provides details about many CSS properties and values.

## Chapters 4 and 5

In these two chapters, we return to HTML elements, with an in-depth look at elements in charge of organizing a page's content (Chapter 4) and a comprehensive treatment of data tables and layout tables (Chapter 5). Chapter 4 focuses on lists, figures, and section-oriented elements, and it weaves in a few CSS details, such as descendent and child selectors, that were not part of Chapter 3's CSS coverage. Chapter 5 focuses on the `table` element and all of its associated elements: `caption`, `tr`, `td`, and so on. As an alternative to using the `table` element, Chapter 5 describes how to achieve table layout with CSS. Specifically, Chapter 5 describes CSS table values, absolute positioning, and relative positioning.

## Chapters 6 and 7

In Chapters 6 and 7, we present what might be considered the seminal features of HTML— links and the ability to embed nontext objects (images, audio, and video) into a web page.

Chapter 6 describes how to implement a link and then discusses navigation techniques that rely on links. Chapter 6 then describes how to navigate to pictures, and presents various details about the img element, bitmap image formats, the SVG image format, and vector graphics.

Chapter 7 continues the discussion of images by describing how to manipulate them with positioning, image sprites, image maps, and so on. Chapter 7 then moves on to a discussion of other embedded objects—audio files and video files.

## Chapters 8 and 9

In Chapters 8 and 9, we present the basics of JavaScript. In building a JavaScript web page, there's a lot to learn. Some books present a huge amount of syntax up front, leaving readers feeling overwhelmed and unable to create JavaScript web pages on their own. Other books introduce a little JavaScript syntax and illustrate what's going on with small, gimmicky web pages that do not comport with standard industry practices. This book strikes a balance between those two strategies. In Chapters 8 and 9, we present enough syntax to build standard-practice JavaScript web pages, but not so much syntax that readers feel overwhelmed. Here's a sample of the key JavaScript constructs introduced in Chapters 8 and 9: functions, variables, the Document Object Model (DOM), event handlers, if statement, strings, operators, and input validation.

In addition to introducing JavaScript constructs, we introduce HTML elements for forms, buttons, and text boxes. Those elements implement input/output functionality, and they enable the web pages to be more "real world."

## Chapters 10, 11, and 12

In Chapters 10 through 12, we introduce JavaScript constructs that are slightly more advanced. Chapter 10 presents while loops and for loops and puts them into practice by looping through form controls like radio buttons, checkboxes, and pull-down menu selections. These form controls could have been introduced earlier with the button and text box form controls, but they fit better in Chapter 10, when loops are introduced. Toward the end of Chapter 10, we describe how to manipulate CSS by using JavaScript and various properties in the DOM.

In Chapter 11, we introduce the concept of object-oriented programming (OOP) and describe how to work with objects in JavaScript. This includes how to implement classes with constructors, properties, and methods; how to instantiate objects; and how to implement inheritance between classes. In JavaScript, arrays are objects, so we wait until after the introduction of OOP to discuss arrays. In our description of arrays, we explain how to instantiate them, how to loop through an array's elements, and how to use an array's methods.

In Chapter 12, we introduce canvas, which is considered to be one of the most important new features of HTML5. We describe how to use the canvas element and JavaScript to draw rectangles, circles, arcs, lines, paths, and text, all within a graphical "canvas" drawing area. After discussing how to draw those graphics objects, the chapter describes how to translate, rotate, and scale them.

# Student Resources

At the book's website, go.jblearning.com/webprogramming, students can view and download these resources:

▶ Student-version lecture slides in PowerPoint format without hidden notes.
  • The student-version slides are identical to the teacher-version slides except that the hidden notes and hidden slides are omitted.
  • Omitting the hidden slides incentivizes students to attend class, where the teacher provides additional content.
▶ Source code and resource files for all the textbook example web pages
▶ Tutorials for web-developer software tools

# Instructor Resources

At the book's website, go.jblearning.com/webprogramming, instructors can view and download these resources:

▶ Teacher-version lecture slides in PowerPoint format with hidden notes
  • Hidden notes provide comments that supplement the displayed text in the lecture slides.
  • For example, if the displayed text asks a question, the hidden notes provide the answer.
▶ Exercise solutions
▶ Project solutions
▶ Test bank questions
▶ Additional projects

# ACKNOWLEDGMENTS

Writing this textbook has been a labor of love, albeit an arduous 3-years-plus labor of love. I am indebted to my team at Jones & Bartlett Learning for their generous commitment to this project. Without them, the content may have been awesome, but no one would have known about it because there would be no book. Our fearless leader, Product Manager Laura Pagluica, kept everyone on track, especially me. She provided sagacious advice in lots of different areas, and on occasion, she (rightfully) reigned in my (sometimes excessive) exuberance. Taylor Maurice gathered and compiled the early-chapter reviews, and Mary Menzemer did the same for the later-chapter reviews. Their work helped greatly in my effort to incorporate reviewer feedback into the book. I'd also like to thank Thais Miller and Vanessa Richards, who did a great job during the production phase.

I'd like to acknowledge the many teachers who provided feedback during the writing phase. Their comments showed attention to detail and tremendous insight, and they led to many improvements in wording and content. So thank you to:

**Simon Baev**
Georgia Southwestern State University

**John Beatty**
La Salle University

**Bill Bennett**
Mt. San Jacinto College

**Noni McCullough Bohonak**
University of South Carolina Lancaster

**Dan Brandon**
Christian Brothers University

**Blase B. Cindric**
University of Mount Union

**Stephen Crandall**
Notre Dame College

**Julius Dichter**
University of Bridgeport

**Zarreen Farooqi**
University of Akron

**Kelly Furnas**
Kansas State University

**Steven Gutierrez**
Lake Erie College

**William J. Hitchcock**
Loras College

**Nanette Hogg**
University of Nebraska at Kearney

**Brian W. Horton**
The University of Texas at Arlington

**Zhenyu Huang**
Central Michigan University

**Deborah J. Hwang**
University of Evansville

**Clara James**
Minneapolis Community & Technical College

**Ravinder Kang**
Highline Community College

**Amitava Karmaker**
University of Wisconsin–Stout

**Gilliean Lee**
Lander University

**Haim Levkowitz**
University of Massachusetts Lowell

**Ted Markowitz**
University of New Haven

**François Neville**
Bemidji State University

**Ralph Phillips**
Central Oregon Community College

**Susan Reeder**
Seattle University

**Jamil Saquer**
Missouri State University

**Ethel Schuster**
Northern Essex Community College

**Derrf Seitz**
Georgia Military College

**Robert Sfarzo**
Cuesta College

**R. Duane Skaggs**
Morehead State University

**Bob Sweeney**
University of South Alabama

**Joo Tan**
Kutztown University of Pennsylvania

**Visa Thiangarajan**
Magnolia Science Academy

**Joe Triplett**
Ohio University

**Marilyn Turmelle**
School for the Talented and Gifted

**Michael Van Hilst**
Nova Southeastern University

**Christopher T. VanOosterhout**
Muskegon Community College

**Sam Vegter**
Western Piedmont Community College

**Jerry Westfall**
Liberty University

My web-programming students have not been shy about making suggestions and finding errors. In particular, thank you Olivia Leung, Matthew Prybyszczuk, Jessica Detweiler, Alexis Fry, Chrisman Miller, and Yves Akanza.

# ABOUT THE AUTHOR

John Dean is an Associate Professor and the Department Chair of the Department of Computer Science and Information Systems at Park University. He earned a PhD degree in computer science from Nova Southeastern University and an MS degree in computer science from the University of Kansas. Dean has worked in industry as a software engineer and project manager, specializing in Java and various web technologies—HTML, CSS, JavaScript, JavaServer Pages, and servlets. He has taught a full range of computer science courses, including client-side and server-side web-programming courses.

## CHAPTER 1

# Introduction to Web Programming

## CHAPTER OBJECTIVES

- ▶ Learn the basics of creating a website.
- ▶ Learn the basics of HTML—elements, tags, attributes.
- ▶ Use structural elements (`html`, `head`, `body`) to form the framework of a web page.
- ▶ Fill in a `head` container with `title` and `meta` elements.
- ▶ Fill in a `body` container with `h1`, `hr`, `p`, `br`, and `div` elements.
- ▶ Learn the basics of Cascading Style Sheets.
- ▶ Learn how HTML, the Web, and web browsers originated.
- ▶ Use the W3C's Markup Validation Service.

# CHAPTER OUTLINE

## 1.1 Introduction

Have you ever perused the Web and wondered how its web pages are made? If so, this book is for you. Actually, even if you haven't thought about how web pages are made, this book can still be for you. All you need is a logical mind and an interest in creating things. This book takes you on a journey where you learn to create informative, attractive, and interactive web pages. So climb on board and enjoy the ride!

To make this book accessible to readers with little background in computers, we start slowly and build upon what comes earlier in the book. If you come to something that you already know, feel free to skip it. If you already know how to program, you'll probably want to skip some of the programming basics when we get to JavaScript. But rest assured that unless you already know HTML, CSS, and JavaScript, the vast majority of this book's content should be new to you. After all, we want you to get your money's worth from this book.

Let's start with a brief description of *the Web*, which is short for *World Wide Web*. Most people say "Web" instead of "World Wide Web," and we'll follow that convention. The Web is a collection of documents, called *web pages*, that are shared (for the most part) by computer users throughout the world. Different types of web pages do different things, but at a minimum, they all display content on computer screens. By "content," we mean text, pictures, and user input mechanisms like text boxes and buttons. **FIGURE 1.1** shows a typical web page. Note the web page's text, pictures, text boxes, and buttons. Also note the web page's address shown in the figure's address bar. The web page address is the location where the web page resides on the *Internet*. Speaking of the Internet, what is it? It's a collection of several billion computers connected throughout the world. Each web page is stored on one of those computers.

Figure 1.1 shows the "TED Talks" website. To visit it, open a browser (e.g., Google Chrome, Microsoft Edge, and FireFox) and enter the web page address shown in the figure's address bar.

At the start of this book, we'll focus on displaying text, like the "2400+ talks to stir your curiosity" at the top of Figure 1.1. Next, we'll focus on the appearance of displayed content. Then on to organizational constructs, pictures, sound clips, and video clips. Finally, we will focus on implementing user input *controls*. For example, in Figure 1.1, note the text boxes and the

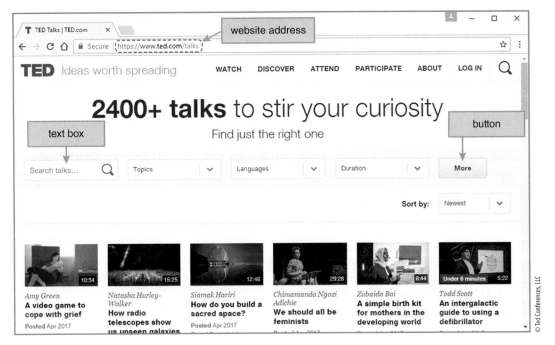

**FIGURE 1.1 A typical web page**

buttons. Those are controls. You'll learn about those controls, plus more controls, in the last several chapters.

In this first chapter, we stick with the basics, so you can get up and running quickly. Specifically, we start with some overarching concepts that explain the process of web page development and dissemination. Then, we introduce the basic constructs that you'll use to describe and display a web page's content. Next, we provide a cursory overview of Cascading Style Sheets (CSS), which you'll use to display a web page's content in a pleasing, formatted manner. Finally, we present a brief history of the primary language used to write all web pages—HTML.

## 1.2 Creating a Website

A *website* is a collection of related web pages that are normally stored on a single web server computer. A *web server* is a computer system that enables users to access web pages stored on the web server's computer. The term "web server" can refer to the web page-accessing software that runs on the computer, or it can refer to the computer itself.

To create a website, you'll need these things: (1) a text editor, (2) an upload/publishing tool, (3) a web hosting service, and (4) a browser. We'll describe them in the upcoming paragraphs.

### Text Editors

There are many different text editors, with varying degrees of functionality. Microsoft's Notepad is free and provides no special web functionality. To use it, the web developer simply enters text, and the text appears as is. Although it's possible to use a plain text editor such as Notepad, most web developers use a fancier type of text editor—a *web authoring tool*. Different web authoring tools have different features that are intended to make the web development process easier. At a minimum, web authoring tools are able to suggest valid code after the user has typed part of a command. This is done by showing a pop-up to the user that suggests valid code that could complete the command currently being entered. This auto-complete mechanism is often called *intellisense* and sometimes called *picklist*. Another feature common to all web authoring tools is *WYSIWYG*, pronounced "wizeewig." It stands for "what you see is what you get." WYSIWYG means that as you're editing your text, you can see what your text will look like after it's eventually uploaded to a website.

On this book's website, we provide a tutorial for learning how to use the Visual Studio web authoring tool. Visual Studio is from Microsoft, so it's not free. But fear not, Microsoftophiles. If you plan to use Visual Studio for nonbusiness purposes, you can download Microsoft Visual Studio Community for free (that means you—students, faculty, and open-source project contributors). Visual Studio Community includes all the functionality of Visual Studio's professional version.[1]

There are a lot of other web authoring tools that you are welcome to learn on your own. Visual Studio and its offshoots run on Windows, but if you have a Mac(intosh) computer, check out Adobe's Dreamweaver web authoring tool. It works on both Windows and Mac. Or, do a Google search for other web authoring tools—most are free and some are quite good!

Normally, web authoring tools enable developers to create not just web pages, but other software as well. Such general-purpose web authoring tools are normally referred to as *integrated development environments*, or *IDEs* for short.

## Web Page Uploads

After you enter your web page text on your local computer with your favorite IDE, you'll probably want to *publish* it. Publishing means that you upload your web page to a web server computer so other users can access it on the Web. Some IDEs, like Dreamweaver, provide built-in uploading capabilities, but other IDEs, like Visual Studio, do not. For IDEs that do not provide built-in uploading capabilities, you'll need to use a separate file upload tool. There are lots of file upload tools. On this book's website, we provide a tutorial for learning how to install and use a free and intuitive file upload tool called WinSCP.

## Web Hosting Service

For a file upload tool such as WinSCP to work, you need to have a web server computer on which to store the uploaded files. For the uploaded files to be accessible as web pages on the Web, your web server computer needs to have a web hosting service in place. The web developer usually doesn't have to worry about the web hosting service software. If the web developer is part of a medium- to large-sized organization, then the organization's information technology (IT)

---

[1] "Visual Studio Community," *Microsoft*, https://www.visualstudio.com/vs/community/.

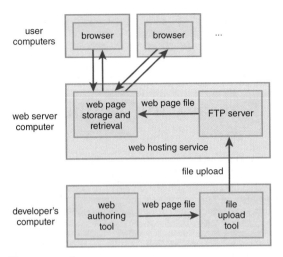

**FIGURE 1.2 Website file processing**

department will install and maintain the web hosting service. On the other hand, if the web developer is part of a very small organization or not part of an organization at all, the developer will need to set up the web hosting service or rely on a generic web-hosting company (e.g., GoDaddy .com) to do so. Regardless of who's in charge of the web hosting service, all web hosting services need to have a mechanism for receiving uploaded files from a file upload tool. Typically, that mechanism is an FTP (file transfer protocol) server, which is a program that runs on the web server computer. **FIGURE 1.2** is a pictorial description of how the FTP server fits in with the rest of the website creation process.

## Browsers

The top of Figure 1.2 shows the final part of the website experience: browser access. A *browser* is a piece of software that enables a user to retrieve and view a web page. According to http:// gs.statcounter.com, the most popular browsers for computers are Google Chrome, Microsoft's browsers (Microsoft Edge and Internet Explorer), and Mozilla[2] Firefox, with Google Chrome at #1. Other browsers are Safari (for Mac devices), Opera, and Android's default browser. Safari and Android are particularly popular with mobile devices.

## 1.3 Web Page Example

Note **FIGURE 1.3**, which shows a simple Kansas City Weather web page. Before showing you the behind-the-scenes code for the Kansas City Weather page, we first need to go over some preliminary concepts. We'll start with the website address. Formally, the website address value is known

---

[2] The name "Mozilla" comes from a combination of the words Mosaic (the first popular graphical browser) and Godzilla (the first known sea monster formed by nuclear radiation).

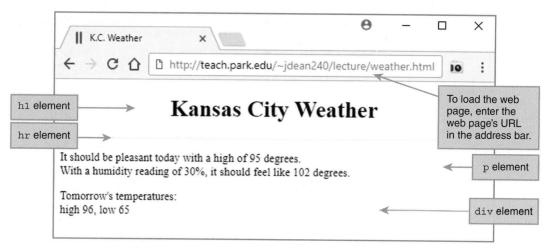

**FIGURE 1.3 Kansas City Weather web page**

as a *URL*, which stands for <u>*Uniform*</u> <u>*Resource*</u> <u>*Locator*</u>. That name is not all that intuitive, so just remember that a URL is a website address. Here's the URL for the Kansas City Weather page in Figure 1.3:

```
http://teach.park.edu/~jdean240/lecture/weather.html
```

The http refers to the <u>*hypertext*</u> <u>*transfer*</u> <u>*protocol*</u>, where a protocol is a set of rules and formats for exchanging messages between computers. After http comes a delimiter, ://, and then the name of the web server computer that stores the web page. For this example, the web server computer is teach. Next comes the domain that describes how the web server can be found on the Internet. For this example, the domain is park.edu. Next, there's a sequence of directories and subdirectories (also called folders and subfolders) that indicate where the web page is stored on the web server computer. That's called the *path*. For this example, the path is ~jdean240/lecture. The ~ (tilde) at the left indicates that the directory is a home directory for a user's account. There's no requirement that you use a ~ for a user's home directory. It's a standard convention at universities, where users (students and teachers) like to do their own thing, but most businesses do not use ~'s. In the example, after the ~jdean240 home directory, there's a / and then lecture. The term lecture is a subdirectory of the home directory, and the / is a delimiter that separates the home directory from the subdirectory.

In the example, after the lecture subdirectory, there's a / and then weather.html. The phrase weather.html is the web page's filename, and the / is another delimiter. This time, the / separates the subdirectory from the web page filename.

In Figure 1.3, all the things you see below the address bar are web page *elements*—h1, hr, p, and div. We'll have more to say about those elements later, but here's just a brief introduction for now.

The h1 element is used to implement a web page heading, with the "h" in h1 standing for "heading." The hr element is used to implement a horizontal line, with the "h" and "r" standing for "horizontal" and "rule," respectively. The p element is used to implement a paragraph. Finally, a div element is used to group words together as part of a division within a web page.

There are additional elements used to implement the Kansas City Weather page, but they're not as intuitive as the elements we've described. For example, there's a body element that forms the entire white area under the address bar. Coming up, we'll show how to implement that element, plus all the other elements in the Kansas City Weather page. But first a tribute to the central role of elements to a web page.

A web page's elements hold the web page's content, which is the most important part of a web page. After deciding on which elements to use and implementing those elements, you'll want to focus on formatting the content. In Chapter 3, we'll describe how to format the content using *CSS*. Optionally, you can add behaviors for some or all the elements. Later in the book, we'll describe how to add behaviors using JavaScript. For example, in the Kansas City Weather page, you could add a behavior to the h1 element, so that when you click it, the subsequent paragraph turns blue. A rather odd scenario, but you get the idea.

## 1.4 HTML Tags

Now we're going to describe how to implement elements for a web page. To implement an element for a web page, you'll need to use tags. For example, if you want to implement a strong element (in order to put emphasis on the element's content and display using boldface), surround the content with <strong> tags. Here's how to implement a strong element for the word "very":

```
Caiden was <strong>very</strong> happy when her tooth finally came out.
```

The use of tags is the key characteristic of a *markup language*. Why is it called "markup"? A markup language "marks up" a document by surrounding parts of its content with tags. Web pages are implemented with HTML, which stands for *Hypertext Markup Language*. You already know what "markup" means. The "hyper" in "Hypertext" refers to HTML's ability to implement hyperlinks. A *hyperlink* (or *link* for short) is where you click on text or an image in order to jump to another web page. So HTML is a language that supports markup tags for formatting and the ability to jump to other web pages.

To simplify the web page creation process, the WYSIWYG option (for web authoring tools) lets you hide the HTML tags. Unfortunately, in hiding the HTML tags, the developer loses some control, and the resulting web pages tend to be sloppy. Even if your web authoring tool generates clean HTML code when in WYSIWIG mode, we strongly recommend that you enter all your tags explicitly, at least for now. That will help you learn HTML details so you'll be able to understand and debug subtle code issues.

Most, but not all, HTML tags come in pairs with a start tag and an end tag. For example, the following code uses an <h1> start tag and an </h1> end tag:

```
<h1>Today's Weather</h1>
```

Note that each tag is surrounded by angled brackets, and the end tag starts with "</". The h1 heading tags cause the enclosed text ("Today's Weather") to display like a heading. That usually means that the enclosed text will be boldfaced, large, and surrounded by blank lines. Note the use of the term "usually." The official HTML standard/specification often doesn't specify precise display characteristics. Consequently, not all browsers display tags in the exact same way.

Besides h1, there are other heading elements—h2 through h6. The element h1 generates the largest heading, and h6 generates the smallest. Use a heading tag whenever you want to display a heading above other text. Headings are usually at the top of the page, but they can be in the middle of the page as well.

The first entity inside a tag is the tag's type. In the previous example, the tag's type is h1. In this simple example, there's only one entity inside the tags—the tag's type. Later, we'll see examples where there are additional entities inside the tags.

When a tag is discussed in general, without reference to a particular tag instance, it is called an element and it is written without the angled brackets. For example, when discussing the <h1> tag in general, refer to it as the h1 element.

There are two types of elements—container elements and void elements. A *container element* (usually called simply a "container") has a start tag and an end tag, and it contains content between its two tags. For example, the h1 element is a container. On the other hand, a *void element* has just one tag, and its content is stored within the tag. We'll see an example of that when we get to the meta element.

## 1.5 Structural Elements

Take a look at **FIGURE 1.4**. It shows the HTML source code that was used to generate the Kansas City Weather web page shown earlier. What's source code, you ask? With many programming languages, two types of code are associated with a single program. There's *source code*, which the programmer enters, and there's *executable code*, which is low-level code that the computer hardware understands and executes (runs). Executable code is generated from the source code with the help of something called a *compiler*. As you learn HTML, there's no need to worry about executable code because it is generated automatically behind the scenes and you never see it. So, why did we bring it up? So you can mention executable code in conversation and impress your techie friends? Yes, there's always that, but also, HTML has source code, and to understand the term source code, it's helpful to understand the term executable code. HTML code is source code because HTML code comes directly from the programming source—the programmer.

Next, we'll describe the different sections of code in Figure 1.4. Let's start with the really important HTML constructs that you'll use as the basic framework for all your web pages—doctype, html, head, and body. The doctype construct is considered to be an instruction, not an element, and it goes at the top of every web page. The html, head, and body elements form the basic structure of a web page, so we'll refer to those elements as *structural elements*. Be aware that that's not a standard term. We made it up because it will make future explanations easier. The doctype instruction plus the structural elements form the skeleton code shown in **FIGURE 1.5**. You can use that skeleton code for all your web pages.

```
<!DOCTYPE html>
<html lang="en">
<head>
<meta charset="utf-8">
<meta name="author" content="John Dean">
<meta name="description" content="Kansas City weather conditions">
<title>K.C. Weather</title>
<style>
  h1 {text-align: center;}
  hr {width: 75%;}
</style>
</head>

<body>
<h1>Kansas City Weather</h1>
<hr>
<p>
  It should be pleasant today with a high of 95 degrees.<br>
  With a humidity reading of 30%, it should feel like 102 degrees.
</p>
<div>
  Tomorrow's temperatures:<br>
  high 96, low 65
</div>
</body>
</html>
```

**FIGURE 1.4** **Source code for Kansas City Weather web page**

```
<!DOCTYPE html>
<html lang="en">
<head>
   ⋮
</head>

<body>
   ⋮
</body>
</html>
```

**FIGURE 1.5** **Skeleton code using just doctype and the structural elements**

The first construct, `<!DOCTYPE html>`, tells the browser what type of document the web page is. Its `html` value (in `<!DOCTYPE html>`) indicates that the document is an HTML document, and more specifically that the document uses the HTML5 standard for its syntax. *Syntax* refers to the words, grammar, and punctuation that make up a language.

After the doctype instruction comes the `html` element. It's a container, and it contains/ surrounds the rest of the web page. Its start tag includes `lang="en"`, which tells the browser that the web page is written in English. The `head` and `body` elements are also containers. The `head` element surrounds elements that provide information associated with the web page as a whole. The `body` element surrounds elements that display content in the web page. Container elements must be properly *nested*, meaning that if you start a container inside another container, you must end the inner container before you end the outer container. Because the `body` element starts inside the `html` element, the `</body>` end tag must come before the `</html>` end tag. In Figure 1.5, note how the `head` and `body` elements are properly nested within the `html` element.

## 1.6 `title` Element

Let's now dig a little deeper into the `head` element. The `head` code in **FIGURE 1.6** comes from the weather page, but in the interest of keeping things simple, we've omitted its `style` element. The `style` element is more complicated, and we'll discuss it later in this chapter.

The `head` element contains two types of elements—`meta` and `title`. In your web pages, you should position them in the order shown in Figure 1.6, `meta` and then `title`. But in the interest of clarity, we'll discuss the `title` element first.

Remember that the `head` element surrounds elements associated with the web page as a whole. The web page's title pertains to the entire web page, so its `title` element goes within the `head` container. The `title` element's contained data (e.g., "K.C. Weather") specifies the label that appears in the browser window's *title bar*. Go back to Figure 1.3 and verify that "K.C. Weather" appears in the tab near the top of the window. With browsers that support tabbed windows, that tab is considered to be the browser's title bar.

The official HTML standard requires that every `head` container contains a `title` element. Besides providing a label for your browser window's title bar, what's the purpose of the `title` element? (1) It provides documentation for someone trying to maintain your web page, and (2) it helps web search engines find your web page. In case you haven't heard of a *web search engine*, it's software that searches the Internet for user-specified information and returns a list of links to web pages that are likely to contain the requested information. Google is the preeminent search

```
<head>
<meta charset="utf-8">
<meta name="author" content="John Dean">
<meta name="description" content="Kansas city weather conditions">
<title>K.C. Weather</title>
</head>
```

**FIGURE 1.6 head container for Kansas City Weather web page**

engine, as evidenced by the use of "google" as a verb. For example, "Did the CIA make up dinosaurs?" "Not sure. I'll google it."

## 1.7 `meta` Element

In Figure 1.6, note the `meta` elements within the `head` container. The `meta` elements provide information about the web page. If you look up "meta" in a standard dictionary, you'll probably see a confusing definition. In everyday speech and in HTML, "meta" means "about itself." As in "Check out this video of two guys watching a how-to video about appreciating videos." "Dude, stop now. You're hurting my brain. That's so meta!"

There are many different types of `meta` elements—some you should always include, but most are just optional. We'll present a few of the more important ones soon, but first some details about the `meta` element's syntax.

The `meta` element is a void element (not a container), so it does not have an end tag. Note how there are no end tags for the three `meta` elements in Figure 1.6. Many web programmers end their void elements with a space and a slash. For example:

```
<meta charset="utf-8" />
```

The space and slash are a bit outdated, and we recommend omitting them. If you decide to include them, be consistent. Don't worry about the meaning of `charset` and `utf-8` for now; we'll discuss them shortly.

## 1.8 HTML Attributes

Before we formally introduce a few of the different types of `meta` elements, we first need to discuss attributes, which are used in all `meta` elements. Container elements provide information between their start and end tags. Void elements (including the `meta` element) have no end tags, so they can't provide information that way. Instead, they provide information using attributes. In the following example, `charset` is an attribute for a `meta` element:

```
<meta charset="utf-8">
```

Most attributes have a value assigned to them. In this example, `charset` is assigned the value `"utf-8"`. Although most attributes have a value assigned to them, some do not. Later on, we'll see some attributes that appear by themselves, without a value. You should always surround attribute values with quotes, thus forming a string. A *string* is a group of zero or more characters surrounded by a pair of double quotes (") or a pair of single quotes ('), with double quotes preferred.

Attributes are more common with void elements, but they can be used with container elements as well. Here's an example of a container element that uses an attribute:

```
<html lang="fr">
   •
   •
   •
</html>
```

The `lang` attribute tells the browser that the element is using a particular language for its content. You can use the `lang` attribute for any element. Here we're using it for the `html` element, so it means that the entire web page uses French. You're not required to use the `lang` attribute, but we recommend that you do include it for the `html` element. For web pages written in English, use `<html lang="en">`.

Why would you want to specify an element's language? The W3C's Internationalization Activity group (https://www.w3.org/International/questions/qa-lang-why.en) provides quite a few good reasons, and here are a few of them:

▶ Help search engines find web pages that use a particular language.
▶ Help spell-checker and grammar-checker tools work more effectively.
▶ Help browsers use appropriate fonts.
▶ Help speech synthesizers pronounce words correctly (we'll discuss speech synthesizers in Chapter 5).

If these benefits haven't convinced you to use the `lang` attribute, consider the fact that as technology has improved, the `lang` attribute's usefulness has grown over the years. That trend will undoubtedly continue. It's hard to know what cool things the `lang` attribute might help with in the future, and you should plan for those cool things by including the `lang` attribute now.

## `meta charset` Element

Now that you've learned syntax details for element attributes, it's time to focus on semantic details. Syntax refers to the punctuation rules for code. *Semantics* refers to the meaning of the code. First up—the semantics for the `meta charset` element.

When a web server transmits a web page's source code to an end-user's computer, the web server doesn't transmit the source code's characters the way you see them in this book or on a keyboard. Instead, it transmits coded representations of the source code's characters. The coded representations are in *binary*, which means a sequence of 0's and 1's, where each 0 and 1 is a *bit* (so 10110011 is a binary sequence of 8 bits). There are different encoding schemes, and in order for the receiving end of a transmission to understand the transmitted binary data, the receiver has to know the encoding scheme used by the sender. For web page transmissions, the `meta charset` element specifies the encoding scheme. Normally, you should use a `charset` value of "utf-8" because all modern browsers understand that value.[3] The encoding scheme is sometimes referred

---

[3] UTF-8 (UCS Transformation Format—8-bit) is a variable-width encoding that can represent every character in the Unicode character set. It encodes each Unicode value using one to four 8-bit bytes.

to as a character set, and that's what `charset` stands for. If you omit the `meta charset` element, your web page will usually work because most browsers assume UTF-8 encoding by default. But don't count on the default. In omitting the `meta charset` element, you run the risk of characters being interpreted incorrectly.

## `meta name` Element

Most of the `meta` elements use the `name` attribute to specify the type of information that's being provided. Common values for the `meta name` attribute are `author`, `description`, and `keywords`. Here's an example with an `author` value for a `name` attribute:

```
<meta name="author" content="John Dean">
```

The `name` and `content` attributes go together. The `name` attribute's value specifies the type of thing that the `content` attribute's value specifies. So in this example, with the `name` attribute specifying "author," the `content` attribute specifies the author's name ("John Dean"). Why is knowing the author's name important? Often, the person who fixes or enhances a web page is different from the person who originally wrote the web page. By specifying the author, the fixer/enhancer knows whom to ask for help.

In the following examples, the `name` attribute uses the values "description" and "keywords":

```
<meta name="description" content="Kansas City weather conditions"
<meta name="keywords" content="KC, weather, meteorology, forecast"
```

The `meta description` element and also the `meta keywords` element help web search engines find your web page. In addition, the `meta description` element helps the person reading the code learn the purpose of the web page.

The `meta description` element isn't as important as the `meta author` and `meta charset` elements. Typically, HTML code is straightforward, so unless you've got tricky code, it's OK to omit the `meta description` tag. Feel free to include it if you feel that it's beneficial. Likewise, the `meta keywords` element can go either way—include it or omit it.

## 1.9 body Elements: `hr, p, br, div`

In the prior sections, we covered the elements that appear inside the weather page's head container. Now let's cover the elements that appear inside the weather page's body container. In **FIGURE 1.7**, which shows the body container code, note the h1, hr, p, br, and div elements. We've already talked about the h1 heading element, so now let's focus on the other elements.

The hr element is used to *render* a horizontal line. When a browser renders an element, it figures out how the element's code should be displayed. To keep things simple, you can think of "render" as a synonym for "display." Go back to Figure 1.3 and note the horizontal line on the weather page browser window. The "h" in hr stands for horizontal. The "r" in hr stands for rule, presumably because a rule is another name for a ruler, which can be used to make a straight line. The hr element is a void element, so it uses just one tag, <hr>.

```
<body>
<h1>Kansas City Weather</h1>
<hr>
<p>
  It should be pleasant today with a high of 95 degrees.<br>
  With a humidity reading of 30%, it should feel like 102 degrees.
</p>
<div>
  Tomorrow's temperatures:<br>
  high 96, low 65
</div>
</body>
```

**FIGURE 1.7** body **container for Kansas City Weather web page**

The p element is a container for a group of words that form a paragraph. Normally, browsers will render a p element's enclosed text with a blank line above the text and a blank line below it. Go back to Figure 1.3 and note the blank lines above and below the two-sentence paragraph.

In Figure 1.7, note how we indented the text between the <p> start tag and the </p> end tag. Whenever you've got a p element whose enclosed text is greater than one line, you should put the start and end tags on separate lines and indent the enclosed text. That rule is an example of a coding-style convention rule (or style rule for short). Whenever you write a program, including an HTML program, it's important to follow standard coding-style conventions, so your program is easy to read by you and also by future programmers who need to understand your program. Programmers get used to certain conventions, such as when to use uppercase versus lowercase, when to insert blank lines, and when to indent. You don't want to jar someone reading your program by using nonstandard conventions. For a complete list of coding-style conventions used in this book, see the two appendices: Appendix 1, HTML5 and CSS Coding-Style Conventions, and Appendix 2, JavaScript Coding-Style Conventions. You might want to skim the appendices now, but don't worry about the details. We'll cover those details as we proceed through the book.

Even though it's a container, the HTML standard allows p's start tag to appear without its end tag. However, that's considered to be bad style, so don't do it. You should never omit end tags for container elements because then it's more difficult for the browser and for people reading your source code to figure out where the container element ends.

A div element is also a container for a group of words, but it's more generic, so the words don't have to form sentences in a paragraph. div stands for division because a division can refer to a part of something that has been divided, and a div element is indeed a part of a web page. Normally, the div element causes its enclosed text to have single line breaks above and below it. If a div element's enclosed text is greater than one line, then proper style suggests putting the <div> tags on separate lines and indenting the enclosed text.

Except for single line breaks instead of blank lines, the characteristics for a div element are the same as for a p element. So when should you use a p element versus a div element? Use a p element if the enclosed text forms something that would normally be considered paragraph. On the other hand, use a div element if the enclosed text is related in some way, but the text would not normally be considered a paragraph. If you use the p element only for bona fide paragraphs, then the rest of the web page can process p elements as paragraphs, and you avoid including non-paragraphs in that processing. For example, you could use Cascading Style Sheets (described in the next section) to indent each paragraph's first line.

Finally, there's the br element, which is used to render a new line. In Figure 1.7, note this line:

```
It should be pleasant today with a high of 95 degrees.<br>
```

You can see the br element's new line in Figure 1.3's browser window. Specifically, the line "With a humidity reading of 30%, ..." starts on a new line even though there is room for it to start at the end of the previous line.

## 1.10 Cascading Style Sheets Preview

We'll wait until Chapter 3 for a robust presentation of Cascading Style Sheets (CSS), but for now it's appropriate to give you a preview so you're aware of the basic concepts. As you may recall, CSS allows you to add formatting to your web pages. The formatting rules go inside a style container. In the skeleton code for the weather web page in **FIGURE 1.8**, note the style container within the head container. Within the style container, note the two lines that begin with h1 and hr. Those lines are the rules that apply to the h1 and hr elements in the body container. Each rule has a CSS property and a CSS value, separated by a colon. The first rule, for h1, uses a text-align property with a value of center. Other text-align values are left and right. The second rule, for hr, uses a width property with a value of 75%.

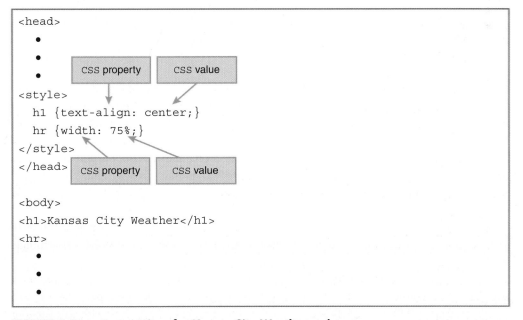

FIGURE 1.8 style container for Kansas City Weather web page

Go back to the web page display in Figure 1.3 and note how `h1` and `hr` are centered. Note how the `hr` element spans 75% of the width of the page. By default, `h1` would be left aligned and the `hr` element would span 100% of the page. Thus, the CSS rules changed the default. If you reduce the `hr` element's width, as in this weather page example, then alignment becomes apparent, and the `hr` element gets center alignment by default. To change its alignment, use `margin-right: 0%` for right alignment or `margin-left: 0%` for left alignment.

## 1.11 History of HTML

In 1989, to help with collaborative research at CERN (the European Laboratory for Particle Physics in Geneva, Switzerland), Tim Berners-Lee came up with the idea of adding "hypertext links" to research papers, so when one paper referred to another, the reader could click the link and quickly go to the other paper. From 1989–1991, Berners-Lee was quite prolific: (1) He designed HTML, with hypertext links as the key feature, (2) he designed the concepts behind the World Wide Web, including the HTTP protocol, and (3) he created a prototype browser for surfing the Internet with HTML web pages. In 1993, Tim Berners-Lee and Dan Connolly submitted the first formal proposal for HTML to the Internet Engineering Task Force (IETF). In 1994, Berners-Lee founded the World Wide Web Consortium (W3C) at the Massachusetts Institute of Technology, with the W3C taking over the stewardship of the HTML standard.

By 1997, the HTML standard evolved to HTML4, with HTML4's last revision appearing in 2000 as HTML 4.01. Bothered by all the poorly formed web pages, the W3C decided to try to force web programmers to conform to stricter syntax rules by introducing XHTML 1.0 Strict in 2000. The "stricter syntax rules" were borrowed from the extensible markup language (XML), and that's what the X in XHTML stands for—XML. XML is not so much a language as a set of rules for how you can define your own language. XHTML 1.0 Strict enforced XML rules such as (1) requiring quoted values for all attributes, (2) requiring a / for all void elements, and (3) requiring an end tag for every container element.

However, even for pages labeled with the new XHTML 1.0 Strict standard, browsers continued to accept poorly formed web pages and render them just fine. Consequently, there was no urgency for programmers to comply with the new XHTML 1.0 Strict standards, and many programmers didn't bother to try to comply.

In 2001, the W3C remedied this browser leniency problem by developing and approving a harsher standard, XHTML 1.1, which specified a new "fail on first error" system. The standard said that if a web page's code does not comply with the standard in any way, the browser should display an error message and not attempt to display the web page's normal content. Internet Explorer (IE), the #1 browser at the time, was unable to render XHTML 1.1 pages. When IE saw the XHTML 1.1 label, it would prompt the user to "Save to disk." Yikes! What a disarmingly worthless message!

Because of this harsh penalty, web programmers avoided using XHTML 1.1, for the most part. The W3C considered XHTML 1.1 to be a stopgap measure that would pave the way to a future standard, XHTML 2.0. XHTML 2.0's goal was to eliminate all problems with past versions of HTML and XHTML. Because XHTML 2.0 development was so slow, and because it was such a departure from what web programmers and browser vendors were used to, some members of the W3C were angered, and in 2004, they left the W3C to make their own new standard. They formed a new working group, *WHATWG*, which stands for *Web Hypertext Application Technology Working Group.*

The primary defectors from the W3C were people from the Mozilla and Opera browser companies. They determined that if XHTML 2.0 came to fruition, they would have to rewrite their browser software. This was doable, but they would end up with a browser that would be incompatible with their customers' existing web pages. Then their customers would defect to other browsers, and with no customers, no money.

The WHATWG spent five years, from 2004 through 2009, creating a Web Apps 1.0 standard. The new standard was a combination of features found in HTML 4.01 and XHTML 1.0, features supported by existing browsers, and new features. Web Apps 1.0 was better than W3C's standards in terms of clearly defining how browsers were supposed to handle errors. Web Apps 1.0 made no attempt to be XML-compliant. It was defined to be more lenient than XHTML; consequently, it was backwards compatible with existing web pages.

In 2009, after making very little progress on XHTML 2.0, the W3C abandoned their XHTML 2.0 efforts and formed a collaborative relationship with the WHATWG, using the Web Apps 1.0 standard as the basis for their current HTML5 standard. In 2011, the W3C came out with a super-cool HTML5 logo, shown here. Display it proudly on all your programmer fashion-wear!

The term "HTML5 standard" is a loose term in that it can refer to any of the W3C's different HTML5 versions. The first version was simply called "HTML5." The next version was called "HTML 5.1," with a space before 5.1. As of 2017, HTML 5.1 was the W3C's official "recommendation," and HTML 5.2 was a "working draft," with the expectation that it would soon become a recommendation. This book presents syntax and semantics from the HTML 5.1 standard, which is a superset of the HTML5 standard. To simplify things, we will use the generic term HTML5 throughout the remainder of the book. If we introduce something that's outside the scope of the original HTML5 standard, we'll point that out, but for the most part, the HTML5 versions are the same.

An indirect benefit of HTML5's rise to prominence is that it has helped to tamp down the *browser wars.* Since the dawn of browsers, to increase their market share, browser manufacturers have added features to their browsers that go above and beyond the HTML standard. This is sometimes a good thing in that end users are treated to cool new features. But from a web programmer's perspective, this is generally a bad thing because programmers are expected to write code that takes advantage of those new features, and writing that code is hard. Specifically, with different users using different browsers and different versions of those browsers, writing and maintaining such *cross-browser-compatible code* is a very time-consuming and messy process. Thus, web programmers refer to the situation disparagingly as the browser wars. In implementing the HTML5 standard, the WHATWG and the W3C incorporated the best added features of the different browsers in order to convince the different browser manufacturers to get on board with the new standard. For the most part, since HTML5's inception, the browser manufacturers have complied with it and have not added as many nonstandard features as in the past. But cross-browser incompatibilities still exist and browser skirmishes continue.

## 1.12 HTML Governing Bodies

As mentioned, the W3C "formed a collaborative relationship with the WHATWG." That was way back in 2009; so did the W3C eventually merge with the WHATWG and form just one governing body? No—there are still two separate organizations even though their roles overlap. They both maintain their own HTML standard. That's a lot of overlap!

The W3C's mission statement says, "To lead the World Wide Web to its full potential by developing protocols and guidelines that ensure the long-term growth of the Web."[4] You can tell from its mission statement that the W3C does a lot more than just maintain its HTML standard. Check out its home page at https://www.w3.org and you'll see a myriad of different tools and articles, all pertaining to the Web. We'll use some of those tools, but for now, we're primarily interested in the HTML standard. More specifically, we're interested in the work done by the W3C's HTML working group (HTMLWG). They publish new versions of the HTML5 standard when they feel their updates are in a stable position.

The WHATWG's mission is narrower in scope than the W3C's mission. WHATWG's home page simply says that they "maintain and evolve HTML." But don't think that they're slackers; maintaining and evolving HTML is a big undertaking. They consider "HTML" to be an umbrella that includes HTML5 (which they refer to as just "HTML"), CSS, and the Document Object Model (DOM), and they provide specifications for each of them. We'll describe each of those technologies as we progress through the book. The W3C also provides specifications for HTML5, CSS, and the DOM. So, what's the difference between the two organizations? The WHATWG's standard is deemed "living," which means the WHATWG is free to make updates at any time, and they don't bother to assign new version numbers to their standard when they do so. That's different from the W3C, which publishes new versions, with version numbers, only after they feel their updates are stable.

Having two HTML standards might seem like a mess, but remember that the Web itself was built organically, with lots of disparate contributors from around the world. The W3C and WHATWG have a vested interest in making sure their standards are pretty close. After all, if one organization goes too far into left field, they'll lose supporters. Some browser manufacturers prefer to follow the W3C's standard because the W3C is a more venerable institution, and they provide stable versions. On the other hand, some browser manufacturers prefer to follow the WHATWG's standard because the WHATWG tends to be more receptive to new trends and suggestions for changes. We'll refer primarily to the W3C standard. But because we use syntax that is common to both standards and supported by all the major browsers, our preference for the W3C standard is pretty much irrelevant. The differences in the standards are prominent only when it comes to the leading-edge stuff.

---

[4] "W3C Mission," *W3C*, https://www.w3.org/Consortium/mission.html.

It's true that the two organizations work collaboratively, but their relationship isn't necessarily a well-oiled machine. Their relationship is more like siblings who grouse every now and then. For example, note this snippet from a WHATWG web page:[5]

> The W3C publishes some forked versions of these specifications. We have requested that they stop publishing these but they have refused. They copy most of our fixes into their forks, but their forks are usually weeks to months behind. They also make intentional changes, and sometimes even unintentional changes, to their versions. We highly recommend not paying any attention to the W3C forks of WHATWG standards.

## 1.13 Differences Between Old HTML and HTML5

In the real world, you'll see a lot of old HTML code. The old code you'll see the most of will probably be XHTML 1.0 because it was the most popular precursor to HTML5. When you see that code, there's no need to be alarmed; today's browsers render XHTML 1.0 code just fine. But in the interest of long-term stability and following your company's coding conventions, you'll sometimes need to convert old HTML code to HTML5. To do so, you need to know the differences between old HTML code and HTML5.

The following differences address the issue of existing web pages that don't match XHTML 1.0's strict syntax. More specifically, the following differences show how HTML5 has loosened up some of its syntax rules as compared to XHTML 1.0:

- ▶ With HTML5, there's no longer a requirement to have a quoted value for every attribute. So for some HTML5 attributes, it's legal to include an attribute by itself, without an equals sign or value attached to it. However, standard coding conventions suggest always including the quotation marks.
- ▶ With HTML5, there's no longer a requirement to have a / for all void elements. For example, the XHTML specification requires writing the `br` void element with a slash, `<br/>`. The HTML5 specification says you can include or omit the slash. Standard coding conventions suggest always omitting the /.
- ▶ With HTML5, there's no longer a requirement to have an end tag for every container. The XHTML specification requires including a `</p>` end tag for every p container element. The HTML5 specification says you can include or omit the end tag. Standard coding conventions suggest always including the end tag.

Old versions of HTML (including XHTML 1.0) include some elements that are deemed outdated. In particular, elements whose purpose is to provide formatting are deemed outdated. This is because formatting is supposed to be taken care of by CSS, not HTML elements. To clean things up, such outdated elements are not a part of the HTML5 standard. For example, the `<font>` and

---

[5] Web Hypertext Application Technology Working Group (WHATWG), "What are the various versions of the HTML spec?" last updated June 14, 2017, https://wiki.whatwg.org/wiki/FAQ#What_are_the _various_versions_of_the_HTML_spec.3F.

`<center>` elements are not supported by HTML5 because they were used to specify font and alignment, which are format-oriented characteristics.

The HTML5 standard includes quite a few new constructs. The following list shows just some of them:

- Structural organization elements—Two examples are the `header` and `footer` elements. We'll cover structural organization elements in Chapter 4.
- Audio and video—The `audio` and `video` elements allow users to play music and video files directly from their browsers without the need of a plug-in. We'll cover `audio` and `video` elements in Chapter 7.
- Canvas—The `canvas` element provides a drawing area and a set of commands that a web programmer can use to draw two-dimensional shapes and animate them. We'll cover the `canvas` element in Chapter 12.
- Drag and drop functionality—The drag and drop constructs provide the ability to drag elements within a web page. This is beyond the scope of this book.
- Web storage functionality—The web storage constructs provide the ability to permanently store data on the browser's computer. This is beyond the scope of this book.
- Geolocation functionality—The geolocation constructs provide the ability to locate the browser's computer. This is beyond the scope of this book.

## 1.14 How to Check Your HTML Code

As described in the previous section, HTML5 contains quite a few differences from earlier HTML standards. So when you're writing your HTML5 code, particularly if you're converting a web page that used an older version of HTML, how do you know if you're following the syntax rules for HTML5? Using this book is a good start, but it doesn't have everything. The formal standards provided by the W3C and WHATWG are comprehensive, but their technical nature and their need to specify details for browser manufacturers make them hard to understand. Here's what we recommend you use for HTML5 reference sites:

https://developers.whatwg.org:
WHATWG's HTML standard for web developers (with browser manufacturer details removed).

https://html.spec.whatwg.org/multipage/semantics.html:
A subset of the WHATWG's standard. It describes all the HTML5 elements.

You'll probably want to refer to one or both of these websites when you have questions about HTML5 syntax.

After you think you've finished creating or modifying a web page, you should check your work by running the W3C's *HTML validation service*, which is formally known as the *Markup Validation Service*. **FIGURE 1.9** shows the validation service's website (https://validator.w3.org). Note the web page's three tabs. With the first tab, **Validate by URI**, the user enters a web address for the page that is to be checked. For that to work, you need the web page to be uploaded to a web

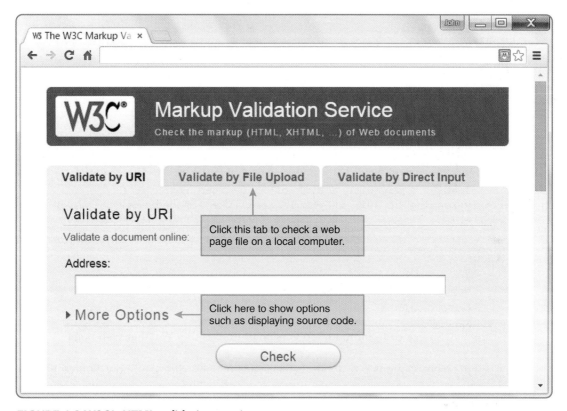

**FIGURE 1.9 W3C's HTML validation service**

server. With the second option, Validate by File Upload, the user selects a file on his or her local computer. With the third option, Validate by Direct Input, the user copies HTML code directly into a large text box. Usually, you'll use the second option, Validate by File Upload, because it's a good idea to test a file stored locally before uploading it. If you upload before testing, you run the risk of having people see your buggy web page.[6]

To get practice with the HTML validation service tool, open your favorite plain text editor or IDE and copy the text from **FIGURE 1.10** into it. That text is a modified version of the code in the original Kansas City Weather page. Save the copied code as a file with the name weatherCheck .html. Go to the W3C's HTML validation service website and select the Validate by File Upload option. That should generate a Choose File button or a Browse button (different for different browsers). Click the button, navigate to your newly saved weatherCheck.html file, and select

---

[6] A web page that's "buggy" has bugs in it, where a *bug* is an error in a computer program. The term "bug" originated from a malfunctioning program run on one of the early computers, the Harvard Mark II. The computer used mechanical relays to store binary values (e.g., a closed relay was a 1 and an open relay was a 0). As the story goes, a programmer found a squashed moth between the contacts of one of the relays, and the moth's body inhibited the flow of electricity through the relay. After removing the bug, the program worked, and the term "debugging" was born.

```
<!DOCTYPE html>
<html lang="en">
<head>
<meta charset="utf-8">
<title>K.C. Weather<title>
</head>

<body>
<h1>Kansas City Weather</h1>
<hr>
<p>
  It should be pleasant today with a high of 95 degrees.<br>
  With a humidity reading of 30%, it should feel like 102 degrees.
<div>
</p>
  Tomorrow's temperatures:<br>
  high 96, low 65
</div>
</body>
</html>
```

**FIGURE 1.10 Source code for modified version of Kansas City Weather web page**

it. Click the **More Options** box. From the generated options, click the **Show Source** box. By turning the show source option on, the file's source code will display with line numbers, which can make debugging easier. Now you're ready to let the validation service do its magic. Click the **Check** button.

The validation service looks for invalid syntax and if it finds any, it prints an error message(s). Here are the error messages the validation service generates for `weatherCheck.html`:

```
Line 20, Column 7: End of file seen when expecting text or an end
tag.
</html>
Line 5, Column 9: Unclosed element title.
   <title>K.C. Weather<title>
```

Unfortunately, error messages can be cryptic, and that is the case for the first of the two error messages. It complains about seeing the end of the file when it's expecting an end tag. Can you figure out what that means? What end tag might be hidden to the validation service? Please do not continue to the next paragraph until after you examine Figure 1.10's code for an end tag problem.

The web page is supposed to display a paragraph first and then a `div` container. To do that, you need start and end tags for a p container and then start and end tags for a `div` container. Unfortunately, Figure 1.10's p and `div` containers overlap. Specifically, p's end tag comes after `div`'s start tag. That prevents the HTML validation service from seeing p's end tag, which explains the "expecting an end tag" error message.

The second error message, "unclosed element title," is easier to figure out. The `title` element is a container; as such, it needs a start tag and an end tag. Unfortunately, the web page uses

`<title>` for the end tag, instead of `</title>` with a slash. Go to your text editor or IDE and fix the two errors in `weatherCheck.html`. Then run the HTML validation service again and note that the two error messages are gone.

You might have noticed that in creating the modified Kansas City Weather page from the original web page, several things were omitted. The `meta author` and `meta description` elements were omitted, but since they are optional, not required, the HTML validation service doesn't complain. Likewise, the CSS rules were omitted, but since they are optional, not required, the HTML validation service doesn't complain.

# 1.15 CASE STUDY: History of Electric Power

## Preview of Ongoing Case Study

This section begins an extended example of iterative construction of a website. This website's theme is a proposed electric-power "microgrid" for the core of a particular small city—Lawrence, Kansas. A microgrid is a small version of a large electrical power network. In normal operation, it provides valued electrical services to local users and the outside world. If disconnected from the outside world, it employs locally generated solar power and previously stored energy to continue providing critical electrical services to local users.

This ongoing case study generates 10 distinct web pages: Electric Power History, Lawrence Hydropower, Area Description, Microgrid Possibilities, Typical Property, Local Energy, Collector Performance, Electric Power Services, Downtown Properties, and Solar Shadowing. For the most part, each of these web pages is developed completely within the case study section at the end of just one chapter. But in some instances, a web page is iteratively enhanced over two or more chapters. For example, the Electric Power History and Lawrence Hydropower web pages are developed separately at the ends of Chapters 1 and 2, respectively, and then enhanced together at the end of Chapter 3. Also, the Area Description web page is developed at the end of Chapter 3, enhanced at the end of Chapter 7, and enhanced again at the end of Chapter 9.

Each chapter's contribution to the ongoing case study highlights material presented in that chapter. The following is an outline of what each chapter's case study section does:

**Chapter 1**: History of Electric Power
> `electricPowerHistory.html` will illustrate HTML structuring (structural elements).

**Chapter 2**: A Local Hydroelectric Power Plant
> `lawrenceHydropower.html` will illustrate HTML styling (block and phrasing elements).

**Chapter 3**: Description of a Small City's Core Area
> `areaDescription.html` (with `lawrenceMicrogrid.css`) will illustrate CSS styling.

**Chapter 4**: Microgrid Possibilities in a Small City
> `microgridPossibilities.html` will illustrate local hypertext navigation.

**Chapter 5**: A Downtown Store's Electrical Generation and Consumption
> `typicalProperty.html` will illustrate use of HTML `table` elements.

**Chapter 6**: Local Energy and Home Page with Website Navigation

`localEnergy.html` will illustrate external hypertext navigation and image display.

`index.html` will implement a primitive home page with website navigation.

**Chapter 7**: Using an Image Map for a Small City's Core Area and Website Navigation with a Generic Home Page

An enhancement of Section 3.21's `areaDescription.html` will illustrate mapped images.

A minimal `index.html` will embed other web pages in a home page's `iframe`.

**Chapter 9**: Dynamic Positioning and Collector Performance Web Page

A further enhanced `areaDescription.html` will reposition images as window size changes.

`collectorPerformance.html` will illustrate local JavaScript reading input from a `form`'s `input` and `select` elements and adding rows of data to a `table`.

**Chapter 10**: Collector Performance Details and Nonredundant Website Navigation

JavaScript functions will employ `if` statements, `Math` functions, and `window` properties to compute data for the table in the previous chapter's case study.

JavaScript in an external file will improve the website navigation employed in Chapter 6's case study.

**Chapter 11**: Downtown Properties Data Processing

`properties.html` will illustrate use of arrays and objects to maintain a sorted database.

**Chapter 12**: Solar Shadowing Dynamics

`solarShadowing.html` will illustrate painting of computed geometric shapes on a `canvas`.

## This Chapter's Web Page

The Electric Power History web page presents a brief text description of the history of electric power, followed by a bullet-point list of five important events. It illustrates the following HTML elements: `html`, `head`, `meta`, `title`, `body`, `h2`, `hr`, `p`, `div`, and `br`. Thus, in one example, it provides a simple review of most of the HTML elements introduced in this chapter. **FIGURE 1.11** contains the source code for this web page.

As in Figure 1.4, the `head` element contains three `meta` elements and a `title` element. The first `meta` element has a `charset` attribute, which helps the local browser interpret the web page's binary coding. The next two `meta` elements have `name` and `content` attributes, which help search engines. In the first of these, the `name` attribute gets the value, `author`, and in the second of these, the `name` attribute gets the value, `description`. The `title` element determines what appears in the tab at the top of the browser's display, and this also helps search engines.

The `body` element contains a heading, a horizontal rule, four text paragraphs, another horizontal rule, and a division with five items, separated by breaks. The selected `h2` heading level avoids overwhelming the page with an excessively large `h1` heading.

In each of the source-code paragraphs in Figure 1.11, text appears as five or six separate lines. Each of these lines begins with two blank spaces and ends with a linefeed. In other words, a

```
<!DOCTYPE html>
<html lang="en">
<head>
<meta charset="utf-8">
<meta name="author" content="John Dean">
<title>Electric Power History</title>
</head>

<body>
<h2>Brief History of Electric Power</h2>
<hr>
<p>
  Thomas Edison's first electric power plant generated 110-volt direct
  current (DC) for lighting and variable-speed machinery in nearby
  buildings. But efficient transmission of power over long distances
  requires higher voltages. In those days, the only way to transform DC
  voltage was to use a "genset" - a DC motor driving a DC generator.
  That's two rotating machines, with four windings.
</p>
<p>
  Then Nikola Tesla invented the alternating current(AC)induction
  motor and transformer. With constant AC frequency, an induction
  motor's speed cannot vary, but it is cheaper and more durable than a
  DC motor. Since a transformer has no moving parts and just two
  windings, it is cheaper and more durable than a DC genset. So at the
  dawn of the 20th century, AC won "the war of the currents."
</p>
<p>
  But not forever. In the middle of the 20th Century, computers began
  consuming progressively more DC power. Then came the insulated-gate
  bipolar transistor(IGBT)and the voltage-source converter(VSC). A
  VSC can make variable-frequency AC which runs induction motors at
  variable speed, and it easily transforms DC.
</p>
<p>
  DC power, computer control, and the internet are helping the power
  grid accept variable renewable resources like wind and solar. And
  they are improving electrical distribution systems on campuses, in
  neighborhoods, and in buildings. With local energy generation and
  storage, distribution systems are evolving into robust "microgrids."
</p>
<hr>
<div>
  * 1882: Edison's Pearl Street DC power plant in New York <br>
  * 1884: Tesla invents closed-core AC transformer in Budapest <br>
  * 1886: Thorenberg AC power plant in Lucerne <br>
  * 1985: Insulated-gate bipolar transistor by Toshiba <br>
  * 2012: UCSD 42-megawatt microgrid in southern California
</div>
</body>
</html>
```

**FIGURE 1.11 Source code for Electric Power History web page**

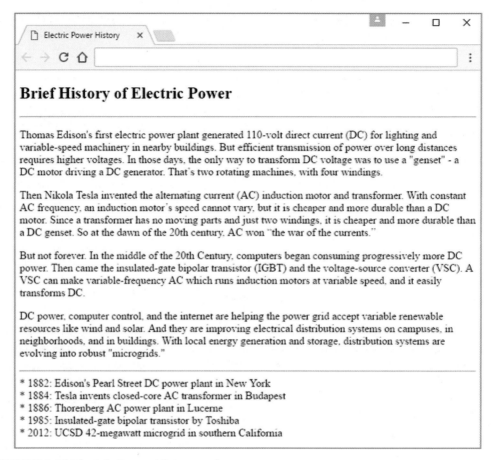

**FIGURE 1.12 Electric Power History web page**

typical text editor would recognize each HTML paragraph as five or six little one-line paragraphs. Distributing a paragraph's text over multiple lines make it easier to read, and each line's initial indentation makes the HTML paragraphing structure easier to recognize.

However, to allow users to resize windows, browsers collapse all contiguous whitespace—including newline characters—into a single-space character. Then they replace one of those single-space characters with a newline character as needed to make running text fit into the current window's width. The browser window in **FIGURE 1.12** shows how this works. Compare the text in Figure 1.12 with that in Figure 1.11, and notice how the browser lengthens and reduces the number of lines as the window's width increases.

Unfortunately, this flexibility comes with a risk. To understand the risk, notice that in Figure 1.11's last text paragraph, at the end of the third line, there is a substantial amount of whitespace. To make your HTML source code more compact, you might be tempted to fill some of this whitespace by hyphenating the word "neighborhoods." Doing that creates more whitespace at the end of the fourth line, and to fill some of this whitespace, you also might be tempted to hyphenate the word "distribution." These changes would make the last text paragraph in Figure 1.11's HTML source code look like this:

```
<p>
   DC power, computer control, and the internet are helping the power grid
   accept variable renewable resources like wind and solar. And they are
   improving electrical distribution systems on campuses, in neighbor-
   hoods, and in buildings. With local energy generation and storage, dis-
   tribution systems are evolving into robust "microgrids."
</p>
```

Then, a browser window whose width is like that in Figure 1.12 would display this modified last text paragraph like this:

DC power, computer control, and the internet are helping the power grid accept variable renewable resources like wind and solar. And they are improving electrical distribution systems on campuses, in neighbor- hoods, and in buildings. With local energy generation and storage, dis- tribution systems are evolving into robust "microgrids."

Uh oh! Look at the last two lines of the preceding paragraph. Notice that even though the words "neighbor- hoods" and "dis- tribution" are no longer split between two lines, they still contain hyphens. Even worse is that after the hyphen, each word contains that internal space character the browser substitutes for the newline character at the end of each HTML source-code line. Because a browser always substitutes a space character for a newline character, in HTML source code, you should not break even a naturally hyphenated word or term at the end of a line of continuing text.

# Review Questions

## 1.2 Creating a Website

1. What is a web server?

2. Name two features of a web authoring tool.

3. What term is used to describe code that is freely available to view and edit?

## 1.3 Web Page Example

4. What does HTTP stand for?

5. What does URL stand for?

## 1.4 HTML Tags

6. What is the name of the HTML element that generates the smallest heading?

## 1.5 Structural Elements

7. What is syntax?

## 1.6 `title` Element

8. What is the purpose of the `title` element?

## 1.8 HTML Attributes

9. For the `meta` element, what is the purpose of the `name` attribute and the `content` attribute?

10. For the `meta charset` element, what does the value `utf-8` stand for? Specifically, what do "u," "t," "f," and "8" stand for individually?

## 1.10 Cascading Style Sheets Preview

11. What does the following CSS rule do?

```
p {text-align: right;}
```

## 1.11 History of HTML

12. Who designed the HTTP protocol?

13. Who founded the W3C? Name one person.

14. Why did users tend to dislike XHTML 1.1?

## 1.13 Differences Between Old HTML and HTML5

15. The HTML5 standard requires every attribute to have a quoted value. True or false.

# Exercises

1.  [after Section 1.2] Search the Internet for a good web hosting service. Describe features of your chosen web hosting service that would make it a good service for your needs (if you don't have any needs, then make some up). You can describe the features in paragraph form or in bullet form, but you must use your own words. Which URL(s) did you use to find your information?

2.  [after Section 1.2] Use the statCounter web page to determine the most popular browsers for mobile devices. List the top three browsers in descending order (most popular first).

3.  [after Section 1.2] Explain all the parts of a URL. For example, in https://mars.jpl.nasa.gov /msl/images/PIA16082_Mitrofanov1F-thm.jpg, what is each of the following?
    https
    mars
    jpl.nasa.gov
    msl/images
    PIA16082_Mitrofanov1F-thm.jpg

4.  [after Section 1.4] What is the difference between a container element and a void element?

5.  [after Section 1.5] What is the purpose of the doctype instruction?

6.  [after Section 1.5] What is wrong with the following body code fragment in terms of the positions of the tags? In your answer, you must (a) use the appropriate term to describe the problem and (b) show how the code should be rearranged.

```
<body>
<p>
  I hate when I'm studying and a velociraptor throws bananas at me.
  Does that happen to anyone else?
  <strong>I hope not!
</p>
</strong>
</body>
```

7.  [after Section 1.8] Provide HTML5 code for a paragraph that contains the following Spanish text from Ernesto Sabato's *On Heroes and Tombs*. As always, use proper coding conventions. You must provide code such that search engines are able to identify the paragraph as containing Spanish. You are to assume that only the one paragraph contains Spanish and not the whole page.

    La vanidad es tan fantastica, que hasta nos induce a preocuparnos de lo que pensaran de nosotros una vez muertos y enterrados.

8. [after Section 1.9] What is the difference between a p element and a div element?

9. [after Section 1.11] Name something important that Ian Hickson did for the Web, and be specific. Ian is not in this book, so you'll need to look him up.

10. [after Section 1.12] This exercise attempts to get you to explore the W3C's website. Find something interesting on the W3C site. You can describe the features in paragraph form or in bullet form, but you must use your own words. Which URL(s) did you use to find your information?

11. [after Section 1.14] Using the text input mode, enter the following code into W3C's HTML validation service. What error messages are generated? Hint: There are three error messages, but only two problems with the code. You may provide the three error messages verbatim or explain the two problems.

```
<!DOCTYPE html>
<html lang="en">
<head>
<title>test title</title>
</head>
<body>
<h7>test heading
</body>
</html>
```

# Projects

1. Create the following web page, and name the file parkBookstore.html. Note that the horizontal line is right aligned. To implement that effect, use the margin-right CSS property with a value of 0.

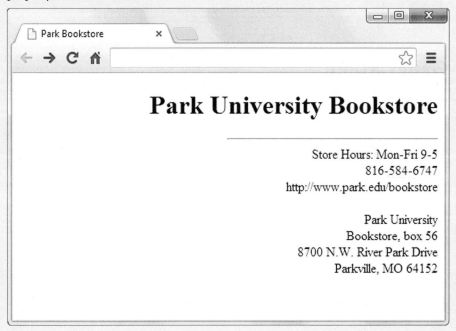

2. Create the following web page, and name the file `galleyMenu.html`. As always, use heading elements for all headings, not just the ones that appear at the top of the page. Note that the horizontal line is left aligned. To implement that effect, use the `margin-left` CSS property with a value of `0`.

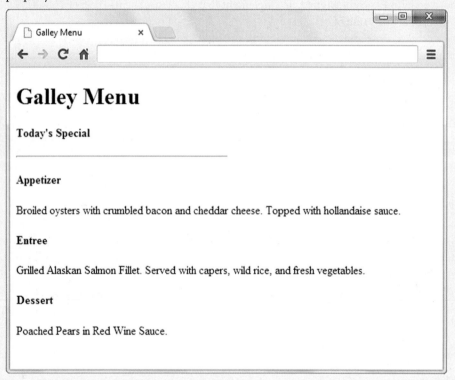

## CHAPTER 2

# Coding Standards, Block Elements, Text Elements, and Character References

## CHAPTER OBJECTIVES

▶ Understand HTML5 coding conventions and learn where they can be found.

▶ Use HTML comments appropriately.

▶ Use the content model categories to determine which elements are allowed inside a given container.

▶ Define a block element.

▶ Understand `blockquote` elements.

▶ Know when whitespace collapsing occurs and how to combat it with the `pre` element.

▶ Understand phrasing elements, like `q`, `cite`, `dfn`, `abbr`, and `time`.

▶ Learn CSS basics.

▶ Learn how and when to use character references.

## CHAPTER OUTLINE

## 2.1 Introduction

In the prior chapter, you were introduced to just enough about HTML elements so you could put together a rudimentary web page. In this chapter, we'll introduce you to additional HTML elements, so your web pages can be more expressive. In presenting the HTML elements, we make a point of using standard coding-style conventions, so your code will be acceptable to the web community as a whole.

Throughout this chapter and the rest of this book, you'll be exposed to lots of HTML elements. If you're like most people, learning lots of things that are all in a single category can be overwhelming. Defining subcategories can make learning easier. For example, rather than trying to memorize every animal species (an impossible task because thousands of new species are discovered each year), biologists remember categories of species, such as reptiles, mammals, and crustaceans, and assign each species to a particular category. Likewise, before you get overwhelmed with element overload, we describe the categorization scheme used by the World Wide Web Consortium (W3C) for organizing HTML elements. A bit confusing at first, but it'll pay off later.

In this chapter, after we present coding-style conventions and the W3C's element categorization scheme, we present elements that span the width of a web page (block elements) and then elements that can be embedded inside a paragraph (phrasing elements). At the end of the chapter, we take a break from HTML elements and introduce character references. Character references allow you to generate characters that are not on a standard keyboard. For example, if you need to display the half character (½) on a web page, you can do that with a character reference.

## 2.2 HTML Coding Conventions

Browsers are very lenient in terms of requiring web developers to write high-quality code. So even if a web page's code uses improper syntax or improper style, web browsers won't display an error message; instead, they'll try to render the code in a reasonable manner. You might think that's a good thing, but it's not. If a web page uses improper syntax, different browsers might render the web page differently. In a worst-case scenario, the web developer tests the web page on a browser where no errors are evident, mistakenly concludes that all is well, and publishes the web page on the Web. And then a user loads the web page using a different browser, and that browser renders the page in an inappropriate manner. So as a web developer, how do you deal with this problem? You should test with multiple browsers and check the syntax using the W3C's HTML validation service.

As you may recall, coding-style convention rules pertain to the format of code. For example, there are rules about when to use uppercase versus lowercase, when to insert blank lines, and when to indent. Those rules help programmers understand the code more easily, but the browsers don't care about such things. Consequently, for all those people who create web pages on their own, there's nothing to stop them from using horrible style. If they want to put the code for their entire web page on one line, browsers will treat that code the same as code with proper newlines and indentations. However, if you are taking a course in web programming, your teacher will (I hope) deduct points for poor style. More importantly, if you create web pages for a company, your company will require you to follow their coding-style conventions.

Companies like their programmers to follow standard coding conventions so the resulting programs are easier to maintain (*program maintenance* means debugging and enhancing a program after it has been released initially). This is particularly true for medium- and large-sized companies, where programs are debugged and enhanced by a larger number of people. With more people involved, there's a greater need to understand other people's code, and adhering to standard coding conventions helps with that.

In this book, we attempt to use coding-style conventions that are as widely agreed upon as possible. And how does one find such conventions? It's the same as for everything else in the world—by googling it. If you google "html style guide," you will get the coding-style conventions used by Google, the company. Because Google is ubiquitous, Google's style rules have gained huge support from the web developer community. Consequently, this book uses coding conventions that match Google's coding conventions. In this section, we'll go over some of the more important style rules, but for a more comprehensive description, see Appendix A, HTML5 and CSS Coding-Style Conventions. For now, it's OK to remember just the following style rules:

- For every container element, include both a start tag and an end tag. So even though it's legal to omit a p element's end tag, don't do it.
- Use lowercase for all tag names (e.g., meta) and attributes (e.g., name).
- Use lowercase for attribute values unless there's a reason for uppercase. For a meta author element, use title case for the author's name because that's how people's names are normally spelled (e.g., name="Dan Connolly").
- For attribute-value assignments, surround the value with quotes, and omit spaces around the equals sign.

The capitalization rule for the doctype instruction is a gray area. Google's Style Guide says "All code has to be lowercase" except when it's appropriate for a value to use uppercase. Based on that, `<!DOCTYPE html>` should be `<!doctype html>`. However, the vast majority of examples on the W3C and WHATWG websites use uppercase for DOCTYPE, and the Google Style Guide uses uppercase for DOCTYPE, so that's what we recommend. If you prefer all lowercase for the doctype instruction, ask your boss or teacher if that's OK; if he or she says it is, go for it. Remember—HTML is case insensitive, and browsers will handle either DOCTYPE or doctype just fine.

The W3C provides a tool named Tidy, at http://services.w3.org/tidy/tidy, which can be used to apply style rules to a web page. Feel free to play around with Tidy, and make up your own mind whether you want to rely on it for formatting your code or rely on careful keyboarding. You can customize Tidy's style rules to match the rules required by your company or your teacher, but be aware that the customization process is nontrivial. Even if you end up using Tidy for all your formatting needs, you should still understand the style rules so you're comfortable reading other people's code.

## 2.3 Comments

As a programmer in the real world, you'll spend lots of time looking at and editing other people's code. And, other people will spend lots of time looking at and editing your code. Therefore, everyone's code needs to be understandable. One key to understanding is good comments. *Comments* are words that humans read but the computer skips. More specifically, for web programming, the browser engine skips HTML comments. The *browser engine* is the software inside a web browser that reads a web page's content (e.g., HTML code, image files) and formatting information (CSS), and then displays the formatted content on the screen.

Usually, HTML code is fairly easy to understand, so there is no need for extensive comments. However, sometimes comments are appropriate. The general rule is to include a comment whenever information is needed to clarify something about nearby HTML code. Here's an example:

```
<!-- The following image should be updated once a month. -->
<img src="januaryPicture.gif" width="400" height="250">
```

In this code fragment, which displays a picture on a web page, the first line is a comment. As you can see, to form a comment, surround commented text with `<!--` and `-->` markers. For comments that are short enough to fit on one line, like above, proper style suggests inserting a space immediately after `<!--` and immediately before `-->`. This is an appropriate comment because without it, it would be harder for the web developer to remember to update the picture.

For comments that are too long to fit on one line, proper style suggests putting the `<!--` and `-->` markers on lines by themselves and indenting the enclosed comment text. Here's an example:

```
<!--
   If the user clicks one of the color buttons, that will cause the
   following paragraph's font color to change to the button's color.
-->
```

If you're curious about the comment's subject matter—changing the color of a paragraph's text—be patient. You'll learn how to do that when we cover *JavaScript* later in the book. For now, all you need to know is that JavaScript is a programming language, but it's more powerful than the HTML programming language. For the most part, HTML just enables you (the programmer) to display stuff on your web page. JavaScript adds quite a bit of functionality by enabling you to read user input and update what the web page displays.

In the world of software development, *documentation* refers to a description of a program. That description can be in the form of a document completely separate from the source code (like a user guide), or it can be embedded in the source code itself. Comments are one form of embedded-code documentation. With HTML, `meta` elements provide another form of embedded-code documentation. As explained in the previous chapter, you should normally always include a `meta` `author` element, so other people in your company know whom to go to when questions arise (or whom to blame when the boss needs a target). The `meta description` and `meta keywords` elements are also popular, but not quite as popular as the `meta author` element.

## 2.4 HTML Elements Should Describe Web Page Content Accurately

An overarching goal in web programming is to use appropriate HTML elements so your web page's content is described accurately. For example, if you have text that forms what would normally be considered a paragraph, then surround the text with a `p` element, not some other element (like `div`). Likewise, if you want to display words as a heading, use a heading element (`h1-h6`), not some other element (like `strong`).

A complementary overarching goal in web programming is to use HTML elements so your web page's content is described fully. For example, if you have a `title` for your web page, it would be legal to enter the title as plain text, and not have it be inside a container. But don't do that. Instead, put the title text inside a `title` element.

So, why is it good practice to describe web page content accurately and fully? It's a form of documentation, and documentation helps programmers understand and maintain the web page code more easily. Another benefit of describing web page content accurately and fully is that it enables you (the programmer) to manipulate the web page more effectively using CSS and JavaScript. For example, if you use `p` elements for all your paragraphs, you can use CSS to make all the paragraphs indented for their first lines. As another example, if you use heading elements (`h1-h6`) for all your headings, you can use JavaScript to make all the headings larger when a button is clicked.

So, how is this goal enforced whereby elements are used to accurately and fully describe the web page's content? Unfortunately, there's nothing in the HTML5 standard or in the W3C's HTML validation service that enforces this goal. Consequently, much of the enforcement is left up to programmers' due diligence. For example, the HTML validation service will allow you to surround a paragraph of text with `h1` tags or no tags at all. It's up to you not to do that; instead, you should surround the text with `p` tags.

## 2.5 Content Model Categories

### What Content Is Allowed Within a Particular Container?

Despite the HTML validation service's shortcomings mentioned in the previous section, it's still a helpful tool, and you should use it. It's good at identifying syntax errors, like misspelling tag names. It's also good at containership rules. For example, the head container must contain a title element, and a p container must not contain a div container. With lots of elements (around 115), there are lots of containership rules (more than 11,000).[1] Rather than having you remember each of those rules, it's easier to assign elements to certain categories and have those categories be the basis for the containership rules. For a given web page, if an element X contains another element Y, all you have to do is look up Y's category and determine whether element X is allowed to contain elements from Y's category.

FIGURE 2.1 shows the W3C's diagram of the different element categories. The diagram becomes useful when you're writing the code for a container and you want to know which elements are allowed inside the container. For example, suppose you're writing the code for a head container. To determine which elements are allowed inside the head container, you can read about the head element in the W3C standard by going to https://www.w3.org/TR/html51. There, scroll through the table of contents to the head element entry (or do a ctrl+f "head element"), and click on its link. That should take you to a description of the head element. Read the "content model" section, which says:

> One or more elements of metadata content, of which exactly one is a title element and no more than one is a base element.[2]

So the head container is allowed to include elements that are in the metadata category. Now go to the content model categories diagram (using the URL from Figure 2.1) and hover your mouse

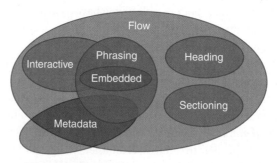

FIGURE 2.1 **Content model categories**

---

[1] "HTML Living Standard," *Web Hypertext Application Technology Working Group (WHATWG)*, last modified June 1, 2017, https://html.spec.whatwg.org/multipage/semantics.html. You can find a complete list of all the HTML elements on this page. The site shows there are 101 container elements and 115 total elements. That means the number of containership relationships is $101 \times 115$, which equals 11,615.
[2] World Wide Web Consortium (W3C), "W3C HTML 5.1 Recommendation: Semantics, structure, and APIs of HTML documents," last modified November 1, 2016, https://www.w3.org/TR/html51/dom.html#kinds-of-content.

over the metadata oval. That generates a list of all the elements in the metadata category—base, link, meta, noscript, script, style, and title.

For another example, suppose you're writing the code for a p element and you want to know what types of elements are allowed inside of it. How should you proceed? Try to do this on your own before reading the next paragraph.

To determine which elements are allowed inside the p container, look up the p element in the W3C standard and read the "content model" section, which says "phrasing content." The p container is allowed to include elements that are in the phrasing category. Now go to the content model categories diagram and hover your mouse over the phrasing oval. That generates a long list of all the content allowed in the phrasing category. That list includes elements that would be appropriate for describing text/phrases inside a paragraph (to remember what phrasing content is for, remember "phrase"). In addition to showing element names, the list also includes the word "text," which is for plain text devoid of markup tags.

As a third example, let's determine what's allowed inside the hr container. When you look up the hr element in the W3C standard and read the "content model" section, it says "empty." That means that the hr element is a void element, so it doesn't have an end tag or any enclosed content.

We'll describe Figure 2.1's categories in depth soon enough, but first note how the categories overlap. If two categories overlap, that means that the categories include some elements that are in both categories. For example, because the interactive and phrasing categories overlap, that means some of the elements in the interactive category are also in the phrasing category. If a category is completely inside another category, then all the enclosed category's elements are also in the surrounding category. For example, because the interactive, phrasing, embedded, heading, and sectioning categories are all inside the flow category, that means all the elements in the enclosed categories are also in the overarching flow category.

## Content Model Category Descriptions

In this subsection, we describe each content model category shown in Figure 2.1. Let's start with the metadata category. The metadata category includes elements that provide information associated with the web page as a whole. That should sound familiar. That's the same description we used for the head container's contents. So an alternative definition of the metadata category is that it includes all the elements that are allowed in the head container.

The flow category includes plain text and all the elements that are allowed in a web page body container. As you can imagine, there are lots of elements in the flow category. We'll discuss quite a few of them later in this chapter, but here's a small sample for now—blockquote, div, hr, p, pre, script, sup. The blockquote, div, hr, p, and pre elements are flow content elements, and they are not in any other content model categories. The script element is for JavaScript. It's in the flow content category as well as the metadata content category (note the intersection of those two categories in the content model categories diagram). You'll normally use script in a head container, but it's legal to use it in a body container as well. The sup element is for superscripting. It's in the flow content category as well as the phrasing content category (note the intersection of those two categories in the content model categories diagram).

We introduced the phrasing category earlier. Here are the phrasing category elements we'll describe later in this chapter—abbr, b, br, cite, code, del, dfn, em, i, ins, kbd, mark, q, s, samp, small, span, strong, sub, sup, time, u, var, wbr.

The embedded category includes elements that refer to a resource that's separate from the current web page. For example, the audio element uses an audio file. Here are the embedded category elements we'll describe later in the book—audio, canvas, iframe, img, and video.

The interactive category includes elements that are intended for user interaction. For example, the textarea element displays a box in which the user can enter text. Here are the interactive category elements we'll describe later in the book—a, button, input, select, textarea.

The heading category includes elements that define a header for a group of related content. For example, the h1 element displays a large header, which would normally go above content that is associated with the header. We already covered the following heading category elements in the previous chapter—h1, h2, h3, h4, h5, h6.

The sectioning category includes elements that define a group of related content. For example, the aside element is for content that's not part of the web page's main flow. Here are the sectioning category elements we'll describe later in the book—article, aside, nav, section.

Now that you've learned about the various content model categories and the content model category diagram, you might feel pretty good about being able to apply the containership rules correctly. But alas, we're human, and we make mistakes every now and then. Therefore, when coding a web page, you should always double-check your work by running the W3C's HTML validation service.

## 2.6 Block Elements

We'll now introduce an element category that is not part of the HTML5 standard. The category is for *block elements*. Even though "block element" is not an official term blessed by the W3C, we'll use it throughout the book because it will make certain explanations easier. A block element expands to fill the width of its container, so for a given container, there will be only one block element for each row in the container. For every example in the first part of this book, each block element's container is the body element, which spans the width of the browser window. So for those examples, the block element also spans the width of the entire browser window. That's different from a *phrasing element* in that (1) a phrasing element's width matches the width of the element's contents and (2) multiple phrasing elements can display in one row. If you're curious, there is a rather convoluted relationship between block elements and the W3C's content model categories: A block element corresponds to an element in the flow category that is not also an element in the phrasing category.

Be aware that a similar term, "block-level element," was part of the HTML4 standard, but it's been omitted from the HTML5 standard. Why? It's probably because the W3C feels that HTML should focus exclusively on content and let the browsers and CSS determine an element's formatting. With its focus on spanning the width of its container, the W3C deemed the block-level element category to be too format-oriented. For block-level element fans, it's disappointing that "block-level element" is no longer part of the official HTML lexicon. However, the term is not completely dead. The W3C's CSS standard uses a block value for the CSS display property (which we'll get to in a later chapter). Mozilla still uses "block" to describe

HTML concepts,[3] and in its coding-style guide, Google uses the similar term "block element" as a synonym for "block-level element."[4] So as not to anger our Google overlords, we follow suit and use the term "block element" instead of "block-level element."

## 2.7 blockquote Element

We've already talked about the div and p elements, which are block elements. Now let's discuss another block element—the blockquote element. You should use a blockquote element when you have a quotation that is too long to embed within surrounding text. It's a block element, so it spans the width of its container. More precisely, its content spans the width of the nonmargin part of its enclosing container.

For a blockquote element example, see **FIGURE 2.2**. In the figure's browser window, note the margins on the four sides of the quote text. Most browsers render a blockquote element by displaying those margins. But as an alternative, a *browser vendor* (an organization that implements a browser) may render a blockquote element by displaying the text with italics and not with margins.

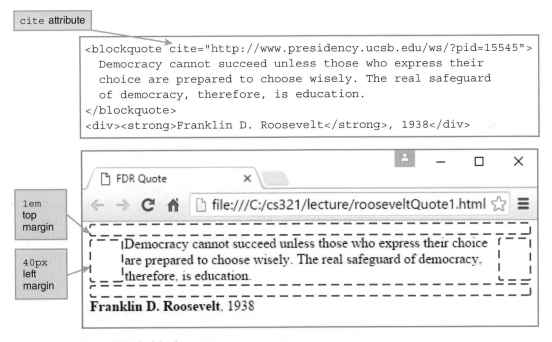

**FIGURE 2.2 An example blockquote**

---

[3] "Block-level elements," *Mozilla Developer Network*, last modified April 21, 2017, https://developer.mozilla.org/en-US/docs/Web/HTML/Block-level_elements.

[4] "Google HTML/CSS Style Guide: 2.2 General Formatting Rules," *Google.com*, http://google.github.io/styleguide/htmlcssguide.html#General_Formatting_Rules.

## Typical Default Display Properties

For each element, the W3C's HTML5 standard provides a "typical default display properties" section that describes the typical format used by the major browsers in displaying the element. Browsers are not forced to follow those guidelines, but they usually do, and as a developer, you should pay attention to the guidelines. For example, **FIGURE 2.3** shows the typical default display properties for the blockquote element.

Do you recognize the format of Figure 2.3's code? It's CSS. The figure shows five CSS rules that are commonly used as defaults when a browser renders a blockquote element. The first CSS rule says to use a block value for the display property. That means that the element the rule applies to, blockquote in this case, will span the width of its container. Thus, the display: block property-value pair matches the characteristics of the block element described earlier.

The second and third CSS rules apply to the top and bottom margins. The 1em values cause each of the two margins to be the height of one line of text. We'll discuss the CSS em unit in more depth in the next chapter, but for now, note the resulting blank lines above and below the blockquote text in Figure 2.2's browser window.

The fourth and fifth CSS rules apply to the left and right margins. The 40px values cause each of the two margins to be 40 pixels wide, where 1 *pixel* is the size of an individually projected dot on a typical computer monitor. We'll discuss the CSS px unit in more depth in the next chapter, but for now, note the resulting margins at the left and right of the blockquote text in Figure 2.2's browser window.

## cite Attribute

In Figure 2.2's blockquote code, did you notice the cite attribute in the element's start tag? For your convenience, here's the start tag again:

```
<blockquote cite="http://www.presidency.ucsb.edu/ws/?pid=15545">
```

The purpose of the cite attribute is to document where the quote can be found on the Internet. The cite attribute's value must be in the form of a URL. Interestingly, browsers do not display the cite attribute's value. That's because the URL value is not for end users. Instead, it serves as documentation for the web developer(s) in charge of maintaining the web page. Presumably, the web developer would check the URL every now and then to make sure it's still active.

```
blockquote {
    display: block;              ◄──  "block" is not part of the HTML5 standard,
    margin-before: 1em;               but it is part of the W3C's CSS standard.
    margin-after: 1em;           ◄──  Top and bottom margins equal the
    margin-start: 40px;               height of a standard line of text.
    margin-end: 40px;            ◄──  Left and right margins
}                                     equal 40 pixels each.
```

**FIGURE 2.3 Typical default display properties for the blockquote element**

Besides providing documentation, another benefit of including the `cite` attribute is that it can be used as a "hook" for adding functionality to the `blockquote` element. Specifically, a web programmer could add JavaScript code that uses the `cite` attribute's URL value to perform some URL-related task (e.g., jumping to the URL's web page when the user hovers his or her mouse over the quote). That will make more sense when we talk about JavaScript later in the book.

By the way, if you think the user might be interested in visiting the web page where the quote came from, you can implement a link. We'll describe how to implement links, using `<a>` and `</a>` tags, in Chapter 4. If you use a link, you may or may not want to also include a `cite` attribute for your `blockquote` element.

## Block Formatting

For a `blockquote` element with enclosed text that's greater than one line, you should use *block formatting*. Block formatting is a coding-style convention where the start and end tags go on their own lines and the enclosed text is indented. For an example, see Figure 2.2's `blockquote` element code, copied here for your convenience:

```
<blockquote cite="http://www.presidency.ucsb.edu/ws/?pid=15545">
   Democracy cannot succeed unless those who express their
   ...
</blockquote>
```

In the previous chapter, we covered the p and `div` elements. Like the `blockquote` element, they are block elements, so they span the width of their containers. For a p element example, see Figure 1.4's p element code, copied here for your convenience:

```
<p>
   It should be pleasant today with a high of 95 degrees.<br>
   With a humidity reading of 30%, it should feel like 102 degrees.
</p>
```

For a `div` element example, see Figure 2.2's `div` element code, copied here for your convenience:

```
<div><strong>Franklin D. Roosevelt</strong>, 1938</div>
```

The p and `div` elements are both block elements. So, in these code fragments, why does the p element use block formatting, but the `div` element does not? The block formatting style rule says to use block formatting for all block elements with content longer than one line. In the preceding p example, the content (plain text) is longer than one line, so block formatting is used. In the preceding `div` example, the content (a `strong` element plus plain text) is shorter than one line, so block formatting is not used.

## Displaying a Web Page Without a Web Server

We'll get back to our discussion of block elements shortly, but for now we should point out something you might have noticed in the Franklin Roosevelt `blockquote` web page shown earlier. In Figure 2.2, note the URL value in the browser window's address bar—file:///C:/cs240/lecture/rooseveltQuote1 .html. The "file" at the beginning of the URL is the protocol. When you see a "file" protocol, that means the web page was generated by simply double clicking on its `.html` file from within Microsoft's File Explorer tool. For example, in the following File Explorer screenshot, imagine double clicking on the `rooseveltQuote1.html` file. That's how we generated Figure 2.2's web page.

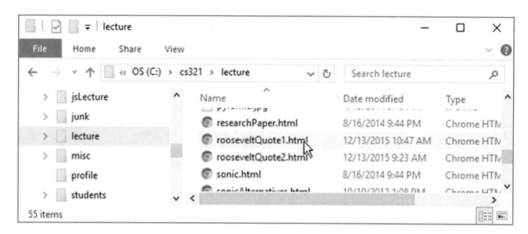

As explained in Chapter 1, if you want a web page to be accessible to everyone on the Web, you'll need to upload its `.html` file to a web server. But for a quick test, it's often easier to generate a web page by just double clicking on its file.

## 2.8 Whitespace Collapsing

The next block element we'll describe is the `pre` element. But for the `pre` element to make sense, we first need to explain whitespace collapsing. *Whitespace* refers to characters that are invisible when displayed on the browser window. The most common whitespace characters are the blank, newline, and tab characters. The web developer generates those characteristics by pressing the spacebar, enter, and tab keys, respectively. Normally, browsers collapse whitespace. In other words, if your HTML code contains consecutive blank spaces, newlines, or tabs, the browser will display the web page with only one whitespace character (usually a blank space).

For an example of whitespace collapsing, let's look at a haiku web page. A haiku is a form of Japanese poetry that consists of three lines—five syllables for the first line, seven syllables for the second line, and five syllables for the third line. In **FIGURE 2.4**, examine the text that comprises the plain text haiku. See how the three lines are centered horizontally? That's common for haikus. In Figure 2.5, note how the plain text haiku is displayed. In particular, note that the haiku's whitespace gets collapsed so that the resulting haiku is no longer centered or on three lines (a major faux pas for haiku fashionistas).

In **FIGURE 2.5**, do you see the newline after "But first"? That is not from collapsing whitespace. The only reason the browser inserts a newline after "But first" is because of line wrap. *Line wrap* is when a word bumps up against the right margin and is automatically moved to the next line.

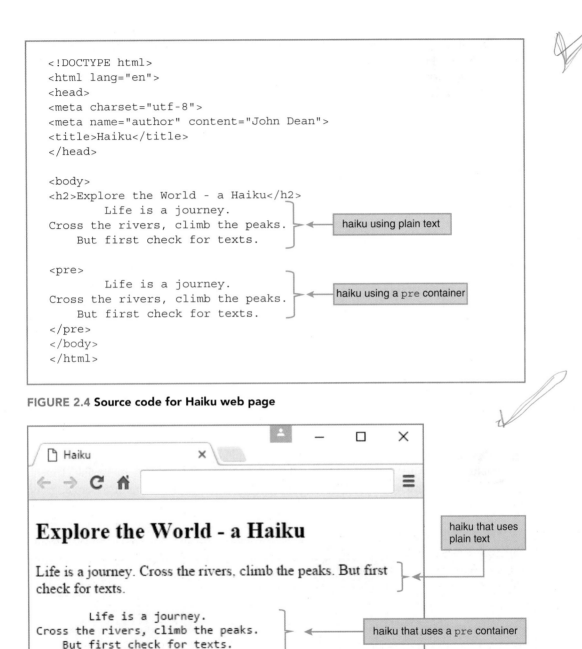

```html
<!DOCTYPE html>
<html lang="en">
<head>
<meta charset="utf-8">
<meta name="author" content="John Dean">
<title>Haiku</title>
</head>

<body>
<h2>Explore the World - a Haiku</h2>
        Life is a journey.
Cross the rivers, climb the peaks.
    But first check for texts.                    ← haiku using plain text

<pre>
        Life is a journey.
Cross the rivers, climb the peaks.                ← haiku using a pre container
    But first check for texts.
</pre>
</body>
</html>
```

FIGURE 2.4 **Source code for Haiku web page**

**Explore the World - a Haiku**

Life is a journey. Cross the rivers, climb the peaks. But first
check for texts.                                    ← haiku that uses plain text

```
        Life is a journey.
Cross the rivers, climb the peaks.                  ← haiku that uses a pre container
    But first check for texts.
```

FIGURE 2.5 **Haiku web page**

   In Figure 2.5, the browser collapses whitespace within the plain text haiku, but the browser preserves whitespace for the rest of the web page. Why is that? Above the plain text haiku, there's a blank line. That's from the preceding h2 element, which displays a noncollapsing blank line above and below its text. Below the plain text haiku, there's another blank line. That's from the pre element, introduced in the next section, which also displays a noncollapsing blank line above and below its text.

Whitespace collapsing can be helpful in many circumstances, but not all. For certain forms of literature, like haikus, line breaks and indentations need to be preserved. Later, we'll show another situation where whitespace needs to be preserved—displaying programming code. The pre element takes care of those situations.

## 2.9 pre Element

You should use the pre element for text that needs to have its whitespace preserved. Formally, pre stands for "preformatted text." However, we prefer to pretend that it stands for "preserved whitespace" because that makes more sense. In Figure 2.5, take a look at the bottom haiku (the one that uses a pre container). Note the blank spaces and newlines. Those are whitespace characters from the source code, and we can thank the pre container for preserving them.

Also in Figure 2.5, note the bottom haiku's monospace font. *Monospace font* is when each character's width is uniform. By default, browsers display pre element text with monospace font. If you don't like the default monospace font, you can use CSS to change the pre element text's font. That will make more sense when we introduce CSS's font property in the next chapter.

## 2.10 Phrasing Elements

Remember phrasing elements? If not, glance back at the content model categories diagram in Figure 2.1.

Phrasing elements are meant for text items that would be deemed acceptable within a typical paragraph. For example, the strong element, introduced in Chapter 1, is a phrasing element. That should make sense when you realize that its purpose is to place emphasis on a word or group of words within a paragraph.

**Cell phone enthusiasts extending their Snapchat streaks**

Just because a phrasing element is defined as something that is "deemed acceptable within a typical paragraph" doesn't mean that phrasing elements can be found only within p containers. On the contrary, phrasing elements are allowed within many container elements besides the p container. In determining whether it's appropriate to use a phrasing element within a given container, think about whether it would be reasonable to put the phrasing element's text within that type of container. For example, in Figure 2.4, the second haiku uses a pre container. In that pre container, would it be reasonable to surround "check for texts" with a strong container? With texting found to be a "necessary component to sustain life,"[5] the answer is an unequivocal yes, and the HTML5 standard does indeed allow `strong` elements within `pre` containers.

As an aside, you can apply the "Would it be reasonable?" test to guess the containership rule for any two container elements. For example, would it be reasonable to embed a p container within another p container? No. So if you nest two p elements and then test your code with the HTML5 validation service, you'll get an error.

In talking about phrasing elements, you should be aware that the term *inline* is sometimes used to describe their nature. That should make sense: It's reasonable for a phrasing element to be contained in a paragraph, so it could be thought of as being "in" one of the paragraph's "lines." Thus the term "inline." Although the W3C appears to have abandoned its use of the term "inline" in its HTML5 standard, the W3C still uses `inline` in its CSS standard as a value for elements that are to be formatted as phrasing elements—where the element's width matches the width of its contents (not the width of its container, like a block element).

The remainder of this chapter focuses on some of the phrasing elements. We'll present about half of them in this chapter, and we'll present some of the other ones later on.

## 2.11 **Editing Elements**

We begin our discussion of individual phrasing elements with two elements that are used to indicate editing changes—the `ins` element (for insertions) and the `del` element (for deletions). First, let's verify that they are indeed phrasing elements. Go to the W3C's content model categories page (https://www.w3.org/TR/html51/dom.html#kinds-of-content) and hover your mouse over the diagram's phrasing area. That should cause a list of all the phrasing elements to appear. In the list, look for the `ins` and `del` elements.

The `ins` element is meant to indicate text that has been inserted. If you're an editor and you're reviewing someone else's written work, you'll probably have suggestions for inserted text every now and then. To make the suggested text stand out, you should format it differently from the original text. That way, the original writer can quickly identify what has been suggested. The `ins` element works the same way.

Typically, browsers display an `ins` container's text with underlining. However, it's up to each browser vendor to determine an element's presentation when it's rendered. *Presentation* refers to the appearance and format of a displayed element. You can assume that browsers will display the text with an appropriate appearance, but that appearance might be different for different browsers.

The `del` element is meant to indicate text that has been deleted. Typically, browsers display a `del` element with strikethrough text. To see an example of that, go to the W3Schools' HTML5 tag reference page at https://www.w3schools.com/tags, click the del tag's link, and then click the **Try it yourself** link. On the try-it-yourself page, enter this:

```
HTML is <del>boring.</del><ins>super exciting!</ins>
```

---

[5] Research findings from 2017 study, "You CANNOT Take Away My Phone!" Research participants: Jordan Dean, Caiden Dean.

After clicking **See Result**, you should see this:

HTML is ~~boring.~~ super exciting!

## 2.12 `q` and `cite` Elements

### `q` Element

Now for another phrasing element—the q element. It's for quoted text that is to be rendered within the flow of surrounding text. That's different from the `blockquote` element, which spans the width of its container. Normally, browsers display a q element by surrounding its text with quotes. In **FIGURE 2.6**, note that there are no quote marks in the code fragment, and note the inserted quote marks in the resulting web browser.

For normal writing, if you have quoted text, the opening quote mark should be right next to the first character in the quoted text, and the closing quote mark should be right next to the last character in the quoted text. When implementing a web page with quoted text, it's a nonissue most of the time because the code that supports that format tends to be intuitive. However, suppose Figure 2.6's code fragment was written as follows, with the `<q>` start tag moved up to the end of the previous line:

```
<p>
   In 1937, President Franklin Roosevelt stated <q>
   The test of our progress is not whether we add more
```

This has been moved up.

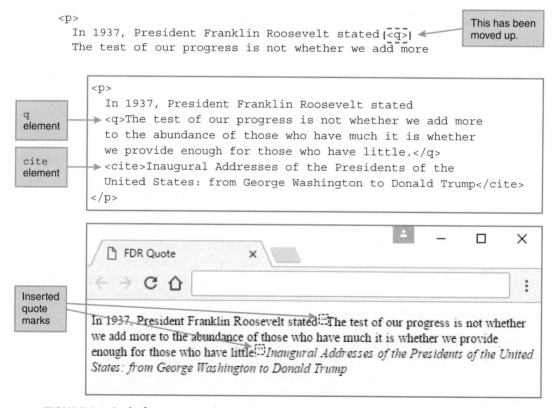

```
<p>
   In 1937, President Franklin Roosevelt stated
   <q>The test of our progress is not whether we add more
   to the abundance of those who have much it is whether
   we provide enough for those who have little.</q>
   <cite>Inaugural Addresses of the Presidents of the
   United States: from George Washington to Donald Trump</cite>
</p>
```

q element

cite element

FDR Quote

Inserted quote marks

In 1937, President Franklin Roosevelt stated "The test of our progress is not whether we add more to the abundance of those who have much it is whether we provide enough for those who have little." *Inaugural Addresses of the Presidents of the United States: from George Washington to Donald Trump*

**FIGURE 2.6 Code fragment with `q` and `cite` elements, plus resulting browser window**

Such a move seems reasonable because there is plenty of room at the end of the previous line. But what do you think happens when the browser renders the code? First, the browser renders the <q> start tag as an opening quote mark. So far, so good. Next, the browser sees the newline and because of whitespace collapsing, it displays a single space before "The test…". Not so good. The moral of the story is to make sure you put the <q> start tag right next to the first character in the quoted text, and you put the </q> end tag right next to the last character in the quoted text.

By the way, this same issue does not apply to the p element. In the preceding code, even though the <p> start tag is on a different line from the paragraph's first character, the browser displays no whitespace at the left of the paragraph's first character. That's because p is a block element, and testing shows that browsers remove whitespace at the left and right of a block element's text.

## cite Element

When you display quoted text, if the text comes from a "work," you should cite the work's title using the cite element. In defining the cite element at https://www.w3.org/TR/html51/textlevel-semantics.html#the-cite-element, the W3C states that a "cite element represents the cited title of a work; for example, the title of a book, paper, essay, poem, score, song, script, film, TV show, game, sculpture, painting, theater production, play, opera, musical, exhibition, legal case report, or other such work." Typically, browsers display a cite container's text with italics.

It's common for a cite element to follow a q element, which is what the example in Figure 2.6 shows. As an alternative, you can have a cite element follow a blockquote element. As another alternative, you can have a cite element appear within a blockquote element, after the blockquote element's text.

Previously, we talked about the cite attribute as part of the blockquote element. What is the difference between the cite element and the cite attribute? The cite element is for a cited work, like a book title, whereas the cite attribute is strictly for a URL value. Another difference is that browsers display the content in a cite element, whereas browsers do not display the content in a cite attribute.

## 2.13 dfn, abbr, and time Elements

In this section, we introduce three elements that aren't used all that often, but they are helpful if you want to manipulate definitions, abbreviations, dates, and times with CSS or JavaScript.

## dfn Element

The dfn element is for a word or expression that is to be defined. It's not for the definition, but rather the thing that is being defined. So, in the following example, dfn tags surround "tooltip," the word being defined, and not "is a pop-up …," which is the definition.

```
<p>
  A <dfn>tooltip</dfn> is a pop-up box that provides information
  about the item that the mouse is hovering over.
</p>
```

You might think that dfn stands for "definition." It's certainly possible that dfn stood for "definition" when HTML was invented. However, the HTML5 standard states that dfn stands for "defining instance," not "definition." "Defining instance" is a mouthful, but it matches the dfn element's functionality pretty well.

Typically, browsers display a dfn element's text with italics. That coincides with standard writing practice, which says to italicize a word if it's being defined.

## abbr Element

The abbr element is for an abbreviation or acronym. For an example, see **FIGURE 2.7**, which surrounds the W3C acronym with abbr tags. In the abbr element's start tag, note the title attribute. It provides the expanded text that the abbreviation represents. So, for the W3C abbr element, its title attribute has the value "World Wide Web Consortium."

Typically, browsers display the abbr element's title value as a *tooltip*. That means that when the mouse hovers over the abbr element's displayed text, the title attribute's value pops up. In Figure 2.7, you can see the "World Wide Web Consortium" tooltip pop-up after the user has hovered the mouse over the abbr element's displayed text, "W3C."

For the W3C Barbeque web page, suppose you want to show not only the expanded form of "W3C" (with the abbr element's title attribute), but you also want to provide a definition of the W3C organization. To do that, you should surround the abbr element with a dfn element, like this:

```
The <dfn><abbr title="World Wide Web Consortium">W3C</abbr></dfn>
is the governing body for various technologies on the Web. It
hosts an annual barbeque fundraiser....
```

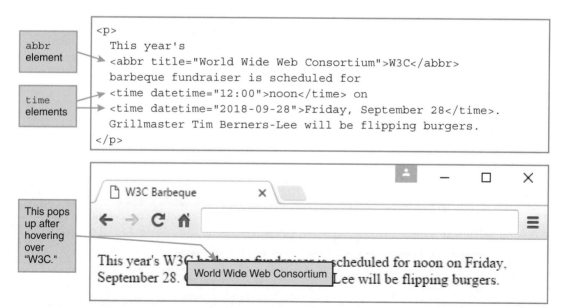

FIGURE 2.7 **Code fragment with abbr and time elements, plus resulting browser window**

## time **Element**

The time element is used to indicate that its text represents a date or time. By using a time element instead of just plain text, you enable the browser engine to recognize the text as a time or date value. That recognition enables CSS and JavaScript to read and/or manipulate the date/time value if there is a need to do so.

The time element's datetime attribute provides a date/time value in a format that the browser engine can understand. The most common format for a date is yyyy-mm-dd. Figure 2.7 shows an example that uses that format. The relevant code is copied here for your convenience:

```
<time datetime="2018-09-28">Friday, September 28</time>
```

The most common format for a time is hh:mm. Figure 2.7 shows an example that uses that format, and here's the relevant code:

```
<time datetime="12:00">noon</time>
```

Here are two additional examples:

```
<time datetime="2019-10-01">Tuesday, October 1</time>
<time datetime="04:00">4 AM</time>
```

Note how the examples follow the preceding formats—4 digits for the year, and 2 digits each for the month, day, hour, and minutes values. If you provide date and time values with fewer digits than 4, 2, 2, 2, and 2, you can't be sure that the browser engine will interpret the values correctly.

Date and time values are not mutually exclusive. It's legal to specify a date and time with one datetime attribute by separating the date and time values with a T. For example:

```
Join us for a rockin' <time datetime="2019-01-01T00:00">New Year's
Eve</time> "Bingo Bash" at the Seniors Center.
All you can drink spiced apple cider!
```

It's legal to omit the datetime attribute, but if you do so, the enclosed content between the time element's tags must use one of the formats prescribed in the HTML5 standard. The preceding formats (yyyy-mm-dd and hh:mm) are in the HTML5 standard, and here are examples that use those formats for the time element's enclosed content:

```
<time>1967-07-15</time>
<time>04:00</time>
```

Browsers do not display the datetime attribute's value, so normally you should include a date and/or time value between the start and end tags, as shown in all the preceding examples. Typically, browsers display a time element's enclosed text with default formatting, which means that the format comes from the element that surrounds the time element.

## 2.14 **Code-Related Elements**

As a programmer, you'll sometimes want to look up coding syntax and coding examples on the Web. It's amazing how much code is out there. To accommodate web developers who want to make web pages that show code, the HTML5 standard provides several coding-related elements— code, kbd, samp, and var.

The code element indicates that its enclosed text is programming code. The kbd element indicates that its enclosed text represents input for a program. The "kbd" stands for "keyboard." The samp element indicates that its enclosed text represents output for a program. The "samp" stands for "sample." The var element indicates that its enclosed text represents a programming variable or a mathematical variable. The "var" stands for "variable."

For an example with all four code-related elements, see **FIGURE 2.8**. It shows a JavaScript code fragment with sample input and output. Specifically, the web page says that if you run the program with "1992" for input, you'll get "The earliest you can receive social security benefits is 2054." If you study the JavaScript code (we'll explain JavaScript syntax later in the book), you'll see that the program adds 62 to the user's entered birth year, and the result is the first year that the user is eligible to receive social security benefits.

Typically, browsers display code element text with monospace font. In **FIGURE 2.9**, note the monospace font used for the code element. Monospace font is appropriate for code element text because when you look at code within a text editor or an IDE, the code uses monospace font. So, on a web page, if you display programming code with monospace font, your code will look more realistic.

Another reason why monospace is appropriate for displaying code is that it enables you to align similar types of things within your program. For example, in Figure 2.9, note the first three lines in the code fragment, copied here for your convenience:

```
var birthYear;     // 4 digit year of birth
var benefitsYear; // The year when social
                   // security benefits can start
```

The preceding code matches what you'd see in an IDE. Because of the monospace font, it was easy to align the //'s. Just press the spacebar until the //'s line up. On the other hand, with the exact same keystrokes as before, if you use a non-monospace font (like Times New Roman), here's what the code looks like:

```
var birthYear;  // 4 digit year of birth
var benefitsYear; // The year when social
        // security benefits can start
```

The reason the //'s don't align like they used to is because the space characters are narrower than the letter characters. If you attempt to fix the alignment in the first and third lines by inserting more space characters in front of the //'s, you probably won't be able to align the //'s perfectly. Even if inserting spaces does generate perfect alignment, the resulting code

```
<!DOCTYPE html>
<html lang="en">
<head>
<meta charset="utf-8">
<meta name="author" content="John Dean">
<title>Coding Elements</title>
<style>
  p {margin-bottom: 0;}
  per {margin-top: 0;}
</style>
</head>

<body>
<p>
  Given the following JavaScript code fragment. If the
  user enters <kbd>1992</kbd>, then <var>benefitsYear</var>
  will be 2054, and the output will be <samp>The earliest
  you can receive social security benefits is 2054</samp>.
</p>
<pre><code>
  var birthYear;      // 4 digit year of birth
  var benefitsYear; // The year when social
                    // security benefits can start
  birthYear = prompt("Enter your birth year:", "");
  benefitsYear = parseInt(birthYear) + 62;
  alert("The earliest you can receive social" +
    " security benefits is " + benefitsYear + ".");
</code></pre>
</body>
```

These CSS rules reduce the gap between the p and pre block elements.

kbd element

var element

samp element

pre and code elements

**FIGURE 2.8 Source code for Coding Elements web page**

will be harder to maintain. For example, assume you have perfect alignment and then you change "benefitsYear" to "benefitYear." To fix the newly introduced misalignment, you might try deleting one or two spaces from each of the other two lines, but that would probably not work perfectly.

As with the code element, browsers typically display kbd and samp text with monospace font. In Figure 2.9, note the monospace font used for the kbd and samp elements. The rationale for monospace font for kbd and samp text is a bit tenuous. Today, most programs display input and output text with fonts that are customizable, and those fonts are usually not in the monospace font category. However, in the old days, programs were rather boring; they were limited to monospace font when displaying input and output. The kbd and samp elements follow that tradition, and that's why they use monospace font by default.

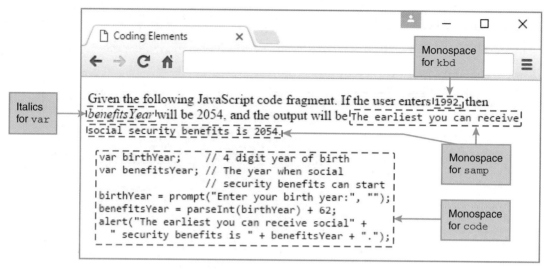

**FIGURE 2.9 Coding Elements web page**

As mentioned earlier, the `var` element is for a programming variable or a mathematical variable. In math books and in equation editors,[6] variables are written with italics. Following suit, browsers typically display `var` elements with italics. For an example, see the variable *benefitsYear* in Figure 2.9.

In this section, we've been examining the source code for the Coding Elements web page. In that source code, there's one last noteworthy item—the CSS rules shown in Figure 2.8 and copied here for your convenience:

```
p {margin-bottom: 0;}
pre {margin-top: 0;}
```

These rules have nothing to do with code-related elements; they help solve a problem. Note the single-line gap between the opening paragraph and the subsequent JavaScript code. Without the CSS rules, that gap would be too large. The opening paragraph and subsequent JavaScript code segments are implemented with p and `pre` elements, respectively. Remember, browsers normally display the p and `pre` elements with blank lines above and below them. To get rid of those blank lines, the CSS rules assign zero-height margins below the p element and above the `pre` element, respectively. Even with those rules in place, you can see in Figure 2.9 that there's still a single blank line between the p element and the `pre` element. That blank line is a result of the newline after `<pre><code>`. Remember that the `pre` element preserves whitespace, so that newline is preserved, thus creating a single blank line.

---

[6] An equation editor is software that helps users write equations within an electronic document.

# 2.15 `br` and `wbr` Elements

In this section, we discuss two elements that deal with line breaks. You already know about the `br` element, which is a void element that causes subsequent text to start on the next line. The `wbr` element (`wbr` stands for "word break") is similar to the `br` element in that it's a void element. But whereas the browser treats `br` as a required break between words, the browser treats `wbr` as a suggested break within a word if the word bumps into the right side of its containing box. So far, the only "containing box" has been the browser window's main box, defined by the `body` element. Later, you'll see how we can create smaller containing boxes within the browser window's main box.

See **FIGURE 2.10** and note the `sup` element. We'll get to that element in the next section. For now, let's focus on the two `wbr` elements within the word "antidisestablishmentarianism." In the resulting browser window, the second `wbr` element causes the browser to insert a break after the "men" syllable in "antidisestablishmentarianism." If the user resizes the window by dragging the right edge to the left, "men" will bump into the right side of the window, and that will cause the browser to insert a break after "anti" in "antidisestablishmentarianism." That's where the first `wbr` element resides.

Using the `wbr` element for regular words, even long ones like antidisestablishmentarianism, is a bit unusual. A more common scenario is when you have a long sequence of nonblank characters that forms a pattern or code of some sort. A URL matches that description. URLs can be quite long, and their dots ( . ) and slashes ( / ) form natural breaking points. Here's an example:

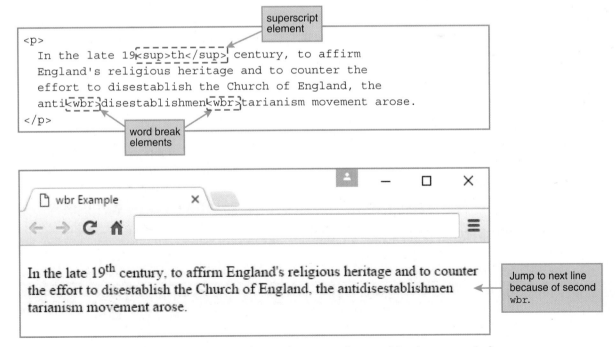

**FIGURE 2.10** Code fragment with `wbr` and `sup` elements, plus resulting browser window

```
To counter an opponent's connected rooks on a closed file, consider
the Bronstein delay
(www<wbr>.chessgeeks<wbr>.com<wbr>/caughtoncamera<wbr>/bronstein.mp4).
```

Note that the `wbr` elements appear before the slashes. Why is it better to position `wbr` elements before a URL's slashes or dots rather than after? If they are positioned after the slashes or dots and there's a line break after one of the URL slashes or dots, readers might mistake it for the end of the URL.

## 2.16 `sub`, `sup`, `s`, `mark`, and `small` Elements

Now for some elements that don't quite fit together, but they're close enough, so we can combine them to avoid ridiculously small sections in the book. The `sub`, `sup`, `s`, `mark`, and `small` elements refer to "things," but for each of them, their most striking characteristic is their appearance and not what they are.

The `sup` element is for a superscript. Typically, browsers display `sup` elements with a slightly raised smaller font. For an example, see Figure 2.10, where the "th" in 19th is superscripted.

The `sub` element is for a subscript. Typically, browsers display `sub` elements with a slightly lowered smaller font. Here's an example with 2 subscripted:

> Why is water sometimes referred to as $H_2O$? Because it's made from two hydrogen atoms and one oxygen atom.

The `s` element indicates something that is no longer accurate or no longer relevant. Typically, browsers display `s` elements with a line-through, like this:

> Corporate lobbyists pay huge sums of money to politicians in order to get them elected and gain access after they're elected. ~~But in America, democracy wins by giving equal say to everyday citizens.~~

Previously, `s` was used to show stricken text for editing purposes, but the W3C now says `s` is not for editing; it's only for something that is no longer accurate or no longer relevant. Remember the phrasing element that indicates a deletion for editing purposes? The `del` element.

The `mark` element is for text that is marked or highlighted so it can be referred to from another place. Typically, browsers display `mark` elements with a yellow background. For an example, see **FIGURE 2.11**, where "Do" and "dew" are marked with a yellow background so they are easy to identify as homonyms.

The `small` element indicates something that would normally be considered "fine print." It's often used for disclaimers. As you would expect, browsers typically display `small` elements with smaller font than the default. For an example, see the medical disclaimer at the bottom of **FIGURE 2.12**.

```
<p>
  Homonymic advertising slogan for Mountain Dew:<br>
  <mark>Do</mark> the <mark>Dew</mark>!          mark element
</p>
```

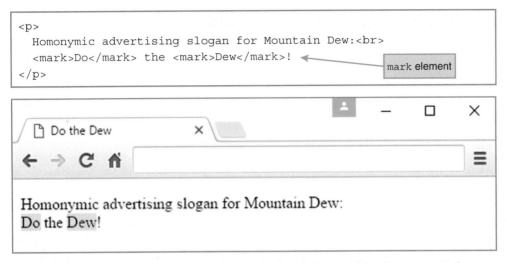

FIGURE 2.11 Code fragment with the mark element, plus resulting browser window

```
<p>
  Do you ever feel tired?<br>
  Don't let lack of sleep get you down. <strong>Fight back!</strong><br>
  Buzz Energy Drink* will get your heart racing and keep you
  <em>going strong</em>!          em element          strong element
</p>
<small>* May cause diarrhea, acute bleeding, and/or sudden death.
  Ask your doctor if it's right for you.</small>          small element
```

FIGURE 2.12 Code fragment with strong, em, and small elements, plus resulting browser window

## 2.17 `strong`, `em`, `b`, `u`, and `i` Elements

The W3C makes it clear that elements should be used according to what they represent and not according to their appearance. In the old days—and even today—web developers violated this credo a lot. That is especially true for this section's elements. As in the previous section, this section's set of elements is loosely coupled. What these elements have in common is that web developers very often use them only for their appearance. You should be a force for good and resist that temptation.

The `strong` element is for text that is supposed to be given strong importance. Typically, browsers display `strong` elements with a boldface font. For an example, see "Fight back!" in Figure 2.12. The `em` element is for text that is supposed to be given emphatic stress (the W3C uses the term "emphatic stress," but most people think of "emphasis"). Typically, browsers display `em` elements with italics. For an example, see "going strong" in Figure 2.12.

Historically, the b, u, and i  elements have been used for presentation exclusively—b for bold, u for underline, and i for italics. Using HTML elements for presentation is anathema to the guiding principles set forth in the HTML5 standard. For presentation, you're supposed to use CSS. Consequently, the W3C doesn't really like the b, u, and i elements. But the elements have been used so much in the past that the organization feels compelled to support them. They are concerned that if the elements are omitted from the HTML5 standard, (1) browsers will still support them, thus undermining the W3C's credibility, or (2) browsers will no longer support them, thus angering web developers and end users when their legacy code breaks. *Legacy code* is code created in the past that uses commands supported by an older standard and not the current standard.

The W3C describes the b element like this:

> The b element represents a span of text to which attention is being drawn for utilitarian purposes without conveying any extra importance and with no implication of an alternate voice or mood, such as key words in a document abstract, product names in a review, actionable words in interactive text-driven software, or an article lede.[7]

The W3C appears to have fudged b's definition to try to make it content-oriented rather than presentation-oriented, but it's a stretch. Bottom line: Try to avoid using the b element, except for the examples mentioned in the previous definition. Instead, try to use other elements or use CSS.

The W3C describes the u element like this:

> The u element represents a span of text with an unarticulated, though explicitly rendered, non-textual annotation, such as labeling the text as being a proper name in Chinese text (a Chinese proper name mark), or labeling the text as being misspelt.[8]

---

[7] World Wide Web Consortium (W3C), "HTML 5.1 W3C Recommendation," *W3C.org*, November 1, 2016, https://www.w3.org/TR/2016/REC-html51-20161101/.
[8] Ibid.

As with the b element, the W3C appears to have fudged u's definition to try to make it content-oriented rather than presentation-oriented. Bottom line: Try to avoid using the u element, except when it comports with the preceding definition. Instead, try to use other elements or use CSS.

The W3C describes the i element like this:

> The i element represents a span of text in an alternate voice or mood, or otherwise offset from the normal prose in a manner indicating a different quality of text, such as a taxonomic designation, a technical term, an idiomatic phrase from another language, transliteration, a thought, or a ship name in Western texts.[9]

Same as with the b and u elements, try to avoid using the i element, except for the examples mentioned in the preceding definition. Instead, try to use other elements or use CSS.

## 2.18 span Element

The span element (like the div block element) has no innate characteristics, either with regard to content or with regard to presentation. Its presentation characteristics are given to it explicitly by CSS. If you want to apply formatting to some text, and the text doesn't coincide with one of the other container elements, then put the text in a span element and apply CSS to the span element.

The next chapter covers CSS in depth, and many of the CSS examples will use the span element. For now, here's a brief overview of the span element.

Think about the u element presented in the previous section. As you know, the u element is frowned upon. For underlining, you should normally avoid using the u element; instead, surround the text that is to be underlined with span tags, and then apply a CSS underline rule to the span element. So if you'd like to underline "Buzz Energy Drink" in Figure 2.12's web page, surround "Buzz Energy Drink" with span tags like this:

```
<span class="underlined">Buzz Energy Drink</span>
```

The class attribute's value (underlined in this case) is the glue that connects an element to a CSS rule. Here's the CSS rule that gets connected to the preceding span element:

```
.underlined {text-decoration: underline;}
```

You can see .underlined, which causes the rule to be connected to the span element. And note text-decoration: underline, which tells the browser to display the span element's text with an underline.

If this example was confusing, don't worry. It'll make more sense when we dig into CSS details in Chapter 3.

---

[9] Ibid.

# 2.19 Character References

A *character reference* is code that you can use in your HTML to display a character that would otherwise be difficult to display. Character references are sometimes called "character entities." We use the term "character reference" because that's the term that the W3C uses. See the table in **FIGURE 2.13**. It contains some of the more popular character references.

## Character Reference Syntax

In Figure 2.13, note the odd-looking syntax, &*name*;, for the character references. Each character reference starts with an ampersand, then a name, and then a semicolon. For example, the table's first character reference is &lt;, where "lt" is the name. The &lt; character reference is for the < symbol, and "lt" stands for "less than." The table shows just a fraction of all the character references defined by the W3C. For a complete list of character references, go to https://www .w3.org/TR/html51/syntax.html#named-character-references. As a sanity check, scroll down to the &lt; character reference for the < symbol.

　　In your HTML source code, you can represent character references in one of two ways. You can use *named character references* or *numeric character references*. For example, you can display the < symbol using the &lt; named character reference or the &#60; numeric character reference. In your web pages, you should use named character references and not numeric character references. Why? Because numeric character references are more cryptic. For example, isn't &#60; harder to figure out than &lt;? After you know "lt" stands for "less than," remembering &lt; is easy. We won't use numeric character references in our examples going forward. With that in mind, we'll keep things simple and use the shortened term "character reference" when referring to a named character reference.

| Character | Character Reference | Description |
|---|---|---|
| < | &lt; | less than |
| > | &gt; | greater than |
| ≤ | &le; | less than or equal |
| ½ | &frac12; | one-half |
| ¼ | &frac14; | one-fourth |
| & | &amp; | ampersand |
| " | &quot; | quote |
| ' | &apos; | apostrophe |
| space |   | nonbreaking space |
| ← | &larr; &leftarrow; | left arrow |
| • | &centerdot; | bullet |
| ✓ | &check; | check mark |
| © | &copy; | copyright |

**FIGURE 2.13 Character references**

In writing the code for a web page, if you want to display a character, normally you just type the character itself. So why are character references necessary? We'll answer that question by examining the character references in Figure 2.13.

## Math-Oriented Character References

The table's first character reference is for the < symbol. If you want to display the < symbol for a math-oriented web page, you might attempt to do so by simply typing the "<" character. But browsers will treat that character as the start of an HTML tag, and the "<" character will not be displayed. So to display the "<" character you must use &lt;. Similar reasoning explains why you need to use &gt; to display the ">" character. If you simply type the ">" character, browsers will treat the ">" character as the end of an HTML tag. The solution is to use &gt;, where "gt" stands for "greater than."

Now for the table's third character reference, &le;. The "le" in "&le;" stands for "less than or equal," and the &le; character reference is for the ≤ symbol. The need for the &le; character reference is pretty clear. There is no ≤ key on a standard keyboard.

There are quite a few math-oriented character references. The table in Figure 2.13 shows five of them, for <, >, ≤, ½, and ¼. Referring to the character reference for ≤, you can probably guess the character reference for ≥. That's right, it's &ge;. Likewise, referring to the character reference for ½, you can probably guess the character references for other fractions, such as ¼ and ⅔. To verify that your fraction guesses are correct, find the fraction character references on the W3C character reference web page mentioned earlier.

## Characters with Special Meaning for HTML

The table's next character reference is for the & symbol. If you want to display it on a web page, you might attempt to do so by simply using the "&" character. But browsers will treat that character as the start of a character reference, and the "&" character will not be displayed. So, to display the "&" character, you must use &amp;.

The table's next two character references are &quot; and &apos;. They can be used to display a quote character (") or an apostrophe character ('), respectively. But normally, if you wish to display a " or ', you should simply use a " or ' and the character will display as is. Can you think of an exception to that rule, when using a " or ' has special meaning and will not display as is? You probably recall that quotes are used in HTML to surround an attribute value. If the attribute value is text that includes a quote mark inside the text, then make sure to use a character reference for the quote mark inside the text. If you use a quote character instead, the browser will treat it as the end of the attribute value's string. For example, this would not work:

> This quote mark indicates the end of the `title` value's string.

```
Originally, <abbr title="⌖Music⌖ Television">MTV</abbr>
actually played music.
```

Here's the corrected code, with `&quot;` character references:

```
Originally, <abbr title="&quot;Music&quot; Television">MTV</abbr>
actually played music.
```

In HTML, you can use single quotes or double quotes to indicate that something is a string. So here's an alternative implementation of the MTV code fragment, with ' characters and `&apos;` character references:

```
Originally, <abbr title='&apos;Music&apos; Television'>MTV</abbr>
actually played music.
```

If you don't like character references because you think they are a form of clutter, you can avoid them by nesting single quotes inside double quotes or double quotes inside single quotes. Note how this example nests single quotes inside double quotes:

```
Originally, <abbr title="'Music' Television">MTV</abbr>
actually played music.
```

## Space Characters

Normally, you should use a regular space character to display a blank space. However, there are two cases where you'll need to use a character reference instead of a space character, and we'll discuss those cases in this subsection.

If you want to display a blank space without allowing a line break, you should use the ` ` character reference, where "nbsp" stands for "nonbreaking space." For example, suppose you're implementing a Motown web page that contains lyrics by the Jackson 5. In the song "ABC," one of the lyrics is "It's easy as 1 2 3." In displaying the lyric, you want 1, 2, and 3 to be on the same line so the reader reads "one two three," as opposed to "one twenty-three" or "twelve three." That means you need to avoid line breaks, and here's the code that does that:

```
It's easy as 1 2 3.
```

If the 1, 2, or 3 bumps against the browser's right edge, then the entire "1 2 3" wraps to the next line.

Remember that if you have consecutive space characters, browsers will collapse those spaces into one space. If you want to display consecutive spaces and avoid that collapsing, you should use one or more consecutive ` ` character references. Here's an example that could be used for a pep rally web page:

```
G O  J A G U A R S  !
```

For the first two-space gap, between "GO" and "JAGUARS," we use two consecutive ` ` character references. For the second two-space gap, between "JAGUARS" and "!," we use a ` ` character reference and then a space character. Both techniques would normally display two consecutive spaces. However, the first technique is usually preferred. Why? Because if the exclamation point bumped up against the right margin, the   space would allow a line break to occur.

## Character References When There's No Choice and When There's a Choice

Figure 2.13's last four character references are &larr;, &centerdot;, &check;, and &copy;. They are used to display the symbols ←, •, √, and ©, respectively. Those character references are just a small sample of character references where there is no key on a standard keyboard for the character reference. With no key, there's no choice. If you want to display the character, you must use the character reference.

On the other hand, if there's a choice, you should use regular characters and not character references. For example, if you want to display an apostrophe for a possessive word, use the apostrophe character (') and do not use &apos;. Why? Because the apostrophe character is more readable. All the displayable keys on a standard keyboard have associated numeric character references. Technically, you could use numeric character references for everything. Here's an ugly example: &#117;&#103;&#108;&#121;.[10] But proper style dictates that if there's a choice, use regular characters and not named character references or numeric character references.

## 2.20 Web Page with Character References and Phrasing Elements

In the past several sections, you learned about phrasing elements and character references. In this section, we put what you learned into practice by examining a complete web page. See the pizzeria web page in **FIGURE 2.14**. Can you figure out what character references and phrasing elements are incorporated into that web page? Try to do that on your own, now, before we analyze the web page together.

### Character References

Let's start with the character references. In the pizzeria web page, can you identify the characters that are implemented with character references? What symbols do you see that are not associated with keys on a standard keyboard? The π, •, and ½ symbols are not associated with keys on a standard keyboard, so they have to use character references. Figure 2.13 shows the character references for • and ½. To get the character reference for π, look it up in the W3C character reference table.

By the way, do you understand the purpose of the • symbol? It's for multiplication, so that means Pi • z • z • a is π times the $z$ variable squared times the $a$ variable.

---

[10] Can you figure out what word is formed by the given code? Hint: Look up "ASCII characters."

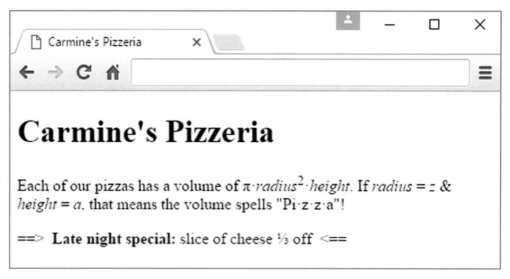

**FIGURE 2.14 Pizzeria web page**

Next are the < and > symbols, which are used to form <== and ==> arrows. Unlike π, •, and ½, the < and > symbols do have associated keys on the keyboard. However, as you know, if you use a "<" character or a ">" character, they will not display as is. To display the < and > symbols, you need to use the character references shown in Figure 2.13.

Note the web page's & symbol. The & symbol is like the < and > symbols in that it has a special meaning in HTML. To display it, you need to use a character reference.

Can you see anything else in the web page that might need a character reference? Think hard before reading on. This one's not so easy.

Do you see where   character references might be helpful? To avoid a line break within "radius = z" and within "height = a," you should use   character references around the equals signs. See Figure 2.14's browser window. With the browser window's width, if regular spaces were used (and not   character references), the browser would have split "height = a." Not a disaster, but somewhat awkward. Another place for   character references is the bottom line. Do you see the two spaces at the right of ==> and also at the left of <==? If regular space characters had been used, then whitespace collapsing would have occurred. But   character references are used and whitespace collapsing is avoided.

**FIGURE 2.15** shows the source code for the Pizzeria web page. The code highlighted in red is for all the character references. As a sanity check, read through the web page's character reference code and make sure it makes sense.

Before we move on to the phrasing elements, there's one more thing to consider in regard to character references. In Figure 2.14, do you see the quote marks around "Pi • z • z • a"? You have a choice of implementing them with either " characters or with character references. Remember, whenever you have a choice, you should use the more straightforward option, which means " characters in this case. You can see the " characters in Figure 2.15.

```
<!DOCTYPE html>
<html lang="en">
<head>
<meta charset="utf-8">
<meta name="author" content="John Dean">
<title>Carmine's Pizzeria</title>
</head>

<body>
<h1>Carmine's Pizzeria</h1>
<p>
  Each of our pizzas has a volume of
  &pi;&centerdot;<var>radius</var><sup>2</sup>&centerdot;<var>height</var>.
  If <var>radius</var> = <var>z</var> &amp;
  <var>height</var> = <var>a</var>, that means the volume spells
  "Pi&centerdot;z&centerdot;z&centerdot;a"!
</p>
<p>
  ==&gt;  <strong>Late night special:</strong> slice of cheese
  &frac13; off  &lt;==
</p>
</body>
</html>
```

```
Character references are in red.
```

```
Phrasing elements are in green.
```

**FIGURE 2.15 Source code for Pizzeria web page**

## Phrasing Elements

Now go back to Figure 2.14 and see if you can figure out what phrasing elements are used in the pizzeria web page. The web page refers to variables named *radius*, *height*, *z*, and *a*. Because they are variables, you should identify them as such by using a separate `var` container for each variable. Note the following line, copied from the pizzeria web page's code, which has a `var` container for each of the two variables, *radius* and *height*:

```
&pi;&centerdot;<var>radius</var><sup>2</sup>&centerdot;<var>height</var>
```

In Figure 2.14, you can see how the `var` containers affect the variables' appearance. The browser displays the variables with italics. Using italics for `var` elements is typical for all the major browsers.

The pizzeria web page displays this formula:

$$\pi \bullet radius^2 \bullet height$$

Because the 2 is a superscript, you should identify it as such by using a `sup` container. That's what the pizzeria web page does, and you can see the relevant code fragment several lines up.

Here's the last noteworthy item in the pizzeria web page. In the web page, do you see the boldfaced "Late night special:"? We want that label to be forceful, so we surround it with a `strong` container, like this:

```
<strong>Late night special:</strong>
```

## 2.21 CASE STUDY: A Local Hydroelectric Power Plant

This section adds another web page to our case study website. The web page describes hydropower produced at a small dam across the Kansas River at Lawrence, Kansas. **FIGURE 2.16** shows the desired result.

Let's partition the task of creating this page. The first five lines of HTML source code should be the same as they were in the previous web page. The `meta description` element should identify this chapter rather than the previous one, and the title element should provide an identifier that describes this page's particular content. That completes the `head` element.

The `body` begins with a `header` whose size is the same as the `header` of the previous web page. As you may recall, that was an `h2` element. Then comes the first text paragraph. Nothing special seems to be happening until we get to the italicized term in parentheses, (*Bowersock*). This is a defined item, whose definition is the preceding quoted string. Now look at the HTML source code in **FIGURE 2.17A**. What puts *Bowersock* in italics is the enclosing `dfn` element (not a deprecated `i` element).

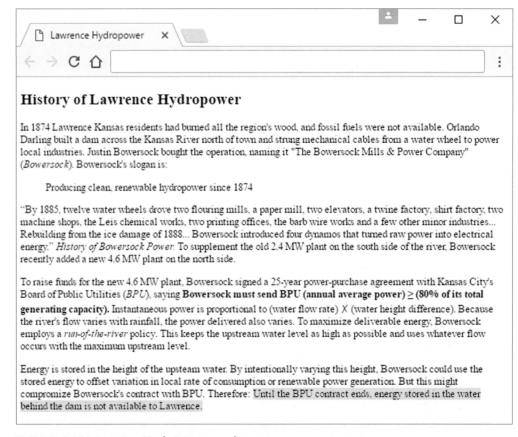

**FIGURE 2.16 Lawrence Hydropower web page**

```
<!DOCTYPE html>
<html lang="en">
<head>
<meta charset="utf-8">
<meta name="author"content=John Dean">
<title>Lawrence Hydropower</title>
</head>

<body>
<h2>History of Lawrence Hydropower</h2>
<p>
   In 1874 Lawrence Kansas residents had burned all the region's wood,and
   fossil fuels were not available. Orlando Darling built a dam across the
   Kansas River north of town and strung mechanical cables from a water
   wheel to power local industries. Justin Bowersock bought the operation,
   naming it "The Bowersock Mills & Power Company" (<dfn>Bowersock</dfn>).
   Bowersock's slogan is:
</p>
<blockquote cite="http://www.bowersockpower.com">
   Producing clean, renewable hydropower since 1874
</blockquote>
```

**FIGURE 2.17A Source code for Lawrence Hydropower web page**

Back in Figure 2.16, notice that Bowersock's slogan stands out because it has space around it. An easy way to get this effect is to use `blockquote` element. Since it's just a short string and the preceding colon indicates it's logically a continuation of the preceding paragraph, it's tempting to put it before that paragraph's closing `</p>`. But if you try that, the W3C Markup Validator will complain with the rather cryptic error message "No p element in scope but a p end tag seen." The problem is that because both `p` and `blockquote` are block elements, neither can fit inside the other. So the `blockquote` element should go after the first paragraph's closing `<\p>`.

In Figure 2.17A, also notice that the `blockquote` includes something that does not appear in the browser's presentation—a `cite` attribute. This hidden documentation tells future website maintainers where this (and other related) information might be found.

Back in Figure 2.16, the second paragraph begins with a long quotation, followed by an italicized title. What's going on here? The paragraph at the top of **FIGURE 2.17B** shows it's just an ordinary quotation followed by a citation identifying the source of that quotation. But this paragraph also has other features. In the HTML source code, the first instance of the abbreviation, MW, is contained in an `abbr` element, which includes a `title` attribute whose value is "megawatt." In some browsers, there is no initial indication of this documentation, but if you hover the mouse over this particular "MW" abbreviation, after a while a box will pop up and display the "megawatt" expansion of this abbreviation. This paragraph also contains another hidden feature: Enclosing the general term "recently" in a `time` element, whose `datetime` attribute specifies "recently" as May 10, 2013, documents the exact date of start of construction of the new plant.

In Figure 2.16's third paragraph, in the middle of the second line, notice the italicized term, *BPU*. Like the first paragraph's italicized *Bowersock*, this italicized *BPU* indicates a defined item, whose definition is the preceding string, "Board of Public Utilities." Shortly after the *BPU* definition, notice the bold-faced clause, **Bowersock ... capacity)**. Figure 2.17B shows this to be a

```
<p>
  <q>By 1885, twelve water wheels drove two flouring mills, a paper mill,
  two elevators, a twine factory, shirt factory, two machine shops, the
  Leis chemical works, two printing offices, the barb wire works and a
  few other minor industries... Rebuilding from the ice damage of 1888...
  Bowersock introduced four dynamos that turned raw power into electrical
  energy.</q> <cite>History of Bowersock Power.</cite> To supplement the
  old 2.4 <abbr title="megawatt">MW</abbr> plant on the south side of the
  river, Bowersock <time datetime="2013-05-10">recently</time> added a
  new 4.6 MW plant on the north side.
</p>
<p>
  To raise funds for the new 4.6 MW plant, Bowersock signed a 25-year
  power-purchase agreement with Kansas City's Board of Public Utilities
  (<dfn>BPU</dfn>), saying <strong>Bowersock must send BPU (annual
  average power) &ge; (80% of its total generating capacity).</strong>
  Instantaneous power is proportional to (water flow rate) &cross;
  (water height difference). Because the river's flow varies with
  rainfall, the power delivered also varies. To maximize deliverable
  energy, Bowersock employs a <em>run-of-the-river</em> policy. This
  keeps the upstream water level as high as possible and uses whatever
  flow occurs with the maximum upstream level.
</p>
<p>
  Energy is stored in the height of the upsteam water. By intentionally
  varying this height, Bowersock could use the stored energy to offset
  variation in local rate of consumption or renewable power generation.
  But this might compromize Bowersock's contract with BPU. Therefore:
  <mark>Until the BPU contract ends, energy stored in the water
  behind the dam is not available to Lawrence.</mark>
</p>
</body>
</html>
```

**FIGURE 2.17B Source code for Lawrence Hydropower web page**

strong element, and this strong element contains the embedded &ge; character reference for the ≥ symbol. The informal multiplication symbol on the next line is a &cross; character. Alternative multiplication symbols are 'X', 'x', '*', and the &centerdot; character. Near the end of Figure 2.16's third paragraph, notice the italicized term, *run-of-the-river*. Figure 2.17B shows that this emphasis comes from the em element, not the deprecated i element.

   In Figure 2.16's final paragraph, notice the highlighting of the last sentence. This indicates a caveat—a caution to remember while reading other material. Figure 2.17B's last text rows show how a mark element flags this warning.

# Review Questions

### 2.2 HTML Coding Conventions

1. Web browsers are strict in terms of forcing developers to write good code. True or false.

2. Who developed the original HTML Tidy tool? Name one person.

### 2.3 Comments

3. What is a browser engine?

4. What is documentation?

### 2.5 Content Model Categories

5. Using the Content model categories diagram, specify five categories that are completely inside the flow category.

### 2.6 Block Elements

6. Provide two characteristics of a block element.

### 2.7 blockquote Element

7. What are the typical default display properties for a blockquote element?

### 2.8 Whitespace Collapsing

8. What are three characters that are subject to whitespace collapsing?

### 2.11 Editing Elements

9. In the world of web programming, what does "presentation" mean?

### 2.12 q and cite Elements

10. What is the difference between a q element and a blockquote element?

### 2.14 Code-Related Elements

11. Times New Roman is an appropriate font for displaying code because it enables you to align similar types of things within your program. True or false.

### 2.15 br and wbr Elements

12. What does "wbr" stand for?

### 2.19 Character References

13. When you want to display a quote character (") on a web page, you should normally use the &quot; character reference. True or false.

# Exercises

1. [after Section 2.2] Why do companies like their programmers to follow standard coding conventions?

2. [after Section 2.2] What does Google's Style Guide have to say about trailing whitespace?

3. [after Section 2.3] Convert the following code so that it is compliant with HTML5 standards and also proper coding conventions. To ensure compliance with the HTML5 standards, I recommend that you enter your converted code into the W3C's HTML validation service. To ensure proper coding conventions, please carefully review the HTML5 coding conventions document.

```
<html>
<head>
<meta charset="utf-8">
<meta name="author" content="John Dean">
<title>Mock Trial How-To<title>
</head>

<body>
<H1>Mock Trial Opening Statements</H1>
<hr>
<strong><p>Prosecuting Attorney</strong>:<br>
Good morning, I am the prosecuting attorney, and I represent the
State. I will call three witnesses. At the conclusion of the case,
we will ask you to convict the defendant of the crime as charged,
thank you.
</p>
<p><strong>Defense Attorney</strong>:<br>
Ladies and Gentlemen of the jury, I intend to prove that my
client xxxxxx is innocent of the alleged murder of yyyyyy, and the
evidence presented by the prosecution is circumstantial.
</body>
```

4. [after Section 2.3] Suppose that your company requires you to include this copyright notice at the top of every one of your web pages:

   INVESTMENT INTELLIGENCE SYSTEMS CORP.
   THIS MATERIAL IS COPYRIGHTED AS AN UNPUBLISHED WORK UNDER
   SECTIONS 104 AND 408 OF TITLE 17 OF THE UNITED STATES CODE.
   UNAUTHORIZED USE, COPYING, OR OTHER REPRODUCTION IS PROHIBITED BY
   LAW.

Show an HTML5 comment container that includes this copyright notice. As always, use proper coding conventions. Note that the copyright notice is a comment and, as such, it should not display on your web pages.

5.  [after Section 2.5] This question gives you practice using the HTML5 language specification website to determine the permitted contents of elements. In your answers, specify one or more of the content model categories (such as "phrasing" or "flow"), or specify "empty."

    a)  What are the permitted contents of the `blockquote` element?

    b)  What are the permitted contents of the `br` element?

    c)  What are the permitted contents of the `q` element?

6.  [after Section 2.13] Provide an HTML5 code fragment for a paragraph element that displays this message:

    Attention Walmart shoppers:
    Christmas sales begin September 15 at 5 am, just in time for the holidays.

    You must provide code that enables JavaScript to understand the date and time. There is no need to provide the JavaScript code itself. For the date value, use the current year.

7.  [after Section 2.13] Provide an HTML5 code fragment for a paragraph element that describes a solid-state device (SSD). Your paragraph must include at least two sentences, and in those sentences, you must include the acronym SSD. You must use an element that indicates that SSD is an acronym and another element that indicates that SSD is a term that is being defined. In your paragraph, you must include a definition for SSD. You must provide code that generates a tooltip for the words that SSD stands for.

8.  [after Section 2.17] Using the `b`, `u`, and `i` elements is generally frowned upon. So why does the W3C include them in their HTML5 standard?

9.  [after Section 2.19] Provide a paragraph element that would render the following line. Use the browser's default font face (there is no need to specify a font). There are two spaces between the two sentences. Display both spaces.

    The ampersand symbol is "&."  The greater than or equal symbol is "≥."

10. [after Section 2.19] Provide an HTML code fragment that would render the quadratic equation as follows:

    $x = (-b \pm (b^2 - 4ac)^{\frac{1}{2}}) / 2a$

    Note:
    ▸  You don't have to provide a style container with your answer, but you should assume that the following style container appears at the top of your quadratic equation web page. It causes the entire web page to use monospace font.

```
<style>
  body {font-family: monospace;}
</style>
```

▶ To further the goal of describing your web page's content, you must surround each variable (*x*, *a*, *b*, and *c*) individually with proper tags.

▶ Insert single spaces on each side of the equals sign, at the left of the ± symbol, on each side of the minus sign, and on each side of the / sign. Do not insert spaces elsewhere.

▶ You don't need to worry about the equation being too long to fit on one line and exhibiting line wrap. That means you don't need to use   character references.

▶ In the preceding equation, note how ½ is one character, with the 1 on top of the /, not 1 at the left of the /.

# Project

Create a web page with a filename of pgmExplanation.html that explains something interesting about a program. Your explanation must make sense. You must use grammatically correct sentences that provide a reasonable flow through your web page. Creativity and aesthetics are part of web programming, and they are part of this assignment. Follow these guidelines:

▶ Include at least one heading (h1, h2, etc.) in your web page.

▶ Display a code fragment from the program, or display the whole program, if appropriate. Feel free to create the program yourself or use a program that you find in a book or on the Internet.

▶ Refer to a specific variable in the program, specific input, and specific output.

▶ Provide a quote from a book that refers to the program or to a concept illustrated by the program, and provide a citation for the book's title. Feel free to use a real quote from a real book or make up a fictional quote from a fictional book.

▶ Provide an acronym (real or made up) or a definition that somehow relates to the web page's discussion.

▶ Include a total of at least 10 different types of phrasing elements in your web page. You must use appropriate phrasing elements that fit the flow of your web page. You will lose points if any of your elements are inappropriate (e.g., using wbr in a normal-length word).

For future projects, you will use CSS for formatting. But for practice purposes, for this project, use only HTML5 elements and not CSS.

# CHAPTER 3

# Cascading Style Sheets (CSS)

## CHAPTER OBJECTIVES

- ▶ Understand the philosophy of how HTML and CSS should fit together.
- ▶ Know when to use the different selectors—type selectors, the universal selector, class selectors, ID selectors.
- ▶ Know the syntax for the different selectors.
- ▶ Apply CSS rules to the span and div elements.
- ▶ Understand the different cascading levels for CSS rules.
- ▶ Implement external CSS files.

- ▶ Understand the syntax and meaning of the color properties and their values.
- ▶ Understand the syntax and meaning of the font properties and their values.
- ▶ Understand the syntax and meaning of the text properties and their values.
- ▶ Understand the syntax and meaning of the border properties and their values.
- ▶ Understand the syntax and meaning of the padding and margin properties and their values.

## CHAPTER OUTLINE

## 3.1 Introduction

In the last chapter, we focused primarily on how to implement web page content. In this chapter, we focus on presentation of web page content. As you may recall, presentation refers to appearance and format. If you think appearance and format aren't all that important, think again. If your web page doesn't look good, people might go to it, but they'll leave quickly. An early exit might be OK if you're helping Grandma post her cat videos, but it's unacceptable for a business trying to generate revenue.

In this chapter, we start with an overview of Cascading Style Sheets (CSS) concepts and CSS basic syntax. We put those things into practice by applying CSS rules to various elements, including span and div elements. We show you how to position those rules (1) at the top of the web page's main file or (2) in an external file. In the second half of the chapter, we describe *CSS properties*. Properties are the hooks used to specify the appearance of the elements within a web page. Specifically, we introduce CSS properties for color, font, and line height. Also, we introduce CSS properties for borders, padding, and margins.

## 3.2 CSS Overview

The W3C's philosophy in terms of how HTML and CSS should fit together is (1) use HTML elements to specify a web page's content, and (2) use CSS to specify a web page's appearance. There are lots and lots of CSS properties that enable you to determine a web page's appearance. In this chapter, we'll cover quite a few of those properties, but not even close to all of them. When implementing a web page, if you need a particular format for an element and you can't find an appropriate CSS property in this book, don't give up right away. Search the Web for additional CSS properties to see if you can find one that suits your needs.

As you'll see shortly, and as you may recall from Figure 1.8's Kansas City Weather web page in Chapter 1, CSS code is normally separated from web page content code. Specifically, web page content code goes in the `body` container, whereas CSS code goes either at the top of the web page in the `head` container or in an external file. Why is that separation strategy a good thing? Because if you want to change the appearance of something, it's easy to find the CSS code—at the top of the web page or in an external file.

The current version of CSS is CSS3, and all major browsers support it. In 2009, the W3C started work on CSS4. There is no single, unified CSS4 specification. Instead, it's maintained as separate modules. Unfortunately, CSS4 is not fully supported by the major browsers yet. Thus, in this book, we stick with CSS3.

## 3.3 CSS Rules

The way CSS works is that CSS rules are applied to elements within a web page. Browsers determine which elements to apply the CSS rules to with the help of selectors. There are quite a few different types of selectors. For now, we'll introduce type selectors and the universal selector. Type selectors are very popular. The universal selector is not as popular, but it's important to understand it because you'll see it referred to on various websites, including the W3C's CSS website at https://www.w3.org/Style/CSS.

With a *type selector*, you use an element type (e.g., `hr`) to match all instances of that element type and then apply specified formatting features to those instances. For example, the following CSS rule uses a type selector with the `hr` element type and applies a width of 50% to all the `hr` elements in the current web page:

```
hr {width: 50%;}
```

A "width of 50%" means that for each `hr` element, its horizontal line will span 50% of the width of its enclosing container. Usually, but not always, the enclosing container will be the web page's `body` container.

Now for another type of selector—the universal selector. The *universal selector* uses the same syntax as the type selector, except that instead of specifying an element type, you specify `*`. The asterisk is a wildcard. In general, a *wildcard* is something that matches every item in a collection of things. For CSS selector rules, the `*` matches every element in a web page's collection of elements. Here's an example universal selector CSS rule that centers the text for every text-oriented element in the web page:

```
* {text-align: center;}
```

Even though the rule matches every element, because the property (`text-align`) deals with text, the rule affects only the elements that contain text.

## 3.4 Example with Type Selectors and the Universal Selector

Now let's look at a complete web page where we put into practice what's been covered so far in regard to CSS rules. Study the source code in **FIGURE 3.1**'s Tree Poem web page. Notice the three CSS rules inside the `style` container. The first two rules should look familiar because they were presented in the previous section. The third rule uses a type selector with a slightly different syntax than before—there's a comma between two element types, `h2` and `p`. If you want to apply the same formatting feature(s) to more than one type of element, you can implement that with one rule, where the element types appear at the left, as part of a comma-separated list.

In Figure 3.1's three CSS rules, notice the four property-value pairs inside the { }'s, and copied here for your convenience:

▶ `text-align: center`
▶ `width: 50%`
▶ `font-style: italic`
▶ `color: blue`

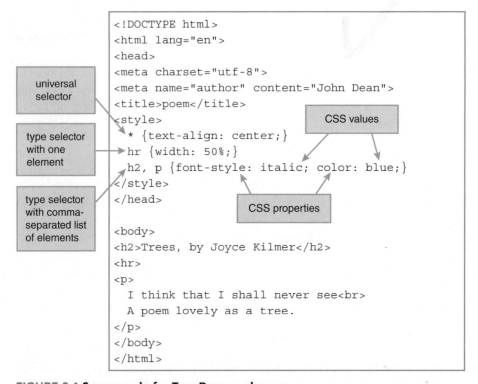

**FIGURE 3.1 Source code for Tree Poem web page**

FIGURE 3.2 **Tree Poem web page**

We'll cover those properties in detail later on, but for now, go ahead and guess what they are for and how they affect the appearance of the Tree Poem web page. After you've made your guess, take a look at the resulting web page in **FIGURE 3.2**.

In the Tree Poem web page, the `* {text-align: center;}` rule causes the elements that contain text to be centered. The `hr` element does not contain text, so it's not affected by the `textalign` property. Nonetheless, as you can see, it's also centered. That's because `hr` elements are centered by default.

The `hr {width: 50%;}` rule causes the horizontal line to render with a width that's 50% of the web page `body`'s width.

Finally, the `h2, p {font-style: italic; color: blue;}` rule causes the heading and paragraph elements to be italicized and blue.

# 3.5 CSS Syntax and Style

## CSS Syntax

In this section, we address CSS syntax details. First—the syntax for the `style` container. Refer back to Figure 3.1 and note how the three CSS rules are enclosed in a `style` container. Here's the relevant code:

```
<style>
  * {text-align: center;}
  hr {width: 50%;}
  h2, p {font-style: italic; color: blue;}
</style>
```

If you go back to the figure, you can see the `style` container positioned at the bottom of the web page's `head` container. It's legal to position it in the `body` container, but don't do it. Coding conventions suggest positioning it at the bottom of the web page's `head` container. By following that convention, other web developers will be able to find your CSS rules quickly.

In the `style` start tag, it's legal to include a `type` attribute with a value of `"text/css"`, like this:

```
<style type="text/css">
```

In the Tree Poem web page, you can see that the `type` attribute is omitted. Currently, `text/css` is the only legal value for the `type` attribute, and it's the default value for the `type` attribute. So why did the HTML designers include a `type` attribute at all if there's only one type? They wanted to leave open the possibility of having different `style` types in the future. Google's Style Guide, which covers both HTML and CSS, recommends that you reduce the size of your web page file by omitting the `type` attribute, and we follow that convention in this book.

## CSS Style

Now we'll look at some CSS guidelines that are not enforced by browsers or the HTML5 standard. They are style guidelines, and you should follow them so your code is easy to understand and maintain.

For short CSS rules, use this format:

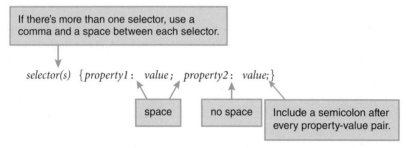

Remember in Chapter 2 when we introduced block formatting for multi-line container elements? That's where the start tag and end tag are aligned at the left, and interior lines are indented. Block formatting for CSS rules is similar in that the first and last lines are aligned at the left, and interior lines are indented. If you have a CSS rule that's kind of long (at least two or three property-value pairs), you should use block formatting like this:

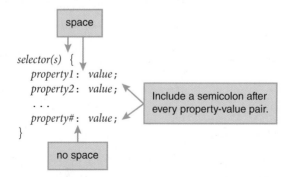

With both short and long CSS rules, the W3C CSS standard allows you to omit the semicolon after the last property-value pair. However, coding conventions suggest that you should not omit the last semicolon—you should include it. That way, if another property-value pair is added later on, there will be less likelihood of accidentally forgetting to add a semicolon in front of the new property-value pair.

## 3.6 Class Selectors

### Class Selector Overview

So far, we've talked about type selectors and the universal selector. We're now going to talk about a third type of CSS selector—a *class selector*. Let's jump right into an example. Here's a class selector rule with .red for its class selector and a background tomato color for matched elements:

```
.red {background-color: tomato;}
```
class selector

The dot thing (.red in this example) is called a class selector because its purpose is to <u>select</u> elements that have a particular value for their <u>class</u> attribute. So the class selector rule would select/match the following element because it has a class attribute with a value of red:

```
<q class="red">It is better to keep your mouth closed and let people
    think you are a fool than to open it and remove all doubt.</q>
```

In applying the class selector rule to this element, the quote gets displayed with a tomato background color.

As with type selectors, you can have more than one class selector share one CSS rule. Just separate the selectors with commas and spaces, like this:

```
.red, .conspicuous, h1 {background-color: tomato;}
```

Note that in addition to a second class selector (.conspicuous), there's also a type selector (h1). In a single CSS rule, you can have as many comma-separated selectors as you like, all sharing the same set of property-value pairs.

With a type selector, your selector name (h1 in the this example) comes from the set of predefined HTML element names. But for a class selector, you make up the selector name. When you make up the selector name, make it descriptive, as is the case for red and conspicuous in the preceding example. As an alternative for red, you could get even more descriptive and use tomato. If you use tomato, that will be the same as the name used by the property value. There isn't anything wrong with that. Consistency is good.

Now let's look at class selectors in the context of a complete web page. In **FIGURE 3.3**, note the three CSS rules with their class selectors .red, .white, and .blue. Then take a look at the three q elements and their class attribute clauses class="red", class="white", and class="blue". Try to figure out what the web page will display before moving on to the next paragraph.

In Figure 3.3, the first q element has a class attribute value of red, which means the .red CSS rule applies. That causes the browser to display the first q element with a tomato-colored

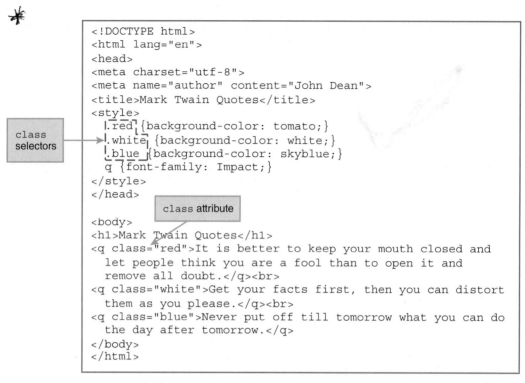

```
<!DOCTYPE html>
<html lang="en">
<head>
<meta charset="utf-8">
<meta name="author" content="John Dean">
<title>Mark Twain Quotes</title>
<style>
  .red {background-color: tomato;}
  .white {background-color: white;}
  .blue {background-color: skyblue;}
  q {font-family: Impact;}
</style>
</head>

<body>
<h1>Mark Twain Quotes</h1>
<q class="red">It is better to keep your mouth closed and
  let people think you are a fool than to open it and
  remove all doubt.</q><br>
<q class="white">Get your facts first, then you can distort
  them as you please.</q><br>
<q class="blue">Never put off till tomorrow what you can do
  the day after tomorrow.</q>
</body>
</html>
```

class selectors

class attribute

**FIGURE 3.3 Source code for Mark Twain Quotes web page**

background. I used a standard red background initially, but I found that the black text didn't show up very well. Thus, I chose tomato red, since it's lighter, and the color reminds me of my cherished home-grown tomatoes. Moral of the story: Get used to trying things out, viewing the result, and changing your code if appropriate.

The second and third q elements have class attribute values of white and blue. As you can see from the source code, that means they get matched with the .white and .blue class selector rules, and they get rendered with white and skyblue backgrounds, respectively. Take a look at **FIGURE 3.4** and note the red, white, and blue background colors for the three quotes.

In addition to the three class selector rules, the Mark Twain Quotes web page also has a type selector rule, q {font-family: Impact;}. We'll discuss the font-family property later in this chapter, but for now, look at the Mark Twain quotes web page and observe the thick block lettering for the three q elements. That lettering is from the Impact font.

Usually, browsers use a default background color of white, so why did we specify white for the second q element's background color? One benefit is that it's a form of self-documentation. Another benefit is that it would handle a rogue browser with a nonwhite default background color. With such a browser, if there were no explicit CSS rule for the white background color, then the user would see red, nonwhite, and blue. That isn't very patriotic for an American folk hero's quotes.

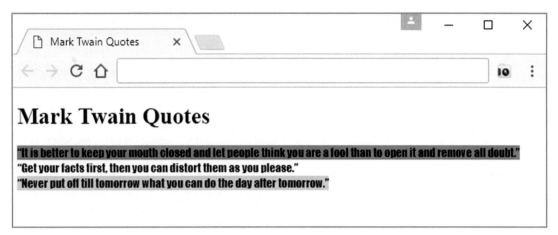

FIGURE 3.4 **Mark Twain Quotes web page**

## `class` Selectors with Element Type Prefixes

Let's now discuss a specialized type of class selector—a class selector with an element type prefix. Here's the syntax:

*element-type* . *class-value* {*property1* : *value* ; *property2* : *value;*}

And here's an example CSS rule that uses a class selector with an element type prefix:

```
q.blue {background-color: skyblue;}
```

Because `q.blue` has `.blue` in it, `q.blue` matches elements that have a `class` attribute value of `"blue"`. But it's more granular than a standard class selector in that it looks for `class="blue"` only in q elements.

**FIGURE 3.5** shows a modified version of the `style` container for the Mark Twain Quotes web page. It uses four class selectors with element type prefixes. How will that code change the appearance of the web page, compared to what's shown in Figure 3.4? The original `style` container used the simple class selector rule `.blue {background-color: skyblue;}`. That caused all elements with `class="blue"` to use the CSS color named `skyblue`. But suppose

```
<style>
  h1.blue {color: blue;}
  q.red {background-color: tomato;}
  q.white {background-color: white;}
  q.blue {background-color: skyblue;}
  q {font-family: Impact;}
</style>
```

FIGURE 3.5 **Improved style container for Mark Twain Quotes web page**

you want a different shade of blue for the "Mark Twain Quotes" header. You could use a distinct class attribute value for the header, like "header-blue," but having such a specific class attribute value would be considered poor style because it would lead to code that is harder to maintain. Specifically, it would be hard to remember a rather obscure name like "header-blue." So, what's the better approach? As shown in Figure 3.5, it's better to use separate h1.blue and q.blue class selectors with element type prefixes. Note how the h1.blue rule specifies a background color of blue, and the q.blue rule specifies a background color of skyblue.

Figure 3.5's style container uses a class selector with an element prefix, q.red, whereas the original style container used a simple class selector, .red. Because there's only one element that uses class="red", the .red class selector was sufficient by itself; however, using q.red (and also q.white) makes the code parallel for the three q element colors. More importantly, using a class selector with an element prefix makes the code more maintainable. *Maintainable* code is code that is relatively easy to make changes to in the future. For example, suppose you decide later that you want a different shade of red for an h2 element. You can do that by using q.red and h2.red.

## Class Selectors with * Prefixes

Instead of prefacing a class selector with an element type, as an alternative, you can preface a class selector with an *. Because * is the universal selector, it matches all elements. Therefore, the following CSS rule is equivalent to a standard class selector rule (with no prefix):

*.*class-value* {*property1*: *value*; *property2*: *value*;}

So what would the following CSS rule do?

*.big-warning {font-size: x-large; color: red;}

It would match all elements in the web page that have a class attribute value of big-warning, and it would display those elements with extra-large red font.

In the preceding CSS rule, note the hyphen in the *.big-warning class selector rule. The HTML5 standard does not allow spaces within class attribute values, so it would have been illegal to use *.big warning. If you want to use multiple words for a class attribute value, coding conventions suggest that you use hyphens to separate the words, as in big-warning.

CSS property names and CSS property values are built into the browser engine, so their naming is not subject to the discretion of web developers. Nonetheless, it's still good to know their naming conventions so it's easier to remember how to spell them. CSS property names follow the same coding convention as developer-defined class attribute values—if there are multiple words, use hyphens to separate the words (e.g., font-size). CSS property values usually follow the same use-hyphens-to-separate-multiple-words coding convention (e.g., x-large in the preceding code fragment). But sometimes nothing separates the words (e.g., skyblue in the Mark Twain Quotes web page).

# 3.7 **ID Selectors**

It's time for another type of selector—an ID selector. An ID selector is similar to a class selector in that it relies on an element attribute value in searching for element matches. As you might guess, an ID selector uses an element's `id` attribute (as opposed to a class selector, which uses an element's `class` attribute). A significant feature of an `id` attribute is that its value must be unique within a particular web page. That's different from a `class` attribute's value, which does not have to be unique within a particular web page. The ID selector's unique-value feature means that an ID selector's CSS rule matches only one element on a web page. This single-element matching mechanism is particularly helpful with links and with JavaScript, but we won't get to those things until later in the book. So why introduce the ID selector now instead of waiting for the links and JavaScript chapters? Because ID selectors are an important part of CSS.

Suppose you want the user to be able to link/jump to the "Lizard's Lounge" section of your web page. To do that, you'd need a link element (which we'll discuss in a later chapter) and also an element that serves as the target of the link. Here's a heading element that could serve as the target of the link:

```
<h3 id="lizards-lounge">Lizards Lounge</h3>
```

In this code, note the `id` attribute. The link element (not shown) would use the `id` attribute's value to indicate which element the user jumps to when the user clicks the link. For the jump to work, there must be no confusion as to which element to jump to. That means the target element must be unique. Using an `id` attribute ensures that the target element is unique.

Now that you have a rudimentary understanding of links and a motivation for using the `id` attribute, let's examine how to apply CSS formatting to an element with an `id` attribute. As always with CSS, you need a CSS rule. To match an element with an `id` attribute, you need an ID selector rule, and here's the syntax:

*#id-value* { *property1*:  *value*;  *property2*:  *value*; }

⌐— ID selector

The syntax is the same as for a class selector rule, except that you use a pound sign (#) instead of a dot (.), and you use an `id` attribute value instead of a `class` attribute value.

Remember the Lizard's Lounge heading element shown earlier? How would the following ID selector rule affect the appearance of the Lizard's Lounge heading?

```
#lizards-lounge {color: green;}
```

This rule would cause browsers to display the Lizards Lounge heading with green font.

Note the spelling of `lizards-lounge`. If you want to use multiple words for an `id` attribute value, the HTML5 standard states that it's illegal to use space characters to separate the words. Coding conventions suggest that you use hyphens to separate the words. That should sound familiar—`class` attribute values also use hyphens to separate words.

## 3.8 `span` and `div` Elements

So far, we've discussed different types of selectors—type selectors, the universal selector, class selectors, and ID selectors. No matter which selector you choose, you can apply it only if there's an element in the web page body that matches it. But suppose you want to apply CSS to text that doesn't coincide with any of the HTML5 elements. What should you do?

If you want to apply CSS to text that doesn't coincide with any of the HTML5 elements, put the text in a `span` element or a `div` element. If you want the affected text embedded within surrounding text, use `span` (since `span` is a phrasing element). On the other hand, if you want the text to span the width of its enclosing container, use `div` (since `div` is a block element).

See **FIGURE 3.6** and note how the `div` and `span` elements surround text that doesn't fit very well with other elements. Specifically, the `div` element surrounds several advertising phrases that describe Parkville's world-famous Halloween on the River celebration, and the two `span` elements surround the two costs, $10 and $15. None of those things (a group of advertising phrases,

a cost, and another cost) corresponds to any of the standard HTML elements, so `div` and `span` are the way to go if you want to apply CSS formatting.

The `div` and `span` elements are generic elements in that they don't provide any special meaning when they're used by themselves. They are simply placeholders to which CSS is applied. Think of `div` and `span` as vanilla ice cream and CSS as the various toppings you can add to the ice cream, such as chocolate chips, mint flavoring, and Oreos. Yummm!

In Figure 3.6, note the `span` element's `class` attribute, copied here for your convenience:

```
<span class="white orange-background">$10</span>
```

In particular, note that there are two class selectors for the `class` attribute's value—`white` and `orangebackground`. As you'd expect, that means that both the `white` and `orangebackground` CSS rules get applied to the `span` element's content. Note that the two class selectors are separated with spaces. The delimiter spaces are required whenever you have multiple `class` selectors for one `class` attribute.

In the Pumpkin Patch web page, there are competing CSS rules for the two costs, $10 and $15. The `div` container surrounds the entire web page body, so it surrounds both costs, and it attempts to apply its orange text rule to both costs.[1] The first `span` container surrounds the first cost; consequently, the first `span` container attempts to apply its white text rule to the first cost. Likewise, the second `span` container surrounds the second cost; consequently, the second `span` container attempts to apply its black text rule to the second cost. So, what colors are used for the `span` text—white and black from the `span` containers or orange from the `div` container? As you can see in **FIGURE 3.7**'s browser window, the "$10" cost text is white, and the

---

[1] The "attempt to apply its orange text rule to both costs" is due to inheritance. We'll introduce CSS inheritance formally in the next chapter.

"\$15" cost text is black. That means that the more local CSS rules (the two span rules) take pre-
cedence over the more global CSS rule (the div rule). The span rules are considered to be more
*local* because their start and end tags immediately surround the cost content. In other words, their
tags surround only their cost content and no other content. The div rule is considered to be more
*global* because its start and end tags do not immediately surround the cost content. In other words,

```
<!DOCTYPE html>
<html lang="en">
<head>
<meta charset="utf-8">
<meta name="author" content="John Dean">
<title>Halloween on the River</title>
<style>
  .orange {color: darkorange;}
  .white {color: white;}
  .black {color: black;}
  .orange-background {background-color: orange;}
</style>
</head>

<body>
<div class="orange">
   Parkville's Halloween on the River, every weekend in October.<br>
   Corn maze: <span class="white orange-background">$10</span><br>
   All you can eat pumpkins:
   <span class="black orange-background">$15</span>
</div>
</body>
</html>
```

div

span

Multiple class selectors for
a class attribute's value.

**FIGURE 3.6 Source code for Pumpkin Patch web page**

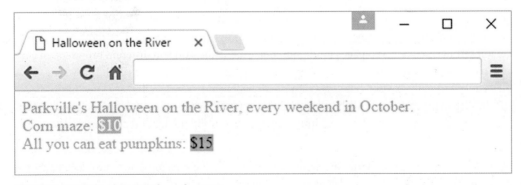

**FIGURE 3.7 Pumpkin Patch web page**

their tags surround not only the cost content, but also additional content. This *principle of locality*, where local things override global things, parallels the nature of the "cascading" that takes place in applying CSS rules. We'll discuss that concept in the next section.

# 3.9 Cascading

Have you wondered about the significance of the words in "Cascading Style Sheets"? Traditionally, a "style sheet" is a collection of rules that assign appearance properties to structural elements in a document. For a web page, a style sheet "rule" refers to a value assigned to a particular display property of a particular HTML element. The "cascading" part of Cascading Style Sheets is the subject of this section. If you look up the word "cascade" online or in a dictionary,[2] you'll see something like "a series of stages in a process." Likewise, CSS uses a series of stages. More specifically, there are different stages/places where CSS rules can be defined. Each stage/place has its own set of rules, and each set of rules is referred to as a style sheet. With multiple style sheets organized in a staged structure, together it's referred to as Cascading Style Sheets.

To handle the possibility of conflicting rules at different places, different priorities are given to the different places. See **FIGURE 3.8**, which shows the places where CSS rules can be defined. The higher priority places are at the top, so an element's `style` attribute (shown at the top of the CSS rules list) has the highest priority. We'll explain the `style` attribute in the next section, but let's first do a cursory run-through of the other items in Figure 3.8's list.

Figure 3.8 shows that the second place for CSS rules is in a `style` container. That placement should sound familiar because we've been using `style` containers for all the prior CSS examples. The next place for CSS rules is in an external file. We'll discuss external files later in this chapter.

The next place for CSS rules is in the settings defined by a user for a particular browser installation. We won't discuss that technique because there's nothing for you, the programmer, to learn or to do. Instead, the user may choose the settings he or she is interested in. If you'd like to learn how to choose the settings, you're on your own, and be aware that different browsers have different interfaces for adjusting their settings.

The last place for CSS rules, and the place with the lowest priority, is in the native default settings for the browser that's being used. As a programmer, there's nothing you can do to modify a browser's native default settings. But you should be aware of those default settings so you know what to expect when none of the first four cascading techniques is employed. In Chapter 2, we described "typical default display properties" for each HTML element presented. Those properties come from the major browsers' native default settings. Different browsers can have different default settings, so your web pages might not look exactly the same on different browsers. In general, try not to rely on browser defaults because it's hard to gauge the whims of the browser gods as they churn out new browser versions (with possibly new browser defaults) at a precipitous pace.

In displaying an element, a browser will check for CSS rules that match the element, starting the search at the top of the cascading CSS rules list in Figure 3.8 and continuing the search

---

[2] A *dictionary* was an ancient form of communication, used as a means to record word definitions. The definitions appeared on thin sheets of compressed wood fiber.

| Places Where CSS Rules Can Be Defined, Highest to Lowest Priority |
|---|
| 1. In an element's `style` attribute. |
| 2. In a `style` element in the web page's head section. |
| 3. In an external file. |
| 4. In the settings defined by a user for a particular browser installation. |
| 5. In the browser's native default settings. |

**FIGURE 3.8 Places where CSS rules can be defined**

down the list, as necessary. When there is a CSS rule match, the CSS rule's properties will be applied to the element, and the search down the list stops for those properties.

# 3.10 `style` Attribute, `style` Container

## `style` Attribute

The `style` attribute is at the top of Figure 3.8's cascading CSS rules list; as such, when you use the `style` attribute for CSS rules, those rules are given the highest priority. Here's an example element that uses a `style` attribute:

```
<h2 style="text-decoration:underline;">Welcome!</h2>
```

As you can see, using the `style` attribute lets you insert CSS property-value pairs directly in the code for an individual element. So the preceding h2 element—but no other h2 elements—would be rendered with an underline.

The `style` attribute is a *global attribute*, which means it can be used with any element. Even though it's legal to use it with every element, and you'll see it used in lots of legacy code, you should avoid using it in your pages. Why? Because it defeats the purpose of CSS—keeping presentation separate from content.

Let's imagine a scenario that demonstrates why the `style` attribute is bad. Suppose you embed a `style` attribute in each of your p elements so they display their first lines with an indentation (later on, you'll learn how to do that with the `text-indent` property). If you want to change the indentation width, you'd have to edit every p element. On the other hand, making such a change is much easier when the CSS code is at the top of the page in the head container because you only have to make the change in one place—in the p element's class selector rule. If you make the change there, it affects the entire web page.

Using the `style` attribute used to be referred to as "inline styles," but the W3C no longer uses that term, and we won't use it either. However, you should recognize the term "inline styles" because you'll hear it being used every now and then.

### `style` **Container**

As you know from prior examples, the `style` element is a container for CSS rules that apply to the entire current web page. The browser applies the CSS rules' property values by matching the CSS rules' selectors with elements in the web page. Normally, you should have just one `style` container per page, and you should put it in a web page's `head` container. It's legal to put a `style` container in the `body`, but don't do it because then it's harder to find the CSS rules.

In Figure 3.8's cascading CSS rules list, note how the higher priority places are more specific. More specific rules beat more general rules. For example, if a `style` attribute designates a paragraph as blue, but a rule in a `style` container designates paragraphs as red, then what color will the browser use to render the paragraph? The `style` attribute's blue color wins, and the browser renders that particular paragraph with blue text. This principle of more specific rules beating more general rules should sound familiar. It parallels the principle introduced earlier that says local things override global things.

## 3.11 External CSS Files

### Overview

In general, splitting up a big thing into smaller parts makes the thing easier to understand. To improve understandability, you should consider moving your CSS rules to an external file. There are two steps necessary to tie a web page to an external file that contains CSS rules. First, for the external file to be recognized as a CSS file, the external file must be named with a `.css` extension. For example, in an upcoming web page, we'll use the filename `pumpkinPatch.css`. Second, for the web page to access a CSS file's CSS rules, the web page must use a `link` element in the web page's `head` container. The `link` element is a void element, so it's comprised of just one tag, with no end tag. Here's the syntax:

```
<link rel="stylesheet" href="name-of-external-file">
```

In this code fragment, note the `href="name-of-external-file"` attribute-value pair. The W3C does not specify what `href` stands for, but the most common belief is that it stands for "hypertext reference." The `href` attribute's value specifies the name of the file that holds the CSS rules (e.g., `pumpkinPatch.css`).

Note the `rel="stylesheet"` attribute-value pair. `rel` stands for "relationship," and its value tells the browser engine what to do with the `href` file. Having a `rel` value of `stylesheet` tells the browser engine to look for CSS rules in the `href` file and apply them to the current web page.

To justify the extra work of adding a `link` element to handle an external CSS file, typically an external CSS file will be nontrivial. That means the file will contain at least five CSS rules (usually a lot more), or it will be shared by more than one web page.

Why is sharing an external CSS file helpful? With a shared external CSS file, it's easy to ensure that all the web pages on your site follow the same common CSS rules. And if you want to change those rules, you change them in one place, in the external file, and the change affects all the web pages that share the external file.

External CSS files used to be referred to as "external style sheets," but the W3C no longer uses that term, and we won't use it either. However, you should recognize the term "external style sheets" because you'll hear it being used every now and then.

## Example

Let's put what you've learned into practice by examining the source code for a modified version of the Pumpkin Patch web page—a version that uses an external CSS file instead of a `style` container. See **FIGURE 3.9**, which shows the `head` container for the modified Pumpkin Patch web page. Note that there's no `style` container; instead there's a `link` element that connects to an external CSS file.

See **FIGURE 3.10**. It shows the source code for the `pumpkinPatch.css` external CSS file, which gets loaded into the new Pumpkin Patch web page. The external CSS file's CSS rules are identical to those found in the original Pumpkin Patch web page, so, as you'd expect, there is no difference in how the two web pages render.

Normally, external CSS files are rather sparse. They include CSS rules, with blank lines to separate logical groups of rules, and that's pretty much it. Optionally, you can include comments to explain nonintuitive characteristics of the CSS file. In the previous chapters, you've learned to include a `meta author` element at the top of your HTML files, so other people in your company know whom to go to when questions arise. Likewise, for each external CSS file, you should include a comment at the top that shows the author's name. Here's an example author's-name comment, copied from the top of the `pumpkinPatch.css` source code:

```
/* John Dean */
```

```
<head>
<meta charset="utf-8">
<meta name="author" content="John Dean">
<title>Halloween on the River</title>
<link rel="stylesheet" href="pumpkinPatch.css">
</head>
```
This `link` element connects the web page to its external CSS file.

**FIGURE 3.9** `head` **container for the Pumpkin Patch web page that uses an external CSS file**

```
/* John Dean */
.orange {color: darkorange;}
.white {color: white;}
.black {color: black;}
.orange-background {background-color: orange;}
```
CSS comment

**FIGURE 3.10 Source code for external CSS file that gets loaded into the Pumpkin Patch web page**

Note the comment syntax. You must start with a /* and end with a */.

If you have a long comment, you should have the comment span several lines, like this:

```
/* The following rules are for a CSS image sprite that enables hover
   effects for the navigation bar at the left. */
```

This comment mentions a "CSS image sprite." We'll describe them in detail later in the book, but for now, just realize that a CSS image sprite is a rather complicated coding construct that requires CSS rules that are nonintuitive. Thus, it provides a good example of something where a CSS comment is appropriate.

## CSS Validation Service

Remember the HTML validation service mentioned in Chapter 1? It's a great tool for verifying that the code in an HTML file comports with the W3C's HTML standard. Likewise, there's a *CSS validation service* tool for verifying that the code in an external CSS file comports with the W3C's CSS standard. You can find the CSS validation service at https://jigsaw.w3.org/css-validator. See **FIGURE 3.11** for a screenshot of the CSS validation service's home page. We'll discuss home pages in more depth in a later chapter, but for now, just know that a *home page* is the default first page a user sees when the user visits a website.

In Figure 3.11, note the CSS validation service's three tabs. With the first tab, **By URI**, the user enters a web address for the external file that is to be checked. For that to work, you need the web

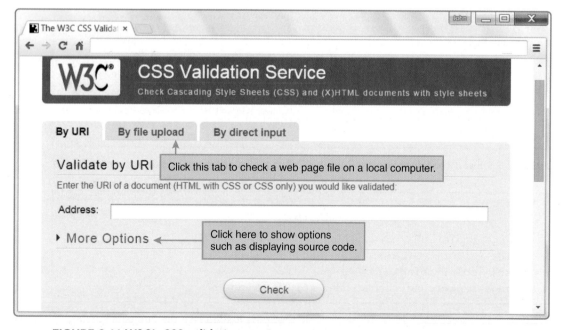

**FIGURE 3.11 W3C's CSS validation service**

page to be uploaded to a web server. With the second option, **By file upload**, the user selects a file on his or her local computer. With the third option, **By direct input**, the user copies HTML code directly into a large text box. Usually, you will use the second option, **By file upload**, because it's a good idea to test a file stored locally before uploading it.

We recommend that you use the CSS validation service to check all your external CSS files. Go ahead and try it out now on the Pumpkin Patch external CSS file. Specifically, retrieve the `pumpkinPatch.css` file from the book's resource center and save it to your hard disk or to a flash drive. Alternatively, you can create the file yourself by loading an IDE, opening a new file, copying Figure 3.10's code into the file, and saving the file with the name `pumpkinPatch.css`. After saving the file, go to the CSS validation service and click the **By file upload** tab. In the **Local CSS file** box, search for and select the `pumpkinPatch.css` file. Click the **Check** button, and that should generate a message indicating success.

## 3.12 **CSS Properties**

For the remainder of this chapter, we'll focus on CSS properties. As you know from prior examples, a CSS property specifies one aspect of an HTML element's appearance. The W3C's CSS3 standard provides many CSS properties (more than a hundred), so there is great flexibility in terms of specifying appearances. Remembering all those properties and the types of values associated with them can be daunting. Unless you've got the memory of a sea lion,[3] you'll probably need to use a CSS reference and look things up every now and then.

The W3C and the WHATWG have CSS references, but, unfortunately, they're rather disjointed, which can make them difficult to navigate. The Mozilla Developer Network has a more user-friendly CSS reference at https://developer.mozilla.org/en-US/docs/Web/CSS /Reference. Take a look at **FIGURE 3.12**, which shows the keyword index part of the reference. Keywords are the words that form the syntax of a language, so the figure's keyword index shows the words that form the CSS language. Note the first keyword entry, `:active`. The keywords that start with a colon are known as pseudo-elements (we'll describe a few of them in later chapters). The non-colonated[4] words are properties. To get details on any of the keywords, click on the keyword. Time for a short field trip: Go to Mozilla's CSS reference and click on the `font-size` property. That takes you to a page with details about the `font-size` property.

We'll discuss quite a few of the CSS properties later in the book, but for this chapter, we'll limit our discussion to the properties shown in **FIGURE 3.13**. Those properties fall into five property groups—color, font, text, border, and margin/padding. We'll discuss the properties in those groups in the upcoming sections.

---

[3] James Randerson, "Sea Lion Scores Top for Memory," *New Scientist*, October 23, 2003, https://www .newscientist.com/article/dn2960-sea-lion-scores-top-for-memory.
[4] "Colonated" isn't a word, but it should be. When the *Oxford English Dictionary* folks get around to approving my word submission, colonated will mean "something that has a colon."

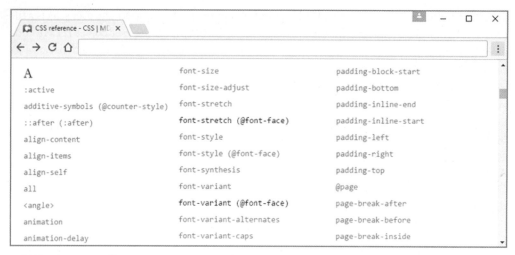

**FIGURE 3.12 Mozilla's CSS properties reference**

| Color properties | `color, background color` |
|---|---|
| Font properties | `font-style, font-variant, font-weight, font-size, font-family, font` |
| Text properties | `line-height, text-align, text-decoration, text-transform, text-indent` |
| Border properties | `border-bottom, border-bottom-color, ...` |
| Margin and padding properties | `margin-bottom, margin-left, ...`<br>`padding-bottom, padding-left, ...` |

**FIGURE 3.13 CSS properties introduced in this chapter**

Note: Ellipses are used here because there are too many border, margin, and padding properties to show in this figure.

## 3.13 Color Properties

In Figure 3.13, you can see two color properties—`color` and `background-color`. The `color` property specifies the color of an element's text. The `background-color` property specifies the background color of an element. The color properties are pretty straightforward, right? It's the *values* for the color properties that require more attention.

There's quite a bit of flexibility when it comes to specifying color values. You can specify a color value using one of five different formats. We'll describe the formats in detail, but first, here's a teaser of what you can look forward to:

color name—for example, red
RGB value—specifies amounts of red, green, and blue

RGBA value—specifies red, green, and blue, plus amount of opacity
HSL value—specifies amounts of hue, saturation, and lightness
HSLA value—specifies hue, saturation, and lightness, plus amount of opacity

## Color Names

The CSS3 specification defines 147 color names, and the major browsers support all those colors. To view the color names and their associated colors, go to https://www.w3.org/TR/css3-color/#svg-color. On that web page, you should recognize a few of the color names, like `orange` and `darkorange`, from previous web page examples in this book. An example of a more obscure color name is `darkslategray`. Note how we use `darkslategray` in this code fragment's class selector rule:

```
<head>
<style>
  .roofColor {color: darkslategray;}
</style>
</head>
                        ↑
                  ┌───────────────┐
                  │  color name   │
                  └───────────────┘
<body>
<p>
  Mackay Hall's roof is
  <span class="roofColor">dark slate gray</span>.
</p>
</body>
```

# 3.14 RGB Values for Color

RGB stands for red, green, and blue. An RGB value specifies the amounts of red, green, and blue that mix together to form the displayed color. To specify an amount of a color, you can use a percentage, an integer, or a hexadecimal number (we'll explain hexadecimal shortly). We'll provide explanations and examples coming up, but for now, here are the allowable ranges for each technique:

percentage—0% to 100% for each color
integer—0 to 255 for each color
hexadecimal—00 to ff for each color

## RGB Values with Percentages

To specify an RGB value with percentages, use this format:

`rgb(`*red-percent*`,` *green-percent*`,` *blue-percent*`)`

Each percent value must be between 0% and 100%. Here's an example class selector rule that uses an RGB value with percentages:

```
<style>
  .eggplant {background-color: rgb(52%,20%,45%);}
</style>
```

What background color does the preceding rule generate? 20% for the second value means that there is very little green in the color mixture. 52% for the first value means that there is a significant amount of red—52% of the maximum amount of red. 45% for the third value means that there is a bit less blue than there is red. Mixing approximately 50% red, approximately 50% blue, and not much green leads to this dark purple color:

Eggplants are dark purple, and that's why we use `eggplant` in the preceding class selector rule.

If you want to specify black, then you need to use the least intensity (a value of `0%`) for each of the three colors. That should make sense because, as any physics major will tell you, black is the absence of all light. Therefore, here's the CSS rule for a black background:

```
.black {background-color: rgb(0%,0%,0%);}
```

To specify white, you need to use the greatest intensity (a value of `100%`) for each of the three colors. That should make sense because white is the combination of all colors.[5] Therefore, here's the CSS rule for white text (which would work nicely with the preceding black background):

```
.white {color: rgb(100%,100%,100%);}
```

## RGB Values with Integers

To specify an RGB value with integers, use this format:

rgb (*red-integer*, *green-integer*, *blue-integer*)

Each integer value must be between 0 and 255, with 0 providing the least intensity and 255 providing the most. Here are two class selector rules that use RGB values with integers:

```
<style>
  .favorite1 {color: rgb(144,238,144);}
  .favorite2 {color: rgb(127,127,127);}
</style>
```

What text color does the `favorite1` class selector rule produce? The larger value, 238, is for green, so it produces a shade of green. The red and blue color values are 144, which is more than halfway to the maximum value of 255. That means the green color will be closer to white than black. The result is a light green. By the way, if you go to the W3C's CSS color names web page, you can find a `lightgreen` color name, and you can see that it matches the preceding `rgb(144,238,144)` value.

What text color does the `favorite2` class selector rule produce? All three color values (127, 127, 127) are the same, so it produces a color somewhere between white and black. Since 127 is halfway to the maximum value of 255, `favorite2` produces a medium gray color.

---

[5] In 1666, Isaac Newton discovered that white light is composed of all the colors in the color spectrum. He showed that when white light passes through a triangular prism, it separates into different colors. And when the resulting colors pass through a second triangular prism, they are recombined to form the original white light.

## RGB Values with Hexadecimal

With many programming languages, including HTML and CSS, numbers can be represented not only with base-10 decimal numbers, but also with base-16 hexadecimal (hex) numbers. A number system's "base" indicates the number of unique symbols in the number system. So base 10 (for the decimal number system) means there are 10 unique symbols—0, 1, 2, 3, 4, 5, 6, 7, 8, and 9. And base 16 (for the hexadecimal number system) means there are 16 unique symbols—0, 1, 2, 3, 4, 5, 6, 7, 8, 9, A, B, C, D, E, and F.

When specifying an RGB color value, you have choices. You can use percentages or standard integers as described earlier, or you can use hexadecimal values. For hexadecimal RGB values, you'll need to use the format #rrggbb where:

rr = two hexadecimal digits that specify the amount of red
gg = two hexadecimal digits that specify the amount of green
bb = two hexadecimal digits that specify the amount of blue

With the percentage and integer RGB values, a smaller number for a particular color means less of that color. Likewise, with hexadecimal RGB values, a smaller number means less of a particular color. The smallest hexadecimal digit is 0, so 00 represents the absence of a particular color. If all colors are absent, that's black. Therefore, #000000 (00 for each of the three colors) indicates black. The largest hexadecimal digit is f, so ff represents the greatest intensity of a particular color. If all colors are maximally intense, that's white. Therefore, #ffffff (ff for each of the three colors) indicates white.

So you now know how to make black and white using hexadecimal numbers. Those are easy. Using hexadecimal numbers that are between the two extremes is a bit trickier. What color does the following value represent?

#ffbbbb

Note ff for the first two digits. The first two digits are for red, so #ffbbbb is a shade of red. Light red or dark red? To figure that out, you need to know whether the other two colors are less than or greater than halfway between 00 and ff. The other two colors both have values of bb. The b hex digit (which represents eleven) is closer to f (which represents fifteen) than 0, so the other two colors are closer to white than black. That means #ffbbbb is light red (otherwise known as pink), and it looks like this:

Here's an example CSS rule with a hexadecimal RGB value:

```
<style>
  .sapphire {background-color: #0f42ba;}
</style>
```

In the #0f42ba color value, which is the most intense—red, green, or blue? The red portion's value, 0f, has an f in it, and we know f represents fifteen, so maybe red is the most intense? No. With good old-fashioned base-10 decimal numbers, 09 is a small number (as compared to, say, 95) because digits at the left (0 in this case) have greater significance than digits at the right (9 in this case).

It's the same in the hexadecimal number system. The red portion of `#0f42ba` is 0f, and now we know that 0f is a small number; consequently, there's very little red in the resulting color. The green portion of `#0f42ba` is 42, and 42 is a relatively small number; consequently, there's not much green in the resulting color. The blue portion of `#0f42ba` is ba, and ba is a relatively large number;[6] consequently, there's quite a bit of blue in the resulting color. Here's what the color looks like:

That is the color of a sapphire gemstone, and that's why the preceding CSS rule uses `sapphire` for its class selector.

The W3C's CSS3 standard says that RGB hexadecimal digits are case insensitive. So in this example, `#0F42BA` (with uppercase F, B, and A) would also work. You'll see lowercase and uppercase on the W3C site and in the real world. Use lowercase to be consistent with standard HTML coding conventions, which say to use lowercase values unless there's a reason to do otherwise. But if you're reading this book as part of a course, and your teacher says to use uppercase hexadecimal digits, then use uppercase hexadecimal digits.

## 3.15 Opacity Values for Color

In the previous section, you learned how to produce a color by using the `rgb` construct with values for red, green, and blue. In this section, you'll learn how to produce a partially transparent color by using the `rgba` construct with values for red, green, blue, and opacity. The fourth value, opacity, determines how opaque the color is, where opaque refers to the inability to see through something. It's the opposite of transparency. If the opacity value is 100%, that means the color is completely opaque, and if there is content behind the color, that content gets covered up. At the other extreme, if the opacity value is 0%, that means the color is completely transparent.

The A in RGBA stands for alpha. Why alpha? There's no official documentation on alpha's etymology, but perhaps the CSS3 standards people chose it simply because it's the first letter in the Greek alphabet.

To specify an RGBA value, use one of these two formats:

`rgba` (*red-integer*, *green-integer*, *blue-integer*, *opacity-number-between-0-and-1*)
`rgba` (*red-percent*, *green-percent*, *blue-percent*, *opacity-number-between-0-and-1*)

For both formats, the fourth value specifies the opacity. The opacity value must be in the form of a decimal number between 0 and 1, with 0 being completely transparent, 1 being completely opaque, and .5 in between.

For the first format, each integer value must be between 0 and 255, with 0 providing the least intensity and 255 providing the most. That should sound familiar because that was also the case for integers with the `rgb` construct. For the second format, each percent value must be between 0% and 100%.

---

[6] To calculate the decimal equivalent of a two-digit hexadecimal number, multiply the left digit by 16 and then add the right digit. So, hexadecimal 0f is 15 (0 × 16 + 15 = 15), hexadecimal 42 is 66 (4 × 16 + 2 = 66), and hexadecimal ba is 186 (11 × 16 + 10 = 186).

You can use the `rgba` construct with the `color` property, which specifies the color of an element's foreground (e.g., text). However, it's more common to use it with the `background-color` property, as you will see in the following example.

FIGURE 3.14's Opacity Example web page illustrates what happens when a transparent yellow color is placed on top of a red background—orange is formed. Before looking at the CSS rules that generate the yellow colors, let's first examine the CSS rule that generates the window's red background color:

```
.red {background-color: red;}
```

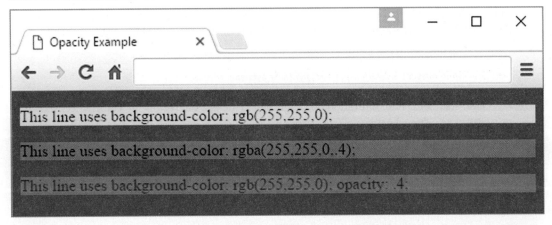

```
<!DOCTYPE html>
<html lang="en">
<head>
<meta charset="utf-8">
<meta name="author" content="John Dean">
<title>Opacity Example</title>
<style>
   .red {background-color: red;}
   .yellow-bg {background-color: rgb(255,255,0);}
   .yellow-bg2 {background-color: rgba(255,255,0,.4);}          rgba construct
   .yellow-bg3 {background-color: rgb(255,255,0); opacity: .4;}
</style>
</head>
<body class="red">                                                opacity property
<p class="yellow-bg">This line uses background-color: rgb(255,255,0);</p>
<p class="yellow-bg2">
  This line uses background-color: rgba(255,255,0,.4);
</p>
<p class="yellow-bg3">
  This line uses background-color: rgb(255,255,0); opacity: .4;
</p>
</body>
</html>
```

FIGURE 3.14 **An opacity example that illustrates the `rgba` construct and the `opacity` property**

Note the browser window's first sentence and the CSS rule that generates its yellow background:

```
.yellow-bg {background-color: rgb(255,255,0);}
```

The `rgb` value's `255` values indicate maximum amounts of red and green, and that forms yellow. The web page's red background is blocked by the sentence's yellow background, which is 100% opaque by default.

Next, note the browser window's second sentence and the CSS rule that generates its orange background:

```
.yellow-bg2 {background-color: rgba(255,255,0,.4);}
```

The .4 indicates that the yellow color will be 40% opaque and 60% transparent. That transparency allows the yellow background to mix with the web page's red background to form orange.

As an alternative to using `rgba`, you can use `rgb` in conjunction with the `opacity` property. Here's the third class selector rule from the Opacity Example web page:

```
.yellow-bg3 {background-color: rgb(255,255,0); opacity: .4;}
```

This rule matches up with the web page's third sentence. With an opacity value of .4, that sentence gets 40% opacity for both its `color` property and its `background-color` property. For the sentence's `color` property, which determines the text's color, the default color is black, and the web page's background color is red. They mix to form a reddish gray. Note the reddish-gray text for the Opacity Example web page's third sentence. For the sentence's `background-color` property, the preceding CSS rule specifies yellow, and the web page's background color is red. They mix to form orange. Note the orange background color for the Opacity Example web page's third sentence.

## 3.16 HSL and HSLA Values for Color

With CSS (and also with HTML), there are sometimes multiple ways to accomplish the same thing. That point is particularly pertinent when it comes to specifying colors. You've already learned how to specify color values with names, the `rgb` construct, and the `rgba` construct. Now for the `hsl` construct. Here's the syntax:

```
hsl(hue-integer, saturation-percent, lightness-percent)
```

HSL stands for hue, saturation, and lightness. Hue is a degree on the color wheel shown in **FIGURE 3.15**. The wheel is a circle, so the wheel's degrees go from 0 to 360. As you can see in the figure, 0 degrees is for red, 120 degrees is for green, and 240 degrees is for blue. For a circle, 0 degrees is equivalent to 360 degrees. So, to specify red, you can use 360 as an alternative to 0.

The second value in the `hsl` construct is the color's percentage of saturation. The W3C says 0% means a shade of gray, and 100% is the full color. For an alternative way to think about it, if you look up "saturation" on Google, you should find something like "the extent to which something is dissolved or absorbed compared with the maximum possible absorption." Suppose there's a girl

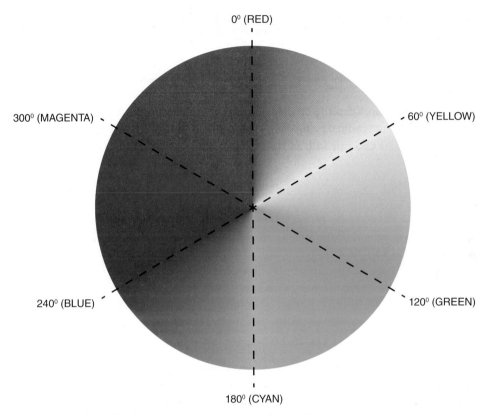

**FIGURE 3.15 Color wheel for the `hsl` construct's hue value**

named Caiden on her middle school cheer team. She washes her new $50 uniform and forgets to remove her cherry nail polish from the uniform's skirt pocket. The result? (1) A big blotch of "maximum possible absorption" red near the pocket due to a saturation value of 100%, (2) a bit of reddish coloring added to the rest of the uniform due to a saturation value near 25%, and (3) a month's worth of Caiden doing the whole family's laundry, nail polish excluded.

The third value in the `hsl` construct is the color's percentage of lightness. A lightness value of 0% generates black, regardless of the values for hue and saturation. A lightness value of 100% generates white, regardless of the values for hue and saturation. A lightness value of 50% generates a "normal" color.

Here's an example CSS rule with an HSL color value:

```
<style>
    p {background-color: hsl(120,50%,75%);}
</style>
```

That color forms a light shade of grayish green, and here's what it looks like:

In the previous section, you learned how to add transparency to an RGB value by using the `rgba` construct. Likewise, to add transparency to an HSL value, you can use the `hsla` construct. Here's the syntax:

`hsla` (*hue-integer*, *saturation-percent*, *lightness-percent*, *opacity-number-between-0-and-1*)

The fourth argument specifies the opacity. The opacity value must be in the form of a decimal number between 0 and 1, with 0 being completely transparent and 1 being completely opaque. Here's an example CSS rule with an HSLA color value:

```
<style>
  .background {background-color: hsla(120,50%,75%,.5);}
</style>
```

What color is specified? It's the same as the earlier grayish-green color, except that this time, the grayish green blends with the web page's background color as a result of the 50% opacity value. With a default white web page background, the result would be a lighter shade of grayish green, like this:

## 3.17 **Font Properties**

In this section, we describe how to display text with different font characteristics. You've probably heard of the term "font," but if not, *font* refers to the characteristics of text characters—height, width, thickness, slantedness,[7] body curvatures, and endpoint decorations. That should make more sense later on when we present CSS font property details and show examples. Specifically, you'll learn about the `font-style`, `font-variant`, `font-weight`, `font-size`, `font-family`, and `font` shorthand properties.

### `font-style` **Property**

The `font-style` property specifies whether the text is to be displayed normally or slanted. Here are the valid values for the `font-style` property:

| `font-style` Values | Description |
|---|---|
| `normal` | Upright characters (not slanted). |
| `oblique` | Use the same font as the current font, but slant the characters. |
| `italic` | Use a cursive font (which tends to be slanted and is supposed to look like handwriting). |

---

[7] Apparently "slantedness" is not a word, but it should be. If it becomes a word, you heard it here first.

These descriptions indicate a slight difference between the `oblique` and `italic` properties, with `italic` tending to be more decorative. Most web developers use the value `italic`. Because italics are so common, you should memorize the following technique for generating italics:

```
.italics {font-style: italic;}
```

As always, choose a name for the class selector that's descriptive. Here, we chose the name `italics` because it's descriptive and easy.

Upright (normal) characters are the default, so why would you ever want to specify normal for the `font-style` property? Suppose you have a whole paragraph that's italicized and you want one word in the paragraph not italicized. To make that word normal (not italicized), you can use `font-style: normal`.

The W3C provides default values for all CSS properties, and to force the default value to be used for a particular property, you can specify `initial` for that property. So, given the situation described with an italicized paragraph, to make one word not italicized, you can apply the following rule to that word:

```
.not-italicized {font-style: initial;}
```

## `font-variant` Property

The `font-variant` property specifies how lowercase letters are displayed. Here are the valid values for the `font-variant` property:

| `font-variant` Values | Description |
|---|---|
| `normal` | Display lowercase letters normally. |
| `small-caps` | Display lowercase letters with smaller-font uppercase letters. |

Here's an example that uses a `small-caps` CSS rule:

```
.title {font-variant: small-caps;}
...
<div class="title">The Great Gatsby</div>
```

And here's the resulting displayed text:

THE GREAT GATSBY

## `font-weight` Property

The `font-weight` property specifies the boldness of the text characters. Here are the valid values for the `font-weight` property:

| `font-weight` Values | Description |
|---|---|
| `normal`, `bold` | It's up to the browser to determine a font weight that can be described as normal or bold. |
| `bolder`, `lighter` | Using a value of `bolder` causes its targeted text to have thicker characters than the text that surrounds it.<br>Using a value of `lighter` causes its targeted text to have thinner characters than the text that surrounds it. |
| `100`, `200`, `300`, `400`, `500`, `600`, `700`, `800`, `900` | 100 generates the thinnest characters and 900 the thickest characters.<br>400 is the same as `normal`, and 700 is the same as `bold`. |

These descriptions for `bolder` and `lighter` are probably all you need to know, but you may want to dig a little deeper. With `bolder` and `lighter`, the targeted text inherits a default `font-weight` value from its surrounding text, and then the targeted text's weight gets adjusted up or down relative to that inherited weight. For example, if you specify a `bold` font weight for a paragraph, you can make a particular word within the paragraph even bolder by specifying `bolder` for that word's font weight.

Because boldfacing is such a common need, you should memorize the following technique for making something bold:

```
.bold {font-weight: bold;}
```

## `font-size` Property

The `font-size` property specifies the size of the text characters. There are quite a few values allowed for the `font-size` property. Here are the most appropriate ones:

| `font-size` Values | Description |
|---|---|
| `xx-small`, `x-small`, `small`, `medium`, `large`, `x-large`, `xx-large` | It's up to the browser to determine a font size that can be reasonably described as `xx-small`, `x-small`, `small`, etc. |
| `smaller`, `larger` | Using a value of `smaller` causes its targeted text to have smaller characters than the text that surrounds it.<br>Using a value of `larger` causes its targeted text to have larger characters than the text that surrounds it. |
| `number of em units` | One em unit is the height of the element's normal font size. |

Here's an example class selector rule that uses the `font-size` property with an `xx-large` value:

```
.huge-font {font-size: xx-large;}
```

So far, most of the CSS property values you've seen have consisted of a text description, such as xx-large. As an alternative, some properties have values that are comprised of two parts—a number and a unit. For example, for the font-size property, you can use a value with a number next to em, where one em unit is the height of a typical character. The em unit's name comes from the letter M. Originally, one em unit equaled the height of the letter M. However, there are fonts for languages that don't use the English alphabet, so it was deemed inappropriate for em to rely on the letter M. Thus, em is no longer tied to the letter M, and testing shows that a single em unit is a bit taller than the height of M.

Here are class selector rules that use the font-size property with em values:

```
.disclaimer {font-size: .5em;}
.advertisement {font-size: 3em;}
```

The first rule is for disclaimer text, which is supposed to be annoyingly small to avoid scrutiny, and its .5em value displays text that is half the size of normal text. The second rule is for advertisement text, which is supposed to be annoyingly large to draw attention, and its 3em value displays text that is three times the size of normal text.

Here, for each font-size value, note that there is no blank space separating the number from em. Likewise, for all CSS values that consist of a number and a unit, you should not have a blank space. Having no blank space is a requirement of the CSS standard.

## Absolute Units

There are quite a few other techniques for specifying font size. For example, you can specify a number along with an in, cm, mm, pt (point), or pc (pica) unit. The W3C refers to those units rather disdainfully as "so-called absolute units." Although they're still used every now and then, and you should understand them, absolute units have fallen out of favor for everyday needs. This is because it's good to allow users to adjust the size of things, particularly people with impaired eyesight. Also, with regular monitors, testing shows that the "absolute units" are not absolute; their sizes vary with different resolutions, different monitors, and zooming in and out.

The W3C says absolute units are required to have absolute lengths only when the target device has a high resolution; that usually means just printers, but it can also mean high-resolution monitors. For a scenario where a fixed size is essential and absolute units are appropriate, picture your wedding preparations. Suppose you're tasked with printing your wedding invitations on pre-cut pink cherub-adorned cards. To avoid agitating a stressed-out fiancé(e), you'll want to use absolute units to make sure the words fits perfectly on the cards.

## font-family Property

The prior font properties allow the web developer to choose values for specific font characteristics (font-weight for characters' thickness, font-size for characters' height, etc.). The next font property, `font-family`, is more holistic in nature. The `font-family` property allows the web developer to choose the set of characters that the browser uses when displaying the element's text. As you'd expect, the characters in a particular character set are similar in appearance—same basic height, width, body curvature, and so on.

Here's an example class selector rule that uses the `font-family` property:

```
.ascii-art {font-family: Courier, Prestige, monospace;}
```

Note that with the `font-family` property, you should normally have a comma-separated list of fonts, not just one font. In applying the preceding rule to elements that use "asci-art" for their `class` attribute, the browser works its way through the `font-family` list from left to right, and uses the first font value it finds installed on the browser's computer and skips the other fonts. So if `Courier` and `Prestige` are both installed on a computer, the browser uses the Courier font because it appears further left in the list.

There are lots of fonts, and different browsers support different ones. Users are able to install fonts in addition to the ones provided by their browsers. For a small sample of popular font names, see https://www.w3.org/TR/css-fonts-3/#generic-font-families. On that website, you can see that most font names use title case (the first letter of each word is capitalized), but a few use all lowercase letters. Font names are case sensitive on some operating systems, so you should take care to use the proper case. The font names that use all lowercase letters are special, and they are known as generic fonts.

A *generic font* is a name that represents a group of fonts that are similar in appearance. For example, `monospace` is a generic font, and it represents all the fonts where each character's width is uniform. Whenever you use a `font-family` CSS rule, you should include a generic font at the end of the rule's list of font names. In the following CSS rule (copied from earlier for your convenience), note the `monospace` font at the end of the list of font names:

```
.ascii-art {font-family: Courier, Prestige, monospace;}
```

The generic font name provides a *fallback mechanism*. If a user's browser doesn't support any of the fonts at the left of the generic font name, the browser uses the generic font to display a font that the browser does support. Generic font names are not actual fonts with specific appearance characteristics; they are just placeholders that tell the browser to look for an actual font in a particular family of fonts. So in the `ascii-art` CSS rule, if a browser does not support the `Courier` or `Prestige` fonts, the browser digs up a monospace font that it does support and uses it. To ensure that a web page's font looks pretty much the same on different browsers, for each `font-family` CSS rule, you should always use fonts that are similar, which means that they are associated with the same generic font. Referring once again to the preceding `ascii-art` CSS rule, `Courier` and `Prestige` both display uniform-width characters, and they are both associated with the same `monospace` generic font.

The `monospace` font is one of five generic fonts that all browsers recognize and support. Here's a list of the five generic fonts with descriptions and examples:

| Generic Font Names | Description | Example Font |
|---|---|---|
| monospace | All characters have the same width. | `Courier New looks like this.` |
| serif | Characters have decorative embellishments on their endpoints. | Times New Roman looks like this. |
| sans-serif | Characters do not have decorative embellishments on their endpoints. | Arial looks like this. |
| cursive | Supposed to mimic cursive handwriting, such that the characters are partially or completely connected. | *Monotype Corsiva looks like this.* |
| fantasy | Supposed to be decorative and playful. | **Impact looks like this.** |

As mentioned earlier, generic font names use lowercase, and you can verify that for the five generic fonts shown. On the other hand, specific font names use title case. You can verify that by examining the five example fonts shown in the right column (e.g., `Courier New`).

When specifying a multiple-word font name, surround the name with quotes. For example, in **FIGURE 3.16**, note the quotes around `New Century Schoolbook`. In addition, note the coding convention of inserting a blank space after each comma in a `font-family` list of font names.

Suppose a web page includes the code in Figure 3.16. If a user's computer has the `New Century Schoolbook` font and also the `Times` font installed on it, which font will the browser use to display the paragraph? It will use `New Century Schoolbook`, because it's the first font in the list and it's installed on the user's computer.

```
<style>
  blockquote {font-family: "New Century Schoolbook", Times, serif;}
</style>
                              quotes                    spaces

<blockquote>
  Call me Ishmael. Some years ago-never mind how long precisely-
  having little or no money in my purse, and nothing particular to
  interest me on shore, I thought I would sail about a little and
  see the watery part of the world.
</blockquote>
<cite>Moby Dick</cite>
```

**FIGURE 3.16 An example font-family CSS rule**

## font Shorthand Property

Fairly often as a web programmer, you'll want to apply more than one of the prior font-related properties to an element. You could specify each of those font properties separately, but there's an easier way. The font property can be used to specify all these more granular font properties—font-style, font-variant, font-weight, font-size, line-height, and font-family. Previously, we mentioned all these font properties except for line-height. We'll cover line-height shortly, but first we'll discuss some overarching details about the font property.

Here's the syntax for a font property-value pair:

font: [*font-style-value*]  [*font-variant-value*]  [*font-weight-value*]
    *font-size-value* [*/line-height-value*]  *font-family-value*

As usual, the italics are the book's way of telling you that the italicized thing is a description of what goes there, so for a font property-value pair in a CSS rule, you would replace *font-style-value* with one of the font-style values, such as italic. The square brackets are the book's way of telling you that the bracketed thing is optional, so the font-style, font-variant, font-weight, and line-height values are all optional. On the other hand, the font-size and font-family values have no square brackets, so you must include them whenever you use the font property. For the property values you decide to include, they must appear in the order previously shown. If a line-height value is included, you must position it at the right of the font-size value, with a / separating the two values.

Here's an example type selector rule that uses a font property:

```
blockquote {
    font: italic large "Arial Black", Helvetica, sans-serif;
}
```

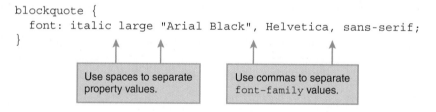

Use spaces to separate property values.

Use commas to separate font-family values.

In the preceding rule, how many types of font properties are specified and what are they? Glancing at the font property's value, you can see there are five items in the list, so you might think there are five types of font properties. Upon closer inspection, you should notice the commas between the last three items. Those commas are delimiters for a sublist, where the sublist is the value for the font-family property. At the left of the font-family property's list, you can see two other property values—italic and large—separated by spaces. Those values are for the font-style and font-size properties.

By the way, the W3C refers to the font property as a *shorthand property* because it's a time-saving construct for handling multiple font characteristics. Later, we'll introduce additional shorthand properties for other groups of related CSS properties. When given a choice between using a shorthand property and using a set of more granular properties, some web programmers prefer using the shorthand property because of its compactness, whereas others prefer using the more granular properties because of their clarity. In this book, we use both techniques and let the situation dictate our preference.

## 3.18 `line-height` **Property**

We mentioned the `line-height` property in the previous Font Properties section as part of our discussion of the `font` shorthand property. We postponed our discussion of the `line-height` property until now because, although it can be part of a `font` shorthand property's value, it's not really a font property. It's used to specify the vertical separation between each line of text in an element. For example, in **FIGURE 3.17**, note the `sentence1` CSS rule with `line-height: 2em`. That rule causes its matching element to display its lines with a vertical separation equal to twice the height of a normal character (remember, an em unit represents the height of a normal character). Note the resulting double-spaced line heights in **FIGURE 3.18**'s displayed text.

```
<!DOCTYPE html>
<html lang="en">
<head>                      A line height of 2em generates double spacing.
<meta charset="utf-8">
<meta name="author" content="John Dean">
<title>Declaration of Independence</title>
<style>
   .sentence1 {line-height: 2em; font-family: Times, serif;}
   .sentence2 {font: 1em/2em Times, serif;}
</style>
</head>
                            This specifies font size and then line height.

<body>
<h2>Declaration of Independence, working draft v. 2.01</h2>
<p>
  <span class="sentence1">We hold these truths to be self-evident,
     that <del>every man is</del><ins>all men are</ins>
     created equal.</span>
  <br>
  <span class="sentence2">That they are endowed by their Creator
     with certain unalienable Rights, that among these are Life,
     Liberty and the pursuit of Happiness.</span>
</p>
</body>
</html>
```

**FIGURE 3.17 Source code for Declaration of Independence web page**

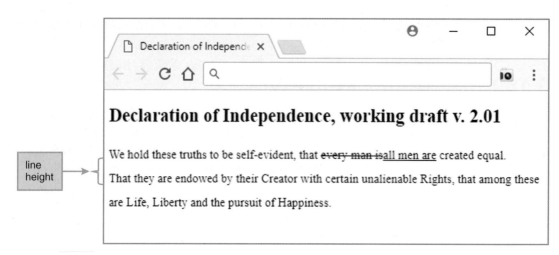

**FIGURE 3.18 Declaration of Independence web page**

In Figure 3.17, note the sentence2 CSS rule with `font: 1em/2em`. You might recall that with the shorthand `font` property, the / separates a `font-size` value from a `line-height` value. So in the sentence2 CSS rule, the `1em` value tells the browser to display text characters with their normal size and the `2em` value tells the browser to display lines with a vertical separation equal to twice the heig0ht of a normal character. That's the same thing that happens with the sentence1 CSS rule. You can verify that the two CSS rules are functionally equivalent by comparing the two sentences in Figure 3.18—they are formatted the same.

Does the font property's *font-size-value/line-height-value* syntax strike you as odd-looking? The way to remember the slash is to think of *font-size-value/line-height-value* as a fraction, where `font-size` is the character height. So `2em/4em` means the characters take up half of the vertical distance between two lines.

As an alternative to using an em value for the `line-height` property, you can use a percentage value. Note this example:

```
.proof-reading {line-height: 300%;}
```

The percentage value is relative to the element's font size, so the preceding rule tells the browser to display matching elements with a line height that is three times the height of a normal character. As you might have surmised, that's the same as if you had used a `3em` value.

## 3.19 Text Properties

If you glance back at the CSS property categories in Figure 3.13, you can see that we've finished with the color properties and the font properties and next are the text properties. With the font properties, we focused on appearance characteristics of individual characters. Now, with text properties, we'll focus on appearance characteristics of groups of characters. We've already talked about `line-height`, which is a text property. We won't bother to cover all the text properties, just the more important ones. Specifically, here's what's on the agenda—text-align, text-decoration, text-transform, and text-indent.

## text-align Property

The text-align property specifies the horizontal alignment for a block of text. Here are the valid values for the text-align property:

| text-align Values | Description |
|---|---|
| left | Align the text at the left. |
| right | Align the text at the right. |
| center | Center the text. |
| justify | Stretch the lines so that each line extends to the left edge and the right edge. |

If you use justify for the text-align property, the browser stretches all the lines in a block of text, except for the block of text's bottom line. The bottom line uses left justification. That behavior mimics what you see for paragraphs in newspapers and magazines, and that's why justify is used primarily for p elements.

## text-decoration Property

The text-decoration property specifies something decorative that is added to text. Here are the valid values for the text-decoration property:

| text-decoration Values | Description |
|---|---|
| none | This displays normal text (no decoration added). |
| underline | Draw a line below the text. |
| overline | Draw a line above the text. |
| line-through | Draw a line through the text. |
| blink | This causes the text to blink. |

Because underlining is so common, you should memorize the following technique for generating an underline:

```
.underlined {text-decoration: underline;}
```

Normally, you should avoid using the `blink` value because it can be very annoying. But if your aim is to antagonize, go for it!

## `text-transform` Property

The `text-transform` property controls the text's capitalization. Here are the valid values for the `text-transform` property:

| `text-transform` Values | Description |
|---|---|
| none | The text renders the same as the original text. |
| capitalize | Transform the first character of each word to uppercase. |
| uppercase | Transform all characters to uppercase. |
| lowercase | Transform all characters to lowercase. |

What's the point of `text-transform`? Why not just use the desired case in the original HTML code? You might want to provide uppercase and lowercase buttons on your web page that allow users to dynamically change the page so it displays all uppercase or all lowercase. You can implement that with JavaScript and the `text-transform` property. You'll learn how to do that later when we get to the JavaScript portion of the book.

## `text-indent` Property

The `text-indent` property specifies the size of the indentation of the first line in a block of text. The block's second and third lines (and so on) are unchanged; that is, they do not get indented. If you want to adjust all the lines in a block of text, use the `margin` property, not the `text-indent` property. You'll learn about the `margin` property later in this chapter.

The most appropriate way to specify a value for the `text-indent` property is to use `em` units. Here's an example type selector rule that uses the `text-indent` property:

```
p {text-indent: 4em;}
```

## 3.20 Border Properties

Now onto the next category of CSS properties—border properties. As expected, the border properties allow you to specify the appearance of borders that surround elements. We won't bother to cover all the border properties, just the more important ones. Specifically, we'll describe the `border-style`, `border-width`, and `border-color` properties. Then we'll finish with the `border` shorthand property.

## `border-style` Property

The `border-style` property specifies the type of border that surrounds the matched element. Here are the valid values for the `border-style` property:

| `border-style` Values | Appearance |
|---|---|
| none | The browser displays no border. This is the default. |
| solid | |
| dashed | |
| dotted | |
| double | |

Here's an example class selector rule that uses the `border-style` property to draw a dashed border:

```
.coupon {border-style: dashed;}
```

We used "coupon" for the class selector because we want the matched element to look like a coupon, with a traditional dashed border surrounding it.

## `border-width` Property

The `border-width` property specifies the width of the border that surrounds the matched element. There are quite a few values allowed for the `border-width` property. Here are the most appropriate ones:

| `border-width` Values | Description |
|---|---|
| thin, medium, thick | The browser determines a border width that can be reasonably described as `thin`, `medium`, or `thick`. The default is `medium`. |
| number of px units | A CSS pixel unit is the size of a single projected dot on a computer monitor when the monitor's zooming factor is at its default position of 100%. |

If you ever use the `border-width` property, remember to use it in conjunction with the `border-style` property. If you forget to provide a `border-style` property, then the default `border-style` value kicks in, and the default value is `none`. With a `border-style` value of none, no border will be displayed. Forgetting the `border-style` property is a very common bug.

CSS pixel values use `px` units. As with all the other CSS size values, CSS pixel values are relative. If a user reduces the monitor's resolution or zooms in on his or her browser, then each CSS pixel expands, and elements that use CSS pixel units will likewise expand.

It's pretty rare to need different widths for the different border sides, but be aware that the feature does exist. If you specify four values for the `border-width` property, the four values get applied to the border's four sides in clockwise order, starting at the top. For example:

```
.boxed {
  border-style: solid;
  border-width: 4px 2px 0px 2px;
}
```

Note what happens when you apply the preceding CSS rule to the following HTML code fragment:

```
My idol is <span class="boxed">Tim Berners-Lee</span>. He rocks!
```

The border's top side is thickest due to the `4px` value. The right and left sides are both two pixels, and the bottom side is missing due to the `0px` value.

Google's Style Guide says if you have a zero value for a CSS property, you should omit the unit in order to make the code more compact. So in the earlier code, that means using `0` instead of `0px`. However, in the interest of parallelism with the other three values, I felt that keeping the `px` unit was appropriate.

With CSS properties that involve four sides (i.e., the preceding `border-width` property, and the `margin` and `padding` properties coming up), there are shortcut techniques for specifying the values. If you specify three values, then the first value applies to the top side, the second value applies to the left and right sides, and the third value applies to the bottom side. Thus, the preceding `border-width` property value pair could have been written as follows and the result would be the same:

```
border-width: 4px 2px 0px;
```

If you specify just two values, then the first value applies to the top and bottom sides and the second value applies to the left and right sides.

In addition to its shortcut techniques, the `border-width` property also has techniques that are more verbose. Specifically, you can use a separate font property (`border-top-width`, `border-right-width`, `border-bottom-width`, and `border-left-width`) for each side's border width. Google's Style Guide recommends not using those properties—too wordy—and we'll follow that recommendation for the most part.

Whew! There are a lot of alternative syntax techniques for the `border-width` property. Thankfully, borders should normally have the same width for all four sides, and to make that happen, the syntax is easy. Just specify one value for the `border-width` property, and that single value applies to all four sides.

## `border-color` Property

The `border-color` property specifies the color of the border that surrounds the matched element. There's no new syntax to learn for the `border-color` property because it uses the same values as the `color` property and the `background-color` property. Remember the types of values that those properties use? Color values can be in the form of a color name, an RGB value, an RGBA value, an HSL value, or an HSLA value.

For the `border-color` property to work, you must use it in conjunction with a `border-style` property. That should sound familiar because we said the same thing about the `border-width` property. In order to change the border's color or change the border's width, you must have a visible border, and that's done by using a `border-style` property.

## `border` Shorthand Property

If you want to apply more than one of the prior border-related properties to an element, you could specify each of those properties separately, but there's a more compact technique. The `border` property is a shorthand notation for specifying a border's width, style, and color in that order. Here are two examples:

```
.understated-box {border: thin dotted blue;}
.in-your-face-box {border: 10px solid;}
```

In the second example, there isn't a color value. You can omit the width and/or color values, but if you omit the style value, then there will be no visible border. You have to include the style value; if you don't, then `border-style`'s default value of none will be used. In both examples, style values are included (`dotted` and `solid`), so the borders are visible.

# 3.21 **Element Box,** `padding` **Property,** `margin` **Property**

In the previous section, you learned how to display a border around an element. Usually, borders have no gaps inside or outside of them. Sometimes that's appropriate, but usually you'll want to introduce gaps to make the elements look comfortable, not cramped. To introduce gaps around

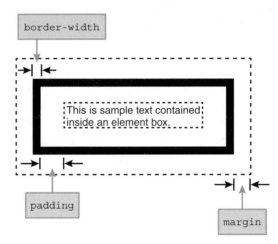

**FIGURE 3.19** **An element box's margin, border, and padding**

an element's border, you need to take advantage of the element's element box. Every web page element has an element box associated with it. As you can see in **FIGURE 3.19**, an element box has a border, padding inside the border, and a margin outside the border. For most elements, but not all, the default border, padding, and margin widths are zero. You can adjust the widths with the border-width, padding, and margin properties.

In Figure 3.19, the dashed lines indicate the perimeters of the margin and padding areas. When a web page is displayed, only the border can be made visible; the dashed lines shown in the figure are only for illustration purposes.

If you have trouble keeping track of which property is inside the border, padding or margin, think of a package you get in the mail. You put padding on the inside of a fragile package's box, so the padding property is for inside the border. Therefore, the margin property must be for outside the border.

## padding and margin Properties

The padding property specifies the width of the area on the interior of an element's border, whereas the margin property specifies the width of the area on the exterior of an element's border. Usually, the most appropriate type of value for the padding and margin properties is a CSS pixel value. Here's an example CSS rule that uses padding and margin properties:

```
.label {border: solid; padding: 20px; margin: 20px;}
```

Just as with the border-width property, you can specify different padding widths for the four different sides. You can use multiple values with one padding property. Or you can use separate padding side properties—padding-top, padding-right, padding-bottom, and padding-left. Likewise, you can specify different margin widths for the four different sides. You can use multiple values with one margin property. Or you can use separate margin side properties—margin-top, margin-right, margin-bottom, and margin-left.

The `margin` and `padding` properties allow negative values. While a positive value forces two elements to be separated by a specified amount, a negative value causes two elements to overlap by a specified amount.

## Example That Uses `padding` and `margin` Properties

Let's put this padding and margin stuff into practice in the context of a complete web page. FIGURE 3.20's browser window shows `span` elements that could serve as labels for water faucet handles. The borders are curved to form ovals. We'll get to the implementation of the curved borders shortly, but let's first focus on the padding and margins.

FIGURE 3.21 shows the code for the Hot and Cold web page. Here's the relevant code for the padding and margins, where `label` is the class attribute value for both of the `span` elements:

```
.label {
  padding: 20px;
  margin: 20px;
  display: inline-block;
}
```

The `padding` and `margin` properties both use values of `20px`, which provides significant space on the interior and exterior of the borders. For the web page's first-cut implementation, there was no `display` property (as shown), and there was no space provided above the two ovals—the ovals bumped up against the top edge of the browser window, which looked ugly. Figuring out the solution required some serious head-scratching. After much trial and error and googling, I learned that vertical margins do not work for standard phrasing elements, such as the `span` element. On the other hand, vertical margins do work for block elements. So, the trick was to turn the label's `span` element into a block element—well, sort of. To help with the explanation, we'll use some different nomenclature. In the world of CSS, we'll refer to phrasing elements as *inline elements* because CSS uses the `inline` value to describe elements that are to be formatted as phrasing elements (where the element's width matches the width of its contents). We'll also refer to elements that have

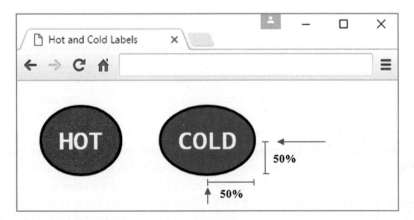

**FIGURE 3.20 Hot and Cold web page**

```html
<!DOCTYPE html>
<html lang="en">
<head>
<meta charset="utf-8">
<meta name="author" content="John Dean">
<title>Hot and Cold Labels</title>
<style>
  .hot {background-color: red;}
  .cold {background-color: blue;}
  .label {
    color: white;
    font: bold xx-large Lucida, monospace;
    border: solid black;
    border-radius: 50%;              ◄——— This implements curved corners.
    padding: 20px;
    margin: 20px;
    display: inline-block;           ◄——— This is necessary for the vertical
  }                                        margins to work.
</style>
</head>

<body>
<span class="hot label">HOT</span>
<span class="cold label">COLD</span>
</body>
</html>
```

**FIGURE 3.21 Source code for Hot and Cold web page**

characteristics of both phrasing and block elements as *inline block elements*. So here's the deal—vertical margins do work for inline block elements. The span element is considered to be a standard inline element by default. By adding the preceding `display: inlineblock` property-value pair to the `label` CSS rule, we make the span element more "blockish," and the browser accommodates by adding space above the ovals. This is another example where research and tweaking are necessary.

Now onto the curved borders. The `border-radius` property allows you to specify how much curvature you want at each of the four corners of an element. The default, of course, is to have no curvature. To achieve curved corners, you need to specify the focal point for each of the corners' curves. Often, you'll have different focal points for each of the four corners, but for both oval elements in the Hot and Cold web page, all four focal points are in the same place—at the center of the oval. To understand how the blue oval's lower-right-corner curve is drawn, imagine a compass with its pointy arm stuck at the center of the blue oval and its free arm sweeping from the bottom of the blue oval toward the right edge of the blue oval. As it moves to the right and up, the compass arm will have to swivel open slightly in order to reach the far right edge of the oval. That sweeping motion forms the lower-right corner's curvature.

So, where does the CSS rule come into play? As you can see in Figure 3.21, the `border-radius` property has a value of `50%`. That `50%` value is used to form the spanning lines shown in Figure 3.20. The specified percentage (50% in this case) is relative to the width and height of the element. So for the lower-right corner, one spanning line goes to the left by 50% of the element's width and the other spanning line goes up by 50% of the element's height. As you can see in Figure 3.20, the ends of the two spanning lines determine the starts of the two arrows that intersect within the element. That intersection point serves as the focal point for the lower-right corner's curved border.

Yes, the `border-radius` property is somewhat complex. If you want to learn all its behaviors and its different syntax options, check out the W3C's explanation at https://www.w3.org/TR/css3-background/#the-border-radius.

## Using a Percentage for a Web Page's Margin

As indicated, you'll normally want to use CSS pixel values for margin widths. However, it's sometimes appropriate to use percentage values instead of pixel values. Case in point—specifying the margin around the entire web page.

Typically, browsers leave a small blank area on the four sides of the window, which is a result of the `body` element having a default margin value of around 8 pixels. To change the body's margin from the default, you can provide a CSS rule for the `body` element's `margin` property. It's OK to use a CSS pixel value, but if you want to have the web page's margin shrink and grow when the user resizes the browser window by dragging a corner, use a percentage value, like this:

```
body {margin: 10%;}
```

The `10%` value indicates that the web page's left and right sides will have margin widths that each span 10% of the web page's width. Likewise, the web page's top and bottom sides will have margin heights that each span 10% of the web page's height.

## When to Use the Different Length Units

In this chapter, we introduced various CSS units that are used for specifying the size, distance, or length of something. Specifically, we described `em`, `px`, `%`, and several absolute units such as `pc`, `in`, `cm`, and so forth. All those units are called *length units*. What follows is a summary of when to use each of the different length units:

▷ Use `em` for font-related properties (like `font-size`).
▷ Use `px` for properties that should be fixed for a given resolution, even if the element's font size changes or even if the containing element's size changes. Typically, that means using `px` for things like border properties and layout.
▷ Use `%` for properties that should grow and shrink with the size of the containing element (like margins for the `body` element).
▷ Use absolute units sparingly—only when a fixed size is essential and the target device has a high resolution.

## 3.22 CASE STUDY: Description of a Small City's Core Area

### This Chapter's Web Page

This section adds another page to our case study website. This page describes the core area of Lawrence, Kansas: (1) downtown Lawrence; (2) East Lawrence, an old residential and industrial area east of downtown; (3) Old West Lawrence, an old residential area west of downtown; and (4) the University of Kansas (KU), a large university southwest of Old West Lawrence. **FIGURE 3.22** shows the desired result.

When you compare this web page with the case study web pages at the ends of Chapter 1 and Chapter 2, suddenly you see color and a centered heading. To promote coherence, it would be nice to repeat such common presentation features on all of this website's web pages. It's best to specify common presentation features like these in an external CSS file, and we'll get to that shortly. But first, let's look at the HTML file that specifies this particular web page's content and

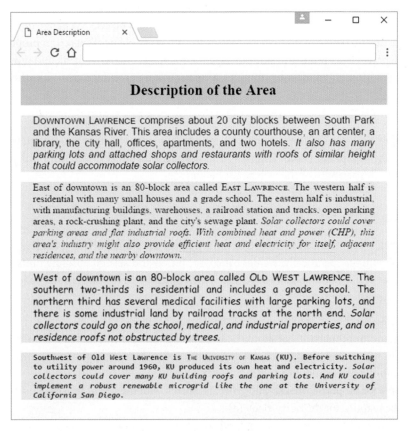

**FIGURE 3.22 Area Description web page describing the core area of Lawrence, Kansas**

the presentation features that are peculiar to this particular web page. **FIGURE 3.23A** shows the first part of this web page's HTML file, `areaDescription.html`.

The first five elements are exactly the same as the first five elements in the HTML files at the ends of Chapter 1 and Chapter 2. The final `meta` element and the `title` element are what you might expect for the current web page. The `link` element is new. It creates a linkage between the current HTML file and the `lawrenceMicrogrid.css` file that specifies our website's common presentation features—like the green background color and the centered heading. Because the filename is preceded by `../Library/`, this CSS file is in a folder that is a sibling of the current folder; both folders are in the same parent folder.

The last `head` element is a `style` element. Using CSS syntax, it specifies presentation features that are specific to the current web page. The first four selectors, `.downtown`, `.eastLawrence`, `.westLawrence`, and `.ku` specify the fonts in the four corresponding paragraphs in Figure 3.22. The different font styles convey subjective feelings for what the different sections of the city are like. The `.downtown` and `.eastLawrence` selectors provide comma-separated lists of font names, one of which, `"Times New Roman"`, is enclosed in quotes because it's a multiword name. The `.westLawrence` and `.ku` selectors include additional `line-height` and `font-weight`

```
<!DOCTYPE html>
<html lang="en">
<head>
<meta charset="utf-8">
<meta name="author" content="John Dean">
<meta name="description" content="Chapter 3. Cascading Style Sheets
   (CSS)">
<title>Area Description</title>
<link rel="stylesheet" href="../Library/lawrenceMicrogrid.css">   ⬅
<style>
  .downtown {font-family: Helvetica, sans-serif;}
  .eastLawrence {font-family: "Times New Roman", serif;}
  .westLawrence {
    font-family: cursive;
    line-height: 1.2em;                                      ┌──────────────┐
  }                                                          │ link to an   │
  .ku {                                                      │ external     │
    font-family: monospace;                                  │ CSS file     │
    font-weight: bold;                                       └──────────────┘
  }
  span.title {font-variant: small-caps;}
  span.opportunity {font-style: italic;}
</style>
</head>
```

**FIGURE 3.23A Source code for the Area Description web page**

properties to compensate for default font features that would otherwise make the overall presentation too chaotic. Notice how additional properties motivate a coding-style switch to block format.

The last two selectors, `span.title` and `span.opportunity`, could just as well have been written more simply as `.title` and `.opportunity`. The element-type prefix, `span`, says that they apply only to presentations within `span` phrasing elements.

**FIGURE 3.23B** contains the rest of the HTML file. Each paragraph's opening `<p>` tag includes a `class` attribute whose value is a corresponding presentation selector defined in the `style` element in the current file's `head` element. Each paragraph also contains two `span` elements, whose "title" and "opportunity" class-attribute values specify `small-caps` and `italic` values

```
<body>
<h2>Description of the Area</h2>
<p class="downtown">
  <span class="title">Downtown Lawrence</span> comprises about 20 city
  blocks between South Park and the Kansas River. This area includes a
  county courthouse, an art center, a library, the city hall, offices,
  apartments, and two hotels. <span class="opportunity">It also has
  many parking lots and attached shops and restaurants with roofs of
  similar height that could accommodate solar collectors.</span>
</p>
<p class="eastLawrence">
  East of downtown is an 80-block area called <span class="title">East
  Lawrence</span>. The western half is residential with many small
  houses and a grade school. The eastern half is industrial, with
  manufacturing buildings, warehouses, a railroad station and tracks,
  open parking areas, a rock-crushing plant, and the city's sewage
  plant. <span class="opportunity">Solar collectors could cover parking
  areas and flat industrial roofs. With combined heat and power (CHP),
  this area's industry might also provide efficient heat and
  electricity for itself, adjacent residences, and the nearby downtown.
  </span>
</p>
<p class="westLawrence">
  West of downtown is an 80-block area called <span class="title">Old
  West Lawrence</span>. The southern two-thirds is residential and
  includes a grade school. The northern third has several medical
  facilities with large parking lots, and there is some industrial land
  by railroad tracks at the north end. <span class="opportunity">Solar
  collectors could go on the school, medical, and industrial
  properties, and on residence roofs not obstructed by trees.</span>
</p>
<p class="ku">
  Southwest of Old West Lawrence is <span class="title">The University
  of Kansas</span> (KU). Before switching to utility power around 1960,
  KU produced its own heat and electricity. <span class="opportunity">
  Solar collectors could cover many KU building roofs and parking lots.
  And KU could implement a robust renewable microgrid like the one at
  the University of California San Diego.</span>
</p>
</body>
</html>
```

**FIGURE 3.23B Source code for Area Description web page**

font-variant and font-style properties, respectively. Go back and look again at Figure 3.22 to see the presentation effects produced by these CSS specifications.

Now it's time to look at the external CSS file responsible for what are to be the website's common coloring, common heading, and other common presentation features. **FIGURE 3.24** shows what this lawrenceMicrogrid.css file looks like. The body selector specifies three properties, a background color, a padding, and a maximum width.

The body type selector's background-color property applies to all parts of the window that are not covered by something else. Its value, azure, is an extremely light blue. The padding property surrounds the body's contents with a 10-pixel-wide buffering strip. In particular, it guarantees that some of that light azure coloring separates the green h2 and p elements from the edges of the window.

The h1 and h2 type selector's margin property reduces the whitespace above headings. Its background-color property specifies the color behind the text in headings. Its value, light-green, is the name of a standard CSS color. Alternative ways to specify this color include #90EE90; rgb(144, 238, 144); and hsl(120, 80%, 75%);. The padding property guarantees that heading text will be surrounded with a 10-pixel-wide strip of light green coloring. The text-align property centers the heading text within this light green background.

The p type selector's background-color property specifies the color behind the text in the web page's paragraphs. As you can see in Figure 3.22, this background color is slightly lighter than the header's background color. It's not one of CSS's standard color values. We get this color value by increasing the last of the three components in the hsl alternative lightgreen color value from 75% to 90%. Notice that the p type selector's padding property value has two components. The first component, 0px, specifies no padding above and below the enclosed text. This avoids increasing the vertical spacing between text in adjacent paragraphs. The second component, 20px, establishes the padding you see at the left and right of the enclosed text in the paragraphs in Figure 3.22. The text-align property value, justify, expands each line of text horizontally to provide both left and right vertical alignment.

```
/* Rules for all web pages */
body {
  background-color: azure;
  padding: 10px;
}
h1, h2 {
  margin: 0px;
  background-color: lightgreen;
  padding: 10px;
  text-align: center;
}
p {
  background-color: hsl(120,80%,90%); /*lighter lightgreen*/
  padding: 0px 20px;
  text-align: justify;
}
```

**FIGURE 3.24 Source code for external CSS file for the Lawrence hydropower website**

## Upgrading Previous Web Pages

With an appropriate CSS file now in hand, it's relatively easy to fulfill a desire expressed near the start of this section: "To promote coherence, it would be nice to repeat such common presentation features on all of this website's web pages." To give previously created HTML files the newly created "common presentation features," go back to those previously HTML files and insert a link to the common CSS file. In particular, go back to Figure 1.11 (HTML source code for the Electric Power History web page) and to Figure 2.17A (source code for the Lawrence Hydropower web page). Then, into each of those source-code files, immediately after the `title` element, paste a copy of the `link` element found immediately after the `title` element in Figure 3.23A's HTML source code for the Area Description web page. Here is that line of HTML source code to copy and paste:

```
<link rel="stylesheet" href="../lawrenceMicrogrid.css">
```

This simple alteration changes what you saw in Figure 1.12 to what you see in **FIGURE 3.25**.

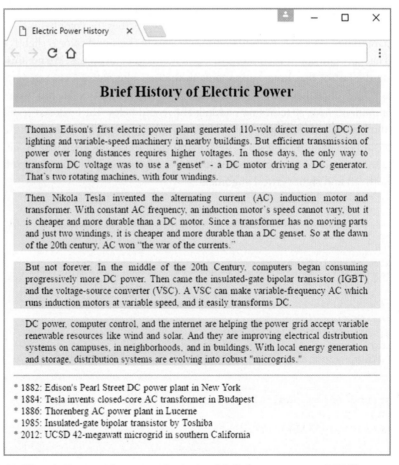

**FIGURE 3.25 Electric Power History web page with link to common CSS file**

And it changes what you saw in Figure 2.16 to what you see in **FIGURE 3.26**.

Including the same link in future case study web pages will give those pages these same presentation features.

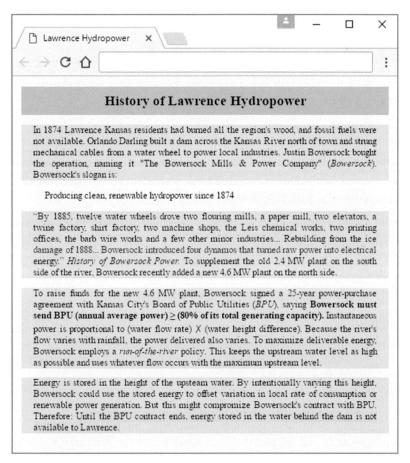

**FIGURE 3.26 Lawrence Hydropower web page with link to common CSS file**

# Review Questions

### 3.3 CSS Rules

1. What is the universal selector's syntax, and which elements does it match?

2. If you specify an element at the left of a selector, that selector is referred to as which type of selector? Here's an example:

```
blockquote {color: red;}
```

### 3.5 CSS Syntax and Style

3. In a CSS rule, you should always include a semicolon after every property-value pair, even the last property-value pair. True or false.

### 3.6 Class Selectors

4. Why are selectors that use the dot syntax (e.g., .in-your-face) referred to as "class selectors"?

### 3.7 ID Selectors

5. What is the symbol used to preface an ID selector?

### 3.9 Cascading

6. What does "cascading" mean in the term "Cascading Style Sheets"?

### 3.10 style Attribute, style Container

7. What is a global attribute?

### 3.11 External CSS Files

8. What is the syntax for the element that links a web page to an external CSS file?

### 3.14 RGB Values for Color

9. If you use an RGB value with integers, what is the valid range for each integer?

### 3.15 Opacity Values for Color

10. If you apply the property-value pair opacity: .5; to a word, what happens?

### 3.16 HSL and HSLA Values for Color

11. What does HSL stand for?

### 3.17 Font Properties

12. What is the CSS property-value pair that causes lowercase letters to be displayed with smaller-font uppercase letters?

13. For the font-family property, why is it good to have a list of values rather than only one value?

**3.19 Text Properties**

**14.** What is the CSS property-value pair that causes underlining to take place?

**3.20 Border Properties**

**15.** If you use the `border-width` property, what other property should you use in conjunction with it?

**16.** The `border` shorthand property can be used to specify which border attributes?

**3.21 Element Box, `padding` Property, `margin` Property**

**17.** What does the `border-radius` property do?

# Exercises

**1.** [after Section 3.8] Suppose you have two CSS selectors—one named `scary-font` and one named `boxed`. If you want to apply both selectors to one `class` attribute, which of the following will you use?

 a)  `class = "scary-font boxed"`

 b)  `class = "scary-font, boxed"`

 c)  Nothing (it's impossible to apply two selectors to one `class` attribute)

**2.** [after Section 3.8] What is special about the `span` element that makes it a good candidate for using CSS?

**3.** [after Section 3.14] For an RGB color value, each of the three colors uses 8 bits. RGB values can be used to represent approximately 16 million different colors. Provide the math that explains why RGB values can be used to represent approximately 16 million different colors.

**4.** [after Section 3.16] Provide a class selector rule that specifies the foreground and background colors shown in the following "Feliz Navidad!" text. For the foreground color, use an HSLA value with 80% opacity. For the background color, use an HSL value. For your class selector, use `christmas` as the `class` attribute value.

Feliz Navidad!

**5.** [after Section 3.17] What's wrong with the following rule?

```
h1 {font-family: Helvetica;}
```

**6.** [after Section 3.17] Specify a class selector rule that attempts to use a font named `Cracked`. If that font is unavailable, then the rule attempts to use a font named `Comic Sans MS`. Your rule should handle the possibility that neither font is available. For your class selector, use fun-font as the class attribute value. Make sure you choose a generic font that is appropriate for Cracked and Comic Sans MS.

7. [after Section 3.20] What does the book's HTML coding conventions appendix say about specifying zero values for CSS properties? Provide the general rule and also the rule for color values.

8. [after Section 3.21] What's wrong with the following rule?

```
p {margin: 2 px;}
```

# Projects

1. Provide complete code for an implementation of the following web page and name the file `cssPractice_societalQuotes.html`:

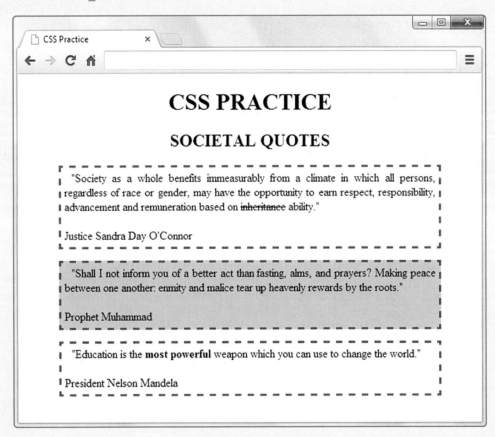

You must use the HTML `body` container code provided (you are not allowed to modify it). To support the HTML `body` container code, you must include a `style` container. Your `style` container must:

▸ Implement an appropriate type selector rule that would apply to <u>all possible heading elements</u> (not just the ones shown).

▸ Implement appropriate class selector rules with `bold` and `strike-through` selectors.

▸ Implement an appropriate type.class selector rule for `p` elements that use a `gray-background` selector.

▶ Implement a type selector rule for all p elements. The rule should specify:
- A 5-pixel padding
- 50-pixel left and right margins
- A dashed red border
- Times New Roman or serif font text that is justified with both the left and right sides
- 10-pixel indentation

```
<body>
<h1>css practice</h1>
<h2>societal quotes</h2>
<p>
  "Society as a whole benefits immeasurably from a climate in
  which all persons, regardless of race or gender, may have the
  opportunity to earn respect, responsibility, advancement and
  remuneration based on <span class="strike-through">inheritance</span>
  ability."
  <br><br>
  Justice Sandra Day O'Connor
</p>
<p class="gray-background">
  "Shall I not inform you of a better act than fasting, alms, and
  prayers? Making peace between one another: enmity and malice tear
  up heavenly rewards by the roots."
  <br><br>
  Prophet Muhammad
</p>
<p>
  "Education is the <span class="bold">most powerful</span>
  weapon which you can use to change the world."
  <br><br>
  President Nelson Mandela
</p>
</body>
```

2.  Create the following web page, and name the file `newspaper.html`:

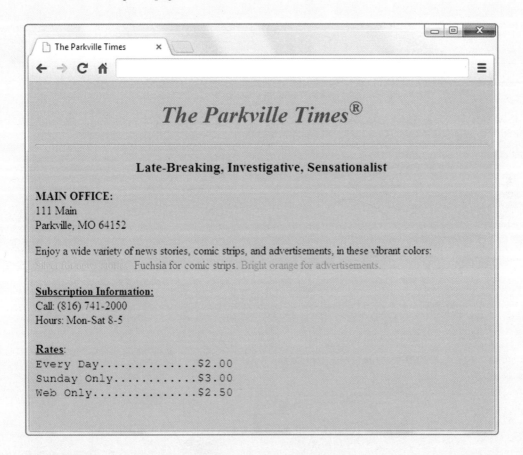

The window background must render using the color cyan. The top heading must render using the color blue. For the sake of getting practice with different color value formats, you must use different techniques to specify each of the three color messages:

silver—use an HSL value
fuchsia—use a hexadecimal RGB value
bright orange—use an integer RGB value

# CHAPTER 4

# Organizing a Page's Content with Lists, Figures, and Various Organizational Elements

## CHAPTER OBJECTIVES

- ▶ Implement a list with items that are unordered (e.g., use bullets for list items).
- ▶ Understand the concept of a nested list and be able to implement a nested list.
- ▶ Understand the syntax and semantics for a descendant selector.
- ▶ Implement a list with items that are ordered (e.g., use letters or numbers for list items).
- ▶ Implement a figure with a picture and a caption.

- ▶ Understand the purpose of organizational elements like section, article, and aside.
- ▶ Implement a navigation bar using nav and a elements.
- ▶ Implement headers and footers.
- ▶ Be familiar with a user agent style sheet.
- ▶ Understand the syntax and semantics for a child selector.
- ▶ Understand how CSS inheritance works.

**131**

## CHAPTER OUTLINE

## 4.1 Introduction

The first three chapters were all about getting you started. With that knowledge base, you should be able to implement simple web pages that display relatively small amounts of text in a pleasing manner. That'll accommodate some of your needs, but more often than not, you'll want to display more than just a "small amount of text." With web pages that have more content, you'll want to present that content in an organized manner so that readers will be able to figure out more easily what's going on. You probably wouldn't enjoy reading a web page with row upon row of text that describes boring plumbing fixture minutia. But how about a web page with a bulleted list of plumbing fixture dos and don'ts, a nested numbered list of plumbing regulations, a figure with a "Mr. Fix-It" plumber picture, and a box at the right with the plumber's contact information? Now that's an exciting web page! In this chapter, you learn how to do all that and more.

Specifically, in this chapter, you'll first learn how to implement lists, so you can display a group of items with bullets, numbers, or letters at the left of each list item. Then you'll learn how to implement figures, which include the figure's main content, plus a caption. The list and figure container elements organize their content with clearly defined display characteristics—lists have symbols next to each of their list items, and figures have captions. On the other hand, the remaining container elements in this chapter do not have clearly defined display characteristics. They are called organizational elements and their purpose is only for grouping content, not for making the grouped content look a particular way. For example, if you want to display an article (i.e., an essay) on a web page, you should group the article's text in an `article` element. For the different sections in an article, you should group each section's text in a `section` element. If you have a navigation bar, you should group the navigation bar's links in a `nav` element. That's just a sample of HTML5's organizational elements. You'll learn about those elements and more as you proceed through the chapter.

## 4.2 Unordered Lists

We start this chapter by learning how to implement lists. Let's jump right into an example. In **FIGURE 4.1**'s web page, note the *unordered list* that shows my weekday routine. It's called

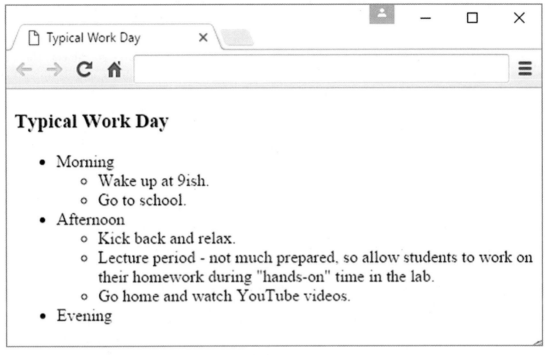

FIGURE 4.1 **Work Day web page**

"unordered" because the list items have bullets and circles next to them, and bullets and circles do not imply any order. If you prefer to have the list items ordered, you can replace the bullets and circles with numbers and letters, as explained in a later section.

To create an unordered list, you surround the entire list with a ul container (ul for unordered list) and use li containers for the individual list items. Here's an example:

```
<ul>
  <li>Wake up at 9ish.</li>
  <li>Go to school.</li>
</ul>
```

Note that it is legal to omit the </li> end tag for list elements, so this is valid HTML as well:

```
<ul>
  <li>Wake up at 9ish.
  <li>Go to school.
</ul>
```

However, in the interest of readability and maintenance, coding conventions suggest that you do not omit the </li> end tag.[1]

---

[1] According to the HTML5 standard, it's also legal to omit the p container's </p> end tag. But once again, to help with readability and maintenance, coding conventions suggest that you always include the </p> end tag.

## Parent and Child Elements

Let's now examine the complete source code for the Work Day web page. In **FIGURE 4.2**, note the outermost ul container and the dashed boxes that show its three li containers. The ul container is considered to be a *parent* element for the three li containers, and the three li containers are considered to be *child* elements of the ul container. The parent–child relationship exists between two elements when the parent element's start tag and end tag surround the child element and there are no other container elements inside the parent element that

```
<!DOCTYPE html>
<html lang="en">
<head>
<meta charset="utf-8">
<meta name= "author" content="John Dean">
<title>Typical Work Day</title>
</head>

<body>
<h3>Typical Work Day</h3>
<ul>
  <li>
    Morning
    <ul>
      <li>Wake up at 9ish.</li>
      <li>Go to school.</li>
    </ul>
  </li>
  <li>
    Afternoon
    <ul>
      <li>Kick back and relax.</li>
      <li>
        Lecture period - not much prepared, so allow students to
        work on their homework during "hands-on" time in the lab.
      </li>
      <li>Go home and watch YouTube videos.</li>
    </ul>
  </li>
  <li>Evening</li>
</ul>
</body>
</html>
```

The big ul container has three child li containers.

**FIGURE 4.2 Source code for Work Day web page**

surround the child element. By examining the Work Day web page's source code, you should be able to verify that the outermost `ul` container and the three boxed `li` containers match that description.

## Nested Lists

In Figure 4.2, each of the first two child `li` containers contains its own sublist. Those are examples of *nested lists*, where you have a list inside a list. In attempting to create a nested list, beginning web programmers often insert a `ul` container immediately inside another `ul` container, so the inner `ul` container is a child of the outer `ul` container. The HTML5 standard does not allow that. The only element that's allowed to be a child of a `ul` element is an `li` element. Thus, to implement a nested list, you need to have an `li` container in between the outer and inner `ul` containers. Can you see that this is the case in the Work Day web page's source code?

Now go back to Figure 4.1 and note the first bullet, labeled "Morning." In implementing that bullet and the subsequent sublist, your first thought might be to do this:

```
<ul>
  <li>Morning</li>
  <ul>
    <li>Wake up at 9ish.</li>
    <li>Go to school.</li>
  </ul>
  ...
```

But if you do that, then the inner `ul` container is a child element of the outer `ul` container. And that violates the rule mentioned that says `ul` containers can have only `li` elements for their child elements. So, what's the proper way to implement the "Morning" label and its subsequent sublist? As shown in Figure 4.2, you need to move the `</li>` end tag down below the sublist's `</ul>` end tag. That way, the inner `ul` list is a child of the `li` container and is not a child of the outer `ul` container.

As you might have noticed, there are lots of indentations with HTML lists. We use the same rule as always—indent when you're logically inside something else. Because each `li` element is logically inside a `ul` container, each `li` element should be indented. If an `li` element contains a sublist, then the sublist's `ul` container should be indented further. Study Figure 4.2 to verify that the Work Day web page's code follows these indentation rules.

## Symbols for Unordered List Items

According to the W3C, the default symbol for unordered list items is a bullet for all levels in a nested list, but the major browsers typically use bullet, circle, and square symbols for the different levels in a nested list. Because the official symbol defaults and the browser symbol defaults are different, you should avoid relying on them. Instead, you should use CSS's `list-style-type` property to explicitly specify the symbols used in your web page lists.

For unordered lists, the most popular values for the `list-style-type` property are none, disc, circle, and square. As you'd expect, the none value means that the browser displays no symbol next to each list item. The `disc` value generates bullet symbols, which you can see next to the outer list items in Figure 4.1's Work Day web page. The `circle` and `square` values generate hollow circles and filled-in squares, respectively. See **FIGURE 4.3**, which shows a second version of the Work Day web page, this time with circle and square symbols for the list items.

For Figure 4.3's second-version Work Day web page, here's the `style` container that generates the list's circle and square symbols:

```
<style>
  ul {list-style-type: circle;}
  ul ul {list-style-type: square;}
</style>
```

The first rule causes the browser to generate circle symbols for the list items in the outer list (e.g., see the figure's "Morning" list item). The second rule causes the browser to generate square symbols for the list items in the two sublists (e.g., see the figure's "Wake up at 9ish" list item). The second rule, with its two ul type selectors, is a descendant selector rule, and we'll explain what that means in the next section.

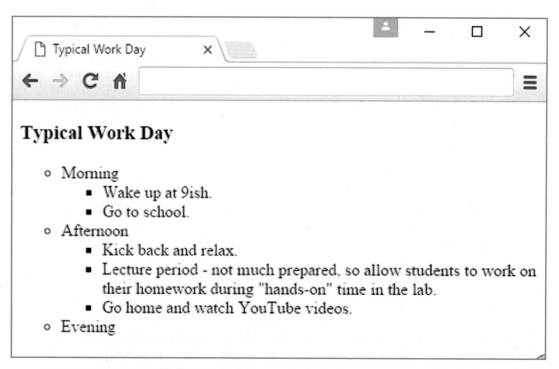

**FIGURE 4.3 Second version of Work Day web page**

# 4.3 Descendant Selectors

A *descendant selector* is when you specify a series of two or more selectors separated by spaces. For each pair of adjacent selectors, the browser searches for a pair of elements that match the selectors such that the second element is contained within the first element's start tag and end tag. When an element is inside another element's start tag and end tag, we say that the element is a *descendant* of the outer element.

To better understand the descendant selector, let's look at an example. The following structure shows how the Work Day web page's ul and li elements are related:

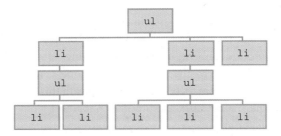

The ul element at the top is for the outer list. The three li elements below it are for the morning, afternoon, and evening list items. Each of the first two list elements contains a sublist, built with its own ul and li elements. The descendant relationship between two elements mimics the descendant relationships you can find in a family tree. Imagine that this structure shown is a family tree of bacteria organisms. Why bacteria? Because bacteria have only one parent, just as HTML elements have only one parent. All the elements below the top ul element are considered to be descendants of the top ul element. On the other hand, only the three li elements immediately below the top ul element are considered to be child elements of that ul element. So for an element to be a child of another element and not just a descendant, it has to be immediately below the other element.

Here's the syntax for a descendant selector rule:

*space-separated-list-of-elements* {*property1* : *value* ; *property2* : *value* ; }

In the following style container, note how the second and third rules use that syntax:

```
<style>
  ul {list-style-type: disc;}
  ul ul {list-style-type: square;}
  ul ul ul {list-style-type: none;}
</style>
```

In applying the three preceding rules to a web page, the browser would use the first rule to generate bullet symbols for list items at the outer level of an unordered outline. It would use the second rule to generate square symbols for list items at the first level of nesting within an unordered outline. And it would use the third rule to display no symbols for list items at the next level of nesting within an unordered outline.

If you ever have two or more CSS rules that conflict, the more specific rule wins.[2] That's a general principle of programming and you should remember it—the more specific rule wins. In the preceding `style` container, the first rule (the one with `ul` for its selector) applies to all `ul` elements, regardless of where they occur. On the other hand, the second rule (the one with `ul ul` for its selector) applies only to `ul` elements that are descendants of another `ul` element. Those rules conflict because they both apply to `ul` elements that are descendants of another `ul` element. For those cases, the second rule wins because the second rule is more specific. The third rule introduces another conflict—this time when there is a `ul` element that is a descendant of another `ul` element, and that other `ul` element is a descendant of a third `ul` element. For those cases, the third rule wins because the third rule is more specific.

In the preceding examples, we use descendant selectors to specify the different levels for nested lists. But be aware that you can use descendant selectors for any element types where one element is contained in another element. In expository writing,[3] if you use a new word in a paragraph, it's common practice to italicize the word and then define it. What descendant selector CSS rule could you use to support this practice? Try to come up with this on your own before you look down.... Assuming you have spent sufficient time trying to figure it out on your own, now you're allowed to proceed. Here's the answer:

```
p dfn {font-style: italic;}
```

## 4.4 Ordered Lists

Next, you'll learn how to generate list items that have numbers and letters next to them. Numbers and letters indicate that the order of the list items is important, and that changing the order would change the list's meaning. Those types of lists are referred to as *ordered lists*.

For an example of an ordered list, see **FIGURE 4.4**. It's a three-level nested list, with roman numerals for the outer list, uppercase letters for the middle-level list, and Arabic numbers for the most interior list.

---

[2] When two or more CSS rules apply to the same element, the browser goes through a rather complex calculation to determine which CSS rule is more "specific," and therefore which CSS rule wins. In describing this process at https://www.w3.org/wiki/Inheritance_and_cascade, the W3C says, "It can be easily shown how to calculate the specificity of a selector." Normally, when you read a technical article that prefaces a subject with something like, "It can be easily shown," get ready to be confused. For particularly complex calculations that can be "easily shown," the author probably had a hard time figuring things out and realized he'd have an even harder time explaining it. So his solution is to say that the calculation is too easy to warrant an explanation. Nonetheless, the W3C's aforementioned web page does provide an explanation, and it's actually pretty good. If you're curious about selector specificity calculation details, check it out.

[3] *Expository* refers to something whose purpose is to explain. So what you're reading now is an example of expository writing.

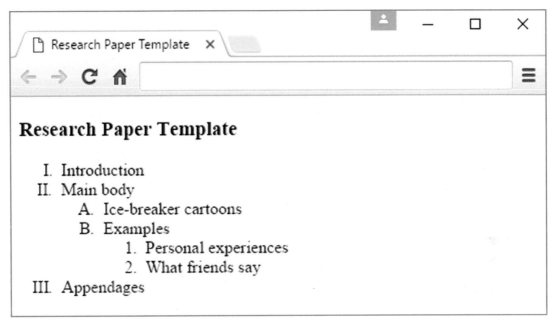

FIGURE 4.4 **Research Paper Template web page**

To create an ordered list, you surround the entire list with an `ol` container (`ol` for ordered list). As with unordered lists, you use `li` containers for the individual list items and you should indent the `li` containers within the `ol` container. Here's the code for the most interior list in the Research Paper Template web page:

```
<ol>
  <li>Personal experiences</li>
  <li>What friends say</li>
</ol>
```

To create sublists for an ordered list, use the same technique that you learned earlier for unordered lists—within the outer list's `ol` container, insert an `li` container, and in that `li` container, insert an `ol` container with its own list items. See examples of that in **FIGURE 4.5**'s source code for the Research Paper Template web page.

Typically, the major browsers display Arabic numbers by default for items in an ordered list, even when the ordered list is nested inside another ordered list. In other words, for the Research Paper Template web page, the default would be to use Arabic numbers (1, 2, 3) for the outer list's Introduction, Main body, and Appendages items and also to use Arabic numbers (1, 2) for the sublist's Ice-breaker cartoons and Examples items.

```
<!DOCTYPE html>
<html lang="en">
<head>
<meta charset="utf-8">
<meta name= "author" content="John Dean">
<title>Research Paper Template</title>
<style>
ol {list-style-type: upper-roman;}
ol ol {list-style-type: upper-alpha;}
ol ol ol {list-style-type: decimal;}
</style>
</head>

<body>
<h3>Research Paper Template</h3>
<ol>
  <li>Introduction</li>
  <li>
    Main body
    <ol>
      <li>Ice-breaker cartoons</li>
      <li>
        Examples
        <ol>
          <li>Personal experiences</li>
          <li>What friends say</li>
        </ol>
      </li>
    </ol>
  </li>
  <li>Appendages</li>
</ol>
</body>
</html>
```

These rules tell the browser how to label the different levels of the nested list.

**FIGURE 4.5 Source code for Research Paper Template web page**

As with unordered lists, you should avoid relying on the default symbols. Instead, you should use CSS's `list-style-type` property. There are lots of `list-style-type` property values for ordered lists. Some of the more popular values are `decimal`, `upper-alpha`, `lower-alpha`, `upper-roman`, and `lower-roman`. In Figures 4.4 and 4.5, you can see `upper-roman`, `upper-alpha`, and `decimal` lists and the CSS rules that generate those lists.

Although they're not used all that often, you should be aware of the `ol` element's `reversed` and `start` attributes. As its name implies, the `reversed` attribute causes list item labels to be in reverse order. For example, the following code fragment's list items[4] get displayed with the labels 3, 2, and 1:

```
<body>
Top Three Least-Loved Christmas Stories
<ol reversed>
  <li>A Holiday Visit from Salmonella</li>
  <li>Jack Frost Loses the Feeling in His Extremities</li>
  <li>The Teddy Bear Who Came to Life and Mauled a Retail Clerk</li>
</ol>
</body>
```

The default is for list item labels to start at position 1. The `start` attribute causes list item labels to start at a specified position. So in the following code fragment, the `ol` element's `start="52"` means that the first list item displays a label associated with the 52nd position. The `style` container's `.roman-list` rule specifies uppercase roman numerals for the list items. Therefore, the three list items get displayed with the labels LII, LIII, and LIV (which are the roman numerals for 52, 53, and 54).

```
<style>
  .roman-list {list-style-type: upper-roman;}
</style>
...
<body>
Super Bowl host cities starting in 2019
<ol class="roman-list" start="52">
  <li>Atlanta, Georgia</li>
  <li>Miami, Florida</li>
  <li>Wakeeny, Kansas</li>
</ol>
</body>
```

# 4.5 Figures

In this section, you'll learn how to implement a figure. Typically, a figure holds text, programming code, an illustration, a picture, or a data table. As with all figures, the `figure` element's content should be self-contained, and it should be referenced from elsewhere in the web page.

## Figure with a Code Fragment

Take a look at **FIGURE 4.6**. It uses the `figure` element to display a listing of programming code that's offset from the regular flow of the web page. The programming code is in JavaScript,

---

[4] Inspired by "Best of The David Letterman Top 10 Lists," http://www.textfiles.com/humor/letter.txt.

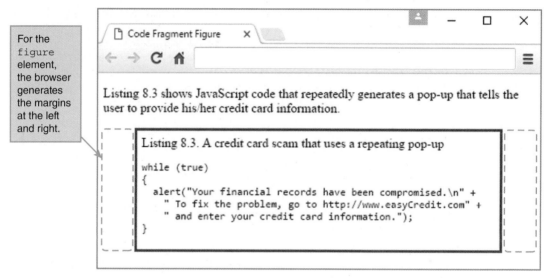

For the figure element, the browser generates the margins at the left and right.

Code Fragment Figure    ✕

Listing 8.3 shows JavaScript code that repeatedly generates a pop-up that tells the user to provide his/her credit card information.

```
Listing 8.3. A credit card scam that uses a repeating pop-up

while (true)
{
  alert("Your financial records have been compromised.\n" +
    " To fix the problem, go to http://www.easyCredit.com" +
    " and enter your credit card information.");
}
```

FIGURE 4.6 **Code Fragment Figure web page**

which you'll learn about in later chapters. For now, there's no need to worry about what the JavaScript code means. Instead, just focus on the `figure` element's syntax. In **FIGURE 4.7**, note the `figure` element's start tag and end tag. Also, note the `figcaption` element inside the `figure` container. As its name implies, the `figcaption` element causes the browser to display a caption for a figure. In the browser window's red-bordered figure, you can see the caption at the top of the figure.

In Figure 4.6's browser window, note how the red-bordered figure has expansive equal-sized margins at the left and right. The browser generates those margins by default for the `figure` element. But what's not a default is the visibility of the `figure` element's border. To make the border visible with a reddish color and a reasonable amount of padding inside it, it was necessary to add this CSS rule:

```
figure {
  border: solid crimson;
  padding: 6px;
}
```

## Figure with an Image

Next, let's use the `figure` element to display a picture with a caption. For an example, see the Final Tag web page in **FIGURE 4.8** and its source code in **FIGURE 4.9**. The `figure` element code and the `figcaption` element code should look familiar. That code is the same as for the Code Fragment Figure web page, except that the `figcaption` element is at the bottom of the `figure`

```
<!DOCTYPE html>
<html lang="en">
<head>
<meta charset="utf-8">
<meta name="author" content="John Dean">
<title>Code Fragment Figure</title>
<style>
  figure {
    border: solid crimson;
    padding: 6px;
  }
</style>
</head>
```

> If you have a figcaption element, it must be inside a figure element.

```
<body>
<p>
  Listing 8.3 shows JavaScript code that repeatedly generates a pop-up
  that tells the user to provide his/her credit card information.
</p>
<figure>
  <figcaption>Listing 8.3. A credit card scam that uses a repeating
    pop-up</figcaption>
  <pre><code>while (true)

  alert("Your financial records have been compromised.\n" +
    " To fix the problem, go to http://www.easyCredit.com" +
    " and enter your credit card information.");
}</code></pre>
</figure>
</body>
</html>
```

> With the pre element, its enclosed text should be at the left. In other words, there is no attempt to follow the usual practice of indenting inside a block element (pre is a block element).

**FIGURE 4.7 Source code for the Code Fragment Figure web page**

container instead of at the top. Consequently, in the browser window, you can see that the caption displays below the picture.

The Final Tag web page's primary focus is its picture. To display a picture, you'll need to use the img element. We will present the img element formally in Chapter 6, but for now, we'll introduce just a few details to explain what's going on in the Final Tag web page. Here's the relevant source code:

```
<img src="finalTag.png" alt="&lt;/life&gt; headstone">
```

Note the img element's src attribute—that's how you specify the location and name of an image file. If you don't specify a path in front of the image file's name, then the default is to look

**FIGURE 4.8 Final Tag web page**

for the file in the same directory that holds the web page's .html file. Later, you'll see how to load a picture from a different directory, but we're keeping things simple here with the web page and the picture file in the same directory.

In the preceding code fragment, note the img element's alt attribute. The HTML5 standard requires that for every img element, you provide an alt (for alternative) attribute. The alt attribute's value should normally be a description of the picture, and it serves two purposes. It provides *fallback content* for the image in case the image is unviewable. As you'll learn in Chapter 5, fallback content is particularly useful for visually impaired users who have *screen readers*. Screen readers can read the alt text aloud using synthesized speech. The preceding code fragment's alt value is rather odd-looking. It contains character references for the < and > symbols. When those character references are replaced with their symbols, the result looks like this:

```
</life> headstone
```

That text provides an accurate description of the picture's content, so the alt value is appropriate.

```
<!DOCTYPE html>
<html lang="en">
<head>
<meta charset="utf-8">
<meta name="author" content="John Dean">
<title>Final Tag Figure</title>
<style>
  body {text-align: center;}
</style>
</head>

<body>                  [src attribute]           [alt attribute]
<figure>
   <img src="finalTag.png" alt="&lt;/life&gt; headstone">  ◄── [img element]
   <figcaption>The Final HTML Tag</figcaption>
</figure>
</body>
</html>
```

**FIGURE 4.9 Source code for Final Tag web page**

# 4.6 Organizational Elements

So far in this chapter, we've organized web page content using lists and figures. Those organizational structures are pretty straightforward because they have physical manifestations—list items in an outline and a caption above or below a figure. The rest of this chapter covers organizational elements that don't have obvious physical manifestations. Their purpose is to group web page content into sections so that you can use CSS and JavaScript to manipulate their content more effectively. Here are the organizational elements you'll be introduced to:

- section
- article
- aside
- nav
- header
- footer

There's usually no need to use these organizational elements for small web pages, but when you have a multipage website, you should try to use them consistently. For example, you should use a common header for all web pages on a particular website. Being consistent will make your web pages look uniform, and that will give your users a comfortable feeling. In addition, consistency leads to web pages that are easier to maintain and update.

We could explain the organizational elements by showing code fragments or a series of small web pages, but that wouldn't illustrate the concepts very well. It's probably better to jump in with a complete web page where there are different areas of content that can be compartmentalized.

Take a look at **FIGURE 4.10**'s web page. It showcases Mangie's List, a tongue-in-cheek service that features reviews of dining and clothing venues from a manly man's perspective. You can see two headings at the top with a light blue background color. The headings are surrounded by a `header` container. Below the headings you can see two links that are surrounded by a `nav` (stands for <u>nav</u>igation) container. Then comes dining content and clothing content, each with its own `section` container. At the right, you can see a red box, which is implemented with an `aside` container. Finally, at the bottom, you can see content enclosed in a `footer` container.

**FIGURES 4.11A** and **4.11B** show the Mangie's List source code. We'll describe the code in detail in the upcoming sections, but for now just peruse the callouts that show where the organizational elements are used.

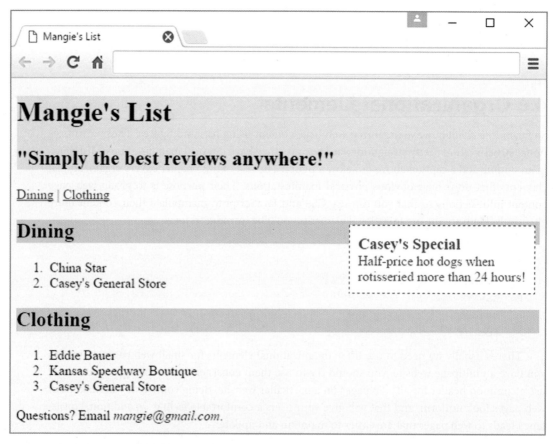

**FIGURE 4.10 Mangie's List web page**

```
<!DOCTYPE html>
<html lang="en">
<head>
<meta charset="utf-8">
<meta name= "author" content="John Dean">
<title>Mangie's List</title>
<style>
   body {background-color: lightyellow;}
   header {background-color: powderblue;}
   section > h2 {background-color: palegreen;}
   aside > h3 {margin: 0;}
   aside {
      border: thin dashed red;
      color: red;
      background-color: white;
      float: right;
      width: 200px;
      margin: 5px;
      padding: 10px;
   }
   address {display: inline;}
</style>
</head>
```

child selectors

Use the `float` property to position an element at the left or right edge of its surrounding container.

Use the `width`, `margin`, and `padding` properties to make the aside box look good.

display property

**FIGURE 4.11A Source code for Mangie's List web page**

# 4.7 `section`, `article`, and `aside` Elements

In this section, we describe three of the organizational elements—section, article, and aside. As with all the organizational elements, the section element is a container. It's used to group together a section of a web page. Yes, that is indeed a circular definition—the section container groups together a section of a web page. Sorry about that, but that's how the HTML5 standard defines the section element. Even though your English teachers might cringe at such circularity, it gets the point across pretty well. The HTML5 standard also describes the section element as a thematic grouping of content. In other words, the content is related in some way with a common theme. Typically, a section will contain a heading and one or more paragraphs, with the heading saying something about the common theme. For example, if you use a section element for a chapter, you would use a heading element for the chapter's title.

Take a look at the two section containers in Figure 4.11B. The first section is for dining, and the second section is for clothing. Note the two h2 heading elements for the two sections. Also note the two ordered lists for the two sections. We said it's common for a section to have one or more paragraphs, but that's not a requirement. Having lists instead of paragraphs is perfectly acceptable.

By default, all the organizational elements span the width of their surrounding containers. As such, they are "block elements" (like p, div , and blockquote). So in the Mangie's List web page,

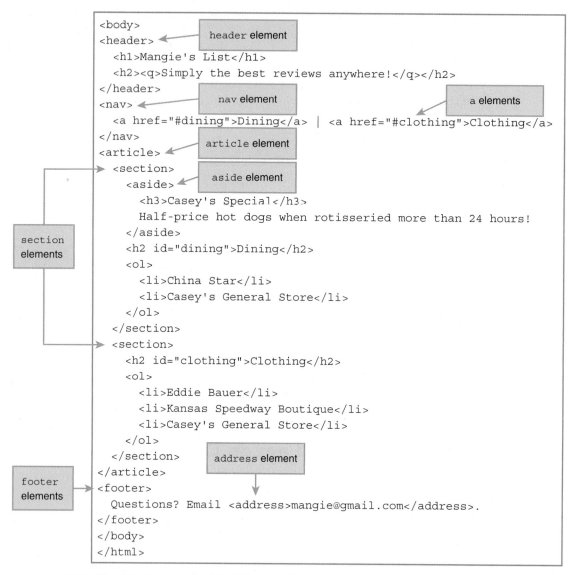

**FIGURE 4.11B Source code for Mangie's List web page**

the section containers span all the way to the right edge of the browser window. You can verify that by glancing back at Figure 4.10 and observing the green background color for the section headings—the green color spans the entire width of the browser window.

Next is the article element. The article element is for grouping together one or more sections such that the group of sections form an independent part of a web page. So if there are three related sections, it would be inappropriate to surround two of the sections with an article container. Why? Because the article would not be independent of the excluded section.

Go back to Figure 4.11B and take a look at the `article` container, which surrounds the web page's two sections. There's just one article because the sections are related. Can you think of an example where you should use multiple `article` elements in a web page? If you implement an online magazine, then you could have multiple magazine articles per page, and each article should be implemented with an HTML `article` container.

Next on the agenda—the `aside` element. Its purpose is to group together content that has something to do with the rest of the web page, but it isn't part of the main flow. Typically, you should position an `aside` element at the right or left. On the Mangie's List web page, note the red box. It contains advertising text, which is not part of the web page's main content, and it's positioned at the right side of the first section. With those characteristics, it's a perfect candidate for the `aside` element. As you can see in Figure 4.11B, we do indeed use the `aside` element for its implementation.

As mentioned earlier, organizational elements are block elements, so they span the entire width of the web page by default. A common way to undo that default behavior for the `aside` element is to "float" the `aside` element to the left or right by using the CSS `float` property. The following CSS rule is for the `aside` element in the Mangie's List web page. In particular, note the `float: right;` property-value pair:

```
aside {
   border: thin dashed red;
   color: red;
   background-color: white;
   float: right;
   width: 200px;
   margin: 5px;
   padding: 10px;
}
```

Go back to Figure 4.10 and observe the `aside` element's position, which is at the right of "Dining," an `h2` heading element. Getting the `aside` element to look good took a bit more effort than just slapping on the `float: right;` property-value pair. Originally, the `aside` element's box was too short and wide, with all of its text appearing on one line. To remedy that situation, we added a `width: 200px;` property-value pair to the `aside` CSS rule (see the earlier CSS rule).

The way the `float` property works is that the floated element gets positioned on the same line as the content that precedes it or on the next line if the preceding content is a block element, and the floated content gets moved to the surrounding container's left or right edge, depending on the `float` property's value. In the Mangie's List web page, the `aside` element is the first element in its surrounding `section` container, so it appears at the top of the `section` container. The dining `h2` element follows the `aside` element, and the `aside` element gets positioned at its right, in the same row. Originally, the `aside` element's top border was aligned precisely with the `h2` element's top border. To nudge the aside element slightly down and to the left (which exposes the `h2` element's green background perimeter in a pleasing manner), we add a `margin: 5px;` property-value pair to the `aside` CSS rule. Also, to avoid having the `aside` element's text too close to its border, we add a `padding: 10px;` property-value pair to the `aside` CSS rule.

## 4.8 nav and a Elements

In this section, we describe another organizational element—nav. The nav element is a container that normally contains links to other web pages or to other parts of the current web page. The nav element gets its name from na̲vigate because you use links to navigate to (jump to) other locations.

Go back to Figure 4.10 and note the two purple links near the top of the web page labeled "Dining" and "Clothing." Here's the nav code that contains those links:

```
<nav>
  <a href="#dining">Dining</a> | <a href="#clothing">Clothing</a>
</nav>
```

Note the two a elements, each with its own pair of start and end tags. Each a element implements a link. When the user clicks on a link, the browser jumps to the value specified by the href attribute. Later we'll use a URL value to jump to a separate web page, but for now, we're keeping things simple and just jumping to a location within the current web page. When jumping to a location within the current web page, the web page scrolls within the browser window so the target is at the top of the web page.

In the preceding code, note how the href's value starts with #. The # indicates that the target is within the current web page. To find that target, the browser looks for an element having an id value equal to the text that follows the # sign. For example, the preceding href value is #dining, so the browser looks for an element with "dining" for its id value. In Figure 4.11B, you can see this heading code for the web page's dining section:

```
<h2 id="dining">Dining</h2>
```

So with an id value of "dining," that heading serves as a target when the user clicks on the nav container's first link.

Originally, the a element's name stood for "a̲nchor" and people would sometimes refer to an a element as an anchor element. But the HTML5 standard no longer uses the word "anchor" in describing the a element. The href attribute's name stands for h̲yperlink re̲ference, since the a element implements a hyperlink.

## 4.9 header and footer Elements

So far, we've covered four organizational elements—section, article, aside, and nav. In this section, we cover two more—header and footer.

### header Element

The header element is for grouping together one or more heading elements (h1-h6) such that the group of heading elements form a unified header for nearby content. Normally, the header is associated with a section, an article, or the entire web page. To form that association, the header element must be positioned within its associated content container. Typically, that means at the top of the container, but it is legal and sometimes appropriate to have it positioned lower.

For the Mangie's List web page, we use a `header` element to group together an `h1` title and an `h2` quote above all of the other content. Go back to Figure 4.10 and find those header items. It's easy to identify them because we use CSS to apply a light blue background color to the header's content. Here's the code for the CSS rule and for the `header` container:

```
<style>
   header {background-color: powderblue;}
   ...
</style>

<header>
   <h1>Mangie's List</h1>
   <h2><q>Simply the best reviews anywhere!</q></h2>
</header>
```

As an alternative, we could have used this CSS rule:

```
h1, h2 {background-color: powderblue;}
```

But why is the original CSS rule—with the `header` type selector—better? First, it leads to more maintainable code because it still works later on if a different-sized heading element is used, like `h3` or `h4`. Second, it leads to a uniform background color for the entire header content. In other words, if you use the preceding CSS rule with `h1`, `h2` for the selector, you'll get blue backgrounds for the two heading elements (good) and a narrow white background in the margin area between them (not so good). Feel free to verify this phenomenon by entering the CSS rule into a copy of the Mangie's List source code and displaying the result.

## footer Element (with address Element Inside It)

The `footer` element is for grouping together information to form a footer. Typically, the footer holds content such as copyright data, author information, or related links. The footer should be associated with a `section`, an `article`, or the entire web page. To form that association, the `footer` element must be positioned within its associated content container. Typically, that means at the bottom of the container, but it is legal and sometimes appropriate to have it positioned elsewhere.

For the Mangie's List web page, we use a `footer` element for contact information. Here's the relevant code:

```
<footer>
   Questions? Email <address>mangie@gmail.com</address>.
</footer>
```

Note how the `footer` container has an `address` element inside of it. The `address` element is for contact information. Here, we show an e-mail address, but the `address` element also works for phone numbers, postal addresses, and so on. If the `address` element is within an `article` container, then the `address` element supplies contact information for the article. Otherwise, the `address` element supplies contact information for the web page as a whole.

## `display` Property, User Agent Style Sheets

The `address` element is a block element, so by default, browsers display it on a line by itself. But sometimes (actually, pretty often), you're going to want to display an address in an inline manner within a sentence. If you look at the Mangie's List web page, you can see that the address is embedded within the footer's sentence. To implement that inline behavior, the web page uses this CSS rule:

```
address {display: inline;}
```

Without that rule, the browsers' native default settings would apply, and the address would appear on a line by itself. You might recall from Chapter 3 that a browser's "native default settings" are one rung in the cascade of places where CSS rules can be defined. If you need a refresher, see Figure 3.8. The formal term for a browser's native default settings is a *user agent style sheet*, where *user agent* is the formal name for a browser. A user agent style sheet forms the lowest priority rung in the cascade of places where CSS rules can be defined. So if there's no higher priority CSS rule for a particular element, then the user agent style sheet's rule will apply. Unfortunately, it can be rather difficult to find the user agent style sheets for the various browsers. But don't lose sleep over that. As a web programmer, if you want certain formatting for a particular element, you should explicitly provide the rule in your source code. Nonetheless, if you're curious, you can go to https://www.w3.org/TR/html51/rendering.html to see the recommended user agent style sheet for all browsers. On that web page, the W3C says "The CSS rules [shown here] are expected to be used as part of the user-agent level style sheet defaults for all documents that contain HTML elements." That doesn't mean that all browsers follow the W3C's user agent style sheet exactly, but they follow it pretty closely.

## 4.10 Child Selectors

There are still a few Mangie's List CSS details that need to be covered. In this section, we tackle child selectors. In introducing child selectors, it's helpful to compare them to descendant selectors. Remember how descendant selectors work? That's when you have two selectors separated by a space, and the browser searches for a pair of elements that match the selectors such that the second element is a descendant of the first element (i.e., the second element is contained anywhere within the first element). A *child selector* is a more refined version of a descendant selector. Instead of allowing the second element to be any descendant of the first element, the second element must be a child of the first matched element (i.e., the second element must be within the first element, and there are no other container elements inside the first element that surround the second element).

The syntax for a child selector is the same as the syntax for a descendant selector, except that > symbols are used instead of spaces. Here's the syntax:

*list-of-elements-separated-with->'s* {property1: value; property2: value; }

For an example, look at this CSS rule from the Mangie's List web page:

```
section > h2 {background-color: palegreen;}
```

That rule matches each h2 element that is a child element of a section element. Go back to Figure 4.11B and look for the h2 elements inside the section containers. Those h2 elements say "Dining" and "Clothing." Thus, the preceding CSS rule causes browsers to display those two words with pale green background colors.

The > symbol is called a *combinator*. We won't use that term all that often, but if you're perusing the W3C literature (a good bedtime read, by the way), you'll run into it every now and then. The > symbol is called a "combinator" because it's used to combine the element at its left with the element at its right. There are other combinator symbols, and if you're interested, you can learn about them by searching for them on the W3C website.

## What Happens When There Are Conflicting CSS Rules

For the section > h2 CSS rule shown in the previous section, why was the combinator necessary? Why not use the following simpler CSS rule?

```
h2 {background-color: palegreen;}
```

If you look back at the Mangie's List web page source code, you can see that there are three h2 elements. Without "section >" at the left of h2, all three h2 elements would be matched. That means the h2 element at the top (inside the header container) would be pale green, and we don't want that. We want the h2 element at the top to use one of the other CSS rules in the Mangie's List web page so it gets a powder blue background. Here's that rule:

```
header {background-color: powderblue;}
```

Both CSS rules (the h2 selector rule and the header selector rule) attempt to assign the background color for the h2 element at the top of the Mangie's List web page. The first rule clearly impacts the h2 element because the selector is h2. The second rule also impacts the h2 element, but the connection is less straightforward. The second rule's selector is header, so it sets the background color for the header container. By default, that background color applies to all of the elements inside the header container, including the h2 element.

So with both rules attempting to assign the background color of the h2 element at the top, which rule takes precedence? The pale green h2 rule has higher precedence because it's more specific—its h2 selector precisely matches the h2 element that is being targeted. But as stated earlier, we don't want the pale green rule to win for the h2 element at the top. The solution is to tighten up the pale green rule's selector. Instead of matching all h2 elements, we match just those elements inside of a section container by prefacing the selector with "section >". Here's the result, copied from the Mangie's List web page source code:

```
section > h2 {background-color: palegreen;}
```

## Tweaking the Aside Box

Here's another child selector CSS rule from the Mangie's List web page:

```
aside > h3 {margin: 0;}
```

By default, browsers display heading elements, including h3, with rather large margins above and below the heading. We already added padding inside the aside element's border, so the additional default spacing from the h3 element creates gaps that are too big. Thus, we specify a margin width of 0 for the h3 element. This is another example where tweaking was necessary. It would be ideal if you could always write code that displays perfectly. But in the real world, most of the time your first-cut code won't be perfect, and you're going to have to go back and improve it incrementally. That's what tweaking is all about.

Since the Mangie's List web page has only one h3 element, we could have used a simple h3 type selector rule (without aside >), but we're planning for the future. If someone adds an h3 element later on, we want it to have a 0 margin only if the h3 element is inside an aside element. That type of thinking and coding makes your web pages more maintainable, which is very important in the real world. Making something easy to maintain means cost savings down the road.

# 4.11 **CSS Inheritance**

Now for one last CSS concept in this chapter—inheritance. CSS *inheritance* is when a CSS property value flows down from a parent element to one or more of its child elements. That should sound familiar. It parallels the inheritance of genetic characteristics (e.g., height and eye color) from a biological parent to a child.

Some CSS properties are inheritable and some are not. To determine whether a particular CSS property is inheritable, go to Mozilla's list of CSS keywords at https://developer.mozilla.org/en-US/docs/Web/CSS/Reference and click on the property you're interested in. That should take you to a description of that property, including its inheritability. Of the CSS properties covered so far in this book, here are the ones that are inheritable:

- color
- font (and all of its more granular properties, like font-size)
- line-height
- list-style (and all of its more granular properties, like list-style-type)
- text-align
- text-transform

To explain CSS inheritance, we'll refer once again to the Mangie's List web page. Specifically, we'll refer to this aside element:

```
<aside>
  <h3>Casey's Special</h3>
  Half-price hot dogs when rotisseried more than 24 hours!
</aside>
```

Also, we'll refer to this associated CSS rule:

```
aside {
  border: thin dashed red;
  color: red;
  background-color: white;
  float: right;
  width: 200px;
  padding: 10px;
  margin: 5px;
}
```

In this rule, the only inheritable CSS property is `color`. If you specify `papayawhip` (look it up; it's real) for a `body` element's color, all the elements inside the `body` container would inherit that color. That would cause the browser to use that color when displaying all the text within the web page. So for the Mangie's List web page, the `red` color gets inherited by the `h3` element that is a child of the `aside` element.

Inheritance is blocked for an inheritable property when an element explicitly specifies a new value for that property. In other words, if a parent element and its child element have two different CSS rules with the same property specified, then the child element's property-value pair (and not the parent element's property-value pair) gets applied to the child element. Formally, we say that the child element's property-value pair *overrides* the inherited property-value pair. So, for the Mangie's List web page, if `color: blue;` was specified for the `h3` element inside the `aside` element, then the browser would display blue text for the `h3` element.

For the other properties shown in the preceding `aside` type selector rule, their values do not flow down via inheritance. Thus, inside the `aside` element, the `h3` element does not get its own border. But it does get a background color of white, and it gets floated to the right. Why? Those properties are not inherited, but by applying those properties to the `aside` element, the `h3` child element is naturally affected.

# 4.12 CASE STUDY: Microgrid Possibilities in a Small City

This section adds another page to our case study website. The desired web page, shown in **FIGURE 4.12**, describes microgrid possibilities. This web page illustrates local navigation, ordered and unordered lists, an aside box, and a footnote.

As implied by the scrollbar at the right side of Figure 4.12, the browser window is too small to display all of the web page's content. To see the lower content, you can use the scroll bar to scroll down. But there's another way that provides quicker access. Note the three local navigation links just below the page header. Clicking one of these links changes what's displayed in the window to let you see the start of the material identified by that link's label. For example, suppose you click the "Typical Microgrid Features" link. Then the window's display changes immediately to what's

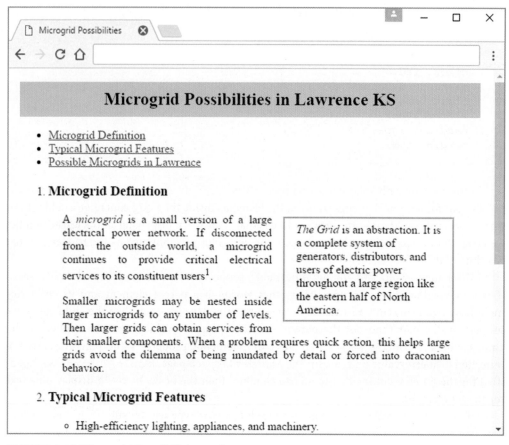

FIGURE 4.12 **Microgrid Possibilities web page**

shown in **FIGURE 4.13**—it's the content identified by the clicked link's label. After reading that content, you could click the browser's back button to return to the original positioning at the top of the web page.

Now let's look at the details. **FIGURE 4.14A** shows the top part of the HTML source code. The first few elements are either the same as before or altered, as you should expect, to describe this particular page. As in the last chapter's case study web page (and in all future case study web pages), there is a link to the common external CSS file. If you compare the main heading of this web page (in Figure 4.12) with the heading in the previous chapter's Figure 3.22, you'll see that this web page's heading has the same `lightgreen` background.

But the green colored paragraph backgrounds in the previous chapter's Figure 3.22 do not appear in this web page. Because this chapter's web page includes an `aside` box and lists as well as paragraphs, and because the external CSS file does not color the backgrounds of these new elements, if we simply accepted the external CSS file's coloring of paragraph backgrounds, the overall appearance would be jumbled. The easiest way to avoid such a jumbled appearance is to include

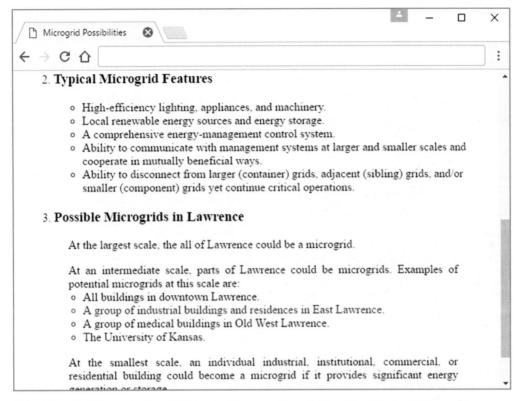

FIGURE 4.13 **Microgrid Possibilities web page after clicking the "Typical Microgrid Features" link**

a counteracting `style` specification in the current web page—a specification that changes the background coloring of paragraphs to match the default background coloring of the other (new) element types. Therefore, the current web page's `style` element includes the following style specification:

```
p {background-color: azure;}
```

The first `aside` property makes the box "float" on the right side of the page. The other `aside` properties should be familiar. The `15px` left and right margins keep it away from adjacent text on the left and move it farther away from the window's edge on the right. Similarly, the `ol` specification increases the space between the right side of ordered-list text and the right side of the window. And the `footer` specification increases the space between the left side of the window and the start of a footnote.

Finally, look at the `#removeLineAbove` selector's `margin-top` property. What's going on there? By default, each block element (like a paragraph or list) is separated from other block elements above and below by one blank line. But in Figure 4.13, look at the bulleted list after the second paragraph under **3. Possible Microgrids in Lawrence**. Conceptually, this bulleted list is not

```
<!DOCTYPE html>
<html lang="en">
<head>
<meta charset="utf-8">
<meta name="author" content="John Dean">
<title>Microgrid Possibilities</title>
<link rel="stylesheet" href="../library/microgrid.css">
<style>
  p {background-color: azure;}
  aside {
    float: right;
    width: 200px;
    margin: 5px 15px;
    border-style: groove;
    padding: 5px 15px;
  }
  ol {margin-right: 20px;}
  footer {margin-left: 20px;}
  #removeLineAbove {margin-top: -1em;}
</style>
</head>
```

**FIGURE 4.14A Source code for Microgrid Possibilities web page**

independent. It is a continuation of the paragraph immediately above it. So, logically, there should not be a blank line above this particular list. The #removeLineAbove selector's margin-top: -1em; property value removes that blank line.

FIGURE 4.14B contains the next section of HTML source code. The nav element includes three a elements with id selectors, which appear later in this HTML source code. (The first one is two lines below the </nav> end tag.) Usually we create an a element by putting <a href=...> and </a> tags around a word or phrase in running text. To jump to that location, the user clicks on that marked-up word or text. The present case, however, calls for a more dramatic representation—the three raised buttons just below the banner at the top of the browser window in Figure 4.12 or the left side of Figure 4.13. A good way to invoke this special presentation is to embed these a elements as list items in an unordered or ordered list within the nav element, as you see near the top of the HTML code in Figure 4.14B.

As you can see in Figures 4.12 and 4.13, the web page is one big ordered list, with three list items, numbered 1., 2., and 3. The first of these items includes a header, an aside box, and two paragraphs. Because it's an ordered list, browsers automatically insert the appropriate number before the first line of material in each list item. Figure 4.14B shows the code for the first li element in the ordered list, and the line in that element is the "Microgrid Definition" header. So, the browser does indeed prepend the number, 1., to that header. The other HTML features in Figure 4.14B are two em elements and a sup element.

```
<body>
<h2>Microgrid Possibilities in Lawrence KS</h2>
<nav>
  <ul>
    <li> <a href="#definition">Microgrid Definition</a> </li>
    <li> <a href="#features">Typical Microgrid Features</a> </li>
    <li> <a href="#examples">Possible Microgrids in Lawrence</a> </li>
  </ul>
</nav>
<ol>
  <li id="definition">
    <h3>Microgrid Definition</h3>
    <aside>
      <em>The Grid</em> is an abstraction. It is a complete system of
      generators, distributors, and users of electric power throughout
      a large region like the eastern half of North America.
    </aside>
    <p>
      A <em>microgrid</em> is a small version of a large electrical
      power network. If disconnected from the outside world, a
      microgrid continues to provide critical electrical services to
      its constituent users<sup>1</sup>.
    </p>
    <p>
      Smaller microgrids may be nested inside larger microgrids to
      any number of levels. Then larger grids can obtain services
      from their smaller components. When a problem requires quick
      action, this helps large grids avoid the dilemma of being
      inundated by detail or forced into draconian behavior.
    </p>
  </li>
```

**FIGURE 4.14B Source code for Microgrid Possibilities web page**

The remainder of the HTML code for this web page appears in **FIGURE 4.14C**. The second ordered list li element contains the header for this element followed by an unordered list that contains five list items. The third ordered list li element contains the header for this element followed by two paragraphs, another unordered list, and another paragraph. The previously described id="removeLineAbove" attribute removes the browser's default blank line immediately above this second subordinate unordered list. Finally, the footer illustrates HTML source code for the footer element, the sup element, and an a element with an href attribute that references an external web page. Notice how the format of this external reference value, http://www. ..., differs from the format of the previous local reference values, like, for example, #definition. Also notice the target="_blank" attribute. This tells the browser

```
  <li id="features">
    <h3>Typical Microgrid Features</h3>
    <ul>
      <li>High-efficiency lighting, appliances, and machinery.</li>
      <li>Local renewable energy sources and energy storage.</li>
      <li>A comprehensive energy-management control system.</li>
      <li>Ability to communicate with management systems at larger and
          smaller scales and cooperate in mutually beneficial ways.</li>
      <li>Ability to disconnect from larger (container) grids,
          adjacent (sibling) grids, and/or smaller (component) grids yet
          continue critical operations. </li>
    </ul>
  </li>
  <li id="examples">
    <h3>Possible Microgrids in Lawrence</h3>
    <p>
      At the largest scale, the all of Lawrence could be a microgrid.
    </p>
    <p>
      At an intermediate scale, parts of Lawrence could be microgrids.
      Examples of potential microgrids at this scale are:
    </p>
    <ul id="removeLineAbove">
      <li>All buildings in downtown Lawrence.</li>
      <li>A group of industrial buildings and residences in East
          Lawrence.</li>
      <li>A group of medical buildings in Old West Lawrence.</li>
      <li>The University of Kansas.</li>
    </ul>
    <p>
      At the smallest scale, an individual industrial, institutional,
      commercial, or residential building could become a microgrid if
      it provides significant energy generation or storage.
    </p>
  </li>
</ol>
<footer id="references">
  <sup>1</sup> For another description of microgrids, see
  <a href="http://www.microgridinstitute.org/" target="_blank">
  Microgrid Institute</a>.
</footer>
</body>
</html>
```

**FIGURE 4.14C Source code for Microgrid Possibilities web page**

to open the referenced external web page in a separate window. If `target="_self"` or the `target` attribute is missing, the referenced web page replaces the web page in the current window.

# Review Questions

### 4.2 Unordered Lists

1. Within a `ul` container, what is the only type of child element allowed?

2. What CSS property-value pair should you use to indicate that a list's items are to be displayed with no labels/symbols at their left?

### 4.3 Descendant Selectors

3. Fill in the blank: When an element is inside an outer element's start tag and end tag, we say that the element is a _____ of the outer element.

### 4.4 Ordered Lists

4. For the `list-style-type` CSS property, what value should you use to generate lowercase roman numerals for list items?

5. For the `ul` element, what does the `start` attribute do?

### 4.5 Figures

6. To make a figure caption display at the bottom of the figure's main content, you must position the `figcaption` element below the `figure` container. True or false.

7. What `img` attribute is used to specify fallback content for an image?

### 4.7 `section`, `article`, and `aside` Elements

8. In general, what is the relationship between `section` and `article`? Just one article in a `section` container? One or more sections in an `article` container? Or something else?

### 4.8 `nav` and `a` Elements

9. Normally, what does a `nav` container contain?

### 4.9 `header` and `footer` Elements

10. Suppose you have a `header` container that contains three heading elements. Suppose you want to assign a background color for the entire heading area. In terms of what is displayed, what problem would arise if you apply the background color to the individual heading elements rather than to the `header` container element?

### 4.11 CSS Inheritance

11. What is CSS inheritance?

12. What does "overriding" mean in the context of CSS inheritance?

# Exercises

1.  [after Section 4.2] Provide a type selector CSS rule for the `ul` element that causes list items to be displayed with check mark symbols (✓) at the left. The `list-style-type` property does not include a value for the check mark symbol. To display check mark symbols, you will need to use the `list-style-image` property, which was not covered in the book. In your answer, use the filename `checkMark.gif`.

2.  [after Section 4.4] Provide a `style` container that could be used to produce this web page:

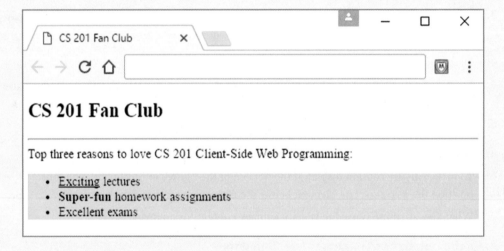

Your `style` container must:

▶ Implement an appropriate type selector rule that renders the outline with a yellow background color.

▶ Implement appropriate class selector rules for the underlined and boldfaced words.

Your `style` container must work in conjunction with the following `body` container. You are to use the `body` container as is; you are not allowed to modify it.

```
<body>
<h2>CS 201 Fan Club</h2>
<hr />
<div>
   Top three reasons to love CS 201 Client-Side Web Programming:
   <ul>
     <li><span class="underlined">Exciting</span> lectures</li>
     <li><span class="superFun">Super-fun</span> homework assignments</li>
     <li>Excellent exams</li>
```

```
    </ul>
  </div>
</body>
</html>
```

3. [after Section 4.4] In addition to unordered and ordered lists, there's also a *description list*, which was not covered in the book. A description list can be used to implement a glossary of terms and definitions. Provide the code for a description list that defines three or more video game terms.

4. [after Section 4.7] By default, an `aside` element displays on a line (or lines) by itself. What CSS property should you use to make it display next to another element, so the two elements share the same line?

5. [after Section 4.9] What entity forms the lowest priority rung in the cascade of places where CSS rules can be defined?

6. [after Section 4.10] What is the difference between a child selector and a descendant selector? In your answer, you must (1) explain what they are for, (2) provide an example child selector, and (3) provide an example descendant selector.

7. [after Section 4.10] Assuming the rest of the web page's code is valid, the following code fragments generate a nested list with three borders.

    a)  Describe what each of the three borders surrounds (for your description, it's OK to provide only a screenshot).

    b)  For each rule, describe which element(s) the rule applies to.

```
<style>
  ul li {border-style: solid;}
  ul > li {border-color: red;}
</style>

<body>
<ul>
  <li>one</li>
  <li>two
    <ol>
      <li>three</li>
    </ol>
  </li>
</ul>
</body>
```

8.  [after Section 4.11] Assuming the rest of the web page's code is valid, the following code fragments generate a nested list.

    a)  Describe the font size and color for each of the three list items (for your description, it's OK to provide only a screenshot).

    b)  For each rule, describe which element(s) the rule affects and whether the effect comes from the rule directly matching that element or whether it comes from CSS inheritance.

```
<style>
  ol > li {font-size: 200%;}
  ul {color: blue;}
  .green {color: green;}
</style>

<body>
<ul>
  <li>one
    <ol>
      <li>two
        <ul>
          <li class="green">three</li>
        </ul>
      </li>
    </ol>
  </li>
</ul>
</body>
```

# Project

Provide complete code for an implementation of the following web page and name the file wealth.html. To make each of the two figures, you can generate a line graph with Microsoft Excel, copy the result to Microsoft Paint, and save the pasted image as a .png file. As an option, feel free to insert a third graph above the other two graphs that shows how the average number of hours worked per week affects retirement wealth.

In the web page, note the superscripted "[1]" in the third line. That is a link to the message at the bottom of the web page. The W3C recommends implementing a footnote by using a link. The link contents should be a square-bracketed number, and the link should be superscripted. To make the link look good, the web page uses these CSS rules:

```
a {color: white; text-decoration: none;}
a:hover {text-decoration: underline;}
```

As always, make sure you use appropriate containers so that your web page's content is properly defined. In particular, you should include aside, header, article, section, and figure elements.

# The American Dream

TNN News, Tuesday March 6, 8pm EST
Author Robert Strausser presents "Survival of the Wealthiest"

## Work hard and become wealthy?
## Maybe so, but work alone might not cut it. The following graphs[1] show various paths to prosperity.

### Education

More advanced schooling helps. If you can avoid the crushing debt of student loans, all the better. Try to find a major that you're good at and that is good to you.

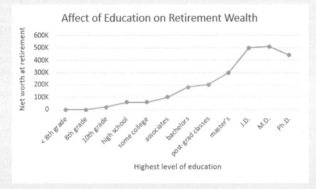

### Birthright

For accruing wealth, what's even better than education? Being born wealthy. In the graph below, note how the birthright high enders are able to become more wealthy than the education high enders. So before being born, shop around.

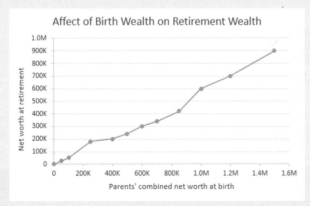

1. Although the graphs' data is fabricated, the trends are real. See Lisa Keister's "Getting Rich: America's New Rich and How They Got That Way" and Pew Charitable Trusts' "Economic Mobility Project."

# CHAPTER 5

# Tables and CSS Layout

## CHAPTER OBJECTIVES

▶ Learn the difference between data tables and layout tables.

▶ Use `table` elements to implement data tables.

▶ Use CSS to format table cells with alignment and padding.

▶ Partition a table with the `thead` and `tbody` elements.

▶ Appreciate the benefits of web accessibility, and make your tables more web accessible.

▶ Learn how to span cells across multiple columns or multiple rows.

▶ Use CSS to implement layout tables.

▶ Use CSS to position an element relative to its containing block.

▶ Use CSS to position an element relative to its normal flow.

## CHAPTER OUTLINE

# 5.1 Introduction

In Chapter 4, we focused on different ways to organize a web page's content. We discussed organizational elements that have clear physical manifestations—list and figure elements. We also discussed several organizational elements that are less clear-cut in terms of their physical manifestations—header, footer, nav, section, article, and so on. In this chapter, we present another organizational construct, but this construct is so popular and important that it merits an entire chapter. In this chapter, we discuss tables.

At its core, a table is a group of cells organized in a two-dimensional structure with rows and columns. Normally, we think of a table's cells as holding data, but tables can also be used purely for presentation purposes. To use a table for presentation purposes, you position content at particular locations on the web page using a row-column layout scheme. An example would be putting a navigation menu at the left, putting pictures at the right, and putting contact information at the bottom. We devote about half of this chapter to tables whose purpose is to hold data. We devote most of the rest of the chapter to tables whose purpose is to provide a row-column layout scheme.

Data tables very often hold numbers, but they can hold text and other types of content as well. The following data table holds text. More specifically, it holds descriptions for the 16 personality types defined by the Myers–Briggs Type Indicator (MBTI) instrument.[1] We created the table using Microsoft Word. One of the projects at the end of this chapter asks you to implement it using HTML.

In the MBTI table, the letters (ST, IJ, etc.) at the top and at the left are headers that show how a person's preferences indicate the person's personality type. The letters represent the contrasting pairs: Introversion (I) / Extroversion (E); Judging (J) / Perceiving (P); Sensing (S) / Intuition (N); Thinking (T) / Feeling (F). So in answering the MBTI questions, if a person indicates preferences

---

[1] Isabel Briggs Myers, *Introduction to Type: A Guide to Understanding Your Results on the MBTI Instrument* (Mountain View, CA: CPP, Inc., 1998). The personality descriptions in Myers's book are quite a bit longer than the ones shown. We shortened the descriptions to save space.

|    | ST | SF | NF | NT |
|----|----|----|----|----|
| **IJ** | Quiet and serious | Quiet, friendly, and responsible | Insightful, committed to their values | Independent-minded and hard-working |
| **IP** | Tolerant and analytical | Quiet, friendly, and sensitive | Idealistic and loyal | Has a desire to develop logical explanations |
| **EP** | Flexible and pragmatic | Outgoing, friendly, and accepting | Enthusiastic and imaginative | Quick, ingenious, and stimulating |
| **EJ** | Practical and realistic | Conscientious and cooperative | Warm, empathetic, and responsive | Decisive and quick to assume leadership |

for sensing, thinking, introversion, and judging, then the table would suggest that the person's personality type is quiet and serious. For more details, see https://www.opp.com/en/tools/MBTI /MBTI-personality-Types.

Unlike data tables, layout tables are not limited to holding data—they are allowed to hold any type of content. Their purpose is to position that content with a row-column layout scheme. Consider this graphic:

Pictures permissions granted by Brad Biles, Park University Director of Communications and Public Relations

To implement this graphic as part of a web page, you would probably want to use a two-row, three-column layout table. The "SEASONS ON THE HILL" heading would be implemented as a table caption. The pictures and season names would be positioned by placing them in the layout table's six cells.

We begin this chapter by describing data tables and the HTML table elements used to implement them such as `table`, `tr`, `th`, `td`, and so on. As part of our discussion of data tables, we describe cell spanning, where adjacent cells are merged to form larger cells. Next, we discuss web accessibility techniques that make it easier for disabled users to understand data table content. We then move on to a discussion of layout tables. We first describe how to implement layout tables using CSS's `display` property with various values such as `table`, `table-caption`, `table-row`, and so on. We then describe how to implement layout tables using CSS's `position` property. We show how to use the `position` property for absolute positioning, where an element gets positioned relative to its containing block, and we show how to use the `position` property for relative positioning, where an element gets positioned relative to its normal position in the web page.

## 5.2 Table Elements

Let's start by looking at a simple data table—the wind disasters table in **FIGURE 5.1**. It's a data table in that it displays data, the names of famous tornadoes and hurricanes, in a row-column format. Headers are not required for a data table, but they are common, and the wind disasters table has two column headers, labeled "Tornadoes" and "Hurricanes."

To create a data table, start with a `table` container element, fill the `table` element with a `tr` element for each of its rows, and fill each `tr` element with `th` elements for header cells and `td` elements for data cells. **FIGURE 5.2** shows the code used to implement Figure 5.1's Wind Disasters web page. Note Figure 5.2's `table` element and its four `tr` elements. The top `tr` element contains `th` elements for the column header cells. The bottom three `tr` elements contain `td` elements for the data cells.

If you'd like to display a title for a table, embed a `caption` element within the `table` container. For example, note the `caption` element in Figure 5.2 and the resulting "Wind Disasters"

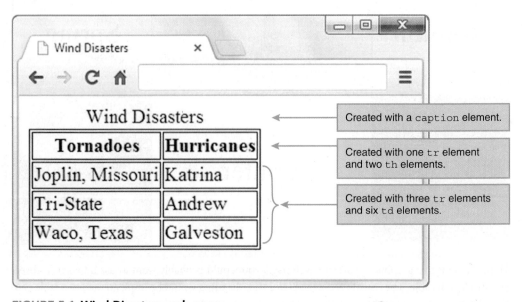

**FIGURE 5.1 Wind Disasters web page**

```
<!DOCTYPE html>
<html lang="en">
<head>
<meta charset="utf-8">
<meta name="author" content="John Dean">
<title>Wind Disasters</title>
<style>
   table, th, td {border: thin solid;}
</style>
</head>

<body>
<table>
  <caption>Wind Disasters</caption>
  <tr><th>Tornadoes</th><th>Hurricanes</th></tr>
  <tr><td>Joplin, Missouri</td><td>Katrina</td></tr>
  <tr><td>Tri-State</td><td>Andrew</td></tr>
  <tr><td>Waco, Texas</td><td>Galveston</td></tr>
</table>
</body>
</html>
```

Explicitly apply a border around the entire table and around each cell.

Indent all the code that appears within the `table` start and end tags.

**FIGURE 5.2 Source code for Wind Disasters web page**

title in Figure 5.1. If you include a `caption` element within a `table` container, the `caption` element must be the first element within the table. As you'd expect, a table's caption displays above the table's grid by default. If you want the caption's text displayed at the bottom, you can use the following CSS type selector rule:

```
caption {caption-side:  bottom;}
```

By default, browsers use boldface font for table header cells. You can see this behavior in Figure 5.1, where the "Tornadoes" and "Hurricanes" headers (implemented with `th` elements) are bolder than the text values below the headers. That default behavior should make sense because table headers are often boldfaced in business reports.

Beginning web programmers sometimes have trouble deciding when to use `th` elements and when to use `td` elements. Use `th` for a cell that is a description for other cells' content; use `td` for all other cells in the table.

The `table` element is a block element. As you learned earlier, unless all the code in a block element can fit on one line (and that's very unlikely with a `table` element), you should indent all of the block element's contained code. For example, in Figure 5.2, note how the `caption` and `tr` elements are indented inside the `table` element's start and end tags.

# 5.3 Formatting a Data Table: Borders, Alignment, and Padding

In this section, we'll describe how to format data tables in terms of their borders, cell alignment, and cell padding. Before HTML5, older versions of HTML allowed you to specify those presentation features using HTML attributes. But in sticking to its goal of keeping content and presentation separate, HTML5 has made those attributes obsolete. The solution? As usual, you should use CSS for presentation.

To specify whether or not you want borders for a table, you should use CSS's `border-style` property. To specify the border's width, you should use CSS's `border-width` property. For example, here's the CSS type selector rule used in the Wind Disasters web page:

```
table, th, td {border: thin solid;}
```

Oops. Why are there no `border-style` and `border-width` properties? That's a trick question. You might recall from Chapter 3 that `border` is a shorthand property that handles a set of border-related properties. In this example, the `border` property's first value is `thin`, which goes with the `border-width` property, and the `border` property's second value is `solid`, which goes with the `border-style` property. With `table`, `th`, and `td` all listed in the rule, the resulting web page displays a thin solid border around the entire table (except for the table's caption), around each header cell, and around each data cell. As a sanity check, glance back at Figure 5.1's Wind Disasters web page and verify that those borders exist.

Now onto the next two formatting features—cell alignment and cell padding. If you add no CSS to a table, then you'll end up using the browser's default CSS values. Table header cells (`th`) have a default alignment of center and a default weight of bold. Table data cells (`td`) have a default alignment of left. Both `th` and `td` cells have a default padding of none. Look at the Wind Disasters web page in Figure 5.1 and verify that the table uses those default CSS values. To adjust the horizontal alignment of text in table cells, use CSS's `text-align` property with a value of `left`, `right`, or `center`. To adjust the padding around the text in table cells, use CSS's `padding` property with a pixel value (e.g., `5px`).

Look at the Wind Disasters web page in **FIGURE 5.3**. Note how the header text ("Tornadoes" and "Hurricanes") is left aligned. Note how there's padding around every cell's text. Also note the border widths—the outer border is thicker than the cell borders, and there's an even thicker border below the header cells. To hone your problem-solving skills, see if you can figure out what CSS rules need to be added in order to implement those formatting features. Please do not continue reading until you try.

Have you got the CSS figured out? To add left alignment and padding to every cell, use this type selector rule:

```
th, td {
  text-align: left;
  padding: 10px;
}
```

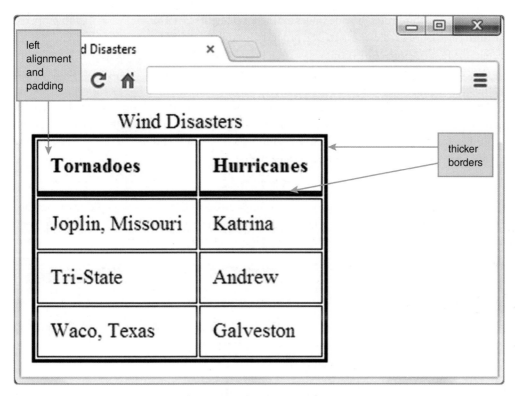

**FIGURE 5.3 Wind Disasters web page with improved formatting**

This rule specifies left alignment for the `td` element, even though the `td` element uses left alignment by default. That's OK. The code is *self-documenting*—it explicitly shows the web developer's intent without needing a comment.

Figure 5.2's `style` container contains the following CSS rule, which creates thin border lines around the entire table and also around each cell:

```
table, th, td {border: thin solid;}
```

To assign a medium width to the table's outer border and to assign a thick width to the header cells' bottom borders, add the following type selector rules below the rule:

```
table {border-width: medium;}
th {border-bottom-width: thick;}
```

Note that all three rules deal with borders. The first and second rules both provide values for the `table` element's `border-width` property. The second rule's `border-width` property is explicit (`border-width: medium`), whereas the first rule's `border-width` property is built into the `border` shorthand property (`border: thin`). So will the table's border width be `medium` or `thin`? If two CSS rules refer to the same property, the rule that appears later overrides the prior rule's property value. Therefore, because the `border-width: medium` rule appears later, it wins and the table's border width will be `medium`.

The first and third rules provide values for the th element's border-bottom-width property. The third rule's border-bottom-width property is explicit (border-bottom-width: thick), whereas the first rule's border-bottom-width property is built into the border shorthand property (border: thin). Because the border-bottom-width: thick rule appears later, it wins and the th elements' bottom border widths will be thick.

In Figure 5.3, note how there's a gap between each of the borders. More specifically, there's a gap between the table's exterior border and the individual cells' borders, and there's a gap between the borders for adjacent cells. If you'd like to eliminate those gaps and merge the borders, use the border-collapse CSS property with a value of collapse, like this:

```
table {border-collapse: collapse;}
```

The default value for border-collapse is separate, and the separate value causes gaps to appear between adjacent borders. On the other hand, if you add the CSS rule to the "improved formatting" Wind Disasters web page shown in Figure 5.3, here's the result:

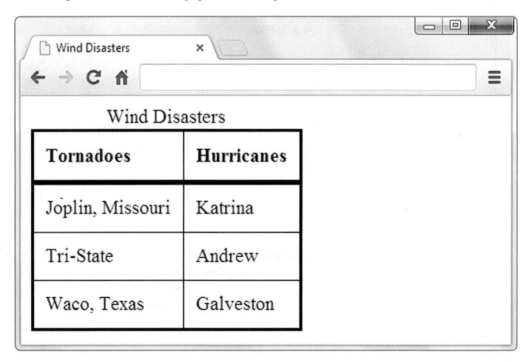

## 5.4 CSS Structural Pseudo-Class Selectors

The previous chapter described lists, and this chapter describes tables and tabular formatting. All of these things involve collections of elements. When you have a collection of elements, sometimes you want to display one or more of those elements differently from the rest. You could do that by including class attributes in each element that you want to display differently. You would then use the class attribute's value as a class selector in a CSS rule. But if the number of elements that you want to display with a special format is large, then quite a few class="*value*" code insertions would be required.

When there is regularity in the locations of certain elements within a collection of elements, you can avoid the class=*"value"* code insertions described and, instead, implement that functionality with a structural pseudo-class CSS rule. *Pseudo-classes* conditionally select elements from a group of elements specified by a standard selector. For example, the following code uses a standard tr type selector to select all the tr elements in a web page, and the :first-of-type pseudo-class checks each of those elements to see if it is a first tr element within a particular table:

```
tr:first-of-type {background-color: palegreen;}
```

For each conditionally selected tr element (i.e., for each first-row tr element), the browser displays the element with a pale green background color.

A pseudo-class is called a "pseudo-class" because using a pseudo-class is similar to using a class attribute, but the two entities are not identical. A pseudo-class is like a class selector in that it matches particular instances of elements (that's what happens with elements that use class attributes). But they are different from class selectors in that they don't rely on the class attribute.

When we describe pseudo-class selectors, we'll very often use the terms sibling and parent. For the preceding CSS rule, we formally say that the pseudo-class checks for a first tr element from among a group of sibling tr elements. *Sibling* elements are elements that have the same parent element. An element is considered to be a parent of another element if it contains the other element with just one level of nesting. This mimics the notion of a human parent. A human is a parent of its children, but is not a parent of its grandchildren.

The W3C defines 12 structural pseudo-classes, but we'll focus on three of the most popular ones; they are :first-of-type, :last-of-type, and :nth-of-type(). See **FIGURE 5.4** for a short description of each one. As indicated in the figure, all pseudo-classes start with a colon. The purpose of a pseudo-class is to qualify a standard selector. More specifically, it provides a condition for selecting an element(s) from among the elements selected by a standard selector.

We've already discussed :first-of-type. Now let's discuss its partner, :last-of-type. As you might guess, the :last-of-type pseudo-class checks each of the elements selected by a standard selector to see if the element is a last element from among a group of sibling elements. So the following example selects li elements that are at the bottom of unordered lists:

```
ul > li:last-of-type {background-color: palegreen;}
```

| Pseudo-Class | Description |
|---|---|
| :first-of-type | Selects first element in sibling group of a particular type. |
| :last-of-type | Selects last element in sibling group of a particular type. |
| :nth-of-type() | Uses parentheses value to select an element or group of elements. |

**FIGURE 5.4 Popular structural pseudo-class selectors**

Note the ul > li child selector notation, which means that an li element is selected only if it is a child of a ul element. Note that there are no spaces on either side of the pseudo-class's colon. That's a style rule. The rationale is that having no spaces serves as a visual reminder that the last-of-type pseudo-class qualifies the li selector. In the CSS rule, it would be legal to qualify ul with its own pseudo-class. If you did so, there should be no space between ul and the newly added pseudo-class.

Now for the more challenging pseudo-class, which is :nth-of-type(). Unlike the other pseudo-classes so far, the :nth-of-type() pseudo-class has parentheses. Inside the parentheses, you provide a value that indicates which element or group of elements you want to select. For example, in the following CSS rule, we put 3 in the parentheses to select the third data cell within a row of sibling data cells:

```
td:nth-of-type(3) {text-align: right;}
```

That rule matches every third td element within each row of td elements and causes those td elements to be right-aligned. Effectively, that causes tables to display their third columns with right-aligned data (which works nicely for money values). As an alternative to putting a number in the parentheses, you can specify even or odd. For example, in the following CSS rule, we put even in the parentheses to select every even-numbered row:

```
tr:nth-of-type(even) {background-color: lightblue;}
```

That rule causes tables to display their even-numbered rows (second, fourth, and so on) with a light blue background color.

As an alternative to putting a number, even, or odd in the parentheses, you can use an expression of the form $an + b$, where $a$ and $b$ are constant integers and $n$ is a variable named $n$. By using such an expression, you can specify interleaved groups of elements. This is better explained with an example:

```
tr:nth-of-type(5n+2) {background-color: red;}
```

That rule selects every fifth tr element starting with the second row. In other words, it selects rows 2, 7, 12, 17, and so on. The way it works is you plug in values for $n$ by starting with $n$ equals 0 and incrementing $n$ by 1 each time. So when $n$ equals 0, row 2 is selected. When $n$ equals 1, row 7 is selected. Make sense?

**FIGURE 5.5** shows code for a simple example that presents electrical power generated by a small store's rooftop photovoltaic solar collectors, plus that store's immediate electrical consumption and electrical and thermal storage. This example includes three structural pseudo-class rules. The first uses nth-of-type selectors to right-align data in the third and fourth columns of the table. The second uses :first-of-type to color the background of the table's header row pale green. The third uses :nth-of-type(2n+3) to color alternate data rows pale goldenrod.

**FIGURE 5.6** shows what this code displays. The optional case study at the end of this chapter expands a variation of this example and includes other material before and after this table.

```html
<!DOCTYPE html>
<html lang="en">
<head>
<meta charset="utf-8">
<meta name="author" content="John Dean">
<title>Local Power Generation and Consumption</title>
<style>
  h3 {text-align: center;}
  table {border-collapse: collapse; margin: 0 auto;}
  th, td {border: thin solid; padding: 2px 5px;}
  td:nth-of-type(3), td:nth-of-type(4) {text-align: right;}
  tr:first-of-type {background-color: palegreen;}
  tr:nth-of-type(2n+3) {background-color: palegoldenrod;}
</style>
</head>

<body>
<table>
  <caption>
    <h3>Noon Power Generation (positive) and Consumption (negative)</h3>
  </caption>
  <tr>
    <th>Component Description</th> <th>Overall Size</th>
    <th>Noon Power</th> <th>Installed Cost</th>
  </tr>
  <tr>
    <td>PV Solar Collectors</td> <td>137 m<sup>2</sup> panel area</td>
    <td>+18 kW</td> <td>$45,000</td>
  </tr>
  <tr>
    <td>Immediate Consumption</td> <td>274 m<sup>2</sup> floor area</td>
    <td>-5 kW</td><td> </td>
  </tr>
  <tr>
    <td>Chilled Water Storage</td> <td>2.3 m diameter x 2.1 m high</td>
    <td>-2 kW</td> <td>$1000</td>
  </tr>
  <tr>
    <td>Battery Storage</td> <td>1.3 m x 1.0 m x 1.1 m high, 1250kg</td>
    <td>+18 kW</td> <td>$6000</td>
  </tr>
</table>
</body>
</html>
```

These rules use structural pseudo-class selectors.

**FIGURE 5.5 Source code for Power Table web page**

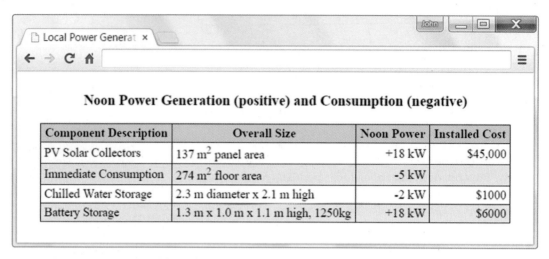

FIGURE 5.6 **Power Table web page**

## 5.5 `thead` and `tbody` Elements

Normally, you'll put table header cells at the top of a table's columns, but sometimes you'll also want to put them at the left of each row. For example, in the Global Temperatures web page in **FIGURE 5.7**, note the year values in header cells at the left. If you have header cells at the left, very often you'll want to differentiate those header cells from the ones at the top. The preferred way to differentiate is to put the top cells' row (or rows) in a `thead` element and put the subsequent rows in a `tbody` element. In the Global Temperatures web page, why would you need to differentiate between the header cells at the left and the ones at the top? So you can apply different CSS background-color rules to the different groups of header cells—midnight blue for the top cells and violet red for the left-side cells.

Take a look at the Global Temperatures `thead` and `tbody` code in **FIGURE 5.8**. The `thead` element contains a `tr` element and three `th` elements within the `tr` element. The `tbody` element contains several `tr` elements, with each `tr` element holding a `th` element and two `td` elements. Here are simplified versions of the descendant selector rules used to color `thead`'s header cells differently from `tbody`'s header cells:

```
thead th {background-color: midnightblue;}
tbody th {background-color: mediumvioletred;}
```

In Figure 5.8, note the indentations for the `thead`, `tbody`, and `tr` containers. They are all block elements, and unless all the code in a block element can fit on one line, you should indent all of the block element's contained code. For example, note how the `tr` elements are indented inside the `thead` and `tbody` containers. Also, inside the first `tr` container, note how the three `th` elements are indented even more so.

Besides using `thead` and `tbody`, there are other ways to distinguish the top header cells from the left-side header cells. For example, you could use `class` attributes with one value for

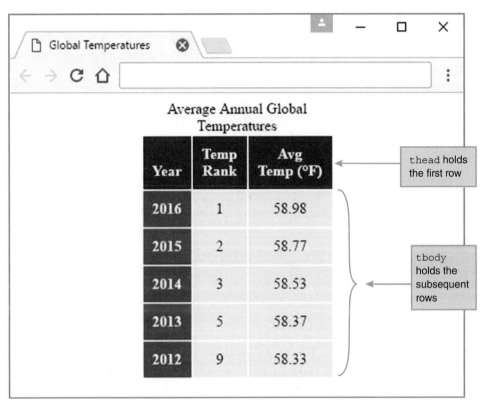

**FIGURE 5.7 Global Temperatures web page**

Note: The web page's table data refers to global land-ocean surface air temperatures. Data from the National Oceanic and Atmospheric Administration (NOAA), "Global Climate Report—Annual 2016," National Oceanic and Atmospheric Administration (NOAA), January 2017, https://www.ncdc.noaa.gov/sotc/global/201613.

the top header cells and a different value for the left-side header cells. However, that would lead to cluttered code—a class attribute for every th cell. On the other hand, the Global Temperatures web page uses thead and tbody, which means less clutter because no class attributes are necessary.

Let's now examine a few noteworthy CSS rules from the Global Temperatures web page that are unrelated to thead and tbody. Here's the first such rule:

```
body {display: flex; justify-content: center;}
```

That rule tells the browser to center all the elements in the body container horizontally within the browser window's borders. Go back to Figure 5.8 and confirm that the body container has only one child element—the table element. So the table gets centered. Go back to Figure 5.7 and confirm that the table is indeed centered. In the CSS rule, the display: flex; property-value pair creates a *flexbox* layout (also called a *flexible box* layout). It provides the ability to add certain formatting features to a standard block element. The formatting feature we're interested in now is horizontal centering, and the justify-content: center property-value pair takes care of that.

```
<!DOCTYPE html>
<html lang="en">
<head>
<meta charset="utf-8">
<meta name="author" content="John Dean">
<title>Global Temperatures</title>
<style>
  body {display: flex; justify-content: center;}
  table, th, td {border: none;}
  th, td {padding: 10px;}
  thead th {
    background-color: midnightblue;
    color: white;
    vertical-align: bottom;
  }
  tbody th {
    background-color: mediumvioletred;
    color: white;
  }
  td {
    background-color: mistyrose;
    text-align: center;
  }
</style>
</head>

<body>
<table>
  <caption>Average Annual Global Temperatures</caption>
  <thead>
    <tr>
      <th>Year</th>
      <th>Temp<br>Rank</th>
      <th>Avg<br>Temp (&deg;F)</th>
    </tr>
  </thead>
  <tbody>
    <tr><th>2016</th><td>1</td><td>58.98</td></tr>
    <tr><th>2015</th><td>2</td><td>58.77</td></tr>
    <tr><th>2014</th><td>3</td><td>58.53</td></tr>
    <tr><th>2013</th><td>5</td><td>58.37</td></tr>
    <tr><th>2012</th><td>9</td><td>58.33</td></tr>
  </tbody>
</table>
</body>
</html>
```

To center a block element (like `table`), apply this CSS code to the element's parent container.

To position text vertically within its container, use the `vertical-align` property.

If a row's content is too long to fit on one line, then put indented cell elements on separate lines.

**FIGURE 5.8 Source code for Global Temperatures web page**

In the CSS rule, note that the selector is body, not table. To center an element, you apply the rule to the element's parent container, not to the element itself.

Because the flexbox layout is fairly new (the W3C introduced it to its CSS specification in 2016), older browsers don't support it. Therefore, you should be familiar with this alternative technique, which is pervasive throughout the web page universe:

```
table {margin: 0 auto;}
```

The code shows two values for the margin property—0 and auto. You might recall from Chapter 3 that if you provide two values, the first value specifies the top and bottom margins and the second value specifies the left and right margins. So with the first value being 0 in the CSS rule, there are no margins above and below the table. The auto value requires some additional explanation. For any block element (including a table element), if the left margin and right margin are both set to auto, that will force the browser to make the margins equal, which forces the browser to center the block element. Thus, the CSS rule causes the table to be centered.

Here's a simplified version of another rule from the Global Temperatures web page that deserves some attention:

```
thead th {vertical-align: bottom;}
```

What is the vertical-align property for? Before answering that question, look back at Figure 5.7's Global Temperatures web page. Note how the top heading values are aligned at the bottom of their cells. Using a bottom value for the vertical-align property causes a cell's text to be aligned at the bottom. If you need top or middle vertical alignment, use the vertical-align property with a value of top or middle, respectively.

Note this additional CSS rule from the Global Temperatures web page, copied here for your convenience:

```
table, th, td {border: none;}
```

The border: none property-value pair means that the browser will not draw border lines. That means the web page's background color appears where the border lines would normally appear. For the Global Temperatures web page, the cells use a different background color than the web page's background. So with border none, the borders display as white lines, from the web page's default white background color. Although the default is for a table to have no visible borders, it's fairly unusual to stick with that default. Thus, we include the rule to make it clear to someone looking at the code that having no borders is intentional. This is a form of self-documentation.

There is one final noteworthy item in the code for the Global Temperatures web page. The table's first row contains this th container code:

```
<th>Avg<br>Temp (&deg;F)</th>
```

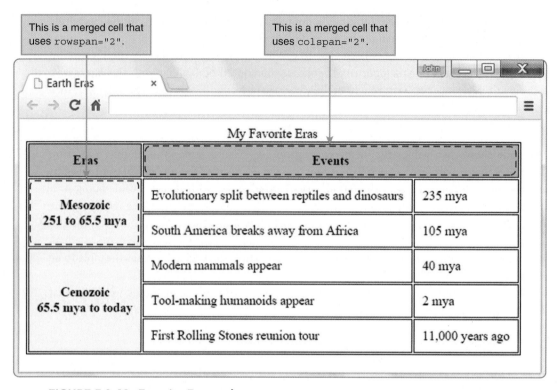

FIGURE 5.9 **My Favorite Eras web page**

What is `&deg;`? It's a character reference for the degree character (°). To verify, see the "Avg Temp (°F)" header in Figure 5.7.

## 5.6 Cell Spanning

So far, all of our data table examples have used a standard grid pattern, with one cell for each row-column intersection. But sometimes data tables will have cells that span more than one of the intersections in a standard grid. For example, see the My Favorite Eras table in **FIGURE 5.9**. We implemented it using a table element with six rows and three columns. The Events cell at the top is a merged version of two cells in the first row. The Mesozoic cell at the left is a merged version of two cells in the first column. Below the Mesozoic cell, the Cenozoic cell is a merged version of the next three cells in the first column.

If you want to create a merged cell that spans more than one column, you'll need to add a `colspan` attribute to a `th` or `td` element. **FIGURE 5.10** shows the code for the My Favorite Eras web page. In particular, examine the code for the table's first row, and note `colspan="2"`, which creates a merged cell that spans two columns. We've copied the code here for your convenience:

```
<tr><th>Eras</th><th colspan="2">Events</th></tr>
```

```
<!DOCTYPE html>
<html lang="en">
<head>
<meta charset="utf-8">
<meta name="author" content="John Dean">
<title>Earth Eras</title>
<style>
  table {border: thin solid;}
  th, td {border: thin solid; padding: 10px;}
  thead th (background-color: lawngreen;}
  tbody th (background-color: lightcyan;}
</style>
</head>

<body>
<table>
  <caption>My Favorite Eras</caption>                    colspan attribute
  <thead>
    <tr><th>Eras</th><th colspan="2">Events</th></tr>
  </thead>                      rowspan attribute
  <tbody>
    <tr>
      <th rowspan="2">Mesozoic<br>251 to 65.5 mya</th>
      <td>Evolutionary split between reptiles and dinosaurs</td>
      <td>235 mya</td>
    </tr>
    <tr>
      <td>South America breaks away from Africa</td>
      <td>105 mya</td>
    </tr>
    <tr>
      <th rowspan="3">Cenozoic<br>65.5 mya to today</th>
      <td>Modern mammals appear</td>
      <td>40 mya</td>
    </tr>
    <tr><td>Tool-making humanoids appear</td><td>2 mya</td></tr>
    <tr>
      <td>First Rolling Stones reunion tour</td>
      <td>11,000 years ago</td>
    </tr>
  </tbody>
</table>
</body>
</html>
```

**FIGURE 5.10 Source code for My Favorite Eras web page**

Note how this row has two cells—an Eras header cell and an Events header cell. On the other hand, the table's next row has three cells—a Mesozoic header cell and two data cells:

```
<tr>
  <th rowspan="2">Mesozoic<br>251 to 65.5 mya</th>
  <td>Evolutionary split between reptiles and dinosaurs</td>
  <td>235 mya</td>
</tr>
```

The different number of cells in the two rows should make sense when you realize that the first row's second cell is formed by spanning two cells in the table's original grid pattern.

In this code fragment, note `rowspan="2"` in the first cell. If you want to create a merged cell that spans more than one row, add a `rowspan` attribute to the cell's `th` or `td` element. Thus, as shown in Figure 5.9, the Mesozoic header cell spans two rows.

Here's the code for the table's next row:

```
<tr>
  <td>South America breaks away from Africa</td>
  <td>105 mya</td>
</tr>
```

Remember that the prior row has three cells. Can you figure out why this row has only two cells rather than three? It's because the prior row's first cell (the Mesozoic header cell) spans down and replaces the next row's first cell.

Refer back to Figure 5.9's My Favorite Eras web page. In the light blue header cells at the left, note how each era's name appears on a separate line from its range of years. We induced that separation by adding `<br>` elements after the words "Mesozoic" and "Cenozoic." If there were no `<br>` elements, then each era's name and range of years would appear on one line, unbroken, and the left-side column would widen to accommodate the longer lines of text. Having such a wide left-side column would look rather odd because of all the unused space within the Mesozoic and Cenozoic header cells. An important takeaway from this is that a table column will conform to the width of the column cell with the widest content. An exception to that rule occurs when a table's natural width is greater than the browser window's width. In that case, the browser will shrink one or more of the table's columns so that the entire table displays in the browser window. In shrinking a column(s), the browser will initiate line wrap in the cell(s) with the widest content. To get a better appreciation for this phenomenon, you should experience it for yourself. Load the My Favorite Eras web page in a browser. Use your mouse to decrease the browser's width, and as you do so, in the first data cell, you should see "dinosaurs" wrap to a second line. The browser chooses to wrap that data cell's text because that data cell contains the widest content from among all the cells in the second column. The rules that determine which columns to shrink first are slightly different for the different browsers. The rules can get pretty complicated, but don't worry—there's no need to understand them fully just yet.

Having different rules about which columns to shrink first can lead to slightly different layouts for users with different browsers. That inconsistency might run counter to your tendency to want to make everything look identical on all browsers. Consistency is indeed a worthy goal. Nonetheless, sometimes attempting to achieve that goal is not worth the effort.

# 5.7 Web Accessibility

In this section, we'll digress a bit and discuss *web accessibility*—a subject that is important for tables specifically, but also for programming in general. Web accessibility means that disabled users can use the Web effectively. Most web accessibility efforts go toward helping users with visual disabilities, but web accessibility also attempts to address the needs of users with hearing, cognitive, and motor skills disabilities.

Many countries have laws that regulate accessibility for websites. For example, https://www .access-board.gov/guidelines-and-standards/communications-and-it describes web accessibility guidelines that U.S. government agencies are required to follow.

To promote the social good (through equal opportunities for disabled people) and to promote their own businesses, many companies have policies that require web developers and software purchasers to follow web accessibility standards. Such policies can promote the company's business not only by attracting people who fall into the traditional disabled categories, but also by providing added value to other people. For example, accessible websites tend to be better for users with slow Internet connections and for users who need glasses.

Typically, visually impaired users have screen readers to read web pages. A *screen reader* is software that figures out what the user's screen is displaying and sends a text description of it to a speech synthesizer. The speech synthesizer then reads the text aloud.

The easiest way to understand a table is to look at it. If you can't see the table and you rely on someone else reading the table's content to you, you'll probably have a harder time understanding what's going on. Likewise, because their output is purely auditory and not visual, screen readers are a bit challenged when it comes to describing a table's content. To overcome that challenge, screen readers rely on the fact that most data tables have header cells in the first row or the first column. When screen readers see such "simple" data tables, they assume that each header in the first row describes the data cells that are below it. Likewise, if there are headers in the first column, screen readers assume that each of those headers describes the data cells that are at the right of the header.

If you have a data table in which one or more header cells are not in the first row or column (i.e., it's not a simple table), then you should consider adding code to make the table more web accessible. In particular, you should consider embedding a `details` element in the table's `caption` element. The `details` element provides a description of the table's content so that a screen reader can read the description and get a better understanding of the nature of the table's organization.

The Grading Weights table in **FIGURE 5.11** has header cells in its second row, so the table is a good candidate for a web accessibility makeover.[2] In the figure, note the right-facing triangle under the table's title. If the user clicks the triangle, the browser will display "help" details that describe the table's content. The triangle and the text that describes the table both come from a `details` element embedded in the table's `caption` element. Take a look at **FIGURE 5.12A** and find the `details` element and its enclosed text. Screen readers will use that text to describe the table's organization. The HTML5 standard requires that you preface the `details` element's text

---

[2] The Grading Weights web page is excerpted from the #1 hit television series "Extreme Makeover: Web Page Accessibility Edition."

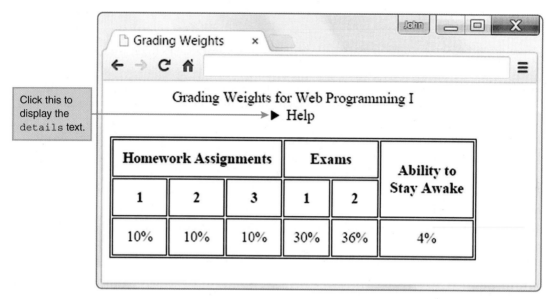

FIGURE 5.11 **Grading Weights web page**

with a `summary` element. In Figure 5.12A, the `summary` element contains one word—"Help." In Figure 5.11, you can see that "Help" serves as a label for the clickable details triangle.

The `details` element is new with HTML5, and, as such, older browsers don't support it. Besides the `details` element, another way to help screen readers understand complicated data tables (where one or more header cells are not in the first row or first column) is to use the `headers` attribute. With a `headers` attribute, you specify the header cell(s) that each data cell or subheader cell is associated with. For example, in the Grading Weights table, the 36% data cell is associated with the Exams header cell and also the 2 subheader cell immediately above the 36% cell. So to help with web accessibility, the 36% cell has a `headers` attribute that specifies those two header cells. Here's the relevant code from **FIGURE 5.12B**:

```
<td headers="exams exam2">36%</td>
```

In this `headers` attribute, the "exams" and "exam2" values match the `id` values for the Exams header cell and the 2 subheader cell immediately above the 36% cell. Here's the relevant code from Figure 5.12B:

```
<th colspan="2" id="exams">Exams</th>
...
<th id="exam2" headers="exams">2</th>
```

In this `headers` attribute, the "exams" value matches the `id` value for the Exams header cell. This stuff can be kind of tricky, so spend time studying the Grading Weights web page and source code until you're comfortable with it.

The `details` element and `headers` attribute make things easier for screen readers by indicating how the cells are organized by rows and columns and how the data cells relate to the header

```
<!DOCTYPE html>
<html lang="en">
<head>
<meta charset="utf-8">
<meta name="author" content="John Dean">
<title>Grading Weights</title>
<style>
  table, th, td {border: thin solid;}
  th, td {
    text-align: center;
    padding: 10px;
  }
  caption {margin-bottom: 15px;}
</style>
</head>

<body>
<table>
  <caption>
    Grading Weights for Web Programming I
    <details>
      <summary>Help</summary>
      The first 3 columns show weights for the 3 homework assignments.
      The next 2 columns show weights for the 2 exams.
      The last column shows the weight for staying awake during class.
    </details>
  </caption>
```

`details` element, embedded in a `caption` element

`summary` element, embedded in the `details` element

**FIGURE 5.12A** **Source code for Grading Weights web page**

cells. But what if a `table` element is used for layout purposes, and the cells are not organized by rows and columns? If a screen reader reads such a table and doesn't know that it's a layout table, there's a good chance that it will provide unhelpful (and possibly confusing) information. For example, before verbalizing each row's content, it might preface the content with a row number, even though the user won't care about row numbers. To avoid this problem, if you have a table element being used for layout purposes, you should add a `role` attribute to the `table` element's start tag, like this:

```
<table role="presentation">
```

That tells the screen reader that the table is for presentation/layout purposes, not for storing data, and the screen reader should then be able to do a better job describing the table's content.

Even though `role="presentation"` is part of the HTML5 specification, the W3C is not particularly fond of it. The W3C states that you should implement layout with CSS and not

```
    <tr>
      <th colspan="3" id="hw">Homework Assignments</th>
      <th colspan="2" id="exams">Exams</th>
      <th rowspan="2" id="awake">Ability to<br>Stay Awake</th>
    </tr>
    <tr>
      <th id="hw1" headers="hw">1</th>
      <th id="hw2" headers="hw">2</th>
      <th id="hw3" headers="hw">3</th>
      <th id="exam1" headers="exams">1</th>
      <th id="exam2" headers="exams">2</th>
    </tr>
    <tr>
      <td headers="hw hw1">10%</td>
      <td headers="hw hw2">10%</td>
      <td headers="hw hw3">10%</td>
      <td headers="exams exam1">30%</td>
      <td headers="exams exam2">36%</td>
      <td headers="awake">4%</td>
    </tr>
    </table>
  </body>
</html>
```

**FIGURE 5.12B Source code for Grading Weights web page**

with the `table` element. That wasn't always the case. In older versions of HTML, the `table` element was used not only for holding data, but also for layout. Consequently, many web developers have gotten used to using the `table` element for layout purposes. Knowing that it's hard to "teach an old dog new tricks," the W3C realizes that this nonconforming practice will continue for the foreseeable future. The `role="presentation"` solution somewhat mitigates the problem.

This section provided a brief introduction to the rather large field of web accessibility. If you'd like additional details, check out the W3C's accessibility page at https://www.w3.org/WAI/intro /accessibility.php.

# 5.8 CSS `display` Property with Table Values

In the previous section, we told you not to use the `table` element for layout tables, but if you do so, you should use `role="presentation"` to avoid incurring the wrath of the W3C police. Now it's time to discuss how to implement layout tables the right way—using CSS rather than the `table` element. There are two main ways to implement layout tables with CSS. If you want the layout boundaries to grow and shrink the way they do for an HTML `table` element, then use the CSS `display` property with table values. On the other hand, if you want the layout boundaries to be fixed (no growing or shrinking), then use CSS position properties. In this section, we discuss the first technique, using the CSS `display` property with table values, and in the next section, we discuss the second technique, using CSS position properties.

# The `display` Property's Table Values

In Chapter 4, you learned about the CSS `display` property. Specifically, you used a `display: inline` property-value pair to display an `address` element (which is normally a block element) in the flow of its surrounding sentence. The `display` property can be used for much more than just inlining block element content. It can also be used to emulate the various parts of a table. Review **FIGURE 5.13**. It shows values for the `display` property that enable elements to behave like the parts of a table. Figure 5.13's first `display` property value is `table`. The `table` value enables an element, like a `div` element, to behave like a table. Here's how you can do that:

```
<style>
  .table {display: table;}
  ...
</style>

<body>
<div class="table">
  ...
</div>
</body>
```

In this code, the selector name, `table`, is a good descriptive name, but you don't have to use it for your selector. You can use any selector name you want, but it should be descriptive.

In Figure 5.13, the descriptions for the `display` property values are pretty straightforward. The only description that needs clarification is the one for `table-header-group`. The `table-header-group` value causes its rows to display before all other rows and after any table captions (even if the `table-header-group` element code appears below any `table-row` element code). If a table contains multiple elements with `table-header-group` values, only the first such element behaves like a `thead` element; the others behave like `tbody` elements.

| Table Values for the `display` Property | Description |
|---|---|
| table | Used to mimic a `table` element. |
| table-caption | Used to mimic a `caption` element. |
| table-row | Used to mimic a `tr` element. |
| table-cell | Used to mimic a `td` element or a `th` element. |
| table-header-group | Used to mimic a `thead` element. |
| table-row-group | Used to mimic a `tbody` element. |

**FIGURE 5.13** Table values for the CSS `display` property

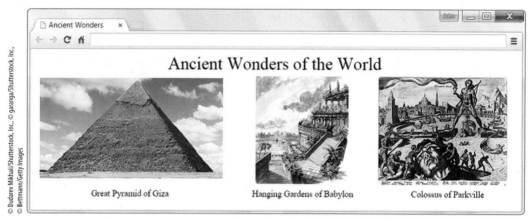

**FIGURE 5.14 Ancient Wonders web page**

One thing you might notice that's missing from Figure 5.13—there are no `display` property values that mimic the functionality of `rowspan` or `colspan`. Sorry, if you want that functionality, the most straightforward solution is to use the real-deal `rowspan` and `colspan` attributes in conjunction with a `table` element. As you might recall, you're supposed to use the `table` element only for data tables and not for table layout. But we'll let you in on a little secret: Browsers don't care. So if you don't mind getting razzed by Tim Berners-Lee at your next W3C cocktail party, you can use the `table`, `rowspan`, and `colspan` elements for table layout. If you do so, as was suggested in Section 5.7, you should add `role="presentation"` to the `table` element's start tag.

## Example Web Page

Take a look at the Ancient Wonders web page in **FIGURE 5.14**. The pictures and the labels under the pictures are displayed using a two-row, three-column layout scheme. You could implement that layout scheme with either a `table` element or with CSS, so which is more appropriate? Because the web page does not contain data,[3] you should use CSS. To have the table's column widths accommodate the widths of the pictures, you should use the CSS `display` property with table values. Using the `display` property with table values makes the web page easy to maintain. As the web developer, if you decide to replace one of the pictures with a wider or narrower picture, the picture's column will grow or shrink to accommodate the new picture.

---

[3] The WHATWG states, "The table element represents data with more than one dimension." The WHATWG doesn't define what "data" is, so there is some ambiguity as to when it's appropriate to use the `table` element. But one thing that's clear is the desire of the standards committees to have web developers use a particular element only when its content coincides with the meaning that the element's tag name implies. Although it's a close call, in our opinion most nonprogrammers would refer to the Ancient Wonders web page as three pictures with labels, and they would not refer to it as a table. Therefore, given that assessment, we feel it would be inappropriate to use the `table` element for the Ancient Wonders web page.

In Figure 5.14, note that there are no borders for the table's exterior and no borders for the table's cells. That's the default for tables created with CSS. If we had wanted borders, we would have applied the CSS `border` property to the element we designate as a table and to the elements we designate as table cells. Now let's examine how we designate table elements with the CSS `display` property.

In **FIGURE 5.15**'s Ancient Wonders `style` container, note the CSS rules that use the `.table`, `.caption`, and `.row` class selectors. In the `body` container, note how those selector names are used to implement a table using `div` elements—`<div class="table">`, `<div class="caption">`, and `<div class="row">`. The `div` element is good for implementing table components because, with one exception, it's generic. That means it doesn't add any formatting features of its own. The exception to that rule is that browsers generate newlines around `div` elements. That works great for implementing tables, captions, and rows because each of those entities is supposed to be surrounded by newlines.

Our implementation of the table cells in the Ancient Wonders web page requires some extra attention. As shown in Figure 5.13, to implement table cells with the `display` property, you need to use the `table-cell` value. In the Ancient Wonders table, each cell in the first row holds a picture, so our first implementation effort attempted to use the pictures' `img` elements as the targets for a `table-cell` rule, like this:

```
img {display: table-cell;}
```

Testing shows that this does not work. That should make sense when you think about what a table cell is supposed to be—a container for content. The `img` element is a void element, not a container, so it's inappropriate to try to use CSS to turn it into a table cell. The solution is to surround the `img` elements with `span` containers and use `span` as the target for a `table-cell` rule. Here's the most straightforward way to apply a `table-cell` value to a `span` element:

```
span {display: table-cell;},
```

If we were to use the CSS rule, then every `span` element would be implemented as a table cell. That's OK for the current version of the Ancient Wonders web page, but as a web developer, you should think about making your web pages maintainable. That means you should accommodate the possibility that you or someone else adds to your web page sometime in the future. If a `span` element is added that's not part of a table, the CSS rule would attempt to make it behave like a table cell, which would be inappropriate. In general, to avoid this kind of problem, you should not use a generic element, `span` or `div`, as the type for a type selector CSS rule.

So rather than using a type selector rule with `span`, we use a more elegant technique. We use a child selector rule that matches every element that is a child of a row element. This is justified because it's reasonable to assume that within a row element, every child element is a data cell. Here's the relevant rule from Figure 5.12's Ancient Wonders source code:

```
.row > * {display: table-cell;}
```

```
<!DOCTYPE html>
<html lang="en">
<head>
<meta charset="utf-8">
<meta name="author" content="John Dean">
<title>Ancient Wonders</title>
<style>
  .table {
    display: table;            ←——————  For table behavior.
    border-spacing: 20px;
  }
  .caption {
    display: table-caption;    ←——————  For caption behavior.
    font-size: xx-large;
    text-align: center;                   For tr behavior.
  }
  .row {display: table-row;}             This causes all children
  .row > * {               ←——————      of .row elements to
    display: table-cell;                 behave like table cells
    text-align: center;                  (i.e., td or th elements).
  }
</style>                   This causes this div element
</head>                    to behave like a table.

                                        This causes this div element
                                        to behave like a caption.
<body>
<div class="table">
  <div class="caption">Ancient Wonders of the World</div>
  <div class="row">
    <span><img src="pyramid.jpg" alt=""></span>
    <span><img src="hangingGardens.jpg" alt=""></span>
    <span><img src= "colossus.jpg" alt=""></span>
  </div>
                                        This causes this
  <div class="row">      ←——————       div element to
    <span>Great Pyramid of Giza</span>  behave like a row.
    <span>Hanging Gardens of Babylon</span>
    <span>Colossus of Parkville</span>
</div>
</body>
</html>
```

**FIGURE 5.15 Source code for Ancient Wonders web page**

You might recall that the > symbol is known as a combinator because it combines two selectors into one. The selector at the left, .row, matches all the elements in the Ancient Wonders web page that have class="row". The universal selector at the right, *, matches any element. When the two selectors are combined with >, the resulting child selector matches every element that is a child of a row element.

As explained earlier, the Ancient Wonders web page uses `div` elements to implement the table's table, caption, and row components. On the other hand, the Ancient Wonders web page uses `span` elements to implement the table's cells (which hold the table's pictures and labels). Like the `div` element, the `span` element is generic. Actually, even more generic. Browsers do not surround `span` elements with line breaks. That's a good thing for table cells because they should be displayed inline, without line breaks surrounding them.

## The `border-spacing` Property

By default, tables created with the `display` property are displayed with no gaps between their cells. For the Ancient Wonders web page, that default behavior would have led to pictures that were touching. To avoid that ugliness, you can use the `border-spacing` property, and that's what we did in the Ancient Wonders `style` container:

```
.table {
  display: table;
  border-spacing: 20px;
}
```

Go back to Figure 5.14 and note the space between the pictures and text in the Ancient Wonders web page. That is due to the `border-spacing` code.

When you use the `border-spacing` property, you should apply it to the entire table, not to the table's individual cells. Consequently, in the Ancient Wonders web page, we apply the `border-spacing` property shown to a `div` element that forms the entire table. In that example, we apply the `border-spacing` property to a table created with CSS. As an alternative, you can apply the `border-spacing` property to an old-fashioned HTML `table` element, and the effect is the same—space gets added between the table's cells.

The `border-spacing` property allows you to specify horizontal and vertical cell spacing separately. Here's an example:

```
border-spacing: 15px; 25px;
```

The first value, `15px`, specifies horizontal spacing, and the second value, `25px`, specifies vertical spacing. Horizontal spacing refers to the width of the gap between adjacent cells in the same row. Vertical spacing refers to the height of the gap between adjacent cells in the same column.

The `border-spacing` property adds space outside each cell's border. On the other hand, the `padding` property adds space inside each cell's border. If you want to see how the two properties differ, feel free to enter the Ancient Wonders web page code into your favorite web authoring tool, add `border-spacing` and `padding` property-value pairs to the table cell selector rule, and view the resulting web page.

In the past, we used the margin property to specify the space outside an element's border. So, can we use the margin property to specify the space outside an individual table cell's border? No, the margin property has no effect when used with elements that are defined to be table cells. That anomaly should make sense when you think about it. If the margin property was able to specify the space outside individual table cell borders, then you could specify different gap sizes between every pair of adjacent cells Yikes. What an unsightly table that would be! So the moral of the story is to use the border-spacing property to specify consistent horizontal and vertical gaps between table cells.

# 5.9 Absolute Positioning with CSS Position Properties

If you want table layout where content controls the size of the table's cells, then use the CSS display property with table values. But if you want table layout where the table's cell sizes are fixed, you should use CSS position properties. For **FIGURE 5.16**'s Imprint Express web page, which technique would be better—using the CSS display property with table values or using CSS position properties?

The Imprint Express web page implements an online newspaper, and newspapers should normally have columns with uniform widths. Using the CSS display property with table values wouldn't satisfy that goal. On the contrary, that technique would cause the column widths to be different. Why is that, you ask? Because the right column's natural width is greater than the left column's natural width. By "natural width," we mean the width of the columns if the window were wide enough to display both columns' content in a single row. The right column

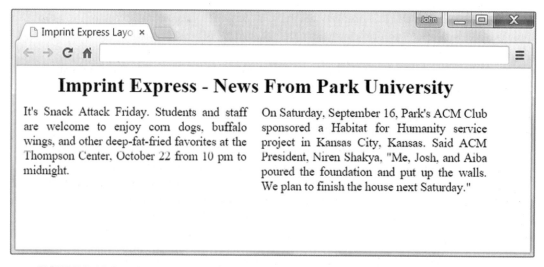

**FIGURE 5.16 Imprint Express web page**

contains more text than the left column, so the right column would be wider. If you then narrowed the window to induce line wrap, the browser would scale down both column widths, but it would continue to display the right column with a greater width than the left column. Note: You could force the two columns' natural widths to be the same by inserting `<br>` tags at the break points shown in the browser window ("staff," "buffalo," "the," etc.), but that would be a nightmare to maintain.

Thus, for the Imprint Express web page, using the CSS `display` property with table values would be inappropriate. Let's now see how CSS position properties would be more appropriate.

Browsers use a default layout scheme known as *normal flow*. With normal flow, within a container, block elements are laid out from top to bottom, one block element per row, and phrasing elements are laid out from left to right in the available space. To remove an element from the normal flow, you can use the CSS position properties shown in **FIGURE 5.17**. In the figure, note that the first position property is named "position." It's confusing to have a group of CSS properties referred to collectively as "position properties" and then have one of those properties—the most important one—use the name "position." Use the `position` property with a value of `absolute` to change the layout scheme from the default normal flow to *absolute positioning*. With absolute positioning, you use the `top` and `left` properties to specify where

| CSS Position Properties | Description |
|---|---|
| `position: absolute` | Tells the browser to position the element relative to the containing block. Normally, the containing block is the web page's `html` element. |
| `left: value*` | Specifies the distance between the containing block's left edge and the element's left edge (where left edge means at the left of any padding, border, or margin). |
| `top: value*` | Specifies the distance between the containing block's top edge and the element's top edge (where top edge means above any padding, border, or margin). |
| `width: value*` | Specifies the width of the invisible box that constrains the element's contents. The width does not include padding, border, or margin. |
| `height: value*` | Specifies the height of the invisible box that constrains the element's text. The height does not include padding, border, or margin. |

**FIGURE 5.17 CSS position properties**

* For the `left`, `top`, `width`, and `height` properties, you should normally provide number-of-pixels values, with px for the unit. But as an alternative, you can provide percentage-of-the-containing-block values, with % for the unit.

the target element's top-left corner is positioned relative to the element's *containing block*. Typically, an element's containing block resolves to the web page's `html` element. We'll talk later about how to designate a different containing block than the `html` element, but don't worry about that for now.

Note the bottom two properties in Figure 5.17—width and `height`. For an absolute positioned element, if you do not specify the element's width (with the `width` property), then the element's width will be determined by the natural width of the element's content. If the content is a picture, that's appropriate, because normally you will want the picture to display with its original dimensions. On the other hand, if the content is a significant amount of text, you should probably specify the element's width. Why? If you don't specify the width, the browser will try to widen the element to display all the text in a single line without any breaks. The `height` property is like the `width` property in that you might want to omit it (e.g., for pictures), but in many cases, you'll want to include it. If you want absolute positioned boxes to be aligned vertically at their bottoms, then for each box you should include not only the `top` property (with the same value for each box), but also the `height` property (with the same value for each box).

Now back to the Imprint Express web page. Before showing you how we implement that web page's layout with CSS position properties, let's design the layout with a drawing. See the drawing in **FIGURE 5.18**. Can you visualize the title positioned in the top region and the two newspaper articles positioned in the left and right regions?

Normally, when designing a web page with CSS position properties, you should start by drawing the layout using paper and a pencil. In your drawing, show pixel measurements for the dimensions of your web page's regions (as in Figure 5.18). By looking at a drawing that's roughly scaled to pixel measurements, you can get a pretty good idea of whether the resulting web page's layout will be aesthetically pleasing. It's good to know that in advance before writing the code and wasting time with recoding efforts if the result looks bad.

To position the Imprint Express web page's left and right newspaper articles using the layout shown in Figure 5.18, you could use `.left-article` and `.right-article` selector rules like this:

```
.left-article {                      .right-article {
  position: absolute;                  position: absolute;
  top: 50px; left: 10px;               top: 50px; left: 330px;
  width: 300px; height: 180px;         width: 300px; height: 180px;
}                                    }
```

As a sanity check, verify that the rules' pixel values agree with the figure's pixel values. For instance, in the rules, the `top` property has a value of 50px, and in the figure, the measurements above the two newspaper article regions add up to 50 (10 + 30 + 10 = 50).

The problem with the rules shown is that there's quite a bit of *code redundancy*. Both rules contain identical (redundant) values, except for the `left` property's value. With code redundancy, if you later decide to make a change (or someone else decides to make a change), you have to remember to make the change in both places. Thus, code redundancy makes web page maintenance more difficult.

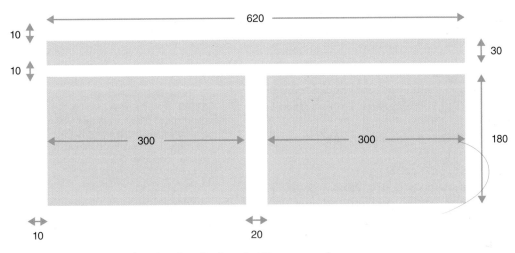

**FIGURE 5.18** **Layout drawing for the Imprint Express web page**

In the actual web page, we avoid code redundancy by putting the property-value pairs that are common to both newspaper article regions in a CSS rule that applies to both of the regions. We also put the `left` property-value pairs in CSS rules that apply to each newspaper article region separately. To see those rules and the rest of the Imprint Express web page code, examine **FIGURE 5.19**. In particular, note how we use an `article` type selector for the rule that applies to both of the newspaper article regions. Note also how we use `article.left` and `article.right` class selectors for the rules that apply to each newspaper article region separately. Prefacing `.left` and `.right` with `article` is not required, but we use the `article` prefix as a form of self-documentation. Also, it allows you to have `left` and `right` `class` attributes for an element different from the `article` element where the two sets of `left` and `right` `class` attributes have different presentation characteristics.

In Figure 5.19's code for the Imprint Express web page, note this CSS rule:

```
* {margin: 0; padding: 0;}
```

We use the universal selector, `*`, to assign a value of 0 to every element's margin and padding areas. In doing so, we enable the CSS position property values to be applied without interference from default margins or borders. If we did not zero out the margin and padding values, then the title's `h1` element would use its default nonzero value for the top margin, and that would cause the title to move down and slightly overlap the two articles. That wouldn't be good.

There's one additional noteworthy item in the Imprint Express web page code. Normally, for the `font-size` property, we've been using values with em units (where em is the height of the letter M in the current context). For the Imprint Express web page, we use units of `pt` (for points) for the `font-size` properties because the web page is supposed to mimic a newspaper. We use 20-point font for the heading and 12-point font for the article text because those are standard sizes for newspapers.

```
<!DOCTYPE html>
<html lang="en">
<head>
<meta charset="utf-8">
<meta name="author" content="John Dean">
<title>Imprint Express Layout</title>
<style>
  * {margin: 0; padding: 0;}
  .title {
    position: absolute;
    left: 10px; top: 10px;
    width: 620px; height: 30px;
    text-align: center;
    font-size: 20pt;
  }
  article {
    position: absolute;
    top: 50px;
    width: 300px; height: 180px;
    text-align: justify;
    font-size: 12pt;
  }
  article.left {left: 10px;}
  article.right {left: 330px;}
</style>
</head>

<body>
<h1 class="title">Imprint Express - News From Park University</h1>
<article class="left">
  It's Snack Attack Friday. Students and staff are welcome to
  enjoy corn dogs, buffalo wings, and other deep-fat-fried favorites
  at the Thompson Center, October 22 from 10 pm to midnight.
</article>
<article class="right">
  On Saturday, September 16, Park's ACM Club sponsored a Habitat for
  Humanity service project in Kansas City, Kansas. Said ACM President,
  Niren Shakya, "Me, Josh, and Aiba poured the foundation and put up
  the walls. We plan to finish the house next Saturday."
</article>
</body>
</html>
```

Set all elements' margins and paddings to 0 so the content positioning relies solely on the absolute position values without interference from default margins or borders.

This `article` type selector rule specifies the CSS properties that apply to both articles.

These class selector rules specify the `left` property, which has a different value for each article.

**FIGURE 5.19 Source code for Imprint Express web page**

# 5.10 **Relative Positioning**

In the previous section, you learned about absolute positioning, where you specify `position: absolute` in a CSS rule in order to position an element relative to the top-left corner of its containing block. As an alternative, you can position an element relative to its normal flow within its surrounding content. That's called *relative positioning*. Take a look at the Divine Comedy web page in **FIGURE 5.20**, where we use relative positioning to move "height of ecstasy" up and "depths of despair" down.

In the Divine Comedy web page's CSS rules, note the `position: relative` property-value pairs. That's how relative positioning is established. In the `.down` CSS rule, note the property-value pairs `top: 2em` and `left: 2em`. Positive values for the `top` property move the element down, and positive values for the `left` property move the element to the right. Thus, in the web page, you can see that "depths of despair" moves 2 font size positions down and 2 font size positions to the right. When applying relative positioning to an element, the element

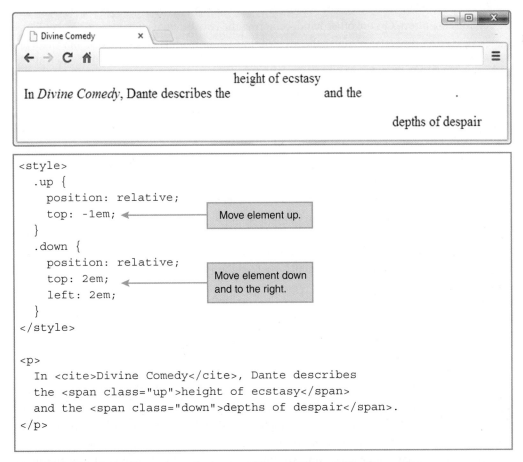

**FIGURE 5.20** **Divine Comedy web page and its relative positioning code**

moves, but the content after the element behaves as if the element stayed in its normal flow position. The web page illustrates this phenomenon by positioning the sentence's period at the right of the normal flow position of "depths of despair." In the web page's .up CSS rule, note the property-value pair top: -1em. The -1em value causes "height of ecstasy" to move up by one font size position.

Using relative positioning to position an element within its normal flow can look strange, so it's not used all that often. But it can be useful for positioning the body element.

## Centering the Entire Page Within a Browser Window

After creating the Imprint Express web page as shown in Figure 5.16, suppose you get the urge to center the page's contents. Centering the heading by itself would be easy. In the h1 element's .title CSS rule, scrap all the absolute positioning property-value pairs and retain only the text-align: center property-value pair. The text-align: center property-value pair would work great for the h1 element because the text-align property's target is plain text, and h1 contains plain text. On the other hand, centering the two articles is not as easy. You could use the text-align property to center the text within each individual article's block, but that's not helpful. You need to center the blocks themselves within the browser window, with the two blocks side-by-side. To do that, the two article elements need to be wrapped in a container, and the container needs to be repositioned so its contents are centered.

In the Imprint Express web page, is there already a container that surrounds the two article elements? Yes, indeed! The body container surrounds them, and as an added bonus, it also surrounds the h1 element. The goal is to reposition the body element within the browser window, so its enclosed elements (the h1 element and the two article elements) become centered horizontally in the browser window.

Do you remember how we centered the table element in the Global Temperatures web page? We used CSS to turn the table's parent container (the body element) into a flexbox, and then we applied justify-content: center to that parent container. We'll do the same thing here, but this time the element that needs centering is the body element. So, what is the body element's containing element? That's right; it's the html element. Here's what we need:

```
html {
  display: flex;
  justify-content: center;
}
```

We want the body's enclosed elements to use absolute positioning relative to the repositioned body. To do that, we need the body container to be the containing block for its enclosed elements. That sounds like it should be the default, but not so. In the previous section, we said that an element's containing block normally resolves to the web page's html element. For this particular situation, we don't want the containing block to be the html element. To force the body container to be the containing block for the body's enclosed elements, we need to apply a `position: relative` CSS rule to the `body` element. Specifically, here's what's needed:

```
body {
  position: relative;
  width: 620px;
  height: 220px;
}
```

In the rule, the `width` and `height` properties (whose values come from the dimensions shown in Figure 5.18) are necessary so the browser engine can establish a framework to which other elements can be added. For example, later you'll see how we position the web page's second newspaper article at the right side of the web page by specifying 0 for the property that indicates distance from the right side of the `body` element. Without the `width` value, the browser won't know the location of the right side.[4] For this particular web page, there's no need to position any elements using the page's bottom edge as the starting point, so it's OK to omit the `height` property. On the other hand, you might want to keep it as a form of self-documentation.

To center the web page's contents, not only do you need a `body` CSS rule with `position: relative` as shown, you also need a CSS rule with `position: absolute` for each of the elements inside the `body` container. **FIGURE 5.21** shows the CSS code for the centered version of the Imprint Express web page. The CSS rules that start with `.title` and `article` apply to the `title` element and the `article` elements, respectively. To have the body container's centered position take effect, both rules include `position: absolute`.

In Figure 5.21, the `body` CSS rule is slightly different from the `body` CSS rule presented earlier. We add a `top` property with a value of 30 pixels in order to shift the `body` container down (notice the expanded blank area at the top of Figure 5.21's web page display). Also, to reduce clutter, we omit the `height` property.

By using relative positioning for the web page's body, we are able to simplify the CSS code for the elements inside the `body` container. Specifically, there is no need for `left` and `top` properties in the `title` element's CSS rule because the `title` element now uses `left` and `top` positioning from the repositioned `body` container. Likewise, there is no need for an `article.left` CSS rule because the left article's element now uses left positioning from the repositioned `body` container. For the `article.right` CSS rule, we could have used `left: 320px` to position the right article 320 pixels from the left edge of the centered body. As a more elegant alternative, we use `right: 0` to position the right article at the right edge of the centered body. The `right` property, not shown in Figure 5.17's table of CSS position properties, works as expected—it specifies the distance between the containing block's right edge and the current element's right edge.

---

[4] Without relative positioning, there's no need to specify the `body` element's dimensions because the browser can calculate the body's default dimensions from the size of the browser window's *viewport* (where the viewport is the large area below the address bar where web page content displays). But with relative positioning, the page dimensions are 0's by default, and that's not helpful for positioning purposes.

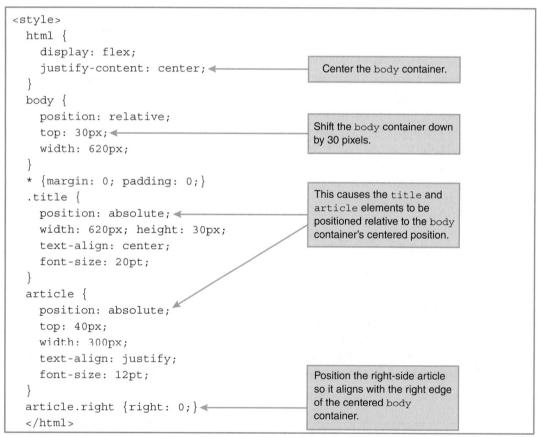

```
<style>
  html {
    display: flex;
    justify-content: center;     ◄──── Center the body container.
  }
  body {
    position: relative;
    top: 30px;     ◄──── Shift the body container down by 30 pixels.
    width: 620px;
  }
  * {margin: 0; padding: 0;}
  .title {
    position: absolute;     ◄──── This causes the title and article elements to be positioned relative to the body container's centered position.
    width: 620px; height: 30px;
    text-align: center;
    font-size: 20pt;
  }
  article {
    position: absolute;
    top: 40px;
    width: 300px;
    text-align: justify;
    font-size: 12pt;
  }
  article.right {right: 0;}     ◄──── Position the right-side article so it aligns with the right edge of the centered body container.
</html>
```

**FIGURE 5.21 Centered Imprint Express web page and its CSS code**

## Relative Positioning for an Element Without Adjusting the Element's Position

So far, we've used the `position: relative` property-value pair to adjust an element's position relative to its normal flow position. You can also use the `position: relative` property-value pair without adjusting the element's position. In that case, the purpose of the `position: relative` property-value pair is to designate the element as a containing block for absolute positioned elements inside it. For example, suppose you want to display several business cards on a web page. Each business card displays a person's name, phone number, and email address. You implement each business card with a `div` element and within each `div`, you use `span` elements for the name, phone number, and email values. For each business card `div` element, you apply a `position: relative` CSS rule. For each `span` element, you apply a `position: absolute` CSS rule with values for the `left`, `top`, `width`, and/or `height` properties. Because of the surrounding `div` element's `position: relative` CSS rule, the `left` and `top` values position the `span` element relative to the `div` element. Each business card's `span` elements are positioned in the same places within the card, so you use the same set of CSS `span` rules for all the business cards. Sharing the CSS `span` rules (and sharing code in general) can lead to a more maintainable web page. If you have to change the positions of the `span` elements within each business card, you make the change in one place—in the shared set of CSS `span` rules—rather than making changes to separate CSS `span` rules for each business card.

To illustrate relative positioning in the context of a complete web page, we could provide the code for the aforementioned business card web page, but that would spoil the fun. This chapter has a project that describes the business card web page in greater detail, and we encourage you to implement it.

## 5.11 CASE STUDY: A Downtown Store's Electrical Generation and Consumption

The web page for this segment of our ongoing case study describes the smallest kind of electrical microgrid—the electrical system for a single small shop or restaurant. Rather than try to specify everything at the start, we'll develop this web page in a sequence of iterations. This strategy minimizes the number of new problems faced at each stage of the design process, and it produces alternative options for different hardware platforms.

For style consistency, we'll continue to format the page header with the external CSS file introduced in Chapter 3, `microgrid.css`. This file specifies the body's width, padding, and background color. After the header, the web page contains an introductory block of text. Next, a table contains the salient features of a typical electrical microgrid. After the table, there are two blocks of text for a system description and an identification of key assumptions used. At the bottom of the web page, there is a one-line summary of the savings produced by the local system's own renewable energy source.

In our first design iteration, we'll focus on the table and use simple paragraphs for the subsequent blocks of text. **FIGURE 5.22** shows the resulting Typical Downtown Property web page.

As in previous segments of this case study, the text in the top banner is an h2 header. The table caption and the headers below the table are in h3 elements. For formatting, they use `text-align: center`, as specified in the external CSS file. The text blocks are in p containers with `text-align: justify` formatting. As expected, the table uses a table container with a caption element, followed by tr elements with embedded th elements.

The only subtleties are in the `style` container's CSS code that formats the table:

```css
.center {
  display: flex; justify-content: center;
}
table {border-collapse: collapse;}
th, td {
  border: thin solid;
  padding: 2px 5px;
}
td:nth-child(3), td:nth-child(4) {
  text-align: right;
}
```

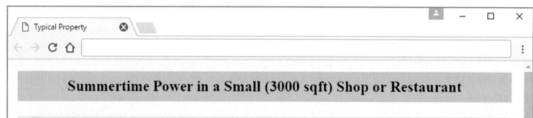

### Summertime Power in a Small (3000 sqft) Shop or Restaurant

The smallest electrical system in Lawrence's downtown is the electrical system in one small shop or restaurant, which typically occupies one lot and is two stories tall. One lot is 25 feet wide and 120 feet deep. Most of the downtown properties are this size. However, some are taller and/or occupy two or more lots. For one of these larger properties, scale up the values in the table below.

### Noon Power Generation (positive) and Consumption (negative)

| Component Description | Overall Size | Noon Power | Installed Cost |
|---|---|---|---|
| PV Solar Collectors | 137 m$^2$ panel area | +15 kW | $45,000 |
| Electrical Consumption | 274 m$^2$ floor area | -5 kW | |
| Chilled Water Storage | 2.3 m diameter x 2.1 m high | -2 kW | $1000 |
| Battery Storage | 1.3 m x 1.0 m x 1.1 m high, 1250kg | -6 kW | $6000 |

**Typical System Description**

To avoid rooftop HVAC clutter, maximize efficiency, and facilitate thermal storage, a ground-source heat pump heats and cools water for HVAC and provides free heat for domestic hot water during the cooling season. Peak electrical consumption (at 4:00 PM) is about 7.5 kW. At peak cooling load, the HVAC equipment consumes 4 kW. At noon, the HVAC cooling equipment uses 2 kW to cool spaces and 2 kW to chill water for storage and use at a later time. Chilled-water storage between 9:00 AM and 3:00 PM stores enough cooling to provide maximum cooling for 3 evening hours. With 15% capacity factor (50% clouds), solar collectors rated at 18 kW save $3300/year.

**FIGURE 5.22 Case Study: Typical Downtown Property web page, first design iteration**

As you learned earlier, to center an element (like a table) horizontally, you can position the element in a flexbox and apply `justify-content: center` to the flexbox. In this code, you can see how we use that CSS property-value pair as part of a `.center` selector rule. We apply that rule to a `div` container that surrounds the table. In the `table` rule, the `border-collapse: collapse` property-value pair makes the table cleaner. The `th, td` rule causes cell borders to be visible and adds padding for each cell. Finally, the `:nth-child()` pseudo-class selectors rule specifies right alignment for the numerical data in the last two columns without changing the default left alignment for the text data in the first two columns.

We suggest that you now write the code for this first-iteration Typical Downtown Property web page using the suggestions. No need to worry about the text that's out of view at the bottom of Figure 5.22. When you're done, you should retrieve the `typicalPropertyFirstCut.html` file from the book's website and compare its source code to yours.

If you load the Typical Downtown Property web page in a browser, you can see that the content remains fairly readable if you reduce the page's width. On the other hand, if you expand the page's width too much, you can get to the point where the lines of text become longer than what you'd want for a comfortable reading experience. If you feel a web page is likely to appear in wide windows, you might want to consider organizing the text in columns, as in a newspaper. **FIGURE 5.23** shows the same information presented in Figure 5.22, but each block of text is split into two columns.

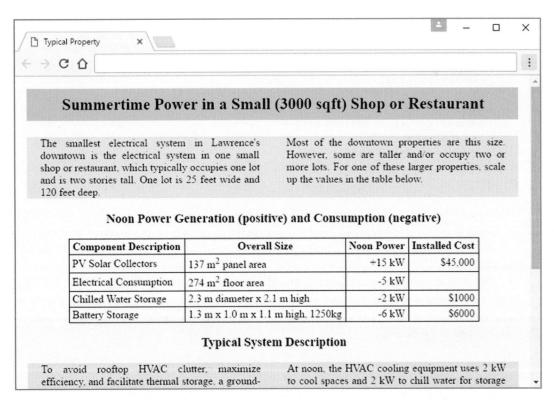

**FIGURE 5.23  Case Study: Typical Downtown Property web page, second design iteration**

For our second design iteration, we'll split each block of text into two columns by replacing each p element in the first iteration with a div element containing a pair of subordinate div elements—one for each column. Thus, for example, for the first block of text, instead of using this:

```
<p>
   The smallest electrical system in Lawrence's downtown ...
        ... values in the table below.
</p>
```

We'll use this:

```
<div class="row">
   <div class="cell">
      The smallest electrical system in Lawrence's downtown ...
          ... occupies a single lot.
   </div>
   <div class="cell">
      One lot is 25 feet wide and 120 feet deep. Most of the ...
          ... values in the table below.
   </div>
</div>
```

This requires two CSS rules. So the style element at the top of the web page will get these two additional components:

```
.row {
   display: table-row;
}
.cell {
   display: table-cell;
   width: 40%;
   padding: 0px 20px;
   text-align: justify;
}
```

This causes the new outer div element to display like a table row, and it causes the new inner div elements to display like table cells. The two cells are the two columns. In the course of doing this, we also insert a text-align: justify property to straighten the ragged right sides in the text blocks.

Now we suggest that you use this method to modify the text blocks in your first-iteration code so that your web page generates a display like that shown in Figure 5.23. When you're done, you should retrieve the typicalProperty.html file from the book's website and compare its source code to yours.

# Review Questions

## 5.2 Table Elements

1. For each of the following elements, what is its HTML start tag?

    a) A table row element

    b) An element within a table row that holds data

    c) An element in the top row of a table that describes the data in the column below

## 5.3 Formatting a Data Table: Borders, Alignment, and Padding

2. Using type selectors, write a CSS rule that creates a thin solid single-line border around all tables and uses a single line to separate adjacent columns and adjacent rows.

3. Using type selectors, write a CSS rule that puts 5 pixels of padding around the text in each table header and data cell.

## 5.4 CSS Structural Pseudo-Class Selectors

4. Write a CSS structural pseudo-class selector that selects the odd table row elements, starting with the third one.

## 5.5 `thead` and `tbody` Elements

5. What is the purpose of the `thead` element, and what is the purpose of the `tbody` element?

6. What does the following CSS rule do?

```
body {display: flex; justify-content: center;}
```

## 5.6 Cell Spanning

7. Assume the following `style` and `body` elements are part of a complete html5 document. Provide a sketch that shows what the code displays.

```
<style>
  th, td {padding: 5px 20px;}
  table, th, td {border: solid thin; border-collapse: collapse;}
</style>

<body>
<table>
  <tr> <th></th> <th colspan="2"></th> <th></th> </tr>
  <tr> <td></td> <td></td> <td></td> <td></td> </tr>
  <tr>
    <td rowspan="3"></td> <td></td> <td></td>
    <td rowspan="3"></td>
  </tr>
```

```
    <tr> <td></td> <td></td> </tr>
    <tr> <td></td> <td></td> </tr>
</table>
</body>
```

### 5.7 Web Accessibility

8.   What is a screen reader?

### 5.8 CSS `display` Property with Table Values

9.   For each HTML element, provide a CSS property-value pair that implements its presentation functionality.

   **a)**   `table`

   **b)**   `caption`

   **c)**   `tr`

   **d)**   `td`

10.   Why is the `div` element a good choice for CSS implementation of table and row components?

11.   The `display: table-cell` property does not work well with elements in the embedded category like `img`, `audio`, and `video`. How can you work around this problem?

### 5.9 Absolute Positioning with CSS Position Properties

12.   Describe how to apply absolute positioning to an element.

13.   With absolute positioning, the `top` and `left` properties indicate the position of the target element's top-left corner relative to what?

14.   What CSS properties establish offsets from container sides to corresponding component sides?

### 5.10 Relative Positioning

15.   With relative positioning, the `top` and `left` properties indicate the position of the target element's top-left corner relative to what?

16.   If you apply the `position: relative` property-value pair to a container, that container can then serve as a containing block for absolute positioned elements inside it. True or false.

## Exercises

1.   [after Section 5.3] Suppose you have a table implemented with a `table` element, and borders are displayed around each table cell and around the table's perimeter. Provide a CSS type selector rule that eliminates the gaps between each of the adjacent borders.

2.  [after Section 5.3] There are quite a few syntax details in HTML5 and in CSS. This book covers a lot of those details, but certainly not all of them. One thing we skipped in this chapter is the `colgroup` element, which is used in conjunction with the `table` element. For this exercise, you'll need to learn about the `colgroup` element by looking it up on the W3C's website.

Given this code:

```
<style>
  table {border-collapse: collapse;}
  th, td {
    padding: .5em;
    text-align: center;
    vertical-align: bottom;
  }
  th {background: lightskyblue;}
</style>
</head>

<body>
<table>
  <caption>Bank Accounts</caption>
  <tr>
    <th>Account<br></th>
    <th>Starting<br>Balance</th>
    <th>Expenditures</th>
    <th>Remaining</th>
  </tr>
  <tr>
    <td>324014</td>
    <td>$2,990.55</td>
    <td>$550.55</td>
    <td>$2,440.00</td>
  </tr>
  <tr>
    <td>361102</td>
    <td>$4,075.00</td>
    <td>$0.00</td>
    <td>$4,075.00</td>
  </tr>
</table>
</body>
```

What `colgroup` element code and CSS code need to be added to this code in order to produce the following web page? As its name implies, the purpose of the `colgroup` element is to group together a set of columns. In this case, you must provide three `colgroup` elements—one for the first column, one for the second and third columns combined, and one for the fourth column. In your answer, you must make it clear where your added code should be inserted in the code.

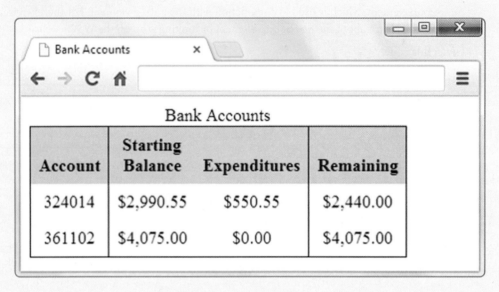

3. [after Section 5.4] What is the purpose of a pseudo-class?

4. [after Section 5.4] Describe the effect of this CSS rule:

   ```
   tr:nth-of-type(odd) {color: red;}
   ```

5. [after Section 5.5] Refer to the Global Temperatures source code in Figure 5.8. Provide a modified table that uses two tbody elements—one for the two most recent years (2015 and 2016) and one for the earlier years. Assign "recentYears" to the class attribute of the tbody containing the two most recent years. Provide a CSS rule for the recent-years data cells that changes the text from black to red. Hint: Use a class selector in conjunction with a descendant selector.

6. [after Section 5.7] Refer to the My Favorite Eras source code in Figure 5.10. Provide a modified table that is more accessible. Specifically, add an id attribute value to the th element at the head of each column and each row. Also, add a header attribute to the Mesozoic and Cenozoic th elements and to every td element.

**7.** [after Section 5.8] A `table` is embedded inside one cell of a larger structure formed using `display: table`, `display: table-row`, and `display: table-cell`. The embedded `table` is the middle cell in the three bordered cells in this screenshot:

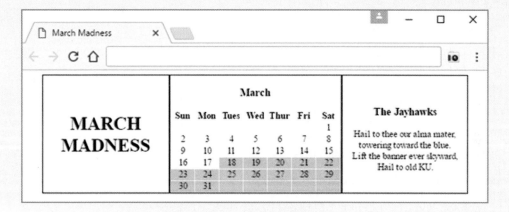

This exercise also provides practice using structural pseudo-class selectors. The selectors apply gold background to the days on the calendar during which NCAA basketball tournament games are played. Your display will look like the screenshot, except for the calendar dates. Use the current year, which means March dates will probably fall on different days of the week. Also, the cell on the right should contain material related to *your* favorite team.

Provide complete source code for the March Madness web page. The following template provides most of the code, so use it as a starting point. In the left section, you'll need to add "MARCH MADNESS." In the middle section, you'll need to provide content for the calendar by adding March, Sun, Mon, …, 1, 2, etc. In the right section, you'll need to replace "Jayhawks" and the fight song with text for your favorite team. In the structural pseudo-class CSS rule, you'll need to provide appropriate values in the selectors' parentheses. Figuring out those values is a bit tricky. Here's a hint: To do something to a particular row and all subsequent rows or a particular cell within a row and all subsequent cells, use the formula, 1n+#, where # is the starting row number or starting cell number.

```html
<!DOCTYPE html>
<html lang="en">
<head>
<meta charset="utf-8">
<meta name="author" content="John Dean">
<title>March Madness</title>
<style>
  html {display: flex; justify-content: center;}
  body {display: table;}
  .row {display: table-row;}
  .cell {
    display: table-cell;
    border: thin solid;
    text-align: center;
    vertical-align: middle;
  }
  .end {width: 200px; padding: 10px;}
  th {width: 40px;}
  tr:nth-of-type() td:nth-of-type(), tr:nth-of-type() {
    background-color: gold;
  }
</style>
</head>

<body>
  <div class="row">
    <div class="end cell">
      <h1></h1>
    </div>
    <table class="cell">
      <caption><h3></h3></caption>
      <tr>
        <th></th><th></th><th></th><th></th><th></th><th></th><th></th>
      </tr>
      <tr>
        <td></td><td></td><td></td><td></td><td></td><td></td><td></td>
      </tr>
      <tr>
        <td></td><td></td><td></td><td></td><td></td><td></td><td></td>
      </tr>
      <tr>
        <td></td><td></td><td></td><td></td><td></td><td></td><td></td>
      </tr>
```

```
    <tr>
      <td></td><td></td><td></td><td></td><td></td><td></td><td></td>
    </tr>
    <tr>
      <td></td><td></td><td></td><td></td><td></td><td></td><td></td>
    </tr>
    <tr>
      <td></td><td></td><td></td><td></td><td></td><td></td><td></td>
    </tr>
    <tr>
      <td></td><td></td><td></td><td></td><td></td><td></td><td></td>
    </tr>
    <tr>
      <td></td><td></td><td></td><td></td><td></td><td></td><td></td>
    </tr>
    <tr>
      <td></td><td></td><td></td><td></td><td></td><td></td><td></td>
    </tr>
  </table>
  <article class="end cell">
    <h3></h3>
  </article>
 </div>
</body>
</html>
```

8. [After section 5.9] Given this `img` element:

```
<img class="cow-picture" src="cowInPond.jpg" alt="cow in pond"
  width="200" height="145">
```

Provide a CSS rule that uses absolute positioning to position the image in the top-right corner of the image's surrounding container, 10 pixels from the top edge and 10 pixels from the right edge.

# Projects ✓

1.  Create the following web page and name the file `foodPyramid.html`:

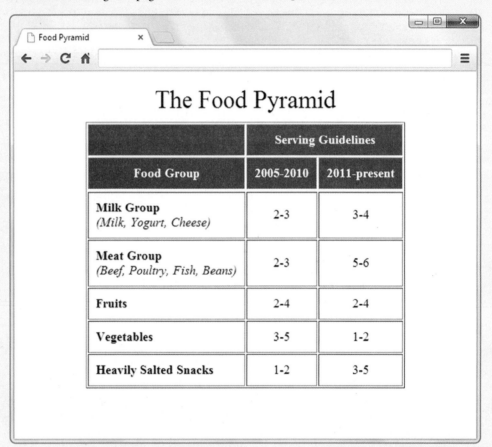

Note:
▶  Use a `table` element with appropriate other elements, including `thead` and `tbody` elements.
▶  The table should be horizontally centered with respect to the browser window.
▶  Look carefully—padding has been added to the table's caption.

2. Create the following web page and name the file `gymnastics.html`:

You are required to use appropriate organizational elements. Use a `header` container for the top two headings. Use two `section` containers—one for the female gymnasts content and one for the male gymnasts content. Use a `figure` container for the image and caption. You are required to use absolute positioning for the `header`, `section`, and `figure` containers.

**Extra Credit**

Modify the gymnastics page so that there is a 20-pixel gap around the page's contents. Hint: For an elegant implementation, you'll need to use the `position: relative;` property-value pair.

Modify the gymnastics page so that the female gymnast list items are numbered continuously and the male gymnast list items are numbered continuously. See the display for details.

# CHAPTER 6

# Links and Images

## CHAPTER OBJECTIVES

▶ Implement a link with the a element.

▶ Learn the different types of `href` attribute values.

▶ Use relative URLs to navigate up and down a directory tree structure.

▶ Implement home page files.

▶ Learn the basics of web design, including the different strategies for organizing your web pages.

▶ Implement a link that jumps to a particular location within a web page.

▶ Use CSS to adjust and tweak a nontrivial web page and its links so it looks good.

▶ Use the a element's `target` attribute to specify the environment in which a web page opens.

▶ Understand the concepts behind GIF, JPEG, and PNG bitmap image formats.

▶ Learn how to implement bitmap image elements within a web page.

▶ Understand the concepts behind SVG image formats.

▶ Learn how to implement SVG image elements within a web page.

▶ Implement responsive-image web pages with the resolution switching and art direction techniques.

## CHAPTER OUTLINE

## 6.1 Introduction

This chapter presents two web page features—links and images—that are emblematic of what it means to be a web page. Almost all web pages include links and images, and they are usually crucial to the web page's popularity. And if you're a web page, popularity is everything.[1]

In Chapter 4, you learned a few link syntax details while implementing a nav container. In this chapter, you'll learn more link syntax details, plus various techniques for jumping to different link targets. In particular, you'll learn how to jump to a target location on a different web page, as well as to a target location on the current web page. Next, you'll learn how to download a file. For all the jumping and downloading operations, you can use a path to identify the location of your target, and you'll learn different techniques for specifying paths. You'll also learn techniques for formatting the links, using various CSS rules.

After learning about links, next you'll learn about another basic building block—images. You can implement a link to an image, but in this chapter, we focus on standalone images. In Chapter 4, you learned a few image syntax details while implementing a figure container. In this chapter, you'll learn a few more image syntax details, but most of the image discussion in this chapter will be about the different types of images that are available. In particular, you'll learn about bitmap image file formats (GIF, JPEG, and PNG) and a vector graphics file format (SVG).

## 6.2 a Element

To implement a link, you'll need to use the a element. Here's an example a element that implements a link to Park University's website:

```
<a href="http://www.park.edu">Park University</a>
```

---

[1] This rather shallow notion of success is particularly prevalent with younger web pages, where getting invited to the "popular" web pages' parties is paramount.

The text that appears between an a element's start tag and end tag forms the link label that the user sees and clicks on. So in this code, the link label is "Park University." By default, browsers display link labels with underlines. So this code renders like this:

Park University

The blue color indicates that the linked-to page has not been visited. We'll discuss visited and unvisited links later on.

When the user clicks on a link, the browser loads the resource specified by the href attribute. For this example, the "resource" is another web page, so when the user clicks on the "Park University" link, the browser loads that web page—the one at http://www.park.edu. As an alternative to specifying a web page for the href attribute's resource, you can specify an image file for the href attribute's resource. We'll show an example of that in the next chapter.

Besides enabling a user to load a resource (which usually means jumping to another web page), the a element can be used as a mechanism that enables a user to download a file of any type—image file, video file, PDF file, Microsoft Word file, and so on. To implement that download functionality, include a download attribute as shown here:

```
<a download href="http://www.park.edu/catalogs/catalog2018-2019.pdf">
  Park University 2018-2019 catalog</a>
```

As always for the a element, the browser displays the text that appears between the start tag and end tag; in this case, that's "Park University 2018–2019 catalog." When the user clicks on that text, the browser downloads the file specified by the href attribute. The user can then choose to view it or save it. Normally, the download attribute has no value, but if you (as the web programmer) want the end user to save the file using a different filename than that specified by the href atttibute, then you should include a filename for the download attribute's value, such as download="Park University 2018-2019 catalog.pdf". But be aware that the browser might override your download attribute's filename and use the href attribute's filename instead.

## Continuation Rule for Elements that Span Multiple Lines

Did you notice that the preceding a element code fragment spans two lines and the second line is indented? This subsection explains that indentation. It's a style thing, and the explanation is not specific to the a element. This subsection is a digression from the rest of this chapter, and it's relevant for examples throughout the rest of the book.

The a element is a phrasing element (which means that it displays "inline," like a phrase within a paragraph). Most phrasing element code is short and can easily fit on one line, but the preceding a element is rather long and spans two lines. The solution was to press enter at the end of the a element's start tag and indent the next line. We use that same solution for other elements that are too long to fit on one line. Here's a meta element example:

```
<meta name="description"
  content="This web page presents Dean family highlights.">
```

Note that we press enter after the `name` attribute-value pair. In the `a` element example, we pressed enter after the `a` element's start tag. The goal is to press enter at a reasonable breaking point. For the preceding example, if we wait to press enter until after "Dean family," that would not be a "reasonable breaking point." It would split the `content` attribute's value across two lines. Doing so would make the code slightly harder to understand and thus defeat one of the primary purposes behind good style—understandability.

Back in Chapter 2, we introduced you to block formatting for block elements, which means the start and end tags go on lines by themselves. The `p` element is a block element, and here's a properly formatted `p` element:

```
<p>
  Known for its Computer Science program,                    Press enter.
  <a href="http://www.park.edu/informationAndComputerScience/accolades">
  Park University</a> is tied for first in the number of Turing Award
  winners among all Missouri universities whose motto is "Fides es Labor."
</p>
```

Align the a element's continuation line with the prior line.

Within the `p` container, there's an `a` element that spans more than one line, and we align its continuation line with the line above it (we don't indent further). That's different from the prior `a` element example. Indenting continuation lines is a bit of a gray area. If the continuation line is in a container that represents something that is supposed to look like a paragraph (e.g., `p` or `blockquote`), then do not indent. Otherwise indent.

Note the line break in the source code after "program,". We inserted a line break so we could fit the `a` element's entire start tag on one line. If we attempt to put the `a` element's entire start tag on the same line as "program," then *line wrap* would occur if we printed the code on paper. Here's what that would look like:

```
<p>
  Known for its Computer Science program, <a
href="http://www.park.edu/informationAndComputerScience/accolades">
  Park University</a> is tied for first in the number of Turing Award
  winners among all Missouri universities whose motto is "Fides et Labor."
</p>
```

line wrap

Note how `href` wraps to the next line where it's not indented. The `href` is aligned with the `<p>` start tag, and that implies that `href` is separate from the `p` element rather than a part of it. And that implication makes the logic hard to follow. The moral of the story is, for statements that might be too long to fit onto one line, press enter at an appropriate breaking point to avoid line wrap.

| Types of `href` Attribute Values | Where the Link Jumps To |
|---|---|
| absolute URL | Find the resource on a different web server than the current web page. |
| relative URL | Find the resource on the same web server as the current web page. Specify the location of the resource by providing a path from the current web page's directory to the destination web page. |
| jump within current web page | Find the resource within the current web page. Specify the location of the resource by providing an `id` value for an element in the web page. |

**FIGURE 6.1** `href` **attribute values**

## Different Types of `href` Values

As you know, the a element's `href` attribute value specifies the resource that is to be loaded. In addition to specifying the resource, the `href` attribute value indicates where the link jumps to in order to find the resource. Indicating where the link jumps to is not a trivial task. Take a look at **FIGURE 6.1**, which provides an overview of the different link-jumping techniques employed by the `href` attribute's value.

For an example that uses an *absolute URL*, suppose you want to add a link on a Facebook page that directs the user to an Instagram page. Here's the link code to do that for a subscriber named Hannah Davis:

```
<a href=" https://www.instagram.com/hannahDavis.html">
   Hannah's Instagram</a>
```

Note the https value for the `href` attribute. You've seen http in the past; https is another popular protocol that you can use with the `href` attribute. It stands for hypertext transfer protocol secure. So the https protocol provides more security for communications than does http.

To jump to a web page that resides on the same web server as the current web page, for the link's `href` attribute, use a relative URL. The relative URL specifies a path from the current web page's directory to the destination web page. The next section provides complete details and examples.

To jump to a designated location within the current web page, for the link's `href` attribute, use a value starting with # such that that value matches an `id` attribute's value for an element in the web page. We introduced this technique earlier, and we'll provide more details and examples later in this chapter.

## 6.3 **Relative URLs**

As promised, in this section we provide additional details about relative URLs. A relative URL value allows you to jump to a web page that resides on the same web server as the current web page. It does so by specifying a path from the current directory to the destination web page. The

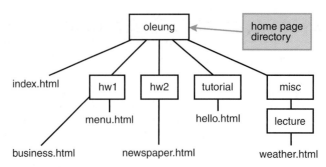

**FIGURE 6.2 Example directory tree**

*current directory* is the directory where the current web page resides. The destination web page is the page that the user jumps to after clicking on the link.

In forming a path for a relative URL value, you'll need to understand how files and directories are organized in a *directory tree* structure. Note the example directory tree in **FIGURE 6.2**. It shows the container relationships between all the files and directories that are within the oleung directory. The oleung directory is the home page directory for student Olivia Leung. A *home page* is the default first page a user sees when the user visits a website. We'll have more to say about home pages shortly, but for now, just realize that a *home page directory* is the directory where a home page resides, and a home page is the starting point for a user's browsing experience on a particular website. A *subdirectory* (also called a subfolder or a child folder) is a directory that is contained within another directory. Thus, in Figure 6.2, there are four subdirectories within the oleung home page directory and one subdirectory within the misc subdirectory. The other entities in Figure 6.2 (the words without borders) are files. The index.html file is in the oleung directory, and the other files are in the tree's subdirectories. Because oleung is the home page directory, you might have guessed that index.html is the home page file. That is indeed the case.

In forming a path for a relative URL value, you'll need to navigate between a starting directory and a target file. In doing so, you'll need to follow these rules:

▷    Use /'s to separate directories and files.
▷    Use "..." to go from a directory to the directory's parent directory.

In the second bullet, what does *parent directory* mean? In Figure 6.2, oleung is the parent directory of hw1 because oleung and hw1 are connected by a single line with oleung on the top. That should make sense because it parallels how human parents are displayed in a genealogy tree. The point of all this is that if you're in a directory and you want to go to that directory's parent directory, you need to use .. For example, suppose you want to provide a link on the newspaper page that takes a user to the home page, index.html. Because the newspaper page is in the hw2 directory, the hw2 directory is considered to be the current directory. The home page is in the oleung directory. The oleung directory is the parent directory of hw2, so you need to use .. in order to navigate up to the oleung directory. Here's the relevant a element code:

```
<a href="../index.html">Olivia's Home Page</a>
```

Note the / (forward slash) between .. and index.html. As explained earlier, the / is a delimiter that separates directories and files. The .. refers to a directory and index.html is a file, so the / is necessary to separate them. Does it make sense that `..` refers to a directory? Remember that `..` navigates from the current directory (`hw2` in this example) to its parent directory (`oleung` in this example), so the result is indeed a directory.

## Relative Path Examples

Using Figure 6.2's directory tree, can you try to come up with the code for an a element that resides in the `index.html` file and takes the user to the business page? See if you can do that on your own without glancing down at the answer.

Assuming you've tried to work it out on your own, now you may look at the answer:

```
<a href="hw1/business.html">Business Page</a>
```

Note that `href`'s value starts with `hw1`. In coming up with the answer on your own, did you start with `..` instead? It's a common error among beginning web programmers to feel the need to use `..` to go up from the current web page to that web page's directory. Try to avoid that misconception. There's no need to go up. If you're in a web page, then you're already in that web page's directory. So to go from the `index.html` page to the business page, you simply go down from `oleung` to `hw1` by specifying `hw1`, then down to the business page by specifying `/business.html`.

The `index.html` page is the website's home page, and as such, it's the first page that you look at when you visit a website. To help with a user's viewing experience, home pages should normally contain links to other pages on the website. So for your next challenge, you should implement another link from the home page—this time, have the link go to the weather page. Try to come up with the code on your own. Assuming you've made an honest attempt, now you can look at the answer:

```
<a href="misc/lecture/weather.html">Weather Page</a>
```

Because the link resides on the home page, the path originates from the home page directory, `oleung`. To get to the weather page, you have to go down to the `misc` directory and then down to the `lecture` directory. In the example code, notice the `/`'s separating the two directories and the `weather.html` filename.

For one last relative URL challenge, try to come up with the code for an a element that resides in the business page and takes the user to the menu page. Once again, see if you can do that on your own without glancing down at the answer. Here's the answer:

```
<a href="menu.html">Menu Page</a>
```

Note that there is no directory in the `href` value—only the filename by itself. With the business and menu pages both in the same `hw1` directory, there's no need to change directories and therefore no need for a path in front of the filename.

## Path-Absolute URLs

As stated previously, a relative URL is for jumping to a web page when the current web page and the target web page are on the same web server. In the prior examples, the relative URL's path started at the current web page's directory. As an alternative, you can have the relative URL's path start at the web server's root directory. A web server's *root directory* is the directory on the web server that contains all the directories and files that are considered to be part of the web server. [2] If you want to have the relative URL's path start at the web server's root directory, preface the URL value with /. For example, using Figure 6.2's directory tree, if oleung is immediately below the web server's root directory, the following code could be added to any of the web pages shown, and it would implement a link to the index.html page:

```
<a href="/oleung/index.html">Olivia's Website</a>
```

A URL value that starts with a / is referred to as a *path-absolute URL*, and it's a special type of relative URL (it's considered a relative URL because the path is relative to the current web server's root directory). The term path-absolute URL comes from the WHATWG. Remember the WHATWG? It stands for Web Hypertext Application Technology Working Group. It's the organization that keeps track of the HTML5 standard with a living document. Its standard aligns very closely with the W3C's HTML5 standard, but because it's a living document, the WHATWG is free to update things at any time it sees fit. Unfortunately, the W3C does not have a formal term for a path that starts with /. But rest assured that the path-absolute URL syntax is valid—all major browsers have supported it for many years. By the way, if you see the term *root-relative path*, that's just another way to refer to a path-absolute URL. In the real world, both terms are popular.

## 6.4 `index.html` File

If a user specifies a URL address that ends with a directory name, then the web server will automatically look for a file named index.html or index.htm and attempt to load it into a browser. This occurs when you specify a URL for a link's href value and also when you enter a URL in a web browser's address box. [3]

The default searched-for file can be reconfigured by the web server's administrator. It's common for Microsoft IIS web server administrators to use default.htm as another default filename for displaying a web page when the URL address ends with a directory name. According to the coding-style conventions in Appendix A, we recommend that you use index.html for your home page file names because that name is the most standard. We prefer .html to .htm because .html is more descriptive—after all, "html" describes the code contained in the file.

If a user specifies a URL address that ends with a directory name, and the web server cannot find a file named index.html or index.htm (or possibly default.htm) in the specified

---

[2] As you might recall, the term "web server" can refer to (1) the physical computer that stores the web page files or (2) the program that runs on the computer that enables clients to retrieve the web pages. When talking about a "web server's root directory," we're not referring to the computer's hard drive root directory. We're referring to the directory that the web server program designates as the top-level container directory for all the web-related files that the web server computer uses.

[3] During the development process, you'll probably want to implement your web pages on your local computer's hard drive. You can load most of your hard drive web pages to a browser by simply double clicking on the file within Microsoft's File Explorer tool. But if you double click on a directory, the index.html file won't load by default. Why? Because the web server is the thing that knows to look for the index.html file (i.e., it knows to search for it if it sees a directory name). And you bypass the web server if you double click a web page file within File Explorer.

directory, then the web server will either (1) load a web page that shows the contents of the specified directory, or (2) display an error page (e.g., "Directory Listing Denied" or "HTTP 404 - Page Not Found"). To avoid the directory contents web page (which is rather ugly) or the error page, you should include an `index.html` file in every directory that might be specified as part of a URL. It might seem a bit weird to have multiple `index.html` files within your website, but for larger websites, get used to it. Clearly, you need an `index.html` file in the directory that sits at the top of your website's directory tree structure—that particular `index.html` file is your website's home page. The other `index.html` files are not the official home page, but you can think of them as "home pages" for different areas within your website.

# 6.5 Web Design

Because a home page is the default first page a user sees when the user visits a website, it's the web developer's first—and possibly only—opportunity to make a good impression on users. So try to get it right, or your users might leave and never come back. In this section, you will learn a few tips on how to make a good first impression. These tips are part of a software area known as *web design*, which is comprised of these subareas: user interface design, user experience design, graphic design, and search engine optimization. Sorry, explaining all that is beyond the scope of this book. But we do explain some of it—we scratch the surface on user interface design and user experience design. That's a surface that needs to be scratched, so let's begin.

## User Interface Design

In a general sense, *user interface design* (UID) refers to the mechanisms by which users of a product can use the product. For web pages, the mechanisms are things like text, color, pictures, buttons, text boxes, and progress bars. A good UID designer will anticipate users' needs and create an interface that meets those needs by incorporating components that are easy to understand and use.

After the home page downloads, users will want to identify the web page's main content quickly. To help in that regard, you should try to avoid clutter, and focus on clear, concise words (and graphics, if appropriate) that describe the web page's main content. Remember that for a nontrivial website, the home page is only for the main content and links to other web pages, not for lots of details. If you need to provide lots of details for something, you should put those details on a separate web page and link to that page from the home page. The link labels themselves are important. For each link label, use only one word or a few words that get to the point quickly. Don't be afraid to remove unnecessary text and to have whitespace on your home page. Whitespace can provide a nice respite for stressed-out web surfers.

In presenting the web page's content, it's important to be consistent with your text and colors. For text, you should limit the number of text fonts used. Pick pleasing fonts that go together well for your main content and your subsidiary content. Make sure that the foreground text colors contrast with the background colors so the text is easy to read. Normally, that means the contrasting colors should be different in terms of lightness and darkness. You should pick a set of colors for your text, background, and graphics that complement each other. Apply a consistent strategy for choosing which colors go to which type of content.

## User Experience Design

*User experience design* is a bit more nuanced than user interface design. For a car, its user interface might be the power steering, the heated leather seats, and the wireless Internet communication. The user experience might be a feeling of calm comfortable control. For a web page, the UID incorporates the elements described in the previous subsection, whereas the user experience design is the feeling produced by those UID elements. For example, you should choose colors and fonts that generate the proper feeling for the user's browsing experience. The user experience design's feeling comes not only from UID elements, but also from things that enhance the user's ability to digest the web page's content, such as helpful pictures, familiar controls, fast downloads, and efficient navigation between web pages.

The first thing a web user notices when visiting a web page is how long it takes to load the page. So in designing your home page, pay heed to the size of the web page file and all its resource files. In particular, image files and video files tend to be large. Later on, you'll learn how to load such resource files without slowing the download for the web page's other content. But for a positive user experience, you should still try to avoid having your home page built with large files.

Most home pages will have links to other web pages within the website. You should use the nav container to group those links. Normally, users navigate to other web pages by clicking links at the top and left, so that's where your nav containers should go. Suppose your website has lots of web pages. On the home page, you could include a link to every one of those web pages, but that might lead to a cluttered home page. As part of the web design process, you need to determine how many links to put on your home page and how to navigate to other pages after clicking on those links. Let's look at some different strategies.

See **FIGURE 6.3**, which shows the organization for a website whose pages are organized with a *linear structure*. That means the home page links to one other page, and that second page links to one other page, and so on. That type of strategy might be used for a website whose purpose is to present a long article. By splitting up the article into separate pages and connecting them with links, the user doesn't have to scroll so far down while reading. Other examples where a linear structure is beneficial are a shopping cart that steps through the transaction or a tutorial with a specific sequence of steps. But be aware that pure linear structures are not all that common. Why? It's difficult for users to go backwards. To return to the beginning, the user has to click the back button multiple times. Another reason linear structures have fallen out of favor is because people are now used to scrolling feverishly on their phones. Using the scroll bar to scroll through a lengthy web page doesn't seem all that bad when compared to lots of link clicking and back button clicking.

Now take a look at **FIGURE 6.4**, which shows a website whose pages are organized with a *hierarchical structure*. That means the home page links to several other pages where those pages serve as pseudo-home pages for the different areas within the website. When compared to linear

FIGURE 6.3 **Website with a linear structure for its web pages**

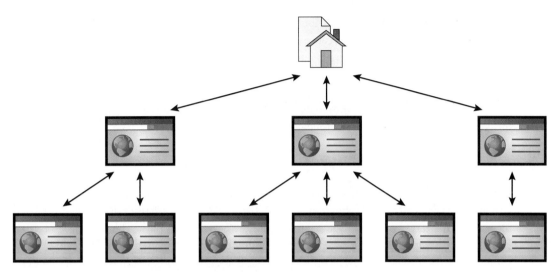

**FIGURE 6.4 Website with a hierarchical structure for its web pages**

structure websites, hierarchical structure websites tend to reduce the number of clicks needed to navigate through a website's web pages.

With hierarchical structures, the home page is often called the *top-level page*, and the next-level pages are often called *second-level pages*. Second-level pages have links to the other pages in their areas. Both top-level and second-level pages are sometimes referred to as landing pages because they can be targets (or "landing places") of links that reside outside the website.

Finally, take a look at **FIGURE 6.5**, which shows a website whose pages are organized with a mixed structure. There's a hierarchical structure for compartmentalizing the website's main areas, plus additional links that (1) connect from within the areas to other areas and (2) connect pages

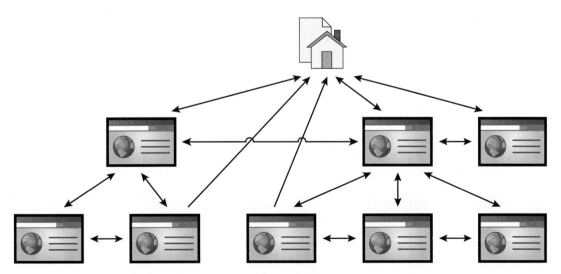

**FIGURE 6.5 Website with a mixed structure for its web pages**

back to the website's home page. For nontrivial websites, this sort of mixed structure is by far the most common type of structure because it leads to the best user experience—fewer clicks to drill down to the different pages within a given area (due to the hierarchical structure) and fewer clicks to jump from within one area to get to a different area. The ability to go from one area to another area is particularly useful when there's an area that serves as a repository for information needed by multiple other areas. To accommodate that scenario, just add a link from each of those areas to the common repository's second-level page.

## 6.6 Navigation Within a Web Page

You might recall from Figure 6.1 that there are three basic types of values for an a element's `href` attribute. We've already talked about an absolute URL value and a relative URL value. In both of those cases, the target is a web page separate from the current web page. The third type of `href` value shown in Figure 6.1 is for when you want a link that takes the user to some specified point within the current web page. That can be particularly useful for long web pages, so the user can quickly jump to designated destinations within the web page. For example, note the blue links near the top of the Clock Tower web page in **FIGURE 6.6**. If the user clicks the **Clock Tower Photograph** link, then the web page scrolls within the browser window so that the link's target (the clock tower photograph itself) gets positioned at the top of the browser window. In Figure 6.6, there is no scroll bar, so no scrolling takes place if the link is clicked. But don't think that this situation (no scrolling) is normal. If a web page has internal links, then the web page will normally be sufficiently long so as to justify the internal links. We'll show the code used to implement those internal links, but first, let's describe the web page's other links.

Note the **Back to the Top** link at the bottom of the page. With a long web page, it's common to have such a link so the user can quickly get back to the top after scrolling to the bottom. Once again, because there is no scroll bar in Figure 6.6's browser window, no scrolling takes place if the link is clicked.

Note the yellow sidebar at the left of the Clock Tower web page. It forms the navigation area with links to other web pages. For example, clicking on **Zombie Bloodbath** takes users to a web page that describes Park University's ill-fated foray into the brain-eating movie production business back in 1978.

### Syntax for Internal Link

Now it's time to show the code used to implement the internal links in the Clock Tower web page. To jump to a designated location within the current web page, you need to use a value starting with # such that that value matches an `id` attribute's value for an element in the web page. Here's the Clock Tower web page's code that links to the pledge drive section:

```
<a href="#pledge-drive">Pledge Drive</a>
```

And here's the element that that link jumps to:

```
<h3 id="pledge-drive">Pledge Drive</h3>
```

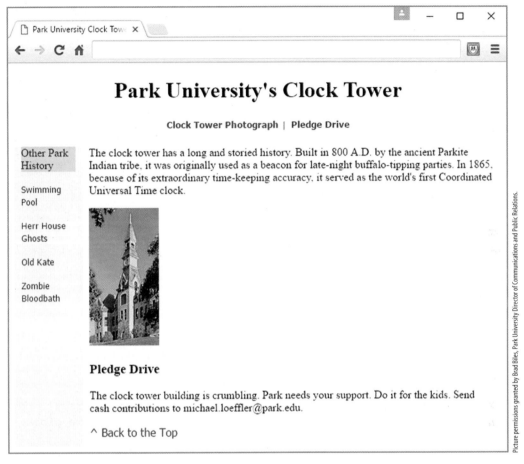

**FIGURE 6.6 Clock Tower web page**

Note the spelling for `pledge-drive`. Standard coding conventions suggest using hyphens to separate multiple words in an `id` value. That should look familiar because you've already learned to use hyphens with multiple-word `class` attribute values.

For a given web page, you can have only one element with a particular `id` value. So because `pledge-drive` appears in this `h3` statement, `pledge-drive` cannot be used as an `id` value anywhere else within the Clock Tower web page. That should make sense—after all, if another element used that same `id` value, then the browser engine would be confused as to which target element to link to when the user clicks the `a` element (with `href="#pledge-drive"`) shown. If you accidentally use the same `id` value for more than one element, don't worry, the validation service will flag it as an error.[4]

Look for the `a` element code and the `h3` element code in **FIGURE 6.7A**'s Clock Tower web page source code. Also, look for two other internal links in the source code. Specifically, can you

---

[4] Of course, this works only if you use the W3C's validation service. You've been using the validation service for all of your web pages, right?

```
<body>
<header>
  <h1 id="top">Park University's Clock Tower</h1>
  <h5>
    <a href="#tower-photo">Clock Tower Photograph</a>   |   
    <a href="#pledge-drive">Pledge Drive</a>
  </h5>
</header>

<div class="table">
  <nav class="cell">
    <div class="nav-heading">Other Park History</div>
    <div><a>Swimming Pool</a></div>
    <div><a>Herr House Ghosts</a></div>
    <div><a>Old Kate</a></div>
    <div><a>Zombie Bloodbath</a></div>
  </nav>

  <section class="cell">
    <p>
      The clock tower has a long and storied history.
      Built in 800 A.D. by the ancient Parkite Indian tribe,
      it was originally used as a beacon for late-night
      buffalo-tipping parties.
      In 1865, because of its extraordinary time-keeping accuracy,
      it served as the world's first Coordinated Universal Time clock.
    </p>
    <p>
      <img id="tower-photo" src="../images/clockTower.jpg"
      alt="Clock Tower Photograph">
    </p>
    <h3 id="pledge-drive">Pledge Drive</h3>
    <p>
      The clock tower building is crumbling.
      Park needs your support. Do it for the kids.
      Send cash contributions to michael.loeffler@park.edu.
    </p>
    <a href="#top">^ Back to the Top</a>
  </section>
</div>
</body>
</html>
```

> It's common to use a vertical bar to separate internal links.

> Note the character references to ensure two spaces on each side of the vertical bar.

**FIGURE 6.7A Source code body container for Clock Tower web page**

find the link that jumps down to the `tower-photo img` element? And how about the link at the bottom that jumps up to the top of the page?

## Walking Through the Clock Tower Web Page's Source Code

There are quite a few details in the Clock Tower web page that are worth looking at. They're not specific to the main point of this section (internal links within a web page), but they are noteworthy nonetheless. The Clock Tower web page's code is long, requiring two figures to show it all. Figure 6.7A shows the web page's `body` container, and **FIGURE 6.7B** shows the `head` container. It might seem odd to have the first figure display the `body` code and the second figure display the `head` code, even though the clockTower.html file positions the `head` container above the `body` container (of course). In the book's figures, we position the two containers in reverse order because when we examine the web page, it'll make more sense to look at the `body` container before the `head` container.

Let's start by examining the `body` container code that separates the `tower-photo` and `pledge-drive` links:

```
   |   
```

Using a vertical bar ( | ) to separate internal links is a very common technique. The vertical bar has no impact on the web page's functionality; it's just for appearance purposes. It's a way to indicate a separation between internal links. Using common techniques helps users to feel comfortable, and that in turn might encourage users to buy what the web page is selling.

Also in Figure 6.7A, note the ` ` character references and the blank spaces surrounding the vertical bar. By inserting a ` ` character reference next to a space character at the left of the vertical bar and also at the right of the vertical bar, that causes two spaces to display on each side of the vertical bar, which looks nicer than single spaces.

Below the vertical-bar-separated links, you can see a `nav` container and also a `section` container, both with `class="cell"`. Can you figure out the purpose of `class="cell"`? We're using a simple CSS table for layout with only one row and two cells—one cell for the navigation bar at the left and one cell for the web page's main content. As you probably already know, a *navigation bar* is a group of links that enable users to navigate (link to) the various pages on a website. To make the user feel comfortable, the navigation bar should look the same on each web page. Typically, navigation bars go at the left, but top and bottom are common as well.

In the Clock Tower `nav` container, note the a elements and the fact that they have no `href` attributes. An a element that has no `href` attribute is called a *placeholder link*. Although the `nav` container's placeholder links currently go nowhere, the idea is that they will be replaced later on with active links. For now, each link is "holding a place" for a future link.

Now let's focus on the web page's table layout. As you can see in Figure 6.7A, the `nav` and `section` elements both contain `class="cell"` attribute-value pairs. As you'll confirm later when we examine the CSS rules, that causes the `nav` and `section` elements to act like table cells. What element acts like the surrounding table? The `div` element, with `class="table"`.

```
<!DOCTYPE html>
<html lang="en">
<head>
<meta charset="utf-8">
<meta name="author" content="John Dean">
<title>Park University Clock Tower</title>
<style>
  header {text-align: center;}
  .table {display: table;}
  .cell {
    display: table-cell;
    padding: 0px 10px 10px;
  }
  nav.cell {width: 80px;}

  /* Avoid yellow background at left extending above the
     page's main content. */
  .cell > :nth-child(1) {margin-top: 0;}
  nav {
    color: darkred;
    background-color: lemonchiffon;
  }
  .nav-heading {background-color: gold;}

  /* Adjust link appearances. */
  a {
    text-decoration: none;
    font-family: Tahoma, Geneva, sans-serif;
  }
  a:hover {text-decoration: underline;}
  nav a {font-size: .8em;}
  nav > * {margin: 1em 0;}
</style>
</head>
```

The `.table` and `.cell` rules form a table that holds the navigation bar at the left and the main content at the right.

Fixed width for the navigation area at the left.

`:nth-child()` selector

**FIGURE 6.7B Source code `head` container for Clock Tower web page**

## Clock Tower Web Page's CSS Rules

Now let's work our way through some of the more interesting details in the web page's CSS rules in the head section. Note the `.table` and `.cell` selectors in Figure 6.7B. As you learned in Chapter 5, they use the `display` property with `table` and `cell` values to implement a table and the cells of a table, respectively. But note that there is no `.row` selector. For a browser to render a table, the cells need to be inside rows, so how can there be no `.row` selector that implements the rows? Here's the deal: if you have `table-cell` elements that are not surrounded by a `table-row` element (or even a `table` element), then the browser engine generates an anonymous (hidden) `table-row` element around those `table-cell` elements. For the Clock Tower web page, there are indeed `table-cell` elements that are not surrounded by a `table-row` element. Can you find where the anonymous `table-row` element tags are inserted in the web page body code? Here's the relevant code from Figure 6.7A:

```
<div class="table">
  <nav class="cell">          Anonymous table-row
                             element start tag goes here.
  . . .
  <section class="cell">
                             Anonymous table-row
  . . .                      element end tag goes here.
</div>
```

Note the callouts that show where the anonymous table-row element tags get inserted in the code.

Now let's turn to the web page's CSS rules. Here's the CSS rule for the navigation area's cell:

```
nav.cell {width: 80px;}
```

Remember what the dot means in the `nav.cell` selector? It means that the browser engine locates all `nav` elements and then matches only those `nav` elements that use `cell` as a `class` attribute value. If you look at the web page body's source code, you'll see that `cell` appears as a `class` attribute value in two places—in the `nav` container (which implements the navigation bar at the left) and also in the `section` container (which holds the page's main content). The `nav.cell` selector matches only the cell in the navigation area at the left. And after matching that navigation area cell, it specifies a fixed width for it. Why do you need a fixed width for the navigation area, but not for the main content area? If the user expands or shrinks the window size, the user would normally expect the paragraphs at the right to expand and shrink, not the navigation area at the left. And that's what happens for the Clock Tower web page.

In the following CSS rule, we already talked about the `table-cell` value for the `display` property. Now let's talk about its `padding` property:

```
.cell {
  display: table-cell;
  padding: 0px 10px 10px;
}
```

The rule applies to both table cells (the navigation bar cell and the main content cell). It specifies that there's no padding on the top, 10 pixels of padding on the left and right (from the second value), and 10 pixels at the bottom. Why is it appropriate to have no padding on the top? As you can see in the nav CSS rule, the left cell has a yellow background and the right cell has no background. If there was padding at the top of the navigation bar's cell, then it would show up as a yellow area jutting above the navigation bar's text. Because the main content area has no background color, there would be no comparable color jutting above the main content area's text, and that asymmetry would look weird. So that's why it's appropriate to have no padding on the top of the navigation bar cell. Knowing to specify 0 pixels for the top of the navigation bar cell is not all that intuitive. Coming up with that solution took some tweaking. Get used to such tweaking when trying to make your web pages look good.

The issue previously described (avoiding a yellow area jutting above the navigation bar's text) actually requires even more tweaking than just setting the top padding to 0 pixels. It also requires setting no margin above each of the top elements in the navigation bar cell and the main content area cell. Here's the relevant CSS rule from the Clock Tower web page's code:

```
.cell > :nth-child(1) {margin-top: 0;}
```

As you know, this rule is known as a child selector, where child selectors use the > symbol to match elements that are child elements of other elements. In processing this rule, the browser engine searches for child elements whose parents use cell for their class attribute value. The :nth-child() selector is a special child selector in that it allows you to specify which child element is selected. This particular rule selects immediate children of "cell" elements where the child is a first child (the 1 value is for the first child).

The :nth-child() selector thing is a *pseudo-class*. In Chapter 5, you learned that a pseudo-class begins with a colon and it conditionally selects elements from a group of elements specified by the selector at the immediate left of the colon. For the :nth-child example, there is no type selector at the immediate left of the colon. So, why's that? If you don't specify a type selector, then the browser inserts the * universal selector as the implicit type selector. So behind the scenes, that rule converts to this rule:

```
.cell > *:nth-child(1) {margin-top: 0;}
```

As you may recall, the * universal selector matches all elements, so all elements are matched (that are children of elements with a class attribute value of cell) and the browser then applies the :nth-child(1) pseudo-class to those matches.

By the way, as an alternative to using :nth-child(1), you can use the :first-child pseudo-class, which also selects the first child from among a list of child elements. We'll use the :first-child pseudo-class in a later chapter.

There are still a few Clock Tower web page CSS rules that we have not yet talked about, but before we describe them, let's take a short break from rules and talk about everyone's favorite topic—style. You'll need to view the CSS code in Figure 6.7B to appreciate the following style commentary, so be prepared to jump back and forth.

The `nth-child` rule is kind of tricky, so you should include a comment for it. The comment is too long to fit at the right of the `nth-child` rule, so the comment appears above the rule. Note the indentation on the comment's line continuation.

Because there are so many CSS rules for the Clock Tower web page, you should separate the rule groups with blank lines. For each rule group that is nonintuitive, you should preface the group with a comment above the rule group. Note the rule group comments in the Clock Tower web page's source code.

In the Clock Tower web page, the last four CSS rules deal with links (see the a element in each rule). We'll wait until the next section to cover those rules, because CSS for links is a big enough subject that it deserves its own section.

# 6.7 CSS for Links

Have you ever noticed that after clicking on a link and returning later, the link's color is different? For example, note the different colored links at the top of the Clock Tower web page in Figure 6.6. The left link, labeled **Clock Tower Photograph**, is blue, indicating that the link has not been clicked. On the other hand, the right link, labeled **Clock Tower Photograph**, is purple, indicating that the link has been clicked in the past. By default, the major browsers use blue text for unclicked links and purple text for clicked links. More formally, those links are referred to as *unvisited links* and *visited links*, respectively. The HTML5 standard does not mention blue and purple as typical defaults, but those colors have been used for decades, so it's reasonable to assume they'll remain as defaults for many more years down the road.

A link is defined as a "visited link" if it leads to a location that the computer's browser has been to recently. Browsers have different time limits to determine whether a location has been visited "recently." If you clear your browser's history, the browser will consider all links to be unvisited, so they will go back to their unvisited color. That can be useful for testing a link's color during development because once you load a page, it no longer displays the unvisited link color.

Be aware that end users have the ability to override the link colors specified by the browser by adjusting their browser's settings. But also be aware that as a developer, you have even more power than the user in this regard. You can use CSS to override the link colors specified by the browser, and those CSS rules override the user's link color browser settings as well.

Now for the CSS that enables you to specify link colors. For unvisited links, use this syntax:

```
a:link {color: color-value;}
```

The a is the element type for a link element. The `:link` thing is a pseudo-class. It qualifies the a element type by searching only for links that have not been visited. As you'd expect, the `a:link` selector is known as a *pseudo-class selector*.

You now know to use `a:link` for unvisited links. For visited links, use `a:visited`, like this:

```
a:visited {color: color-value;}
```

Here are a couple of examples. The first rule specifies burlywood for unvisited links, and the second rule specifies light blue for visited links:

```
a:link {color: burlywood;}
a:visited {color: #aaaaff;}
```

Despite the undeniable excitement of being able to change web page link colors with CSS, please try to show restraint. Using different colors might confuse your end users. They might not consciously realize that a web page's link colors are different, but they might realize it at a subconscious level. That can be particularly annoying for users who explicitly configure their browser's link colors.

In addition to being able to change the colors in your web page's links, you can also change your links' underline scheme. By default, browsers display links with underlines. If that leads to visual clutter or confusion with regular text that's underlined, and you'd like to have no link underlining, then use text-decoration: none, like this:

```
a {text-decoration: none;}
```

If link underlines are disabled using this CSS rule, but you want to display underlines when the mouse hovers over a link, use the a:hover pseudo-class selector with text-decoration: underline, like this:

```
a:hover {text-decoration: underline;}
```

In case you were wondering, the :hover selector matches any element that is being hovered over, not just links, so to limit the matches to just links, you need to preface :hover with a, as shown in the example.

When using both of these rules, there's a conflict in that they both apply to link elements. How is that conflict resolved? Because the a:hover selector is more specific than the a selector, the a:hover selector overrides the a selector for links that are being hovered over.

We encourage you to find these CSS rules in the Clock Tower web page code in Figure 6.7B. While you're there, also note the two nav element CSS rules, which are copied here for your convenience:

```
nav a {font-size: .8em;}
nav > * {margin: 1em 0;}
```

The first rule specifies a smallish font size of .8em for all link elements in the nav container. The second rule adds a 1em margin to the top and bottom of all elements that are child elements of the nav container. We hope those rules make sense—you want the navigation bar links to be unobtrusive (with a smaller font size), but to make them easily clickable, you want them separated vertically (with added margin space at the top and bottom of each link).

As with all the book's web page examples, we encourage you to retrieve the Clock Tower web page's source code from the book's website and play around with it. After loading the page in a browser, try hovering your mouse over the top links. That should cause your standard mouse pointer to change to a hand icon, indicating an active link. Then hover your mouse over the placeholder links. That should cause your mouse pointer to change to an I-bar icon. That's a bit confusing, so to improve the user's experience, you could add this CSS rule:

```
nav a {cursor: not-allowed;}
```

With that rule in place, hovering your mouse over the placeholder links causes your mouse pointer to change to a blocked icon (⊘), indicating that the link is inactive.

# 6.8 a Element Additional Details

There are just a couple more things to discuss about links that don't quite fit with the earlier sections. Previously, we discussed how to link to a different web page and also how to link to a specified location within the current web page. It's also legal to combine those techniques and link to a specified location within a different web page.

## Linking to a Specified Location Within a Different Web Page

To link to a specified location within a different web page, use the href attribute to specify the other page (using an absolute url with http or a relative URL) and then append a # value to specify the location within that page. To explain that more fully, we need an example. Given the following directory tree, can you provide a link from the home page to the clock tower photograph? The photograph's img element resides in the clockTower.html web page, and it uses an id value of tower-photo. Try to come up with the code for the link element before you glance down at the answer.

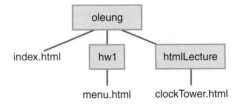

As shown, student Olivia Leung has an index.html home page in her oleung home page directory. In implementing a link from the home page to the clock tower photograph, don't fall into the trap of thinking you need to use .. to first go <u>up</u> to the oleung home directory. Remember: when you're in the index.html home page, the "current directory" is the oleung directory. So the path to the clock tower photograph starts by going down (from the oleung directory) to the htmlLecture directory. Here's the link code:

```
<a href="htmlLecture/clockTower.html#tower-photo">
   Park University Clock Tower Photograph</a>
```

| Values for the a Element's target Attribute | Description |
|---|---|
| `_self` | Overlay the current web page with the target web page. |
| `_blank` | Open the target web page in a new browser window or in a new tab within the current browser window. |
| `_parent` | Open the target web page in the current web page's parent document, which is typically the browser window that caused the current web page to open. |

**FIGURE 6.8** **Specifying the environment in which the web page opens**

After the target web page's filename (`clockTower.html`), you can see `#tower-photo`. Go back to Figure 6.7A and find `id="tower-photo"` in the clock tower photograph's `img` element. Remember: to link to a particular element, you preface the element's `id` value with #.

## `target` Attribute

So far, we've discussed only one attribute for the a element—the `href` attribute. Now let's discuss the `target` attribute. The a element's `target` attribute value specifies where to open the linked-to web page. Note the three values listed in **FIGURE 6.8**.

The `target` attribute's default value is `_self`. As noted in the figure, if you have a link that uses the `_self` value and the link is clicked, the specified new page loads within the current web browser and overlays the previous page. Most links omit the `target` attribute and stick with the `_self` default behavior. But every now and then, you might want to open a targeted web page in a new browser window or in a new tab, and we address that next.

As noted in the figure, if you have a link that uses the `_blank` value and the link is clicked, the specified new page loads in a new browser window or in a new tab within the current browser window. With the `_blank` value, it's up to the browser to decide whether to use a new window or a new tab. Here's an example link element that uses the `_blank` value:

```
<a href="https://www.youtube.com/watch?v=zm48WoRs0hA&noredirect=1"
   target="_blank">Bethany Mota: Perfect Back to School Hair, Makeup
   &amp; Outfit!</a>
```

Here's a coding conventions refresher: In the code, note that `target` is indented. That's because it's a continuation of the a start tag that began on the previous line. Note, `&amp; Outfit` is also indented, to the same column as the second line. Both lines are a continuation of the a element, so they both get indented one level.

So with a `target="_blank"` link, if the link is clicked, the specified new page loads in a new browser window or in a new tab within the current browser window. Can you think of a disadvantage of that behavior? Clicking the back arrow won't take the user back to the previous page. Maybe that's OK if you want to give prominence to a particularly important linked-to page (like Bethany Mota's classic 2013 video "Perfect Back to School Hair, Makeup & Outfit!"[5]), but if you want to counteract that behavior, the `target` attribute's `_parent` value can come to your rescue.

As noted in Figure 6.8, if you have a link that uses the `_parent` value and the link is clicked, the target web page loads in the current web page's *parent document*, which is typically the browser window that caused the current web page to open. Effectively, that means if you use `target="_blank"` to open a web page in to a new window or new tab, you can use `target="_parent"` to open another web page in the original window or tab. If you return to the original web page with `_parent`, you'll often want to use JavaScript to close the newly opened window or tab after you leave it. We'll discuss JavaScript extensively later in the book.

## 6.9 Bitmap Image Formats: GIF, JPEG, PNG

So far, you've seen examples where if the user clicks a link, the browser opens a new page. It's also possible to create a link where if the user clicks it, the browser opens an image. Usually, "opening an image" causes the image to fill the entire browser window. Normally, that's inappropriate, but as you'll learn in the next chapter, you can use an `iframe` element to create a window "frame," which allows you to open/display an image within just the frame part of the window. But before we talk about the `iframe` element in the next chapter, first we need to talk about image file formats and `img` element details. That will take a while, and the rest of this chapter is devoted to that.

There are two basic categories of image files—bitmap image files and vector graphics files. We'll have more to say about vector graphics files soon enough, but for now we'll focus on bitmap image files. With bitmap image files, an image is comprised of a group of pixels. For example, an *icon*, which is simply a small image file, typically has 16 rows with 16 pixels in each row. Within a bitmap image file, every pixel gets mapped to a particular color value, and each color value is a sequence of bits (where a bit is a 0 or a 1[6]). For a browser to display a bitmap image, it displays each pixel's mapped color. This reliance on mapping color bit values to pixels is the basis for the name *bitmap image*.

The three most common formats for bitmap image files (also called raster image files) on the Web are GIF, JPEG, and PNG. You can see brief descriptions of those formats in **FIGURE 6.9**. We'll provide more details shortly, but first, you should be aware of two other file formats—BMP (for bitmap) and TIFF (for tagged image file format). They're both very popular for graphics applications, but they're generally not used with web pages. Why? BMP files are too large, and TIFF files cannot be viewed by web browsers without a plug-in.[7] Since we're focusing on web pages, we'll refrain from providing details about them.

---

[5] According to my middle school and high school daughters, vlogger Bethany Mota is the coolest, barely twentysomething in the whole world. Formerly bullied, she's now a *motavatour* megastar.

[6] For the purpose of this discussion about bitmap images, all you need to know about bits is that they are 0's and 1's. But from a computer hardware perspective, 0's and 1's are high-energy signals versus low-energy signals. When a computer generates a low-energy signal, that's a 0. When a computer generates a high-energy signal, that's a 1.

[7] A *plug-in* is a software component that adds functionality to an existing software application, like a browser.

| Bitmap Image Formats | Description |
|---|---|
| GIF | Good for limited-color images such as line drawings, icons, and cartoon-like illustrations. |
| JPEG | Good for high-quality photographs. |
| PNG | Flexible; good for limited-color images and also high-quality photographs. |

FIGURE 6.9 **Common formats for web page bitmap image files**

## GIF Image File Format

Let's begin our discussion of image file formats with GIF files. GIF files use a filename extension of .gif. GIF stands for Graphics Interchange Format. Because the G in GIF stands for "graphics" and graphics is pronounced with a hard g, many people in industry (most?) pronounce GIF files

with a hard g, so it sounds like the "gif" part of "gift." But don't jump on that bandwagon just yet. For a full pronunciation explanation, see http://www.olsenhome .com/gif. That web page points out that CompuServe, the company that invented the GIF format, documented GIF's pronunciation as "jif," with a soft g, like the peanut butter.[8] If you're reading this book without a teacher, we recommend that you pronounce GIF files as "jif." However, if you've got a teacher, you should follow your teacher's lead.

In creating a GIF file from an original picture, the original picture's colors are mapped to an 8-bit palette of colors. That means each pixel uses 8 bits, and those 8 bits determine the pixel's color. And the entire set of colors forms the image's *color palette*. Each image has its own color palette with its own set of colors. So for the peanut butter image seen here you'd need to capture colors such as red, brown, and blue. Each of those colors would have an 8-bit sequence associated with them, such as 01011010 for red, 11011001 for brown, and 00010110 for blue.

With 8 bits for each color value, there are 256 different ways to arrange the 0's and 1's. You can prove this to yourself by writing all the different permutations of eight bits, or you can just remember that the number of permutations is equal to 2 raised to the power of the number of bits, where $2^8 = 256$. That means each GIF image file can handle a maximum of 256 distinct colors. If a picture has more than 256 distinct colors, then when creating the GIF file from the picture, some of the colors won't be stored accurately. Instead they'll be stored with similar colors that are part of the GIF file's color palette, and that leads to the GIF file's image being a degraded version of the original photograph. Color degradation is nonexistent or imperceptible for limited-color images such as line drawings, icons, or cartoon-like illustrations, and that's why GIF files are good for those types of things and not good for color photographs.

---

[8] A comment from one of that web page's readers is particularly insightful: "No *decent* coder would pass up an opportunity to inflict a horrid pun on the world. And seeing as peanut butter is one of the principal three programmer foods (the other two being Pepsi and nacho cheese Doritos), the reference is immediately obvious."

By using only 8 bits of storage for each pixel, GIF files are able to achieve relatively small file sizes. That's the main benefit of using the GIF file format—small file sizes. File sizes can be reduced further by applying a compression scheme. The GIF file compression algorithm is *lossless* because it does not introduce any color degradation. But be aware that the compression is applied to the GIF file's 256-color-palette image, not to the original picture. As already mentioned, if the original picture has more than 256 distinct colors, then there is indeed information loss in going from the original picture to the GIF file image.

A fun feature of the GIF file format is that it supports simple animation. In rendering an *animated GIF*, the browser displays a sequence of image frames in quick succession. Normally, animated GIF files are configured to display their frame sequences in continuous loops rather than only one time.

## JPEG Image File Format

Next up, the JPEG image file format. JPEG stands for Joint Photographic Experts Group, and JPEG is pronounced "jay-peg." JPEG files use a filename extension of `.jpeg` or `.jpg`.

In creating a JPEG file from an original picture, the original picture's colors are mapped to a 24-bit palette of colors. With 24 bits, there are approximately 16 million permutations of 0's and 1's in each color value ($2^{24}$ = 16,777,216). That means approximately 16 million unique colors can be represented, and that's more colors than the human eye can discern. So unless you're an eagle with the ability to distinguish between more than 16,000,000 colors, you should be in good shape with the quality of colors in JPEG files. In other words, for humans, there is effectively no information loss in 24-bit palette JPEG images.

Note this picture of the New York Catskills' famed fall foliage:

Photo courtesy of Allegany County, New York.

**Fall on Alma Pond in the Catskills**

With the picture's wide variety of colors, a GIF file would have to approximate many of the colors in order to conform to the constraints of its relatively small color palette. But with the JPEG format, all the photograph's original colors can be displayed accurately.

In attempting to produce optimized JPEG files, "lossy" compression schemes are applied. The person who creates the JPEG image file chooses the lossiness of the compression scheme—higher loss means greater color degradation and greater file size reduction. With that in mind, JPEG images can vary widely in terms of color degradation and file size. Nonetheless, for photographs, optimized JPEG files almost always produce a better balance between file size and quality than the other file formats.

## PNG Image File Format

PNG stands for Portable Network Graphics, and PNG is pronounced "ping." PNG files use a file-name extension of .png.

The PNG format was invented in 1996 as an open-source alternative to the GIF format because the GIF format was copyright protected with a patent owned by Unisys. So each time someone made a new GIF file, they were supposed to pay a license fee to Unisys. Oftentimes, GIF file creators didn't bother to pay the license fee, which was illegal. To avoid such illicit activity, the web community eventually invented their own open-source format for image files, and the PNG format was born. After the PNG format's inception in 1996, the GIF copyright expired, so it's now legal to create and use GIF files without fear of retribution. Although the PNG format no longer serves as a licit alternative to the illicit use of the GIF format, the PNG format remains very popular, as it improved upon the GIF format in several ways.

The PNG format provides more flexibility in terms of clarity versus file size. In creating a PNG file from an original picture, you can choose to map each pixel to only a few bits (to create an image file that doesn't require much storage) all the way up to 64 bits per pixel (to create an image file that is very clear). As mentioned earlier, only 24 bits are needed to represent approximately 16 million unique colors, and that's all that most humans can discern. The additional bits for 64-bits-per-pixel PNG files are for things like multiple channels and opacity/transparency levels. Those details are quite technical, and they're beyond the scope of this book.

The PNG format provides more flexibility in terms of transparency. You can create images with different levels of transparency for different parts of an image. GIF images can have only two levels of transparency—completely opaque or completely transparent. PNG images can have 256 levels of transparency.

Note the web page in **FIGURE 6.10**. In particular, note the yellow stucco background behind the aquarium.[9] The background comes from the web page and not from the image file. You can't see the image's original area outside of the aquarium (and the image's rectangular edges) because it's covered over by the web page's background. The browser is able to "cover over" that area because the PNG file is configured to be transparent there. The PNG format allows that sort of complete transparency, but it also allows partial transparency. In the figure, notice the partially transparent glass near the top of the aquarium and the partially transparent water within the aquarium. Note how the glass area is more transparent than the water area. That should make sense when you realize that the glass area is filled with air, which is clearer than the murky aquarium water.

Learning how to create and edit images and add different levels of transparency to them is beyond the scope of this book, but if you're interested, feel free to learn about such things on your own. To get started, you could purchase one of the popular graphics software packages, such as

---

[9] The yellow stucco might not be the most attractive, but the web page takes its cue from the official PNG website. The PNG authors are known for their creativity and attention to detail...not so much for their fashion sense.

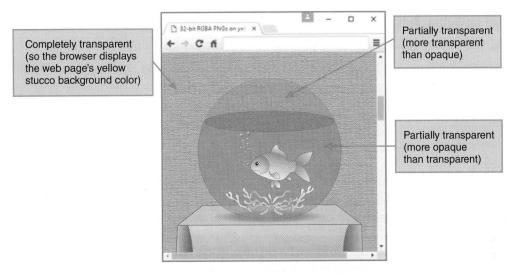

Completely transparent (so the browser displays the web page's yellow stucco background color)

Partially transparent (more transparent than opaque)

Partially transparent (more opaque than transparent)

**FIGURE 6.10 Aquarium PNG image with multiple levels of transparency**

Adobe Photoshop or Corel PaintShop Pro. Or as an alternative, you could download and use the GIMP graphics software package for free.

## Image Format Comparison

When you implement a web page with an image(s), you'll need to decide which image format is most appropriate. There are no absolute rules. What follows are guidelines.

If your image is a photograph, you should normally choose the JPEG format because a JPEG file will yield a higher quality image, and it will tend to be smaller in size. How can a JPEG file be smaller than a GIF file when a JPEG file uses 24 bits for each color and a GIF file uses 8 bits for each color? For photographs, the JPEG compression scheme is much more effective than the GIF compression scheme. The JPEG compression often reduces the size so it's less than the size of a comparable original GIF file and even less than a compressed version of the GIF file.

For limited-color images such as line drawings, icons, and cartoon-like illustrations, choose the GIF or PNG format because that will lead to smaller files than if the JPEG format is used. The PNG format is flexible—in addition to being a good choice for limited-color images, it can also be used for high-quality photographic images.

As mentioned earlier, the GIF format supports simple animation. The PNG format does not support animation, but in 2001, an offshoot of the PNG working group formally introduced an extension to the PNG format called MNG that does support animation. Here are a few advantages that MNG files have over animated GIF files:

- ▶ Significantly improved compression
- ▶ Ability to move images relative to the other images in the animation's sequence of images
- ▶ Ability to use not only PNG images, but also JPEG-oriented (JNG format) images

## 6.10 img Element

Now that you know about image file formats, it's time to focus on the nuts and bolts of how to display an image on a web page. In Chapter 4, we introduced the img element, which displays images. In this section, we'll review what you learned and provide more details.

Let's jump right into an img element example:

```
<img src="../images/winkingSmiley.gif"
  alt="Winking Smiley Face" width="50" height="50">
```

The src attribute specifies the image's filename and the location of the image's file. In this img element, the filename is winkingSmiley.gif. The location is indicated by the path that comes before the filename. The path that comes before winkingSmiley.gif is ../images/. Do you remember what the .. is for? The .. says to move up to the parent directory of the current directory. After .. comes /images, which says to go down to the images directory. That's where the winkingSmiley.gif file is supposed to reside.

Quick quiz: How would you specify src's value if winkingSmiley.gif was in the same directory as the current web page? Before reading on, try to figure it out for yourself. The answer is... src="winkingSmiley.gif". The key is to realize that if the image file and current web page are in the same directory, then there's no need for a path.

Referring back to the img code fragment, note the alt attribute and its "Winking Smiley Face" value. The HTML5 standard states that the alt attribute is required. The alt attribute's value should normally be a description of the picture. The alt stands for "alternative" because it provides an alternative for displaying the image in case the image is unviewable. Formally, we refer to the alt attribute as a *fallback mechanism* because it provides content for the browser to fall back on if the image can't be displayed. That content is referred to as *fallback content*.

Earlier, we said the image might be unviewable. There could be a problem with the file, such as it might not exist, it might be corrupted, or it might be in a different location than what's specified in the src attribute's path. Other reasons for not being able to view a file have nothing to do with the file; they have to do with the user. To make web page downloads faster, users might disable the ability to download images on their browsers. Some users are visually impaired and use screen readers to process web page content. Screen readers ignore displayable things like images and instead rely on the fallback content to know what to read aloud to the user.

Browsers are free to use the alt fallback content as they see fit. Before HTML5, prior versions of HTML specified that the alt attribute's value should be displayed as a *tooltip* (text that pops up when the user hovers the mouse over an item), but that's no longer the case. With HTML5, it's the title attribute that is used for tooltips. Well, formally, the HTML5 standard says the title attribute is for "advisory information," and that has led browsers to use the title attribute for tooltips. To avoid redundancy, current browsers no longer use the alt attribute for tooltips. Instead, they use the alt attribute as fallback content for things like screen readers attempting to render img elements.

An img element's width and height attributes specify the image's size in pixels. In implementing an img element, you should find the image's actual width and height values and use those values for the img element's width and height attributes. Perhaps the easiest way to find an image's actual

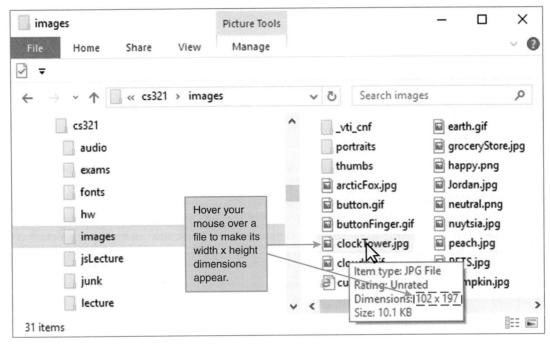

**FIGURE 6.11 How to find pixel dimensions for an image file**

width and height values is to find the image file in File Explorer, hover your mouse over it, and look for its dimensions. **FIGURE 6.11** shows how that's done for the Clock Tower web page's image file.

If you omit the img element's width and height attributes, then the image will display with its natural size, which is a good thing. But specifying its natural size explicitly is better because that improves download speed. How is that, you ask? The size and position of the image affects the layout of the other items on the web page. For example, the width of an image determines whether the subsequent item on the web page gets positioned at the right of the image or on the next row. If the image's dimensions are known early during the web page download process, then those dimensions can be used to display the web page's other items in their proper positions. On the other hand, if the image's dimensions are not specified, then the browser has to wait for the image file to be downloaded and displayed before it knows where to position the other items. Avoiding the wait can be very helpful because, typically, image files (and audio and video files, covered in the next chapter) take much longer to download than other items on the web page. If you specify width and height values that don't match the image's original pixel dimensions, the picture will be displayed with the specified dimensions, but the quality of the resulting picture normally will degrade. So try to always use the correct dimensions.

# 6.11 **Vector Graphics**

GIF, JPEG, and PNG are formats for bitmap images. As discussed earlier, a bitmap image works with the help of a map that assigns a color to each pixel in the image's rectangular grid of pixels. If you attempt to resize a bitmap image (by using an img element's width and height attributes or by zooming in/out), pixels are dropped or added, and those changes can degrade the image's quality. That's a problem, and in this section we address that problem by introducing a different type of image file format. With the vector graphics image file format, images are created from mathematical formulas and are not dependent on mapping colors to individual pixels. So if you resize a vector graphics image, the image is redrawn (using the image's formulas) to accommodate the grid's new rectangular grid of pixels—and no degradation occurs. Yay!

## SVG Image Format

SVG is the most popular type of vector graphics format, and that's the format we'll focus on. SVG stands for Scalable Vector Graphics. SVG files use a filename extension of .svg, but after compression, the resulting compressed file has an extension of .svgz.

As mentioned, one of the primary benefits of the SVG format over bitmap image formats is that there's no degradation when an SVG file is resized. To see what we're talking about, study **FIGURE 6.12**. The two pictures at the top show what happens when a PNG file and an SVG file

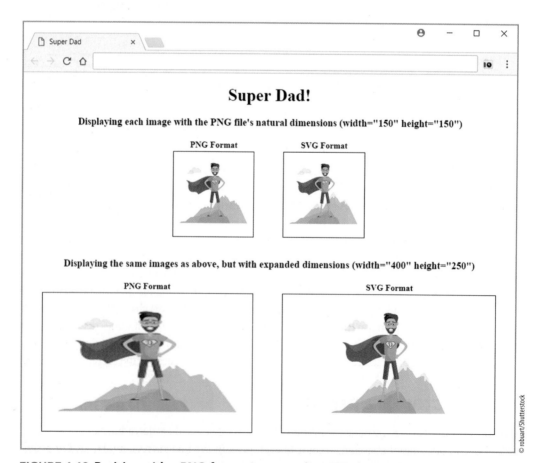

**FIGURE 6.12 Resizing with a PNG-format image and an SVG-format image**

use their actual dimension values (150 pixels wide and 150 pixels tall) in their img elements—they both display accurately with no degradation. The two pictures at the bottom show what happens when the same two files use expanded dimension values (400 pixels wide and 250 pixels tall) in their img elements. You can see that in the PNG-version web page, Super Dad looks like he's put on a few pounds and his lines are a bit fuzzy. That's because the PNG-version web page adds more pixels at the left and right than at the top and bottom to accommodate going from 150 pixels to 400 pixels in terms of width, and from 150 pixels to 250 pixels in terms of height. On the other hand, the SVG-version web page uses its underlying mathematical formulas to draw Super Dad accurately, regardless of the img element's width and height attribute values.

Not only can you degrade a PNG file by using width and height attribute values that are scaled improperly, you can also degrade a PNG file by zooming in on your browser window. If you'd like to verify that phenomenon, go to the book's website, find the superDad.html file, and open it in a browser. To zoom in, press ctrl+plus (hold down the control key while tapping the + key) about eight times. Note that the smaller PNG picture degrades, and the smaller SVG picture does not degrade.

In addition to enabling accurate resizing, the SVG format provides several other benefits over the bitmap image format. SVG files tend to be smaller, and that leads to faster web page downloads. An SVG file's formulas are built with SVG code, and as with HTML code, you can use JavaScript to dynamically manipulate any of the elements in the SVG file's code. Starting in Chapter 8, you'll learn how to use JavaScript to manipulate the elements in an HTML page. At that point, you'll be ready to learn on your own how to use JavaScript to manipulate SVG files as well. With the ability to manipulate SVG files, you will then be able to animate your SVG images.

Unfortunately, the SVG format is not perfect. It does not lend itself well to accurately displaying most photographs. Most photographs have lots of different colors and lines, and it's difficult for (SVG-format) formulas to describe all of that complexity. The SVG format is not supported by older browsers, but this is becoming a nonissue, as all current and fairly recent browsers do support the SVG format. Another drawback is that there are relatively few prebuilt SVG files to choose from (if you go to the Google Images site, you can find lots of bitmap images, but way fewer SVG images). Because it can be very difficult to find freely available SVG files that fit your needs, as a web developer, you might want to install an SVG editor tool and create your own SVG files.

## Displaying an SVG File with an img Element

There are several techniques for using SVG to display an image in a web page. If you already have an SVG file, the easiest way to display it is to use the standard img element with a src attribute that specifies the SVG file's name. **FIGURE 6.13** shows the complete source code for the Super Dad web page. In the body container, note the second and fourth img elements, with their superDad.svg filenames.

## Displaying an SVG Code Fragment with an svg Element

If you want to use SVG to display an image in a web page, but you don't have an SVG file, you can embed SVG code within an svg element. **FIGURE 6.14** shows a Voting Sticker web

```
<!DOCTYPE html>
<html lang="en">
<head>
<meta charset="utf-8">
<meta name="author" content="John Dean">
<title>Super Dad</title>
<style>
  h1, h3 {text-align: center;}
  td {border: thin solid;}
  .center {display: flex; justify-content: center;}
  .gap {width: 50px; border: none;}
</style>
</head>

<body>
<h1>Super Dad!</h1>
<h3>Displaying each image with the PNG file's natural
  dimensions (width="150" height="150")</h3>
<div class="center">
  <table>
    <tr><th>PNG Format</th><th></th><th>SVG Format</th></tr>
    <tr>
      <td><img src="../images/superDad.png" alt="Super Dad standing"
        width="150" height="150"></td>
      <td class="gap"></td> <!-- can't adjust table cell margins -->
      <td><img src="../images/superDad.svg" alt="Super Dad standing"
        width="150" height="150"></td>
    </tr>
  </table>
</div>
<br>
<h3>Displaying the same images as above, but with
  expanded dimensions (width="400" height="250")</h3>
<div class="center">
  <table>
    <tr><th>PNG Format</th><th></th><th>SVG Format</th></tr>
    <tr>
      <td><img src="../images/superDad.png" alt="Super Dad standing"
        width="400" height="250"></td>
      <td class="gap"></td> <!-- can't adjust table cell margins -->
      <td><img src="../images/superDad.svg" alt="Super Dad standing"
        width="400" height="250"></td>
    </tr>
  </table>
</div>
</body>
</html>
```

SVG file

SVG file

**FIGURE 6.13 Source code for Super Dad web page**

page and its source code. In the source code, note the svg element's tags and the SVG code between the svg element's start and end tags. SVG code uses XML (extensible markup language) format, which is the format used by HTML5's precursor language, XHTML. HTML5 still uses XML format for the most part, but sometimes slacks off in order to support real-world web programmer practices. A formal discussion of XML syntax is beyond the scope of this book, but in perusing the figure's SVG code, you can see that the syntax format is pretty

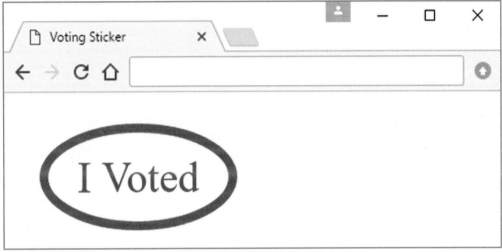

FIGURE 6.14 **Voting Sticker web page and its source code**

much the same as what you've seen with HTML5. SVG code (and XML syntax in general) uses start tags and end tags (e.g., <tag>...</tag>) to describe element content within the SVG image.

If you're interested in learning how to write SVG code, feel free to start with Mozilla's main SVG documentation page at https://developer.mozilla.org/en-US/docs/Web/SVG. For our purposes, we just want to show an example that gives you an idea of what it's all about. In Figure 6.14's Voting Sticker web page source code, note the svg container. Its start tag provides width and height attributes for the SVG code's drawing area. Inside the svg container, you can see two SVG code elements—ellipse and text.

The SVG ellipse element's cx and cy attributes specify the position in pixels of the ellipse's center point. All pixel values are in reference to the (0, 0) point at the top-left corner of the SVG drawing area. So in the Voting Sticker web page, the cx="120" and cy="70" attribute-value pairs mean the ellipse's center is 120 pixels to the right of the drawing area's left edge and 70 pixels down from the drawing area's top edge. The rx and ry attributes specify the ellipse's horizontal and vertical radius values, respectively. The fill, stroke, and stroke-width attributes specify the interior color, the border color, and the border width, respectively.

The SVG text element's text-anchor and alignment-baseline attributes specify the text's horizontal and vertical alignment. The x and y attributes specify the reference point for positioning the text. With the Voting Sticker's middle and central values for horizontal and vertical alignment, the reference point is in the center of the text. The font-size attribute specifies the size of the text's font in pixels. Finally, in the Voting Sticker's text element, the fill attribute specifies the color of the ellipse's interior.

Using SVG code to create the Voting Sticker image was pretty straightforward, but trying to create more complicated drawings can be a daunting task if you attempt to write the code by hand. That's why we found an existing SVG file for the Super Dad web page. That file was probably created by an SVG editor tool rather than by hand. A downside of using an SVG file is that you can't manipulate the SVG file's content with JavaScript. On the other hand, if you insert the SVG code within an svg container in an HTML file, then you can manipulate the SVG code with JavaScript. That means, with some programming know-how, you can translate, rotate, scale, and animate the SVG image.

## 6.12 Responsive Images

As you know, users view web pages on different types of platforms—desktops, laptops, tablets,[10] and smartphones. In this book, we focus on general-purpose programming concepts and syntax, and you should be able to use what you've learned to tailor your code for any of the platforms. However, if you want your code to be "responsive" (i.e., you want it to dynamically generate different layouts and images for different platforms), you'll need to learn responsive web design.

---

[10] A tablet is a computer that uses a touchscreen for its primary input device, rather than a keyboard and mouse.

© MPFphotography/Shutterstock Inc.

**FIGURE 6.15 How a responsive web page's layout can display differently on different platforms**

*Responsive web design* (RWD) is the practice of writing code that dynamically generates web pages that conform to different screen sizes and viewing orientations (portrait or landscape). For example, **FIGURE 6.15** shows how a responsive web page could be displayed with a customized layout for each of the four platforms.

RWD is a rather large subject and, for the most part, beyond the scope of this book, but in this section, we give you a small taste of what's out there. Specifically, we present a brief overview of *responsive images*, which are images that display differently in different environments. At http://usecases .responsiveimages.org, the W3C describes various situations where responsive images are appropriate. We'll provide implementation strategies for two of those situations. Specifically, we'll describe how to implement responsive images using the resolution switching technique and the art direction technique.

## Resolution Switching

*Resolution switching* is when you provide a list of images for different versions of the same picture where the images are identical in terms of *aspect ratio*, where aspect ratio is the ratio of an image's width to height. **FIGURE 6.16** shows the img element for a web page that employs resolution switching to display one of three different pictures on a web page. Note the srcset attribute, which provides a comma-separated list of image filenames with an image width next to each filename. The image width values are the pixel values you see when you hover your mouse over the file in File Explorer (refer back to Figure 6.11 for an example). When specifying an image width value, insert a space before the value and append a w after the value.

In Figure 6.16, note the sizes attribute. Its value helps the browser choose the most appropriate file from among the srcset attribute's list of image files. The sizes attribute provides a

```
<img
   srcset="pigeons-320w.jpg 320w,
           pigeons-480w.jpg 480w,
           pigeons-800w.jpg 800w"
   sizes=" (max-width: 340px) 90vw,
           (max-width: 500px) 90vw,
           800px"
   src="pigeons-800w.jpg" alt="feeding pigeons in St. Mark's Square">
```

The `srcset` attribute holds the image filenames and their widths.

The `sizes` attribute holds viewport width conditions and associated image-slot widths.

**FIGURE 6.16 Code fragment for resolution-switching `img` element**

comma-separated list of values. Each value has two parts—a condition that checks the width of the browser window's viewport and the width of the slot in which the image displays. The *viewport* is the area below the address bar where web page content displays. As you can imagine, mobile devices have the smallest viewports, whereas laptops and desktop monitors have the largest viewports.

From Figure 6.16, here's the `sizes` attribute's first value:

```
(max-width: 340px) 90vw
```

The `max width: 340px` condition means that if the device's viewport is less than or equal to 340 pixels, then the web page uses `90vw` for its image slot width. The `vw` unit stands for viewport window, and it's used for specifying an image slot width as a percentage of the viewport's width. The `90vw` value means that the image slot width spans 90% of the viewport's width. You can use other units rather than vw (such as px), but vw can make maintenance chores easier.

In the figure, the `sizes` attribute's third value has just one part—the width of the slot in which the image displays. There's no viewport width condition because the last value in the list serves as the default. If the viewport width does not match any of the prior conditions, then the default image slot width applies.

In Figure 6.16, note the `src` attribute at the bottom of the `img` element. It's a required attribute, and it serves as a backup for browsers that don't support the responsive attributes, `srcset` and `sizes`.

Normally, one of the first things a browser does in loading a web page is to download all the web page's image files. But with responsive-image web pages, to save time, only the image files that are needed are downloaded. More specifically, in processing a resolution-switching `img` element, the browser finds the `sizes` attribute's first condition that's true, and it remembers that condition's image slot width. It then finds the image file referenced in the `srcset` list that most closely matches that image slot width. Then it loads that image file and ignores the other files.

## Art Direction

Now for another responsive-image implementation technique—*art direction*. For both resolution switching and art direction, you provide a list of images for different versions of the same picture. With resolution switching, the different versions are different sizes, but they have the same aspect ratio. On the other hand, with art direction, the different versions can have different aspect ratios as a result of cropping the original picture in different ways. For example, for a desktop computer layout, the browser's viewport would be wider, so having a wide landscape-oriented picture should be OK. But for a mobile device layout, the browser's viewport would be narrower, so using that same landscape-version image would probably make the picture's main subject too small. The solution is to use a portrait-version image where the main subject can be zoomed in.

To implement responsive images with the art direction technique, you wrap the images in a `picture` container. Specifically, the `picture` container holds a group of `source` elements, where each `source` element value has two parts—a condition that checks the width of the browser window's viewport and an image filename. For an example, see the `picture` element and its two `source` elements in **FIGURE 6.17**. The `source` element's `media` attribute provides the condition that checks the viewport's width, and the `source` element's `srcset` attribute provides the image filename. In the figure, the first `source` element uses the condition `max-width: 799px` to check for a viewport width of less than or equal to 799 pixels. The second `source` element uses the condition `max-width: 800px` to check for a viewport width of greater than or equal to 800 pixels.

```
<!DOCTYPE html>
<html lang="en">
<head>
<meta charset="utf-8">
<meta name="author" content="John Dean">
<title>Dominican Republic</title>
</head>

<body>
<h1>Joe Hartman School in the Dominican Republic</h1>
<picture>
  <source media="(max-width: 799px)" srcset="../images/drKids-450w.jpg">
  <source media="(min-width: 800px)" srcset="../images/drKids-800w.jpg">
  <img src="../images/drKids-800w.jpg" alt="Jordan with kids at recess">
</picture>
<p>
  During this past spring break, Jordan participated in a service trip to
  the Dominican Republic. One of the group's primary activities was
  helping to build an annex to a grade school. In the above picture, you
  can see Jordan with some of the kids. She's the one wearing sunglasses.
</p>
</body>
</html>
```

The `media` attribute holds a viewport width condition.

The `srcset` attribute holds an image filename.

**FIGURE 6.17 Source code for Dominican Republic Kids web page**

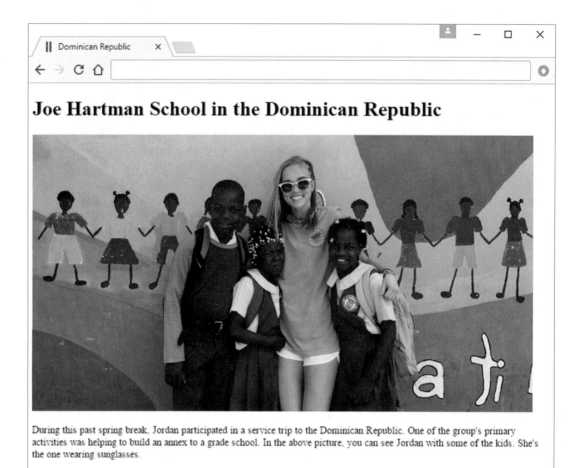

**FIGURE 6.18** Dominican Republic Kids web page on a desktop monitor

**FIGURE 6.19 Dominican Republic Kids web page on a smartphone**

In processing a picture element, the browser checks for the first source element whose condition is true and loads that source element's associated image file. In Figure 6.17, note the required img element below the source elements. The img element's src attribute provides an image file that the browser loads if none of the source element conditions are true. Regardless of the conditions, the img element's alt attribute does its usual thing—it provides fallback content in case the selected image cannot be displayed.

**FIGURES 6.18** and **6.19** show what the Dominican Republic Kids web page looks like on a desktop monitor and a smartphone, respectively. Note that the desktop, with its wider viewport, displays the landscape-version image, and the phone, with its narrower viewport, displays the portrait-version image. Cool!

# 6.13 **CASE STUDY:** Local Energy and Home Page with Website Navigation

In this section, we add another web page to our case study website—a web page that describes some of the technology and benefits of local energy generation and storage. Then we present a home page for the case study website that includes links to the new local energy web page, plus links to web pages introduced in earlier chapters' case study sections.

## Local Energy Web page

Let's get right to it. **FIGURE 6.20** shows a Local Energy web page, which provides information about local energy generation and storage. This includes electricity from photovoltaic (PV) solar collectors, support for electric utilities, cogeneration, and energy storage.

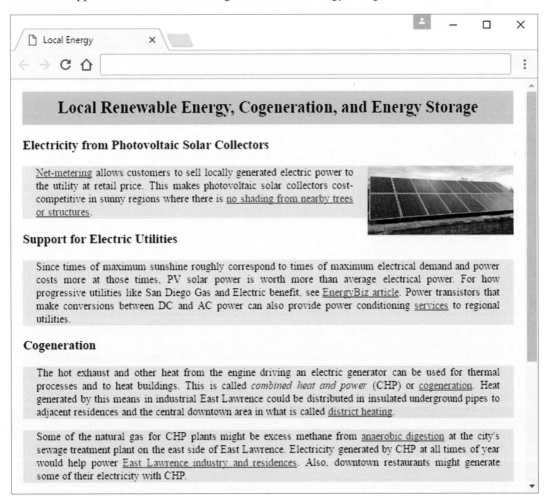

**FIGURE 6.20 Display of Local Energy web page**

In the Local Energy web page's source code, the following `style` container specifies the position and size of an `img` element:

```
<style>
  img {float: right; margin-left: 20px; width: 30%;}
</style>
```

The type selector rule floats the `img` element to the right side of the element in which it is embedded, and its top edge aligns with the top edge of the element that follows the `img` element.

The source code's `body` element contains an h2 page heading and four `section` elements, each with an h3 heading and one or two paragraphs. In this implementation, the `section` elements don't actually do anything except provide organizational structure, but they might be helpful in later enhancements. **FIGURE 6.21A** shows the first two sections. In the first `section`, you can see its h3 heading and then an `img` element. After that comes a p element,

```
<body>
<h2>Local Renewable Energy, Cogeneration, and Energy Storage</h2>
<section>
  <h3>Electricity from Photovoltaic Solar Collectors</h3>
  <img src="../images/generatingPanels.jpg" alt="Photovoltaic Solar
    Collectors"/>
  <p>
    <a href="http://www.seia.org/policy/distributed-solar/net-metering"
    target="_blank">Net-metering</a> allows customers to sell locally
    generated electric power to the utility at retail price. This makes
    photovoltaic solar collectors cost-competitive in sunny regions
    where there is <a href="areaDescription.html">no shading from
    nearby trees or structures</a>.
  </p>
</section>
<section>
  <h3>Support for Electric Utilities</h3>
  <p>
    Since times of maximum sunshine roughly correspond to times of
    maximum electrical demand and power costs more at those times,
    PV solar power is worth more than average electrical power. For
    how progressive utilities like San Diego Gas and Electric benefit,
    see <a href=
    "http://www.energybiz.com/magazine/article/325109/dawn-microgrids"
    target="_blank">EnergyBiz article</a>. Power transistors that make
    conversions between DC and AC power can also provide power
    conditioning <a href="services.html">services</a> to regional
    utilities.
  </p>
</section>
```

**FIGURE 6.21A** body **container of Local Energy web page**

so the image's top aligns with the top of that paragraph, and its right side aligns with the right side of that paragraph.

Note the a element links within the first `section` container. The "Net-metering" a element links to a remote-site web page, and its `target="_blank"` attribute tells the browser to display that remote-site page in a new browser window or in a new tab within the current browser window. The "no shading from nearby trees or structures" element refers to a different web page on the current site—the web page described at the end of Chapter 3. Since this element does not contain an explicit `target` attribute, the referenced web page replaces the web page from which it was called.

**FIGURE 6.21B** contains the third and fourth `section` containers. Skim those sections on your own and pay attention to the links. In particular, note its first section's second paragraph, which contains this link:

```
<a href="microgridPossibilities.html#examples">
```

This link jumps to the `microgridPossibilities.html` web page and looks for an element with `id="examples"` on that web page. It then positions that element at the top of the web page.

The development of the Local Energy web page left a dangling loose end. Near the bottom of Figure 6.21A, the reference in the tag, `<a href="services.html">`, refers to an Electric

```
<section>
  <h3>Cogeneration</h3>
  <p>
    The hot exhaust and other heat from the engine driving an electric
    generator can be used for thermal processes and to heat buildings.
    This is called <em>combined heat and power</em> (CHP) or
    <a href="http://en.wikipedia.org/wiki/Cogeneration" target="_blank">
    cogeneration</a>. Heat generated by this means in industrial East
    Lawrence could be distributed in insulated underground pipes to
    adjacent residences and the central downtown area in what is called
    <a href="http://en.wikipedia.org/wiki/District_heating" target=
    "_blank"> district heating</a>.
  </p>
  <p>
    Some of the natural gas for CHP plants might be excess methane from
    <a href="http://www.energy.ca.gov/biomass/anaerobic.html" target=
    "_blank"> anaerobic digestion</a> at the city's sewage treatment
    plant on the east side of East Lawrence. Electricity generated by
    CHP at all times of year would help power
    <a href="microgridPossibilities.html#examples">East Lawrence
    industry and residences</a>. Also, downtown restaurants might
    generate some of their electricity with CHP.
  </p>
</section>
```

**FIGURE 6.21B** body **container for Local Energy web page**

**(continues)**

```
<section>
  <h3>Energy Storage</h3>
  <p>
    In summer, electricity generated by PV can
    <a href="typicalProperty.html">chill water</a> in storage tanks for
    later cooling. This shifts the noon peak in PV generation to the
    later peak in consumption. The storage rate can be varied to offset
    variations in PV output created by passing clouds. In winter, heat
    from CHP making electricity can heat water in (the same) storage
    tanks. This transfers excess heat generated in the day when
    electricity is most needed to night when heat is most needed.
  </p>
  <p>
    Large low-cost centrally located molten-salt <a
    href="http://en.wikipedia.org/wiki/Sodium%E2%80%93sulfur_battery"
    target="_blank">sodium-sulfur batteries</a> or room-temperature
    <a href="http://www.sciencemag.org/content/349/6255/1529.abstract"
    target="_blank">quinone-based flow batteries</a> or smaller
    <a href="http://en.wikipedia.org/wiki/Sodium-ion_battery" target=
    "_blank">sodium-ion</a> batteries in local shops and restaurants
    can smooth variations in load and PV generation and provide
    emergency power.
    <a href="http://en.wikipedia.org/wiki/Lithium-ion_battery" target=
    "_blank">Lithium-ion</a> batteries in electric vehicles can be
    wirelessly recharged through inductive coils in <a href=
    "http://pluglesspower.com" target="_blank">parking lots</a> or at
    <a href="http://www.waveipt.com" target="_blank">bus stops</a>.
  </p>
</section>
</body>
```

**FIGURE 6.21B** body **container for Local Energy web page (*continued*)**

Power Services web page that does not yet exist. If a user were to use a browser to open the Local Energy web page and click on the services link down near the end of the second paragraph, the browser would respond unhappily, with a message something like, "This web page is not found." That web page would not be found because it hadn't been created yet. It won't be created until Chapter 10.

Meanwhile, to avoid user frustration, you could create a "stub" web page that displays only a title. But there's a better strategy. Create a stub web page that redirects the browser to a place that already exists and that might provide some satisfaction. In this case, a plausible surrogate is the "definition" list item on the Microgrid Possibilities web page developed in the case study section at the end of Chapter 4. **FIGURE 6.22** contains the HTML code for a redirecting stub for the not-yet-developed Electric Power Services web page, services.html. In the figure, the dashed box surrounds the element that does the redirection. It's a "refresh" meta element. In the refresh content the 0; indicates the time delay before refreshing occurs, and the url identifies the new destination. The next subsection includes another illustration of redirection.

```
<!DOCTYPE html>
<html lang="en">
<head>
  <meta charset="utf-8">
  <meta name="author" content="John Dean">
  <meta name="description" content="Services Redirection">
  <meta http-equiv="refresh" content="0;
    url=microgridPossibilities.html#definition">
  <title>Electric Power Services Stub</title>
</head>
</html>
```

Redirection to a different web page.

**FIGURE 6.22 Redirecting "stub" of Electric Power Services web page, `services.html`**

## Home Page with Simple Website Navigation

Chapter 4's case study section showed how to create local navigation links that help users to jump within a web page, and it included one reference to a remote site. The Local Energy web page includes references to other pages and places on the current site and to pages on remote sites. This subsection begins an ongoing investigation of ways to use a home page to consolidate references to other pages on the same website.

For our case study, we use a directory named `microgrid` that stores all the files necessary for the case study's website. To keep the files organized, we use a subdirectory named `pages` that holds the `.html` files, a subdirectory named `images` that holds the image files, and a subdirectory named `library` that holds the CSS files. Assuming the `microgrid` directory is within a `deanWebBook` directory on the hard drive's root directory, here is what you would enter in a browser's address box in order to view the pages directory in the browser window:

```
file:///C:/deanWebBook/microgrid/pages
```

**FIGURE 6.23** shows the result of entering that address in a browser window. You could click on any of the displayed filenames—or the parent directory—and the browser would display it in a new window. For example, if you clicked on the electricPowerHistory.html link, the browser would display the Brief History of Electric Power web page shown in Chapter 3's case study section.

Most people would say that Figure 6.23's directory listing would not get high marks as a "home page." It's just a default. To avoid this default and generate a real home page, a directory needs an `index.html` file. To preserve the integrity of original files in the `pages` directory, copy the files in that directory and paste the copies in a new directory named `microgrid2`, and make all adjustments on the copies in the new directory. When that development is done, insert a very simple `index.html` file in the original directory that automatically redirects user queries from the original directory to the new directory.

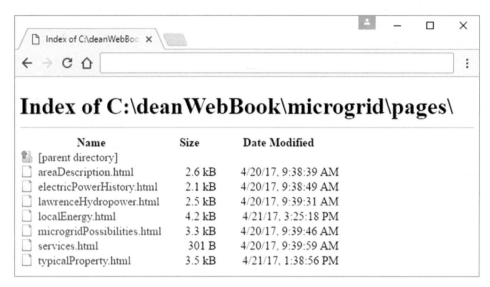

**FIGURE 6.23** **Representative browser window of a directory with no `index.html` file**

The new directory will also have an `index.html` file, but this one will be more comprehensive. It will display a full-fledged home page. This home page should portray the character of the whole website and reflect its sponsor's objectives. What you've seen so far suggests two plausible alternatives: The website might be sponsored by a city government promoting "green" enterprise, or it might be sponsored by an organization promoting modernization of electric power systems. If it's the former, the home page might present the material in the Area Description web page shown in Chapter 3's case study section. If it's the latter, the home page might present the material in the Local Energy web page shown in Figure 6.20.

Suppose it's the former, and the sponsor is the city government. Because the new directory's `index.html` file will contain all the information in the old directory's `areaDescription.html` file, the `areaDescription.html` file itself need not be present in the new directory. So when copying the individual files from the original directory to the new directory, save the `areaDescription.html` file into the new directory as `index.html`. Then, in the `head` element, change the `title` element to this:

```
<title>Lawrence Microgrid</title>
```

**FIGURE 6.24** shows the proposed new home page. The HTML source code for most of the material on this page (the "Description of Area" header and everything below it) is what came from the original directory's `areaDescription.html` file.

The new material in the top quarter of Figure 6.24 requires a new `h1` element for the large website title at the top and a new `nav` element for the buttons just below it. **FIGURE 6.25** shows this additional HTML source code, which goes immediately after the opening `<body>` tag.

To implement the new website header and the navigation buttons, you need to add the CSS rules in **FIGURE 6.26**. Note the `li` type selector rule and all its property-value pairs. They make the links look like buttons. To make the buttons look three-dimensional and raised, we use the

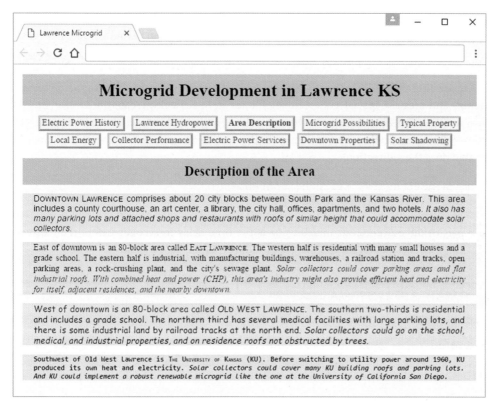

**FIGURE 6.24** **Lawrence Microgrid website's home page,** `index.html`

```
<header>
  <h1>Microgrid Development in Lawrence KS</h1>
  <nav>
    <ul>
      <li><a href="electricPowerHistory.html">Electric Power History</a>
        </li>
      <li><a href="lawrenceHydropower.html">Lawrence Hydropower</a></li>
      <li><a href="index.html"><strong>Area Description</strong></a>
        </li>
      <li><a href="microgridPossibilities.html">Microgrid Possibilities
        </a></li>
      <li><a href="typicalProperty.html">Typical Property</a></li>
      <li><a href="localEnergy.html">Local Energy</a></li>
      <li><a href="#">Collector Performance</a></li>
      <li><a href="#">Electric Power Services</a></li>
      <li><a href="#">Downtown Properties</a></li>
      <li><a href="#">Solar Shadowing</a></li>
    </ul>
  </nav>
</header>
```

**FIGURE 6.25** **Source code for the navigation section of the website's home page**

`border: outset` property-value pair. You could add the rules to the `style` element that already exists in the head element in the new directory's `index.html` file, but it would be nice if these same rules could apply also to other files. So it's better to add them to the common `microgrid.css` file.

After testing all the files in the new `microgrid2` directory, go back to the original `microgrid` directory and create a special `index.html` file for it. Specifically, create the `index.html` file shown in **FIGURE 6.27** and stick it in the original `microgrid` directory. That home page has one purpose—it automatically redirects control to the new `microgrid2` directory. Here's the magic code that does the redirection:

```
<meta http-equiv="refresh" content="0;
  url-../microgrid2/index.html">
```

The 0 part of the `content` attribute's value is the time delay in seconds before the redirecting (refreshing) will occur, and the `url` part is the address of the page to load.

```
/* Rules for interpage navigation */
nav ul {
  list-style-type: none;
  text-align: center;
  padding-left: 0px;
}
nav li {
  display: inline-block;
  padding: 0px 4px 2px 4px;
  margin: 2px 4px 2px 4px;
  background-color: lightgoldenrodyellow;
  border: outset;
  border-color: lightgreen;
}
nav a {text-decoration: none;}
```

**FIGURE 6.26 Additional CSS rules in `microgrid.css` needed for the home page's navigation**

```
<!DOCTYPE html>
<html lang="en">
<head>
<meta charset="utf-8">
<meta name="author" content="John Dean">
<meta http-equiv="refresh" content="0;
  url=../microgrid2/index.html">
<title>Lawrence Microgrid Redirection</title>
</head>
</html>
```

**FIGURE 6.27 `microgrid`'s `index.html` file that redirects to `microgrid2`'s `index.html` file**

Now when a user employs a browser to search for `microgrid`, instead of getting what you see in Figure 6.23, the user gets what you see in Figure 6.24. The latter is a more attractive home page. When this home page appears, a user can explore the website by clicking one of the ten raised buttons under the website title. Clicking one of the last four buttons—Collector Performance, Electric Power Services, Downtown Properties, and Solar Shadowing—doesn't do anything because those web pages do not yet exist. (The four instances of `href="#"` in Figure 6.25 are dummy references.) The `strong` "Area Description" text in the third button suggests that this button corresponds to the (currently displayed) home page. Clicking this Area Description button refreshes this page.

Clicking either the first, second, fourth, fifth, or sixth button causes the user to jump to a page containing material identified by the words on that button. For example, if you click the Electric Power History button, the browser jumps to the Electric Power History page. Notice that elements in Figure 6.25 do not have `target` attributes. So, where will a referenced page display? It will display on the current web page, completely replacing it, and the website title and navigation buttons will be gone. It's not a disaster, because the user can use the back arrow in the upper left corner of the browser window to return to the home page and go to other pages from there.

## Enhanced Home Page with Website Navigation

Although it's not a disaster, the previous subsection's proposal produces a result that is not as user-friendly as it might be. It would be friendlier if the overall website name and navigation buttons were visible and accessible on every web page. This would help the user remember the context and enable the user to visit any subset of the website's pages in any order. And it would preserve the user's ability to retrace steps using the browser's back arrows. How might you get this friendlier presentation?

Conceptually, it's pretty simple. Just copy the `header` element in Figure 6.25 from the top of the `body` element in the new `index.html` file, and insert it at the same place (as the first item in the `body` element) in each of the other files in the website directory.

For an additional user benefit, you might also insert the `footer` element in **FIGURE 6.28** as the last item in each file's `body` element. This puts two more navigation buttons at the bottom of each page. The first button's `href="#"` attribute tells the browser to jump to the top of the current page. The second button tells the browser to jump to the home page. Because they are embedded in the same types of elements as the header buttons, these additional buttons automatically utilize the same common CSS rules as the buttons at the tops of the web pages.

```
<footer>
  <nav><ul>
    <li><a href="#">Top</a></li>
    <li><a href="index.html">Home</a></li>
  </ul></nav>
</footer>
```

**FIGURE 6.28  Insert this footer at the bottom of each web page's `<body>` element**

FIGURE 6.29 shows the result. Although this enhanced website navigation is indeed user-friendly, it still leaves something to be desired. There is substantial duplication of headers and footers. And it's not just the duplication. Do you remember those `href="#"` destination addresses for the last four buttons in Figure 6.25? Each time a new page is added to the website, the developer must remember to replace that # with the address of the new page on *all* previous pages. You'll see how to solve this problem later in the case study section at the end of Chapter 10. Meanwhile, the case study section at the end of Chapter 7 will introduce an alternative approach that does not exhibit the current redundancy problem.

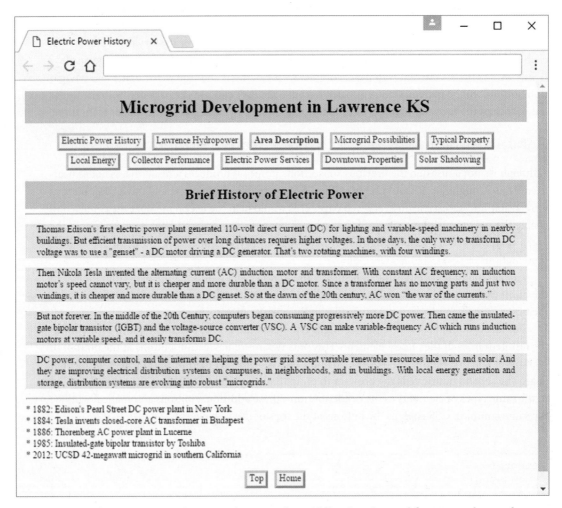

**FIGURE 6.29** Electric Power History web page after adding header and footer to that web page

# Review Questions

### 6.2 a Element

1. In the a element, what attribute specifies the resource that is to be loaded when the user clicks the link?

### 6.3 Relative URLs

2. What is a home page?

3. In a path, what is the purpose of "..."?

### 6.5 Web Design

4. What is the difference between user interface design and user experience design?

5. For nontrivial websites, which sort of navigation organizational structure is the most popular: linear, hierarchical, or mixed?

### 6.6 Navigation Within a Web Page

6. What is a placeholder link?

7. What happens if you have a CSS table with `table-cell` elements that are not surrounded by a `table-row` element?

### 6.7 CSS for Links

8. What are the traditional default colors for unvisited and visited links?

9. What selector matches links that the mouse is hovering over?

### 6.8 a Element Additional Details

10. What attribute-value pair should you use to cause a link to open its linked-to page in a separate window or tab?

11. The default functionality for clicking a link is for the new page to load within the current web browser and overlay the previous page. True or false.

### 6.9 Bitmap Image Formats: GIF, JPEG, PNG

12. What is the meaning of the word "bitmap" for bitmap image files?

13. What is a color palette?

14. Which type of image format is usually better for photographs—GIF or JPG?

15. An offshoot of the PNG working group created an image file format that supports animation. What is the name of that image file format?

### 6.10 `img` Element

16. Why is the `img` element's `alt` attribute particularly important for end users who are visually impaired?

17. Why is it good to always include an `img` element's `width` and `height` attributes?

### 6.11 Vector Graphics

18. When a vector graphics image gets resized, why does it avoid the degradation experienced by bitmap images?

19. Beside the ability to resize without degradation, what is a benefit of using an SVG file over a bitmap image file?

20. For SVG images, what is an advantage of using an `svg` element as opposed to an `img` element?

### 6.12 Responsive Images

21. What is responsive web design?

# Exercises

1. [after Section 6.2] Provide a link element (and nothing else) that, when clicked, causes an end user to download an image file of a dog in a tree. Search for a real image and use its URL.

2. [after Section 6.3] Provide proper HTML5 container code (start tag, enclosed content, end tag) for a link that takes the user to a page named `hawaii.html` that's located in a directory named `vacation`. The `vacation` directory is a subdirectory in the current directory's parent directory. The link should display a label that says, "Hawaii pictures."

3. [after Section 6.3] How are an absolute URL and a path-absolute URL different?

4. [after Section 6.6] Given the following web page. Clicking the <u>Drivers education classes</u> link (underlined) causes the browser to jump to the **Drivers education classes** heading. Provide the code for that link element. Also provide the code for the h4 heading element that is the target of that link. You do not have to provide code for the entire web page, only the link element and the h4 element. As usual, use proper style.

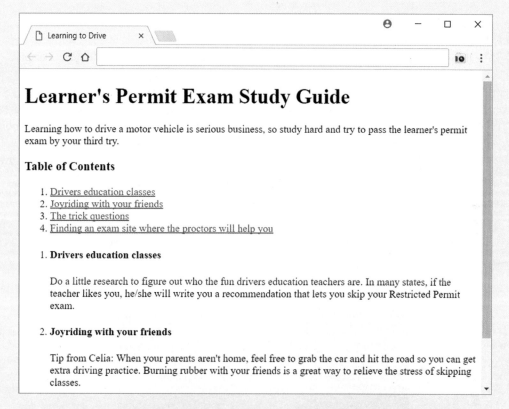

5.  [after Section 6.7] Provide three CSS rules that implement links as follows. All links should have no underlining. Unvisited links should be dark green. Visited links should be pink.

6.  [after Section 6.9] How many different levels of transparency can a PNG image have?

7.  [after Section 6.9] Download and install GIMP on your home computer. Use GIMP to create a red-bordered heart icon with a transparent outer background and a white interior. Paste your heart icon on top of other text such that the heart's transparent background is obvious. Note the following example, with two of the hearts pasted on top of some arbitrary large-font text:

# Some arbitrary♡large-font text

8.  [after Section 6.12] Find a device emulator website that shows what responsive web pages look like on different user-specified platforms. Load Figure 6.17's Dominican Republic Kids web page into an emulator for the latest iPhone. Provide a screenshot of the result.

# Project

Create a web page named `weather.html` that mimics the following displayed page, except:

▷ Use a picture different from the one shown.
▷ Use cities different from those shown continents can be the same or different).

Near the top of the web page, Africa, Australia, and South America are links to their associated areas below the picture. The links have their underlines turned off. When the user's mouse hovers over one of the links, the background color turns to silver. To implement that effect, use CSS, not JavaScript. In the web page, the user is hovering over the South America link, and that's why its background is silver and there's a South America URL at the bottom of the page (the URL appears by default).

Note:

▷ You must include at least three continents. For each continent, you must include at least two links to city weather pages.
▷ Your city weather links must link to working web pages (use a search engine to find such pages).
▷ You must use CSS table properties (not a `table` element) to position the continent and city names.

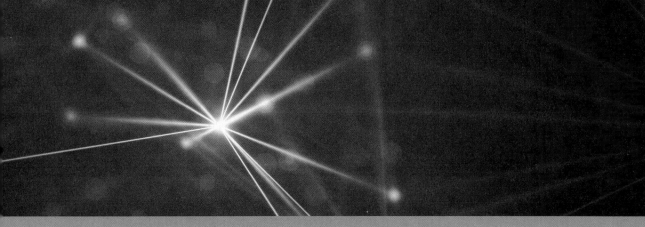

# CHAPTER 7

# Image Manipulations, Audio, and Video

## CHAPTER OBJECTIVES

- ▶ Position an image at the left or right with text displayed at its other border.
- ▶ Learn how to display a shortcut icon in a browser's tab area.
- ▶ Implement an `iframe` element with the ability to display a web page or an image in it.
- ▶ Create an image sprite file and use it in a web page.
- ▶ Implement an audio player using the `audio` element.

- ▶ Handle different audio file formats.
- ▶ Cover a web page's background with an image.
- ▶ Understand how to use web fonts.
- ▶ Implement a video player using the `video` element.
- ▶ Center a web page's content.
- ▶ Cover a web page's background with a color gradient.

## CHAPTER OUTLINE

## 7.1 Introduction

In the previous chapter, you learned about images, but only the basics. Specifically, you learned about their formats and how to display them. In this chapter, you'll learn how to do additional things with images, such as position them. By default, images are displayed inline, which means that they are positioned in the normal left-to-right, top-down flow of their web page host. As an alternative, you can position them at the left or the right of the web page. If you want an icon image to appear in the tab at the top of the browser window, you can do that. Or, if you want to display an image within a frame within the browser window—yep, you can do that too. In this chapter, you'll learn how to do those things, plus you'll learn about more advanced image-related topics, such as implementing a rollover with an image sprite and implementing a clickable image map with multiple hotspots.

In addition to learning about images, you'll also learn about other media types—audio and video. We start with an introduction to the different audio and video file formats. Then we dig into the details of how to implement audio and video players with the `audio` and `video` elements and their attributes. Along the way, in presenting the audio and video web page example, you'll be introduced to several CSS properties that enable you to spruce things up. With CSS, you can import and use customized fonts that are not part of the W3C's standards, you can use an image file as the background for your web page, and you can create a color gradient (a smooth transition between two or more colors) and use it as the background for your web page.

## 7.2 Positioning Images

The `img` element is an inline element (more formally, a phrasing element), so it gets displayed within the normal flow of its surrounding text. That works well for small images (icons), but not so well for medium and large images. See the smiley face image in **FIGURE 7.1**. It's a small image, an icon, and its default inline positioning works well. But the tree photographs? They're taller and their default inline positioning causes the browser to generate quite a bit of dead space above the text lines in which they're embedded. In general, you should avoid such dead space.

To avoid wasted space around a medium or large image, you might want to display it on a line by itself by surrounding it with a block element. We do that in an upcoming example,

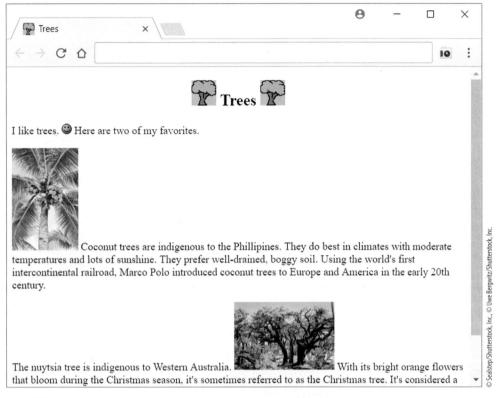

© Sealstep/Shutterstock, Inc., © Uwe Bergwitz/Shutterstock, Inc.

**FIGURE 7.1 Trees web page with default picture positioning**

but for now, let's focus on another technique—"floating" an image to the left or to the right, so its adjacent text displays along its right or left border, respectively. In **FIGURE 7.2**, note how the tree photographs are floated to the left and to the right with the text wrapping around the photographs' borders.

To float an image, you apply a CSS rule to the img element, where the CSS rule uses the float property and a value of left or right. You can see the complete source code for the Trees web page in **FIGURE 7.3**, but, for your convenience, here are the CSS rules in charge of floating the two tree photographs:

```
.left {float: left; margin: 8px;}
.right {float: right; margin: 8px;}
```

The margin property in this example is not required for floating, but without it, the image's adjacent text will display uncomfortably close to the image. Here are the img elements that use these CSS rules:

```
<img class="left" src="../images/coconut.jpg"
  width="100" height="150" alt="">
<img class="right" src="../images/nuytsia.jpg"
  width="150" height="100" alt="">
```

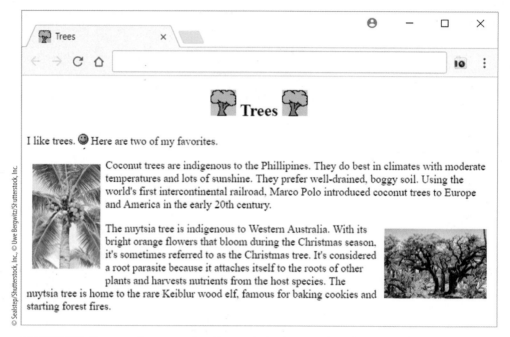

FIGURE 7.2 **Trees web page using the `float` property for picture positioning**

Now let's focus on the h2 heading element at the top of the Trees web page. Go back to Figure 7.2, and verify that the heading's "Trees" text and the surrounding tree icons are centered horizontally on the web page. In the past, we've centered a heading element's text with a `text-align: center` CSS rule. As you can see in Figure 7.3's source code, we use that same technique for the Trees web page heading, even though the h2 element includes more than just text—it includes two img elements, as well. Despite its name, the `text-align` property is in charge of aligning not just text, but all inline content within the element to which the `text-align` property is being applied. The img element is an inline element. So applying `text-align: center` to the h2 heading works great for centering the "Trees" text and the surrounding tree icons.

# 7.3 Shortcut Icon

When you open a new tab in a browser, do you notice the icon that appears in the tab area at the top of the window? For an example, go back to Figure 7.2 and find the tree icon in the tab area of the Trees web page. Those icons are called *shortcut icons*. In this section, you'll learn about shortcut icons.

To mark your web page with a shortcut icon in the browser's tab area, in your web page's head container, include a link element with `rel="icon"`. For example, here's the code from the Trees web page that causes the tree shortcut icon to be displayed:

```
<link rel="icon" href="../images/tree.png">
```

```
<!DOCTYPE html>
<html lang="en">
<head>
<meta charset="utf-8">
<meta name="author" content="John Dean">
<title>Trees</title>
<link rel="icon" href="../images/tree.png">
<style>
h2 {text-align: center;}                      ◄──── Center the heading's contents.
.xleft {float: left; margin: 8px;}
.xright {float: right; margin: 8px;}          ◄──── Float the photographs to the
</style>                                              left and to the right.
</head>

<body>
<h2>
  <img src="../images/tree.png" width="37" height="37" alt="">
  Trees
  <img src="../images/tree.png" width="37" height="37" alt="">
</h2>
<p>
  I like trees.
  <img src="../images/smiley.gif" width="15" height="15" alt="">
  Here are two of my favorites.
</p>
<p>
  <img class="left" src="../images/coconut.jpg"
  width="100" height="150" alt="">
  Coconut trees are indigenous to the Phillipines. They do...
</p>
<p>
  The nuytsia tree is indigenous to Western Australia.
  <img class="right" src="../images/nuytsia.jpg"
  width="150" height="100" alt="">
  With its bright orange flowers that bloom during the Christmas...
</p>
</body>
</html>
```

**FIGURE 7.3 Source code for Trees web page**

The rel attribute specifies the relationship between the current web page and the linked-to entity. So for a shortcut icon, the rel attribute specifies icon. Do you recall what else the link element has been used for? It's used for linking to an external CSS file. In that case, the rel attribute specifies stylesheet (rel="stylesheet").

For shortcut icons, the W3C recommends using a GIF or PNG file with dimensions of 16 × 16 pixels or 32 × 32 pixels. If you use an image file with dimensions different from 16 × 16 or 32 × 32, the browser will adjust its size, so it fits in the small square area reserved for the shortcut icon in the browser window's tab. But as you know, degradation occurs when an image file's size gets adjusted, particularly if the original file's size does not scale perfectly with the new file's size.

Normally, for the sake of consistency, you should use the same shortcut icon for all the web pages on your website. That's why shortcut icons are sometimes called *website icons*. Shortcut icons are also called *bookmark icons* because when you display your bookmarks/favorites list, the icons appear next to the names in the list. Finally, shortcut icons are also called *favicons*, for favorite icons. There's no official pronunciation, but most people say "FAV-ih-con." Sometimes "FAVE-ih-con."

## 7.4 `iframe` Element

You've learned how to display an image in the body of a web page and also in the tab area at the top of the browser window. In this section, you learn to display an image in a frame that's embedded within the browser window. Specifically, you'll use an `iframe` (short for inline frame) element to create a *browsing context*. A browsing context is an area within a web page that can display an embedded *web document*, where a web document is something with a URL (i.e., a web page or a stored image).

Instead of loading an entire web page within an `iframe`'s browsing context, it's more common to load a stored image into a browsing context. For example, in the Art Exhibit web page in **FIGURE 7.4**, an `iframe` element is used to display the large picture in the center. The Art Exhibit web page's website stores image files for that picture and three other pictures that all have the same dimensions. In addition, the website stores image files for the four smaller pictures at the left of Figure 7.4. Those pictures are smaller versions of the larger pictures. When the user clicks one of the smaller images, the browser grabs the larger version of the clicked image and copies it to the browsing context area. To make sure you understand what's going on, please find the Art Exhibit web page on the student resources website and try it out for yourself. The smaller images are known as thumbnails. A *thumbnail* is a smallish image that serves as a representative for a larger version of that same image. Thumbnails are often used to help with the organization of a group of images. In conjunction with that effort, they can help users to identify and select standard-size images.

Take a look at the Art Exhibit web page's source code in **FIGURE 7.5A**. In particular, note the `iframe` code, copied here for your convenience:

```
<iframe class="cell" name="full-size" width="480" height="320"
   src="../images/houseRenderings/kitchen.jpg"></iframe>
```

The `iframe` element's `width` and `height` attributes are self-explanatory. The `iframe` element's `src` attribute specifies the web document that initially appears within the `iframe`'s browsing context. The `src` attribute can specify a path to another web page, in which case the browser

*Drawings courtesy of Beth Pennekamp*

**FIGURE 7.4 Art Exhibit web page**

displays the entire specified web page in the browsing context area. But the prior code doesn't specify a path to another web page. Instead, it specifies an image file, man.jpg. And when a user clicks one of the thumbnails, the image gets replaced by the image specified by the thumbnail. We'll get to the thumbnail details soon enough, but first let's finish going over the iframe's attributes.

In order to load a new image into the browsing context area, we need to be able to refer to the iframe element, and the name attribute's value allows us to do that. As you can see in the previous code, the iframe element's name attribute has a value of full-size. In the Art Exhibit web page, the a elements specify target="full-size" to connect to the iframe element. In the following code (from the Art Exhibit web page), note the target attribute and its full-size value:

```
<a href="../images/houseRenderings/kitchen.jpg" target="full-size">
  <img src="../images/thumbs/kitchenThumb.jpg" alt="kitchen"></a>
```

```
<body>
<h1>Modular House Exhibit, Park University's Graphic Design Program</h1>
<h3>
  Click a thumbnail at the left in order to move it to the viewing frame
  at the right.
</h3>
<div class="table">
  <nav class="cell">
    <a href="../images/houseRenderings/kitchen.jpg" target="full-size">
      <img src="../images/thumbs/kitchenThumb.jpg" alt="kitchen"></a>
    <a href="../images/houseRenderings/living.jpg" target="full-size">
      <img src="../images/thumbs/livingThumb.jpg" alt="living space"></a>
    <a href="../images/houseRenderings/stairway.jpg" target="full-size">
      <img src="../images/thumbs/stairwayThumb.jpg" alt="stairway"></a>
  </nav>
  <iframe class="cell" name="full-size" width="480" height="320"
    src="../images/houseRenderings/kitchen.jpg"></iframe>
</div>
</body>
</html>
```

FIGURE 7.5A **Source code body container for Art Exhibit web page**

As always for an a element, the href attribute indicates what to load when the user clicks the link. In the past, we've only loaded another web page, but you can also load an image with the href attribute, and that's what the prior a element code indicates. If there were no target attribute, the browser would implicitly use the value _self for the target attribute, which tells the browser to overlay the current web page with the href value. But with target="full-size", the target attribute tells the browser to open the man.jpg image in the full-size browsing context.

Remember that with the a element, it's the content between the start and end tags that provides the interface for the user to click on. Normally, that content is simply text, so the user clicks text to activate the link. But as you can see in Figure 7.5A, we're using a thumbnail image instead of text for the user to click on.

## Formatting

Before leaving the Art Exhibit web page, there are a few formatting issues that are worth noting. To get the thumbnails to appear vertically at the left of the iframe's browsing context area, we use a one-row two-cell table. We use a nav container to hold all the thumbnails and form the left cell. We use the iframe to form the right cell. Go to Figure 7.5A to verify the table structure. You'll see that the two-cell table is built with the CSS display property and table values. You'll see that there is no element for the table's row, which means we're using an anonymous table-row element.

Peruse **FIGURE 7.5B** to see all the CSS rules. Here's the rule that implements the table:

```css
.table {
  display: table;
  display: flex;
  align-items: flex-start;
}
```

```
<!DOCTYPE html>
<html lang="en">
<head>
<meta charset="utf-8">
<meta name="author" content="John Dean">
<title>Modular House Exhibit</title>
<style>
  body {
    font-family: Garamond, serif;
    background-color: lavender;
    color: navy;
  }
  h1 {
    font-family: Papyrus, fantasy;
    font-size: 36px;
  }
  .table {
    display: table;
    display: flex;                      ◀——— Align table cells at their tops.
    align-items: flex-start;
  }
  .cell {display: table-cell;}
  nav > * {
    display: block;                     ◀——— Block formatting for the a elements.
    margin: 18px 25px 18px 0;
  }
  a > img {                                    Promotes seamless integration of
    width: 120px;                              iframe's browsing context with
    height: 80px;                              rest of web page.
  }
  iframe {border: none; overflow: hidden;}
</style>
</head>
```

**FIGURE 7.5B** Source code `head` container for Art Exhibit web page

The `display: table` property-value pair converts a `div` container to a table, which is pretty straightforward. But the other two property-value pairs took quite a bit of head scratching to come up with. Initially, the top thumbnail's bottom edge aligned with the large picture's bottom edge, which made for a lot of dead space above the top thumbnail. To get the top thumbnail's top to align with the large picture's top, we introduced the flexible box layout (using `display: flex`) and the `align-items: flex-start` property-value pair. The horribly named `flex-start` value indicates top alignment.

Here's the rule that causes the `nav` and `iframe` elements to become table cells, and it should look familiar:

```
.cell {display: table-cell;}
```

And here's the rule that formats the individual `a` elements within the `nav` container:

```
nav > * {
  display: block;
  margin: 18px 25px 18px 0;
}
```

The rule matches all of the `nav` container's child elements, which are `a` elements. By default, `a` elements use inline formatting. So without this rule, the browser displays the thumbnail links horizontally. To convert the `a` elements to block formatting, we use the `display: block` property-value pair. The `margin: 15px 25px 15px 0` property-value pair prevents the pictures from touching each other.

Next is the rule that specifies the thumbnail pictures' dimensions:

```
a > img {
  width: 120px;
  height: 80px;
}
```

The `width` and `height` properties serve as an alternative to including `width` and `height` attribute-value pairs for each of the thumbnail `img` elements. By using a CSS rule, we avoid redundant attribute-value pairs, and avoiding redundancy means the code is easier to maintain.

Typically, browsers display a faint border around the `iframe`'s browsing context that distinguishes it from the rest the web page's content. Normally, you're going to want to avoid that behavior. To get the browsing context to integrate seamlessly with the rest of the Art Exhibit web page, we use the following CSS rule:

```
iframe {border: none; overflow: hidden;}
```

The `border-none` property-value pair makes the `iframe`'s browsing context border invisible. Normally, if the `iframe`'s content is larger than the `iframe`'s dimensions, the browser displays scrollbars so all of the content can be accessed. The `overflow-hidden` property-value pair clips the content so no scrollbars display.

# 7.5 **CSS Image Sprites**

In the previous section, we used the a element not for its standard purpose of linking to a separate web page, but rather for loading an image into a frame within the current web page. In this section, we once again use the a element for something other than its standard purpose. We use it to implement a rollover. A *rollover* is when an image file changes due to the user moving the mouse over the image. Rollovers have been around for quite a long time. Early on, web programmers were limited in their ability to implement rollovers. They had to use JavaScript, which we'll get to in the next chapter. In this section, you'll take advantage of advances in CSS and learn how to implement rollovers without JavaScript. All you need is a link and a little CSS.

Remember the a:hover pseudo-class selector introduced in the last chapter? We used it to change the link's color and the link's underlining when the user's mouse hovers over the link. To implement a rollover, we'll once again use the a:hover pseudo-class selector, but this time we'll get fancier than just changing the link's color and underlining. We'll use CSS to overlay an image with a new image. You might think that the two images come from two different image files. *Au contraire!* It's quicker to download one file rather than two, so we stuff both images into one file and use CSS to view only one of the images at a time. How cool is that?

A *CSS image sprite* is when you have an image file with more than one image in it, and the browser animates the images so the user views only one image at a time. You might have heard the term "sprite" from game programming, where a sprite is a bitmap file that gets integrated into a larger scene to help with animations. Sorry—no mutant cyborg space alien motorcycle chase scene animations here. Just simple image overlays when the mouse hovers over an image. But it's still cool!

## Example

Let's jump right into an example. See **FIGURE 7.6**. At the right side of the figure, you can see the scratchSprite.png image file that contains three images of Scratch[1] the cat. When the web page first loads, the browser displays the first image, which you can see in the screenshot at the left of the figure. If the user hovers the mouse over Scratch, the browser displays the second image (with the speech balloon). If the user clicks Scratch, the browser displays the third image (with the clothing). For a rollover, all you need are two images, not three. We add a third image here to show how you can capture and process a mouse click. In this case, during the rollover, Scratch does what all new programmers do when they write their first program—he exclaims "Hello World!" If the user responds with a mouse click, Scratch shows off his (hello) worldly bona fides by donning his snappy Austrian lederhosen.

Take a look at the Scratch web page source code in **FIGURE 7.7**. In particular, note the a element code, copied here for your convenience:

```
<a id="scratch"></a>
```

[1] First released in 2005, Scratch is a programming language environment intended to turn kids on to the joy of programming, animation, and video game building. It was designed by Mitchel Resnick at the Massachusetts Institute of Technology. It's maintained by the MIT Media Lab Lifelong Kindergarten Group.

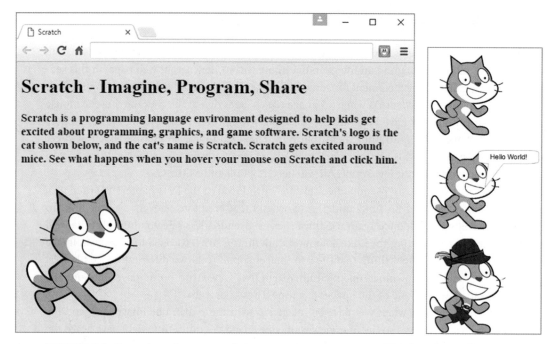

**FIGURE 7.6 Scratch web page and the `scratchSprite.png` file that the web page relies on**

Pretty bare-bones. All the work is done by the CSS rules. Here's the first CSS rule, which determines what happens when the web page first loads:

```
#scratch {
    display: block;
    width: 300px;
    height: 242px;
    background-image: url(../images/scratchSprite.png);
    background-position: 0 0;
}
```

Remember how the # works for the `#scratch` selector? `#scratch` is an ID selector that matches elements that have `id="scratch"`. The web page's a element has `id="scratch"`, so this rule applies to that a element.

You probably noticed that the Scratch web page a element consists of two tags and no content between them. That means, by default, the link would display nothing. The CSS rule comes to the rescue by displaying the image file's first image in the place where the link resides on the web page. The image file comes from the `background-image` property. Note the rather odd-looking `url` (*filename*) syntax for the `background-position` property's value. The CSS rule's `display: block` property-value pair, together with the `width` and `height` properties and their values, tell the browser to display the background image within a 300 × 242

```
<!DOCTYPE html>
<html lang="en">
<head>
<meta charset="utf-8">
<meta name="author" content="John Dean">
<title>Scratch</title>
<style>
  body {background-color: #f1daf1;}
  #scratch {
    display: block;
    width: 300px;
    height: 242px;
    background-image: url(../images/scratchSprite.png);
    background-position: 0 0;
  }
  #scratch:hover {background-position: 0 -244px;}
  #scratch:active {background-position: 0 -488px;}
</style>
</head>

<body>
<h1>Scratch - Imagine, Program, Share</h1>
<h3>
  Scratch is a programming language environment designed to help
  kids get excited about programming, graphics, and game software.
  Scratch's logo is the cat shown below, and the cat's name is
  Scratch. Scratch gets excited around mice. See what happens
  when you hover your mouse on Scratch and click him.
</h3>
<a id="scratch"></a>
</body>
</html>
```

**FIGURE 7.7 Source code for Scratch web page**

rectangular area. The 300 × 242 dimensions match the dimensions of each of the three images in the image file.

And now for the property that does all the magic—the background-position property. It's in charge of specifying the $x$ and $y$ coordinates for where the image file content's top-left corner gets positioned in relation to the background image's element. The "background image's element" is the a element link, which the CSS rule formats as a 300 × 242 block. So the background position values of 0 and 0 indicate that the image file content's top-left corner gets positioned at the top-left corner of the link's block. The image file's first image (and the other two images, as well) is 242 pixels tall, so the browser displays only the first image and crops off the bottom two images. *Cropping* means to cut something off so the browser doesn't display it.

The next two CSS rules take care of displaying the bottom two images:

```
#scratch:hover {background-position: 0 -244px;}
#scratch:active {background-position: 0 -488px;}
```

The `#scratch:hover` pseudo-class rule indicates that when the mouse hovers over the link's block, the image file content's top-left corner gets positioned 244 pixels above the top-left corner of the link's block. With each image being 242 pixels tall and with a 2-pixel gap between images, that means the browser displays the middle image and crops off the top and bottom images.

Referring back to the prior pair of rules, the second rule uses the `:active` pseudo-class selector. When used with an a element, that selector matches any link that is currently active. A link is "currently active" when the user holds the mouse button down on the link. The `:active` pseudo-class selector isn't used much, but every now and then, it can be helpful.

## Making a CSS Image Sprite File

To make a sprite image file, you can draw the file's images directly using a graphics application like Adobe Photoshop or GIMP. As an alternative, you can find separate images, resize them so they have the same dimensions, and then use a tool to merge the images into one file. For the remainder of this subsection, we describe the latter approach.

For the `scratchSprite.png` file shown in Figure 7.6, we found the three royalty-free Scratch images on the Google Images website and copied each image to its own file. We used GIMP to (1) resize each file to 300 × 242 pixels and (2) add transparency to each image's background. The transparency isn't required, but in Figure 7.6's screen capture, you should be able to appreciate the simple elegance of Scratch's transparent background being overlaid with pink from the `body` element's `backgroundcolor` property. If you don't want to bother with downloading and installing GIMP, you can use Microsoft Paint instead (which comes with Windows) to resize each file, but Paint doesn't support the ability to add transparency.

After creating the three image files, we used a tool to merge the images into one file. Specifically, we used the CSS Sprites Generator tool found at https://www.giftofspeed.com/sprite -generator/. See **FIGURE 7.8**, which shows the tool's prompts for image files, generated file's type, alignment, and padding. After you press the **Build** button, the tool generates a downloadable sprite image file. Plus, it displays the `background-position` CSS rules that you can paste into your web page source code file. That's very handy, because the *x* and *y* position values for those rules, while not super complicated, normally require some thinking (and thinking is best left to computers, not to us humans).

## 7.6 Audio

So far in this chapter, we've focused on visual media with images. Now it's time to move on to audio media. In this section, you'll learn how to implement an audio player with the `audio` element.

Prior to HTML5, end users had to install a plug-in to play sound from a web page. Now there's no need for that. Today's browsers include a built-in audio player that's used in conjunction with the `audio` element. Here's a simple `audio` element example:

```
<audio src="../audio/witchesCackle.mp3" preload="auto" controls>
  </audio>
```

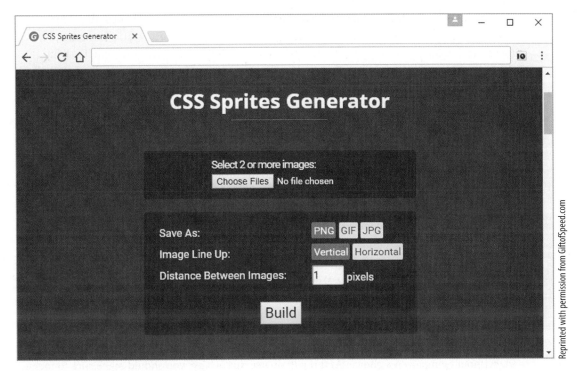

**FIGURE 7.8 CSS Sprites Generator**

Note that the `audio` element requires a start tag and an end tag, even though there's no content between the tags. Later you'll see an example where there is content between the tags.

## `audio` **Element Attributes**

In the prior `audio` element code fragment, note the `src` attribute. It specifies a path to an audio file named `witchesCackle.mp3`. As you'd expect, the filename's `.mp3` extension indicates that the file is an mp3 file. Soon, we'll talk about different audio file types, but for now let's focus on the `audio` element's attributes.

The `controls` attribute tells the browser to display an audio control bar (for starting, pausing, and adjusting the volume) for the audio player. You should always include the `controls` attribute. If you don't, some users will be annoyed that they are unable to stop the sound. In the code fragment, note how the `controls` attribute isn't assigned a value. When you specify an attribute by itself, that's known as an *empty attribute*. As an alternative, it's legal to specify a dummy value or empty string like this:

```
controls="controls"
controls=""
```

But proper style suggests using `controls` by itself because that's less code, and less code means quicker downloads, and quicker downloads mean more customers.

The `preload` attribute indicates whether the browser should download audio information when the web page first loads, or wait to download if and when the user starts the audio player. If there's a `preload` value of `auto` (as shown in the prior code example) or the empty string (`""`), the browser takes that as a suggestion to download the audio file when the page loads initially. If there's a `preload` value of `meta`, the browser takes that as a suggestion to download the metadata (e.g., duration) when the page loads initially. If there's a preload value of `none`, the browser downloads no audio information when the page loads initially.

Why might preloading be helpful? By starting the download right away, you can reduce the wait time when the user clicks the play button. But be aware that the browser uses the `preload` attribute only as a suggestion. It's ultimately up to the browser to decide whether to download the audio file or its meta information before the user clicks the play button.

So, what's the benefit of not preloading? If there's limited bandwidth on the web server, and the user does not end up choosing to play the audio file, preloading will cause other downloads to slow down. Preloading is particularly detrimental if you do it for lots of `audio` elements on the same web page.

The `audio` element's `autoplay` attribute tells the browser to start playing the audio file when the page first downloads. If you provide an `autoplay` attribute, there's no need to specify `preload` because preloading occurs regardless of the `preload` attribute's value. Typically, `autoplay` is used for sounds that are meant to be played in the background. You should use the `autoplay` attribute sparingly because some users might get annoyed having to listen to the audio file without being given a choice. And if you do use `autoplay`, you should make sure to include the `controls` attribute, so the user can turn off the sound if necessary.

The `audio` element's `loop` attribute tells the browser to play the audio file repeatedly. Use the `loop` attribute sparingly—only if it's appropriate to repeat the sound.

## Audio File Formats

Unfortunately, different browsers support different audio file formats. To handle that situation, you can omit the `audio` element's `src` attribute and, instead, include `source` elements between the `audio` element's start and end tags. Here's an example that uses multiple `source` elements to make it extremely likely that the browser supports at least one of the rainstorm audio file formats:

```
<audio autoplay controls loop>
  <source src="../audio/rainStorm.mp3" type="audio/mpeg">
  <source src="../audio/rainStorm.wav" type="audio/wav">
  <source src="../audio/rainStorm.ogg" type="audio/ogg">
</audio>
```

For maximum browser compatibility, you should include `source` elements for these three popular audio file formats—`.mp3`, `.wav`, `.ogg`. At the time of this book's writing, Chrome and Firefox support all three audio formats, but Internet Explorer supports only the mp3 format. Older browsers have less support, so for the next several years, you should provide multiple `source` elements with multiple file formats. To help the browser determine whether it's capable of displaying a particular audio file, you should include a `type` attribute with each `source` element. You can see examples of that in the prior code fragment: `type="audio/mpeg"`, and so on. The browser loads the first file that uses a format that the browser supports, so in processing the code fragment, if a browser supports all three file formats, the browser will use the mp3 file.

If there's a particular sound you need for a web page, and you can find only one file for it (as opposed to finding three files, with the three file formats), you should use a file converter to create files with the other formats. You should be able to use free file converters on the Web. For example, http://www.online-convert.com works well and is easy to use.

## Halloween Sounds Web Page

The rainstorm `audio` element shown earlier produces the background sound for the Halloween Sounds web page shown in **FIGURE 7.9**. In the figure, note the rainstorm sound's audio player, and note the two other players for the witch's cackle sound and the werewolf sound. The rainstorm sound's `audio` element includes `autoplay` and `loop` attributes. That tells the browser to start playing the rainstorm sound when the page first downloads and to replay the sound in a loop. As an indication that the rainstorm sound is currently playing, you can see that the rainstorm audio player displays a pause button. The other players are not currently playing, so you can see that they display play buttons.

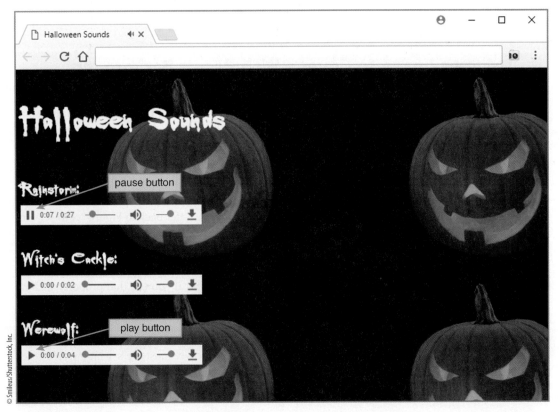

**FIGURE 7.9 Halloween Sounds web page**

It's reasonable to assume that the user will want to play all three Halloween sounds. As you'll see later (in the web page's source code figure), the bottom two `audio` elements include `preload` attributes in order to speed things up. We want the rainstorm audio file to be preloaded as well, but there's no `preload` attribute in its `audio` element. Why? Because its `autoplay` attribute tells the browser to preload the audio file regardless of the presence of a `preload` attribute.

# 7.7 **Background Images**

In the Halloween Sounds web page, we use a jack-o'-lantern image as the background for the web page's `body` element. Specifically, we use the `background-image` property to specify a URL to an image file. You can see the entire Halloween Sounds web page source code in **FIGURE 7.10**, but we've copied the `background-image` property CSS rule here for your convenience:

```
body {background-image: url(../images/pumpkin.jpg);}
```

The `background-image` property uses a URL value to specify the background image's file. Note the URL value's syntax—`url` and then parentheses around a path and a filename. As an option, you can surround the path and filename with single quotes or double quotes.

When you use a background image, you should pick an image that won't blend in with or hide your page's text. For example, in Figure 7.9's Halloween Sounds web page, note how the text's white color contrasts nicely with the dark background.

## Using an Image to Cover a Web Page's Background

As you know through personal experience, end users resize their browser windows all the time. So if you use a background image for a web page, you can't count on the image's dimensions matching the browser window's dimensions. Actually, it's the viewport's dimensions that matter. Suppose that a web page's background image is smaller than the browser window's viewport. That can lead to boring dead space surrounding the background image. There are several strategies for overcoming that potential problem.

The first strategy is to rely on the default behavior where the browser fills the entire viewport by displaying multiple copies of the image using a *tiled layout*. Refer back to Figure 7.9 to see four tiled jack-o'-lantern images. That's called "tiling" because it's similar in appearance to tiles on a bathroom floor. It can make your web page look kind of amateurish, so allow that behavior only if you're sure that's what you want. A simple way to avoid tiled background images is to apply `background-repeat: no-repeat` to the body element, but if you use that property with no other background properties, you're left with the dead space problem.

Another strategy for overcoming the dead space problem is to use an image large enough to cover most monitors. As of this book's writing, if you choose a picture that's 1600 pixels wide and 1200 pixels tall, the result should look pretty good because the picture will cover most users' windows. However, the tendency is for newer monitors to have greater resolution, so you should plan accordingly. A drawback of using a large fixed image is that the background image will often be cropped significantly.

```
<!DOCTYPE html>
<html lang="en">
<head>
<meta charset="utf-8">
<meta name="author" content="John Dean">
<title>Halloween Sounds</title>
<style>
  @font-face {
    font-family: Buffied;
    src: url(../fonts/buffied.woff) format("woff"),
         url(../fonts/buffied.ttf) format("opentype");
  }
  h1, h3 {color: white; font-family: Buffied, serif;}
  h1 {font-size: 5em;}
  h3 {font-size: 3em; margin-bottom: 0;}
  body {background-image: url(../images/pumpkin.jpg);}
</style>
</head>

<body>
<h1>Halloween Sounds</h1>
<h3>Rainstorm:</h3>
<audio autoplay controls loop>
  <source src="../audio/rainStorm.mp3" type="audio/mpeg">
  <source src="../audio/rainStorm.wav" type="audio/wav">
  <source src="../audio/rainStorm.ogg" type="audio/ogg">
</audio>
<h3>Witch's Cackle:</h3>
<audio src="../audio/witchesCackle.mp3" preload="auto" controls></audio>
<h3>Werewolf:</h3>
<audio src="../audio/werewolf.mp3" preload="auto" controls></audio>
</body>
</html>
```

> Better to have multiple file formats (with `source` elements) than just one file format (with the `src` attribute).

**FIGURE 7.10 Source code for Halloween Sounds web page**

A third strategy for overcoming the dead space problem is to have the browser automatically expand the background image to conform to the size of the viewport while maintaining the background image's original shape. Sounds like magic, eh? Well, browsers can do that, and it's called *scaling*. See **FIGURE 7.11** for an improved version of the Halloween Sounds web page, where the background image is scaled.

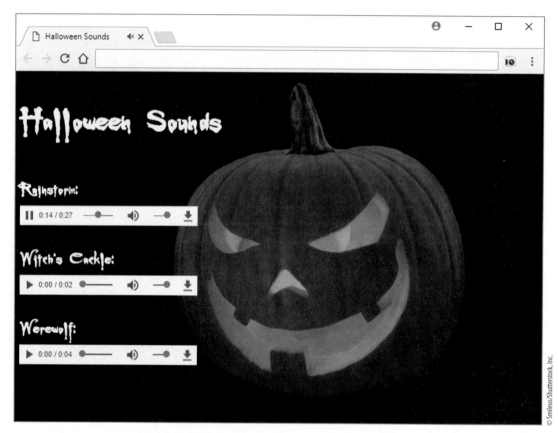

**FIGURE 7.11 Improved Halloween Sounds web page with scaling**

The improved Halloween Sounds web page uses the same code as before, except for its body CSS rule. Here's that rule:

```
body {
  background-image: url(../images/pumpkin.jpg);
  background-size: cover;
  background-attachment: fixed;
  background-position: center;
}
```

Note the `background-size: cover` property-value pair. It tells the browser to initiate the scaling process for the background image. Specifically, the browser attempts to "cover" the web page's background by scaling the image such that its larger dimension matches the width or height of the viewport. As for the smaller dimension, unless the image's dimensions and the viewport's dimensions scale perfectly (which is highly unlikely), the smaller dimension won't match the viewport. If the user resizes the browser window to make its small dimension even smaller, that can lead to a cropped image. But with a typically sized browser window, instead of

FIGURE 7.12 **Effect of different background properties on the Halloween Sounds web page**

cropping, you get uncovered dead space in the viewport. You can see that situation at the left side of **FIGURE 7.12** where the background image's vertical dimension is smaller than the viewport. That might be acceptable, particularly if you have a background color that matches the color at the image's perimeter, but if you don't like it, there's another background property that can help.

In the prior body CSS rule, note the background-attachment: fixed property-value pair. Its primary purpose is to "fix" the background so if there's a scrollbar and the user scrolls, the background remains stationary. A secondary purpose is to help with covering the viewport if it's used in conjunction with the background-size: cover property value pair. Specifically, if both property-value pairs are used (as is the case for the improved Halloween Sounds web page), and if the viewport is larger than the background image's native size, the browser expands the background image so there is no uncovered space in either dimension. The end result is that one of the background image's dimensions will match the viewport and the other dimension will be greater than the viewport. Unfortunately, that will cause the image to get cropped along the dimension that's larger than the viewport. To see examples of such cropping, study the middle and right-side browser windows in Figure 7.12. So if you want your background image to completely cover the browser's viewport, you'll have to live with a little cropping. Remember that life is full of trade-offs ("Should I answer my cell phone, or should I check for oncoming traffic?"), and sometimes web programming has trade-offs as well.

Another background property that you should be aware of is the background-position property. In the improved Halloween Sounds web page, we use a value of center for that property, which tells the browser to center the background image horizontally. If you omit the background-position property, the browser positions the background image with its top-left corner in the top-left corner of the browser window's viewport. To see the difference between those two scenarios, study the middle and right-side browser windows in Figure 7.12.

In the improved Halloween Sounds web page, we use the background-position property to specify the image's horizontal position. As for the vertical position, the default is to position the image with center alignment, and that works fine most of the time. If you want a different vertical alignment, you can specify a second value for the background-position property. Here's an example that positions a background image with its right edge at the viewport's right edge and its bottom edge at the viewport's bottom edge:

```
body {
  background-image: url(../images/pumpkin.jpg);
  background-size: cover;
  background-attachment: fixed;
  background-position: right bottom;
}
```

For the `background-position` property's first value, you can specify pixels from the left edge or you can specify `left`, `center`, or `right`. For the `background-position` property's second value, you can specify pixels from the top edge or you can specify `top`, `center`, or `bottom`.

## 7.8 Web Fonts

In the Halloween Sounds web page, did you notice the scary-looking font for the text? In this section, we explore how you can incorporate such nonstandard fonts, called *web fonts*, into your web pages.

For standard fonts (such as Tahoma and Courier New), you can be reasonably confident that those fonts will be installed on users' computers and they will work. But to be safe, you should always include a generic font family in each of your CSS `font-family` rules. On the other hand, nonstandard fonts will not normally be preinstalled on users' computers, so to get them to work, you'll need to use a CSS `@font-face` rule. They're called *at-rules* because they use the @ symbol.

The W3C states that at-rules "define special processing rules or values for the CSS document." Using such a rule means that when the user loads the web page, the web server sends the web page file plus a web font file. Here's the at-rule used in the Halloween Sounds web page:

```
@font-face {
  font-family: Buffied;          ← newly created font
  src: url(../fonts/buffied.woff2) format("woff2"),
       url(../fonts/buffied.woff) format("woff");
}
```

Note the at-rule's first line: `@font-face`. All `at-rules` begin that way, with "@" and then an identifier that specifies the type of at rule that's being defined. Note also the `font-family` property and its value of `Buffied`.[2] The `font-family` property's value provides the name with which later code can refer to the new font. So in the following example (also from the Halloween Sounds web page), note how the h1 and h3 elements are able to use the `Buffied` font:

```
h1, h3 {color: white; font-family: Buffied, serif;}
```

Even though the `Buffied` web font will most likely be downloaded and utilized successfully, to be safe you should still include a generic font family, as shown with `serif` in the h1, h3 rule.

Now let's examine the `src` attribute in the `Buffied` at-rule. In particular, note the two web font files with `.woff` and `.woff2` extensions. Those two files use the WOFF (Web Open Font

---

[2] The name "Buffied" comes from the 1997–2003 television series *Buffy the Vampire Slayer*—a postmodern Gothic pastiche with panache. The Buffied font comes from Online Web Fonts at https://www.onlinewebfonts.com.

Format) and WOFF 2.0 web font formats, introduced in 2010 and 2016, respectively. The WOFF 2.0 web font format does a better job with compression, with WOFF 2.0 files showing a 30% reduction in file size when compared to WOFF files. Current browsers support WOFF 2.0 files, but to accommodate older browsers, you should probably include both WOFF and WOFF 2.0 files in your at-rules, as is the case with the Halloween Sounds at-rule.

For an at-rule's `src` property, you should include not only a `url` value for the filename, but also a `format` value that indicates the file's format type. For a WOFF file, you should use `format("woff")`, and for a WOFF 2.0 file, you should use `format("woff2")`. To see the `url` value and the `format` value in action, study the `src` property in the `Buffied` at-rule.

There's no need to worry that including multiple web font filenames in your source code will slow things down by having both files downloaded. The browser looks at the `format` value and downloads the associated file only if the browser supports that format. The browser looks at `format` values in the order they appear in the code. After the browser finds a format it supports, it attempts to download that file and ignores any other web font files. So if you have a WOFF 2.0 file, it should go first in the code. Why? Because WOFF 2.0 files are smaller, and you want to give priority to smaller files.

When searching for web fonts on the Internet, you'll probably have a hard time finding WOFF and WOFF 2.0 files. But it's easy to find files with the extension `.ttf`, where ttf stands for TrueType font. If you'd like to use a TrueType font file on your web page, you can do so by adding it to an at-rule's `src` attribute like this:

```
url(../fonts/Buffied.ttf) format("truetype");
```

That's OK, but with WOFF and WOFF 2.0 files both showing a significant reduction in file size when compared to TrueType font files, you're better off using a file converter tool to create WOFF and WOFF 2.0 versions of the TrueType font file, and using the newly created files in your web page. You should be able to find free file converter tools on the Web. For example, https://font-converter.net works well and is easy to use.

## 7.9 Video

In this section, you'll learn how to implement a video player with the `video` element. The `video` element is fairly similar to the `audio` element, so much of this discussion should sound familiar.

### video Element Syntax

In the old days, end users had to install a plug-in to play a video from a web page. Fortunately, that's no longer the case. Today's browsers include a built-in video player that's used in conjunction with HTML5's `video` element. Here's a `video` element example:

```
<video src="stBernardClimbsFlagPole.mp4"
  width="350" height="260"
  preload="metadata" controls
  poster="stBernardClimbsFlagPole.jpg"></video>
```

Like the audio element, the video element requires a start tag and an end tag even when there's no content between the tags. In this example, there's no content between the tags. Later, you'll see an example where there is such content.

Let's run through the attributes for the video element. As is customary, the src attribute specifies a path to a file. In this example, the src attribute's file is an mp4 video file. Later, we'll describe the different video file formats.

The width and height attributes specify the size of the video's display box in pixels. As with the img element, you should always include the width and height attributes. That allows the browser to download the rest of the web page right away. Without the width and height attributes, the browser has to wait for the video file to download to know the video's dimensions, which affect the position of the surrounding content. If you specify larger dimensions for the video box than the video object's natural dimensions, the browser will display the video with the specified dimensions. That's fine, as long as you specify dimensions that are scaled versions of the video's natural dimensions. If you use dimensions that are not properly scaled, the browser will display the video with the correct proportions, but you'll have blank areas along the edges to fill in the video box to the specified dimensions.

The preload attribute tells the browser whether to download the video or its meta information when the page initially loads (as opposed to waiting for the user to click the play button). But the preload attribute is only a suggestion—it's up to the browser to decide what to do. If you specify preload="metadata", that asks the browser to download information about the video file (dimensions, duration, etc.), the first frame, and possibly a few additional frames. By preloading the first frame, the browser can display the first frame in the video box whenever the video is not playing. To decrease the delay when the user clicks the play button, you can specify preload="auto", which asks the browser to preload the entire video, not just the video's metadata information. To avoid possibly unnecessary bandwidth usage, you can specify preload="none", which asks the browser to download no video information when the page initially loads.

The poster attribute specifies an image that displays while the video is not playing, thus overriding the default behavior of using the video's first frame for the paused video display.

The controls attribute causes a control bar to display. The control bar allows the user to start and pause the video and adjust the volume. You should always include the controls attribute with the video element because without it, users will probably get annoyed at not being able to control the video.

Unfortunately, different browsers support different video file formats. To handle that situation, you can omit the video element's src attribute and, instead, include multiple source elements between the video element's start and end tags. For example:

```
<video width="397" height="225" preload="metadata" controls
   poster="../images/groceryStore.jpg">
   <source src="../video/swedishAd.mp4" type="video/mp4">
   <source src="../video/swedishAd.webm" type="video/webm"></video>
```

You can see two source elements that utilize an .mp4 file (swedishAd.mp4) and a .webm file (swedishAd.webm). The W3C recommends that you use those types of files (.mp4 and .webm) because they're popular and well supported by today's browsers. Formally, those file types use the MPEG-4 format and the WebM format.

To help the browser determine whether it's capable of displaying a particular video file, you should include a `type` attribute with each `source` element. For example, in the prior `video` element, the first `source` element uses `type="video/mp4"`.

If you find only one file format for a particular video, you should use a file converter to create a file(s) with the other format(s). You should be able to use free file converters on the Web. For example, http://www.online-convert.com works well and is easy to use. That's the same converter that was suggested earlier for use with audio files.

## TV Advertisements Web Page

The `video` code fragment shown earlier produces the video at the left side of the TV Advertisements web page shown in **FIGURE 7.13**. In the figure, note the two videos (they're empty here, but the real web page displays first-frame images within the video boxes), note how everything is centered horizontally and vertically within the web page, and note the background color spectrum. We'll focus on the videos for now and get to the other things in the next section.

The TV Advertisements web page's code is rather long, requiring two figures to show it all. **FIGURE 7.14A** shows the web page's body container and Figure 7.14B (in the next section) shows the `head` container. The body container implements two videos. The first video is implemented with a `video` container and uses the code described earlier. The second video is implemented with an `iframe` container, and it deserves an explanation.

© Lyudmyla Kharlamova/Shutterstock, Inc.

**FIGURE 7.13 TV Advertisements web page**

```
<body>
<div class="table">
  <div class="caption">Television Advertisements</div>
  <div class="cell">
    <h3>Kid in a Swedish Grocery Store:</h3>
    <video width="397" height="225" preload="metadata" controls
      poster="../images/groceryStore.jpg">
      <source src="../video/swedishAd.mp4" type="video/mp4">
      <source src="../video/swedishAd.webm" type="video/webm"></video>
  </div>
  <div class="cell">
    <h3>Doritos Kid:</h3>
    <iframe width="400" height="225" allowfullscreen
      src="http://www.youtube.com/embed/VxzhGPrHCKI?rcl=0"></iframe>
  </div>
</div>
</body>
</html>
```

**FIGURE 7.14A Source code body container for TV Advertisements web page**

As an alternative to playing a video directly from a web page with a `video` element, you can use an `iframe` element to play a video on an external web page. Here's an example, copied from the TV Advertisements web page:

```
<iframe width="400" height="225" allowfullscreen
  src="http://www.youtube.com/embed/VxzhGPrHCKI?rel=0"></iframe>
```

Note the `allowfullscreen` attribute, which enables users to expand the video to full-screen mode.

There are plusses and minuses to using the `iframe` element to play a video on an external web page versus using the `video` element. First, the advantages of using the `iframe` element: You don't have to create your own video files or find video files you can copy. Instead, you just find web pages that host videos, and that's pretty easy (heard of YouTube?). You don't have to use up storage space on your own web server.

On the other hand, here are advantages of using the `video` element: Users are not required to install a video player plug-in. Also, you're not dependent on an external web server continuing to host the video. Finally, you can use JavaScript to customize your video, and you can avoid an external web page's customizations (like advertisements). You'll learn about JavaScript starting in the next chapter. How exciting!

## 7.10 Centering Content Within the Viewport, Color Gradients

In this section, we describe the formatting used in the TV Advertisements web page. We'll discuss the web page's layout, including how to center the web page's content within the viewport. Then we'll discuss how to generate a color spectrum for the web page's background.

## Web Page's Layout

Let's start with something that should be a review—using the CSS `display` property with table values. In Figure 7.13, note that the two video boxes and their headings are side-by-side. We achieved that look by using CSS. Specifically, we defined a table with the `display: table` property-value pair and two table cells with `display: table-cell` property-value pairs. Take a look at the TV Advertisements `head` container in **FIGURE 7.14B**, and find those property-value pairs. Also, find their associated `class="table"`, `class="cell"` attribute-value pairs in Figure 7.14A's body container.

Next up—centering the web page's content within the web page. In the Trees web page presented earlier, do you recall centering the heading's contents? We used `text-align: center` to center the heading's tree icons and text horizontally within the heading. That worked great for that

```
<!DOCTYPE html>
<html lang="en">
<head>
<meta charset="utf-8">
<meta name="author" content="John Dean">
<title>TV Ads</title>
<style>
  html {
    height: 100vh;
    display: flex;                          The html type selector rule
    justify-content: center;                centers the body element
    align-items: center;                    within the viewport.
  }
  body {
    background-image: linear-gradient(to right, blue, #00ffff, #ff7700);
    background-attachment: fixed;
    text-align: center;                     This creates a color gradient.
  }
  .table {
    display: table;                         This creates a table layout.
    border-spacing: 20px;
  }
  .caption {
    display: table-caption;
    font-size: xx-large;
  }
  .cell {display: table-cell;}
</style>
</head>
```

**FIGURE 7.14B Source code head container for TV Advertisements web page**

situation because the `text-align` property centers inline objects within a block container, and the heading's tree icons and text are inline objects. But for the TV Advertisements web page, we want to center the web page's entire contents within the browser window's viewport. And the entire contents consist of more than just block containers with inline objects inside them. Specifically, we want to center the contents of the table we created for the adjacent video objects. As you can verify by examining the source code, the table is a `div` block element and each video object is part of its own `div` block element. So the `text-align` property won't help to center the table of two video objects.

To center the contents of a block element when the block contains other block elements, we first need to convert the outer block element to a *flexbox*, which generates a *flexible box layout* for the outer block element. To create a flexbox, we apply a `display: flex` property-value pair to the outer block element. Now, let's apply that strategy to the TV Advertisements web page.

For the TV Advertisements web page, the goal is to center the page's entire contents. The easiest way to do that is to center the `body` element within its container. So, what contains the `body` element? The `html` element. So the solution is to use `display: flex` to turn the `html` element into a flexbox, and then we add the magic centering property-value pairs to the html element. Specifically, we add `justify-content: center` to the `html` type selector rule to center the `html` element's contents horizontally. And we add `align-items: center` to the `html` type selector rule to center the `html` element's contents vertically. That centers the `body` element within the viewport.

Take a look at the `html` type selector rule in Figure 7.14B, and you'll see the three property-value pairs just mentioned, plus a fourth property-value pair, `height: 100vh`. As you might guess, the `height` property assigns a height to an element. Normally, the height of the `html` element is the height of the web page's content. That's not what we want. Because we're interested in using the `html` container to center the body element within the browser window, we need the `html` container's dimensions to match the viewport's dimensions. Fortunately, the `html` container's default width does equal the viewport's width. But we need to do a little work for the `html` container's height. Specifically, we use `height: 100vh` to force the `html` container's height to match the viewport's height. The `100vh` value tells the browser to use 100% of the viewport's height. The `vh` in `100vh` is a relative unit, where vh stands for <u>v</u>iewport <u>h</u>eight, and `1vh` equals 1% of the height of the viewport.

## Using a Color Gradient to Cover a Web Page's Background

For the Halloween Sounds web page, we used an image file for the web page's background. That's quite common and works nicely, but using an image file has its drawbacks—files can take a while to download, and some users disable file downloads. To avoid those problems, you can specify a color gradient value for the background image. A *color gradient* value displays a smooth transition between two or more colors.

Look back at the TV Advertisements web page in Figure 7.13. For the background, you can see a color gradient that transitions from blue to blue-green to orange. Here's the code that implements that color gradient:

```
body {
  background-image: linear-gradient(to right, blue, #00ffff, #ff7700);
}
```

Note the `background-image` property. In the Halloween Sounds web page, we used `background-image` with a `url` value (for specifying an image file), and here we're using it with a `linear-gradient` value (for specifying a color gradient). You can use a `linear-gradient` value anywhere you can use an image file value. The most common place to use an image file value is with the `background-image` property, but be aware that you can also use it with the `list-style-image` property, which provides content for the markers that go next to the items in a list.

In the prior code fragment, the `linear-gradient`'s last three arguments specify the gradient's colors. The colors are blue, green-blue, and reddish orange. The `linear-gradient`'s first argument, `to right`, specifies the direction that the gradient's colors flow. The word after "to" specifies the target, where you can use `right`, `left`, `bottom`, or `top` for the target value. Or you can use a combination of those values to specify a corner target (e.g., `to right bottom`). Look back at the TV Advertisements web page and verify that blue, green-blue, and reddish orange are positioned left to right. If you omit the `linear-gradient`'s first argument, the default is for the colors to be positioned top to bottom. You can specify as many colors as you'd like. The browser positions the first color at the starting point and the last color at the ending point, and intermediate colors are equally spaced in between.

There are quite a few options when it comes to color gradients. In this discussion, we only scratched the surface. If you have time, you might want to review the W3C's CSS standard on your own and learn how to repeat a color pattern, generate a radial color gradient, and specify the locations for the colors within a color gradient.

## 7.11 CASE STUDY: Using an Image Map for a Small City's Core Area and Website Navigation with a Generic Home Page

This section starts by enhancing the Area Description web page developed at the end of Chapter 3. It adds mapped images to the `areaDescription.html` file in the initial `LawrenceMicrogrid` folder described in the case study section at the end of Chapter 6. Remember, the files in that original folder did not receive the additional `header` and `footer` interpage navigation elements added in Chapter 6's case study section. In the same spirit, this section's enhanced Area Description page will not have `header` and `footer` interpage navigation elements. Moreover, all new web pages developed in subsequent end-of-chapter case study sections will go into that same folder in the same condition—without `header` and `footer` interpage navigation elements.

After developing this new page, we will return to the website navigation problem and propose another navigation system that is easier to maintain than the enhanced website navigation system described at the end of Chapter 6. This new alternative will make it possible to add new pages to the website without having to add duplicate header and footer elements, and without having to update `href="#"` references in header elements on previous pages.

## This Chapter's Web Page

Take a look at **FIGURE 7.15**, which shows the enhanced Area Description web page. The heading at the top and the text at the bottom are the same as the heading and text in Chapter 3's case study web page. The street map and the image and the caption below them are new.

As the web page's caption indicates, the street map contains six regions. When the user's mouse moves onto one of the regions, the browser displays a pop-up box that identifies the entered region. In the figure, note the hand cursor hovering over the downtown area and the resulting "Downtown Lawrence" pop-up box. If the user clicks on the map, the browser detects which region was clicked and displays a picture of the region in the area at the right of the map. Note the click-induced Downtown Lawrence picture at the right of the map.

This enhancement to Chapter 3's Area Description web page requires additional code in the web page's body container. **FIGURE 7.16** shows what to insert after the body container's h2 element and before the subsequent p class="downtown" element.

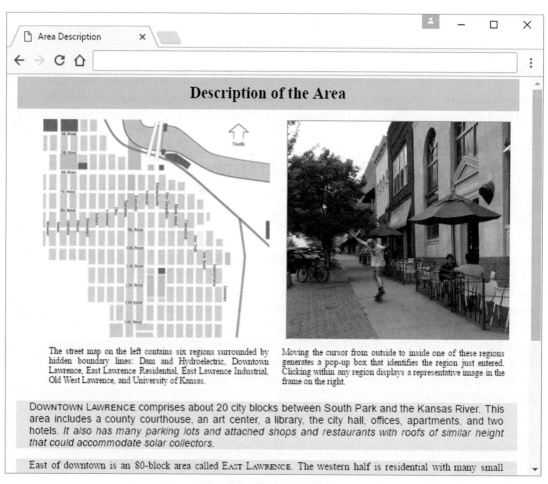

**FIGURE 7.15 Enhanced Area Description web page**

> This provides a hook for usemap in the img element.

```
<map name="oldLawrence" id="oldLawrence">
  <area href="../images/bowersockDam.jpg" shape="rect"
    coords="175,4,192,52" target="photo" alt ="Dam and Hydroelectric"
    title="Dam and Hydroelectric">
  <area href="../images/downtownView.jpg" shape="poly"
    coords="136,85,136,235,198,235,198,175,225,97,225,65,195,50"
    target="photo" alt ="Downtown Lawrence" title="Downtown Lawrence">
  <area href="../images/eastLawrence.jpg" shape="poly" coords=
    "199,170,199,350,280,350,280,185,225,107" target="photo"
    alt="East Lawrence Residential" title="East Lawrence Residential">
  <area href="../images/industrialPark.jpg" shape="poly" coords=
    "225,95,295,200,295,240,355,225,355,100,250,85" target="photo"
    alt="East Lawrence Industrial" title="East Lawrence Industrial">
  <area href="../images/oldWestLawrence.jpg"
    shape="poly" coords=
    "6,0,6,217,66,217,66,279,101,279,101,350,135,350,135,70,80,0"
    target="photo" alt ="Old West Lawrence" title="Old West Lawrence">
  <area href="../images/kansasUniv.jpg" shape="poly"
    coords="0,218,0,330,100,330,100,280,65,280,65,218" target=
    "photo" alt="University of Kansas" title="University of Kansas">
</map>
<figure id="figure">
  <img id="streetMap" src="../images/lawrenceMap.jpg"
    alt="Map of Old Part of Lawrence" usemap="#oldLawrence">
  <iframe name="photo" src="../images/downtownView.jpg"></iframe>
  <figcaption>
    <div>
      The street map on the left contains six regions surrounded by
      hidden boundary lines: Dam and Hydroelectric, Downtown Lawrence,
      East Lawrence Residential, East Lawrence Industrial, Old West
      Lawrence, and University of Kansas.
    </div>
    <div>
      Moving the cursor from outside to inside one of these regions
      generates a pop-up box that identifies the region just entered.
      Clicking within any region displays a representative image in
      the frame on the right.
    </div>
  </figcaption>
</figure>
```

> Connect the image to the map.

**FIGURE 7.16 Additional source code for enhanced Area Description web page**

In Figure 7.16, find the map container and the street map `img` element within the `figure` container. Together, they implement an *image map*. If you've ever been on the Web (if not, now's a good time), you've probably used an image map. It's when you move your mouse over an image and different pop-ups occur at different areas on the image. Those different areas are called *hotspots*. Clicking on a hotspot takes you to another web page or another place within the current web page.

Because the `map` element works in conjunction with an `img` element, you should normally position it near the `img` element, but that's not a syntactic requirement. To associate an `img` element with a `map` element, the `img` element must include a `usemap` attribute with the `map` element's `id` value for `usemap` attribute's value. For example, in Figure 7.16, find the `map` element's `id` value of `oldLawrence`. And then find the `img` element's `usemap="#oldLawrence"` attribute-value pair.

Within the `map` element, an `area` element's `coords` attribute defines the outline of a region on the `img` that uses the image map. When `shape="rect"`, subsequent coordinate pairs are the *x* and *y* positions of the upper-left and lower-right corners of a rectangle. When `shape="poly"`, subsequent coordinate pairs are the *x* and *y* positions of successive points on a polygon. Distances are in pixels right and down from the upper-left corner of the user element. A mouse click in the identified region copies what's referenced by the `area` element's `href` attribute to what's referenced by its `target` attribute.

The `figure` element has three subordinate elements: The `img` element contains the mapped image. The `iframe` element, which gets a photograph, is the `area` elements' `target`. Notice that `target`'s value matches the value of `iframe`'s `name` attribute. The `figcaption` element contains two columns of text describing the mapped image and target photograph.

All of this requires additional CSS rules. **FIGURE 7.17** shows the additional code to insert in the `style` element in Chapter 3's Area Description web page. The `#figure` rule's `position: relative` property establishes a reference for position offsets specified in subsequent rules that include the `position: absolute` property. The `#figure` rule's `height` property determines the starting point of material coming after the `figure` element. It does not, however, affect the dimensions of any of the `figure` element's contents (`img id="streetMap"`, `iframe class="photo"`, and `figcaption`), because other rules establish their heights and widths. The final `div` rule creates a two-column format for the figure caption.

There is a residual problem, however. In Figure 7.15, the code does not center the figure because in a narrow window like that shown, centering would push part of the map out of view to the left. So the gap between the left side of the browser window and the left side of the figure does not change as the user resizes the browser window. That's good for narrow windows, but it looks odd when the window is wide, as in **FIGURE 7.18**. In the case study section of Chapter 9, you'll see how to get the best of both worlds: (1) Hold the left side of the figure a constant distance away from the left side of the window when the window is narrower than the combined width of the map and the picture. (2) Horizontally center the map and picture in the window when the window width is greater than the combined width of the map and the picture.

```
#figure {
  position: relative;
  height: 405px;
}
#streetMap {
  position: absolute;
  top: 0px; left: 0px;
  width: 350px;
}
iframe {
  position: absolute;
  top: 0px; left: 370px;
  width: 340px;
  height: 325px;
  margin: 0px 5px;
}
figcaption {
  position: absolute;
  top: 340px;
  width: 720px;
  font-size: small;
  text-align: justify;
}
div {
  width: 360px;
  padding: 0px 10px;
  display: table-cell;
}
```

**FIGURE 7.17** **Additional style rules for enhanced Area Description web page**

## Website Navigation Using a Generic Home Page

The enhanced website navigation system described in the case study section at the end of Chapter 6 made user-friendly navigation available no matter where the user was within the website. However, source code duplication made that user-friendly navigation hard to maintain. Now, you'll see another way to make user-friendly interpage navigation continuously available without having to duplicate `header` and `footer` elements and without having to update previous pages' `href="#"` attributes.

The key is to implement an `index.html` home page that includes the previously developed navigation header, plus an `iframe` element. **FIGURE 7.19** contains the source code for the new frame-based `index.html` file.

The heart of the new `index.html` file is the `iframe` element near the bottom of the code in Figure 7.19. All of the website's pages will go into this `iframe` element. Notice that in addition to having an `id="page"` attribute-value pair, the `iframe` element also has a `name="page"` attribute-value pair. As you'll see shortly, the `name` attribute's value provides a "hook" for the a elements to link to. Compare the `header` element in Figure 7.18 with the new `header` element

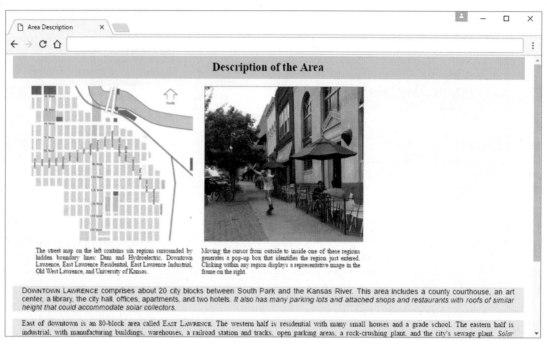

**FIGURE 7.18 Enhanced Area Description web page in wide window**

in Figure 7.19. In the new `header` element, the `a` elements include new `target="page"` attributes. These tell browsers to put user-selected pages into the `iframe` (because the `iframe` has a `name="page"` attribute-value pair).

The new `header` element also includes a little `h5` heading element between the navigation buttons and the `iframe`. In case users might want to bookmark or save the current contents of the `iframe`, this little heading element provides advice on how to do it.

The new `index.html` file's `head` element starts with the usual `meta` elements and the now-familiar `link` to the common external CSS file. Then it provides a `style` element with two rules. In the rule for the new little `h5` element, the `margin` property centers its text vertically between the bottom(s) of the navigation buttons above and the top of the heading of the default or user-selected website page in the `iframe` below.

The new `index.html` does not itself contain any home-page content beyond the common website title, the interpage navigation buttons, and the advice in the little `h5` element. All the rest of the content comes from whatever is displayed in the `iframe` element. The `iframe` element's `src` attribute initializes the frame with the content in the Area Description web page.

Take a look at the resulting frame-based home page in **FIGURE 7.20**. The inner scroll bar is for the contents of the `iframe` element. Initially, that scroll bar started slightly above the h2 header's text. That's because of the h2 header's top margin. To get the h2 header's text and the scroll bar to align, we had to add this additional rule to the common external CSS file:

```
h2 {margin-top: -15px;}
```

```html
<!DOCTYPE html>
<html lang="en">
<head>
<meta charset="utf-8">
<meta name="author" content="John Dean">
<title>Lawrence Microgrid</title>
<link rel="stylesheet" href="../library/microgrid.css">
<style>
  h5 {
    margin: -10px auto 10px;
    text-align: center;
  }
  #page {
    width: 100%;
    height: 500px;
    border: none;
  }
</style>
</head>

<body>
<header>
  <h1>Microgrid Development in Lawrence KS</h1>
  <nav>
    <ul>
      <li><a href="electricPowerHistory.html" target="page">
        Electric Power History</a></li>
      <li><a href="lawrenceHydropower.html" target="page">
        Lawrence Hydropower</a></li>
      <li><a href="areaDescription.html" target="page">
        <strong>Area Description</strong></a></li>
      <li><a href="microgridPossibilities.html" target="page">
        Microgrid Possibilities</a></li>
      <li><a href="typicalProperty.html" target="page">
        Typical Property</a></li>
      <li><a href="localEnergy.html" target="page">Local Energy</a></li>
      <li><a href="#">Collector Performance</a></li>
      <li><a href="#">Electric Power Services</a></li>
      <li><a href="#">Downtown Properties</a></li>
      <li><a href="#">Solar Shadowing</a></li>
    </ul>
  </nav>
  <h5>To bookmark or save content below, open it in a new tab by
    right-clicking the corresponding button above.</h5>
</header>
<iframe id="page" name="page" src="areaDescription.html"></iframe>
</body>
</html>
```

**FIGURE 7.19** Frame-based `index.html` file for Lawrence Microgrid website

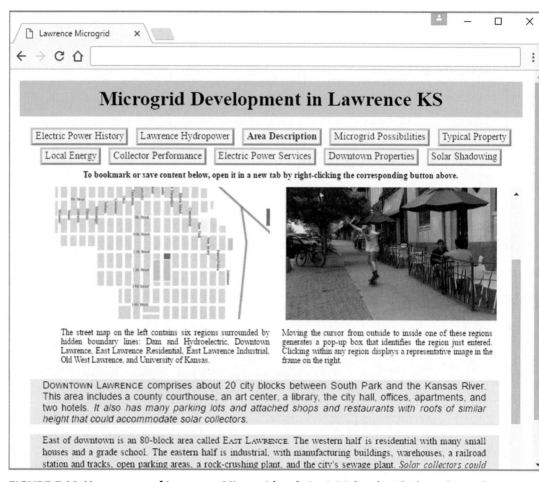

**FIGURE 7.20** **Home page of Lawrence Microgrid website initialized with the enhanced Area Description web page in** `iframe` **after scrolling** `iframe`**'s content**

Because scrolling down just scrolls down within the `iframe` element, it does not drive the website title and top navigation buttons out of view. Consequently, from any place on the home page, a user can click any top navigation button and jump to any other page. That click replaces the material in the `iframe` element with the material in the web page corresponding to the clicked button, but the navigational buttons above the `iframe` remain continuously visible. Clicking one of those top navigation buttons displays the top part of the corresponding web page. A user who is near the bottom of a web page and wants to jump immediately to the top of that same page can click the header's continuously visible button for that page. Of course, the vertical scroll bar provides another way to get back to the top of the current page. In any event, "Top" and "Home" buttons at the bottoms of pages are now unnecessary and redundant.

Now suppose a user clicks the "Local Energy" navigation button, and the `iframe` element displays this website's Local Energy web page. Then, under "Electricity from Photovoltaic Solar

Collectors," suppose the user clicks the underlined term, <u>Net-metering</u>. If (on the Local Energy web page) the <u>Net-metering</u> a element did not contain a `target="_blank"` attribute, that click on <u>Net-metering</u> would replace the `iframe`'s display with the remote page referenced in <u>Net-metering</u>'s a element. But because the <u>Net-metering</u> a element does contain a `target="_blank"` attribute, the browser displays the referenced web page in a new window with a corresponding new tab. The browser retains a tab for the original window, and the user can click that tab to go back to the "Microgrid Development in Lawrence KS" website and its 10 navigation buttons. To optimize user overview and search control, the browser maintains appropriate backtracking navigation in each window. The user can continue clicking any sequence of browser tabs, local and/or remote navigation buttons, and/or underlined hypertext references. At any time, the user can click either tab and use the arrows in the corresponding window's upper-left corner to backtrack or retrace within the scope of that tab.

When looking at the Lawrence Microgrid home page, if the user performs a bookmark operation, the page that gets bookmarked is the `index.html` page—not the page currently visible in its `iframe` element. This behavior continuously highlights the current website and promotes its sponsor rather than particular details. Users who are more interested in the particular details on one of the subordinate pages normally displayed in the `iframe` can always follow the advice in the little `h5` element and right-click that page's continuously visible navigation button, and select from the browser's pop-up window to open that page in a new tab or window. Then, the user can bookmark that subordinate page.

The `iframe` element's precursor was the `frame` element. With the advent of HTML5, the W3C got rid of the `frame` element because of various problems. The `iframe` element is a much improved construct and it serves a useful purpose, but it's not perfect. As mentioned earlier, it can make bookmarking rather cumbersome. Also, it can be detrimental to *search engine optimization* (SEO). Typically, search engines downplay the content within `iframe` elements and they don't bother to save that content as part of their indexing systems. Thus, if you care about your web page's popularity, try to avoid putting searchable content in an `iframe`. In later chapters' case studies, we redo the Lawrence Microgrid home page without using an `iframe` element.

# Review Questions

**7.2 Positioning Images**

1. Using `float: right` causes text to display (float) along an image's right boundary. True or false.

2. The `align-text` property can be used to align images within a block element. True or false.

**7.3 Shortcut Icon**

3. When implementing a shortcut icon, why should the icon have small square dimensions?

**7.4 `iframe` Element**

4. What is a browsing context?

5. What is a thumbnail?

**7.5 CSS Image Sprites**

6. What is a rollover?

7. In implementing an image sprite, what does the `background-position` property do?

**7.6 Audio**

8. For a user to play an audio clip supplied by an HTML5 `audio` element, what audio plug-in will the user need to install?

9. What happens if an `audio` element includes `preload="auto"`?

10. For the `audio` element, it's usually a good idea to include a `loop` attribute. True or false.

**7.7 Background Images**

11. Suppose a web page uses the `background-image` property to cover the web page's background with an image. By default, if the image is smaller than the viewport, what does the browser do to cover the web page's background?

**7.8 Web Fonts**

12. How does every at-rule begin?

13. In implementing web fonts for your web pages, what are the two most useful web font formats?

14. In defining a web font, why is it good to use multiple versions of the web font's file?

**7.9 Video**

15. For a `video` element, what is the purpose of the `poster` attribute?

16. For a `video` element, why might you want to specify `preload="none"`?

### 7.10 Centering Content Within the Viewport, Color Gradients

17. Assume you have an element with a flexible box layout. What CSS property-value pair is needed to center the element's content vertically?

18. What is the default direction for positioning a linear gradient's colors?

# Exercises

1. [after Section 7.2] Provide an `img` element and an associated CSS rule (two separate things) that could be used to render the following sun image. Do not use a `style` attribute. Your code should cause surrounding text to flow down on the right of the sun image. You're welcome to create an entire web page for testing purposes, but the only thing you're required to submit is the image tag and the CSS rule. If you want to create an entire web page, you'll need to find an actual sun-image file. Otherwise, feel free to dream up a sun-image filename and appropriate size values. You should assume that the image file is stored in the same directory as the web page.

2. [after Section 7.4] Suppose you have an `a` element and an `iframe` element, and you want the `a` element's `href` value to load within the `iframe` element. How can you make that happen? In your answer, you must mention the attributes in the `a` and `iframe` elements that are used to tie the two elements together.

3. [after Section 7.4] Given an `img` element with `class="block-image"`. Provide a CSS rule that causes the image to display using block formatting.

4. [after Section 7.5] Implement a CSS image sprite that toggles between a stationary cartoon animal (a kangaroo?) and that same animal jumping. The toggling occurs when the mouse moves over the image and when the mouse moves away.

5. [after Section 7.7] Given this body element start tag:

```
<body class="honey-bunny">
```

Provide a class selector rule that uses scaling to cover the web page completely with an image file named goldenLagomorph.jpg. Your code should position the background image with its top-left corner in the top-left corner of the browser window's viewport. Assume the web page and the image file are stored in the same directory.

6. [after Section 7.10] Provide a background-image property-value pair that could be used to generate this radial gradient background:

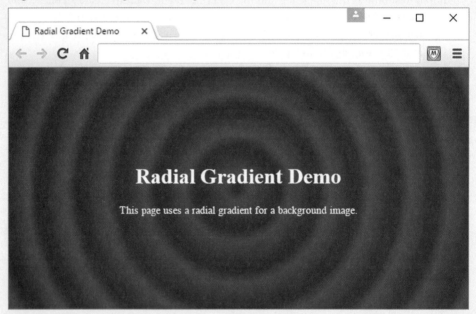

If you want to test your CSS rule, you would of course need to have HTML code for the "Radial Gradient Demo" text, but that code and testing are not required—you need only to provide a CSS rule.

## Project

Create a web page named rowing.html that mimics the following displayed page, except that you must use a background picture different from the one shown, and you must use your own shortcut icon (not my JD shortcut icon).

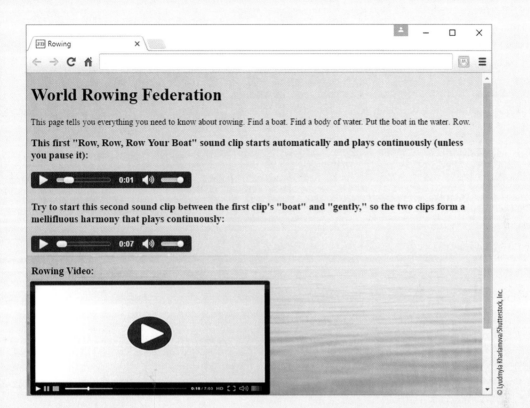

© Lyudmyla Kharlamova/Shutterstock, Inc.

Note:
- Each of the audio control bars shown should refer to two audio files that play "Row, Row, Row Your Boat." The two files should use two of the three main audio formats supported by the major browsers. Feel free to use a file converter program to create a second audio file. Store your background image file in `images`, a subdirectory of your `hw` directory.
- Search for an audio file that plays "Row, Row, Row Your Boat." My audio file is a piano recording, with no vocals, but you are welcome to use any type of music. Store your audio files in `audio`, a subdirectory of your `hw` directory.
- To know what attributes to use for your `audio` elements, study the words shown above each control bar.
- Find a video about rowing and add it to your web page.

You must use a background picture that has something to do with a body of water or boats. Your text must be easy to read—don't let it blend in with the background image. Use one of these strategies:
- Use a picture large enough to cover most monitors (1280 × 1024 is sufficient).
- Apply CSS so the browser scales the picture dynamically to cover the viewport entirely.
- Repeat the picture (do this only if the result looks reasonably good).

# CHAPTER 8

# Introduction to JavaScript: Functions, DOM, Forms, and Event Handlers

## CHAPTER OBJECTIVES

▶ Learn how JavaScript came to be.

▶ Implement a button control with an event handler.

▶ Understand syntax rules for functions, variables, identifiers, and assignments.

▶ Learn about the Document Object Model.

▶ Implement a form with a text control and a button.

▶ Learn how to update a web page with dynamic HTML.

▶ Understand proper JavaScript coding conventions.

▶ Learn about event-handler attributes.

▶ Implement a rollover using mouse events.

▶ Accommodate disabled JavaScript.

## CHAPTER OUTLINE

## 8.1 Introduction

So far, the HTML/CSS ride has been fairly smooth. It's now time to learn JavaScript, and you may experience some turbulence along the way. But don't worry. If your seat belts are securely fastened and you're prepared to go slowly and think things through, you should be fine. Actually, you should be more than fine because using JavaScript is exhilarating. With JavaScript, you can make your web pages come alive by having them interact with the user. In the previous chapter, you got a small taste of interaction with image sprites, where CSS rules are used to implement rollover effects. But JavaScript is a full-blown programming language, and, as such, anything is possible.

In this chapter, we start with a brief history of the JavaScript language and then quickly move to an example web page where we use JavaScript to display a message when the user clicks a button. In presenting the example, we describe the web page's underlying mechanisms—buttons, functions, and variables.

Next, we describe the basics of the *document object model* (the *DOM*), which will provide a solid foundation for understanding JavaScript constructs that are introduced in this chapter and throughout the rest of the book. The DOM provides hooks that enable various web page objects to do things. For example, web page forms are built with the DOM's underlying framework, and that framework enables forms to process user-entered data when the user clicks a button. In talking about forms and buttons, we describe event handlers, which connect a user's interaction with instructions that tell the browser what to do when the interaction occurs. For example, when a user clicks a button, the browser might display a message. When a user moves the mouse over an image, the browser might swap in a different image.

# 8.2 **History of JavaScript**

HTML's first version, designed by Tim Berners-Lee from 1989 to 1991, was fairly static in nature. Except for link jumps with the a element, web pages simply displayed content, and the content was fixed. In 1995, the dominant browser manufacturer was Netscape, and one of its employees, Brendan Eich, thought that it would be useful to add dynamic functionality to web pages. So he designed the JavaScript programming language, which adds dynamic functionality to web pages when used in conjunction with HTML. For example, JavaScript provides the ability to update a web page's content when an event occurs, such as when a user clicks a button. It also provides the ability to retrieve a user's input and process that input.

It took Eich only 10 days in May 1995 to implement the JavaScript programming language—a truly remarkable feat. Marc Andreessen, one of Netscape's founders, originally named the new language Mocha and then LiveScript. But for marketing purposes, Andreessen really wanted the name JavaScript. At the time, the software industry was excited about the hot new programming language, Java. Andreessen figured that all the Java bandwagon devotees would gravitate to their new browser programming language if it had the name Java in it. In December 1995, Andreessen got his wish when Netscape obtained a trademark license from Java manufacturer, Sun Microsystems, and LiveScript's name was changed to JavaScript. Unfortunately, many, many people over the years have made the mistake of assuming that JavaScript is the same as Java or very close to it. Don't be fooled by the name—JavaScript is not all that similar to Java. Actually, C++ and other popular programming languages are closer to Java than JavaScript is.

In 1996, Netscape submitted JavaScript to the Ecma International[1] standards organization to promote JavaScript's influence on all browsers (not just Netscape's browser). Ecma International used JavaScript as the basis for creating the ECMAScript standard. As hoped, ECMAScript now serves as the standard for the interactive programming languages embedded in all of today's popular browsers. At the time of this book's printing, the most recent ECMAScript version is version 7, published in 2016. Coming up with the name ECMAScript was a difficult process, with different browser manufacturers having strong opposing views. JavaScript creator Brendan Eich has stated that the result, ECMAScript, is "an unwanted trade name that sounds like a skin disease."[2]

In 1998, Netscape formed the Mozilla free-software community, which eventually implemented Firefox, one of today's premier browsers. Brendan Eich moved to Mozilla, where he and others have continued to update JavaScript over the years, following the ECMAScript standard as set forth by Ecma International.

Other browser manufacturers support their own versions of JavaScript. For their Internet Explorer and Edge browsers, Microsoft uses JScript. For their Chrome browser, Google uses the V8 JavaScript Engine. Fortunately, all the browser manufacturers attempt to follow the ECMAScript

---

[1] Ecma International is a standards organization for information and communication systems. The organization's former name was the European Computer Manufacturers Association (ECMA), but they changed their name to Ecma International (with Ecma no longer being an acronym) to broaden their appeal to those outside of Europe.

[2] Eich, Brendan, "Will there be a suggested file suffix for es4?," Mail.mozilla.org, October 3, 2016, https://mail .mozilla.org/pipermail/es-discuss/2006-October/000133.html.

standard, so for most tasks, programmers can write one version of their code and it will work for all the different browsers. In this book, we stick with standard ECMAScript code that works the same on all browsers. As with almost everyone in the web-programming community, we refer to our code as JavaScript, even though JavaScript is just one of several ECMAScript implementations (JavaScript is the implementation used in Mozilla's Firefox).

## 8.3 Hello World Web Page

When learning a new programming language, your first program is supposed to simply print "Hello, world!" That's the traditional Hello World program. Because the program's task is so simple, the code is short and it gives the learner an opportunity to focus on the syntax basics and not get bogged down with too many details. With that said, your first JavaScript "program" is embedded in **FIGURE 8.1**'s Hello web page, which displays "Hello, world!" when the user clicks the button.

For the book's web pages that use JavaScript, as in the Hello web page shown in Figure 8.1, you'll need to enter the web page's URL in a browser and interact with the web page to fully appreciate how the web page works. The book's preface provides the URL where you can find the book's web pages. So go ahead and find the Hello web page's URL, enter it in a browser, click the web page's button, and be amazed as the "To see the ..." text gets replaced by the large "Hello, world!" text.

Now take a look at the Hello web page's source code in **FIGURE 8.2**. You can see that there's not much JavaScript—it's just the code in the `script` container and the code that follows the `onclick` attribute. The rest of the web page is HTML code. Later, we'll explain the JavaScript

**FIGURE 8.1 Initial display and what happens after the user clicks the button on the Hello web page**

```
<!DOCTYPE html>
<html lang="en">
<head>
<meta charset="utf-8">
<meta name="author" content="John Dean">
<title>Hello</title>
<script>
  function displayHello() {
    var msg;
    msg = document.getElementById("message");
    msg.outerHTML = "<h1>Hello, world!</h1>";
  }
</script>
</head>

<body>
<h3 id="message">
  To see the traditional first-program greeting, click below.
</h3>
<input type="button" value="Click Me!" onclick="displayHello();">
</body>
</html>
```

JavaScript code

**FIGURE 8.2 Source code for Hello web page**

code that handles the text replacement when the user clicks the button, but let's first examine the HTML code that's in charge of displaying the web page's button.

# 8.4 Buttons

There are different types of buttons, each with its own syntax. To keep things simple, we'll start with just one type of button, and here's its syntax:

```
<input type="button"
  value="button-label"
  onclick="click-event-handler">
```

Note that the code is a void element that uses the input tag. As its name suggests, the input tag implements elements that handle user input. You might not think of a button as user input, but it is—the user chooses to do something by clicking a button. Later, we'll introduce other user input elements (e.g., text controls and checkboxes) that also use the input tag.

As we've done throughout the book when introducing new constructs, the prior code fragment shows only the most important syntax details, so you don't get overwhelmed with too much to remember. We're showing the input element's most common attributes—type, value, and onclick. Note how the input element at the bottom of Figure 8.2 follows this syntax pattern and includes those three attributes.

The `input` element is used for different types of user input, and its `type` attribute specifies which type of user input. More formally, the `type` attribute specifies the type of *control* that's being implemented, where a control is a user input entity such as a button, text control, or checkbox. In the Hello web page source code, note that the `type` attribute gets the value `button`, which tells the browser to display a button. If you don't provide a `type` attribute, the browser will display a text control, because that's the default type of control for the `input` element. We'll describe text controls later in this chapter. For now, just know that a *text control* is a box that a user can enter text into, and this is what a (filled-in) text control (with a prompt at its left) looks like:

First Name:   | Ahmed |

Because it uses a box, many web developers refer to text controls as "text boxes." We use the term "text control" because that's the term used more often by the HTML standards organizations.

The `input` element's `value` attribute specifies the button's label. If you don't provide a `value` attribute, the button will have no label. If you want a button with no label, rather than just omitting the `value` attribute, we recommend that you specify `value=""`. That's a form of self-documentation, and it makes your code more understandable.

The `input` element's `onclick` attribute specifies the JavaScript instructions that the JavaScript engine executes when the user clicks the button. What's a JavaScript engine, you ask? A *JavaScript engine* is the part of the browser software that runs a web page's JavaScript. In the Hello web page, the `onclick` attribute's value is JavaScript code that "handles" what's supposed to happen when the user clicks the button. Clicking the button is considered to be an *event*, so the `onclick` attribute's JavaScript code is known as an *event handler*. Besides `onclick`, there are other attributes that call event handlers, like `onfocus` and `onload`, but they aren't used much for buttons, so they won't be introduced until later, when they will be more useful with other types of controls.

In the Hello web page source code, note that the `onclick` attribute's value is simply `displayHello();`. That calls the `displayHello` function, which is defined in the web page's `script` block. We'll discuss function calls and function definitions in the next section.

## 8.5 Functions

A function in JavaScript is similar to a mathematical function. A mathematical function receives arguments, performs a calculation, and returns an answer. For example, the sin(*x*) mathematical function receives the *x* argument, calculates the sine of the given *x* angle, and returns the calculated sine of *x*. Likewise, a JavaScript function might receive arguments, will perform a calculation, and might return an answer. Here's the syntax for calling a function:

*function-name(zero-or-more-arguments-separated-by-commas)* ;

As mentioned earlier, the **Hello web page** button has an `onclick` attribute with a value of `displayHello();`. That's a JavaScript function call, and its syntax matches the preceding syntax. Note the parentheses are empty because there's no need to pass any argument values to the `displayHello` function. If there were arguments, they would need to be separated by commas, and proper style suggests that you insert a space after each comma.

Here's the syntax for a function definition:

```
function function-name (zero-or-more-parameters-separated-by-commas) {
    statement-1;
    statement-2;
    ...
    last-statement;
}
```

And here's the `displayHello` function definition from the Hello web page:

```
function displayHello() {                           ← function heading
    var msg;
    msg = document.getElementById("message");
    msg.outerHTML = "<h1>Hello, world!</h1>";       ← function body
}
```

You should be able to recognize that the `displayHello` function definition follows the prior syntax. The parentheses in the *function heading* are empty because the function call's parentheses are empty (the function call was `displayHello();`). If there are arguments in the function call, then you'll normally have the same number of parameters in the function heading—one parameter to receive each argument's value. Note how we're using the term *argument* for the values in a function call's parentheses and the term *parameter* for the associated words in a function definition heading's parentheses. Some people use the term argument for both, but to make it easier to distinguish between the function call and the function definition, we'll stick with the separate formal names—argument and parameter.

Normally, function definitions should be placed (1) in a `script` container in the web page's `head` container or (2) in an external JavaScript file. Go back to the Hello web page code in Figure 8.2 and verify that the `displayHello` function definition is in a `script` container. You'll want to use an external JavaScript file if you have lots of JavaScript code. We'll show a web page that uses an external JavaScript file later in the book.

Looking at the previous code fragment, you can see three lines in the function's body. Each line is a JavaScript *statement*, where a statement performs a task. Note the semicolons at the end of all three statements. Semicolons are required at the end of a JavaScript statement only if the JavaScript statement is followed by another JavaScript statement, so it would have been legal to omit the semicolon after the last statement. However, coding conventions dictate that you terminate every statement with a semicolon, even the last one. Why? Suppose there's no semicolon at the end of the last statement and someone later adds a new statement after the last statement. If they forget to insert a semicolon between the two statements, that creates a bug. Another reason to insert a semicolon after the last statement is that if you don't do it, the JavaScript engine does it for you behind the scenes, and that slows things down slightly.

## 8.6 **Variables**

Let's continue working our way through the code in the Hello web page's function. Here's the function's first statement:

```
var msg;
```

The `msg` thing is a variable. You should already be familiar with variables in algebra. You can think of a variable as a box that holds a value. In this case, the `msg` variable will hold a string that forms a message.

Before you use a variable in JavaScript code, you should use `var` to declare the variable in a *declaration statement*. For example:

```
var name;
var careerGoals;
```

Words that are part of the JavaScript language are known as *keywords*. The word `var` is a keyword. On the other hand, `name` and `careerGoals` are not keywords because they are specific to a particular web page's code and not to the JavaScript language in general. In the previous section, we showed the `displayHello` function. In that function, besides `var`, can you identify another keyword? The function heading uses the word `function` and `function` is a keyword. With most of JavaScript's keywords, it's illegal for you as a programmer to redefine them to mean something else. So you cannot use "function" as the name of a variable. Those keywords are "reserved" for the JavaScript language, and they are known as *reserved words*. There are a few keywords that can be redefined by a programmer, but an explanation is beyond the scope of this book. Many programmers use the terms "keywords" and "reserved words" interchangeably, but there is a slight difference, as not all keywords are reserved words.

In most programming languages, when you declare a variable, you specify the type of values that the variable will be allowed to hold—numbers, strings, and so on. However, with JavaScript, you do not specify the variable's type as part of the declaration. The variable's type is determined dynamically by the type of the value that's assigned into the variable. For example:

```
name = "Mia Hamm";
careerGoals = 158;
```

What type of value is `"Mia Hamm"`? A string, since a *string* consists of zero or more characters surrounded by a pair of double quotes (`"`) or a pair of single quotes (`'`). What type of value is 158?[3] A number, since a number consists of digits with an optional decimal point. JavaScript is known as a *loosely typed language*, or a *dynamically typed language*, which means that you do not declare a variable's data type explicitly, and you can assign different types of values into a variable at

---

[3] Mia Hamm held the record of 158 goals in women's international soccer team play until fellow American Abby Wambach broke the record in 2013.

different times during the execution of a program. For example, it would be legal to assign a string to `name` and then later assign a number to `name`. But proper coding conventions dictate that you don't do that, because it can lead to code that's difficult to understand.

## 8.7 Identifiers

An identifier is the technical term for a program component's name—the name of a function, the name of a variable, and the names of other program components we'll get to later on. In the Hello web page, `displayHello` was the identifier for the function name, and `msg` was the identifier for a variable. In naming your variables and functions, the JavaScript engine requires that you follow certain rules. Identifiers must consist entirely of letters, digits, dollar signs (`$`), and/or underscore (`_`) characters. The first character must not be a digit. If you do not follow these rules, your JavaScript code won't work.

Coding-convention rules are narrower than the preceding rules. Coding conventions suggest that you use letters and digits only, not dollar signs or underscores. They also suggest that all letters should be lowercase except the first letter in the second word, third word, and so on. That's referred to as *camel case*, and here are a few examples: `firstName`, `message`, `daysInMonth`. Notice that the identifiers' words are descriptive. Coding conventions suggest that you use descriptive words for your identifiers. Beginning programmers have a tendency to use names like `x`, `y`, and `num`. Normally, those are bad variable names. However, if you have a situation in which you're supposed to read in a number and the number doesn't represent anything special, then `x` or `num` is OK.

If any of the coding conventions are broken, it won't affect your web page's ability to work properly, but your code will be harder to understand and maintain. If your code is harder to understand and maintain, that means programmers who work on the code in the future will have to spend more time in their efforts, and their time costs money. Normally, programmers spend more time working on old code (making bug fixes and making improvements) rather than writing new code, and all that work on old code costs money. So to help with your present or future company's bottom line (profit and world domination), put in the time up front writing good code.

## 8.8 Assignment Statements and Objects

We still haven't finished with the Hello web page. Actually, we still haven't explained the magic behind how the web page replaces the initial message with "Hello, world!" when the user clicks the button. To understand how that works, we need to talk about assignment statements and objects.

Once again, here's the Hello web page's `displayHello` function:

```
function displayHello() {
  var msg;
  msg = document.getElementById("message");
  msg.outerHTML = "<h1>Hello, world!</h1>";
}
```

variable declaration

assignment statements

In the function's body, the first statement is a variable declaration for the `msg` variable. After you declare a variable, you'll want to use it, and the first step in using a variable is to put a value inside it. An assignment statement puts/assigns a value into a variable. As you can see in the preceding example, the function body's second and third statements are assignment statements. The assignment operator (=) assigns the value at the right into a variable at the left. So in the first assignment statement, the `document.getElementById("message")` thing gets assigned into the `msg` variable. In the second assignment statement, the `"<h1>Hello, world!</h1>"` thing gets assigned into the `msg.outerHTML` variable.

Those two assignment statements are pretty confusing. To understand the syntax requires an understanding of objects. An *object* is a software entity that represents something tangible. The fact that it's software means that it can be manipulated with JavaScript code, which provides you, the programmer, with great power!

Behind the scenes, all of the elements in a web page are represented as objects. When a browser loads the Hello web page, the browser software generates objects for the `head` element, the `body` element, the `h3` element, and so on. There's also an object associated with the entire web page, and that object's name is `document`. Each object has a set of related properties, plus a set of behaviors. A *property* is an attribute of an object. A behavior is a task that the object can perform. The `document` object contains properties like the web page's type. Most web pages these days (and all the web pages in this book) have a value of HTML5 for the `document` object's `type` property. But it's possible to have other types, like HTML 4.01 or XHTML 1.0 Strict. The `type` property's value comes from the doctype instruction, which should appear at the top of every web page. Here's the Hello web page's doctype instruction:

```
<!DOCTYPE html>
```

The `html` value indicates that the `document` object's type is HTML5.[4] To access an object's property, you specify the object name, a dot, and then the property name. So to access the current web page's document type, use `document` for the object name, . for dot, and `doctype` for the property. Here's the JavaScript code:

```
document.doctype
```

Remember that an object is not only a set of properties, but also a set of behaviors. One of the `document` object's behaviors is its ability to retrieve an element using the element's `id` value. In JavaScript (and many other programming languages, as well), an object's behaviors are referred to as *methods*. To retrieve an element, the `document` object uses its `getElemementById` method. To call an object's method, you specify the object name, a dot, the method name, and

---

[4] It might seem odd that the `html` value indicates HTML5, but as you might recall, the standards organizations worked very hard to move from older versions of HTML to HTML5. By having `html` indicate HTML5, the W3C makes HTML5 the default and furthers HTML5's position as king. If you want another version of HTML, like HTML 4.01, you have to provide a doctype instruction with a value different from `html`—a value too painfully long and ugly to show here.

then parentheses around any arguments you want to pass to the method. For example, here's the `getElemementById` method call from the Hello web page's `displayHello` function:

```
document.getElementById("message")
```

See how the method call includes `"message"` for its argument? In executing the method call, the JavaScript engine searches for an element with `id="message"`. There is such an element in the Hello web page, and here it is:

```
<h3 id="message">
  To see the traditional first-program greeting, click below.
</h3>
```

So the `getElementById` method call retrieves that `h3` element.

The HTML5 standard says that an `id` attribute's value must be unique for a particular web page. You might recall how we used an `id` attribute to identify a target for a link within a web page. Using an `id` attribute is necessary in that situation because we need a link's target to be unique. Likewise, we use an `id` attribute to retrieve an element (with `getElementById`) so there won't be any confusion in terms of which element to retrieve.

Let's get back to explaining the `displayHello` function. Here it is again:

```
function displayHello() {
  var msg;
  msg = document.getElementById("message");
  msg.outerHTML = "<h1>Hello, world!</h1>";
}
```

Previously, we said the `getElementById` method call retrieves the `h3` element. Well, almost. Actually, the `getElementById` method retrieves the object associated with the `h3` element. In the `displayHello` function, you can see that the `getElementById` method call is on the right-hand side of an assignment statement, so the method's returned value (the `h3` element's object) gets assigned into the variable at the left of the assignment statement. After `msg` gets the `h3` element's object, that object gets updated with this assignment statement:

```
msg.outerHTML = "<h1>Hello, world!</h1>";
```

Note `msg.outerHTML`. All element objects have an `outerHTML` property, which stores the element's code, including the element's start and end tags. The `msg` variable holds the `h3` element's object, so `msg.outerHTML` holds the `h3` element's code. Assigning `<h1>Hello, world!</h1>` to `msg.outerHTML` causes `msg`'s code to be replaced with `<h1>Hello, world!</h1>`. Thus, when the button is clicked, the original `h3` message gets replaced with an `h1` "Hello, world!" message. Go back to Figure 8.1 and confirm that the "Hello, world!" text is larger than the original "To see the …" text. That should make sense, now that you realize that the `h3` start and end tags get replaced with `h1` start and end tags.

As you might have guessed, in addition to `outerHTML`, there's also an `innerHTML` property. It accesses the content that's between the element's start and end tags, and it does not include the element's start and end tags. Later on, we'll use `innerHTML` in a separate web page example.

# 8.9 Document Object Model

Whew! We've finally finished examining the Hello web page code. The examination process required getting down in the weeds and learning about objects. Now let's step back and look at a big-picture issue related to objects. Let's examine how a web page's objects are organized.

The Document Object Model, which is normally referred to as the DOM, models all of the parts of a web page document as nodes in a node tree. A node tree is similar to a directory tree, except instead of showing directories that include other directories (and files), it shows web page elements that include other elements (and text and attributes). Each node represents either (1) an element, (2) a text item that appears between an element's start and end tags, or (3) an attribute within one of the elements. If that doesn't make sense, no worries. See the node tree example in **FIGURE 8.3**, and you should be able to understand things better by examining how the code maps to the nodes in the node tree.

The figure's code is a stripped-down version of the Hello web page code shown earlier, with some of its elements and attributes (e.g., the meta and script elements) removed. The node tree shows blue nodes for each element in the web page code (e.g., head and title). It shows yellow nodes for each text item that appears between an element's start and end tags (e.g., "Hello"). And it shows green nodes for each attribute in the web page document's elements (e.g., h3's id attribute).

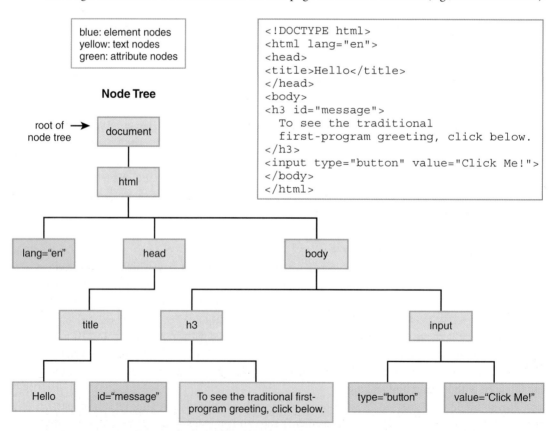

FIGURE 8.3 **Node tree for simplified Hello web page**

Note that the nodes are arranged in a hierarchical fashion, where nodes at the top contain the nodes below them (e.g., the head node contains the title node). The node at the top of the node tree is the document object, which we discussed earlier. Using computer science terminology, the node at the top of a tree is called the *root node*.

The term *dynamic HTML* refers to updating the web page's content by manipulating the DOM's nodes. Assigning a value to an element object's outerHTML property (as in the Hello web page) is one way to implement dynamic HTML. We'll see other techniques later.

The main point of explaining the DOM is for you to get a better grasp of how everything in a web page is represented behind the scenes as an object. As a web programmer, you can use the DOM's hierarchical structure to access and update different parts of the web page. The DOM provides different ways to access the nodes in the node tree. Here are three common techniques:

1.  You can retrieve the node tree's root by using document (for the document object) in your code and then use the root object as a starting point in traversing down the tree.
2.  You can retrieve the node that the user just interacted with (e.g. a button that was clicked) and use that node object as a starting point in traversing up or down the tree.
3.  You can retrieve a particular element node by calling the document object's getElementById method with the element's id value as an argument.

In the Hello web page, we used the third technique, calling getElementById. Later on, we'll provide web page examples that use the first two techniques. We hope you're excited to know what you have to look forward to![5]

# 8.10 Forms and How They're Processed: Client-Side Versus Server-Side

Have you ever filled out input boxes on a web page and clicked submit in order to have some task performed, like converting miles to kilometers or buying a canine selfie stick? If so, you've used a form. A *form* is a mechanism for grouping input controls (e.g., buttons, text controls, and checkboxes) within a web page.

If you've spent much time on the Internet, you probably know that forms are very popular. So why did we wait until now to introduce them? Before this chapter, all you knew was HTML, which is very limited in terms of processing capabilities. With HTML, you can implement forms and controls, but HTML won't help you process the user's input. To make forms useful, you need to read the user's input, process it, and display the results. And to do all that, you need JavaScript.

Before we dig into the details of how to implement a form with HTML and how to process the input with JavaScript, let's look at an example web page that uses a form. **FIGURE 8.4** shows a temperature conversion calculator. Note the quantity text control at the top, the result text control at

---

[5] If you read about those techniques in the later chapters and that doesn't satiate your quest for knowledge, you can learn yet another technique on your own. Using a node object from the DOM node tree, you can call getElementsByTagName to retrieve all of the node's descendant elements that are of a particular type (e.g., all the div elements).

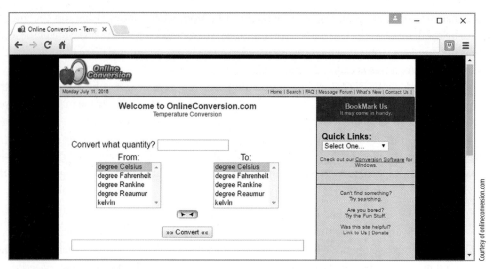

**FIGURE 8.4 Web page that performs temperature conversions**

the bottom, the two list boxes at the sides, and the convert button in the center. All those controls are inside a form. Behind the scenes, the convert button has a JavaScript event handler. When the user clicks the button and submits the form, the event handler code reads the form's input values, does the calculation, and displays the result.

There are two basic strategies for processing a form's input data. The calculations may occur on the *client side* (on the browser's computer) or on the *server side* (on the web server's computer). With server-side processing, the form input values are transmitted across the Internet to the server computer. The server then does the calculations and transmits the answers back to the client computer. The answers are in the form of a new web page or an updated version of the original web page. With client-side processing, there's no need to go back and forth across the Internet with user input and generated results. After the web page downloads, the client computer does all the work. Therefore, client-side processing tends to be faster. So normally, you should use client-side processing for relatively simple web pages.

On the other hand, there are several reasons why server-side processing is sometimes preferable:

▶ When the calculations require a lot of programming code. If client-side processing were used, all the calculation code would have to be downloaded to the client, and that would slow things down. Slowdowns can lead to impatient users giving up and going away.

▶ When the calculations require the use of large amounts of data, which usually means using a database. The rationale is basically the same as for the case where there's lots of programming code. With large amounts of data, you don't want to have to download it across the Internet to the browser because that would slow things down. Therefore, you should keep the data on the server side and do all the processing there.

▶ When the code is proprietary. *Proprietary code* is code that gives the programmer (or, more often, the programmer's company) a competitive advantage. You should keep proprietary code on the server side, where it's more difficult for a competitor or hacker to access it.

▶  When the inputs and/or calculation results need to be shared by other users. In order for the data to be shared, it needs to be transmitted to the server so it can be later transmitted to other users.

▶  When user information needs to be processed securely behind the scenes on the server. For example, credit card numbers and passwords should be processed on the server side.

Quiz time: For Figure 8.4's temperature conversion web page, should processing take place on the client side or the server side? Think before you read on.

The calculations are simple enough that all the programming can be done on the client side, and client-side would lead to a slightly faster experience, so client-side processing is preferred. Be aware that some developers like to use server-side for almost all their web pages. Although that's not recommended, you should be aware that that's sometimes the case. If someone knows a server-side tool really well (e.g., ASP.NET or PHP, which are beyond the scope of this book), they might be inclined to use it for everything. After all, if your only tool is a hammer, everything looks like a nail.

Let's look at a second example web page that uses a form. **FIGURE 8.5** shows a web page that manages the phone numbers for employees at a company. Once again, should processing take

**FIGURE 8.5 Web page that manages the phone numbers for a company's employees**

place on the client side or the server side? With a large company, there would be a large number of employees, a large amount of data, and a database would be appropriate, so server-side processing is the way to go. With a small company, there wouldn't be a large amount of data, but, regardless, you need to save the data permanently on the server side, so the updated employee phone data can be viewed later by other users. So with a small company, server-side processing is still the way to go.

## 8.11 `form` Element

Let's now discuss the `form` element, which is in charge of grouping a form's controls. Here's a template for the `form` element's syntax:

```
<form>
  label
  text-box, list-box, check-box, etc.
  label
  text-box, list-box, check-box, etc.
  ...
  submit-button
</form>
```

Note how there's a submit button control at the bottom and other controls above it. That's probably the most common layout because it encourages the user to first provide input for the controls at the top before clicking the button at the bottom. However, you should not try to pigeonhole every one of your web page forms into the template. If it's more appropriate to have your submit button at the top or in the middle, then you should put your submit button at the top or in the middle. One other thing to note in the template is the labels. The labels are text prompts that tell the user what to enter in the subsequent controls.

The following code implements a form with two text controls and a submit button:

```
<form>
  First Name:
  <input type="text" id="first" size="15"><br>
  Last Name:
  <input type="text" id="last" size="15"><br><br>
  <input type="button" value="Generate Email"
    onclick="generateEmail(this.form);">
</form>
```

Notice how this code matches the template provided earlier. The first two controls are text controls that hold first name and last name user entries. We'll cover text control syntax details shortly, but not quite yet. The bottom control is a button. When the button is clicked, its `onclick` event handler calls the `generateEmail` function that combines the entered first and last names to form an email address. We'll explain the event handler's `this.form` argument later, when we present the web page that this form is part of. But first, let's finish talking about forms.

Although it's legal to use `input` elements—like text controls and buttons—without surrounding them with a `form` element, you'll usually want to use a form. Here are some reasons for doing so:

▶ Forms can lead to faster JavaScript processing of the input elements. Understanding why that's the case will make sense after we explain the JavaScript code in an upcoming web page later in this chapter.

▶ Forms provide support for being able to check user input to make sure it follows a particular format. That's called *input validation*, and we'll spend a considerable amount of time on it in the next chapter.

▶ Forms provide the ability to add a reset button to assign all the form controls to their original values. To implement a reset button, specify `reset` for the `type` attribute, like this:

```
<input type="reset" value="Reset">
```

## 8.12 Controls

There's lots more syntax to cover when it comes to HTML controls, but before returning to the syntax jungle, a controls overview might be helpful. It's rather difficult to keep track of which controls use which elements, and this section attempts to make the learning process easier. Read it now and use it as a reference later.

**FIGURE 8.6** shows some of the more popular controls and the elements used to implement them. As you can see, most of the controls use the `input` element for their implementation. But just to make things difficult,[6] not all controls use the `input` element. Some important controls use the `select` and `textarea` elements.

In the figure, note the controls in the first table that use the `input` element. You've already learned about the button control. You've been introduced to the text control, and you'll learn its syntax details in the next section. You'll learn about the number control in Chapter 9. For now,

| input Element |
| --- |
| button |
| text control |
| number |
| radio button |
| checkbox |
| password |
| date |
| color |

| select Element |
| --- |
| pull-down menu |
| list box |

| textarea Element |
| --- |
| textarea control |

**FIGURE 8.6 Some of the more popular controls and the elements used to implement them**

[6] Although difficulty is generally not fun, it's not *always* bad. As difficulty goes up, web programmer wages go up.

just know that the number control provides a mechanism for users to enter a number for input, and it has built-in checking to make sure the input is a properly formatted number. You'll learn about the radio button and checkbox controls in Chapter 10. You've probably seen those controls many times on the Web, so we'll forgo a preliminary explanation at this point.

At this point, we're not providing code examples for the password, date, and color controls, but you should understand what they do. The password control allows the user to enter text into a box where, to help with privacy, the entered characters are obscured. Typically, that means the characters display as bullets. The date control allows the user to enter a month-day-year value for a date. Most browsers implement the date control with a drop-down calendar where the user picks a date from it. Note **FIGURE 8.7**, which shows a calendar displayed after the user clicks the down arrow on the date control's top-right corner. The color control enables the user to select a color from a *color picker* tool. Figure 8.7 shows a color picker displayed after the user clicks the color control's black button.

Be aware that you might run into older browsers that don't support the date and color controls fully. Instead of displaying date and color pickers, they just display boxes that users can enter text into.[7]

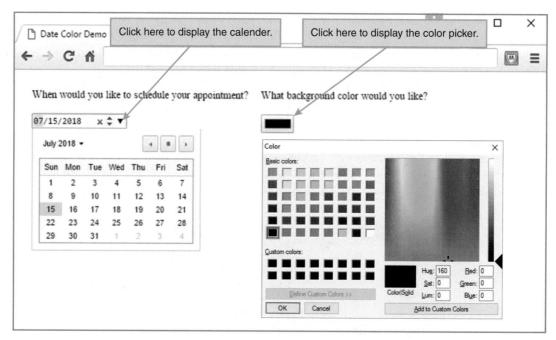

**FIGURE 8.7 Web page that illustrates the date and color controls**

[7] Web Hypertext Application Technology Working Group (WHATWG), "The `input` element," https://html.spec.whatwg.org/#the-input-element. We encourage you to peruse the WHATWG's `input` element page for more details about the password, date, and color controls, and to learn about all the other controls that use the `input` element.

In Figure 8.6, note the two controls that use the `select` element—the pull-down menu and list box controls. You'll learn about those controls in Chapter 10. Both controls allow the user to select an item(s) from a list of items. The pull-down menu control normally displays just one item at a time from the list and displays the rest of the list only after the user clicks the control's down arrow. On the other hand, the list box control displays multiple list items simultaneously without requiring the user to click a down arrow.

And finally, in Figure 8.6, note the control that uses the `textarea` element—the textarea control. You'll learn about the textarea control in Chapter 10. For now, just know that it allows the user to enter text into a multiline box. So it's the same as the text control except for the height of the box. We cover the text control in all its glory in the next section.

## 8.13 **Text Control**

Earlier, we described the text control as a box that a user can enter text into. Now it's time to dig into text control details. Here's a template for the text control's syntax:

```
<input type="text" id="text-box-identifier"
  placeholder="user-entry-description"
  size="box-width" maxlength="maximum-typed-characters">
```

As you can see, and as you might recall from our description of the button control, the `input` element is a void element, so there's just one tag and no end tag.

The preceding text control template does not include all the attributes for a text control—just the more important ones. We'll describe the attributes shown, plus a few others shortly, but let's first look at an example text control code fragment:

```
<input type="text" id="ssn"
  placeholder="#########" size="9" maxlength="9">
```

Note how the example follows the syntax pattern shown earlier. The text control is for storing a Social Security number, so the `id` attribute's `ssn` value is an abbreviation for Social Security number. What's the purpose of the nine #'s for the `placeholder` attribute? Social Security numbers have nine digits, so the nine #'s implicitly tell the user to enter nine digits with no hyphens.

### Attributes

Here are the text control attributes we'll talk about in this subsection:

| Text Control Attributes | | | | | | | | |
|---|---|---|---|---|---|---|---|---|
| type | id | placeholder | size | maxlength | value | autofocus | disabled | readonly |

As mentioned earlier (when describing the `input` element for the button control), the `type` attribute specifies the type of control. For a text control, use `type="text"`. The default value for the `type` attribute is `text`, so if you omit the `type` attribute, you'll get a text control. But for self-documentation purposes, we recommend that you always include `type="text"` for your text controls.

The `id` attribute's value serves as an identifier for the text control, so it can be accessed with JavaScript. Previously, in the Hello web page, we used an `h3` element's id value and called `getElementById` to retrieve the object associated with the `h3` element. In an upcoming example, we'll do the same thing using a text control's `id` value.

The `placeholder` attribute provides a word or a short description that helps the user to know what to enter into the text control. When the page loads, the browser puts the `placeholder`'s value in the text control. As soon as the user enters a character into the text control, the entire `placeholder` value disappears.

The `size` attribute specifies the text control's width, where the width value is an integer that approximates the number of average-size characters that can fit in the box. So `size="5"` means approximately 5 characters could display in the box simultaneously. The default size is 20.

The `maxlength` attribute specifies the maximum number of characters that can be entered in the box. By default, an unlimited number of characters is allowed. Entries that exceed the box's width cause input scrolling to occur.

The next four attributes are popular, but not quite as popular as the prior attributes, and that's why they don't appear in the previous text control example. Like the other attributes, they are not required by the HTML5 standard. Use them if you need them.

The `value` attribute specifies an initial value for the text control. The `value` attribute's value is treated as user input. If the user wants a different input, the user must first delete the `value` attribute's value. If the user does nothing and there's JavaScript code that retrieves the user input, it gets the `value` attribute's value by default.

The `autofocus` attribute specifies that after the page has loaded, the browser engine positions the cursor in the text control. To achieve autofocus, specify `autofocus` by itself. As you may recall, when you specify an attribute by itself, that's known as an *empty attribute*.

The `disabled` attribute specifies that the text control cannot receive the focus, and, therefore, the user cannot copy or edit the text control's value. To disable a control, specify `disabled` by itself. The `readonly` attribute specifies that the user can highlight the control's value and copy it, but the user cannot edit it. To make a control read-only, specify `readonly` by itself. For disabled and read-only text controls, the only way to change their values is to use JavaScript assignment statements. You'll see an example of that later in this chapter.

## 8.14 Email Address Generator Web Page

In this section, we examine a web page that uses text controls for a person's first and last names. In **FIGURE 8.8**, you can see what happens on that web page when the user clicks the **Generate Email** button. The underlying JavaScript code retrieves the text controls' user-entered values and displays an email address that's built with those values.

In dissecting the Email Address Generator web page's implementation, let's start with the body container, which you can see in **FIGURE 8.9A**. Note the `form` container and the `h3`

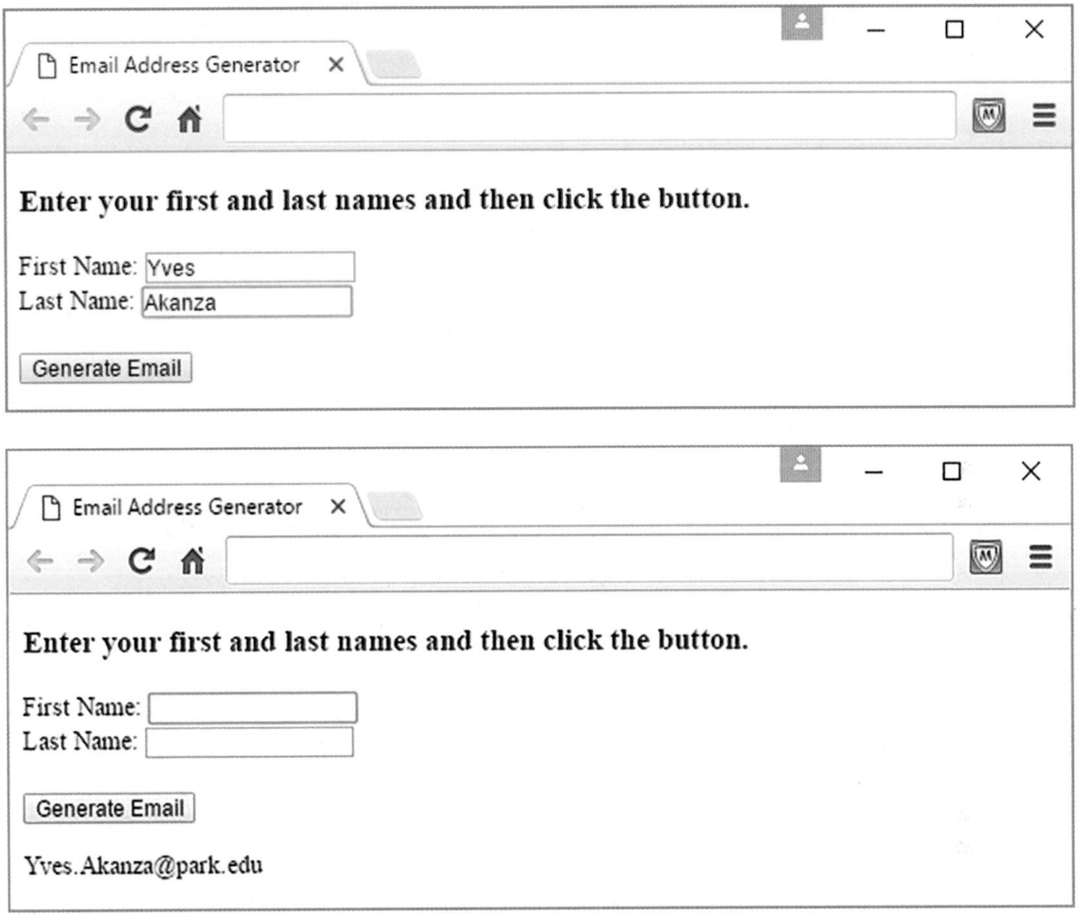

**FIGURE 8.8** Email Address Generator web page—what happens after the user enters first and last names and what happens after the user clicks the **Generate Email** button

element above the form. It would be legal to move the h3 element inside the form, but we recommend not doing so. It's good to keep the form clean, with just control elements and their labels inside it. As you'll see later, having less content within a form can lead to faster retrieval of user input.

Note the two text controls with `size="15"`. So are the user entries limited to 15 characters each? No. The boxes are 15 characters wide, but the user can enter as many characters as desired. Note the first-name text control's `autofocus` attribute. That causes the browser to load the web page with the cursor in that text control.

Note the p element below the form. It's a placeholder for the generated email address. When the user clicks the button, the JavaScript engine calls the `generateEmail` function, which assigns the generated email address to the empty area between the p element's start and end tags.

```
<body>
<h3>
  Enter your first and last names and then click the button.
</h3>
<form>
  First Name:
  <input type="text" id="first" size="15" autofocus>
  <br>
  Last Name:
  <input type="text" id="last" size="15">
  <br><br>
  <input type="button" value="Generate Email"
    onclick="generateEmail(this.form);">
</form>
<p id="email"></p>
</body>
</html>
```

Use `autofocus` for the first-name text control.

The `this` keyword refers to the object that contains the JavaScript in which `this` appears. In this example, the enclosing object is the button element's object.

**FIGURE 8.9A** body **container for Email Address Generator web page**

Note the `this.form` argument in the button event handler's `generateEmail` function call. The `this.form` argument requires some in-depth explanation. In the `generateEmail` function (which we'll examine later), we'll need to retrieve the user inputs from the form. To make that possible, when the user clicks the button, we need to pass the form to the `generateEmail` function. So why `this.form` for the generateEmail function call's argument? In general, the `this` keyword refers to the object that contains the JavaScript in which `this` appears. Specifically in this example, the enclosing object is the button element's object. The button element's object has a `form` property that holds the form that surrounds the button. Therefore, we can pass the form object to the `generateEmail` function by calling `generateEmail(this.form)`.

## 8.15 Accessing a Form's Control Values

In the previous section, you learned how the Email Address Generator's button event handler passes its form object to the `generateEmail` function by using `this.form`. In this section, we'll examine the function itself and learn how to use the form object to access control values within the form.

As you learned earlier, whenever you pass an argument to a function, you should have an associated parameter in the function's heading. Therefore, to receive the form object passed to the `generateEmail` function, there's a `form` parameter in the function's heading, as you can see here:

```
function generateEmail(form)
```

**FIGURE 8.9B** shows the head container for the Email Address Generator web page. Note the form parameter in the generateEmail function's heading. Be aware that you're not required to use the word "form" for the parameter. We could have used a different parameter name, like "namesForm," but then everywhere you see form within the function body, we'd need to change it to the new parameter name.

Within the generateEmail function body, we use the form parameter to retrieve the text control user inputs. Here's the code for retrieving the user input from the first-name text control:

```
form.elements["first"].value
```

To access the controls that are within a form, we use the form object's elements property. The elements property holds a collection of controls, where a *collection* is a group of items that are of the same type. To access a control within the elements collection, you put quotes around the control's id value and surround the quoted value with []'s. So in the preceding code, you can see first within the []'s, and first is the value for the control's id attribute. Go back to Figure 8.9A and verify that the first-name text control uses id="first". After retrieving the control, there's still one more step (which people forget all the time). To get the user input, you need more than just the control by itself; you need to access the control's value property as shown.

As an alternative to using form.elements["first"], you can use form["first"]. We don't use the form[] syntax in the book's examples because it uses quirky syntax that works with JavaScript, but not with other programming languages. You should get used to standard

```
<!DOCTYPE html>
<html lang="en">
<head>
<meta charset="utf-8">
<meta name="author" content="John Dean">
<title>Email Address Generator</title>
<script>
  // This function generates an email address.

  function generateEmail(form)
    document.getElementById("email").innerHTML =
      form.elements["first"].value + "." +
      form.elements["last"].value + "@park.edu";
    form.reset();
    form.elements["first"].focus();
  } // end generateEmail
</script>
</head>
```

Parameter that holds the form object.

**FIGURE 8.9B** head **container for Email Address Generator web page**

programming language syntax. The `elements` property is a collection of things, and in JavaScript, to access an element within a collection, you use `[]`'s. On the other hand, `form["first"]` relies on the form object somehow morphing into a collection so `[]`'s are used—very odd indeed! But on the other other hand (assuming you have three hands), if you feel comfortable using the `form[]` syntax, go for it. It uses less code, which leads to slightly faster downloads.

## JavaScript Object Properties and HTML Element Attributes

In the `form.elements["first"].value` code fragment shown in the previous section, the `value` property returns the text control's user-entered value. If there's no user entry, then the value of the text control's `value` attribute is returned. If there's no user entry and there's also no `value` attribute, then the value property holds the empty string by default. Having a corresponding JavaScript `value` property for the HTML `value` attribute is indicative of a pattern. There's a parallel world between JavaScript properties and HTML element attributes. In our earlier presentation of the text control element's syntax, we showed these text control element attributes:

```
type, placeholder, size, maxlength, value, autofocus, disabled,
readonly
```

Here are the corresponding JavaScript properties for a text control element object:

```
type, placeholder, size, maxLength, value, autofocus, disabled,
readOnly
```

Note that HTML attributes use all lowercase, whereas JavaScript properties use camel case, which means the two-word properties are spelled `maxLength` and `readOnly`. Get used to that weirdness—use all lowercase for HTML attributes, but camel case for JavaScript properties. JavaScript is case sensitive, so you must use camel case for your code to work. HTML is not case sensitive, but you should use all lowercase in order to exhibit proper style.

## Control Elements' `innerHTML` Property

In the Email Address Generator web page's `generateEmail` function, the goal is to update the following p element by replacing its empty content with a generated email address:

```
<p id="email"></p>
```

To do that, we retrieve the p element's object and then use its `innerHTML` property, like this:

```
document.getElementById("email").innerHTML
```

Remember the `outerHTML` property? It accesses the control element's code, including its start and end tags. The `innerHTML` property accesses the content within the control element's code, not including its start and end tags.

In the `generateEmail` function, here's the assignment statement that uses `innerHTML` to update the p element with a generated email address:

```
document.getElementById("email").innerHTML =
   form.elements["first"].value + "." +
   form.elements["last"].value + "@park.edu";
```

↑

| string concatenation operator |

To connect a string to something else (e.g., another string, a number), you need to use the concatenation operator, +. The resulting connected value forms a string. So in the preceding assignment statement, the three concatenation operations form a single string, and that string gets assigned into the `innerHTML` part of the retrieved p element.

In the `generateEmail` function, we use `form.elements` to retrieve the two text controls. As an alternative, we could have used `document.getElementById` to retrieve the controls (e.g., `document.getElementById["first"]`). Why is it better to use `form.elements`? Because `document.getElementById` has to search through all the element nodes in the web page's entire node tree, whereas `form.elements` has to search through only the control nodes in the form part of the web page's node tree. This difference in speed won't be noticeable with web pages that don't use much code (like the Email Address Generator web page), but it's good to use coding practices that *scale* well to web pages with lots of code.

## 8.16 `reset` and `focus` Methods

Go back to Figure 8.9B, and you can see that we still haven't talked about the last two lines in the generateEmail function. Here are those lines:

```
form.reset();
form.elements["first"].focus();
```

The form object's `reset` method reassigns the form's controls to their original values. Because the Email Address Generator web page has no `value` attributes for its text controls, the `reset` method call assigns empty strings to the text controls, thereby blanking them out.

When an element object calls the `focus` method, the browser puts the focus on the element's control if it's possible to do so. For text control elements, like the first-name text control retrieved in the preceding code, putting the focus on it means the browser positions the cursor in the text control.

## 8.17 Comments and Coding Conventions

In prior chapters, you learned about various coding conventions for HTML and CSS. Earlier in this chapter, you learned a few coding conventions for JavaScript, such as needing to use descriptive variable names. In this section, you'll get a deeper immersion into JavaScript coding conventions. Remember—it's important to follow coding conventions so your code is understandable, robust, and easy to maintain.

## Comments

Let's start with a very important coding convention—use appropriate comments. JavaScript has two types of comments: one type for short comments and one type for longer comments. The syntax for short comments is simply two forward slashes (//) at the left of the descriptive text. Here's an example:

```
// An "admin" user can create and edit accounts.
form.elements["username"].value = "admin";
```

The JavaScript engine ignores JavaScript comments, so why bother to include them? One of the primary purposes of comments is to explain tricky code so programmers can understand the code more easily. Some programmers might find the preceding `focus` method call confusing, and the comment attempts to alleviate some of that confusion.

If you have a comment that spans multiple lines, you can preface each line of the comment with its own //, but that can get cumbersome for long comments. For long comments, you'll normally want to use the other JavaScript comment syntax. Here's the syntax for the other type of comment:

```
/* descriptive-text-goes-here */
```

Typically, this syntax is used for comments that span multiple lines, but it's legal to use it for single-line comments as well. Here's an example comment that spans multiple lines:

```
/* After entering an invalid password 3 times, disable the
    password control so the user cannot try again this session.*/
form.elements["password"].readOnly = true;
```

The /* ... */ syntax should look familiar. CSS uses the same syntax for its comments.

In all of these examples, note the blank spaces next to each of the comment characters (after //, after /*, and before */). The spaces are not required by the JavaScript language, but coding conventions suggest that you include them. Why? So the words in your comments stand out and are clear.

## Code Skeleton That Illustrates Coding Conventions

There are quite a few coding conventions that we'd like to introduce in rapid-fire succession. To help with the explanations, we'll refer you to the code skeleton shown in **FIGURE 8.10**.

As stated earlier, you should use comments to explain tricky code. In addition, you should include a comment above every function to describe the function's purpose. To make a function's preliminary comment and its subsequent function heading stand out, you should insert a blank line between them. In Figure 8.10, note the two functions and the comments with blank lines above them.

As you read the following coding conventions, for each convention, go to Figure 8.10 and verify that the code skeleton follows that convention:

▸ If there are two or more functions, separate each adjacent pair of functions with a line of *'s surrounded by blank lines.

- ▶ Put all variable declarations at the top of a function's body, and for each variable declaration, provide a comment that describes the variable.
- ▶ Provide an "end ..." comment for each function's closing brace.
- ▶ Position a function's opening brace ({) at the right of the function heading, separated by a space.
- ▶ Position a function's closing brace (}) in the same column as the function heading's first character.
- ▶ Between a function's opening and closing braces, indent each statement with two spaces.

We'll introduce coding conventions throughout the book's remaining chapters. Appendix B describes all of the JavaScript coding conventions used in this book. Go ahead and skim through it now, and refer back to it later on as questions arise.

## Why You Should Use `var` for Variable Declarations

Earlier in the chapter, you were told that before you use a variable, you should use `var` to declare the variable in a declaration statement. Unfortunately, many JavaScript programmers do not use `var`, and you should understand why it's better to use `var`.

Using `var` helps programmers to identify the variables in a function quickly, and that makes the function easier to understand and maintain. If `var` is not used for a variable, then the JavaScript engine creates a *global variable*. A global variable is a variable that's shared between all the functions for a particular web page. Such sharing can be dangerous in that if you coincidentally use same-named variables in different functions, changing the variable's value in one function affects the variable in the other function.

By using `var`, you can use same-named variables in different functions, and the JavaScript engine creates separate local variables. A local variable is a variable that can be used only within the function in which it is declared (with `var`). The *scope* of a variable refers to where the variable

```
// Check whether the entered username is valid.

function validUsername(form) {
  var username; // object for username text control
  ...
} // end validUsername

//**************************************

// Check whether the entered password is valid.

function validPassword(form) {
  var password; // object for username text control
  ...
} // end validPassword
```

**FIGURE 8.10 Code skeleton that illustrates coding conventions**

can be used, so the scope of a function's local variables is limited to the function's body. If you have same-named local variables in different functions, changing one of the variables won't affect the other variable because each variable is a separate entity. Such separation is normally considered a good thing because that makes it harder for the programmer to accidentally mess things up.

## 8.18 Event-Handler Attributes

Remember the `onclick` attribute for the button control's input element? That attribute is known as an *event-handler attribute* because its value is an event handler. As you know, an event handler is JavaScript code that tells the JavaScript engine what to do when a particular event takes place. When an event takes place, we say that the event *fires*. For the button control's `onclick` attribute, the event is clicking the button.

Take a look at the table of event-handler attributes and their associated events in **FIGURE 8.11**. We'll provide a brief overview of those event-handler attributes in this section and put them to use in web page examples later on.[8]

The first event-handler attribute shown in Figure 8.11's table is `onclick`, which you should already be familiar with. It's very common to use `onclick` with a button, but the HTML5 standard indicates that you can use it with any element.

The next event-handler attribute is `onfocus`. You can use `onfocus` to do something special when a control gains focus. For example, when the user clicks within a text control, you could implement an `onfocus` event handler to make the text control's text become blue.

The next event-handler attribute is `onchange`. You can use `onchange` to do something special when a control's value changes. For example, when the user clicks a radio button, you could implement an `onchange` event handler that displays an "Are you sure you want to change your selection?" message.

| Event-Handler Attributes | Events |
|---|---|
| onclick | User clicks on an element. |
| onfocus | An element gains focus. |
| onchange | The value of a form control has been changed. |
| onmouseover | Mouse moves over an element. |
| onmouseout | Mouse moves off an element. |
| onload | An element finishes loading. |

FIGURE 8.11 **Some of the more popular event-handler attributes and their associated events**

---

[8] Web Hypertext Application Technology Working Group (WHATWG), "Event handlers on elements, Document objects, and Window objects," https://html.spec.whatwg.org/multipage/webappapis.html#event -handlers-on-elements,-document-objects,-and-window-objects. If you'd like to learn about additional event-handler attributes, peruse the WHATWG's event handler page.

The next event-handler attributes, `onmouseover` and `onmouseout`, are often used to implement rollovers for `img` elements. The mouseover event is triggered when the mouse moves on top of an element. The mouseout event is triggered when the mouse moves off of an element.

The last event-handler attribute shown in Figure 8.11 is `onload`. The load event is triggered when the browser finishes loading an element. It's common to use the `onload` attribute with the `body` element so you can do something special after the entire web page loads.

## 8.19 `onchange, onmouseover, onmouseout`

In this section, we provide web page examples that put into practice what you learned earlier about event-handler attributes. Specifically, we'll use the `onchange` event-handler attribute to improve the Email Address Generator web page. Then we'll use `onmouseover` and `onmouseout` to implement a rollover in another web page.

### Improving the Email Address Generator Web Page with `onchange`

In the Email Address Generator web page, suppose you want to force the user to enter the first name before the last name. To do that, you can disable the last-name text control initially and remove that restriction after the first-name text control has been filled in. To determine whether the first-name text control has been filled in, you can rely on the text control's change event firing. A text control's change event fires after the user clicks or tabs away from the text control after the user has made changes to the text control. By adding an `onchange` event-handler attribute to the text control's `input` element, the text control can "listen" for the first-name text control being changed and then act accordingly.

In implementing the improvements to the Email Address Generator web page, the first step is to disable the last-name text control when the web page first loads. Note the `disabled` attribute:

```
Last Name:
<input type="text" id="last" size="15" disabled>
```

The next step involves adding an `onchange` event handler to the first-name text control's `input` element. Note the `onchange` event handler:

```
First Name:
<input type="text" id="first" size="15" autofocus
   onchange = "this.form.elements['last'].disabled=false;">
```

| 1. Spaces around = . | 2. Retrieve the form object. | 3. Retrieve the last-name text control object. | 4. Make the control active (not disabled). |

Before we explain the onchange event handler's rather complicated details, let's first appreciate its overall nature. In our previous event-handler examples, the event handler has always been a function call, like this:

```
onclick="generateEmail(this.form)";
```

With a function call, the work is done in the function's body. In the onchange event handler shown earlier, the event handler contains code that does the work "inline." Inline JavaScript is appropriate when there is just one statement and there is only one place on the web page where the code is used. An advantage of using inline JavaScript is that it can lead to code that is easier to understand because all the code (the HTML control code and the event handler JavaScript code) is in one place.

Now let's dig into the details of the onchange event handler shown earlier. The following four items refer to four noteworthy details from the onchange event handler. As you read each item, go to the same-numbered callout next to the onchange event handler code fragment and see where the item is located within the code fragment.

1. For normal attribute-value pairs, you should not surround the = with spaces. But for an event-handler attribute, if its value is not short, separate the value from the attribute with spaces around the =. For the onchange event handler, we have inline JavaScript code and the event handler is not short, so spaces around the = are appropriate.
2. If you're inside a form control, to retrieve the form element's object, use this.form. The example code fragment is for an input element, and the input element is indeed inside a form (as you can verify by going back to the web page's source code in Figure 8.9A).
3. To retrieve the last-name text control object, specify elements['last'] with single quotes around 'last' to avoid terminating the prior opening double quote. In the event-handler code fragment, note the double quote that begins the onchange attribute's value. To nest strings inside strings, you can use double quotes for the outer string and single quotes for the inner string (as shown in the example code fragment) or vice versa.
4. To make the retrieved text control active (not disabled), assign false to the text control object's disabled property.

Suppose you've added the disabled attribute to the last-name text control and the onchange event handler to the first-name text control as described earlier. With the new code added, what happens after a user clicks the **Generate Email** button and wants to enter first and last names for a second email address? Will the user's experience be the same? (Having a consistent experience is a good thing, by the way.) Specifically, will the user again be forced to enter the first name first?

Well… actually no. The onchange event handler activates the last-name text control, and it remains active after that. So, what's the solution? After clicking the button, you need to disable the last-name text control. To do that, you should add this code at the bottom of the `generateEmail` function:

```
form.elements["last"].disabled = true;
```

## Implementing a Rollover with `onmouseover` and `onmouseout`

A rollover is when an image file changes due to the user rolling the mouse over the image. As you learned in the previous chapter, you can implement a rollover with a CSS image sprite. Now, you'll learn how to implement a rollover with `onmouseover` and `onmouseout` event handlers that reassign values to the image object.

Take a look at the Scraps the Dog web page in **FIGURE 8.12**. If the user moves the mouse over the image, the browser swaps out the original picture and displays a picture of Scraps at his third birthday party. If the mouse moves off of the image, the browser swaps out the birthday picture and displays the original picture.

**FIGURE 8.13** shows the source code for the Scraps web page. Let's focus on the event-handler code. The `onmouseover` and `onmouseout` event handlers both rely on the `this` keyword. Read the figure's left callout and make sure you understand why `this` refers to the `img` element. With that in mind, `this.src` refers to the `img` element's `src` attribute, which is in charge of specifying the `img` element's image file. So it's the event handlers' assignment of files to the `src` attribute that implements the rollover functionality.

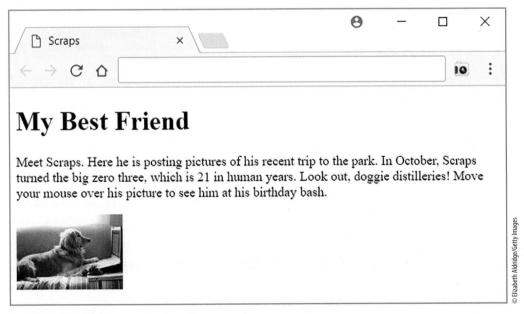

© Elizabeth Aldridge/Getty Images

**FIGURE 8.12 Scraps the Dog web page**

```
<!DOCTYPE html>
<html lang="en">
<head>
<meta charset="utf-8">
<meta name="author" content="John Dean">
<title>Scraps</title>
</head>

<body>
<h1>My Best Friend</h1>
<p>
  Meet Scraps. Here he is posting pictures of his recent
  trip to the park. In October, Scraps turned the big
  zero three, which is 21 in human years. Look out, doggie
  distilleries! Move your mouse over his picture
  to see him at his birthday bash.
</p>
<img scr="../images/scrapsAtWork.jpg"
  width="130" height="90" alt="Scraps"
  onmouseover =
    "this.src='../images/scrapsThirdBirthday.jpg';"
  onmouseout = "this.src='../images/scrapsAtWork.jpg';">
</body>
</html>
```

> The `this` keyword refers to the object that contains the script in which `this` is used. In this example, the enclosing object is the `img` element's object.

> For statements that are too long to fit on one line, press enter at an appropriate breaking point, and indent.

**FIGURE 8.13 Source code for Scraps the Dog web page**

Read the right callout in Figure 8.13 and note the line break in the source code after `onmouseover =`. The line break is necessary because the event-handler code is long enough to run the risk of bumping against the edge of a printer's right margin. If that happens, then line wrap occurs. Several chapters ago, we introduced the concept of line wrap for HTML code, and the concept is the same with JavaScript code. For statements that might be too long to fit onto one line, press enter at an appropriate breaking point, and on the next line, indent past the starting point of the prior line.

## 8.20 Using `noscript` to Accommodate Disabled JavaScript

So far, you might have assumed that all users will be able to take advantage of the cool JavaScript that you've learned. That assumption is valid for the vast majority of users, but with 3.7 billion users in the world and counting,[9] you'll probably run into a lack of JavaScript support every now and then.

Older browsers don't support JavaScript, but the bigger roadblock is that some users intentionally disable JavaScript on their browsers. Typically, they do that because they're concerned that executing JavaScript code can be a security risk. However, most security experts agree that JavaScript is relatively safe. After all, it was/is designed to have limited capabilities. For example, JavaScript is unable to access a user's computer in terms of the computer's files and what's in the computer's memory. Also, JavaScript can send requests to web servers only in a constrained (and safe) manner.

Despite JavaScript's built-in security measures, some users will continue to disable JavaScript on their browsers. For your web pages that use JavaScript, it's good practice to display a warning message on browsers that have JavaScript disabled. To display such a message on only those browsers and not on browsers that have JavaScript enabled, use the `noscript` element. Specifically, add a `noscript` container to the top of your `body` container, and insert explanatory text inside the `noscript` container. Here's an example:

```
<noscript>
  <p>
    This web page uses JavaScript. For proper results,
    you must use a web browser with JavaScript enabled.
  </p>
</noscript>
```

---

[9] InternetLiveStats.com, "*Internet Users*," http://www.internetlivestats.com/internet-users

# Review Questions

**8.2 History of JavaScript**

1.  Which is JavaScript closer to—LiveScript or Java?

2.  What is ECMAScript?

**8.4 Buttons**

3.  For a button control, what does the `input` element's `value` attribute specify?

4.  What is an event handler?

**8.6 Variables**

5.  What is a keyword? Provide two examples.

**8.8 Assignment Statements and Objects**

6.  In JavaScript, what is a property?

7.  An `id` attribute's value must be unique for a particular web page. True or false.

**8.9 Document Object Model**

8.  What are the three types of nodes in the DOM's node tree?

9.  What object is the root node of the DOM's node tree?

**8.13 Text Control**

10.  What's the difference between the text control's `size` attribute and its `maxlength` attribute?

11.  What's an empty attribute?

**8.14 Email Address Generator Web Page**

12.  What is the `this` keyword?

**8.15 Accessing a Form's Control Values**

13.  What operator is in charge of connecting a string to something else to form a larger string?

**8.17 Comments and Coding Conventions**

14.  The most common syntax for comments is `//`. When is it appropriate to use the `/* ... */` syntax for comments?

15.  What is the scope of a local variable?

**8.19 `onchange`, `onmouseover`, `onmouseout`**

16.  To implement a rollover with JavaScript, what two event-handler attributes should you use?

### 8.20 Using `noscript` to Accommodate Disabled JavaScript

**17.** List several security measures that are built into JavaScript.

**18.** What is the purpose of the `noscript` element?

# Exercises

**1.** [after Section 8.5] Why is it appropriate to terminate every statement with a semicolon, even the last one in a function? Provide two reasons.

**2.** [after Section 8.7] For each of the following variable names, indicate (with *Y* or *N*) whether it's legal and whether it uses proper style. Note: You may skip the style question for illegal variable names because style is irrelevant in that case.

                                    legal (Y/N)?        proper style (Y/N)?

```
a)  _totalPages

b)  2ndTeam

c)  car Color

d)  weight#of#specimen

e)  seatNumber

f)  BookCost$
```

**3.** [after Section 8.10] Find a website, or just imagine a website, where users are able to make reservations at restaurants. Should such a website be implemented with client-side technology or server-side technology? Provide at least two reasons that justify your answer.

**4.** [after Section 8.11] Implement a button that, when clicked, reassigns the form's controls to their original values. The button should be labeled "Start over." Your solution should not use an event handler. Just show the `input` element, nothing else.

**5.** [after Section 8.17] The following code is syntactically correct and would work if combined with the usual HTML structural elements, but it has <u>many</u> style mistakes, a few output display mistakes, and a maintainability mistake. Provide an improved <u>function definition</u> with none of those mistakes.

```
<script>
  function displaymessage (name,month,day,year){
  birthdaywish=document.getElementById("msg");
  birthdaywish.innerHTML=name+"was born on"+month+day+", "+year+".
Happy birthday!"}
</script>
```

```
<body>
<input type="button" value="Click me"
  onclick =
    "displaymessage('Taylor Swift', 'December', '13', '1989');">
<br>
<p id="msg"></p>
</body>
```

6. [after Section 8.17] Why is it good to use `var` for same-named variables that are in different functions?

# Project

Create a web page named `compassGame.html` that displays E (for east), S (for south), N (for north), and W (for west) as shown in the sample session's first screenshot, and asks the user to rearrange the four directions so they are positioned correctly for a compass. In the sample session, note how the three bidirectional arrows swap the direction letters. Initially, the text controls and the **Update** button are disabled. When the user clicks the **Restart** button, the four direction letters are erased, and the text controls and **Update** button are activated. When the user clicks the **Update** button, the text control values are copied to the direction letters, and the text controls and **Update** button are disabled.

Note:

▸ To achieve the proper layout for the direction letters and bidirectional arrows, use the CSS `display` property with table values. And for the table rows and cells, use CSS child selector rules, not class selector rules.

▸ The text controls must be as narrow as possible and must hold a maximum of one character each. In the sample session, the text controls are not very narrow, but that is Chrome's fault. Use code that specifies maximally narrow text controls.

▸ In the sample session's browser windows, in the second sentence, note that *Restart* and *Update* are italicized.

▸ Provide code that displays a warning message on browsers that have JavaScript disabled. The warning message should not display on browsers that have JavaScript enabled.

To rotate the top-left and bottom-right arrow buttons, use the following class selector with the `transform` property:

```
.diagonal {transform: rotate(-45deg);}
```

We did not cover the CSS `transform` property. To learn about it, google "css transform property."

**Sample Session**

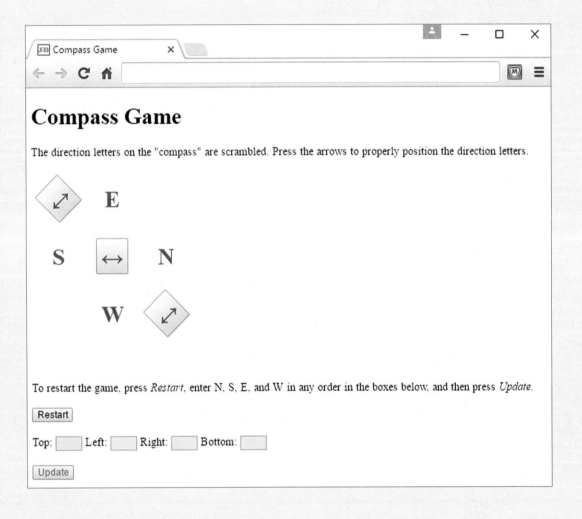

After pressing the bottom-right arrow:

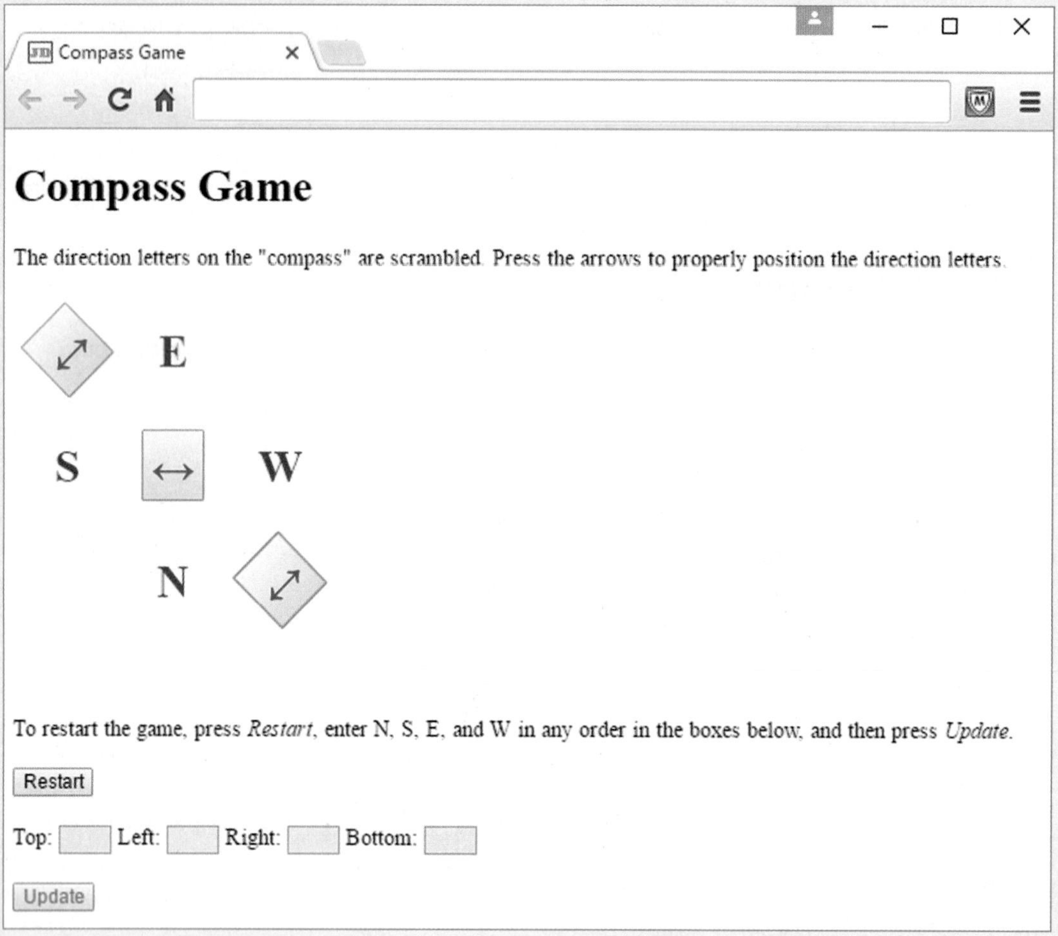

After pressing the **Restart** button:

# Compass Game

The direction letters on the "compass" are scrambled. Press the arrows to properly position the direction letters.

To restart the game, press *Restart*, enter N, S, E, and W in any order in the boxes below, and then press *Update*.

Restart

Top: [ ] Left: [ ] Right: [ ] Bottom: [ ]

Update

After entering S, E, W, and N in the text controls and pressing the **Update** button:

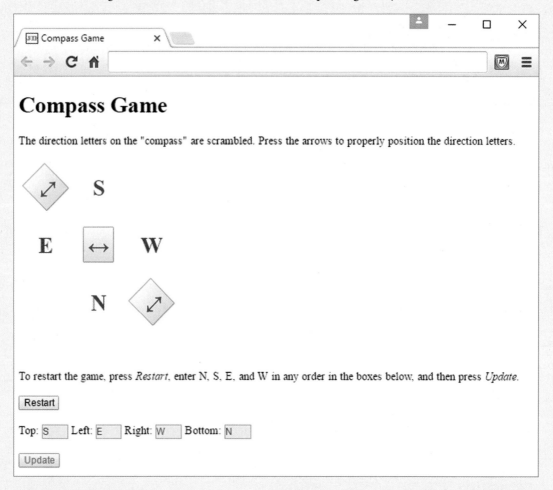

**Extra Credit**

Start with a copy of your regular project's `.html` file. Below the code for your compass table, replace the code that generates the four bottom lines with a single **Shuffle** button. The **Shuffle** button should randomly shuffle the positions of the direction letters N, S, E, and W. To implement the shuffle functionality, you'll need to jump ahead in the book to learn about JavaScript arrays, loops, and random number generation. You must provide output that illustrates the **Shuffle** button's functionality.

# CHAPTER 9

# Additional JavaScript Basics: `window` Object, `if` Statement, Strings, Numbers, and Input Validation

## CHAPTER OBJECTIVES

▶ Use the `window` object to retrieve various properties of the current window.

▶ Display pop-up messages and retrieve user input by calling the `alert`, `confirm`, and `prompt` methods.

▶ Write `if` statements in order to implement branching logic.

▶ Learn string details—how to compare them, concatenate them, and display special characters using escape sequences.

▶ To process strings, learn how to call various string methods.

▶ To process numbers, learn how to use arithmetic operators.

**351**

▶  Call various `Math` object methods.

▶  To help with web accessibility, use `label` elements with your controls.

▶  Implement constraint validation for form controls by adding CSS and JavaScript that tell the user when input is invalid.

▶  To form more complex `if` conditions, learn how to use comparison operators and logical operators.

▶  Understand and use JavaScript's operator precedence table in order to evaluate complex expressions.

## CHAPTER OUTLINE

## 9.1 Introduction

In this chapter, we continue with the introduction to the JavaScript programming language. This time, there are more nuts and bolts about the language itself that are not tied to the HTML environment in which the JavaScript executes.

This book makes no assumptions about prior programming experience. If you're a complete newbie, read this chapter slowly and drink it in. On the other hand, if you already know another programming language (like Java, C++, or Python), then some of what you saw in the prior chapter probably looked familiar (e.g., variables, assignment statements, and functions). Likewise, even more of this chapter will look familiar. But don't skip this chapter! JavaScript has its quirks that you need to learn about.

We start the chapter with a discussion of the `window` object, which allows the programmer to retrieve information about the browser window—the URL of the currently active web page, the type of browser, and so on. Then we turn to dialog boxes, which provide a crude, but effective, means to force the user to answer a question. We introduce the `if` statement in order to do different things, depending on the user's answer to a question. We then talk about strings and numbers. To force users to provide input that makes sense, we describe input constraint validation techniques. Finally, we talk about various operators that can be used with the `if` statement to distinguish between different situations.

# 9.2 `window` Object

In the previous chapter, you learned about the document object model (DOM), which uses the `document` object as the root node of the DOM's node tree. The node tree contains objects for each entity within a web page—elements, attributes, and plain text. You can use JavaScript with the DOM's objects to manipulate the elements, attributes, and plain text in a web page. Usually, as a JavaScript programmer, all you'll need to access are the things within the current web page. But sometimes there's a need to access the window that contains the web page. To do that, you can use the `window` object.

When you launch a browser (e.g., when you double click the Chrome icon on your desktop), or you launch a new tab within a browser window, the browser creates a new `window` object. The `window` object has quite a few properties and methods that JavaScript can use to access and manipulate various characteristics of the window. We'll present a few `window` object methods later. For now, we'll focus on the properties. **FIGURE 9.1** shows some of the more popular

| window Object Properties | Description |
| --- | --- |
| document | Returns the `document` object, which can be used to retrieve information about the web page that's loaded. |
| location | Returns the `location` object, which contains information about the URL of the web page that's being displayed. |
| navigator | Returns the `navigator` object, which contains information about the browser that's being used. |
| screen | Returns the `screen` object, which contains information about the monitor that's being used. |
| history | Returns the `history` object, which can be used to navigate backwards and forward to web pages that have been visited recently. |

**FIGURE 9.1** Some of the more popular properties in the `window` object

properties in the `window` object. All the properties shown are objects. That might seem a bit odd that an object (the `window` object) contains other objects for its properties. By having properties that are objects, the multitude of properties and methods in the `window` object are compartmentalized into their own separate objects. Compartmentalization is good because it makes it easier for programmers to keep track of things.

The first property listed in Figure 9.1 is the `document` property. It returns the `document` object that's at the root of the DOM node tree. Thus, you can think of the `window` object as being on top of the DOM's node tree. Remember in the previous chapter how we called `document` `.getElementById` to retrieve a control object associated with a particular element? Now you know what that `document` thing is—a property of the `window` object.

The next property listed is the `location` property, which holds the URL of the web page that's being displayed. Back in Chapter 1, we explained the different parts of a URL. As a programmer, you might want to retrieve not just the whole URL value, but also its individual parts. For example, to check to see if the https protocol is being used, which is more secure than http, you can use the `location` object's `protocol` property. If the `protocol` property reveals that https is being used, then you can feel more comfortable displaying sensitive information. Another use for the `location` object is to load a different web page by calling the `location` object's `assign` method and pass a URL value as the argument.

The next property listed is the `navigator` property, which holds information about the browser that's being used—Google Chrome, Mozilla Firefox, and so on. The term navigator comes from old-time browser manufacturer Netscape's seminal browser product, Netscape Navigator.

The next property listed is the `screen` property, which holds information about the monitor that's being used, such as the monitor's dimensions. As a programmer, if you know the screen is small, you can use the `screen` property to make sure to display objects that are small enough to fit within its dimensions.

The last property listed is the `history` property. It returns the `history` object that enables the programmer to implement backwards and forward web page navigation event handler code for web pages that the user has visited within the browser's current tab session.

## Example Web Page with `window` Object Properties

Let's put what you've learned about the `window` object into practice with a Window Information web page that displays information retrieved from the `window` object. **FIGURE 9.2** shows the web page's code.

Note the `window.location.href` code embedded in a string concatenation that forms the web page's first message. That code retrieves the web page's URL, and you can go to **FIGURE 9.3**'s Window Information browser window and verify that the first message shows the web page's URL. The way `window.location.href` works is that `window` gets the `window` object, `.location` gets the `window` object's `location` object, and `.href` gets the `location` object's URL value. Note the `window.location.protocol` code embedded in the same string concatenation. It accesses the `location` object's `protocol` property. As you can see in Figure 9.3, that code causes the browser to display the URL's protocol, http:.

```
<!DOCTYPE html>
<html lang="en">
<head>
<meta charset="utf-8">
<meta name="author" content="John Dean">
<title>Window Information</title>
<script>
  // This function displays information about the window.

  function displayWindowInfo() {
    var msg1, msg2, msg3; // they hold window information
    msg1 = document.getElementById("location-info");
    msg1.innerHTML =
      "This page's full URL: " + window.location.href + "<br>" +
      "This page's protocol: " + window.location.protocol;
    msg2 = document.getElementById("browser-info");
    msg2.innerHTML =
      "Browser name: " + window.navigator.userAgent;
    msg3 = document.getElementById("screen-info");
    msg3.innerHTML =
      "Screen width: " + window.screen.availWidth +
      " pixels<br>" +
      "Screen height: " + window.screen.availHeight + " pixels";
  } // end displayWindowInfo
</script>
</head>

<body onload="displayWindowInfo();">
<h2>Getting Information From the Window Object</h2>
<p id="location-info"></p>
<p id="browser-info"></p>
<p id="screen-info"></p>
</body>
</html>
```

Retrieves an object with information about web page's URL.

Retrieves an object with information about user's monitor.

Retrieves an object with information about user's browser.

**FIGURE 9.2 Source code for Window Information web page**

Before moving on to a description of additional window object properties, let's review Figure 9.2's JavaScript to see how the href and protocol properties get displayed. Here's the relevant code from the displayWindowInfo function:

```
msg1 = document.getElementById("location-info");
msg1.innerHTML =
  "This page's full URL: " + window.location.href + "<br>" +
  "This page's protocol: " + window.location.protocol;
```

**FIGURE 9.3 Window Information web page**

The `document.getElementById("location-info")` method call retrieves the object associated with the element that has `id="location-info"`. As you can see in the `body` container, that object is the `p` element with `id="location-info"`. The `href` and `protocol` properties are assigned into the `p` object's `innerHTML` property, which updates the `p` element's content dynamically on the browser window. This same technique is used for additional `window` object properties retrieved in the Window Information web page.

In addition to the `href` and `protocol` properties, the `location` object also has the `hostname` and `pathname` properties. The `hostname` property refers to the name of the web server computer (e.g., teach.park.edu). The `pathname` refers to the directories and subdirectories in between the home page directory (or the web server's root directory) and the web page's filename.

Notice how in Figure 9.2, `msg2` gets assigned the object associated with the web page's second message (using the `p` element with `id="browser-info"`). And the `window` object's `navigator.useragent` property gets assigned into `msg2.innerHTML`. The `navigator.useragent` property holds the name of the browser that's being used. Here's the `useragent` property's browser name, as shown in Figure 9.3's browser window and copied here for your convenience:

```
Mozilla/5.0 (Windows NT 10.0; WOW64) AppleWebKit/537.36 (KHTML, like
Gecko) Chrome/54.0.2840.71 Safari/537.36
```

Ouch! That's rather long and complicated. Unfortunately, the browser's type (Google Chrome version 54) is not obvious from the `useragent` property's displayed information. The `navigator` object's other properties provide even less helpful information. To figure out the user's browser, you must write JavaScript code that examines the string returned by the `userAgent` property. That can get quite messy, and the technique is beyond the scope of this book. If you're interested in learning about it on your own, see http://www.javascriptkit.com /javatutors/navigator.shtml.

In Figure 9.2, note how `msg3` gets assigned the object associated with the web page's third message (using the `p` element with `id="screen-info"`). And the `window.screen` object's `availWidth` and `availHeight` properties get assigned into `msg3.innerHTML`. The `availWidth` and `availHeight` properties hold the dimensions for the user's screen. More specifically, they hold the dimensions in pixels that are available to a window when the window is maximized. The available dimensions do not include user interface features displayed by the operating system, such as the taskbar on Windows computers. If you want to get the dimensions of the current state of the window (not necessarily maximized), don't use the `screen` object. Instead, use the `window` object and its `outerWidth` and `outerHeight` properties. Those dimensions are for the entire window, including the window's borders.

## Global Object

As you learned in the previous chapter, a global variable is a variable that's shared between all the functions for a particular web page. Normally, global variables are to be avoided, because they can lead to inappropriate data sharing. But there are some global variables and global methods that are built into the JavaScript language, and you should feel free to use them when they're needed. The `window` object's *members* (an object's members are its properties and methods) are all global, so when you use them, you're using the current web page's single copy of them.

Because all the `window` object's members are global, the `window` object is special, and it's given a special name—the *global object*. The JavaScript engine generates the `window` object automatically whenever the user launches a new browser instance. If you attempt to access a property or call a method and you don't prepend such attempts with an object dot, then the JavaScript engine automatically inserts the global object (`window`) and a dot in front of the member. For example:

```
document.getElementById["ssn"]    ≡  window.document.getElementById["ssn"]
screen.availWidth                 ≡  window.screen.availWidth
location.assign("url-value")      ≡  window.location.assign("url-value")
```

The ≡ symbol is not part of JavaScript—it's a symbol borrowed from logic that means "is equivalent to."

There's no absolute rule about when to include and when to omit `window` dot in your code. But in general, you should use `window` dot for less common window members, as a form of self-documentation. The `screen`, `location`, and `navigator` properties are less common, and you should prepend them with `window` dot. On the other hand, the `document` object is used so often that most programmers are comfortable with it and use it without `window` dot. The `window` object has three methods—`alert`, `confirm`, and `prompt`—that are used fairly often, and most programmers call them without `window` dot. We'll describe those methods in the upcoming sections.

## 9.3 `alert` and `confirm` Methods

### Dialog Boxes

The `window` object's `alert`, `confirm`, and `prompt` methods generate dialog boxes. A *dialog box* (or dialog for short) is a window that performs one simple task. For example, this dialog simply displays a message:

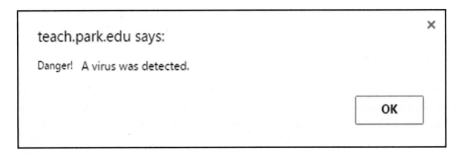

With a standard window, the web programmer has quite a bit of control in terms of customization. The programmer determines the number of controls and the layout of those controls. On the other hand, dialog boxes are pretty plain, and the programmer can't do much about that plainness. Note the plainness in the preceding dialog—there's a message, an **OK** button, and a close-out **X** button in the upper-right corner, and that's it.

The primary way to provide information to a user or get input from a user is to use the main browser window, but if you want to draw sharp attention to a particular output or input task, then using a dialog can sometimes be helpful. Dialogs are able to draw "sharp attention" because they pop up (that's why they're often called "pop-ups"), and they are modal. There are two types of windows—*modeless* and *modal*. Most windows are modeless, which means you can jump back and forth between them simply by clicking your mouse anywhere on the modeless windows. Dialog windows are modal, which means they block users from interacting with anything else on the dialog's parent window. (A dialog's parent window is a window that holds the page that generated the dialog.) You must first close the dialog in order to go back to the parent window. Forcing the user to interact with the dialog draws sharp attention to the dialog.

## `alert` Method

Let's now talk about the different JavaScript methods for generating dialog boxes. First up, the `alert` method. It generates a dialog box that simply displays a specified message. Here is its syntax:

```
alert (message) ;
```

For example, to produce the dialog shown earlier, we used this JavaScript:

```
alert ("Danger! A virus was detected.") ;
```

Note that the example does follow the syntax where the message argument is a string with quotes. After the user reads the alert message, the user clicks the **OK** button to make the dialog disappear.

## `confirm` Method

The `confirm` method generates a dialog box that displays a specified question. The user is expected to answer yes or no to the question (by clicking **OK** or **Cancel**). Here's an example dialog generated by a `confirm` method call:

Here's the syntax for a `confirm` method call:

```
confirm (question) ;
```

What follows is an example `confirm` method call that uses this syntax and produces the dialog shown previously:

```
confirm ("Do you always tell the truth?") ;
```

In response to the dialog box's question, if the user clicks **OK**, then the `confirm` method returns true. Otherwise, if the user clicks **Cancel** or clicks the close-out **X** button, the `confirm` method returns false. The Lie Detector web page, whose source code appears in **FIGURE 9.4**, uses the `confirm` method's return value to display a message indicating the user's self-proclaimed level of truthfulness. The web page uses the `alert` method to display the message, and here's what the message looks like after the user clicks the **OK** button:

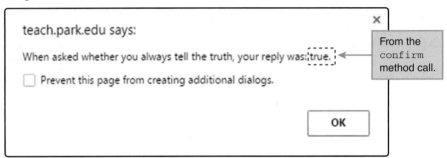

Note the word "true" at the end of the message. That's the value returned from the `confirm` method call after the user clicks the **OK** button.

Study the `askAboutLying` function in Figure 9.4. Note how the `confirm` method call appears at the right side of an assignment statement with the `reply` variable at the left. That means the value returned by the `askAboutLying` function (either true or false) gets assigned into the `reply` variable. Note how the next statement, an `alert` method call, concatenates the `reply` variable's value at the end of the `alert` message.

```
<!DOCTYPE html>
<html lang="en">
<head>
<meta charset="utf-8">
<meta name="author" content="John Dean">
<title>Lie Detector Test</title>
<script>
  function askAboutLying() {
    var reply; // user's reply
    reply = confirm("Do you always tell the truth?");
    alert("When asked whether you always tell" +
      " the truth, your reply was: " + reply + ".");
  } // end askAboutLying
</script>
</head>

<body onload="askAboutLying();">
<h1>Lie Detector Test</h1>
</body>
</html>
```

**FIGURE 9.4 Source code for Lie Detector web page**

Think about the situation where the `alert` message displays "your reply was false." Describe the type of person who would generate that output—someone who always tells the truth, someone who always lies, or some other type of person? This brainteaser is an end-of-chapter exercise question, so no answer is provided here.

Look again at the `alert` method call statement, and note how it spans two lines. It would have been legal to enter the entire method call statement on one line, but if someone printed the code, line wrap would occur. Line wrap is ugly and leads to code that is harder to understand. To avoid line wrap, you should press enter at an appropriate breaking point and on the next line, indent past the starting point of the prior line. That's what we do for the `alert` method call, but the breaking point is in the middle of a string, and that requires a little extra work. To break/split a string, terminate the first part of the string with a closing quote, insert a concatenation operator, +, and start the next line's continuation string with an opening quote.[1] Look at Figure 9.4 and verify that the `alert` method call uses that technique for splitting the `alert` method's message string.

## 9.4 if Statement: if by itself

In the previous section, we didn't do much with the `confirm` method call's returned value—we simply displayed it. That's OK, but rather unusual. Usually, you'll use the `confirm` method call's returned value of true or false as the criterion for making a decision. If the user clicks OK (for yes), then you'll do one thing, or if the user clicks Cancel (for no), then you'll do something else. The easiest way to implement that logic is with an `if` statement.

### Syntax

Let's jump right into an `if` statement example. In the next section, you'll see an `if` statement that uses a `confirm` method call, but for our first example, let's keep things simple. Here's an `if` statement that checks a person's age and displays a message of joy if the age is greater than 16:

```
              ┌───────────┐
              │ condition │
              └───────────┘
                     ↖
if (age > 16) {
   msg = document.getElementById("message");
   msg.innerHTML =
      "You can now drive without parental supervision. Road trip!";
}
```

Note how this example fits the syntax shown at the left of **FIGURE 9.5**. The syntax requires you to have a condition after the word `if`. The *condition* is a question, and it must be surrounded by parentheses. To form a question, you can use the > (greater than) symbol as shown in this example or other comparison operators that we'll talk about later.

In Figure 9.5's syntax at the left, note the braces ({ }) that surround the statements that follow the condition. In JavaScript (and other programming languages as well), braces are used to group

---

[1] As an alternative, you can use the backslash (\) to split a string across two lines. We'll explain that technique later in this chapter.

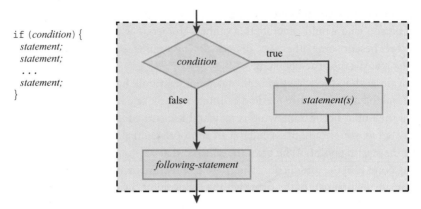

```
if (condition) {
    statement;
    statement;
    ...
    statement;
}
```

**FIGURE 9.5 Syntax and semantics for the "if by itself" form of the if statement**

statements together that are logically inside something else. So they're used for the statements inside an if statement's condition. They're also used for the statements that comprise a function's body. Whenever you use braces (for if statements, function bodies, and other situations introduced later on), you should indent the statements that are inside the braces. This is not a JavaScript language requirement, it's a style thing. By indenting, you make it clear to someone reading your code that the statements inside the braces are logically inside something else. The formal term for zero or more statements surrounded by braces is a *block statement* (or *compound statement* for other languages). A block statement can be used anywhere a standard statement can be used.

## Semantics

The *semantics* of a statement is a description of how the statement works. The diagram at the right side of Figure 9.5 illustrates the semantics of the if statement by showing what happens for different values of the if statement's condition. The diagram is a flowchart. A *flowchart* is a pictorial representation of the logic flow of a computer program. More formally, it shows the program's flow of control, where *flow of control* is the order in which program statements are executed.

In Figure 9.5, note the flowchart's rectangles, diamond, and arrows. The rectangles are for *sequential statements*, which are statements that are executed in the sequence/order in which they are written (i.e., after executing a statement, the computer executes the statement immediately below it). The diamond shapes are for *branching statements* (like if statements), where the answer to a question determines which statement to execute next. They're called branching statements because their decision points (the conditions) generate branches/forks in the code's flow of control. The arrows indicate how the rectangles and diamonds are connected. Branching statements are also known as *selection statements* because in executing those types of statements, the computer selects which path to take.

Study Figure 9.5's flowchart, and make sure you understand the if statement's semantics. If the if statement's condition evaluates to true, then the right-side statements are executed. Otherwise, those statements are skipped, and control flows down to the statements below the if statement.

# 9.5 Game Night Web Page

In the previous section, we examined an `if` statement with a mathematical-expression condition that asked whether the user's age is greater than 16 (`age > 16`). For a condition to work, it has to evaluate to true or false. The `age > 16` condition does indeed evaluate to true or false, with the result depending on `age`'s value. In this section, we examine a web page with an `if` statement where the condition again evaluates to true or false, but this time, it might not be as obvious that the condition evaluates to true or false. This time, we use the `confirm` method call (introduced two sections earlier) for the `if` statement's condition.

Take a look at the Game Night web page in **FIGURE 9.6**. When the user clicks the button, the browser asks whether the user wants to follow the link to the party reservation web page. If the user clicks **OK**, the browser redirects the user to another web page, the Park University ACM Club web page. To implement that functionality, we use an `if` statement.

Take a look at the Game Night web page source code in **FIGURE 9.7**. In particular, note the `partyOn` function's `if` statement. As you can see, the condition is a `confirm` method call, `confirm("Can you handle the excitement?")`. Remember that the condition needs to evaluate to true or false. Because the `confirm` method returns a value of true or false, you can think of the `confirm` method call being physically replaced by a true or false value. Clearly, having true or false in the condition's parentheses satisfies the JavaScript engine's requirement for having

FIGURE 9.6 **Game Night web page**

```html
<!DOCTYPE html>
<html lang="en">
<head>
<meta charset="utf-8">
<meta name="author" content="John Dean">
<title>Game Night</title>
<style>
  body {background-color: rgb(205, 250, 255);}
</style>
<script>
  // Direct the user to the ACM Club page.

  function partyOn() {
    if (confirm("Can you handle the excitement?")) {
      window.location.assign(
        "http://www.park.edu/clubs-and-organizations" +
        "/active-student-clubs.html");
    }
  } // end partyOn
</script>
</head>

<body>
<h1>Park ACM Club Game Night</h1>
<p>
  Join Park's ACM Club for another wild and crazy
  night of computer fun!
</p>
<ul>
  <li>Play computer games!</li>
  <li>Talk about computers!</li>
  <li>Win posters of your favorite computers!</li>
</ul>
<p>Confirm your reservation now by clicking below.</p>
<input type="button" value="Party Reservations" onclick="partyOn();">
</body>
</html>
```

> Returns a value of true or false.

**FIGURE 9.7 Source code for Game Night web page**

the condition evaluate to true or false. So everything works as expected—if the user clicks OK on the confirm dialog, true is returned, the if condition is true, and the browser executes the statement inside the braces. That statement is a window.location.assign method call, which causes the browser to load the web page specified by the method call's URL-value argument.

## 9.6 `prompt` **Method**

As mentioned earlier, the window object has three methods that generate dialog boxes—`alert`, `confirm`, and `prompt`. We've already described `alert` and `confirm`; now it's time for `prompt`.

The `prompt` method generates a dialog box that displays a specified question. The user is expected to answer the question by entering a value in a text control and then clicking OK. Or, the user may click Cancel to avoid answering the question. Here's an example dialog generated by a `prompt` method call:

Here's the syntax for a `prompt` method call:

`prompt (`*prompt-message*`,   "")`

What follows is an example `prompt` method call that uses this syntax and produces the dialog shown previously:

`prompt ("What's your name?",   "");`

The first argument provides the dialog box's prompt. The second argument (the two-quotes-with-nothing-in-between thing) specifies the initial value that appears in the prompt box. For example, this would cause zeros to appear in the prompt box:

`prompt ("What's your student ID?",   "0000000");`

Normally, you'll want to display an empty initial value, and to do that, you specify the *empty string* (`""`) for the second argument. The W3C defines the prompt method with two parameters, so you should always include two arguments. However, and not surprisingly, browsers are lenient and they allow one argument. If you omit the second parameter, the Internet Explorer browser displays "undefined" as the initial value (ugly!), whereas Chrome and Firefox display nothing.

If a user sees a prompt dialog box and clicks Cancel or the close-out X button, the `prompt` method returns the value `null`, which is a JavaScript keyword that indicates the absence of a user entry. Otherwise, if the user clicks OK, then the `prompt` method returns the contents of the prompt box's text control.

## 9.7 Game Night Web Page Revisited

Your mission, if you choose to accept it, is to modify the Game Night web page's button event handler, so instead of linking to another web page, it displays a party reservation pass. More specifically, your task is to edit the partyOn function so it does this:

1. Prompt the user for his/her name.
2. If the user clicks **Cancel**, do nothing. Otherwise, display two dialogs with these messages:

   ▶   The next pop-up will be your party reservation. Print it.
   ▶   Admit one to the ACM Club party: *user's-name.*

The first step is to prompt the user for his/her name, and, not surprisingly, we'll use the prompt method for that. But how should the prompt method be situated? Normally, as a web programmer, you'll want to do something with the prompt method's returned value (i.e., you'll want to do something with the user's input). That means you'll normally want to embed the method call within an assignment statement or an if statement's condition. For the improved Game Night web page, you'll need to save the user's input in a variable, so you can display the user's name on the party reservation pass. To save the user's input, you need an assignment statement, like this:

```
name = prompt("What's your name?", "");
```

Then we need to check the user's input using the name variable and an if statement, like this:

```
if (name != null) {
```

The != thing is JavaScript's inequality operator. It compares its two operands (name and null in this case) and evaluates to true if they are unequal and evaluates to false if they are equal. Remember that null is what's returned by the prompt method when the user clicks the prompt dialog box's **Cancel** button, and the user's string input is returned when the user clicks the **OK** button. So the preceding if condition checks for the user clicking the **OK** button. Inside the if statement, we need two alert method calls that (1) inform the user about the upcoming party reservation pass, and (2) display the party reservation pass. To see the alert method call code, study the partyOn function definition in **FIGURE 9.8**.

### Dialog Boxes—Use Them Sparingly

The "improved" Game Night web page uses a prompt dialog box and two alert dialog boxes. That's probably a bit much. JavaScript's alert, confirm, and prompt methods are OK when used in small doses, but they can be annoying if used too much because their dialog boxes block users from interacting with anything else. Another problem with the three dialog box methods is that users will sometimes configure their browsers to disable pop-up windows (including the pop-ups generated by alert, confirm, and prompt).

```
<script>
  // Print a party reservation pass.

  function partyOn() {
    var name; // user's name

    name = prompt("What's your name?", "");
    if (name != null) {
      alert("The next pop-up will be your party" +
        " reservation. Print it.");
      alert("Admit one to the ACM Club party: " + name);
    }
  } // end partyOn
</script>
```

**FIGURE 9.8 `script` container for improved Game Night web page**

The standard way to generate dynamic output is to use dynamic HTML, and the standard way to get input is to use form controls. So when should you use the `alert`, `confirm`, and `prompt` methods for output and input? Use them only when you want to draw sharp attention to something and to force the user to deal with the issue immediately.

# 9.8 if Statement: `else` and `else if` Clauses

In the Game Night web page, you were introduced to the simplest form of the `if` statement—when the `if` clause is by itself. That form takes care of the case when you want to do something or nothing. But what if you want to do one thing or something else, depending on the value (true or false) of a condition? Or, what if you want to do one thing from among a list of three or more options? In this section, we describe additional forms of the `if` statement that take care of those situations.

**FIGURE 9.9** shows the syntax and semantics for the form of the `if` statement that takes care of the situation where you want to do one thing or something else. It uses the same `if` clause at the top that you've seen before, but it adds an `else` clause. To differentiate, we'll refer to the previous form of the `if` statement as "if by itself" and this new form of the `if` statement as "if, else."

**FIGURE 9.10** shows the syntax and semantics for the form of the `if` statement that takes care of the situation where you want to do one thing from among a list of three or more options. It uses the same `if` clause at the top and the same `else` clause at the bottom that you've seen before, but it adds one or more `else if` clauses in the middle. To distinguish this form of the `if` statement, we'll refer to it as the "if, else if" `if` statement. You may include as many `else if` clauses as you like—more `else if` clauses for more choices. Note that the `else` clause is optional.

In Figure 9.10, note the flowchart's flow of control as indicated by the arrows. After one condition is found to be true, all the other conditions are skipped, and control flows down to the statement below the entire `if` statement. That means that the JavaScript engine executes only

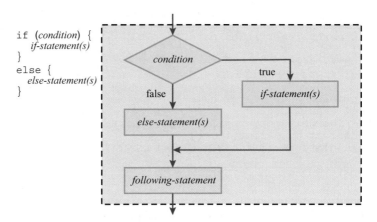

**FIGURE 9.9 Syntax and semantics for the "if, else" form of the `if` statement**

one of the block statements—the one with the condition that's true. If all the conditions are false and there's no "else" block, the JavaScript engine executes none of the block statements.

In this section, you learned about the three forms of the `if` statement. You'll see those forms used in examples throughout the remainder of the book. Here's a summary of the different forms:

- ▶ "if by itself"—use when you want to do one thing or nothing.
- ▶ "if, else"—use when you want to do one thing or another thing.
- ▶ "if, else if"—use when there are three or more possibilities.

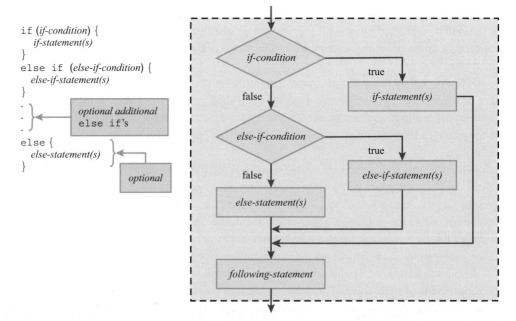

**FIGURE 9.10 Syntax and semantics for the "if, else if, else" form of the `if` statement**

# 9.9 **Strings**

You've been using strings for quite a while now, but you've been using them in a bare-bones fashion. In this section, you'll learn about some of the functionality that JavaScript provides to make working with strings easier. That added functionality is particularly important because strings are used so often for processing user input. In this section, you'll learn about string operators, hard-to-represent string characters (such as the quote character), and also string methods.

## Comparison Operators

In the improved Game Night web page, remember the following prompt for the user's name and the `if` statement that verifies that the user entered something?

```
var name; // user's name
name = prompt("What's your name?");
if (name != null) {
...
```

This `if` statement condition uses the inequality operator, `!=`, to check whether the `name` variable's value is not equal to the `null` value. As an alternative, we could have used the equality operator, `==`, to check whether the `name` variable's value is equal to the `null` value. Here's what that looks like:

```
if (name == null) {
```

Remember that the `prompt` method returns `null` if the user clicks the **Cancel** button. If you want to see if the user clicks the **OK** button with nothing in the input box, you can compare the `name` variable to the empty string, like this:

```
if (name == "") {
```

When testing for equality, you need to use two equals signs, not one. The single equals sign is for the assignment operator. If you accidentally use one equals sign (`=`), the JavaScript engine assigns the value at the right into the variable at the left. That kind of error can be surprisingly hard to find, so try to avoid it. Remember: When testing for equality, use `==`, not `=`.

As you've learned, you can use the `==` and `!=` operators to check whether a string variable holds or does not hold a particular value. If you'd like to check two strings to see which comes first in the dictionary, you can use the `<`, `>`, `<=`, and `>=` operators. In comparing two strings, all the string comparison operators (`<`, `>`, `<=`, `>=`, `==`, `!=`) use *lexicographical ordering*. That means the computer compares the characters in the two strings one at a time until it reaches two characters that are different. Then it uses alphabetical order for those individual characters to determine the ordering. Thus, because the third-letter "i" in "amino acid" comes after the third-letter "a" in "amanuensis" in the alphabet, the expression `"amino acid" > "amanuensis"` evaluates to true and the expression `"amino acid" < "amanuensis"` evaluates to false.[2]

If two strings are compared such that the first string matches the second string's left side and the second string has additional characters at the right, then the first string comes first in the dictionary. For example, `"malaprop" < "malapropism"` evaluates to true.

The `>=` and `<=` operators work as you'd expect, both returning true when the compared strings are equal. In writing `>=` and `<=`, don't forget to put the `=` at the right; `=>` and `=<` are not valid JavaScript operators.

## String Concatenation

As you know, strings are normally concatenated with the + operator. You can also concatenate with the += concatenation assignment operator. Whereas the + operator does not change either of its two string operands (it merely returns the concatenated version of the two strings), the += operator updates the string variable at the left of +=. For example, suppose you have a variable named `consumable` that holds the value "water" and you want to update it by concatenating "melon" at its right. Here's how you can do that:

```
var consumable;
consumable = "water";
consumable += "melon";
```

After this code executes, the `consumable` variable holds "watermelon".

## Escape Sequence Characters and String Continuation with \

In forming a string, you'll sometimes want to use characters that are difficult to represent. For example, let's try to store the following exchange between my daughter Jordan (as a toddler) and Jordan's mother:

```
"Mommy, hurry up and get dressed - go faster than a horse."
"That's pretty fast, Jordan."
"OK, then go faster than a baby hippopotamus." No response.
"OK, then go faster than a wall. You should be able to beat a wall."
```

Most of this code is easy to store—just use the letters and punctuation as is. Note the quote mark (`"`) before "Mommy" and the quote mark after "horse." Storing those quote marks and the other quote marks is a bit of a challenge. Storing the text as four separate lines is also a bit of a challenge. Here's a first-cut attempt at storing the first two lines:

---

[2] Note the space character in "amino acid." Just like in a dictionary, the space character comes before letter characters. For a complete understanding of how the JavaScript engine determines the order of strings, you need to realize that each character in a string is associated with an underlying numeric value. The *Unicode standard* (and the *ASCII table*, which is a subset of the Unicode standard) provide those underlying numeric values. Feel free to peruse the Unicode standard at http://unicode.org/standard/standard.html.

```
var exchange;
exchange = ""Mommy, hurry up and get dressed - go faster than a horse."";
exchange += ""That's pretty fast, Jordan."";
```

In attempting to store the quote marks, this code simply uses the quote marks as is. But in doing so, it messes up the quote marks that signal the beginning and end of the strings. The JavaScript engine interprets `""`Mommy as a completed string (`""`) followed by a variable named Mommy. That's not right. So, what's the solution? As you learned in the last chapter, to nest a string inside a string, you can use single quotes for the inner string and double quotes for the outer string. This second-cut attempt does that:

```
var exchange;
exchange = "'Mommy, hurry up and get dressed - go faster than a horse.'";
exchange += "'That's pretty fast, Jordan.'";
```

With single quotes nested inside the double quotes, if there was an attempt to display exchange's content, the single quotes would display. Displaying single quotes rather than double quotes might bother some users, but that's not a big problem. Can you see a bigger problem? The apostrophe in "That's" acts as a closing quote for the preceding single quote. And that causes the single quote after "Jordan" to be orphaned. Bottom line—the code doesn't work.

There are several solutions. One solution is to replace the apostrophe in "That's" with the special character \ ', like this:

```
exchange += "'That\'s pretty fast, Jordan.'";
```

JavaScript uses the backslash notation for special characters like the single quote. Those characters are called *escape sequence* characters because the backslash "escapes" the subsequent character (the ' in this case) from its normal meaning. For the single quote character, its normal meaning is the start or end of a string. By using the backslash, the single quote is just a normal character that's displayed, so it does not interfere with the opening single quote that appears at its left.

JavaScript was designed to be used with web pages, but it can also be used in other contexts. In those other contexts, there are many escape sequence characters that come in handy. If you want to see all of JavaScript's escape sequences, feel free to peruse http://www.ecma-international .org/ecma-262/5.1/. The characters you find there mirror the escape sequences you'll find in many other programming languages.

For a table of the escape sequences that are useful for web pages, see **FIGURE 9.11**. In addition to the single quote escape sequence, the table shows a double quote escape sequence. The double quote escape sequence works like its single quote counterpart. When you use \ ", the double quote is just a normal character that's displayed, and it does not serve as the start or end of a string. With that in mind, can you think of how you might use double quote escape sequences to fix the original errant exchange += statement? The solution is to replace the single quotes that surround the string with double quote escape sequences, like this:

```
exchange += "\"That's pretty fast, Jordan.\"";
```

| Escape Sequence Characters | Meaning |
|---|---|
| \' | Single quote character with no significance in terms of starting or ending a string. |
| \" | Double quote character with no significance in terms of starting or ending a string. |
| \\ | Single backslash character. |
| \n | Newline character with no relation to the letter *n*. |

**FIGURE 9.11 JavaScript escape sequence characters that are helpful for web pages**

With double quote escape sequences nested inside the regular double quotes, the JavaScript engine would display double quotes around the strings. And that should make everyone happy.

There's still another issue to resolve for the Mommy-Jordan conversation code. We want the result to look like a dialog between two people when it displays on the web page. That means the four quotes should display on four separate lines. To make that happen, we need the JavaScript to generate `<br>` elements. Here's the corrected code with `<br>`'s inserted:

```
var exchange;
exchange =
   "\"Mommy, hurry up and get dressed - go faster than a horse.\"<br>";
exchange += "\"That's pretty fast, Jordan.\"<br>";
```

Figure 9.11's next escape sequence character is \\, which enables a programmer to store a single backslash within a string variable. Can you figure out why the double backslash notation is necessary? Suppose a programmer attempts to store a backslash by using a single backslash, like this:[3]

```
var musicFolder;
musicFolder = "C:\Users\John\Music";
```

When the JavaScript engine sees a backslash, it interprets the backslash as the start of an escape sequence. When the symbol after the backslash isn't one of the symbols indicative of a special character, the JavaScript engine simply replaces the escape sequence with the symbol after the backslash. So in the preceding code fragment, the \U gets replaced with U, the \J

---

[3] Windows software uses backslashes for path delimiters that separate folders and files. Other operating systems and website addresses use forward slashes for their path delimiters. So why is Windows different? Windows was built on top of DOS, and DOS used the forward slash for command line switches. If you've never heard of DOS and command line switches, forget about it! (DOS dinosaurs, like me, are a dying breed.)

gets replaced with J, the \M gets replaced with M, and the `musicFolder` variable ends up with an incorrect path because all the \'s get stripped out. Here's the corrected assignment statement:

```
musicFolder = "C:\\Users\\John\\Music";
```

Figure 9.11's last escape sequence character is \n, for the newline character, which enables a programmer to generate a new line. If you use \n to generate new lines in your HTML code, that won't have an impact on the user's view because browsers collapse source code whitespace when rendering HTML code. If you want the user to see a new line on the browser window, you need to generate `<br>` elements, as shown in the preceding assignment statement. So, why are you reading about the \n escape sequence? Because the \n escape sequence is how you can generate new lines in dialog box messages. For example, in **FIGURE 9.12**, note the four \n's in the code and also note the four new lines for a, b, c, and d in the dialog box. Without those \n's, the dialog box would display the a, b, c, and d choices on one long line. Not a good look.

```
<script>
  prompt("Of the following U.S. Presidents, which one" +
    " did not die on July 4?\n \
    a)  John Adams\n \
    b)  Thomas Jefferson\n \
    c)  James Monroe\n \
    d)  Ronald Reagan", "");
</script>
```

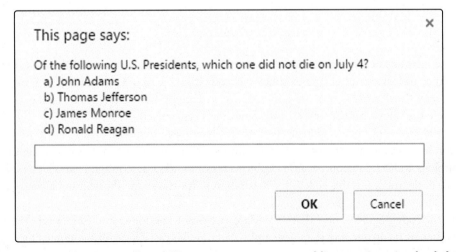

FIGURE 9.12 **Dialog box with newline escape sequences and line continuation backslashes**

In Figure 9.12, the `prompt` method call's prompt message string is quite long and spans six lines. We use two different techniques for continuing the string across multiple lines. To split the first and second lines, we use the technique introduced earlier—a closing quote, a concatenation operator (+), and an opening quote on the next line. At the end of the subsequent lines that need the string to continue, we use a different technique—a backslash by itself with no closing quote for the first line and no opening quote for the second line. With the backslash technique, whitespace is preserved. Specifically, the dialog box displays any whitespace at the left of the \ and any white space at the left of the next line. That's why, in the figure, the a, b, c, and d choices are indented.

So which technique is better for continuing long strings—the close quote, concatenation operator, open quote technique, or the backslash-by-itself technique? Basically, you should use what is appropriate for the particular situation. An end-of-chapter exercise asks you to rewrite the first part of the previous prompt code using the single backslash technique. In doing that, you should be able to discern why the close quote, concatenation operator, open quote technique is more elegant for that particular situation.

## String Methods

Because strings are such an integral part of so many programming tasks, the JavaScript language provides lots of string methods that make it easier to implement solutions for such tasks. We'll introduce more string methods later, but for now, we'll just provide two string methods, and then use them in the next section's web page.

The `toUpperCase` method returns an all-uppercase version of the string that calls the `toUpperCase` method. Likewise, the `toLowerCase` method returns an all-lowercase version of the string that calls the `toLowerCase` method. Here's an example:

```
var exclamation = "Holy Cow!";
var exclamationUpper, exclamationLower;
exclamationUpper = exclamation.toUpperCase();
exclamationLower = exclamation.toLowerCase();
```

initialization statement

Multiple variable declarations with one `var`

The methods do not update the string variables that appear at the left of the method calls. Thus, after the JavaScript engine executes this code, the `exclamation` variable still holds the value "Holy Cow!". And as expected, the `exclamationUpper` and `exclamationLower` variables hold the values "HOLY COW!" and "holy cow!", respectively.

In the preceding code fragment, the first statement is an *initialization statement*. It's a combination of a variable declaration and an assignment. Normally, you should use separate variable declarations and assignments because that provides room for a description comment next to the variable declaration. But this code is for illustration purposes, so the shortcut initialization statement is OK.

In the code fragment, note that we declare `exclamationUpper` and `exclamationLower` on one line by using one `var` statement and separating the variables with a comma. Once again, that leaves less room for description comments. But since the code is for illustration purposes, we won't lose sleep over it.

## 9.10 **Word Ordering Web Page**

In this section, we put into practice what you've learned in the previous two sections by examining a web page that uses (1) an "if, else if, else" form of the `if` statement and (2) various string operations. See the web page in **FIGURE 9.13**. The user enters two words, clicks the < button, and the web page sorts the words.

To start our examination of the Word Ordering web page, let's look at **FIGURE 9.14A**, which shows the web page's `body` container. Note the two `&lt;` character references. The `lt` stands for "less than," and the browser displays those character references as < symbols. The first one is part of the `h3` element's instructions, and the second one is for the button's label. Note the two ` ` nonbreaking spaces above the button and below the button. With back-to-back nonbreaking spaces, they provide more than the default single space of separation between the button and the button's surrounding elements (text controls). Note the `id` values for the two text controls and the

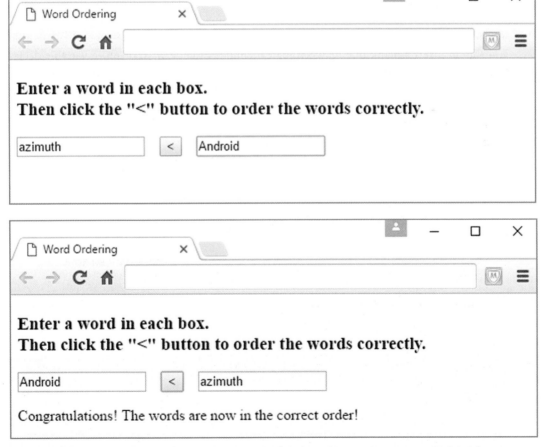

**FIGURE 9.13** **Word Ordering web page after typing words into the text controls and after clicking the < button**

p element. We'll use those `id` values in the button's event handler code. And finally, note how the button's `onclick` event handler calls the `correctWordOrder` function and passes the button's `form` object as an argument.

Let's now study the `correctWordOrder` function's implementation by examining its code in **FIGURE 9.14B**. In Chapter 8, you learned coding conventions that are to be followed when implementing a function. Note how the `correctWordOrder` function follows those conventions:

▶ Indent by two spaces within the `script` start and end tags, and indent by two more spaces inside the function's braces.
▶ Include a descriptive comment above the function heading with a blank line between the comment and the function heading.
▶ Properly position the function's opening and closing braces.
▶ Include an "`end …`" comment for the function's closing brace.
▶ Position all variable declarations at the top of the function's body.
▶ Include a comment for each variable declaration statement and align the comments.

In the `correctWordOrder` function, note the blank line below the variable declarations. The blank line is a gray area in terms of coding conventions. With prior functions, we didn't bother to insert a blank line below variable declarations. The general rule is that you should insert a blank line between logical chunks of code. Two or more variable declaration statements constitute a "chunk of code," and that's why you see the blank line in the `correctWordOrder` function. If you prefer to have a blank line even when there's just one variable declaration, that should be fine, but if you want to be sure, check with your teacher or your work supervisor.

```
<body>
<h3>
  Enter a word in each box.<br>
  Then click the "&lt;" button to order the words correctly.
</h3>
<form>
  <input type="text" id="word1" size="15">
    
  <input type="button" value="&lt;"
    onclick="correctWordOrder(this.form);">
    
  <input type="text" id="word2" size="15">
</form>
<p id="message"></p>
</body>
</html>
```

> Display a < symbol for the instructions and the button's label.

**FIGURE 9.14A** `body` **container for Word Ordering web page**

```
<!DOCTYPE html>
<html lang="en">
<head>
<meta charset="utf-8">
<meta name="author" content="John Dean">
<title>Word Ordering</title>
<script>
  // This function corrects the words' order.

  function correctWordOrder(form) {
    var tb1, tb2;      // text controls for user entries
    var word1, word2;  // user-entered words
    var msg;           // message after button clicked

    tb1 = form.elements["word1"];
    tb2 = form.elements["word2"];
    word1 = tb1.value;
    word2 = tb2.value;
    msg = "Congratulations! The words are now in the" +
      " correct order!";

    if (word1.toLowerCase() > word2.toLowerCase()) {
      tb1.value = word2;
      tb2.value = word1;
    }
    else if (word1.toLowerCase() < word2.toLowerCase()) {
      msg += "<br>(Although they were in the correct order" +
        " to begin with.)";
    }
    else {
      msg += "<br>(Although with the words being the same," +
        " the \"correct order \" doesn't mean much.)";
    }
    document.getElementById("message").innerHTML = msg;
  } // end correctWordOrder
</script>
</head>
```

Annotations:
- Insert a blank line below a group of variable declarations.
- Initialize the output message here. We add to the message later using +=.
- Use the \" escape sequence to display a double quote.

**FIGURE 9.14B** `head` **container for Word Ordering web page**

In the `correctWordOrder` function, note the `if`, `else if`, and `else` blocks of code. Those three blocks of code handle the three possible word orders. The `if` condition checks for the first word coming after the second word in the dictionary. The `else if` condition checks for the first word coming before the second word in the dictionary. The `else` block handles the other case—when the first word equals the second word (with case insensitivity).

Now let's slow down and examine the `if` code block in greater detail. It's in charge of swapping the text control's values when the user enters out-of-order words and the user clicks the `<` button. With text control `id` values of `word1` and `word2`, the following code shows a first-cut attempt at swapping the text control's values:

```
if (form.elements["word1"].value > form.elements["word2"].value) {
   form.elements["word1"].value = form.elements["word2"].value;
   form.elements["word2"].value = form.elements["word1"].value;
}
```

At first glance, this code might look reasonable. The `form.elements["word#"].value` code accesses each text control's user-entered value, so the first assignment statement successfully assigns the second text control's user-entered value to the first text control. The second assignment is supposed to assign the first text control's user-entered value to the second text control, but something goes awry. Can you figure out what happens when the second assignment executes? After the first assignment, the `form.elements["word1"].value` property holds what the user entered in the second text control. So in the second assignment, that second text control user entry gets assigned back into the second text control—which is worthless. So what's the solution? Before executing the first assignment, you should save the second text control's value in a separate variable, so when the second text control gets a new value assigned into it, the second text control's original user entry is safely stored in the separate variable. This is a very important concept, so to make sure you understand it, here's a simplified example where `x` and `y` are the variables whose values are to be swapped, and `temp` is the (temporary) separate variable:

```
temp = x;
x = y;
y = temp;
```

Study Figure 9.14B, and you'll see that we use the variable `word2` as the separate variable that stores the second text control's value. Here's the relevant code (with a few minor modifications that don't affect the logic):

```
word2 = tb2.value;
if (word1.toLowerCase() > word2.toLowerCase()) {
   tb2.value = word1;
   tb1.value = word2;
}
```

The `toLowerCase` method calls mean that the function is able to handle lowercase and uppercase words and sort them with the case ignored. That's why, in Figure 9.13, Android gets moved to the left of azimuth after the user clicks the `<` button.

In the prior code fragment, `tb1` and `tb2` variables store the text control objects. And, as you'd expect, the `word1` variable stores the first text control's value. The `word2` variable is necessary for the sake of the swap. The other three variables (`tb1`, `tb2`, and `word1`) aren't necessary from a logic perspective, but they lead to code that is easier to understand and more efficient. Without those extra variables, you'd have to do something like this:

```
word2 = form.elements["word2"].value;
if (word1.toLowerCase() > word2.toLowerCase()) {
  form.elements["word2"].value = form.elements["word1"].value;
  form.elements["word1"].value = word2;
}
```

All those `form.elements["..."]` code snippets can get confusing, which makes maintenance more difficult. Another reason this code fragment is bad is that with every `form.elements["..."]`, the JavaScript engine has to search through all of the controls in the form, and those searches take a relatively long time to execute. So although this solution works, it's rather inelegant. Strive for elegance! Let your inner swan soar!

Go back to Figure 9.14B and note how we assign the `msg` variable to "Congratulations! The words are now in the correct order!" above the `if` statement. And note how we use `+=` to append different text onto the end of the `msg` string variable within the `else if` and `else` code blocks. That's a fairly common technique where you initialize a string variable and then use the `+=` operator to add text to it later on.

There's one last noteworthy item in the Word Ordering web page's code. Near the bottom of the `correctWordOrder` function, find the `\"` escape sequences that are meant to offset "correct order" within the `msg` variable's assigned string. What's wrong with using regular quotes (`"`) to offset "correct order"? The first regular quote would be interpreted by the JavaScript engine as the terminating quote for the `msg` variable's assigned string, and that would be inappropriate.

## 9.11 **More String Details**

There are two forms for strings—string primitives and string objects. A string primitive is simply a group of characters. String primitives are also known as *string literals*, and they are written with single quotes (as in 'Carpe Diem!') or double quotes (as in "Let's not seize the day—let's have a meeting instead!"). A string object wraps up a string primitive, and in doing so, it adds properties and methods. In this section, we'll introduce one string property and several string methods.

A string object's `length` property returns the number of characters in the string. Note this example, which uses the length property:

```
var musician = "Taylor Swift";
alert("There are " + musician.length + " characters in \"" +
  musician + "\".");
```

The `musician.length` code returns the value 12, so the resulting alert dialog looks like this:

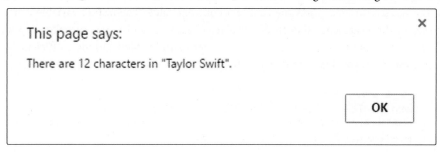

In the prior code fragment, note that `length` does not use parentheses. That's because `length` is a property, not a method.

JavaScript, being the accommodating (and wacky) language that it is, automatically converts a string primitive to a string object if there's an attempt to access a string property or call a string method from a string primitive. In the prior code fragment, `musician` gets assigned a string primitive, "Taylor Swift". When the JavaScript engine sees an attempt to access the `length` property (with `musician.length`), it converts the `musician` variable's primitive value to an object and then it uses the `length` property to return the string's length.

Because strings are such an integral part of so many programming tasks, JavaScript provides lots of string methods to make those programming tasks easier. JavaScript has over 40 string methods. You've already seen the `toLowerCase` and `toUpperCase` methods. **FIGURE 9.15** shows some additional popular string methods. Spend some time reading the methods' descriptions so you get an idea of what's available.

In Figure 9.15, when we describe the methods, we use the term *calling string*. The calling string refers to the string object that appears at the left of the dot when a string method is called. For example, in the following code fragment, which finds the index position of the space between a person's first and last names, `musician` is the calling string for the `indexOf` method call:

```
var musician = "Bob Marley";
var spacePosition;                    calling string

spacePosition = musician.indexOf(" ");
```

Be aware that the characters in a string are numbered starting with 0 for the first character. So, what does `spacePosition` hold after the preceding code fragment executes? It holds the value 3 ('B' is at 0, 'o' is at 1, 'b' is at 2, and the space character is at 3).

In Figure 9.15, note the `[]`'s in the method headings for `indexOf`, `lastIndexOf`, and `substring`. You should not include the `[]`'s in your code when you call one of those methods. The `[]`'s are a standard syntax notation that indicate that something is optional. So, as explained in its description, when you call the `indexOf` method, the second argument is optional. As you can see in the `indexOf` method's heading, if you include a second argument, you need to preface it with a comma.

| |
|---|
| `charAt (`*index*`)`<br>  Return the character at the calling string's index position, where a string's first character is at index position 0. |
| `indexOf (`*search-string* `[,` *from-index*`] )`<br>  Search within the calling string for the specified search string. Return the start position of the first occurrence of the found string, where 0 is the position of the calling string's leftmost character. If there's a second argument, start the search at that argument's index position. Return -1 if the search string is not found. |
| `lastIndexOf (`*search-string* `[,` *from-index*`] )`<br>  Starting from the right side, search within the calling string for the specified search string. Return the start position of the first occurrence of the found string, where 0 is the position of the calling string's leftmost character. If there's a second argument, start the search at that argument's index position. Return -1 if the search string is not found. |
| `replace (`*search-string*`,` *new-string*`)`<br>  Search within the calling string for the specified search string and replace the first occurrence of the found string with the specified new string. Perform the replacement in a new string and return that new string. Do not change the calling string. |
| `substring (`*begin-index* `[,` *after-end-index*`] )`<br>  Return the portion of the calling string from the specified beginning index position to just before the specified ending index position. If the ending index position is omitted, then return the portion of the calling string from the specified beginning index position to the end of the calling string. If either argument is greater than the string's length, it is treated as if it were equal to the string's length. |
| `trim ()`<br>  Return a new string with all whitespace removed from the start and end of the calling string. Do not change the calling string. |

**FIGURE 9.15 Some of the more popular string methods—their headings and descriptions**

At the bottom of Figure 9.15, we describe the simplest version of the `replace` method. For more complex replacements (including multiple replacements within the calling string), you'll need to use a *regular expression* for the first argument. To learn about regular expressions, read Mozilla's description of the `replace` method at https://developer.mozilla.org/en-US/docs/Web/JavaScript/Reference/Global_Objects/String/replace. Regular expressions are kind of tricky, but their power is intoxicating!

# 9.12 Arithmetic Operators

As stated earlier, it's common for web pages to process strings, and that's why JavaScript supports string processing with string operators and quite a few string methods. Likewise, it's common for web pages to process numbers, and that's why JavaScript supports number processing with arithmetic operators and quite a few math-computation methods. In this section, we describe JavaScript's arithmetic operators.

## Addition, Subtraction, Multiplication, and Division

JavaScript uses +, -, and * for addition, subtraction, and multiplication, respectively. They work the same as the addition, subtraction, and multiplication operators you learned in elementary school. The multiplication operator uses the asterisk and not a cross (×) or a dot (·) as in mathematics books, but other than that, there are no differences, so let's move on.

JavaScript supports two forms of division. For regular division (the kind that you do with a calculator), use the *division operator*, which is implemented with the / symbol. For division where you want to find the remainder, use the *remainder operator*, which is implemented with the % symbol.[4] The following examples use the division and the remainder operators, respectively:

```
13 / 5 ⇒ 2.6
13 % 5 ⇒ 3
```

The ⇒ symbol is not part of JavaScript; it's just a notation that helps with the explanations. In this book (and in many mathematics books), the ⇒ symbol indicates "evaluates to." So the first line says that the expression 13 / 5 evaluates to 2.6. The second line says that the expression 13 % 5 evaluates to 3. The remainder operator (%) might need a little more explanation. In elementary school, you probably learned how to divide by using this "long division" notation:[5]

Let's think about the case where the dividend (the thing at the left of the operator) is less than the divisor (the thing at the right of the operator). For the expression 6 % 9, the dividend is 6 and the divisor is 9. Try to evaluate the following expression without looking at the answer further down.

```
6 % 9 ⇒ ?
```

After you've guessed at an answer, take a look at the equivalent grade school arithmetic notation:

---

[4] The remainder operator is sometimes referred to as the modulus operator because that's the name given to the % operator in other programming languages. However, for all math wonks out there, the formal name in JavaScript is the remainder operator because the generated result takes its sign (positive or negative) from the dividend, not from the divisor. A true modulo operation takes its sign from the divisor, not from the dividend. Now, aren't you glad that I cleared up that remainder/modulus operator controversy for you?

[5] If you're from a country other than the United States, then the division notation you grew up with might look different from what's shown here. But we hope you remember how to calculate a remainder. If not, ask your teacher or google it.

Finding the remainder is a requirement for quite a few programming tasks. For example, suppose you want to implement an online multiplayer card game that deals the deck's 52 cards to all the players, such that each player gets the same number of cards and the remaining cards go in the middle (where they're eventually taken by the player who wins the first trick). Note how the remainder operator is used to calculate the cards in the middle:

```
cardsInMiddle = 52 % numOfPlayers;
```

For another example, suppose you want to implement a web page that helps kids to learn even and odd. If the user clicks the **Even** button, the event handler uses the following code to determine if the number in the `myFavoriteNumber` text control is even:

```
if (document.getElementById("myFavoriteNumber") % 2) == 0)
```

This code should make sense when you realize that if you divide an even number by 2, the remainder is zero.

## Exponentiation

JavaScript provides an exponentiation operator, which uses two consecutive asterisks, **, for its implementation. Here's an example that calculates the volume of a ball:

```
var volume; // volume of the ball
var radius; // radius of the ball
...
volume = 4 / 3 * Math.PI * radius ** 3;
```

The volume assignment uses this mathematical formula for the volume of a sphere:

$$V = \frac{4}{3}\pi r^3$$

In the code fragment, `Math.PI` is a property of the `Math` object; as you'd expect, it holds the value of $\pi$, which is approximately 3.14159. `PI` is a *named constant*, which means that it's a special variable whose value is fixed. To indicate their specialness, JavaScript uses uppercase for all of its named constants, and that's why `PI` uses all uppercase. The `Math` object is a global object, and as such, you don't have to declare it with `var`—just use it. The `Math` object is very important. In addition to having the `PI` property, it has many mathematical methods, which we'll talk about in the next section.

In calculating the volume of a sphere (using the formula shown earlier), the exponentiation operation needs to be performed first. In JavaScript, as in the world of mathematics, the exponentiation operator has higher precedence than the / and * operators. So in the preceding JavaScript code fragment, even though the / and * appear at the left of the ** operator, the JavaScript engine does indeed perform the exponentiation operation first. We'll have more to say about operator precedence in an upcoming subsection.

The ECMAScript organization introduced the exponentiation operator fairly recently, as part of its 2016 ECMAScript standard. So be aware that older browsers don't support it.

## Increment and Decrement

It's common for a program to need to count the number of times something occurs. For example, have you ever seen web pages that show the number of visitors to the web page? Keeping track of the number of visitors requires a `count` variable. You can implement counting up by 1 like this:

```
count = count + 1;
```

But because counting up is such a common task, JavaScript provides a special operator for it, the *increment operator*, which is implemented with ++. Standard coding conventions suggest that when you add 1 to a variable, you should use the increment operator, and not the assignment operator. So to add 1 to a `count` variable, here's the preferred technique:

```
count++;
```

Counting down is also a common task, so JavaScript provides a special operator for it, the *decrement operator*, which is implemented with --. Suppose you keep track of the number of remaining coupons with a variable named `remainingCoupons`. After using a coupon, you should implement the decrementation process like this:

```
remainingCoupons--;
```

Standard coding conventions suggest that you always use the decrement operator to decrement a variable by 1 (as shown), but you should be aware of this alternative code:

```
remainingCoupons = remainingCoupons - 1;
```

This code works, but you should avoid using it.

## Compound Assignment Operators

In the previous chapter, we introduced you to the assignment operator. In this chapter, we've introduced you to several arithmetic operators. Now, we present operators that combine those two functions—assignment and arithmetic.

Here's how you can update x by adding 99.9 to it:

```
x = x + 99.9;
```

And here's the alternative way to do the same thing:

```
x += 99.9;
```

The += thing is the *addition assignment operator*. Standard coding conventions suggest that you use the addition assignment operator to add a value to a variable.

The -=, *=, /=, %=, and **= operators parallel the += operator, and they are collectively referred to as *compound assignment operators*. We won't bore you with detailed explanations, because they all work the same as the addition assignment operator, but make sure you understand these examples:

```
x -= 10;         ≡    x = x - 10;
x *= num;        ≡    x = x * num;
x /= 5.5;        ≡    x = x / 5.5;
x %= 3;          ≡    x = x % 3;
x **= 1.5;       ≡    x = x ** 1.5;
x *= num - 2;    ≡    x = x * (num - 2);
```

The examples show compound assignment operator statements on the left and their equivalent long-form statements on the right. The ≡ symbol means "is equivalent to." It's better style to use the forms on the left rather than the forms on the right, but don't ignore the forms on the right. They show how the compound assignment operators work.

The bottom example is the only one in which the compound assignment operator uses an expression rather than a single value; that is, the right of *= is num - 2, not just a single value like num. For cases like these, the compound assignment form is somewhat confusing. Therefore, for those cases, it's acceptable stylewise to use the equivalent long form rather than the compound assignment form.

## Expression Evaluation and Operator Precedence

Now let's think about what happens when a mathematical expression incorporates different types of operators. For a web page that calculates miles per gallon (MPG) for a car trip, the following is a first-cut assignment statement for the MPG calculation:

```
mpg = milesAt2ndFillUp - milesAt1stFillUp / gallonsAt2ndFillup
```

The user is supposed to keep track of his/her car's odometer miles values for two trips to the gas station, subtract the two miles values, and divide the result by the number of gallons purchased during the second trip to the gas station. So, does this assignment statement do what it's supposed to do? To answer that question, you need to know the order of operation for the three operators in the assignment statement. We want subtraction to be performed first, then division, and then assignment. With JavaScript (and all other programming languages), assignment has a lower precedence than the other operators, which is a good thing. But division has a higher precedence than subtraction, so the JavaScript engine divides milesAt2ndFillUp by gallonsAt2ndFillup before performing the subtraction. That's wrong, and mpg gets assigned the wrong value. So what's the solution?

The solution is to add parentheses to force the subtraction to take place first:

```
mpg = (milesAt2ndFillUp - milesAt1stFillUp) / gallonsAt2ndFillup
```

To know when parentheses are necessary, you need to be familiar with JavaScript's operator precedence table, shown in **FIGURE 9.16**. The operators are organized into groups, with the groups at the top having higher precedence than the groups at the bottom. Within a particular operator group, the operators have equal precedence.

Using the operator precedence table might take some practice. Suppose you have an expression that uses * and +. Because the * operator's group is higher in the table than the + operator's group, the JavaScript engine executes the * operator before the + operator. Because parentheses appear at the top of the table, if parentheses appear within an expression, then the JavaScript engine executes the items inside the parentheses before the items outside the parentheses.

| 1. Grouping with parentheses | *(expression)* |
|---|---|
| 2. Increment and decrement operators | `x++`<br>`x--` |
| 3. Exponentiation operator (right-to-left) | `x ** y` |
| 4. Multiplication and division operators (left-to-right) | `x * y`<br>`x / y`<br>`x % y` |
| 5. Addition and subtraction operators (left-to-right) | `x + y`<br>`x - y` |
| 6. Assignment operators (right-to-left): | `y = x`<br>`y += x`<br>`y -= x`<br>`y *= x`<br>`y /= x`<br>`y %= x`<br>`y **= x` |

**FIGURE 9.16 Abbreviated operator precedence table**

In the operator precedence table, note "left-to-right" in the descriptions for the fourth and fifth groups. If an expression has two or more operators from the fourth group (`*`, `/`, and `%`), then the JavaScript engine executes the operators appearing at the left before operators appearing at the right. Likewise, if an expression has two or more operators from the fifth group (`+` and `-`), then the JavaScript engine executes the operators appearing at the left before the operators appearing at the right. In mathematics, that's referred to as left-to-right *associativity*. For example, if `*` and `/` appear in the same expression and `/` appears further to the left than `*` within that expression, the JavaScript engine performs the division before the multiplication.

In the operator precedence table, note "right-to-left" for the exponentiation operator. That indicates right-to-left associativity, which means that if you have an expression with multiple exponentiation operators, the JavaScript engine executes the rightmost exponentiation operators first. So as shown in the following one-step-at-a-time analysis, `2 ** 3 ** 2` evaluates to 512:

```
2 ** 3 ** 2 ⇒
2 ** (3 ** 2)  ⇒
2 ** 9  ⇒
512
```

In the operator precedence table, note that the assignment operators also use right-to-left associativity. So for an expression with multiple assignment operators, the JavaScript engine executes the assignments appearing at the right before the assignments appearing at the left. For example:

```
var pointsTeam1 = pointTeam2 = 0;
```

The JavaScript engine executes the `pointTeam2 = 0;` assignment first. Assignment operations evaluate to the value that gets assigned into the variable, so `pointTeam2 = 0` evaluates to 0. The

JavaScript engine then executes the other assignment operator (the one at the left) by assigning that 0 value to the `pointsTeam1` variable.

# 9.13 `Math` Object Methods

To make processing numbers easier, JavaScript has more than 30 methods that perform mathematical operations. We don't want to overwhelm you with all of them. In this section, we present the ones that tend to be used most often. In the last section, we introduced you to the `Math.PI` constant, which is a property of the `Math` object. This section's methods, not surprisingly, are members of the `Math` object as well.

Take a look at the `Math` methods in **FIGURE 9.17**. They're all pretty straightforward, but one thing you should be aware of is that if you use a variable for one of the arguments, the method calculates a value as described in the figure and returns that calculated value, but the argument variable's value doesn't change. Thus, if you want to change the value of a variable $x$ so it holds the absolute value of its original value, this won't work:

```
Math.abs(x);
```

Instead, you need to do this:

```
x = Math.abs(x);
```

| |
|---|
| `Math.abs` *(number)*<br>　　Returns the absolute value of the given number. |
| `Math.ceil` *(number)*<br>　　Returns the smallest whole number that is greater than or equal to the given number.<br>　　`ceil` stands for "ceiling." |
| `Math.floor` *(number)*<br>　　Returns the largest whole number that is less than or equal to the given number. |
| `Math.max` *(x, y, z, ... )*<br>　　Returns the largest of the given numbers. |
| `Math.min` *(x, y, z, ... )*<br>　　Returns the smallest of the given numbers. |
| `Math.pow` *(base, power)*<br>　　Returns the first argument's value raised to the power of the second argument's value. |
| `Math.random()`<br>　　Returns a uniformly distributed value between 0.0 and 1.0, but not including 1.0. |
| `Math.round` *(number)*<br>　　Returns the whole number that is closest to the given number. |
| `Math.sqrt` *(number)*<br>　　Returns the positive square root of the given number. |

**FIGURE 9.17 Some of the more popular `Math` methods—their headings and descriptions**

The `round` method performs normal rounding—if a number's fractional portion is .5 or greater, then round up; otherwise round down. The `Math` object's `ceil` method always rounds up, and the `floor` method always rounds down. For an example that uses the `floor` method, suppose you're working the checkout line at Walmart (after a year-long internship as a Greeter) and you need to give 87 cents in change to a customer. How do you know how many quarters to dispense? You divide by 25 (the number of pennies in a quarter) and round down. Here's the JavaScript code:

```
numQuarters = Math.floor(change / 25);
```

The `pow` method has been around a long time, so when there's a need to raise a value to a power, many JavaScript programmers use the `pow` method. But remember the new arithmetic operator, `**`, which also raises a value to a power. Using `**` is slightly faster, but the efficiency improvement is so slight that you should feel free to use either technique.

The `random` method uses a uniform distribution in finding a number between 0.0 and 1.0, not including 1.0. A uniform distribution means that there's an equal likelihood of choosing a number anywhere on the number line between 0 and 1.

If you love mathematics and you'd like to see what else the JavaScript `Math` object has to offer, feel free to peruse Mozilla's Math object page at https://developer.mozilla.org/en-US/docs/Web /JavaScript/Reference/Global_Objects/Math.

## 9.14 Parsing Numbers: `parseInt, parseFloat`

When using all the number-crunching constructs you learned about in the previous sections, the first step is usually retrieving numeric input from the user. When the user types into a text control or a `prompt` dialog, JavaScript reads the input as a string. If you need numeric input, then the string must be parsed in order to convert it to a number. This section describes that process.

*Parsing* is the examination of text to determine what the text represents. The functions `parseInt` and `parseFloat` attempt to convert text to integers and decimal numbers, respectively. They are global functions in that they are not associated with an object, and so to call them, there's no need to preface them with an object and a dot (as you've seen with string methods and `Math` methods). For example:

```
balloons = parseInt(prompt("Number of water balloons:", ""));
diameter = parseFloat(prompt(
  "Diameter of each balloon in inches:", ""));
```

The `prompt` methods[6] return the user's input as strings. The `parseInt` function attempts to convert its string argument to an integer, and the integer value is then assigned into the `balloons`

---

[6] Are you bothered by referring to `prompt` as a method even though there's no object dot needed when you call it? It is indeed a method, and the reason the object dot is unnecessary is because `prompt` is one of the methods in the `window` object. Remember that `window` is JavaScript's global object, and you can access its members without needing the object dot syntax.

variable. Using `parseInt` for the number of balloons should make sense because you can't have half of a balloon. The `parseFloat` function attempts to convert its string argument to a decimal number and the decimal value is then assigned into the `diameter` variable. Using a decimal number for a balloon's diameter should make sense because you can have a diameter with a value that's between two integers.

So, why use the word "float" for a method that returns a decimal number? Most programming languages (including JavaScript) use the term *floating point* for a number that uses a decimal point. That's because such a number can be written with different forms by shifting its decimal point. For example, 56001.9 can be written with scientific notation as $5.60019 \times 10^4$. So in rewriting the number, we "floated" the decimal point to the left by four positions.

In the balloons code fragment shown earlier, there's no attempt to verify that the user enters valid input. In an upcoming example, we'll use several techniques to ensure that the user enters an integer when they're supposed to and a decimal number when they're supposed to.

## 9.15 Water Balloons Web Page

In the previous section, we showed you a code fragment that used prompt dialogs to get input for the number of water balloons and the diameter of those balloons. In this section, we examine a complete web page that gets those input values using text controls. See the Water Balloons web page in **FIGURE 9.18**. When the user clicks the **Calculate water** button, the button's event handler reads the user's input from the text controls, calculates the gallons of water needed to fill up

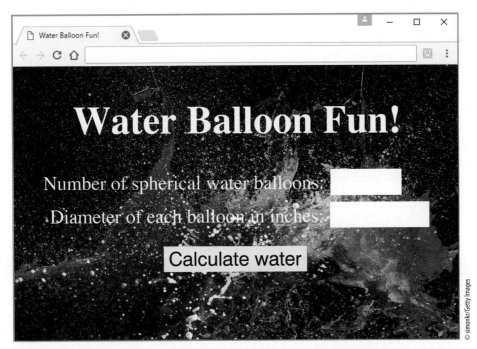

© simonkr/Getty Images

**FIGURE 9.18 Water Balloons web page using text controls for the input**

the balloons, and displays the calculated gallons below the button. The event handler uses arithmetic operators, a `Math` method, `parseInt`, and `parseFloat`.

## body Container

Let's begin our examination of the Water Balloons web page with the `body` container, which you can see in **FIGURE 9.19A**. Note the two text controls for the quantity and diameter user inputs. Also, note the `label` elements that appear before the text controls. As you might have guessed from its name (`label`), the primary purpose of a `label` element is to serve as a prompt (i.e., label) for a text control or some other control within a form.

When using a `label` element, you should connect it to its control by adding an `id` attribute to the control and a `for` attribute to the `label` element with matching values for the two attributes' values. For an example, go to Figure 9.19A and find the first text control and its `id="qty"` attribute-value pair. Then find the preceding `label` element's `for="qty"` attribute-value pair.

Using a `label` element is good for the usual reason—it helps to describe the web page's content. But in addition, the `label` element is particularly helpful for web accessibility. As you may

```
                  To help with accessibility, use the label element for control prompts.

<body>
<h1 class="top">Water Balloon Fun!</h1>
<form class="table" id="myForm">
  <div class="row">                          the form's id value
    <label for="qty">Number of spherical water balloons:</label>
    <input type="text" id="qty" size="3" maxlength="3">
  </div>
  <div class="row">
    <label for="diameter">Diameter of each balloon in inches:</label>
    <input type="text" id="diameter" size="4" maxlength="4">
  </div>
                      To connect the button to the form, use the form
</form>                attribute with a value equal to the form's id value.
<br>
<div class="bottom">
  <input type="button" form="myForm" value="Calculate water"
    onclick="calculateWater(this.form);">
  <br><br>
  <output id="total-water" form="myForm"></output>
</div>
</body>
```

**FIGURE 9.19A body container for Water Balloons web page**

recall, screen readers can help visually impaired users read web pages. By using a `label` element and tying it to a control, you enable a screen reader's speech synthesizer to speak the label's text as a prompt for the control. That way, the visually impaired user knows how and what to input. Very helpful, indeed!

Because a `form` and its submit button are logically connected, normally you should position the button within the `form` container. Initially, that's what we did for the Water Balloons web page. But after using a CSS table layout to center and align the form's labels and text controls, we were stuck with a recalcitrant button that couldn't be centered between the labels column and the text controls column. For such centering to work, we'd have to span the button across those two columns, but CSS table values don't support cell spanning. The solution was to move the button below the form and use a separate CSS rule to center the button. Take a look at Figure 9.19A and verify that the button is positioned below the form and not within it. Notice how the button's event handler calls the `calculateWater` function with `this.form` as its argument. Remember that `this.form` retrieves the form that's associated with the current control. With the button control moved out of the form, you need to do something extra to connect the button to the form. Specifically, you need to add a `form` attribute to the button element where the `form` attribute's value matches the form's `id` attribute value. Look again at the figure and this time note the button's `form="myForm"` attribute-value pair and the form's `id="myForm"` attribute-value pair.

You've probably seen lots of calculator pages on the Web that help you with various calculations. For example, calculating a grade point average (GPA) based on a series of entered grades and course credits. For a calculator page, the `form` and `input` elements do a pretty good job of defining the web page's user-entry content. Likewise, there's an `output` element that does a good job of defining a calculator page's result. The HTML5 standard says you can use the `output` element to hold the result of any user action, but usually you'll use the `output` element to hold the result of a calculation performed by a web page.

The Water Balloons web page is a calculator—when the user clicks the button, the JavaScript engine calculates the total gallons needed for the water balloons and displays the result below the button in an `output` element. For the `output` element to work properly with JavaScript, it needs to be associated with a `form` container. That association is built in if the `output` element is implemented within a `form` container. But with the Water Balloons web page's `output` element below the button, you need to add code to connect the `output` to the form. As you've already seen with the button element, you connect the `output` element to the form by using a `form` attribute with a value equal to the form's `id` value. In the Water Balloons web page, the form's `id` value is `myForm`, so here's the appropriate `output` element code:

```
<output id="total-water" form="myForm"></output>
```

In the upcoming `script` container subsection, you'll learn how the calculated gallons value gets inserted between the `output` element's start and end tags.

## `style` Container

As is the case for most of the web page examples in this book, we store all of the web page's code in just one file. That means the CSS rules go inside a `style` container within the web page's head container, as opposed to having them inside an external CSS file. The book has lots of disparate web pages, and having just one file per web page makes it easier to organize those web pages. But be aware that for a normal organization's website, you should have external CSS files for your nontrivial web pages, and those CSS files will very often be shared by lots of web pages on the website.

Take a look at the Water Balloons web page `style` container in **FIGURE 9.19B**. As you can see, there are quite a few CSS rules. Most are straightforward enough that you should be able to understand them on your own. We'll focus on the ones that are a bit trickier.

```html
<!DOCTYPE html>
<html lang="en">
<head>
<meta charset="utf-8">
<meta name="author" content="John Dean">
<title>Water Balloon Fun!</title>
<style>
  html {display: flex; justify-content: center;}
  body {
    background-color: black;
    background-image: url(../images/waterBalloons.jpg);
    background-size: cover;
    background-repeat: no-repeat;
  }

  .table {display: table;}
  .row {display: table-row;}
  .row > * {display: table-cell;}

  .table {border-spacing: 10px;}
  .row > :first-child {text-align: right;}
  .row > * {font-size: 2em;}

  .top {font-size: 4em; text-align: center;}
  .bottom {text-align: center;}
  .bottom > * {font-size: 2em;}
  *:not(input) {color: white;}
</style>
```

> The `:first-child` pseudo-class matches elements that are the first child of another element. This particular rule selects immediate children of `.row` elements where the child is a first child.

> The `:not` pseudo-class filters the matching elements by omitting the ones described by the value in the parentheses.

**FIGURE 9.19B** `style` **container for Water Balloons web page**

The first CSS rule uses the `display: flex` property-value pair to create a flex box layout for the `html` container and then uses `justify-content: center` to center all of the content within that container. Because the `html` container surrounds the entire web page, all of the web page's content gets centered. Go back to the browser window in Figure 9.18 and verify that the content is centered.

Also in Figure 9.18, note how the form's labels are right aligned, and the form's text controls are left aligned. That alignment is possible because we've implemented a table layout for the form. Go to the `body` container in Figure 9.19A and verify that the form has a `class="table"` attribute-value pair. Also verify that the form's two `div` containers (for the text controls and their labels) have `class="row"` attribute-value pairs. And then note the `.table` and `.row` class selector rules in Figure 9.19B's `style` container. Those rules use `display: table` and `display: table-row` to display the form with a table layout. To complete the table layout, we need to define table cells. We could have added `class="cell"` to the label and text control elements. But that would mean four attribute-value pairs, which is a lot of clutter. So instead, we avoid the `class="cell"` attribute-value pairs by matching the child elements of the already-defined rows. Specifically, we use the child selector `.row > *` to match the label and text control elements, and then apply `display: table-cell` to those elements. Very elegant, indeed!

In Figure 9.19B, note the three CSS rules that establish the form's table layout. Below those rules, you can see three CSS rules that format the table's content. The first of those rules uses the `border-spacing` property to provide gaps between the table's cells. Without those gaps, the labels would butt up against the text controls and the text controls' boxes would touch. No touching, please! The next CSS rule uses `.row > :first-child` for its selector. The `.row >` matches the child elements within the elements that are considered to be rows. Then comes the `:first-child` pseudo-class to narrow the selection further. It's the pseudo-class's job to examine each of the selected elements one at a time and determine if that element fits the condition specified by the pseudo-class. So for this case, the rule selects all children of row elements such that the child is a first child of its parent. In looking at the web page's `body` code, you can see that the first child elements are the `label` elements. The rule uses `text-align: right` to right align the labels' right edges, which is normal for text control prompts.

At the bottom of Figure 9.19B's `style` container, note the `*:not(input)` selector. Once again we're using a pseudo-class. The `:not` pseudo-class removes the specified elements from the current set of matched elements. By using the universal selector (`*`) with `:not(input)`, the rule matches all elements except the `input` elements (i.e., the text controls and the button). The rule uses `color: white` so the matched elements display with a white text color. Their white text contrasts nicely with the background image's black color. On the other hand, the text controls and the button display white backgrounds by default, so we don't want to change their default black text to white.

## `script` Container

Next up—the Water Balloons web page's `script` container. As you can see in **FIGURE 9.19C**, the `script` container contains the `calculateWater` function, which is called by the button's `onclick` event handler.

```
<script>
  // This function calculates and displays the total water
  // needed to fill up water balloons.

  function calculateWater(form) {
    const CUBIC_INCHES_PER_GALLON = 231;  ←——————— named constant
    var qty;        // number of balloons
    var diameter;   // balloon diameter (in inches)
    var gallons;    // total gallons of water needed

    qty = parseInt(form.elements["qty"].value);
    diameter = parseFloat(form.elements["diameter"].value);
    gallons = qty *
      (4 / 3 * Math.PI * Math.pow(diameter / 2, 3) /
      CUBIC_INCHES_PER_GALLON);
    document.getElementById("total-water").innerHTML =
      "Gallons of water needed to fill up the balloons = " +
      gallons.toFixed(1);  ←——————— round to the nearest tenth
  } // end calculateWater
</script>
</head>
```

**FIGURE 9.19C** `script` **container for Water Balloons web page**

As you learned earlier when `Math.PI` was introduced, a named constant is a variable whose value is fixed. The `PI` named constant is built into the `Math` object, and, as such, you don't have to worry about declaring `PI` as a named constant—you just use it. In the `calculateWater` function, the user enters the balloons' diameter value in inches, so when the volume is first calculated, it's in cubic inches. To convert the volume to gallons, the function divides the volume by 231, which is the number of cubic inches per gallon. For a full understanding of the math, study the function's math calculations. The main point here is that 231 is a special value that would be confusing if it appeared in the JavaScript code with no explanation. You could use a comment, but the standard practice is to do something else. When you have a special value that's fixed, you should declare a named constant variable and assign the special value to it. We do that in the `calculateWater` function, and here's the code:

```
const CUBIC_INCHES_PER_GALLON = 231;
```

`const` is a reserved word that declares a variable to be a named constant. So if there's an attempt to reassign a value to `CUBIC_INCHES_PER_GALLON` later on, the JavaScript engine will generate an error and the assignment won't work. To make named constants prominent, you should position their declaration statements at the top of the function (go to Figure 9.19C and verify that the CUBIC_INCHES_PER_GALLON declaration is the first line in the calculateWater function).[7] As you learned for the Math.PI named constant, JavaScript uses uppercase for all of its named constants. Likewise, you should use all uppercase for named constants that you implement. Using uppercase and positioning named constants at the top helps with maintenance. If you ever need to update the named constant's value, it's easy to do so. You go to the top, make the change there, and everywhere the named constant is used, its value gets updated. Easy!

In Figure 9.19C, the code below the named constant declaration should make sense because it uses syntax that you've seen before. Note the way the user's quantity and diameter input values are retrieved using the form.elements property with the elements' qty and diameter id values. As a sanity check, verify those id values in Figure 9.19A. Remember that user input values are always strings. In the calculateWater function, note the way the user's quantity and diameter input values are converted to numbers using parseInt and parseFloat. Also note how the gallons variable gets its value by using arithmetic operators and the Math.pow method. We could have used the exponentiation operator instead of Math.pow, but we wanted to provide an example with Math.pow.

The calculateWater function's last statement assigns the calculated gallons value to the web page's output element. Note how we retrieve the output element's object in the usual way, with form.elements. Note how we use the output object's value property to store a string and the gallons number within the output object. The browser then displays what's stored in the output object's value property.

Most likely, the calculated gallons value will have a fraction that uses multiple digits at the right of the decimal point. To make the calculated gallons value look good, the calculateWater function rounds the result to the nearest tenth position. If the user enters 20 balloons with 5 inch diameters, the code generates a gallon's value of approximately 5.6666534, and with rounding, the web page displays the result as 5.7. At the very bottom of the calculateWater function, note the gallons.toFixed(1) expression. That's the code that rounds the gallons result to the nearest tenth. The way it works is that when the JavaScript engine sees the gallons variable at the left of a dot and a method name, the JavaScript engine converts the number to an object. The object is a number object because it holds a number, and it's a *calling object* because it calls a method, the toFixed method. The toFixed method uses its argument value (1 in this case) as the position where rounding takes place, with 1 being the tenths position, 2 being the hundredths position, and so on. The method performs the rounding and returns the rounded value. If the returned value has fewer digits at the right of the decimal point than indicated by the toFixed method's argument, then 0's are appended at the right. So if gallons holds the value 5.999, gallons.toFixed(1) returns 6.0, not 6. Although the toFixed method performs rounding, the rounding does not affect the calling object, whose value remains unchanged.

---

[7] Although we recommend top-of-function positioning for named constant declarations, it's legal to position them lower down within a function's body. The scope of a named constant is restricted to the block in which the named constant is declared. A *block* refers to a block statement, which is a set of statements surrounded by braces. So if a named constant were declared within an if statement's braces, the named constant could be used only within the if statement's braces.

# 9.16 Constraint Validation for Form Controls

In the Water Balloons web page, we used text controls for the user's quantity and diameter inputs. You can use text controls for lots of different types of input, and that works OK, but you can improve the user's experience if, for each input, you use a control that's specific to the input's type. See **FIGURE 9.20** for six such controls. They all display boxes that look like text controls (the W3C refers to all of them as *one-line plain text edit controls*), but they have the ability to check the user's input to make sure it fits within specific constraints.

Of Figure 9.20's six controls, we'll spend the most time with the number control, which we describe in depth in the next section. For now, to give you a sense of how the other controls work, let's look briefly at an email control example. The following code displays a one-line plain text edit control that checks the user's input to make sure it uses the format "firstname.lastname@park.edu":

```
<input type="email" title="firstname.lastname@park.edu"
  pattern="[A-Za-z0-9]+\.[A-Za-z0-9]+@park.edu">
```

The `pattern` attribute's value is a regular expression that specifies one or more alphabetic or numeric characters, a dot, one or more alphabetic or numeric characters, the @ sign, and then

| input Element | Constraints |
|---|---|
| type="email" | Automatically check the input for a bare-bones email format (e.g., text, @, text). The programmer can provide additional pattern rules so the input matches a more specific email format. |
| type="number" | Automatically check the input for a number. The programmer can provide additional constraints for the input such as being within a certain range and allowing a certain number of digits at the right of the decimal point. |
| type="password" | Enable user to enter text that displays with dots or asterisks so other people cannot see the entered characters. The programmer can provide pattern rules so the input matches a specific password format. |
| type="search" | The programmer can provide pattern rules so the input can be used as a search string. |
| type="tel" | The programmer can provide pattern rules so the input matches a specific telephone number format. |
| type="url" | Automatically check the input for a bare-bones URL format (e.g., text, colon, text). The programmer can provide additional pattern rules so the input matches a specific URL format. |

**FIGURE 9.20 One-line plain text edit controls that are customized to handle specific types of input**

"park.edu". A full understanding of regular expressions is beyond the scope of this book, but if you want to learn on your own, Mozilla provides a nice overview at https://developer.mozilla.org /en-US/docs/Web/JavaScript/Guide/Regular_Expressions.

In the previous code fragment, note the `title` attribute. The HTML5 standard says that whenever you use the `pattern` attribute, you're required to also have a `title` attribute. You might recall that browsers render the `title` attribute's value as a tooltip. So by including a `title` attribute, users can get help in the form of a pop-up message that tells them what to enter in order to satisfy the `pattern` attribute's regular expression.

By the way, the email control provides built-in input validation even without the `pattern` attribute. The email control automatically checks the user's input to see if it follows a standard email format with text, an @ sign, and then more text. With a `pattern` attribute, you can provide additional email formatting requirements that are more specific. Sometimes that's helpful, but often it's unnecessary.

For all of the one-line plain text edit controls, there are several ways in which you can perform input validation. First, use an appropriate form control that has built-in input validation. For the controls shown in Figure 9.20, plus the text control, you can include a `pattern` attribute as part of the control's implementation and provide more specific input requirements that way. As you'll see in the next section, for the number control, you can include additional attributes that constrain different features of the user input. Next, you can add CSS rules that display invalid input in a manner indicative of an error. And finally, you can add JavaScript that executes after the user clicks the form's submit button. The JavaScript displays a warning(s) about any invalid input. Are you now properly stoked to learn about the CSS rules and JavaScript that can turbocharge the input validation on your web page forms? Onward to the next section.

## 9.17 Constraint Validation Using the Number Control's Attributes

With so many web pages that perform numeric calculations, the number control is very popular. Normally, browsers implement a number control with a spinner attached to the usual one-line plain text edit box. To see what we're talking about, look at the spinners in the improved Water Balloons web page in **FIGURE 9.21**. The first number control shows what happens after the user clicks the spinner's up arrow twice. The control shows 2 because the spinner's starting value was 0, and each spinner click increments the value by 1. As an alternative to clicking the spinner arrows to adjust the number control's value, users can enter numbers directly into the box. That's particularly helpful for large numbers. After all, using the spinner to enter a large number would require too many clicks.

Here are the number control's most important attributes:

| Number Control Attributes | | | | | | | | | |
|---|---|---|---|---|---|---|---|---|---|
| type | id | min | max | step | required | value | autofocus | disabled | readonly |

You already know about most of the attributes because you saw them with the text control, and they work the same for the number control. We'll focus on the new attributes—min, max, step, and required. But before digging into the attributes, you should know the starting

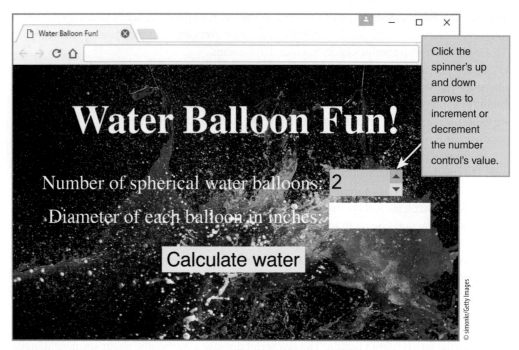

**FIGURE 9.21 Improved Water Balloons web page using number controls for the input**

syntax for the number control. To create a number control, you'll need an `input` element with `type="number"`:

```
<input type="number"...>
```

The `min` and `max` attributes form the range of minimum and maximum values that the user is allowed to enter in the number control's box. Not surprisingly, the HTML5 standard requires the `max` attribute's value to be greater than or equal to the `min` attribute's value. In the improved Water Balloons web page source code in **FIGURE 9.22**, note the `min="0"` and `max="99"` attribute-value pairs for the quantity number control. With that code in place, if the user enters an out-of-range value such as -5, the browser will detect the user entry as being invalid. Some browsers automatically provide a visual signal when invalid input is detected. Most often, those visual signals are in the form of changing the number control's border to red. In addition to that automatic signaling, all modern browsers allow programmers to add CSS and/or JavaScript that provides customized warnings when invalid input is detected. We'll show examples of that in the upcoming sections.

The `min` and `max` attribute values help with the operation of the number control's spinner. It's not specified by the HTML5 standard, but testing shows that when you first click a spinner's up or down arrow, the `min` value determines the starting point. If there's no `min` attribute, then the spinner's starting value is 0. The `max` attribute value prevents the spinner from incrementing to a number greater than the `max` attribute's value.

The number control's `step` attribute specifies (1) the distance between valid values and (2) the value adjustment generated by each spinner click. So in Figure 9.22's quantity number control,

```
<body>
<h1 class="top">Water Balloon Fun!</h1>
<form class="table" id="myForm">
  <div class="row">
    <label for="qty">Number of spherical water balloons:</label>
    <input type="number" id="qty"
      min="0" max="99" step="1" required>
  </div>
  <div class="row">
    <label for="diameter">Diameter of each balloon in inches:</label>
    <input type="number" id="diameter"
      min="0" max="12" step=".01" required>
  </div>
</form>
<br>
<div class="bottom">
  <input type="button" form="myForm" value="Calculate water"
    onclick="calculateWater(this.form);">
  <br><br>
  <output id="total-water" form="myForm"></output>
</div>
</body>
</html>
```

Number control attributes that help with constraint validation.

**FIGURE 9.22** body **container for improved Water Balloons web page**

with a min value of 0 and a step value of 1, two up arrow clicks generate the 2 you can see in Figure 9.21. The diameter number control also has a min value of 0. With a step value of .01, two up arrow clicks would generate a value of .02.

If the user enters a number manually, without using the spinner, the min, max, and step values determine what user entries are deemed valid. For example, because the quantity number control has a min value of 0, a max value of 99, and a step value of 1, only integers between 0 and 99 are deemed valid.

To allow decimal input, use the step attribute with a decimal value. For example, in the following code fragment, step=".01" means each spinner click adjusts the current value up or down by .01, and valid values can have up to 2 digits at the right of a decimal point.

```
<input type="number" id="hourly-pay"
  min="10" max="100" step=".01" required>
```

The min and max attributes can have negative numbers for their values. The step attribute does not allow negative numbers. For the step attribute, you must have a positive number or the value "any." If you specify step="any", that means the user can enter any number between the min and max values with any number of digits at the right of the decimal point. If you don't provide a step attribute, then the default step value is 1. So in the Water Balloons web page, we could have omitted the step="1" attribute-value pair. Including it is a form of self-documentation.

The number control's `required` attribute indicates that the user is required to enter a value, and if there's no value entered, the control's input is deemed invalid. It's an empty attribute, which means you can use it by itself, without needing a value for it. Unlike the `min`, `max`, and `step` attributes, which are used by only some of the controls, the `required` attribute can be used with all the controls.

## 9.18 Constraint Validation Using CSS Pseudo-Classes

In the previous section, you learned how to implement number controls with attributes that define what it means for a user's input to be valid or invalid. When entering into a form's boxes, users sometimes enter invalid information. To help prevent that, you should consider using CSS and JavaScript so that the user is made aware of the problem and then will be inclined to re-enter with valid input. In this section, we describe how you can use CSS to customize the format of controls that have invalid input. In a later section, we describe how you can use JavaScript to display error messages after the user submits the form with invalid input.

To create a CSS rule that matches invalid-input controls, all you have to do is append an `:invalid` pseudo-class to an `input` type selector. For example, to display all invalid input controls with a light red background color, you can use this CSS rule:

```
input:invalid {background-color: rgb(255, 220, 220);}
```

`:invalid` **pseudo-class**

If a form has lots of controls with invalid input, and if all of those controls display with a red background color, that might be a bit overwhelming for the user. To avoid that unpleasantness, you might want to display red only when an invalid-input control has the *focus*. A control gains the web page's focus when the user clicks on the control or tabs the cursor to the control. To have a CSS rule match a control only when the control has focus, you can use the `:focus` pseudo-class. For example, the improved Water Balloons web page uses the following rule to highlight its invalid-input number controls with a light red background when a control has the focus:

```
input:invalid:focus {background-color: rgb(255, 220, 220);}
```

Note how the `:invalid` and `:focus` pseudo-classes are used together by concatenating them both to the `input` type selector.

Here's what the improved Water Balloons web page controls look like when the user enters an invalid value in the diameter number control and the focus is still on that control:

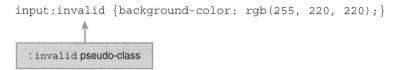

Number of spherical water balloons: 2

Diameter of each balloon in inches: -5

To counteract the negative vibes from red backgrounds on invalid inputs, you might want to make the user feel good by showing soothing light green backgrounds for valid inputs. You can do that with the `:valid` pseudo-class. For example, the improved Water Balloons web page uses the following rule to highlight its valid-input number controls with a light green background when a control has the focus:

```
input:valid:focus {background-color: lightgreen;}
```

To see what the web page looks like when the user enters valid input, go back to Figure 9.21 and note the light green background in the quantity number control.

By the way, the improved Water Balloons web page uses the same `style` container code as the original Water Balloons web page, except for the addition of the two background color CSS rules.

# 9.19 **Comparison Operators and Logical Operators**

We're not done with the improved Water Balloons web page. We still need to present its `calculateWater` function, which checks for valid input and calculates the number of gallons of water needed to fill up the balloons. But all that checking and calculating uses Java Script operators that haven't been introduced, or they've been introduced but not described fully. So in this section, we'll take a little side trip where you learn about those operators, and in the next section, we'll use those operators in implementing the `calculateWater` function.

## Comparison Operators

As you know, an `if` statement's heading includes a condition with parentheses around the condition, like this:

```
if (condition) {
   . . .
```

Usually (but not always), the condition performs some type of comparison, and the comparison uses a *comparison operator*. Here are JavaScript's comparison operators:

```
<, >, <=, >=, ==, !=, ===, !===
```

Each comparison operator compares two operands and returns either true or false, depending on the values of those operands.

The `<`, `>`, `<=`, and `>=` operators are collectively referred to as JavaScript's *relational operators*. They work the same as the operators you've seen in mathematics books, except that you have to use `<=` instead of ≤, and you have to use `>=` instead of ≥. The reason you can't use ≤ or ≥ is because those symbols are not found on standard keyboards, and even if they were there, the JavaScript engine wouldn't understand them.

The `==`, `!=`, `===`, and `!==` operators are collectively referred to as JavaScript's *equality opera-tors*. As you might recall from earlier in this chapter, the `==` operator tests two operands for equal-ity. For example, suppose you have a variable named `floor` that keeps track of an elevator's floor position in a hotel. Because of triskaidekaphobia, many hotels do not have a thirteenth floor.[8] The following code fragment attempts to display a warning if `floor` holds the value 13:

```
if (floor = 13) {                      This is a bug.
   alert("Warning - The elevator indicates floor 13, but there" +
      " is no 13th floor!");
}
```

Do you see the error in the code? It's a very common mistake to use one equals sign instead of two, and that can lead to a particularly pernicious bug. It's pernicious (causing harm in a way that is not easily seen or noticed) in that the browser engine executes the code with no error message, so the programmer might not realize there's an error. With just one equals sign, the `if` statement's condition is an assignment, not a test for equality. And when there's an assignment, the assign-ment expression evaluates to the value that's assigned into the variable. So for this code fragment, the `if` statement's condition evaluates to 13. Having a condition evaluate to 13 might seem odd. Normally, a condition should evaluate to true or false, but this is JavaScript, and—sorry—JavaScript has its quirks. Here's the behind-the-scenes scoop, set off in a box to give it the idiosyn-cratic attention it deserves:

> If a condition evaluates to a non-zero value, the condition is treated as true.
> If a condition evaluates to zero, the condition is treated as false.

So that means that with the prior hotel floor `if` condition evaluating to 13, the condition is treated as true. Which means that regardless of the `floor` variable's original value, after executing the code fragment, `floor` gets assigned the value 13, and the user sees the dialog warning. When the `floor` variable starts out holding something other than 13, that warning is inappropriate. We hope the programmer (you) will catch the bug, but maybe not. So try hard to remember to use `==` and not `=` when testing for equality.

As you might recall from earlier in this chapter, the `!=` operator tests two operands for inequality. The `!=` operator is pronounced "not equal."

It won't affect your programs very often, but you should be aware that in comparing two values with `==` or `!=`, if the values are of different types, the JavaScript engine attempts to convert them to the same type before performing the comparison. That slows things down a bit, but it's normally imperceptible. The attempt to convert the operands to the same type might come in

---

[8] In many countries, the number 13 is considered to be an unlucky number. Some consider the number to be more than unlucky and have an intense fear of 13, which is known as *triskaidekaphobia*. Because architects and builders are aware of this phobia, they may decide to skip 13 when numbering hotel floors. In such hotels, elevators show buttons for floors 1 through 12, then floors 14 through the top floor, with no floor 13. In the United States, many government buildings use their secret 13th floors for surveillance operations conducted in partnership with space aliens.

handy if you retrieve a string value from a text control and you want to know if it equals a particular number. For example, imagine a web page that provides division practice for kids. It prompts the user to enter two numbers in dividend and divisor number controls, and it prompts the user to enter the division result in a text control. A text control is used for the result instead of a number control because we want to allow the user to enter a string for the result. After all, if the user enters a divisor value of 0, then the division operation generates the special numeric value `Infinity`,[9] and for the right answer, the user would need to enter the string "Infinity". The following code checks to see whether the user's entered division result is correct:

```
dividend = form.elements["dividend"].valueAsNumber;
divisor = form.elements["divisor"].valueAsNumber;
result = form.elements["result"].value;
if (dividend / divisor == result) {
    ...
```

The `valueAsNumber` property returns a number from a number control.

The `value` property returns a string.

The point of this example is that the `if` statement's test for equality works fine, even though the left side evaluates to a number and the right side is a string. Note the `valueAsNumber` property for the dividend's number control. If you use the `value` property for a number control, you'll get a string value, which will sometimes be OK. But in most cases (including this case), you'll want to use the `valueAsNumber` property so you can use the retrieved number later on as part of an arithmetic calculation.

Although you'll usually want to use `==` and `!=` for testing equality and inequality, be aware that there are "strict" versions of those operators that do not perform type conversions. The *strict equality operator* (also called the *identity operator*) uses three equals signs, `===`, for its syntax. It evaluates to true only if its two operands are the same value and the same type. The *strict inequality operator* (also called the *non-identity operator*) uses `!==` for its syntax. It evaluates to true if its two operands are different values or they are different types. Most programmers don't use `===` and `!==` very often. They rely instead on the `==` and `!=` operators because they're used to those operators from other programming languages, and unless their operands are different types, `==` works the same as `===` and `!=` works the same as `!==`.

## Logical Operators

You've now seen how to use comparison operators to test a condition for an `if` statement. An `if` statement will sometimes need a condition that involves more than one test. The `&&` (pronounced "and") and `||` (pronounced "or") operators enable you to tie multiple tests together to form a nontrivial `if` condition.

If two criteria both need to be true for a condition to be satisfied, then you should use the `&&` operator to join the two criteria together. For example, suppose you're designing a web

[9] If the user enters a negative number for the dividend and 0 for the divisor, then the division operation generates `-Infinity`. And if the user enters 0 for both the dividend and the divisor, the division operation generates the special numeric value NaN, which stands for "not a number."

page that checks whether a user-entered vehicle speed is legal in the United Kingdom. Different types of roads have different minimum and maximum speeds. For a dual carriageways road, the minimum speed is 40 mph and the maximum speed is 70 mph. If the user enters a speed in a text control and then clicks the **Dual Carriageways** button, the following code uses the && operator to check that the speed is at least 40 mph and the speed is no greater than 70 mph:

```
speed = form.elements["speed"].valueAsNumber;
if (speed >= 40 && speed <= 70) {
  . . .
```

We could have added inner parentheses to make it obvious that the >= and <= operators need to be executed before the && operator:

```
if ((speed >= 40) && (speed <= 70))
```

The additional parentheses might help to make the code more understandable to a human reader, but they're irrelevant to the computer. That's because, due to operator precedence, the JavaScript engine automatically executes the >= and <= operators before the && operator. Note the operator precedence table in **FIGURE 9.23**,[10] and verify that the comparison operators (including >= and <=) have higher precedence than the logical and operator (&&). This table adds comparison operators and logical operators to the operator precedence table presented earlier.

By the way, in checking to see if the user-entered speed is between 40 and 70, you might be tempted to do something like this:

```
if (speed >= 40 && <= 70)
```

Sorry—that's a common error and it doesn't work. If you have a condition where both criteria use the same variable (like when a variable's value needs to be between two other values), you must include the variable on both sides of the &&. In other words, you must include the second speed variable like this:

```
if (speed >= 40 && speed <= 70)
```

As you know, with the && operator, both conditions must be true for the result to be true. If you have a situation where only one of two conditions needs to be true for the result to be true, then you should use the || operator. For example, suppose you're designing a medical advice web page for your astrology practice. The following code uses the || operator to check whether a user-entered blood type is A or B:

---

[10] The table shown in Figure 9.23 has the operators you'll need for most of your JavaScript programming tasks. But if you're an operatorphile, you'll probably want to peruse the complete (and considerably larger) JavaScript operator precedence table at https://developer.mozilla.org/en-US/docs/Web/JavaScript/Reference/Operators/Operator_Precedence.

| Operator Type | Associativity | Specific Operators |
|---|---|---|
| 1. grouping with parentheses | | ( ) |
| 2. logical not | right-to-left | ! |
| 3. increment and decrement | | ++, -- |
| 4. exponentiation | right-to-left | ** |
| 5. multiplication and division | left-to-right | *, /, % |
| 6. addition and subtraction | left-to-right | +, - |
| 7. relational | left-to-right | <, >, <=, and >= |
| 8. equality | left-to-right | ==, !=, ===, and !== |
| 9. logical and | left-to-right | && |
| 10. logical or | left-to-right | \|\| |
| 11. assignment | right-to-left | =, +=, -=, *=, /=, %=, **= |

**FIGURE 9.23** **JavaScript operator precedence table**

```
bloodType = form.elements["bloodType"].value;
sign = form.elements["zodiacSign"].value;
if ((bloodType == "A" || bloodType == "B") && sign == "Taurus") {
   alert("You are susceptible to ACL tears." +
      " Adding myrrh to your incense should help.");
}
```

Note that the `bloodType` variable appears twice in the `if` statement's condition. That's necessary because you must repeat the variable when both sides of an `||` condition involve the same variable. Note that we're using not only the `||` operator, but also the `&&` operator. The code works as expected—if the user has A or B blood and the user is a Taurean, then the entire `if` condition is true.

In the preceding code fragment, note the inner parentheses surrounding the `||` operation. We want the JavaScript engine to execute the `||` operator before the `&&` operator, and the parentheses force that order of operation. But would the code still work even if the parentheses were omitted? Look at the operator precedence table. It indicates that `&&` has higher precedence than `||`, so we do indeed need the parentheses to force the `||` operation to be performed first.

The `&&` and `||` operators are referred to as logical operators because they rely on true and false logic. There's one more logical operator, the `!` (pronounced "not") operator. The `!` operator reverses the truth or falsity of an expression. So if you have an expression that evaluates to true, and you stick a `!` operator in front of it, the resulting expression evaluates to false. For example, suppose the variable `sign` contains the value "Taurus". Then the following `!` operators turn true to false and false to true, respectively:

```
!(sign == "Taurus") ⇒ false
!(sign == "Virgo") ⇒ true
```

If you dislike the three fire zodiac signs (Aries, Leo, and Sagittarius) and want to exclude them using an `if` condition, you can do this:

```
if (!(sign == "Aries" || sign == "Leo" || sign == "Sagittarius"))
```

Note that the `!` is inside one set of parentheses and outside another set. Both sets of parentheses are required. The outer parentheses are necessary because the compiler requires parentheses around the entire condition. The inner parentheses are also necessary because without them, the `!` operator would operate on the `sign` variable instead of on the entire condition. Why? This would happen because the operator precedence table shows that the `!` operator has higher precedence than the `==` and `||` operators. The way to force the `==` and `||` operators to be executed first is to put them inside parentheses.

Try not to get the `!` logical operator confused with the `!=` inequality operator. The `!` operator switches the truth or falsity of a condition. The `!=` operator asks a question—are the two things unequal?

## 9.20 JavaScript for the Improved Water Balloons Web Page

In the last section, we journeyed into the exciting world of comparison operators and logical operators. In this section, we put those operators into practice while we improve the input validation for the Water Balloons web page. Specifically, we add JavaScript to display error messages after the user submits a form with invalid input.

You might recall from our earlier Water Balloons web page discussion that you can use CSS to perform constraint validation before the form is submitted. After the form is submitted (by clicking a button that executes an `onclick` event handler), you can use JavaScript to call the form object's `checkValidity` method. If it returns false, that means at least one of the form's control values is invalid, and you can then display an appropriate warning message. Here's an example that illustrates how the `checkValidity` method could be used to check the inputs in the Water Balloons web page:

```
if (form.checkValidity() == false) {
  alert("Invalid input.\nAs you enter values," +
    " green means valid input and red means invalid input.");
}
else {
  qty = form.elements["qty"].valueAsNumber;
  diameter = form.elements["diameter"].valueAsNumber;
  ...
```

In the preceding code fragment, if the form is found to have invalid input, the `alert` message warns the user by describing the meaning of the green and red background colors. Those background colors are implemented with `:valid` and `:invalid` pseudo-class selectors, which you can see in the Water Balloons web page `style` container in **FIGURE 9.24A**. That message is helpful, but it's pretty generic. If you want more granularity in your warning message, call the `checkValidity` method from individual controls rather than from the form.

```html
<!DOCTYPE html>
<html lang="en">
<head>
<meta charset="utf-8">
<meta name="author" content="John Dean">
<title>Water Balloon Fun!</title>
<style>
  html {display: flex; justify-content: center;}
  body {
    background-color: black;
    background-image: url(../images/waterBalloons.jpg);
    background-size: cover;
    background-repeat: no-repeat;
  }
  .table {display: table;}
  .row {display: table-row;}
  .row > * {display: table-cell;}

  .table {border-spacing: 10px;)
  .row > :first-child {text-align: right;}
  .row > * {font size: 2em;}

  .top {font-size: 4em; text-align: center;}
  .bottom {text-align: center;}
  .bottom > * {font-size; 2em;}
  *:not(input) {color: white;}

  input:valid:focus {background-color: lightgreen;}
  input:invalid:focus {background-color: rgb(255, 220, 220);}
</style>
```

> Display valid input with a green background and invalid input with a red background.

**FIGURE 9.24A** `head` **container for improved Water Balloons web page**

As shown in **FIGURE 9.24B**'s `calculateWater` function, the improved Water Balloons web page checks each control separately for invalid input by calling the `checkValidity` method from individual controls. Here's the code that checks the `qtyBox` control for invalid input:

```
if (!qtyBox.checkValidity() && diameterBox.checkValidity()) {
  alert("Invalid quantity value. Please reenter.");
}
```

Note the `!` operator at the left of `qtyBox.checkValidity()`. If the user enters an invalid value in the `qtyBox` control, the `checkValidity` method returns false, the `!` operator reverses that to true, and `!qtyBox.checkValidity()` returns true. Note the `if` statement's `&&` operator, which ties together two subconditions. That code checks for the user entering an invalid `qtyBox` value and a valid `diameterBox` value. If you look further down in Figure 9.24B's

```
<script>
  // This function calculates and displays the total water
  // needed to fill up water balloons.

  function calculateWater(form) {
    var CUBIC_INCHES_PER_GALLON = 231;
    var qty;        // number of balloons
    var diameter;   // balloon diameter (in inches)
    var gallons;    // total gallons of water needed
    var qtyBox, diameterBox;  // text controls
    var totalWater;            // result message

    qtyBox = form.elements["qty"];
    diameterBox = form.elements["diameter"];
    totalWater = form.elements["total-water"];

    if (!form.checkValidity()) {              [&& operator]
      totalWater.value = "";
      if (!qtyBox.checkValidity() && diameterBox.checkValidity()) {
        alert("Invalid quantity value. Please reenter.");
      }
      else if (!diameterBox.checkValidity() && qtyBox.checkValidity()) {
        alert("Invalid diameter value. Please reenter.");
      }
      else if (!diameterBox.checkValidity() && !qtyBox.checkValidity()) {
        alert("Invalid quantity and diameter values. Please reenter.");
      }
    } // end if
```

**FIGURE 9.24B** `head` **container for improved Water Balloons web page**

`calculateWater` function, you'll see `else if` code blocks that check for the other cases—where the user enters only an invalid `diameterBox` value and where the user enters invalid values for both controls.

Look again at the code that checks the `qtyBox` control for invalid input. We could have written that code without using the `!` operator. We could have done this:

```
if (qtyBox.checkValidity() == false && diameterBox.checkValidity()) {
  alert("Invalid quantity value. Please reenter.");
}
```

Both ways work, but the first way is considered more elegant and most veteran programmers do it that way.

Not wanting to beat a dead horse, but look again at the big `else` code block in **FIGURE 9.24C**. It handles the situation where both user input values are valid. As with the original Water Balloons web page, it calculates the amount of water needed for the water balloons. The only change to the original code is the `if` statement that checks to see if the user entered 0 for the quantity or 0 for the diameter. Note how the `||` operator is used to combine those two subconditions.

```
    // Both user entries are valid.
    else {
      qty = qtyBox.valueAsNumber;
      diameter = diameterBox.valueAsNumber;

      if ((qty == 0) || (diameter == 0)) {
        totalWater.value = "No water is needed.";
      }
      else {                          [|| operator]
        gallons = qty *
          (4 / 3 * Math.PI * Math.pow(diameter / 2, 3) /
          CUBIC_INCHES_PER_GALLON);
        totalWater.value =
          "Gallons of water needed to fill up the" +
          " balloons = " + gallons.toFixed(1);
      }
    } // end else
  } // end calculateWater
</script>
</head>
```

**FIGURE 9.24C** `head` **container for improved Water Balloons web page**

# 9.21 CASE STUDY: Dynamic Positioning and Collector Performance Web Page

## Dynamic Positioning of Area Description Web Page

In Chapter 7's case study section, the `areaDescription.html` code positions its figure near the left side of the window. This provides good access to the map when the browser window is narrow, but when the browser window is wide, that leads to quite a bit of dead space at the right of the figure. The `position` properties needed to perform mapping operations take control away from browsers and inhibit their ability to perform cosmetic repositioning in response to CSS properties. But JavaScript can step in and do such repositioning.

To do the repositioning, you need to edit the `areaDescription.html` file. Specifically, you need to add a `script` container for the `alignFigure` function, as shown in **FIGURE 9.25**. Also, you need to add `onload` and `onresize` event handlers to the `body` element's start tag that call the `alignFigure` function.

The `alignFigure` function initializes the `figure` variable with the `figure` element. It initializes the `winWidth` variable with the browser window's width. And it initializes the `figWidth` variable with a value that matches the window width when the window width is just barely wide enough to show all of the figure.

```
<head>
  ...
<script>
  function alignFigure() {
    var figure = document.getElementById("figure");
    var winWidth = window.innerWidth;
    var figWidth = 765; // emperical fit
    var leftSpace = (winWidth - figWidth) / 2 - 40;

    if (winWidth < figWidth) {
      figure.style.left = "-40px";
    }
    else {
      figure.style.left = leftSpace + "px";
    }
  } // end alignFigure
</script>
</head>

<body onload="alignFigure()" onresize="alignFigure()">
```

**FIGURE 9.25** Repositioning of figure in enhanced Area Description web page

Whenever the window's width is less than the figure's width, the -40px value for `figure.style.left` pushes the figure further left than it would normally be and aligns it with the left side of most of the other material on the left side of the window. In narrow windows, this provides the greatest possible view of the map. On the other hand, when `winWidth` equals or exceeds `figWidth`, `figure.style.left` takes on a value that centers the figure in the window. For that code to work, the JavaScript engine relies on the figure object's style property. We'll provide an in-depth look at the `style` property in the next chapter.

## Collector Performance Web Page

This chapter's web page introduces the subject of solar collector performance by providing a calculator that computes noontime electric power generation of a photovoltaic solar panel as a function of latitude, panel slope, rated capacity, and time of year. **FIGURE 9.26** shows what the

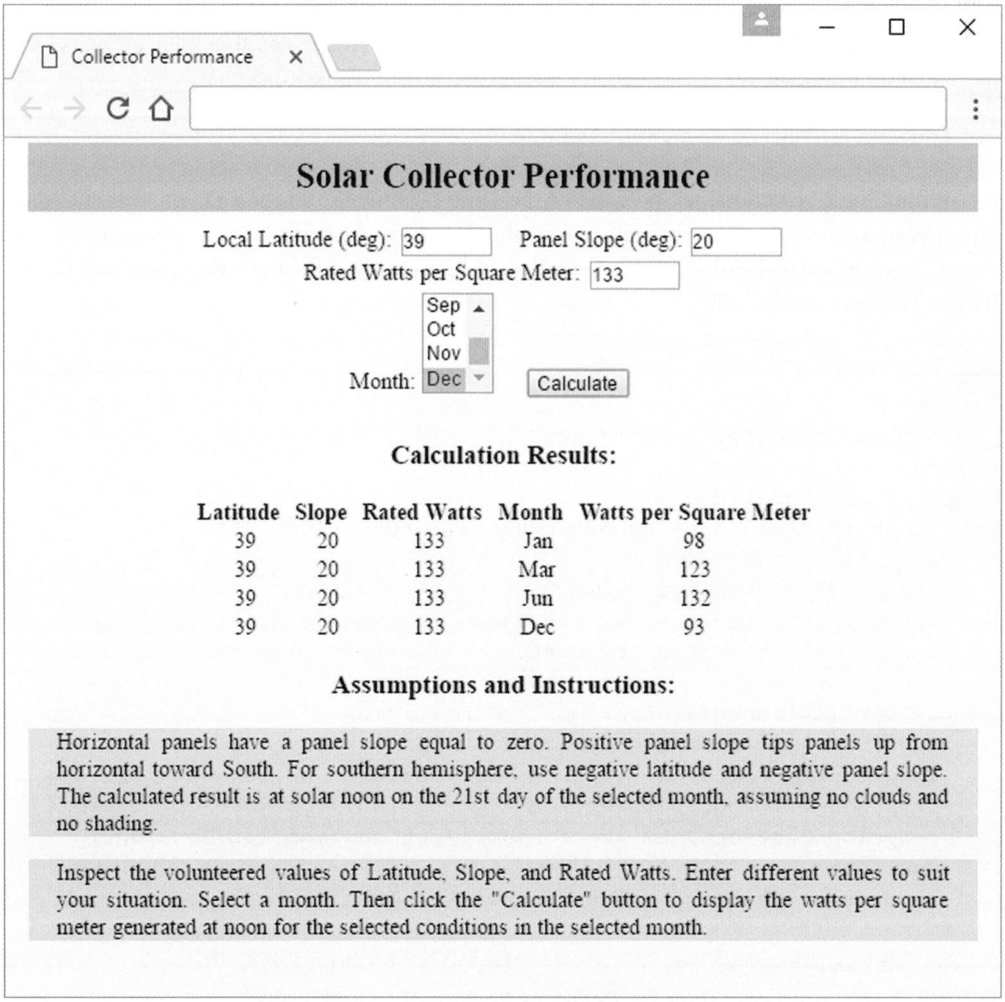

**FIGURE 9.26 Collector Performance web page after four calculations**

result displays after the user performs calculations for January, March, June, and December. This works in the southern hemisphere as well as the northern hemisphere. Just negate the latitude, and negate the slope to specify a north-facing panel.

**FIGURES 9.27A** and **9.27B** show the Collector Performance web page's body container. Within the form, note that there are three input element text controls, and then there's a select element. We'll describe the select element in detail in the next chapter, but for now, just know that it's used here to implement a list box for the user's choice of one or more months. Because of the select element's multiple attribute, the user is able to select multiple values from the list box. Look back at Figure 9.26's browser window and identify the **Month** label and the list box at its right. At the bottom of the browser window, you can see results for Jan, Mar, Jun, and Dec because the user chose those four months from the list box.

The form's select element contains twelve option elements. The text within each option element is the month list box. By default, nothing is selected initially. If a user clicks the "Calculate" button before selecting a month, the Calculation Results under the "Month" and "Watts per Square Meter" headings will be blank. However, the programmer could elect to preselect one particular option (like "Jun") by giving it a selected attribute, like this:

```
<option selected>Jun</option>
```

Within the form container, notice how the input elements and the select element are all preceded by a label element having a for attribute that associates the label with its subsequent control. As you learned earlier, the label element helps to describe the web page's content, and it helps with web accessibility.

```
<body>
<h2>Solar Collector Performance</h2>
<form>
  Local Latitude (deg):
  <input id="latitude" type="text" size="5" value="39">
  Panel Slope (deg):
  <input id="panelSlope" type="text" size="5" value ="20"><br>
  <label for="ratedWatts">Rated Watts per Square Meter:</label>
  <input id="ratedWatts" type="text" size="5" value="133"><br>
  <label for="months">Month:</label>
  <select id="months" name="months" multiple>
    <option>Jan</option> <option>Feb</option> <option>Mar</option>
    <option>Apr</option> <option>May</option> <option>Jun</option>
    <option>Jul</option> <option>Aug</option> <option>Sep</option>
    <option>Oct</option> <option>Nov</option> <option>Dec</option>
  </select>
  <input type="button" value="Calculate" onclick="calc(this.form)">
</form>
```

**FIGURE 9.27A** body **container for Collector Performance web page**

```
<h3>Calculation Results:</h3>
<div class="center">
  <table id="performance">
    <tr>
      <th>Latitude  </th> <th>Slope  </th> <th>Rated Watts
       </th> <th>Month  </th> <th> Watts per Square Meter</th>
    </tr>
  </table>
</div>
<h3>Assumptions and Instructions:</h3>
<p>
  Horizontal panels have a panel slope equal to zero. Positive panel
  slope tips panels up from horizontal toward South. For southern
  hemisphere, use negative latitude and negative panel slope. The
  calculated result is at solar noon on the 21st day of the selected
  month, assuming no clouds and no shading.
</p>
<p>
  Inspect the volunteered values of Latitude, Slope, and Rated Watts.
  Enter different values to suit your situation. Select a month. Then
  click the "Calculate" button to display the watts per square meter
  generated at noon for the selected conditions in the selected month.
</p>
</body>
```

**FIGURE 9.27B** body **container for Collector Performance web page**

Notice that the form's final input element, which is the **Calculate** button, includes onclick="calc(this.form)". This triggers execution of JavaScript that generates one of the rows of output in Figure 9.26 under the "Calculation Results" heading. In the table's tr element, the   characters insert additional space between successive th elements.

**FIGURE 9.28** shows the bottom half of the head element. The top half is not shown because by now it should be either familiar or a straightforward variation of what you have seen before. If you'd like to see the complete code, as always, you should feel free to retrieve it from the book's website. In the style container, the body rule's min-width property keeps a narrow window from wrapping label text in an annoying way. The input:last-child rule puts extra space around the **Calculate** button. The center rule positions the table. Specifically, it adds extra space above and below the table. Also, it horizontally centers the table within its surrounding div container whenever the browser window is greater than the body's minimum width.

The script container in Figure 9.28 illustrates some of this chapter's JavaScript techniques. The global variables, form, altitude, and cosIncidenceAngle, facilitate information transfer from one function to another.

The calc function is what executes when a user presses the "Calculate" button. It starts by declaring and initializing a table variable with a reference to the body's table element. Then

```
<head>
...
<style>
  body {
    text-align: center;
    min-width: 500px;    /* prevents label wrapping */
  }
  form, input:last-child {margin: 10px 20px;}

  /* position the table */
  .center {
    margin: 10px 0;
    display: flex; justify-content: center;
  }
</style>
<script>
  var form;               // html element
  var altitude;           // solar angle above horizon
  var cosIncidenceAngle;       // perpendicular component of radiation

  // This function invoked by user click on Calculate button

  function calc(solarForm) {
    var table;        // table of computed performance values
    var row;          // row in displayed table of calculated values
    var monthIndex;   // index of selected month

    table = document.getElementById("performance");
    row = table.insertRow(table.rows.length);
    form = solarForm;
    computeAngles();            // for altitude and cosIncidenceAngle
    row.insertCell(0).innerHTML = form.elements["latitude"].value;
    row.insertCell(1).innerHTML = form.elements["panelSlope"].value;
    row.insertCell(2).innerHTML = form.elements["ratedWatts"].value;
    monthIndex = form.elements["months"].selectedIndex;
    row.insertCell(3).innerHTML =
      document.getElementsByTagName("option")[monthIndex].innerHTML;
    row.insertCell(4).innerHTML = findWatts();
  } // end calc

  function computeAngles() {
    // presented in case study section at end of next chapter
  } // end computeAngles

  function findWatts() {
    // presented in case study section at end of next chapter
  } // end findWatts
</script>
</head>
```

**FIGURE 9.28** `head` **container for Collector Performance web page**

it declares a `row` variable and initializes it with a new row in the table. After declaring a local `monthIndex` variable to be used later, it initializes the global `form` variable with the parameter's reference to the `body`'s `form` element. Then it calls the `computeAngles` function, which you'll see in the case study section at the end of the next chapter. This function initializes the other two global variables, `altitude` and `cosIncidenceAngle`.

Next, the `calc` function inserts three cells in the newly created table row with copies of user-input values for `latitude`, `panelSlope`, and `ratedWatts`. Notice how the code identifies `input` elements by their `id` values. Then, after initializing the local `monthIndex` variable, it uses that to insert the next cell in the table row with the text displayed in the user-selected `option` in the `select` element. Then it inserts the last cell in the table row with the value returned by the `findWatts` function. Instead of using the index numbers 0, 1, 2, 3, and 4 as arguments for the successive `insertCell` method calls, the `calc` function could have used the same argument, `row.cells.length`, in each of these calls, and `length` would have incremented automatically as cells were added.

The detailed contents of the functions, `computeAngles` and `findWatts`, are not shown here because they contain JavaScript features you have not studied yet. The next chapter will describe these features, and the case study section at the end of the next chapter will present the details of this web page's `computeAngles` and `findWatts` functions.

# Review Questions

### 9.2 `window` Object

1. What property of the `window` object retrieves an object that stores information about the current web page's URL?

2. What's the purpose of the `window` object's `navigator` property?

### 9.3 `alert` and `confirm` Methods

3. Which is the more common way to get information from a user—with a control on a browser window or with a dialog?

4. The `alert` dialog is considered to be a modal window. True or false.

### 9.4 `if` Statement: `if` by itself

5. What is a block statement?

### 9.6 `prompt` Method

6. What are the significant differences between the `confirm` method and the `prompt` method?

7. What is the empty string?

8. If a user sees a `prompt` dialog box and clicks **Cancel** or clicks the close-out **X** button, what value does the `prompt` method return?

### 9.9 Strings

9. What escape sequence should you use to display a double quote within an `alert` dialog message?

10. What is \n?

### 9.11 More String Details

11. For string objects, is `length` a property or a method?

### 9.13 `Math` Object Methods

12. What does `Math.ceil` do?

13. What does `Math.floor` do?

### 9.15 Water Balloons Web Page

14. What does the `:first-child` pseudo-class do?

### 9.17 Constraint Validation Using the Number Control's Attributes

15. For a number control, what attribute indicates that the user must enter a value?

16. For a number control, what attributes determine the range for the number control's spinner?

### 9.18 Constraint Validation Using CSS Pseudo-Classes

17. What does the following selector do?

```
input:valid:focus
```

### 9.19 Comparison Operators and Logical Operators

18. Which operators have right-to-left associativity?

19. Assume the following:

```
var num = 9;
var x = 3.0, y = 6.2;
```

Evaluate the following expressions. Show your work, using a separate line for each evaluation step.

a) `x + num / 2 % 2`

b) `x >= 4 || y < 7 && num != 3 ** 2`

### 9.20 JavaScript for the Improved Water Balloons Web Page

20. If you use a form object to call the `checkValidity` method, what happens?

# Exercises

1. [after Section 9.2] You can use `window.history` to retrieve the `history` object. Using the `history` object, what methods can you call to navigate backwards and forward to web pages that have been visited recently? The answer is not in the book. See https://developer.mozilla.org/en-US/docs/Web/API/History.

2. [after Section 9.3] Refer to the Lie Detector web page's code shown earlier in the chapter. Think about the situation where the alert message displays "your reply was false." Describe the type of person who would generate that output—someone who always tells the truth, someone who always lies, or some other type of person?

3. [after Section 9.9] This code comes from the part of the chapter that describes how to continue a string with \:

```
<script>
  prompt("Of the following U.S. Presidents, which one" +
    " did not die on July 4?\n \
    a)  John Adams\n \
    b)  Thomas Jefferson\n \
    c)  James Monroe\n \
    d)  Ronald Reagan", "");
</script>
```

Provide new code for the first three lines (the first line is `<script>`) such that you use \
instead of + for the string continuation mechanism. Make sure that the resulting dialog's
message looks the same as the original dialog's message. Hint: In order to get the resulting
message to look good, you might have to compromise your coding style a bit.

4. [after Section 9.9] You should get into the habit of writing test code that helps you
understand things. In Section 9.9's String Methods subsection, there's a code fragment that
calls `toUpperCase` and `toLowerCase`. Provide an `alert` method call that shows the code
fragment's effect. Specifically, your `alert` method call should produce the following dialog.
Your code should produce the `alert` message precisely—don't forget the spaces, the quotes,
the new lines, and so on.

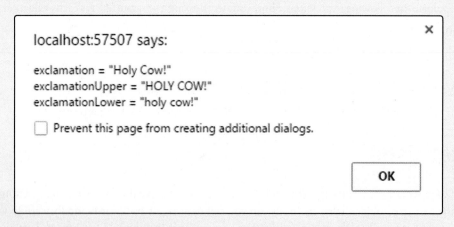

5. [after Section 9.11] Given the following code fragment. What are the resulting values in
`var1`, `var2`, `var3`, `var4`, and `var5`?

```
var name = "Cat in the Hat";
var1 = name.length();
var2 = name.charAt(5);
var3 = name.indexOf(" ");
var4 = name.indexOf("t", 4);
var5 = name.lastIndexOf("t");
```

6. [after Section 9.11] Given the following code fragment. What are the resulting values in `var1`, `var2`, `var3`, and `var4`?

```
var name = "Anna banana";
var1 = name.substring(4, 8) + " ";
var2 = var1.trim();
var3 = name.replace("an", "ri");
var4 = name.substring(5);
```

7. [after Section 9.15] How is the `label` element helpful for web accessibility?

8. [after Section 9.15] Suppose you have a button that is placed outside of a web page's form. What's the best way to associate the button with the form, so that when the user clicks the button, it's straightforward for the form's controls to get processed?

9. [after Section 9.19] Given this code fragment:

```
if (lineSize) {
   alert("There are " + lineSize + " people in line.");
}
else {
   alert("The line is empty.");
}
```

a) If `lineSize` is 0, what's the output?

b) If `lineSize` is 5, what's the output?

10. [after Section 9.19] Sometimes, JavaScript's `==` operator is slightly slower than the identity operator. In what situation is that the case?

11. [after Section 9.19] Assume this:

```
var x = 15;
var y = .4;
```

Evaluate the following expressions. Show your work, using a separate line for each evaluation step.

a) `4 - x / 2 + y`

b) `x % 4 + 4 % x`

c) `2 ** 3 / 2 * 3`

d) `y != 0 && !(y > 4 || true)`

# Project

Create a web page named `rootsCalculator.html` that calculates the roots of the quadratic equation for user-entered integer values for *a*, *b*, and *c*. The quadratic equation is a polynomial of this form where *a* must be nonzero by definition:

$$ax^2 + bx + c = 0$$

The formula for finding *x*'s roots is:

$$x = \frac{-b + \sqrt{b^2 - 4ac}}{2a}$$

In displaying the roots, use this table:

| Situation | Output Message |
|-----------|----------------|
| $b^2 < 4ac$ | Solution: *x*'s roots are imaginary |
| $b^2 = 4ac$ | Solution: *x* = *single-root* |
| $b^2 > 4ac$ | Solution: *x* = *first-root*, *x* = *second-root* |

Use number controls for the a, b, and c user inputs. After the **Calculate roots** button is clicked, if there's valid input, your web page should generate a solution message below the button.

You must include appropriate attributes for your number controls, and that includes appropriate attributes for input validation. In particular, make sure that *a*, *b*, and *c* are integers between –99 and +99 and make sure that *a* is nonzero. Also, when focus is on a number control, display a red border if the number control's value is a noninteger or outside of the range –99 to +99. If the user enters 0 in the *a* number control, there is no need to display a red border around the number control. After the **Calculate roots** button is clicked, if there's invalid input, erase any previous solution message and display an error message dialog that specifies which value(s) is invalid. See the sample session for details.

As always, use proper HTML code for all variables displayed on your web page. Use `label` elements for each of your number control prompts.

### Extra Credit
After the **Calculate roots** button is clicked, if there's invalid input, in addition to displaying an error message dialog, display a red border around all the number controls that contain invalid input.

## Sample Session

After clicking on the first number control:

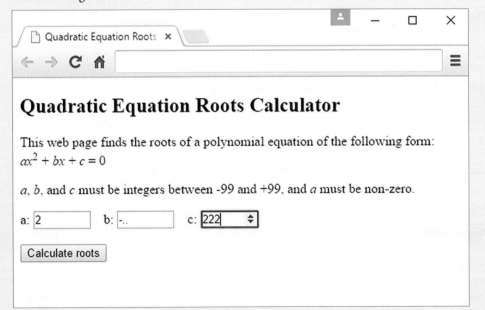

After entering values:

After reentering values and clicking **Calculate roots:**

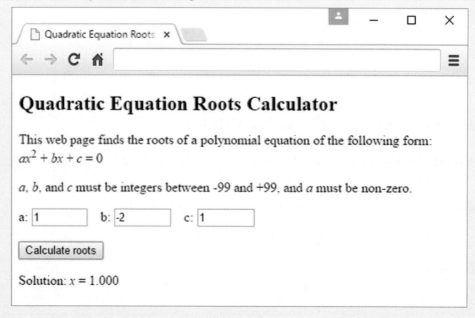

After reentering values and clicking **Calculate roots:**

After reentering values and clicking Calculate roots:

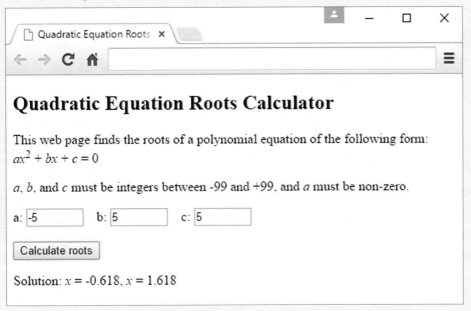

After entering 0 for a, 12.3 for b, and nothing for c, and clicking Calculate roots:

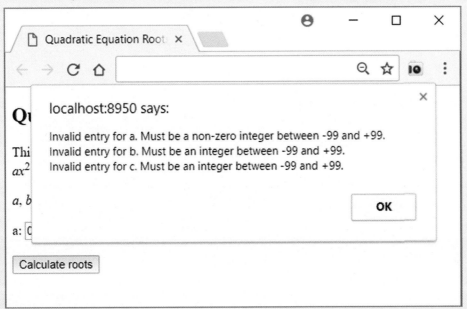

After clicking **OK** to clear the dialog:

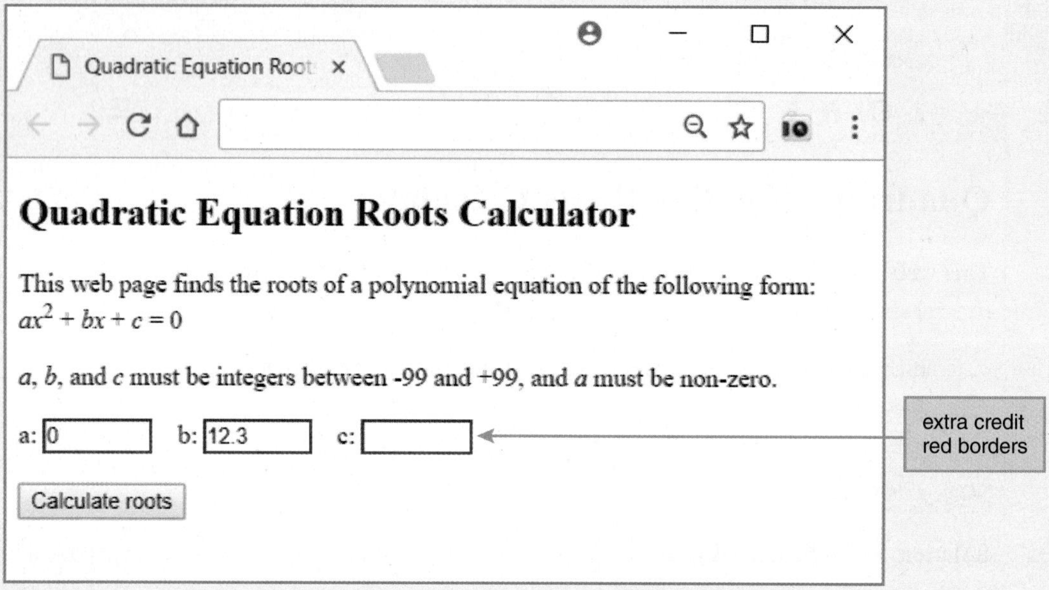

Browser window titled "Quadratic Equation Roots" showing:

# Quadratic Equation Roots Calculator

This web page finds the roots of a polynomial equation of the following form:
$ax^2 + bx + c = 0$

$a$, $b$, and $c$ must be integers between -99 and +99, and $a$ must be non-zero.

a: [0]    b: [12.3]    c: [ ]    ← extra credit red borders

[Calculate roots]

# CHAPTER **10**

# Loops, Additional Controls, Manipulating CSS with JavaScript

## CHAPTER OBJECTIVES

▶ Use a `while` loop to solve problems that require repetition.

▶ For web pages with a significant amount of JavaScript code, move that code to an external file.

▶ Implement a solution using a `do` loop if you're sure that the repeated task needs to be executed at least one time.

▶ Use a radio button group when the user is supposed to select one value from among a list of values.

▶ Use a checkbox when the user is supposed to check or not check an item for selection.

▶ Implement a compact solution for a repetitive task using a `for` loop if you know in advance how many times the loop will execute.

▶ Use the `fieldset` container to make the grouping clear for a group of radio buttons or a group of checkboxes.

▶ Learn techniques for dynamically updating the appearance of a web page using JavaScript and CSS.

▶ Use absolute positioning and the `z-index` property to position elements on top of each other.

▶ Implement a textarea control for multiple-line user entries.

▶ Use the `select` element to implement pull-down menus and list boxes.

## CHAPTER OUTLINE

# 10.1 Introduction

In the previous two chapters, you learned about the basic building blocks needed to implement interactive web pages. Specifically, you learned about forms, buttons, text controls, number controls, event handlers, and JavaScript. In this chapter, you'll add to your tool bag, so you can implement a wider variety of web pages. You'll learn how to make those web pages look better and behave more dynamically.

In this chapter, we introduce controls that can be grouped together, such as radio buttons and checkboxes. You'll learn how to access and update those controls by using JavaScript loop statements to process the individual values within the control's group of values. You'll also use JavaScript to dynamically modify a web page's CSS formatting. You'll learn a new type of formatting with the CSS z-index property. It enables you to stack elements on top of each other, and you'll use JavaScript to modify the stacking order. Finally, you'll learn about pull-down menus and list boxes, which allow users to select one or more values from a list of choices.

# 10.2 while Loop

For many programming tasks, you'll need to perform the same operation repeatedly (e.g., adding a group of numbers to find their sum). To perform operations repeatedly, you'll need to use a loop statement. JavaScript provides three types of loop statements—while loop, do loop, and for loop. We'll cover the while loop in this section, and the do and for loops later in the chapter.

## Syntax and Semantics

The while loop is the most flexible of the three types of loops. You can use it for any task that needs repetitive operations. **FIGURE 10.1** shows the syntax and semantics for the while loop. The syntax at the left of the figure should look familiar because it's similar to the if statement

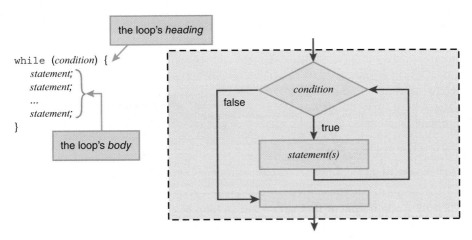

**FIGURE 10.1 Syntax and semantics for the while loop**

syntax. In the while loop's heading, after the reserved word while, you need parentheses, a condition, and an opening brace. As you know, a condition is a question that evaluates to true or false. In the while loop's body, you can have as many statements as you like. Below the body's statements, you indicate the end of the while loop with a closing brace.

In terms of style, the while loop is pretty much the same as the if statement. You should put a space between the condition and the opening brace. Also, don't forget to indent the statements within the braces and align the closing brace with the first character in the loop's heading.

In using loops, you'll need to get comfortable with the jargon. The number of times that a loop repeats is referred to as the number of *iterations*. It's possible for a loop to repeat forever. That's known as an *infinite loop*, and it's usually indicative of a bug. It's also possible for a loop to repeat zero times. There's no special term for the zero iteration occurrence, but it's important to be aware that this sometimes happens.

Study Figure 10.1's flowchart and make sure you understand the while loop's semantics. If the while loop's condition evaluates to true, then the statements within the loop are executed and control then flows back to the top of the loop, where the condition gets checked again. That continues until the condition becomes false. At that point, control flows down to whatever is below the while loop.

## Tracing an Example

The code fragment in **FIGURE 10.2** uses a while loop to calculate the factorial of a user-entered number. The code comes from an exercise at the end of this chapter. The exercise shows the code as part of a complete web page, so go there now if you're curious. The main point of the code fragment is to show how a while loop can be used to implement a solution that requires repetitive operations. As you probably recall from a middle school math class, the factorial of a nonnegative integer $x$ is denoted by $x!$ To calculate the factorial of $x$, you multiply all the integers from 1 up to $x$. So 4! equals 1 • 2 • 3 • 4, which equals 24. In the code fragment, the while loop uses a count variable as the multiplicand for each loop iteration multiplication operation.

```
num = form.elements["number"].valueAsNumber;
factorial = 1;
count = 2;

while (count <= num) {
    factorial *= count;
    count++;
}

form.elements["result"].value = num + "! = " + factorial;
```

The `while` loop performs multiple multiplication operations:
1 * 2 * 3 * ... * num

**FIGURE 10.2 Code fragment that uses a `while` loop to calculate a factorial**

Let's trace the code fragment. *Tracing* is where you essentially pretend you're the computer. You step through the program line by line and carefully record what happens. For many traces, the outcome is dependent on user input. For the factorial web page, the user enters a value into a number box, and when the user clicks the form's button, the JavaScript retrieves the user's entered value. We don't know what a real user will enter, but we need to provide an assumed input value so we can proceed with the trace. Let's assume the user enters 3 into the number box.

The code fragment's first statement uses `form.elements["number"]` to retrieve a control that has an `id` value of `number`. If you look at the complete web page code in the exercise at the end of this chapter, you can see that the number box has an `id` value of `number`. The number box's input value, which we assume to be 3, gets assigned into the `num` variable. The second and third statements assign 1 and 2 to the `factorial` and `count` variables, respectively. Remember, the point of a trace is to carefully record what happens. Here's how you should record the trace after executing the first three lines:

| num | factorial | count | result element |
|-----|-----------|-------|----------------|
| 3   | 1         | 2     |                |

The `while` loop's heading checks the condition `count <= num`. Because 2 is less than 3, the condition is true, and the loop's body gets executed. The loop body's first statement multiplies `factorial` times `count` and puts the result back into the `factorial` variable. The loop body's second statement increments `count`. Here's what your trace should look like after executing those two statements:

| num | factorial | count | result element |
|-----|-----------|-------|----------------|
| 3   | ~~1~~     | ~~2~~ |                |
|     | 2         | 3     |                |

Note how 1 and 2 are crossed off. After a variable's value changes, you should cross off its old value so the old value doesn't accidentally get reused later.

Continuing with the trace, the next step is to jump back to the `while` loop's heading and check the condition again. Is the condition `count` `<=` `num` still true? Yes, `count`, 3, is equal to `num`, 3. So the loop's body gets executed again, and here's what your trace should look like after that execution:

| num | factorial | count | result element |
|-----|-----------|-------|----------------|
| 3   | ~~1~~     | ~~2~~ |                |
|     | ~~2~~     | ~~3~~ |                |
|     | 6         | 4     |                |

Going back to the top of the loop, and checking the condition, `count` is 4 and `num` is 3, so the condition is false. The next step is to jump below the loop and execute the bottom statement. The bottom statement concatenates three entities: `num`'s value, "! = ", and `factorial`'s value. The concatenated result is "3! = 6". That string is then assigned into the control specified by `form.elements["result"]`. In the trace, we represent that control with the heading "`result` element." Here's what your final trace should look like:

| num | factorial | count | result element |
|-----|-----------|-------|----------------|
| 3   | ~~1~~     | ~~2~~ |                |
|     | ~~2~~     | ~~3~~ |                |
|     | 6         | 4     |                |
|     |           |       | 3! = 6         |

# 10.3 External JavaScript Files

All the JavaScript function definitions you've seen so far have been positioned within web page head containers. In the real world, web programmers will often use external files to hold their JavaScript function definitions and then have their web pages link to those external JavaScript file(s).

There are several advantages of positioning a web page's JavaScript function definitions in an external file:

▶ If another web page needs the functionality provided by one of the functions, the second web page can link to the external file and share the function. By using the already-written function, the second web page doesn't have to "reinvent the wheel."

▶   If an external JavaScript file and its functions are shared by multiple web pages, maintenance (i.e., fixing bugs and making improvements) becomes easier and storage requirements are reduced. On the other hand, if there were no external JavaScript file, then the web pages would need to have their own copies of the functions. That means redundant code. And why is redundant code bad? If you need to fix or enhance the code, you have to do it in more than one place, and that takes more time, and you might forget.

Implementing and using an external JavaScript file is fairly straightforward. In creating a JavaScript file, you can use the same tool you use to create HTML files: a plain text editor or a fancy IDE—either is fine. You must name your JavaScript file with a `.js` (for JavaScript) file extension. For the file's content, include documentation comments at the top, followed by the code for your function definitions. In the next section, we'll present a complete web page that uses an external JavaScript file, but for now, just glance at the JavaScript file in Figure 10.4 so you get a feel for its content.

To link a web page to an external JavaScript file, include an empty `script` container with a `src` attribute that specifies the location of the file. For example:

```
<script src="compoundInterest.js"></script>
```

The `src` attribute's value specifies that the JavaScript file is stored in the same directory as the HTML file. If you store the JavaScript file elsewhere, then use a path in front of the filename as part of the `src`'s value.

Note that if your `script` tag includes a `src` attribute (as in the preceding example), then it's illegal to also include JavaScript code inside the `script` tags. If you need JavaScript code for your web page that's not part of the external JavaScript file, you should provide a separate `script` container without a `src` attribute and include the additional JavaScript code there.

## 10.4 Compound Interest Web Page

Let's put what you've learned into practice with a complete web page that uses a `while` loop and an external JavaScript file. **FIGURE 10.3**'s Compound Interest web page generates a table of compound interest values for a user-specified number of years. In the figure, note the initial deposit (often referred to as the "principal") of $1000 and the interest rate of 10%. Using those values, the table's year 1 values are calculated as follows. The interest earned is $1000 × 10% = $100, and the ending value is $1000 + $100 = $1100. To verify the table values for years 2 through 4, use the prior ending value as the new starting value and apply the same mathematical calculations.

To start our examination of the Compound Interest web page source code, let's look at **FIGURE 10.4A**, which shows the web page's `body` container. Note the `class="table"` and `class="row"` attribute-value pairs. As you'll see when we get to the CSS rules, those attribute-value pairs apply CSS table values in order to help with the layout. Specifically, they cause the three number boxes and their associated `label` elements to be aligned as shown in Figure 10.3.

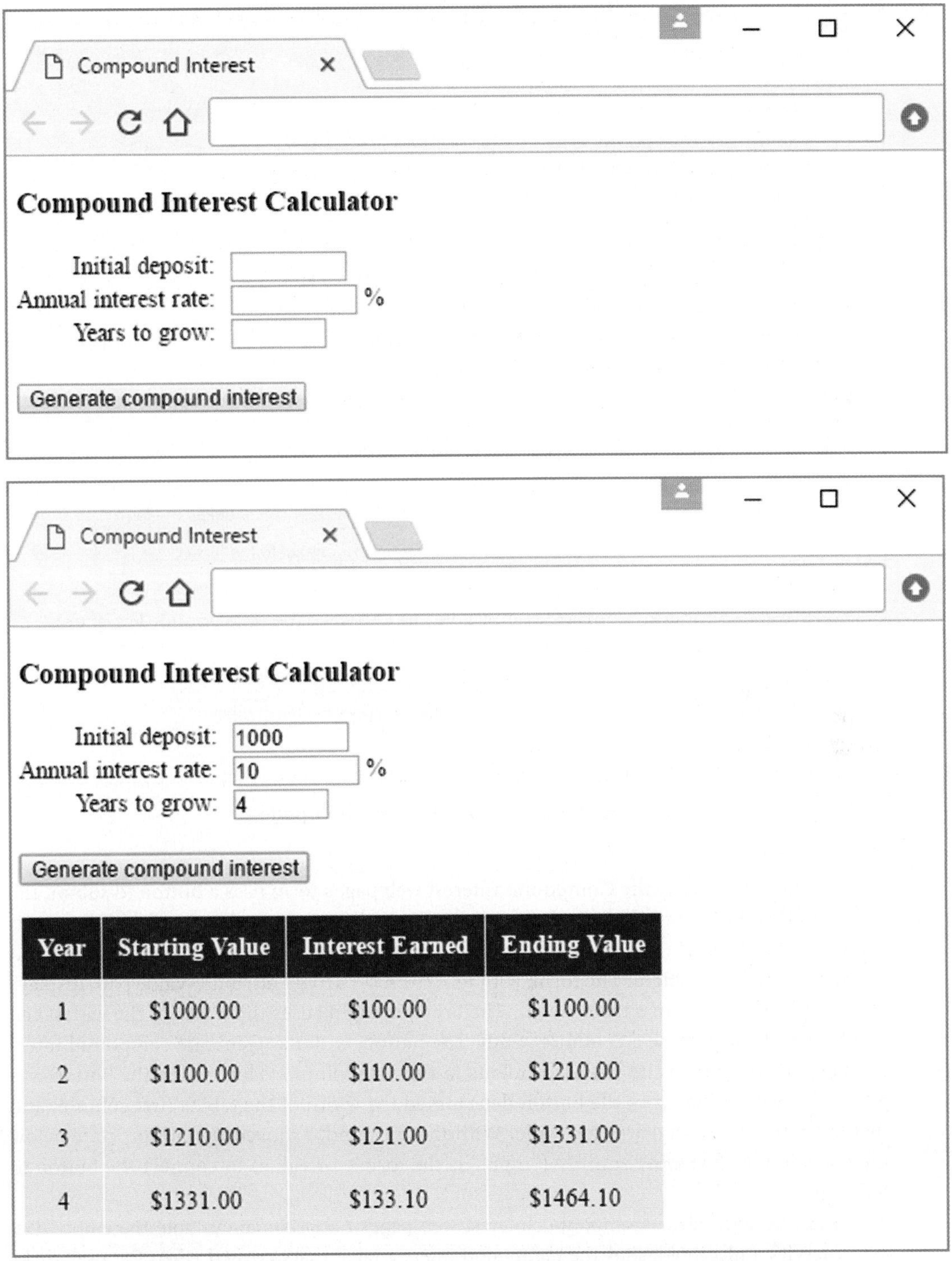

**FIGURE 10.3 Compound Interest web page—initial display and what happens after the user enters values and clicks the button**

```
<body>
<h3>Compound Interest Calculator</h3>
<form class="table" id="input">
  <div class="row">
    <label for="deposit">Initial deposit:</label>
    <input type="number" id="deposit"
      min="1" max="9999" step="1" required>
  </div>
  <div class="row">
    <label for="rate">Annual interest rate:</label>
    <input type="number" id="rate"
      min="0" max="100" step=".1" required>
    <span> %</span>
  </div>
  <div class="row">
    <label for="years">Years to grow:</label>
    <input type="number" id="years"
      min="1" max="20" step="1" required>
  </div>
</form>
<br>
<input type="button" form="input" value="Generate compound interest"
  onclick="generateTable(this.form);">
<br><br>
<div id="result"></div>
</body>
</html>
```

The button is below the form, but uses the `form` attribute to connect to the form.

The `div` element holds the dynamically generated compound interest table.

**FIGURE 10.4A** `body` **container for Compound Interest web page**

As with most forms, the Compound Interest web page's form uses a button to submit the form's input values and calculate the result. In Figure 10.4A, note that the form's button is below the `form` container. Originally, I positioned the button within the `form` container, but that led to a layout problem. The form, with its `class="table"` attribute-value pair, displays its content as cells within a table layout. The browser engine uses the width of the widest cell in a column to determine a column's width. The button, with its "Generate compound interest" label, is wider than the `label` elements in the first column. Thus, when the button was positioned within the form, the button determined the width of the table's first column, and that led to a column that was too wide. With that in mind, I moved the button code below the form and used `form="input"` ("input" is the form's `id` value) to connect the button to the form.

At the bottom of the Compound Interest web page's `body` container, note the empty `div` container. It's a placeholder for the compound interest table that's created when the user clicks the button. We'll see how that table gets built when we examine the JavaScript code. But first, let's examine the CSS code.

## Formatting the Web Page with CSS

**FIGURE 10.4B** shows the Compound Interest web page's style container. Note the .table, .row, and .row > * class selectors that define the table, rows, and cells, respectively, for the form's table layout. The .row > :first-child selector rule selects the first child elements for each of the row elements. Looking at the web page's body code, you can see that the first child elements are the number boxes' labels. The rule uses text-align: right and padding-right: 10px to make the labels align right with a bit of padding.

Next up in the style container are type selector rules for table, th, and td elements. But there are no table, th, and td elements in the original web page, so why do we need to have type selector rules for them? When the user clicks the **Generate compound interest** button, the button's event handler calls the generateTable function, which generates the table, th,

```
<!DOCTYPE html>
<html lang="en">
<head>
<meta charset="utf-8">
<meta name="author" content="John Dean">
<title>Compound Interest</title>
<style>
  .table {display: table;}
  .row {display: table-row;}
  .row > * {display: table-cell;}
  .table {border-spacing: 0 3px;}
  .row > :first-child {
    text-align: right;
    padding-right: 10px;
  }
  table {text-align: center;}
  table, th, td {border: none;}
  th, td {padding: 10px;}
  th {
    background-color: midnightblue;
    color: white;
  }
  td {background-color: mistyrose;}
</style>
<script src="compoundInterest.js"></script>
</head>
```

Load the JavaScript file's contents into this web page.

**FIGURE 10.4B** head **container for Compound Interest web page**

and `td` elements. So we're using JavaScript to dynamically generate a table—pretty cool, right? Before examining the JavaScript, let's finish working our way through the CSS rules in the `style` container.

The `table {text-align: center;}` rule causes all of the table's text to be center aligned. The table's text resides in the `th` and `td` elements, so as an alternative, we could have used a `th, td` type selector instead of the `table` type selector. As you might recall, the `text-align` property is inheritable. That means if you assign a `text-align` value to the `table` element (as we do in the Compound Interest web page), the `text-align` value also gets assigned to the `table` element's descendant elements, which include the `th` and `td` elements.

As you can see in Figure 10.3's browser window, there are no explicit borders around the entire table or the table's cells. The web page delineates the table's cells by applying nonwhite background colors to the cells and letting the web page's default white background color poke through between the cells to form the cell borders. With those lines coming from the web page's background color, there's no need for explicit CSS table borders. The `table, th, td {border: none;}` rule indicates that such borders will be suppressed. The default is for the `table`, `th`, and `td` elements to have no borders, so that rule is technically unnecessary. So why include it? It's a form of self-documentation. Remembering that no borders is the default might be difficult, and the CSS rule makes it clear what's going on.

The Compound Interest web page's remaining CSS rules are pretty straightforward. Go through them on your own, and then note the `script` tags at the bottom of the `head` container. The `script` start tag's `src` attribute points to the external JavaScript file, which we'll discuss next.

## Generating the Table with JavaScript

**FIGURE 10.5** shows the JavaScript file for the Compound Interest web page. Note the prologue section at the top of the file. You should include a prologue at the top of every one of your JavaScript files. A *prologue* is a block comment that provides information about the file, so someone who's interested in the file can quickly get an idea of what the file is all about.

In the figure, note how the prologue begins with `/*` and ends with `*/`. As you know, those characters are required to mark the beginning and end of a JavaScript block comment. To make the prologue's information stand out, it's common to enclose the prologue's information in a box of asterisks. Note how the "box" is formed with an asterisk line at the top, single asterisks at the left edge, and an asterisk line at the bottom. Within the box, include the filename, the programmer's name, a blank line, and a description of the file's code.

Below the prologue, you can see that the file contains just one thing—the `generateTable` function definition. It's common for a JavaScript file to contain multiple function definitions, where the functions are called from different web pages, but in this relatively simple example, there's just one function definition and one web page.

The `generateTable` function starts by retrieving the values from the three number controls. The rest of the function is all about building the code that implements the table that displays the compound interest results. That code gets built by assigning and concatenating code strings into start of the block comment

```
/*****************************************************
* compoundInterest.js
* John Dean
*
* This file contains a function that supports the
* compound interest web page.
******************************************************/
```

end of the block comment

prologue

```
// This function generates a compound interest table.

function generateTable(form) {
  var amount;     // accumulated value for each new year
  var rate;       // interest rate
  var years;      // years for principal to grow
  var interest;   // interest earned each year
  var table;      // compound interest table
  var year = 1;   // the year being calculated

  amount = form.elements["deposit"].valueAsNumber;
  rate = form.elements["rate"].valueAsNumber;
  years = form.elements["years"].valueAsNumber;

  table =
    "<table>" +
    "<tr><th>Year</th><th>Starting Value</th>" +
    "<th>Interest Earned</th><th>Ending Value</th></tr>";

  while (year <= years) {
    table += "<tr>";
    table += "<td>" + year + "</td>";
    table += "<td>$" + amount.toFixed(2) + "</td>";
    interest = amount * rate / 100;
    table += "<td>$" + interest.toFixed(2) + "</td>";
    amount += interest;
    table += "<td>$" + amount.toFixed(2) + "</td>";
    table += "</tr>";
    year++;
  } // end while

  table += "</table>";
  document.getElementById("result").innerHTML = table;
} // end generateTable
```

**FIGURE 10.5 External JavaScript file for Compound Interest web page**

the `table` variable. The first such assignment takes care of the `table` start tag and the first `tr` element with its four `th` cells:

```
table =
  "<table>" +
  "<tr><th>Year</th><th>Starting Value</th>" +
    "<th>Interest Earned</th><th>Ending Value</th></tr>";
```

Go back to Figure 10.3's browser window and verify that the displayed table's first row matches the `<tr>` content in the preceding code.

The subsequent assignments use the `+=` compound assignment operator to concatenate additional code onto the end of the `table` variable. Note how those compound assignment operators are inside a loop. Each loop iteration implements a new `tr` container with its `td` cells. More specifically, each loop iteration starts by concatenating a `tr` start tag and ends by concatenating a `tr` end tag. In between those `+=` operations, you can see `+=` operations for a row's four `td` elements. Those `td` elements contain values for the current year, the year's starting balance, the calculated interest, and the calculated ending balance. Get used to the technique exhibited here when you need to build a rather complicated string value. Start by initializing a string variable and then incrementally append to it by using the `+=` operator. Very useful!

The function's last statement assigns the just-built `table` variable to the placeholder `div` element at the bottom of the web page. Here's that statement:

```
document.getElementById("result").innerHTML = table;
```

The `getElementById` method retrieves the "result" element. Going back to the web page's body container, you can see `id="result"` in the bottom `div` element. As you know, the `innerHTML` property is how you access the interior between the element's start and end tags. So assigning the `table` variable there causes the compound interest table to display. Yay!

## JavaScript Debugging

All of the major browsers have debugging tools built in. Chrome's debugging tool is called "Developer Tools." To load it while viewing a web page with Chrome, you press ctrl+shift+i for Windows computers or cmd+opt+i for Mac computers. To get practice using Developer Tools, you should download the Chrome Developer Tools tutorial on the book's website and work your way through the tutorial's instructions. It uses the Compound Interest web page to illustrate how to use the debugger tool to find bugs and fix them.

If you don't have time to learn all of the debugger's features, that's OK, but you should at least open the debugger and take advantage of its *console frame*. As you execute JavaScript on a web page, if there's a syntax error, the console frame displays a message that describes the error and provides a link to the errant line in the source code. That can be very helpful. Also, to help with debugging, you can call `console.log` with a message as an argument and the message gets displayed in the debugger's console frame. Very helpful again! For example, suppose you've got an event handler that calculates the total cost of a user's purchase, and you want to display the `cost` variable's value. The following `console.log` method call displays the `cost` variable's value in the console frame:

```
console.log("cost = " + cost);
```

# 10.5 do **Loop**

As mentioned earlier, JavaScript has three types of loops—the `while` loop, do loop, and `for` loop. Next up—the do loop.

## Syntax and Semantics

Note the do loop's syntax template at the left of **FIGURE 10.6**. It shows the do loop's condition at the bottom. That contrasts with the `while` loop, where the condition is at the top. Having the condition tested at the bottom guarantees that the do loop executes at least one time. After all, the condition is the only way to terminate the loop, and the JavaScript engine won't check the condition (at the bottom) until after executing the lines above it. In the syntax template, note the semicolon at the right of the condition. That's also different from the `while` loop. Finally, note that the `while` part is on the same line as the closing brace—that's good style. It's legal to put `while` (*condition*) ; on the line after the closing brace, but that would be bad style because it would look like you're trying to start a new `while` loop.

With a `while` loop, with its condition at the top, if the condition starts out with a false value, the JavaScript engine will execute the loop body zero times. For most looping situations, it's appropriate to accommodate the possibility of zero iterations. But for those situations where zero iterations doesn't make sense—that is, when you're sure that the loop body should be executed at least one time—it's more efficient to use a do loop.

## Powers of 2 Web Page

**FIGURE 10.7** shows a web page that uses a do loop as part of its event handler code. Let's start by figuring out why using a do loop is appropriate. The web page asks the user to enter the largest power of 2 he or she can think of. If the user enters a number less than 10, the web page tells the user to enter a larger number. After the user submits an answer, the button's event handler determines whether the entered number is indeed a power of 2. It does so by repeatedly dividing by 2 until the result is

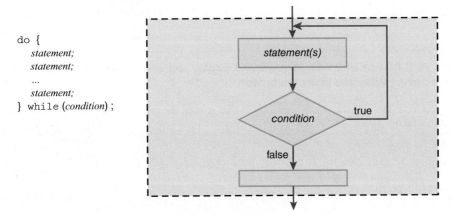

```
do {
    statement;
    statement;
    ...
    statement;
} while (condition) ;
```

**FIGURE 10.6 Syntax and semantics for the do loop**

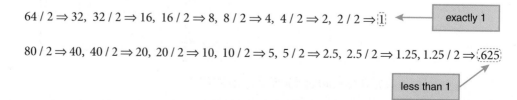

**FIGURE 10.7 Powers of 2 web page—initial display and what happens after the user enters a correct value and clicks the button**

less than or equal to 1. If the result is exactly 1, that means the entered number is a power of 2. For example, the following division operations show that 64 is a power of 2, and 80 is not a power of 2:

$64 / 2 \Rightarrow 32, \ 32 / 2 \Rightarrow 16, \ 16 / 2 \Rightarrow 8, \ 8 / 2 \Rightarrow 4, \ 4 / 2 \Rightarrow 2, \ 2 / 2 \Rightarrow \boxed{1}$ ⟵ exactly 1

$80 / 2 \Rightarrow 40, \ 40 / 2 \Rightarrow 20, \ 20 / 2 \Rightarrow 10, \ 10 / 2 \Rightarrow 5, \ 5 / 2 \Rightarrow 2.5, \ 2.5 / 2 \Rightarrow 1.25, 1.25 / 2 \Rightarrow .625$

less than 1

Because the user is forced to enter a number 10 or greater, you're guaranteed to need to divide by 2 at least once. That means a do loop is appropriate.

We'll get to the do loop code soon enough, but let's examine the HTML and CSS code first. **FIGURE 10.8A** shows the web page's body container. As you skim through it, note the body container's two child elements—a form and an image. By default, a form is a block element, so it would normally span the width of the web page's viewport, causing the image to display below the form. To get the image to display at the right of the form, we use a little CSS magic....

We introduced the flexible box layout in an earlier chapter and used it to center a web page's contents horizontally. This time, we use it to "flex" the size of the body container's two child elements so they conform to the size of their contents. Take a look at **FIGURE 10.8B**'s style container, and note this flexbox CSS rule:

```
body {display: flex; align-items: flex-start;}
```

The display: flex property-value pair converts the body container into a flexbox and causes the form's width to conform to the size of its content (and not span the width of the web page). The align-items: flex-start property value causes the flex container's child elements to be aligned at the top. The style container's next two rules tweak the layout's margins to further improve the layout:

```
form, img {margin: 20px 20px 0;}
h1 {margin-top: 0;}
```

The style container's last CSS rule applies a very light shade of pink to the web page's background:

```
body {background-color: rgb(255, 246, 250);}
```

```
<body>
<form>
  <h1>MATH IS FUN!</h1>
  <label for="number">What is the largest power of 2
    you can think of?</label>
  <br><br>
  <input type="number" id="number"
    min="10" step="1" required>
  <br><br>
  <input type="button" value="Submit"
    onclick="checkForPowerOf2(this.form);">
  <br><br>
  <output id="result"></output>
</form>
<img src="../images/girlJuggling.png" width="128" height="212" alt="">
</body>
</html>
```

**FIGURE 10.8A body container for Powers of 2 web page**

```
<!DOCTYPE html>
<html lang="en">
<head>
<meta charset="utf-8">
<meta name="author" content="John Dean">
<title>Powers of 2</title>
<style>
  body {display: flex; align-items: flex-start;}
  form, img {margin: 20px 20px 0;}
  h1 {margin-top: 0;}
  body {background-color: rgb(255, 246, 250);}
</style>
<script>
  // This function checks whether the user entered a power of 2.

  function checkForPowerOf2(form) {
    var numBox;       // number control
    var output;       // output element that displays the response
    var num;          // user-entered number
    var quotient;     // number that is repeatedly divided by 2
    var wholeNumber;  // is the quotient a whole number?
```

**FIGURE 10.8B** `head` **container for Powers of 2 web page**

The web page's background color applies to the background parts of the image (the parts surrounding the girl and her juggled numbers) because the image's background uses transparent bits there.

Now let's examine the web page's `script` container with its `checkForPowerOf2` function definition. Figure 10.8B shows trivial stuff—the function heading and the variable declarations. **FIGURE 10.8C** shows the good stuff. The function checks the number box and displays an error message for invalid input. If the user enters valid input, the function uses a do loop to repeatedly divide by 2 while the resulting quotient is greater than 1. After the loop, if the final quotient is exactly 1, that means the user entered a power of 2, and the web page displays a congratulatory message.

Note the condition at the bottom of the do loop:

```
} while (wholeNumber && quotient > 1);
```

Previously, we said the loop repeats as long as the resulting quotient is greater than 1. Well, almost. As you can see in the do loop's condition, there's a second thing that must also be true for the loop to repeat—the `wholeNumber` variable must have a value of true. If you start with a power of 2 and you repeatedly divide by 2, each resulting quotient will be a whole number (e.g., $16 / 2 \Rightarrow 8$, $8 / 2 \Rightarrow 4$, $4 / 2 \Rightarrow 2$, $2 / 2 \Rightarrow 1$). On the other hand, if you start with a number that's not a power of 2 and you repeatedly divide by 2, you'll eventually get a quotient that's not a whole number. So to make the function more efficient, with each loop iteration, you can check the resulting quotient to see if it's a whole number. If it's not a whole number, you can immediately terminate the loop and tell the user that his or her entry was not a power of 2. To keep track of whether the resulting quotient is a whole number, we use the `wholeNumber` variable.

```
       numBox = form.elements["number"];
       output = form.elements["result"];

       if (!numBox.checkValidity()) {
         output.value =
           "Invalid input. You must enter an integer 10 or greater.";
       }
       else {
         num = quotient = numBox.valueAsNumber;
         wholeNumber = true;
         do {                    compound assignment operator for division
           quotient /= 2;
           if (quotient != Math.floor(quotient)) {
             wholeNumber = false;          check for quotient not
           }                               being a whole number
         } while (wholeNumber && quotient > 1);

         if (quotient == 1) {
           output.value = "Yes, " + num + " is a power of 2." +
             " You're so awesome!";
         }
         else {
           output.value = "Sorry, " + num + " is not a power of 2.";
         }
       } // end else
     } // end checkForPowerOf2
  </script>
  </head>
```

FIGURE 10.8C `head` **container for Powers of 2 web page**

## Using a Boolean Variable to Terminate the Loop

In the past, we've used variables to store numbers, strings, and objects. The JavaScript language supports those *data types* as well as a few others. The Boolean data type is for variables that hold the value true or the value false, and those variables are referred to as *Boolean variables*. As you might have guessed by now, the wholeNumber variable is a Boolean variable. It holds the value true if the most recently generated quotient is a whole number and false otherwise. In the checkForPowerOf2 function, note how we assign true to wholeNumber above the loop and then inside the loop, we assign false to wholeNumber if the new quotient is not a whole number. Note how we use Math.floor to see if the new quotient is not a whole number:

```
    if (quotient != Math.floor(quotient)) {
```

Remember that the floor method rounds down, so if the quotient is not a whole number, rounding down returns a value different from the original value. And the != operator evaluates to true if the values are different. At the bottom of the loop, we use `wholeNumber` in the do loop's condition:

```
} while (wholeNumber && quotient > 1);
```

If `wholeNumber` has the value false, then the condition pares down to `false && quotient > 1`. Remember that if you use false with the `&&` operator, the result is false, regardless of the other operand's value.

By the way, we didn't have to use a Boolean variable in the `checkForPowerOf2` function. This do loop provides the same functionality without using a Boolean variable:

```
do {
  quotient /= 2;
} while (quotient != Math.floor(quotient) && quotient > 1);
```

So, what's the benefit of using a Boolean variable? It can lead to more readable code, as is the case in the do loop condition in the Powers of 2 web page. Readability can be improved even more dramatically in other cases. In general, a Boolean variable can be used to keep track of a situation in which there's a state with one of two possible values. For example, if you're writing a program that plays a game against the computer, you can keep track of the "state" of whose turn it is by using a Boolean variable named `userTurn`. If `userTurn` holds the value true, it's the user's turn. If `userTurn` holds the value false, it's the computer's turn. In an end-of-chapter exercise, you'll be asked to trace a code fragment that uses such a `userTurn` Boolean variable.

In case you were wondering, the term Boolean comes from George Boole, a 19th-century English mathematician. He invented Boolean algebra, which describes operations that can be performed with true and false values.

## 10.6 Radio Buttons

So far, we've covered several form controls in depth—the button, text, and number controls. Also, we briefly introduced you to several other controls, such as the email and password controls. Now it's time for the radio button control. Radio buttons come in a group, where only one radio button in a group can be selected at a time. When one of the buttons in the group is clicked, it gets selected and the other buttons get unselected. That's different from regular buttons, which are standalone entities.

### HTML Attributes

Here are the radio button control's more important attributes:

| Radio Button Control Attributes | | | | | | |
|---|---|---|---|---|---|---|
| type | name | value | checked | required | disabled | onclick |

To create a radio button control, you'll need an `input` element with `type="radio"`. To group radio buttons together, you'll need the radio buttons to have a `name` attribute with the same value. For example, the following radio buttons form a radio button group because they have the same "color" value for their `name` attribute:

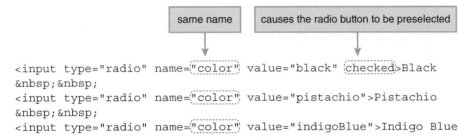

```
<input type="radio" name="color" value="black" checked>Black
  
<input type="radio" name="color" value="pistachio">Pistachio
  
<input type="radio" name="color" value="indigoBlue">Indigo Blue
```

Here's how the preceding code looks when rendered on a browser window:

⦿ Black      ◯ Pistachio      ◯ Indigo Blue

The default is for radio buttons to be unselected, and that's why the second and third radio buttons are unselected. If a radio button has a `checked` attribute, then the browser preselects the radio button. In the preceding code fragment, note the `checked` attribute for the first radio button. That's why there's a selected dot in the black radio button. If the user clicks on a different radio button, then that other radio button gets selected, and the selected dot disappears from the black radio button. If the user clicks on an already selected radio button, nothing happens.

The `value` attribute provides a value that's specific to an individual radio button. Typically, an event handler uses the radio button's value to know what the user selected.

In the prior code fragment, you can see "Black," "Pistachio," and "Indigo Blue" after the three input tags. Those plain-text strings serve as labels for the three radio buttons. If you want your web page to be accessible to the visually impaired, you should use `label` elements instead of plain text for your labels. By using the following `label` element, a visually impaired user's screen reader will say "black" (because "Black" appears within the `label` element, after the `input` element) to indicate what the radio button is for.

```
<label><input type="radio" name="color" value="black" checked>
   Black</label>
```

In the past, we connected a `label` element to its control by using a `for` attribute. This time, as an alternative, we're embedding the control inside the `label` element's start and end tags. Both techniques provide the same functionality.

If a radio button group has one or more radio buttons with a `required` attribute, then the whole radio button group is considered to be required. And if a radio button group is "required," that means one of its radio buttons must be selected; otherwise the radio button group is considered to have invalid input. You can then check for invalid input in an event handler by calling the `checkValidity` method, which should sound familiar because that's what we did for the number control in the previous chapter.

The radio button's `disabled` attribute works the same as for the other controls. It grays out the radio button and makes it unusable.

Typically, radio buttons are like text controls and number controls in that they serve as repositories for user input. Typically, regular buttons are in charge of calling an event handler and processing the user input. But every now and then, you might want a radio button to act more like a regular button, so when the user clicks it, it calls an event handler and processes the user input. To achieve that functionality, include an `onclick` event handler attribute with the radio button element.

## Using JavaScript to Retrieve Radio Button Objects

You've been introduced to the HTML used to create radio buttons. Now it's time to get acquainted with the other side of the coin—the JavaScript used to access and manipulate the radio button object's properties. The first step in your journey toward manipulation mastery is knowing how to retrieve a radio button object.

Before retrieving an individual radio button, you need to retrieve the collection of radio buttons that the radio button is part of. In the past, to retrieve an individual control, we used `form.elements` with `[]`'s around the control's `id` value. To retrieve a collection of radio buttons, we once again use `form.elements`, but this time the `[]`'s go around the `name` value for the radio buttons that are grouped together. For example, here's how you can retrieve the radio button collection for a group of radio buttons where "color" is the name of the radio button group:

```
tshirtRBs = form.elements["color"];
```

Then, to retrieve an individual radio button within the collection, you use the notation *collection*[*index*], where an index value of 0 refers to the collection's first object, an index value of 1 refers to the collection's second object, and so on. For example, you could use the following code to retrieve the second radio button in the `tshirtRBs` collection:

```
pistachioRB = tshirtRBs[1];
```

## JavaScript Properties

See **FIGURE 10.9**. It shows the more popular properties for radio button collections and also for individual radio buttons.

After retrieving a radio button collection, you can get the value of the selected radio button with the help of the collection's `value` property. For example:

```
alert("You ordered a " + tshirtRBs.value + " t-shirt.");
```

If no radio button is selected, then the `value` property returns the empty string.

In Figure 10.9, note how several of the properties' descriptions start with "Returns" and the others start with "Returns/assigns." The properties that start with "Returns" are *read-only*

| |
|---|
| *radio-button-collection*.`value`<br>Returns/assigns the selected radio button's value. |
| *radio-button-collection*.`length`<br>Returns the number of buttons in the radio button collection. |
| *radio-button-collection*[*i*].`value`<br>Returns/assigns the *i*th button's value. |
| *radio-button-collection*[*i*].`defaultChecked`<br>Returns true or false, for whether the *i*th button was preselected. |
| *radio-button-collection*[*i*].`checked`<br>Returns/assigns true or false, for whether the *i*th button is currently selected. |
| *radio-button-collection*[*i*].`disabled`<br>Returns/assigns true or false, for whether the *i*th button is disabled. |

**FIGURE 10.9 Properties for radio button collections and for individual radio buttons**

properties, meaning that you can read the property's value, but you cannot update its value. The properties that start with "Returns/assigns" allow you to read the property's value <u>and</u> update its value. For example, Figure 10.9 says "Returns/assigns" for the radio button collection's `value` property. We've already explained what reading the `value` property does. If you assign a value to a radio button collection's `value` property, the JavaScript engine looks for the first radio button whose `value` property equals the assigned value. If a match is found, then that radio button gets selected and the other ones get deselected. If there's no match, then nothing happens.

The radio button collection's `length` property returns the number of radio buttons in the radio button collection. Sometimes, you'll want to loop through all the radio buttons in a group, and you can use the `length` property to specify the number of loop iterations. For example, if you want to disable all the radio buttons in a group, you can use the `length` property to loop through them. Later on, we'll show a complete web page that uses the `length` property to loop through a collection of controls.

In Figure 10.9, the properties below the `length` property are for individual radio buttons. Each of those properties is prefaced with *radio-button-collection* `[i]`. The *i* is an index value that indicates the radio button's position within the radio button collection. To display the first radio button's value, you can use this code:

```
alert("The first selection is for a " + tshirtRBs[0].value +
  " t-shirt.");
```

Be aware that the `defaultChecked` property is associated with the `checked` attribute, whereas the `checked` property is not associated with the `checked` attribute. A radio button's `checked` property returns true if the radio button is currently selected. If you assign true to a radio button's `checked` property, then false is automatically assigned to the other buttons' `checked` properties, which means they will be deselected.

## 10.7 Checkboxes

Up next is the checkbox control. It's pretty similar to the radio button control, so be prepared for much of the upcoming description to sound familiar.

When a checkbox is clicked, a check appears in the checkbox. When the checkbox is clicked again, the check disappears. Checkboxes are sometimes standalone entities, and sometimes they come in groups. If they're in a group, they're not limited to just one selection (as radio buttons are). None, some, or all of them can be selected.

### HTML Attributes

Here are the checkbox control's more important attributes:

| Checkbox Control Attributes | | | | | | | |
|---|---|---|---|---|---|---|---|
| type | id | name | value | checked | required | disabled | onclick |

To create a checkbox control, you'll need an `input` element with `type="checkbox"`. For a standalone checkbox, you'll normally want to include an `id` attribute, so your event handler JavaScript can use `form.elements[checkbox-id]` to access the checkbox. Here's an example that implements a standalone checkbox:

```
I accept the terms and conditions of this agreement
<span class="barely-visible">(subject to corporate interpretation
  and revision)</span>:
<input type="checkbox" id="accept-terms" required
  onclick="acceptTerms(this.form);">
```

Note the `id` attribute's value, `accept-terms`. The HTML5 standard does not allow spaces within `id` values. If you want to use multiple words for an `id` value, use hyphens to separate the words, as exemplified by `accept-terms`. Can you remember where else you've seen hyphens used to separate words, and spaces not being allowed? We use hyphens for `class` attribute values (e.g., `cleanmodern-font`), CSS property names (e.g., `font-size`), and sometimes CSS property values (e.g., `x-large`). Spaces aren't allowed within `id` attribute values and `class` attribute values because those values need to be available for class selectors. If spaces were allowed, then the browser engine would have to be able to process the following selector rules. With the spaces, that would be difficult, if not impossible.

```
#accept terms {color: red;}
.clean modern font {font-family: "Century Gothic", Geneva, sans-serif;}
```

illegal spaces

In the previous checkbox code fragment, note the `required` attribute. It indicates that the checkbox must be selected; otherwise, the checkbox is considered to have invalid input.

Also in the preceding checkbox code fragment, note the `onclick` event handler attribute. Imagine that the event handler's `acceptTerms` method assigns false to the form's other controls' `disabled` properties so the user can proceed with filling out the form. Having an `onclick` event handler is not all that common for a checkbox, but more common than for a radio button.

To group checkboxes together, you'll need the checkboxes to have the same `name` attribute value. For example, the following checkboxes form a checkbox group because they have the same "jobSkills" value for their `name` attribute:

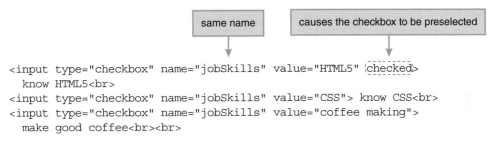

```
<input type="checkbox" name="jobSkills" value="HTML5" checked>
  know HTML5<br>
<input type="checkbox" name="jobSkills" value="CSS"> know CSS<br>
<input type="checkbox" name="jobSkills" value="coffee making">
  make good coffee<br><br>
```

Here's what this code fragment looks like when rendered on a browser window:

> ☑ know HTML5
> ☐ know CSS
> ☐ make good coffee

The HTML5 checkbox is checked because the code fragment's first checkbox element has a `checked` attribute.

In the preceding job skills code fragment, the `name` attribute has a value made with two words—"jobSkills"—and the third checkbox's `value` attribute has a value made with two words, "coffee making." Whereas `id` attribute values use a hyphen to separate words, `name` and `value` attribute values use camel case or spaces to separate words. When would you have a need for a space? If you want to display a checkbox group's name (e.g., "job skills") or a particular checkbox's value (e.g., "good coffee") on a web page, having spaces between the words looks better than camel case. That will make more sense later on when we present a complete Job Skills web page with an event handler that displays the skills checkboxes' values.

## Using JavaScript to Retrieve Checkbox Objects

Having learned how to implement a checkbox with HTML, it's now time to access and manipulate a checkbox's properties with JavaScript. To do that, you first need to retrieve a checkbox object.

To retrieve a standalone checkbox, you use `form.elements` with `[]`'s around the checkbox's `id` value. For example, to retrieve the checkbox presented earlier where the user accepted a form's terms and conditions, you could use the following code, where "accept-terms" is the checkbox's `id` value:

```
acceptTermsCB = form.elements["accept-terms"];
```

To retrieve a checkbox that's part of a group of checkboxes, you first retrieve the checkbox's collection by using `form.elements` with `[]`'s around the checkbox group's `name` value. For example, to retrieve the checkbox collection for the group of checkboxes presented earlier where the user selected his or her job skills, you could use the following code, where "jobSkills" is the name of the checkbox group:

```
jobSkillsCBs = form.elements["jobSkills"];
```

Then, to retrieve an individual checkbox within the collection, you use the notation *collection* [*index*] notation, where an index value of 0 refers to the first object in the collection. For example, you could use the following code to retrieve the third checkbox in the `jobSkillsCBs` collection:

```
coffeeCB = jobSkillsCBs[2];
```

## JavaScript Properties

See **FIGURE 10.10**. It shows the more popular JavaScript properties for checkbox collections and individual checkbox objects.

Figure 10.10's list of properties is pretty much the same as for radio buttons, except there's no `value` property for the collection. Why is there a `value` property for a radio button collection, but not for a checkbox collection? A checkbox collection very often has more than one checkbox that's selected, so returning a single selected value for a checkbox collection doesn't make sense. On the other hand, returning multiple values for a checkbox collection, one for each selected checkbox, does make sense, and web page event handlers do that fairly often.

To help you find the values associated with all the selected checkboxes in a checkbox collection, you can loop through the collection and retrieve the value for each selected checkbox. As you learned in the radio buttons section, the `length` property returns the number of objects in a collection. So you can use the `length` property to specify the number of loop iterations. In the next section, we'll show a complete web page that uses the `length` property to do just that.

| |
|---|
| *checkbox-collection*.`length`<br>    Returns the number of buttons in the checkbox collection. |
| *checkbox*.`value`<br>    Assigns/returns the checkbox's value. |
| *checkbox*.`defaultChecked`<br>    Returns true or false, for whether the checkbox was preselected. |
| *checkbox*.`checked`<br>    Assigns/returns true or false, for whether the checkbox is currently selected. |
| *checkbox*.`disabled`<br>    Assigns/returns true or false, for whether the checkbox is disabled. |

**FIGURE 10.10 Properties for checkbox collections and for individual collections**

In Figure 10.10, the properties below the `length` property apply to individual checkboxes, and they work the same as for individual radio buttons. For example, a checkbox's `checked` property indicates whether the checkbox is selected or not. For a standalone checkbox, like `acceptTermsCB`, you could use this code to know whether the checkbox is selected:

```
if (acceptTermsCB.checked) {
```

For a checkbox in a `jobSkillsCBs` checkbox collection, you could use this code to know whether the third checkbox is selected:

```
if (jobSkillsCBs[2].checked) {
```

## 10.8 Job Skills Web Page

As promised, in this section we present a web page that uses a loop to retrieve the values for each selected checkbox in a checkbox collection. We're using a modified version of the job skills code fragment presented earlier and adding an event handler to it. See the web page's browser window in **FIGURE 10.11**. Initially, the web page displays nothing below the **Submit** button. After the user clicks **Submit**, the web page displays a message below the button.

Peruse the Job Skills web page `body` container in **FIGURE 10.12A**. Note that each checkbox element includes a `required` attribute. That means the user is supposed to select all three checkboxes. Note the Submit button at the bottom, which, when clicked, calls the `checkInput` function.

**FIGURE 10.12B** shows the web page's `checkInput` function. The function examines the checkboxes and displays a message at the bottom that describes whether the applicant is fit for hire. Specifically, if all three job skills checkboxes are selected, the message indicates that the user is hired. Otherwise, the message indicates the user is not hired and displays the values of the skills checkboxes that are not selected.

Because each checkbox element includes the `required` attribute, an unselected checkbox is considered to be invalid input. If any of the form's controls contains invalid input, then the form as a whole is considered to have invalid input. Near the top of the function, note how the form calls the `checkValidity` method. When called from a form object, the `checkValidity` method returns true when every input value in the form is considered valid. For the Job Skills web page, that means the `checkValidity` call returns true if all three checkboxes are selected. When that's the case, the message indicates that the user is hired.

If the form's `checkValidity` method call returns false, that means at least one of the checkboxes is unselected. In that case, the function retrieves the checkbox collection, `jobSkillsCBs`, and loops through the checkbox objects within the collection. The loop knows how many times to repeat by comparing a counter variable `i` to the number of checkboxes in the collection. You should verify that logic by examining the loop's condition, `i < jobSkillsCBs.length`, examining how `i` gets initialized to 0 at the top of the function, and examining how `i` gets incremented at the bottom of the loop.

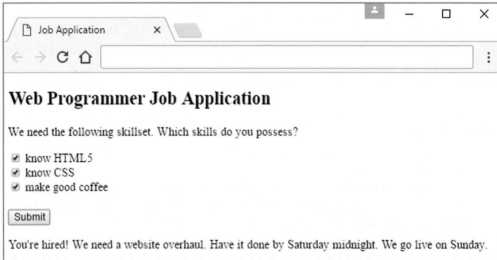

**FIGURE 10.11 Job Skills web page—what happens for a failing applicant and a successful applicant**

To access each checkbox within the loop, we use the checkbox collection with []'s surrounding the variable i. That is, we use jobSkillsCBs[i]. Note how we're using i for two purposes—as a counter variable for the while loop and also as an *index variable* to access the individual checkboxes within the collection. For each checkbox object, we call the checkbox's checkValidity method to see if that checkbox is selected. If it's not selected, we retrieve the checkbox's value (using the checkbox's value property) and append it to the message string

```
<body>
<h2>Web Programmer Job Application</h2>
<p>We need the following skillset. Which skills do you possess?</p>
<form>
  <input type="checkbox" name="jobSkills" value="HTML5" required>
    know HTML5<br>
  <input type="checkbox" name="jobSkills" value="CSS" required>
    know CSS<br>
  <input type="checkbox" name="jobSkills" value="coffee making" required>
    make good coffee<br><br>
  <input type="button" value="Submit" onclick="checkInput(this.form);">
</form>
<p id="message"></p>
</body>
</html>
```

**FIGURE 10.12A** `body` **container for Job Skills web page**

```
<!DOCTYPE html>
<html lang="en">
<head>
<meta charset="utf-8">
<meta name="author" content="John Dean">
<title>Job Application</title>
<script>
  // Evaluate user's job skills and generate hiring plan.

  function checkInput(form) {
    var message; // hiring plan after examining job skills
    var i = 0;

    if (form.checkValidity()) {
      message =
        "You're hired! We need a website overhaul." +
        " Have it done by Saturday midnight. We go live on Sunday.";
    }
    else {
      message = "Sorry we can't hire you." +
        " You are deficient in these areas:";
      jobSkillsCBs = form.elements["jobSkills"];

      while (i < jobSkillsCBs.length) {
        if (!jobSkillsCBs[i].checkValidity()) {
          message += "<br>" + jobSkillsCBs[i].value;
        }
        i++;
      } // end while
    } // end if

    document.getElementById("message").innerHTML = message;
  } // end checkInput
</script>
</head>
```

**FIGURE 10.12B** `head` **container for Job Skills web page**

variable. That's how we create the list of the skills that the user is deficient in. After the loop terminates, we assign the `message` variable to the placeholder p element at the bottom of the web page.

## 10.9 `for` Loop

In the previous section, we used a `while` loop to access all the checkboxes in the collection of job skills checkboxes. Using a `while` loop works OK, but in this section, we use a `for` loop to access the checkboxes, which leads to a more compact implementation.

FIGURE 10.13 shows the `while` loop used in the Job Skills web page and a functionally equivalent `for` loop. Both versions use a counter variable, `i`, that gets initialized to 0 and gets incremented each time through the loop. With a `for` loop, the counter mechanism is implemented within the loop's heading. It's such a foundational part of a `for` loop that the counter variable is given a special name—an *index variable*. Sound familiar? Yep, an index variable is also the name we use for the variable inside `[]`'s when referring to an individual object within a collection. So in Figure 10.13's `for` loop body, the `i` in `jobSkillsCBs[i]` is an index variable not only for the `for` loop, but also for the `jobSkillsCBs` collection.

```
var i = 0;

while (i < jobSkillsCBs.length) {

   if (!jobSkillsCBs[i].checkValidity()) {

      message += "<br>" + jobSkillsCBs[i].value;

   }

   i++;

} // end while
```

```
for (let i=0; i<jobSkillsCBs.length; i++) {

   if (!jobSkillsCBs[i].checkValidity()) {

      message += "<br>" + jobSkillsCBs[i].value;

   }

} // end for
```

FIGURE 10.13 `while` **loop versus** `for` **loop comparison for Job Skills web page**

With a `for` loop, all the looping mechanism code is stuffed into the `for` loop heading. That can make for a rather complicated looking heading when you're new to `for` loops. But for veteran `for` loop users, the `for` loop heading's structure can be comforting because it's compact and it follows a standard format. The `for` loop heading is formed with three components—the initialization, condition, and update components—with the components separated by semicolons:

```
for (initialization; condition; update) {
```

In Figure 10.13, identify those three components in the `for` loop heading. And note the arrows, which show the corresponding component code embedded in the `while` loop. Hopefully, seeing how the `while` loop incorporates the components makes it clear how the components work, but if not, the following list explains how the `for` loop uses the three components:

1. Initialization component

   Before the first pass through the body of the loop, execute the initialization component.
2. Condition component

   Before each loop iteration, evaluate the condition component:
   - If the condition is true, execute the body of the loop.
   - If the condition is false, terminate the loop (exit to the statement below the loop's closing brace).
3. Update component

   After each pass through the body of the loop, return to the loop heading and execute the update component. Then, recheck the continuation condition in the second component, and if it's satisfied, go through the body of the loop again.

Perhaps the hardest part of the `for` loop mechanism to remember is that you have to execute the update component's code after you're done with each loop iteration. It can be hard to remember because the code appears at the top of the loop, even though you execute it after executing the bottom of the loop.

In Figure 10.13, note that we declare the `i` index variable with `let` in the `for` loop heading. When you declare a `for` loop index variable with `let`, that limits the scope of the index variable to just the loop. In other words, whenever a variable is declared in the `for` loop heading, it exists and can be recognized and used only by code that is within the heading or body of that `for` loop. By limiting the index variable's scope, you can redeclare the same-named index variable in a second loop with no fear of one loop's index variable messing up the other loop's index variable. You might think that using `var` instead of `let` for declaring your index variable would accomplish the same thing. Nope. If you declare a variable with `var`, the variable's scope is the entire function. Normally, that won't create problems, but you should do more than strive for acceptable normalcy. You should strive for maximum elegance, and that means using `let` for your index variable declarations.

In the following `for` loop heading (copied from Figure 10.13 for your convenience), note that there are no spaces surrounding the = operator and the < operator:

```
for (let i=0; i<jobSkillsCBs.length; i++) {
```

Why is that good practice? The `for` loop header is inherently complex, so in order to temper that complexity, we add visual cues to compartmentalize the `for` loop header. More specifically, we omit spaces within each of the three sections, and we insert a space after each semicolon to keep the three sections separate.

## When to Use Each Type of Loop

Although you can use any of the three loops for any looping task, you should strive to use the type of loop that fits best for your particular task at hand. If you have a task where you know the exact number of loop iterations before the loop begins, use a `for` loop. For the Job Skills web page, the task was to loop through the checkboxes in a checkbox collection. The number of loop iterations came from the checkbox collection's `length` property. We knew that value before executing the loop, so using a `for` loop worked out nicely. Remember the compound interest web page? The task was to repeatedly generate projected interest and balance values for upcoming years. The number of loop iterations came from the user's input in the "Years to grow" text control (see Figure 10.3 for a refresher). We used a `while` loop for that implementation, but because we knew the number of loop iterations before executing the loop, we could have used a `for` loop and the result would have been slightly more compact. On the other hand, what about the Powers of 2 web page? The task was to repeatedly divide by 2 until the quotient became 1 or less than 1. Before the loop began, we did not know how many times the loop would repeat, so using a `for` loop would have been inappropriate. We knew that the loop should be executed at least one time, so we used a `do` loop, and the JavaScript programming gods smiled down upon us and said, "It was good."

### for...of Loop

Now that you know when to use a `for` loop, let's get fancy and introduce another version of the `for` loop. The for...of loop uses a more compact heading than the traditional `for` loop by eliminating the index variable. For example, here's a for...of loop that is functionally equivalent to the loop used in the Job Skills web page:

```
for (let skill of jobSkillsCBs) {
  if (!skill.checkValidity()) {
    message += "<br>" + skill.value;
  }
} // end for
```

As promised, you can see that the for...of loop uses no index variable. The for...of loop is more compact than the traditional `for` loop because there are no initialization, condition, and update parts you need to worry about. With a traditional `for` loop, those parts implement the loop's counting mechanism. With a for...of loop, the counting functionality is taken care of automatically behind the scenes without you (the developer) having to do anything.

Before you get too excited about the `for...of` loop, you need to realize that it's not as general purpose as the standard `for` loop. The `for...of` loop works only if you have a collection. Here's the syntax for the `for...of` loop's heading:

```
for (let variable of collection) {
```

In the Job Skills `for...of` loop shown here, `jobSkillsCBs` is the collection and `skill` is the variable. The `skill` variable serves as a repository for each object in the `jobSkillsCBs` collection as the loop traverses through the objects. So in the loop's body, to access a value in the collection, you don't need `[]`'s around an index variable. Instead, you simply use the variable declared in the loop's heading. In the Job Skills web page, to access a checkbox object within the loop, we simply use the `skill` variable. "Accessing" the checkbox object means you can read its values or update its values.

# 10.10 `fieldset` and `legend` Elements

In the past several sections, we've used radio button groups and checkbox groups. To make the groupings more obvious to someone viewing the web page, you can add a border around each group and embed a caption within the border. Note the following example, which provides a border and caption for a group of three color-selection radio buttons:

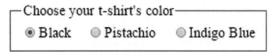

To make a border, surround the radio button elements with a `fieldset` container. To make a caption, include a `legend` element within the `fieldset` container. Here's the relevant code that was used to create the preceding radio button group:

```
<style>
  fieldset {display: inline;}
</style>
...
<fieldset>
  <legend>Choose your t-shirt's color</legend>
  <input type="radio" name="color" value="black">Black
    
  <input type="radio" name="color" value="pistachio">Pistachio
    
  <input type="radio" name="color" value="indigoBlue">Indigo Blue
</fieldset>
```

The `fieldset` element is a block element, so by default, its border spans the web page's entire width. To have its border conform to its contents, convert the `fieldset` element to an inline element by applying a `display: inline` property-value pair to it. See the relevant CSS rule in the `style` container shown earlier. If that rule were not present, the radio button would look like this:

```
┌─Choose your t-shirt's color──────────────────────────────────────────────┐
│  ⦿ Black     ⦾ Pistachio     ⦾ Indigo Blue                                 │
└────────────────────────────────────────────────────────────────────────────┘
```

# 10.11 Manipulating CSS with JavaScript

In this section, we continue to use radio buttons and checkboxes, but our main focus will be on something new and super exciting—using JavaScript to dynamically update a web page's CSS. There are quite a few JavaScript techniques for manipulating a web page's CSS. In this section, we show you two such techniques.

## Assigning a New Value to an Element's `class` Attribute

As you know, you can modify the appearance of an element with the help of the element's `class` attribute and a class selector rule. For example, the following code fragment applies italics to a `div` element by including `class="italic"` in the `div` start tag and providing a `.italic` class selector rule:

```
<style>
  .italic {font-style: italic;}
  .bold {font-weight: bold;}
  .small-caps {font-variant: small-caps;}
</style>
...
<div class="italic" id="message">
  Money is not speech. Corporations are not people.
</div>
```

Given this code fragment, if you want an event handler to dynamically update the `div` element's text so it displays with boldface and small caps, you need to change the `div` element's `class` attribute code from `class="italic"` to `class="bold small-caps"`.[1] Well actually, that's what you should imagine in your head, but as a programmer, you don't write that code. Here's the JavaScript code that you would write as part of an event handler:

```
document.getElementById("message").className = "bold small-caps";
```

The `getElementById("message")` method call retrieves the `div` object, and the `className` property accesses the `div` element's `class` attribute. Then the `bold` and `small-caps` selector names get assigned to the `div` element's `className` property, causing the `div` element to use the `.bold` and `.small-caps` class selector rules in the `style` container.

---

[1] Remember that if a `class` attribute has multiple selector names assigned to it (e.g., `bold` and `small-caps`), then each selector's CSS rule is applied separately to the `class` attribute's element.

Did you notice that the prior `getElementById` code uses a property named `className` to access the `div` element's `class` attribute? It would make more sense if the `class` attribute's associated property were named class, but "class" is already a JavaScript keyword used for something else.[2] Sadly, I often make the mistake of using "class" instead of "className" for the `class` attribute's property. Try to avoid making that mistake, or at least try to recognize the problem after you make it the umpteenth time.

## Assigning a Value to an Element's `style` Property

Now let's explore a second technique for manipulating CSS with JavaScript. Do you remember the `style` attribute introduced back in Chapter 3? It allows you to insert CSS property-value pairs as part of an element's HTML code. For example, the following code applies a font size of 3 em to the `div` element:

```
<div id="message" style="font-size:3em;">
  Money is not speech. Corporations are not people.
</div>
```

Remember that one of the overarching goals of good web programming is to keep presentation separate from content. Using the `style` attribute violates that goal. You'll find that other web developers sometimes use the `style` attribute, but you should avoid using it in your own web pages. We show the `style` attribute in the preceding code fragment because the upcoming JavaScript technique uses a `style` property that is associated with the `style` attribute. To understand the `style` property, you have to understand the `style` attribute first.

The following `div` element is the same as before, but with no `style` attribute:

```
<div id="message">
  Money is not speech. Corporations are not people.
</div>
```

Suppose you want to apply a font size of 3 em to the `div` element, but with the application taking place dynamically, as part of an event handler. Here's the JavaScript assignment statement that will let you do that:

```
document.getElementById("message").style.fontSize = "3em";
```

The `getElementById("message")` method call retrieves the `div` object, and the `style` property accesses the `div` element's `style` attribute. Even when there's no explicit `style` attribute in the `div` element's code, there's still an associated empty `style` property for the `div` element (and every element on a web page). The `style` property is an object that has properties for every CSS property. In the preceding assignment statement, we use the `style` property object's `fontSize` property. The JavaScript `fontSize` property is associated with CSS's

[2] JavaScript uses the word "class" to implement object-oriented programming (OOP) classes. You'll learn about classes and OOP in Chapter 11.

`font-size` property. So `style.fontSize = "3em"` in JavaScript is functionally equivalent to `style="font-size:3em;"` in HTML.

Did you notice that the JavaScript property name `fontSize` is different from the associated CSS property name `font-size`? JavaScript and CSS were developed separately. In coming up with a name for the font size property, JavaScript's designer (Brendan Eich) probably wanted to mimic CSS's `font-size` name, but realized the hyphen would be interpreted as a minus sign in JavaScript and that would mess things up. And thus we're left with the lovable, huggable amalgam that is HTML, CSS, JavaScript syntax.

## Font Styles Web Page

Now that you've learned how to manipulate CSS using JavaScript, let's put your newfound knowledge into practice as part of a complete web page. See the Font Styles web page in **FIGURE 10.14**. The web page prompts the user to select a font size and other font features. When the user clicks the **Done** button, its event handler applies the selected font values to a message at the bottom of the web page, causing the message's appearance to change. More specifically, the event handler

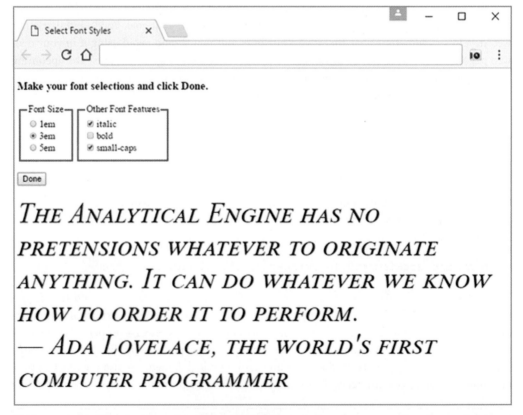

**FIGURE 10.14 Font Styles web page—what happens after the user makes font selections and clicks the Done button**

uses JavaScript to manipulate the CSS that gets applied to the bottom message. In the figure, note that the 3em, italic, and small caps options are selected and the message's text is three times as large as normal, it's italicized, and it uses small caps.

Examine the Font Styles web page's body container in **FIGURE 10.15A**. Note the three radio button elements with their common group name, fontSize, and the three checkbox elements with their common group name, otherFontFeatures. Note how we surround each of the two groups with fieldset containers and put legend elements within those fieldset elements. Below the fieldset containers, note the **Done** button. Its onclick event handler calls the applyFontSelections function, which we'll examine a bit later.

At the bottom of the body container, note the div element with its "The Analytical Engine has no…" text. The div element has a class="hidden" attribute-value pair, which means the

```
<body>
<h3>Make your font selections and click Done.</h3>
<form>
  <fieldset>
    <legend>Font Size</legend>
    <input type="radio" name="fontSize" value="1em" checked>1em<br>
    <input type="radio" name="fontSize" value="3em">3em<br>
    <input type="radio" name="fontSize" value="5em">5em
  </fieldset>
  <fieldset>
    <legend>Other Font Features</legend>
    <input type="checkbox" name="otherFontFeatures"
      value="italic">italic<br>
    <input type="checkbox" name="otherFontFeatures"
      value="bold">bold<br>
    <input type="checkbox" name="otherFontFeatures"
      value="small-caps">small-caps
  </fieldset>
  <br><br>
  <input type="button" value="Done"
    onclick="applyFontSelections(this.form);">
</form>
<br>
<div class="hidden" id="message">
  The Analytical Engine has no pretensions whatever to
  originate anything. It can do whatever we know how to
  order it to perform.<br>
  &mdash; Ada Lovelace, the world's first computer programmer
</div>
</body>
</html>
```

> The hidden selector name (defined in the style container) causes the div element to be invisible.

**FIGURE 10.15A** body **container for Font Styles web page**

`style` container's `.hidden` class selector rule gets applied to the `div` element. That rule makes the `div` element's text invisible when the page first loads. Let's now look at the web page's `head` section and examine the `.hidden` class selector rule.

See the Font Styles web page `style` container in **FIGURE 10.15B**. The `.hidden` class selector rule uses `display: none`, which means the matched element, `div` in this case, does not display. As an alternative to `display: none`, you can use `visibility: hidden` for the property-value pair. The difference is that with `visibility: hidden`, the browser provides layout space for the element, whereas with `display: none`, no space is provided. Note the `style` container's `.italic`, `.bold`, and `.small-caps` class selector rules. The event handler uses those rules to change the bottom text's appearance when the user clicks the **Done** button.

See the `applyFontSelections` function in **FIGURE 10.15C**. It's called when the user clicks the web page's **Done** button. The function first calls `getElementById("message")` to retrieve the `div` element at the bottom of the web page and store the `div` element's object in a variable named `message`. The rest of the function is in charge of retrieving the user's font selections and applying those selections to the bottom `div` element. In processing the radio buttons, we use coding techniques you've seen in prior examples. We use the radio button group's `value` property to retrieve the selected font size value (1em, 3em, or 5em), and we use the `div` element's `style` property to update the `div` object's `fontSize` property.

In processing the checkboxes, the code is a bit more complicated, but we're once again relying on coding techniques that should look familiar. We use a `for...of` statement to loop through the checkboxes, and if a checkbox's `checked` property is true, we append that checkbox's value (italic, bold, or small-caps) to the `selectors` variable. What is the `selectors` variable? The

```
<!DOCTYPE html>
<html lang="en">
<head>
<meta charset="utf-8">
<meta name="author" content="John Dean">
<title>Select Font Styles</title>
<style>
  fieldset {
    display: inline;
    border-color: blue;
  }
  .hidden {display: none;}          This causes the web
  .italic {font-style: italic;}     page's bottom message
  .bold {font-weight: bold;}        to be invisible.
  .small-caps {font-variant: small-caps;}
</style>
```

**FIGURE 10.15B** `style` **container for Font Styles web page**

```
<script>
  // Apply the user's font selections to text at the
  // bottom of the web page.

  function applyFontSelections(form) {
    var fontFeatureCBs;  // collection of checkboxes
    var message;         // message element
    var selectors = "";  // a list of selectors for message

    message = document.getElementById("message");
    message.style.fontSize =
      form.elements["fontSize"].value;

    fontFeatureCBs = form.elements["otherFontFeatures"];
    for (let fontFeature of fontFeatureCBs) {
      if (fontFeature.checked) {
        selectors += fontFeature.value + " ";
      }
    } // end for

    message.className = selectors;
  } // end applyFontSelections
</script>
</head>
```

**FIGURE 10.15C** `script` **container for Font Styles web page**

`selectors` variable stores italic, bold, and/or small-caps selector values—one selector value for each font feature that the user chooses. We initialize `selectors` to the empty string and then we add values to it by using += in the checkbox loop. So if the user selects the italics and small-caps checkboxes, the `selectors` variable ends up with "italics small-caps" for its value.

Here's the function's last statement:

```
message.className = selectors;
```

Remember that `message` stores the bottom `div` element's object. By assigning `selectors` to `message.className`, we're able to update the class selector rules that get applied to the `div` element's text. So if the user selects the italics and small-caps checkboxes, the event handler assigns the `.italics` and `.small-caps` class selector rules to the `div` element's text.

# 10.12 Using `z-index` to Stack Elements on Top of Each Other

In this section, we continue our discussion of manipulating CSS with JavaScript, but now the emphasis is more on the CSS than the JavaScript. You'll be learning about the CSS `z-index` property and then how to change its value using JavaScript.

## z-index **Property**

If you want to stack elements visually on top of each other, use absolute positioning to achieve the overlap, and then use the z-index CSS property to determine the order of elements along the web page's z axis. The z axis comes from the Cartesian coordinate system, which has x, y, and z axes for describing a three-dimensional space. The x and y axes run horizontally and vertically. With CSS, the z axis runs from the monitor and toward the user's eyes. If a web page element has a larger z-index value than another element, then the larger-valued element appears in front of the other element. "In front of" means closer to the user as the user faces the screen. z-index values can be any integer value, positive or negative.

Suppose you have three img elements with class="tiger", class="lemur", and class="red-panda" and the following class selector rules:

```
.tiger {position: absolute; left: 0; top: 0; z-index: -1;}
.lemur {position: absolute; left: 15%; top: 10%; z-index: 0;}
.red-panda {position: absolute; right: 0; bottom: 0; z-index: 1;}
```

Can you figure out how those rules affect the three pictures? Do not read the next paragraph until after you've thoroughly mulled over the rules.

The tiger img element is positioned at the top-left corner of the containing block. The lemur is pushed 15% to the right of the containing block's left edge, and it's pushed 10% down from the containing block's top edge. The red panda is positioned at the bottom-right corner of the containing block. The tiger's z-index value is less than the other z-index values, so the tiger picture displays behind the other pictures. The red panda's z-index value is greater than the other z-index values, so the red panda picture displays in front of the other pictures.

**FIGURE 10.16 Animal Stacking web page—initial display and what happens after the user clicks on the tiger picture**

## Animal Stacking Web Page

Take a look at the Animal Stacking web page in **FIGURE 10.16** and note how the animal pictures are stacked on top of each other (as described in the previous subsection). When the user clicks on a picture, there's an event handler that brings that picture to the front by changing the picture's z-index value.

See **FIGURE 10.17A** and peruse the Animal Stacking web page's body container. Note that there's a div container that surrounds three animal img elements. As you'll see when we look at the web page's style container, we use CSS to get those animal images to stack on top of each other. Note that each img element has an onclick event handler that calls a moveToTop function. As you'll see when we look at the web page's script container, that function adjusts the img element's z-index value so the img element moves to the top of the z-axis stack.

**FIGURE 10.17B** shows the Animal Stacking web page's CSS rules. Note the .tiger, .lemur, and .red-panda class selector rules, which are the same as what you saw in the earlier code fragment, except the z-index values are now 0, 1, and 2, respectively. Those rules ensure that the images overlap and that the red panda is on top of the stack and the tiger is on the bottom.

The class selector rules for the three images all specify absolute positioning. An element with absolute positioning uses its containing block as the reference point for its left, top, right, and bottom property values. You might recall that the default containing block is the web page's html element, and that you can use relative positioning to change the containing block. In the Animal Stacking web page, we want the images to be positioned relative to the div container that surrounds the images. To accomplish that goal, we apply relative positioning to the (class="images") div container like this:

```
.images {position: relative; height: 504px; width: 786px;}
```

In addition to specifying relative positioning, this rule specifies values for the height and width properties. The height and width are necessary because the third image is positioned at the div element's bottom-right corner. If the div element were too small or too large, the third image would be too close to the other images or too far from the other images, respectively.

```
<body>
<h1>Furry Forest Friends</h1>
<div class="images">
  <img src="../images/tiger.jpg" width="400" height="317"
    alt="tiger" class="tiger" onclick="moveToTop(this)">
  <img src="../images/lemur.jpg" width="480" height="411"
    alt="lemur" class="lemur" onclick="moveToTop(this)">
  <img src="../images/redPanda.jpg" width="550" height="403"
    alt="red panda" class="red-panda" onclick="moveToTop(this)">
</div>
</body>
</html>
```

**FIGURE 10.17A** body **container for Animal Stacking web page**

```
<!DOCTYPE html>
<html lang="en">
<head>
<meta charset="utf-8">
<meta name="author" content="John Dean">
<title>Animal Stacking</title>
<style>
  h1 {text-align: center;}
  .images {
    position: relative;
    height: 504px; width: 786px;
  }
  .tiger {
    position: absolute;
    left: 0; top: 0;
    z-index: 0;
  }
  .lemur {
    position: absolute;
    left: 15%; top: 10%;
    z-index: 1;
  }
  .red-panda {
    position: absolute;
    right: 0; bottom: 0;          ←  The right and bottom properties
    z-index: 2;                       specify the offset between the current
  }                                   element and the containing block's right
</style>                              edge and bottom edge, respectively.
<script>
  var topIndex = 2;             ←  global variable

  // This function uses the topIndex global variable to
  // bring the clicked picture to the front.

  function moveToTop(picture) {
    picture.style.zIndex = ++topIndex;
  }                                          ↑
</script>                                    └─ prefix mode increment operator
</head>
```

**FIGURE 10.17B** **head** **container for Animal Stacking web page**

## Global Variables

Now let's figure out how clicking on a picture brings the picture to the front. Here's the first statement in the web page's `script` container:

```
var topIndex = 2;
```

Previously, you were told to use `var` when declaring variables within a function, and if you omit the `var`, the JavaScript engine creates a global variable. In declaring and initializing `topIndex` in the preceding code fragment, we do use `var`, but because the variable is declared above the function and not in the function, `topIndex` is a global variable. Normally, you want to stay away from global variables because they can lead to bugs and code that is hard to maintain. With a global variable, the variable is shared by all of the web page's functions. Formally, we say that the global variable's scope is the entire web page.

The other feature of a global variable (and the salient feature for the Animal Stacking web page) relates to its persistence. *Persistence* refers to how long a variable's value survives before it's wiped out. Global variables persist for as long as the variable's web page is loaded on the browser. That's in contrast to *local variables*, which are declared using `var` within a function. Local variables persist only as long as the JavaScript engine is executing code within the variable's function. After finishing with a function, the JavaScript engine resets the function's local variables back to their original undefined status, so the next time the function is called, the local variables' previous values are forgotten.

## Using JavaScript to Modify the Stacking Order

Now that we've established that `topIndex` is a global variable, we still need to know what it's for and how it works. It keeps track of the `z-index` value for the picture that is currently at the front. When the user clicks a picture, its event handler increments the `topIndex` variable and assigns the new value to the picture element's `z-index` property. Because the picture's `z-index` value is greater than the other pictures' `z-index` values, the clicked picture gets moved to the front.

Let's go back and look at the code that makes all this possible. In the following `img` element, note how the `onclick` event handler calls the `moveToTop` function with a `this` argument:

```
<img src="../images/tiger.jpg" width="400" height="317"
  alt="tiger" class="tiger" onclick="moveToTop(this)">
```

The `this` argument refers to the object associated with the current element, so in the preceding code fragment, `this` refers to the clicked image's object. In the following `moveToTop` function definition, note the `picture` parameter in the function's heading:

```
function moveToTop(picture) {
  picture.style.zIndex = ++topIndex;
}
```

The `picture` parameter receives the clicked image's object. In the function's body, we use the `picture` variable's `style` property to access the clicked image's `zIndex` property. As expected, the `zIndex` property is associated with the image's CSS `z-index` property. Note how the function assigns `++topIndex` to the image's `z-index` property.

The `++` operator should look familiar. It's the increment operator, and it adds 1 to the `topIndex` variable. In previous examples, we put `++` after the variable instead of before it. For example, we used `i++` in the Job Skills web page to increment the `i` index variable.

The increment operator has two different modes—*prefix mode* and *postfix mode*. Prefix mode is when you put the `++` before the variable that is to be incremented. Using prefix mode causes the variable to be incremented before the variable's value is used. For example:

```
y = ++x;    is equivalent to    x = x + 1;
                                 y = x;
```

Postfix mode is when you put the `++` after the variable that is to be incremented. Using postfix mode causes the variable to be incremented after the variable's value is used. For example:

```
y = x++;    is equivalent to    y = x;
                                 x = x + 1;
```

In the Animal Stacking web page's `moveToTop` function, we embed the incrementation operation within an assignment statement, like this:

```
picture.style.zIndex = ++topIndex;
```

When you embed an increment operator expression within another statement, it's important to think about which mode is appropriate—prefix or postfix. In the preceding example, we have to use prefix notation, `++topIndex`, because we need to increment first and then use `topIndex`'s updated value. If you have an incrementation operation that's on a line by itself (i.e., the increment operator expression is not embedded within another statement), then there's no difference in functionality between using prefix mode and postfix mode. When it makes no difference, most programmers use postfix mode by convention.

## 10.13 Textarea Controls

To round out your introduction to HTML's most popular controls, we'll cover textarea controls[3] in this section and pull-down menus and list boxes after that.

The textarea control is similar to the text control in that it enables the user to enter text into a box. The only significant differences in functionality are that the box can have multiple

---

[3] Most web developers use the term "textarea control" to refer to the control described in this section. Unfortunately, the W3C tends to use the term "multiline plain text edit control" instead. It's quite a mouthful, and it's not used much by web developers. Therefore, we'll refrain from adopting their term. Sorry, W3C. We're sticking with "textarea control."

rows, and the box will have a scrollbar if it contains more text than can be seen within the box's borders. There are quite a few differences in syntax, and we'll cover those differences next.

Because of the somewhat disjointed nature of HTML's development (remember the browser wars?), knowing which element to use for a particular control can be a bit of a challenge. Up to this point, all the controls described so far have used the `input` element. The textarea control, on the other hand, uses the `textarea` element. Recall that with the `input` element, we use the `type` attribute to distinguish which type of control is being implemented—a button, a text control, a checkbox, and so on. But with the `textarea` element, there's no uncertainty (the `textarea` element implements the textarea control, and that's it), so no `type` attribute is necessary.

Here's an example `textarea` element:

```
<textarea id="feedback" rows="4" cols="50" maxlength="50"></textarea>
```

Note that the `textarea` element is a container, with an end tag. That's different from the `input` element, which is a void element, with no end tag. If there's any content between the `textarea` element's two tags, that content gets displayed as the textarea control's default user input. Default user input might be appropriate in special circumstances, but normally you'll want your `textarea` controls to start off empty.

If the prior code was indented, to avoid line wrap, you might want to split the code like this:

```
<textarea id="customerFeedback" rows="4" cols="50" maxlength="250">
    </textarea>
```

Pressing enter and indenting on the next line leads to a textarea control that is prepopulated with whitespace.

The updated code looks innocuous, but, beware, a subtle error has been introduced. Remember that any content between the `textarea` element's tags gets displayed as the textarea control's default user input. If the content includes whitespace, that whitespace is (annoyingly) preserved. That means that the preceding code generates a textarea control with a newline character and several space characters for its default text. That's not a disaster, but it can be disconcerting for users who are paying attention. The solution is to make sure there's no gap between the start tag's > and the end tag's <. That means if you have a long `textarea` start tag, you should split it after one of its attributes. Or as an alternative, you could split it right before its closing >, like this:

```
<textarea id="customerFeedback" rows="4" cols="50" maxlength="250"
    ></textarea>
```

This leads to an empty textarea control (which is a good thing).

## HTML Attributes

Here are the textarea control's more important attributes:

| Textarea Control Attributes | | | | | | | | |
|---|---|---|---|---|---|---|---|---|
| id | rows | cols | maxlength | placeholder | spellcheck | disabled | readonly | required |

The `id` attribute works the same for all elements—its value serves as an identifier for the control, so it can be accessed with JavaScript. The `rows` and `cols` attributes are specific to the textarea control, and we'll describe them coming up. The `maxlength`, `placeholder`, and `spellcheck` attributes work the same for the text and textarea controls, and we'll review them shortly. The `disabled`, `readonly`, and `required` attributes work the same for all the controls. If you need a refresher on them, refer back to earlier descriptions of control attributes.

The `rows` attribute specifies the textarea control's height, where the height value is an integer that approximates the number of lines of text that can fit in the box. So `rows="4"` means approximately 4 lines of text can display in the box simultaneously. The default `rows` value is 2, but you should provide an explicit value for the `rows` attribute (and the `cols` attribute) as a form of self-documentation.

The `cols` attribute specifies the textarea control's width, where the width value is an integer that approximates the number of average-size characters that can fit in the box. So `cols="50"` means approximately 50 characters can display in one line of the box. The default `cols` value is 20. If a line in the box is filled with text, and the user attempts to enter more characters for that line, line wrap occurs. In other words, the right-edge text wraps around to the next line.

The textarea control's `maxlength` attribute (and also the text control's `maxlength` attribute) specifies the maximum number of characters that can be entered in the control's box. By default, there is no limit to the amount of text that can be stored in a textarea control. If the user enters more text than can fit in the textarea control's box, a scrollbar appears, and the text at the top scrolls up and out of view. As a programmer, you can prevent or reduce such scrolling behavior by including a `maxlength` attribute.

The textarea control's `placeholder` attribute (and also the text control's `placeholder` attribute) provides text that helps the user to know what to enter into the control. When the user enters text into the control, the `placeholder`'s text disappears.

The textarea control's `spellcheck` attribute (and also the text control's `spellcheck` attribute) determines whether the browser engine should check the entered text for spelling and grammar mistakes. A value of `true` indicates checking should occur, and a value of `false` indicates checking should not occur. A value of `default` or omitting the spellcheck attribute indicates that the browser should check or not check based on its default behavior. The most common developer strategy is to rely on the default behavior, but if you want to allow nonstandard words in a textarea control or text control, then you should consider using `spellcheck="false"`.

## Using JavaScript with the Textarea Control

All of the textarea control's attributes shown earlier (`id`, `rows`, `cols`, `maxlength`, etc.) have an associated property in the JavaScript world. So there are `cols` and `rows` properties you can use to retrieve or update the number of columns and rows in the textarea's box, a `maxLength` property you can use to retrieve or update the maximum number of characters the user can enter into the textarea's box, and so on. As you may recall, HTML attributes use all lowercase, whereas JavaScript properties use camel case, which means there's a `maxlength` attribute and a `maxLength` property. Likewise, there's a `readonly` attribute and a `readOnly` property.

The `textarea` element has a `value` attribute that we didn't bother to mention earlier because it's not used all that often. It works the same for the text and textarea controls—it specifies an initial value for the control, and it's treated as user input. The associated JavaScript `value` property is used a lot—it's how you retrieve or update the textarea control's user input. In an upcoming web page, we implement a textarea control with an `id` value of `newComment`, and we pass the control's form to an event handler function. Within that function, we could use the following code to display the textarea control's user input in a dialog box:

```
newComment = form.elements["newComment"];
alert(newComment.value);
```

And here's how we could clear the textarea control's box so it's empty:

```
newComment.value = "";
```

If you'd like to verify that the user enters something in a textarea control, you can compare the textarea's value to the empty string (e.g., `newComment.value != ""`). Or as a more elegant solution, you can provide a `required` attribute with the textarea control, and then use the control's form object to call its `checkValidity` method. If `checkValidity` returns true, that means the textarea control's value is nonempty. It also means the form's other controls are valid as well. Here's the relevant code:

```
if (form.checkValidity()) {
  . . .
```

## 10.14 Dormitory Blog Web Page

Let's put what we've learned about the textarea control into practice in the context of a complete web page. See the Dormitory Blog web page in **FIGURE 10.18A**. The large box under the main heading is a read-only textarea control that displays a collection of comments about Park University's dorms. The box under "Select a dorm" is a pull-down menu. We'll cover pull-down menus in the next section. For now, just realize that when the user clicks the pull-down menu's down arrow, a list of dorm names appears. The user then selects a dorm from the list. The box under "Your comment" is a textarea control where the user enters a comment about the selected dorm. Because

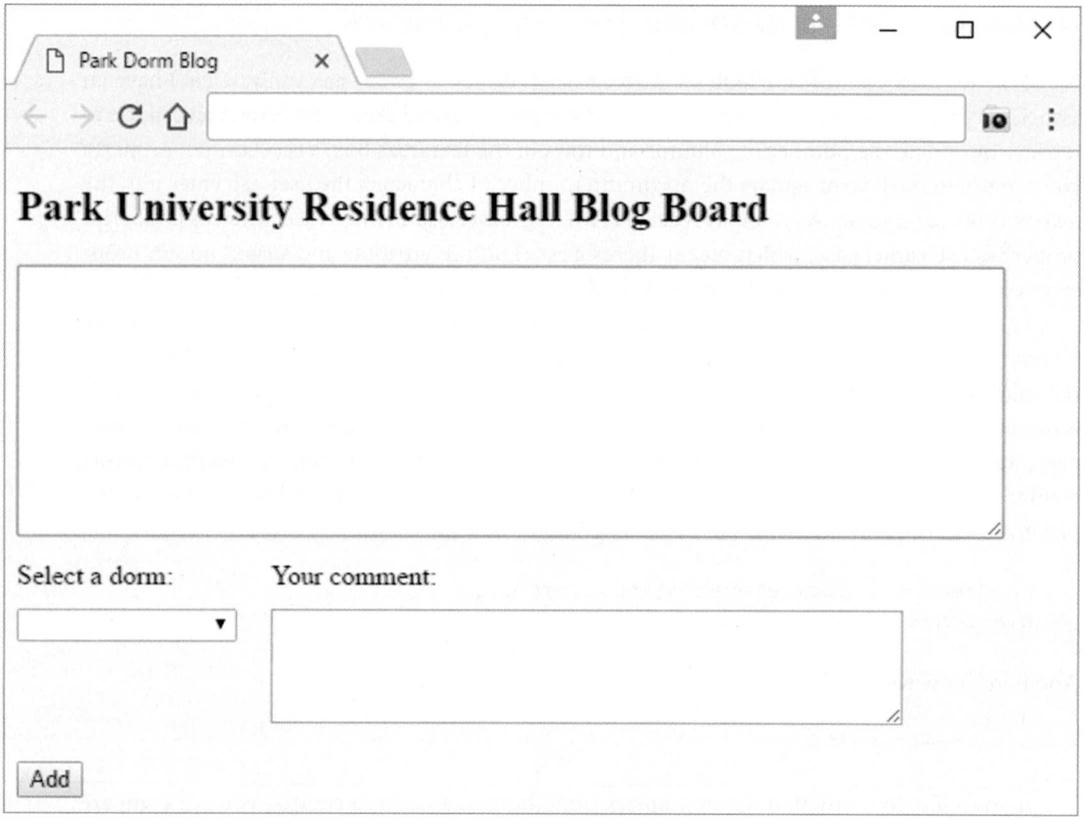

**FIGURE 10.18A  Dormitory Blog web page—initial display**

the pull-down menu and the "Your comment" textarea control are for user input, we'll refer to them as the web page's input controls. To submit a comment, the user must enter something in both input controls and then click the **Add** button.

**FIGURE 10.18B** shows two comment submissions and what the blog page looks like afterwards. In the web page's textarea box at the top, note how new submissions get inserted above prior submissions. And for each submission, note how the dorm name gets displayed above the user's comment. The input controls get cleared after each submission, and that's why the figure shows empty input controls at the bottom of the web page.

## body **Container**

Let's begin our examination of the Dormitory Blog web page's source code with the body container, which you can see in **FIGURE 10.19A**. Find the two textarea elements. The first one is rather large (rows="10" cols="80") and uses a readonly attribute. It's for displaying the collection of submitted comments. The second one is smaller (rows="4" cols="50"), and it's for submitting individual user comments. Between the two textarea elements, you can see the code for a pull-down menu. It uses the select element. We'll describe the select element's

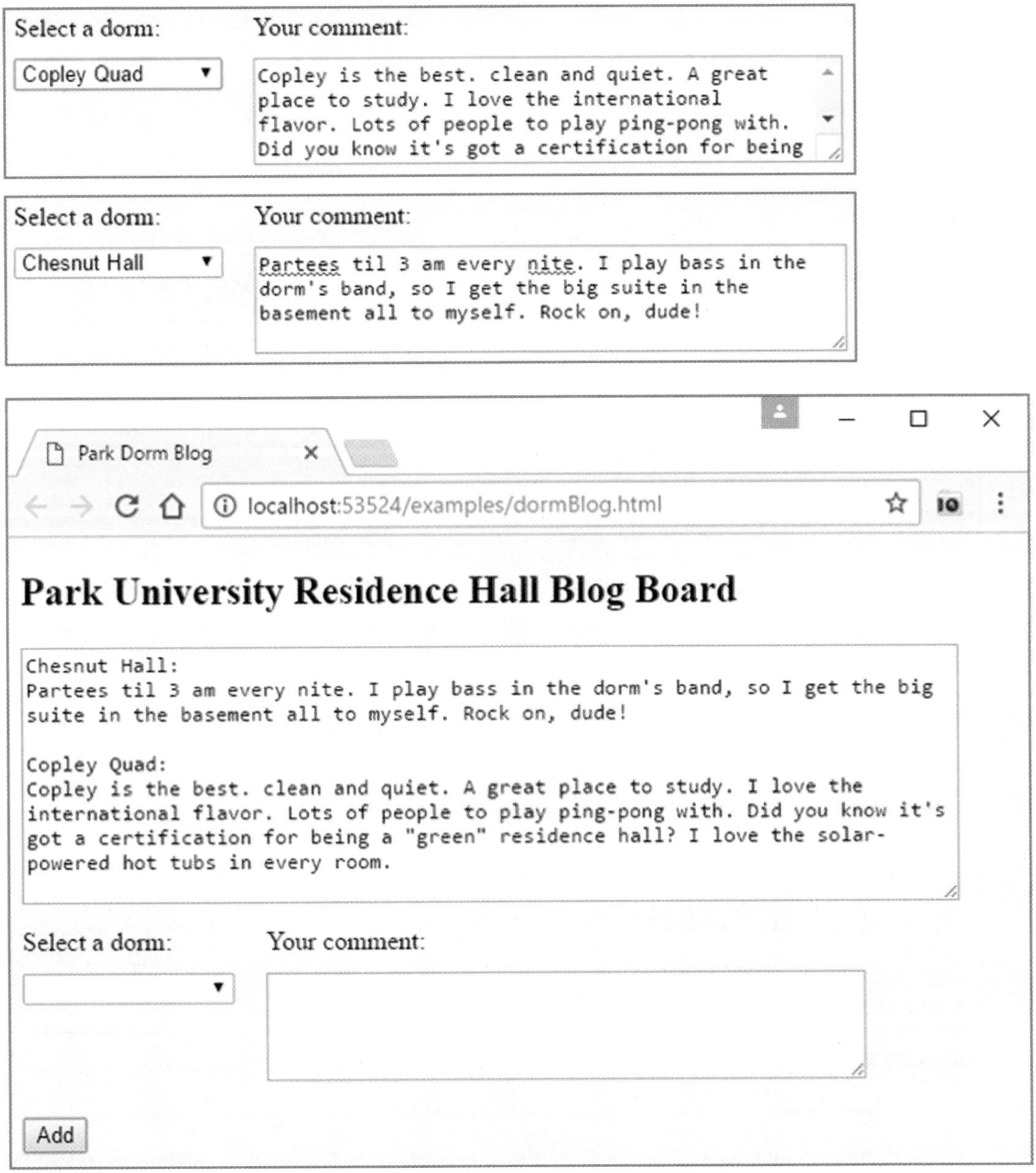
Select a dorm:
Your comment:
Copley Quad
Copley is the best. clean and quiet. A great place to study. I love the international flavor. Lots of people to play ping-pong with. Did you know it's got a certification for being
Select a dorm:
Your comment:
Chesnut Hall
Partees til 3 am every nite. I play bass in the dorm's band, so I get the big suite in the basement all to myself. Rock on, dude!
Park Dorm Blog
localhost:53524/examples/dormBlog.html
Park University Residence Hall Blog Board
Chesnut Hall:
Partees til 3 am every nite. I play bass in the dorm's band, so I get the big suite in the basement all to myself. Rock on, dude!
Copley Quad:
Copley is the best. clean and quiet. A great place to study. I love the international flavor. Lots of people to play ping-pong with. Did you know it's got a certification for being a "green" residence hall? I love the solar-powered hot tubs in every room.
Select a dorm:
Your comment:
Add

**FIGURE 10.18B Dormitory Blog web page—two submissions and what the page looks like afterwards**

syntax and functionality in the next section. When the user clicks the button at the bottom of the form, the button's event handler processes the values in the input controls.

Both input controls include the `required` attribute, which means the event handler can call `checkValidity` to make sure that the input controls contain nonempty values. The textarea

```
<body>
<h2>Park University Residence Hall Blog Board</h2>
<form>
  <textarea id="allComments"
    rows="10" cols="80" readonly></textarea>
  <br>
  <div class="table">
    <div class="row">
      <label for="dorm">Select a dorm:</label>
      <label for="newComment">Your comment:</label>
    </div>
    <div class="row">
      <div>
        <select id="dorm" required>
          <option></option>
          <option>Chesnut Hall</option>
          <option>Copley Quad</option>
          <option>Browning Hall</option>
          <option>Eaton Hall</option>
          <option>Melrose Hall</option>
          <option>Semple Hall</option>
        </select>
      </div>
      <div>
        <textarea id="newComment" rows="4" cols="50"
          required spellcheck="true"></textarea>
      </div>
    </div>
  </div>
  <br>
  <div id="error">You must select a dorm and enter a comment.</div>
  <input type="button" value="Add"
    onclick="addComment(this.form);">
</form>
</body>
</html>
```

readonly attribute for the top textarea box

CSS table layout for the input controls and their headers

required and spellcheck attributes for the textarea input control

This error message is hidden initially.

**FIGURE 10.19A** body **container for Dormitory Blog web page**

control's element includes a `spellcheck` attribute so the user is alerted to spelling mistakes. In Figure 10.18B's second submission, you can see red squiggly underlines for "Partees" and "nite," which indicate spell-checking errors.

Note the `class="table"` and `class="row"` attribute-value pairs for the containers that surround the input controls and their headers. They provide the scaffolding for a CSS table. In the next subsection, we'll review the CSS rules that get applied to those container elements.

Below the CSS table containers, there's a `div` element with an error message inside it. As you'll see when we examine the `style` container, we use CSS to make the error message invisible when the page first loads. As you'll see when we examine the external JavaScript file, the form's event handler makes the error message visible if there's invalid input.

## `style` Container

Go back to Figure 10.18B and verify that the input controls and their headers are aligned. The web page uses a CSS table to achieve that alignment. As you've seen in the past, we implement the table with CSS rules that use the `display` property and `table` values. Specifically, take a look at the `.table`, `.row`, and `.row > *` rules in **FIGURE 10.19B**'s `style` container. The `.table` rule designates a table (for the outer `div` container). The `.row` rule designates table rows (for the two `div` elements within the outer `div` container). The `.row > *` rule designates table cells (for the two headers and their two controls).

As is often the case, tweaking the CSS was necessary to make things look good, even after using a CSS table for layout. To make the pull-down menu and the textarea input control align at their top edges, we use the `vertical-align: top` property-value pair for the table cells. And to make the table's left cells align at the left with the other content on the page, we provide a `padding` rule for the table cells with 0 padding at the left.

```
<!DOCTYPE html>
<html lang="en">
<head>
<meta charset="utf-8">
<meta name="author" content="John Dean">
<title>Park Dorm Blog</title>
<style>
  body {background-color: azure;}
  .table {display: table;}
  .row {display: table-row;}
  .row > * {
    display: table-cell;
    vertical-align: top;
    padding: 10px 20px 0 0;
  }
  #error {
    display: none;
    color: red;
    margin-bottom: 20px;
  }
</style>
<script src="dormBlog.js"></script>
</head>
```

This causes the pull-down menu and the "Your comment" textarea box to be aligned at their top edges.

This causes the "Select a dorm" header and the pull-down menu to align at the left with the other content on the page.

This causes the error message to be hidden initially.

**FIGURE 10.19B** head container for Dormitory Blog web page

Recall that the error message `div` element at the bottom of the web page is supposed to be invisible when the page first loads. We make it invisible with the help of the `style` container's last rule. Go back to the `body` container and verify that the error message `div` element includes an `id="error"` attribute-value pair. Go back to the `style` container and verify that the last CSS rule matches that `div` element by using `#error` for its selector. The `#error` CSS rule makes the error message `div` element invisible by using a `display: none` property-value pair. In the upcoming subsection, you'll see how we use JavaScript to make the element visible when the user submits the form with invalid input.

## addComment **Event Handler Function**

If you go back to Figure 10.19A, you can see that the button's `onclick` attribute calls an `addComment` function. Take a look at the `addComment` function in **FIGURE 10.20**. The function begins by retrieving the read-only textarea control at the top and the two input controls. It stores the controls in local variables so they can be easily accessed later on. The function then calls the form's `checkValidity` method to check for valid input. Because the input controls use the `required` attribute, `checkValidity` returns true only if the controls hold nonempty values. If either control holds an empty value, this code gets executed:

```
document.getElementById("error").style.display = "block";
```

In executing the code, the JavaScript engine assigns `block` to the error message `div` element's CSS `display` property. The `block` value is the default value for a `div` element's `display` property, and it causes the `div` element to be visible. So if there's invalid user input, the error message `div` element becomes visible.

Continuing with our examination of the `addComment` function, if the `checkValidity` method returns true, we want the error message `div` element to return to its initial state and become invisible. Here's the code that does that:

```
document.getElementById("error").style.display = "none";
```

The none value should make sense because that's the value that's used in the CSS rule that gets applied when the page first loads:

```
#error {display: none;}
```

After taking care of the error message `div` element, the `addComment` function assigns the user input controls' values to an `addedVerbiage` local variable. It then inserts the `addedVerbiage` string in front of the existing comments in the read-only textarea control. Here's the code that does that, where `allComments` is the local variable for the read-only textarea control:

```
allComments.value = addedVerbiage + allComments.value;
```

On the right side of the assignment statement, we use the `value` property to read the string within the textarea control. And on the left side, we use the `value` property to update that string.

```
/*********************************************************
 * dormBlog.js
 * John Dean
 *
 * This file contains a function that supports the dorm blog web page.
 *********************************************************/

// This function posts a new comment in the community textarea.

function addComment(form) {
  var dorm;           // select control for dorm
  var newComment;     // textarea for the new comment
  var allComments;    // textarea for combined comments
  var addedVerbiage;  // text to add to blog

  dorm = form.elements["dorm"];
  newComment = form.elements["newComment"];
  allComments = form.elements["allComments"];

  if (!form.checkValidity()) {
    document.getElementById("error").style.display = "block";
  }
  else {
    document.getElementById("error").style.display = "none";
    if (allComments.value == "") {
      addedVerbiage = dorm.value + ":\n" + newComment.value;
    }
    else {
      addedVerbiage = dorm.value + ":\n" + newComment.value + "\n\n";
    }
    allComments.value = addedVerbiage + allComments.value;
    dorm.selectedIndex = 0;
    newComment.value = "";
  } // end else
} // end addComment
```

Make the error message visible.

Make it invisible.

Clear the input controls.

**FIGURE 10.20** External JavaScript file for Dormitory Blog web page

Next, the addComment function clears the input controls with these assignment statements, where dorm and newComment are the local variables for the input controls:

```
dorm.selectedIndex = 0;
newComment.value = "";
```

Don't worry about the dorm pull-down menu's selectedIndex property for now. We'll tackle pull-down menu details in the next section.

## 10.15 Pull-Down Menus

As promised, in this section we describe pull-down menus. We introduced you to pull-down menu basics in the prior section, so some of this discussion should sound familiar. When a user clicks a pull-down menu's down arrow, that causes a list of selections to appear below the down arrow. When the user clicks one of the selections, the list collapses and the selected value appears next to the down arrow. What follows is an example from the Dormitory Blog web page. It shows what happens when a user clicks the pull-down menu's down arrow and then clicks the Copley Quad selection:

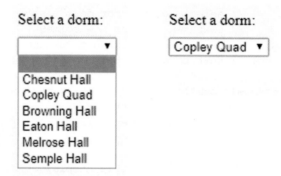

To implement a pull-down menu, you need a `select` element container with `option` elements inside it. Here's the code that implements the dorm selection pull-down menu:

```
<select id="dorm" required>
  <option label=" "></option>
  <option>Chesnut Hall</option>
  <option>Copley Quad</option>
  <option>Browning Hall</option>
  <option>Eaton Hall</option>
  <option>Melrose Hall</option>
  <option>Semple Hall</option>
</select>
```

When a pull-down menu's option list is collapsed, it displays the value associated with the option that's currently selected. By clicking an option, the user determines the current selection. But when the pull-down menu first loads, the default current selection is the first option. In the preceding code fragment, the first `option` element has no content between its tags, so the pull-down menu's initial selection has a value equal to the empty string. Glance up at the pull-down menu pictures, and you can verify that the initial pull-down menu displays nothing (i.e., the empty string) at the left of its down arrow.

It's common practice to have no content for the first `option` element in a pull-down menu's `select` container. That way, it's clear to the user that there's no preferred selection. Also, it encourages the user to make a selection rather than to accept the default selection. Additionally, it provides a hook for JavaScript to perform input validation. Specifically, if an `option` element has no content, then that option's value is the empty string. And if the user selects an option with an empty-string value, and the pull-down menu uses the `required` attribute, then the form's `checkValidity` method indicates invalid input by returning false.

Be aware that if you have no content for an `option` element, then the HTML5 standard requires a `label` attribute for the `option` element. As its name implies, the `label` attribute provides a label for the option when the option is displayed as part of the pull-down menu. In the code fragment shown earlier, note the first option's `label=" "` attribute-value pair.

## HTML Attributes

Typically, `select` element syntax is sparse. Just a few attributes are commonly used with the `select` element for pull-down menus, and here they are:

| Pull-Down Menu `select` Element Attributes | | |
|---|---|---|
| id | disabled | required |

You should be familiar with the `id` and `disabled` attributes since they work the same for all elements. The `required` attribute means that the user has to select an option with a nonempty string value. For the Dormitory Blog web page's pull-down menu, its `select` container defines an empty-string value for its first option, so if that option is selected, the form's `checkValidity` method flags it as an invalid input.

As you know, the `select` element works in conjunction with the `option` element. Like the `select` element, the `option` element's syntax is sparse. Here are the more commonly used attributes for the `option` element when it's positioned within a `select` element:

| Pull-Down Menu `option` Element Attributes | | |
|---|---|---|
| label | selected | value |

We've already described the `label` attribute—it provides a label for the option when the option is displayed as part of the pull-down menu. The `selected` attribute is an empty attribute in that, if it's included, it appears by itself without a value. If an `option` element has a `selected` attribute, the option's value is preselected within the pull-down menu. If no `option` element has a `selected` attribute, then the first option is preselected by default. For pull-down menus, only one option can be selected, so only one `option` element can have the `selected` attribute.

In implementing the Dormitory Blog web page, suppose you have a strong affinity for Browning Hall. In that case, you might want to eliminate the first `option` element (with its empty-string value) and add a `selected` attribute to the Browning Hall `option` element like this:

```
<option selected>Browning Hall</option>
```

An `option` element's `value` attribute provides the value for its pull-down menu when that option is selected. If an `option` element has no `value` attribute, then its value comes from the text content that appears between the `option` element's start and end tags. For the Dormitory Blog web page's pull-down menu, we did not use `value` attributes for any of the `option` elements. Instead, all of the options' values come from the text between the `option` elements' tags.

For the Dormitory Blog web page's pull-down menu, we could have implemented the first `option` element like this:

```
<option value="">Click down arrow</option>
```

That way, the user would be prompted to click the down arrow and display the dorm options. The `value` attribute's empty string ensures that the first option is not a valid selection (because the form's `checkValidity` method returns false for a `required` pull-down menu whose value is the empty string).

## Using JavaScript with Pull-Down Menus

All of the `select` and `option` elements' attributes shown earlier (`id`, `disabled`, etc.) have an associated property in the JavaScript world, but those properties are not used very often. The pull-down menu's more popular properties are `value` and `selectedIndex`, both of which come from the `select` element's object.

The `select` element object's `value` property holds the value associated with the currently selected option. If you go back to the Dormitory Blog web page's `addComment` function in Figure 10.20, you can see how we use the `value` property to retrieve the selected dorm from the dorm pull-down menu. Here's the relevant code:

```
dorm = form.elements["dorm"];
newComment = form.elements["newComment"];
...
addedVerbiage = dorm.value + ":\n" + newComment.value;
```

The `value` property goes both ways—you can use it to read the pull-down menu's selected value, and you can also use it to update the pull-down menu's selected value. So if you want to update the selection to "Eaton Hall," you could do this:

```
dorm.value = "Eaton Hall";
```

The `select` element object's `selectedIndex` property holds the index of the currently selected option. Index values start at 0 for the first option, so for the dorm pull-down menu, the empty option is at index 0, the Chesnut Hall option is at index 1, and so on.

In the Dormitory Blog web page's `addComment` function, we use the `selectedIndex` property to clear the pull-down menu. Specifically, after inserting the user's input into the read-only textarea control at the top of the page, we clear the dorm pull-down menu by assigning 0 to the `selectedIndex` property, where 0 is the index associated with the empty-string option. Here's the relevant code:

```
dorm.selectedIndex = 0;
```

# 10.16 List Boxes

Next up is the list box control. List boxes are similar to pull-down menus, so we won't have to start from scratch in describing them. They both enable the user to select an option from a list of options.

As you know, pull-down menus collapse after the user selects an option. With a list box, the list of options remains viewable after the user selects an option. For example, here's what the dorms input control looks like implemented as a list box instead of a pull-down menu:

A drawback of a list box is that it takes up more space. So if you have lots of options, you should probably use a pull-down menu rather than a list box. But with relatively few options, a list box can be more user friendly—no need to click a down arrow to figure out what's going on. Another list box advantage is that you can configure them to allow users to select more than one option.

The syntax for list boxes is the same as for pull-down menus, but with a few attributes added. Both controls use a `select` container that surrounds `option` elements. For example, here's the code that generates the dorms list box:

```
<select id="dorm" multiple size="6" required>
  <option>Chesnut Hall</option>
  <option>Copley Quad</option>
  <option> Browning Hall</option>
  <option> Eaton Hall</option>
  <option> Melrose Hall</option>
  <option> Semple Hall</option>
</select>
```

That's the same code as for the pull-down menu, except we've added `multiple` and `size` attributes and we've omitted the empty `option` element, which had no content between its tags. We'll get to the `multiple` and `size` attributes in the next subsection. But for now, let's focus on why we no longer need an empty `option` element. It was appropriate for our pull-down menu's first option to be empty because we wanted to encourage the user to click the down arrow and select a dorm from the list of dorm options. On the other hand, with a list box, there's no down arrow and all of the dorm options display when the page loads. So there's no need to clutter up the list with an empty option.

## HTML Attributes

Here are the attributes that are commonly used with the `select` element for list boxes:

| List Box `select` Element Attributes | | | | |
|---|---|---|---|---|
| id | disabled | required | multiple | size |

The `multiple` and `size` attributes are what distinguishes a list box from a pull-down menu. The `multiple` attribute is an empty attribute. If you include it with a `select` element, the user will be able to select multiple options.

The `size` attribute specifies the number of options that display simultaneously. In the list box code fragment shown in the previous subsection, you can see `size="6"` for the `select` start tag, and that's why all six options display simultaneously in the list box. If a `select` element has a `multiple` attribute and there's no `size` attribute, then the default size is 4. So in the list box code fragment, if there were no `size` attribute, the list box would look like this:

If a list box's size is less than the list box's number of options, then the browser engine provides a vertical scroll bar to help with the user's selection process. After making a selection, if the user wants to make another selection, he/she can ctrl+click on the additional selection.

The common attributes for the `option` element are the same for list boxes and pull-down menus, so the following graphic should be unnecessary, but for the sake of parallelism, here you go:

| List Box `option` Element Attributes | | |
|---|---|---|
| label | selected | value |

With pull-down menus, you can add the `selected` attribute to only one `option` element, but with list boxes, you can add the `selected` attribute to as many option elements as you like.

## Using JavaScript with List Boxes

In our earlier discussion of JavaScript with pull-down menus, we focused on the `value` and `selectedIndex` properties. Those properties allow you to read and update the pull-down menu's single selected option. If your list box allows only one selection (because there's no `multiple` attribute), then you're good to go—the `value` property works the same as for pull-down menus. But if your list box allows multiple selections, then the `value` and `selectedIndex` properties access the first selected option and that's it. Normally, that's unacceptable. So if your list box allows multiple selections, you'll want to use a different set of properties to process the user's selections. This table highlights those properties:

| Object | Property | Description |
|---|---|---|
| `select` element's object | `selectedOptions` | Retrieve the collection of options that are currently selected in the list box. |
| `option` element's object | `value` | Access the option's value. |

To process a user's selections from a list box, use the `select` element object's `selectedOptions` property to access the selected options and loop through those selected options. Within the loop, you can access the current option's value by using the option object's `value` property. You can see that strategy put into practice by examining the `addComment` function in **FIGURE 10.21**. That function is part of a `dormBlog2.js` external JavaScript file. As always, we encourage you to play around with the book's web page examples by getting the source code from the book's website. You should be able to get this list box example to work by making slight edits to the `dormBlog.html` file and linking it to the `dormBlog2.js` external JavaScript file.

Here's the loop from the `addComment` function that processes the list box's selected options:

```
for (let option of dorm.selectedOptions) {
  if (dorms != "") {
    dorms += ", ";
  }
  dorms += option.value;
} // end for
```

Note the `dorm` variable, which holds the list box control's object. We use its `selectedOptions` property to retrieve the collection of selected option objects. The `for` loop iterates through the selected options and stores the current option in a local `option` variable. The current option's value is retrieved using the `option` object's `value` property. That value is then appended onto the `dorms` variable, which holds the list of selected options. Note the `if` statement. It ensures that the dorm names are separated by commas. Specifically, it adds a comma after the `dorms` value if the `dorms` value already holds another dorm name(s).

```javascript
// This function posts a new comment in the community textarea.

function addComment(form) {
  var dorm;           // select control for dorm
  var newComment;     // textarea for the new comment
  var allComments;    // textarea for combined comments
  var addedVerbiage;  // text to add to blog
  var dorms;          // for multiple selections

  dorm = form.elements["dorm"];
  newComment = form.elements["newComment"];
  allComments = form.elements["allComments"];

  if (!form.checkValidity()) {
    document.getElementById("error").style.display = "block";
  }
  else {
    document.getElementById("error").style.display = "none";
    dorms = "";
    for (let option of dorm.selectedOptions) {
      if (dorms != "") {
        dorms += ", ";
      }
      dorms += option.value;
    } // end for

    if (allComments.value == "") {
      allComments.value = dorms + ":\n" + newComment.value;
    }
    else {
      allComments.value = dorms + ":\n" + newComment.value +
        "\n\n" + allComments.value;
    }
    dorm.selectedIndex = -1;  // ← Reset list box so no
    newComment.value = "";    //   option is selected.
  } // end else
} // end addComment
```

**FIGURE 10.21** `addComment` **function for list box version of Dormitory Blog web page**

Go back to Figure 10.21 and note this assignment statement at the bottom of the `addComment` function:

```
dorm.selectedIndex = -1;
```

That's how we reset the list box so that no options are selected. You might recall that for the pull-down menu version of `addComment`, we assigned 0 to `dorm.selectedIndex`. Why the difference? For the pull-down menu, we wanted to select the first option, which was empty, so using 0 for `selectedIndex` was appropriate. But for the list box, we need none of the options to be selected and that means assigning the special value -1 to `selectedIndex`.

# 10.17 CASE STUDY: Collector Performance Details and Nonredundant Website Navigation

## Collector Performance Subordinate Function Details

The case study section at the end of Chapter 9 described the Collector Performance web page with HTML source code in the `body` element and top-level JavaScript code in the `head` element. The top-level JavaScript code made calls to subordinate functions whose details were omitted because they employed features not yet described at that point. But after reading this chapter, you should now be able to understand the JavaScript in those subordinate functions.

**FIGURE 10.22** shows the Collector Performance web page's `computeAngles` function. It provides examples of using `if` statements. It also provides examples of using members from the `Math` object—the `Math.PI` constant and various `Math` methods. All of the `Math` methods employed here are based on trigonometric functions used to describe the position of the sun in the sky at various latitudes, times of year, and times of day. The current application focuses on just one time of day—noon. That simplifies things, but only somewhat. We'll use temporary `alert` statements to investigate details and confirm assertions about what's going on.

As you may recall from the case study at the end of the previous chapter, the enclosing `script` declared three global variables—`form`, `altitude`, and `cosIncidenceAngle`. The `calc` function presented in last chapter's case study initialized the `form` variable with a reference to the web page's `form` element. Comments after the `altitude` and `cosIncidenceAngle` declarations said `altitude` is the "solar angle above horizon" and `cosIncidenceAngle` is the "perpendicular component of radiation." These two variables were to be initialized by calculations in this section's `computeAngles` function.

The `computeAngles` function begins by declaring six local variables—`latitude`, `panelSlope`, `month`, `solarDeclination`, `cosAzimuth`, and `sinAltitude`. It initializes `latitude` and `panelSlope` by using `form` and `id` values to retrieve user inputs and then multiplying by `Math.PI/180` to convert input degrees to radians. It initializes `month` by using `form`, `id`, and the `select` element's `selectedIndex` attribute to retrieve the index of the user-selected month. Because the index of the first selected month (Jan) is 0, it adds 1 to generate a month number that accords with common use: January is month 1, February is month 2, and so on.

```
function computeAngles() {
  var latitude;    // earth latitude
  var panelSlope;  // angle of solar panels up from horizontal to south
  var month;       // month number (Jan = 1, Feb = 2, ...)
  // Using 1985 ASHRAE Fundamentals Guide, Chapter 27, Table 1, and
  // approximating earth's elliptical orbit as a circle:
  var solarDeclination; // solar altitude at north pole in radians
  var cosAzimuth;       // at noon, this is always either -1.0 or +1.0
  // Using 1985 ASHRAE Fundamentals Guide, Chapter 27,
  // equation (3), at noon:
  var sinAltitude;      // sin(solar altitude)

  latitude = form.elements["latitude"].value * Math.PI/180;
  panelSlope = form.elements["panelSlope"].value * Math.PI / 180;
  month = form.elements["months"].selectedIndex + 1;
  solarDeclination = (-23.45 * Math.PI/180)
    * Math.cos(month * Math.PI/6);
  cosAzimuth;        // at noon, this is always either -1.0 or +1.0
  sinAltitude =
    Math.cos(latitude) * Math.cos(solarDeclination)
    + Math.sin(latitude) * Math.sin(solarDeclination);
  altitude = Math.asin(sinAltitude);
  if (altitude > 0) {
    // Using 1985 ASHRAE Fundamentals Guide, Chapter 27,
    // equation (4), at noon:
    cosAzimuth =
      (Math.sin(solarDeclination) - sinAltitude * Math.sin(latitude))
      / (Math.cos(altitude) * Math.cos(latitude));
    cosIncidenceAngle = sinAltitude * Math.cos(panelSlope)
      - cosAzimuth * Math.cos(altitude) * Math.sin(panelSlope);
    if (cosIncidenceAngle < 0) {
      cosIncidenceAngle = 0.0;
    }
  } // end if altitude > 0
} // end computeAngles
```

**FIGURE 10.22** `computeAngles` **function for Collector Performance web page**

Solar declination is the angle by which the North Pole tips toward the sun. It maximizes in June at +23.45 degrees, it minimizes in December at −23.45 degrees, and it's near zero in March and September when the earth's tipping is perpendicular to the sun. The multiplication by `Math.PI/180` converts degrees to radians, and the subsequent multiplication by `Math.PI/6` converts months to radians. This latter conversion minimizes the enclosing cosine function when month = 12, which, of course, is equivalent to month = 0. Thus, `solarDeclination` exhibits sinusoidal oscillation between −23.45 degrees in December and +23.45 degrees in June.

Azimuth is the sun's angle from north in the horizontal plane. It's the compass direction. The `cosAzimuth` variable is the cosine of the azimuth. At high northern (positive) latitudes, the noontime sun is due south and `cosAzimuth = -1.0`. At high southern (negative) latitudes, the noontime sun is due north and `cosAzimuth` = +1.0. If all we care about is noon, why do we need azimuth information? It's because at mid latitudes (between Havana, Cuba and Rio De Janeiro, Brazil), things get messy. Whether the noontime sun is north or south depends in a complex way on latitude and time of year, and the formula for azimuth provides the easiest way to untangle this complexity.

The `sinAltitude` variable represents the sine of the solar altitude at noon. This formula is fairly simple. Using one of trigonometry's fundamental identities, it could have been written like this:[4]

```
var sinAltitude = Math.cos(latitude - solarDeclination);
```

Stated another way, the noontime solar altitude is the complement of latitude minus the current solar declination. When latitude equals solar declination, the noontime sun is straight overhead. When latitude is high (near either pole) noontime solar altitude is small—especially in winter, when the sign of the solar declination is opposite to the sign of the latitude and their magnitudes add.

Because noontime sun is either straight south or straight north, the noontime formula for `cosAzimuth` should return either –1.0 or +1.0. Although a full understanding might be difficult, you can verify this phenomenon by temporarily inserting an `alert` statement immediately after Figure 10.22's evaluation of `cosAzimuth`, like this:

```
cosAzimuth =
    (Math.sin(solarDeclination) - sinAltitude * Math.sin(latitude))
    / (Math.cos(altitude) * Math.cos(latitude));
alert("latitude= " + latitude * 180/Math.PI + ", month= " + month +
    ", cosAzimuth= " + cosAzimuth);
cosIncidenceAngle = sinAltitude * Math.cos(panelSlope)
    - cosAzimuth * Math.cos(altitude) * Math.sin(panelSlope);
```

Suppose you set the latitude input at +21 (the latitude of Hawaii). Because this is within the tropical region between –23.45 and +23.45, at noon the sun might be either south or north, depending on time of year. Now, suppose you select the month, "May". After clicking **Calculate** you'll get an `alert` pop-up like this:

```
┌─────────────────────────────────────────────────────────┐
│                                                    ✕       │
│  JavaScript Alert                                          │
│                                                            │
│  latitude= 21, month= 5, cosAzimuth= -1.0000000000004752   │
│  ☐ Prevent this page from creating additional dialogs.     │
│                                                            │
│                                    ┌──────────┐            │
│                                    │    OK    │            │
│                                    └──────────┘            │
└─────────────────────────────────────────────────────────┘
```

---

[4] The longer form is a direct simplification of the more general formula that includes time of day.

The negative value for `cosAzimuth` says the May noontime sun is south of vertical. Next, suppose you select the month, "Jun". After clicking **Calculate** you'll get an `alert` pop-up like this:

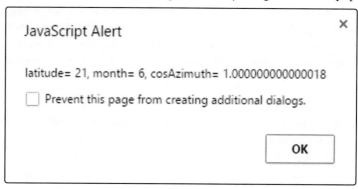

The positive value for `cosAzimuth` says the June noontime sun is north of vertical.

Because the magnitudes of these two values for `cosAzimuth` are indeed very close to 1.0, this test validates the earlier assertion that the `cosAzimuth` formula does a good job of resolving the binary question of whether the noontime sun is north or south of vertical. But notice that in both cases, the magnitudes are slightly greater than unity. This very small anomaly doesn't matter in the present case, but what would happen if you wanted to use `Math.acos` to convert `cosAzimuth` to the angle, `azimuth`?[5] To answer this question, you could replace the temporary `alert` statement shown earlier with a temporary `alert` statement like this:

```
alert("azimuth= " + Math.acos(cosAzimuth));
```

Then if you repeated the experiment, entering +21 for `latitude` and either "May" or "Jun" for `month`, the `alert` pop-up would look like this:

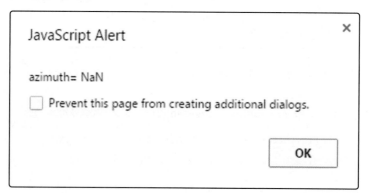

NaN means "not a number." This error occurs because floating-point round-off happened to generate a value for `cosAzimuth` whose magnitude exceeded 1.0, and there is no angle for a sine or cosine whose magnitude exceeds 1.0. After such an attempted evaluation, subsequent calculations would fail, and it might take a while to determine the cause. You can avoid frustration by arbitrarily

---

[5] You'll see this done in the case study section at the end of Chapter 12.

```
function findWatts() {
  var ratedWatts;   // maximum panel output in Watts / square meter
  var watts = 0;    // instantaneous Watts / square meter

  ratedWatts = form.elements["ratedWatts"].value;
  if (altitude > 0) {
    watts = ratedWatts *
      (0.86 * cosIncidenceAngle + 0.14 * Math.sin(altitude));
  }
  return Math.round(watts);
} // end findWatts
```

**FIGURE 10.23** `findWatts` **function for Collector Performance web page**

multiplying all `Math.acos` or `Math.asin` arguments by a round-off error-suppression factor like 0.999999.

Assuming the `cosAzimuth` evaluation in the `computeAngles` function always yields either exactly +1 or exactly –1, the `cosIncidenceAngle` evaluation near the bottom of Figure 10.22 reduces to:

```
cosIncidenceAngle = sinAltitude * Math.cos(panelSlope)
  ± Math.cos(altitude) * Math.sin(panelSlope);
```

Another trigonometric identity says this noontime formula is equivalent to:

```
cosIncidenceAngle = Math.sin(altitude ± panelSlope);
```

The plus sign is for noontime sun south of vertical, and the minus sign is for noontime sun north of vertical. Thus, for example, when noontime sun is south of vertical, `cosIncidenceAngle` maximizes at 1.0 when `altitude` plus `panelSlope` equals 90 degrees.

The last statement in Figure 10.18 zeros `cosIncidenceAngle` when it's less than zero because that means the sun is behind the panel.

**FIGURE 10.23** shows the Collector Performance web page's `findWatts` function. This illustrates another `if` statement, another `Math.sin` operation, and a `Math.round` operation. First it retrieves the user-input value for `ratedWatts`. Then it declares and initializes a local `watts` variable to zero. Then, if `altitude > 0`, it replaces that zero `watts` value by a positive value using an empirical formula involving `cosIncidenceAngle` for direct sunlight and `altitude` for indirect sunlight. Finally, it returns a rounded version of the computed `watts`. The rounding converts the floating-point value generated by the calculation to an integer for cleaner display.

## Nonredundant Website Navigation

The HTML code in Figures 6.25 and 6.28 generated the useful header and footer navigational elements displayed in Figure 6.29. These navigational elements worked well and looked good, but there was substantial duplication—the same header and footer code had to be present on every web page. Moreover, each time the developer added a new page to the website, it was necessary to remember to replace the # in the `href="#"` with the destination address for the new page on *all* previous pages.

The case study section at the end of Chapter 7 used a home page `iframe` to avoid these problems. Unfortunately, that `iframe` approach introduced other problems—it made bookmarking more difficult, and it introduced an unsightly scrollbar.

However, JavaScript provides what many would consider to be a better implementation of website navigational features. To eliminate the redundancy in Chapter 6's website design, put all of the navigational features into one external JavaScript file, and make that one file equally accessible to every web page. JavaScript code in that one file dynamically installs the header and footer features on whatever web page calls it. To make this possible, each individual web page must include (1) a `script` element that references the common JavaScript code file and (2) an `onload` event attribute in the opening `body` tag that calls a function in the JavaScript file.

This approach requires that a small duplicated modification be made to each individual web page, but this modification is simple, and it's not likely to require any maintenance. On each web page, replace these two lines of code:

```
</head>

<body>
```

With these three lines of code:

```
<script src="../library/navigation.js"></script>
</head>

<body onload="createHeaderFooter();">
```

If the `body` start tag already has an `onload` event method call, include another one, like this:

```
<body onload="createHeaderFooter(); initializeColor();">
```

This change makes each web page immediately call the `createHeaderFooter` function in the `navigation.js` file. The new code assumes the `navigation.js` file is in the sibling `library` folder.

The `createHeaderFooter` function simply adds HTML header and footer code to the HTML code that's initially in each bare-bones web page. The function inserts code like that in Chapter 6's Figure 6.25 just after the `body` start tag, and it inserts code like that in Chapter 6's Figure 6.28 just before the closing `body` end tag.

**FIGURE 10.24A** shows the first part of the JavaScript code in the `navigation.js` file. The `createHeaderFooter` function begins by declaring six variables to hold html elements. It initializes the first five. The first two statements after the declarations fill the `h1` element with text and insert it into the new `header` element. (It's "appended" to the beginning of the initially empty element.)

```
function createHeaderFooter() {
  var h1 = document.createElement("h1");
  var header = document.createElement("header");
  var footer = document.createElement("footer");
  var nav = document.createElement("nav");
  var ul = document.createElement("ul");
  var li;

  h1.innerHTML = "Microgrid Development in Lawrence KS";
  header.appendChild(h1);
  li = getli("electricPowerHistory.html", "Electric Power History");
  ul.appendChild(li);
  li = getli("lawrenceHydropower.html", "Lawrence Hydropower");
  ul.appendChild(li);
  li = getli("index.html", "<strong>Area Description</strong>");
  ul.appendChild(li);
  li = getli("microgridPossibilities.html", "Microgrid Possibilities");
  ul.appendChild(li);
  li = getli("typicalProperty.html", "Typical Property");
  ul.appendChild(li);
  li = getli("localEnergy.html", "Local Energy");
  ul.appendChild(li);
  li = getli("collectorPerformance.html", "Collector Performance");
  ul.appendChild(li);
  li = getli("services.html", "Electric Power Services");
  ul.appendChild(li);
  li = getli("#", "Downtown Properties");
  ul.appendChild(li);
  li = getli("#", "Solar Shadowing");
  ul.appendChild(li);
  nav.appendChild(ul);
  header.appendChild(nav);
  document.body.insertBefore(header, document.body.childNodes[0]);
```

**FIGURE 10.24A  JavaScript that adds a heading and adds header and footer navigation buttons to web page being loaded**

In Figure 10.24A, note the ten pairs of statements that have this form:

```
li = getli(...);
ul.appendChild(li);
```

The `getli` function call retrieves a new `li` element from the subordinate `getli` function you'll see shortly. But before getting into that, let's continue with the code in Figure 10.24A. Each of these pairs of statements creates one button and adds it to the unordered list of buttons that will go at the top of the current web page. After the list of buttons is complete, an `appendChild(ul)` call inserts it into the empty `nav` element. Then an `appendChild(nav)` call adds the `nav` element to the `header` element—after the previously inserted `h1` title. The final statement in Figure 10.24A inserts the fully populated `header` element into the body element—before any other material already in the body of the current page. (That other material is all the elements in the `body` of the html code that called this `createHeaderFooter` JavaScript function.)

Before moving on, notice the `"#"` values in the first arguments of the final two `getli` function calls. These are the dummy addresses of web pages that have not yet been created. This `navigation.js` file is the *only* place one needs to go to register a newly created web page! This simple update to the common `navigation.js` file is the only existing-code change needed when a new web page is added.

**FIGURE 10.24B** contains the rest of the `navigation.js` file. The first two statements create new `nav` and `ul` elements and assign them to the previously defined `nav` and `ul` variables. This time, they are for the footer. Then two more pairs of statements create "Top" and "Home" buttons for the bottom of the page and add them to the unordered list for this footer. Then the new `ul` element is inserted into the new `nav` element, and that is inserted into the `footer` element. The last statement in the `createHeaderFooter` function appends the `footer` to all the other material in the body. This other material is now the new `header` followed by the html file's original `body`, so the `footer` is really at the end.

Now look at the subordinate `getli` function called from multiple locations in both figures. This function creates and populates all list items—the buttons at the top and bottom of the browser window. First the function creates new `li` and `a` elements. Then it gives the `a` element a reference and a text label. Then it inserts the `a` element into the `li` element, and finally it returns that `li` element to the calling statement.

```
  nav = document.createElement("nav");   // for another nav element
  ul = document.createElement("ul");      // for another unordered list
  li = getli("#", "Top");
  ul.appendChild(li);
  li = getli("index.html", "Home");
  ul.appendChild(li);
  nav.appendChild(ul);
  footer.appendChild(nav);
  document.body.appendChild(footer);
} // end createHeaderFooter

function getli(ref, label) {
  var li = document.createElement("li");
  var a = document.createElement("a");

  a.setAttribute("href", ref);
  a.innerHTML = label;
  li.appendChild(a);   // insert a into li
  return li;
} // end getli
```

**FIGURE 10.24B JavaScript that adds a heading and adds header and footer navigation buttons to web page being loaded**

# Review Questions

### 10.2 `while` Loop

1. What's the term for a loop that repeats forever?

### 10.3 External JavaScript Files

2. External JavaScript files can help reduce redundant code. Why is redundant code bad?

3. What's the file extension for an external JavaScript file?

### 10.4 Compound Interest Web Page

4. In an external JavaScript file's prologue, what goes inside the asterisk box?

5. With Chrome, which keys do you press to load its debugger tool?

### 10.5 `do` Loop

6. When should you use a `do` loop?

7. What are the two possible values a Boolean variable can hold?

### 10.6 Radio Buttons

8. Suppose you have a collection of radio buttons named `years`. Using `[]` notation, how can you access the first radio button?

9. If you have a radio button group with none of the radio buttons selected, what does the radio button collection's `value` property return?

10. What does a radio button object's `defaultChecked` property return?

### 10.7 Checkboxes

11. If you'd like to form a collection of checkboxes (as opposed to a standalone checkbox), what code do you need to include with each checkbox?

12. Is it legal to have a space within a `class` attribute's value? Within an `id` attribute's value? Within a `name` attribute's value? Within a `value` attribute's value?

### 10.9 `for` Loop

13. What are the three components in a standard `for` loop's heading?

14. When should you use a standard `for` loop?

### 10.11 Manipulating CSS with JavaScript

15. What is the name of the JavaScript property associated with the HTML `class` attribute?

16. What is the name of the JavaScript property associated with the HTML `style` attribute?

17. Both of the `display: none` and `visibility: hidden` property-value pairs cause their matched elements to not display. What's the functionality difference between the property-value pairs?

### 10.12 Using `z-index` to Stack Elements on Top of Each Other

18. If two elements overlap and one element has a `z-index` value of 0 and the other element has a `z-index` value of -1, what happens in terms of how they're displayed?

19. What is a variable's persistence?

20. Suppose a function is called, and it updates a global variable. If the function is called a second time, will the updated variable's value be remembered, or will it be reset to its original undefined value?

### 10.13 Textarea Controls

21. Suppose you have a variable named `recommendation` that holds a textarea object. What code can you use to clear the textarea's box so it's empty?

### 10.14 Dormitory Blog Web Page

22. Where does the Chesnut Hall bass player live?

### 10.16 List Boxes

23. What does it mean if a list box object's `selectedIndex` property is -1?

## Exercises

1. [after Section 10.2] Assume the following code is part of a working web page. What message will the `alert` dialog display?

```
var msg = "Usie:";
var x = 3;
while (x > 0) {
  msg += " " + x
   x--;
}
alert(msg);
```

2. [after Section 10.2] Assume the following code is part of a working web page. The following code is supposed to display the sum of 1 through 4 (with a dialog that says "Sum = 10") and the product of 1 through 4 (with a dialog that says "Product = 24"). Find the errors and fix them.

```
var count = 1;
var sum = 0;
```

```
var product = 0;

while (count < 4) {
  sum += count;
  product *= count;
  if (count == 4)
    alert("Sum = " + sum);
    alert("Product = " + product);
  count++;
}
```

3. [after Section 10.5] Assume the following code is part of a working web page. What message will console.log display?

```
var userTurn = true;
var userTurns = computerPoints = 0;
do {
  if (userTurn) {
    userTurns++;
  }
  else {
    computerPoints++;
  }
  userTurn = !userTurn;
} while (userTurns < 2);
console.log("computer points: " + computerPoints);
```

4. [after Section 10.5] Suppose you have a variable named quantity that holds a number. Provide an if statement heading that checks to see whether quantity holds a whole number.

5. [after Section 10.9] Given the following web page code that generates the factorial for a user-entered number. Provide a standard for loop that could be used to replace the while loop.

```
<!DOCTYPE html>
<html lang="en">
<head>
<meta charset="utf-8">
<meta name="author" content="John Dean">
<title>Factorial Generator</title>
<script>
  // This function generates a factorial.

  function generateFactorial(form) {
    var num;        // a user-entered number
    var factorial;  // factorial of num
    var count;      // multiplicand for factorial calculation

    num = form.elements["number"].valueAsNumber;
```

```
      factorial = 1;
      count = 2;

      while (count <= num) {
        factorial *= count;
        count++;
      }
      form.elements["result"].value = num + "! = " + factorial;
    } // end generateFactorial
  </script>
</head>

<body>
<form>
  <label for="number">Enter a whole number:</label>
  <input type="number" id="number"
    min="0" max="15" step="1" required>
  <br><br>
  <input type="button" value="Generate Factorial"
    onclick="generateFactorial(this.form);">
  <br><br>
  <output id="result"></output>
</form>
</body>
</html>
```

6. [after Section 10.9] The web page code in the prior exercise generates the factorial for a user-entered number. Why would it be inappropriate to replace the `while` loop with a `for...of` loop?

7. [after Section 10.10] Provide code that generates the following radio button group. You don't need to provide code for a complete web page—just the code for a CSS rule and a container that generates the radio buttons, the border, and the border's caption.

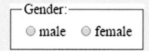

8. [after Section 10.11] CSS uses the name `background-color` for the property that defines the background color for an element. JavaScript uses the name `backgroundColor` for the associated property in the JavaScript world. Using the same spelling would make things easier on web developers. So why didn't JavaScript's inventor use `background-color` for the JavaScript property name?

9. [after Section 10.11] The `className` property stores an element's `class` attribute value as a string. If the class attribute has multiple values, those values are separated by spaces. To add or remove values, you have to process those space separators. The `classList` property stores an element's

class attribute value as a collection of values. To add or remove values, you can call its add or remove methods. How can Figure 10.15C's applyFontSelections function be modified so it uses the classList property to add values to the message element's class attribute?

10. [after Section 10.12] Assume the following code is part of a working web page. The prefix-mode decrement operator works the same as the prefix-mode increment operator, except subtraction is performed instead of addition. What message will console.log display?

```
var a = b = 10;
var c = d = 20;
console.log("a = " + ++a + ", b = " + b++ +
  "\nc = " + --c + ", d = " + d--);
```

# Project

Create a web page named storyGenerator.html and an accompanying external JavaScript file named storyGenerator.js that generates a story[6] by plugging user-entered text values into holes in a story template. For a better understanding of what's wanted, study the following screenshots.

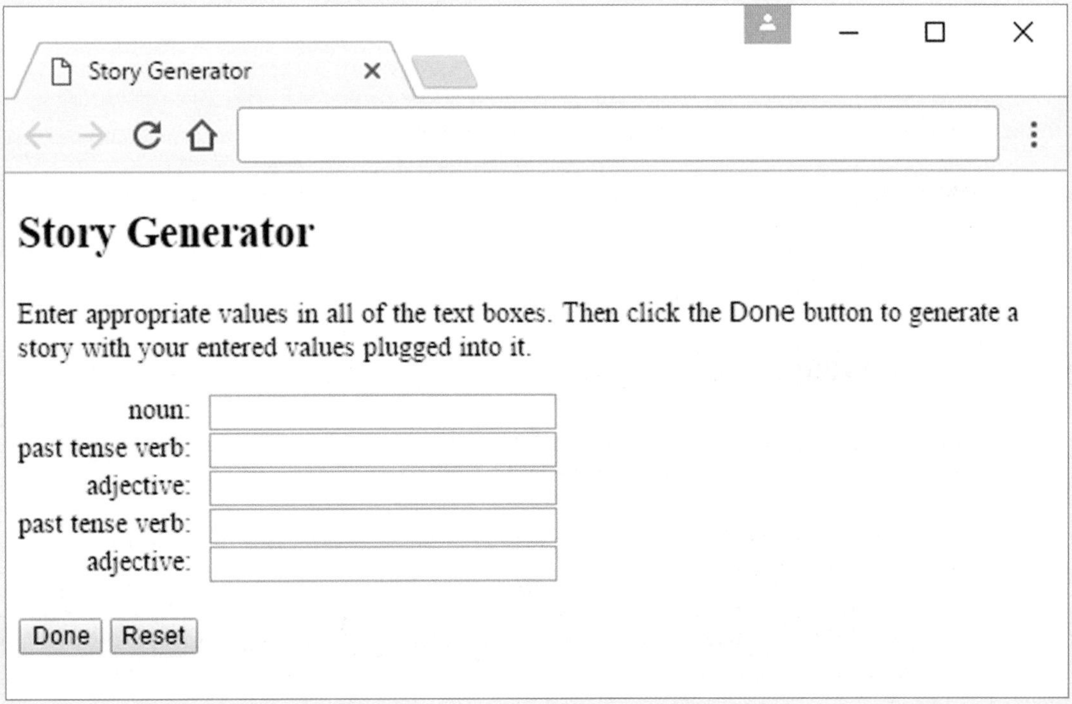

---

[6] The story we use is Charles M. Schulz's, *It Was a Dark and Stormy Night, Snoopy* (New York: Ballantine Books, 2004).

After clicking **Done**:

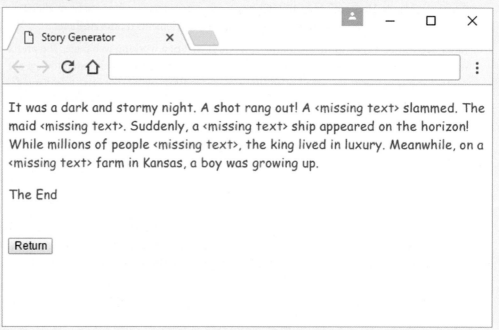

After clicking **Return** and entering values in the text boxes:

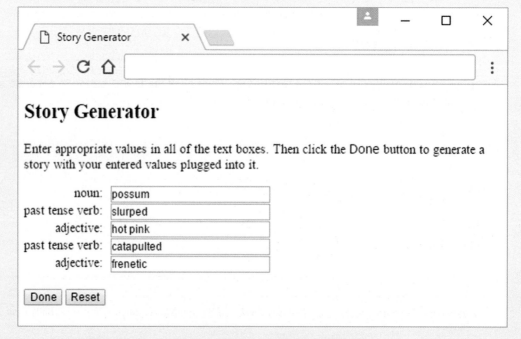

After clicking **Reset**, all the text box values should disappear.

After entering the same values as before and clicking **Done**:

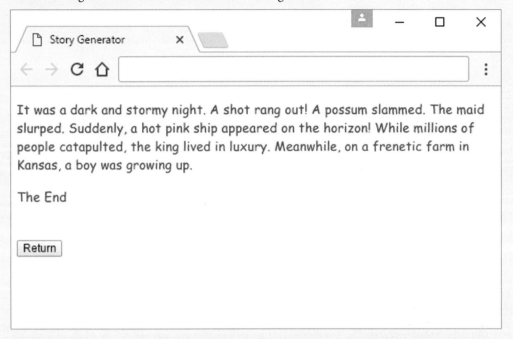

Although the screenshots might imply that there are two pages, there is only one page. Use two `section` containers, and toggle the visibility back and forth between each section.

As always, your implementation should exhibit elegance. In particular, you are required to use a loop to fill in the holes in your story. In your loop, use an index variable to access and transfer each textbox control to its associated story hole. Specifically, use `form.elements[i]` to retrieve each textbox control and use *story*`.children[i]` to retrieve each hole where *story* is the container object that surrounds the story text.

Note:

▸ In the instructions above the text boxes, for the word "Done," use the Tahoma font.
▸ There is a gap between the prompts and their associated text boxes.
▸ You must use a `label` element for each of your text boxes.
▸ You must use an external JavaScript file.

For your generated story:

▸ Use blue text.
▸ Use a Comic Sans MS font.
▸ Use red for "<missing text>" for story holes that have no user entry.

# CHAPTER 11

# Object-Oriented Programming and Arrays

## CHAPTER OBJECTIVES

▶ Learn object-oriented programming basics, such as the concept of a class and the concept of encapsulation.

▶ Implement classes with constructors, properties, and methods.

▶ Instantiate objects using the classes you've defined.

▶ Know when to use class properties versus regular properties.

▶ Know when to use `static` methods versus regular methods.

▶ Implement event handlers where the `event` object helps to process the event.

▶ Learn how to add event handlers dynamically using the `addEventListener` method.

▶ To support older browsers, learn how to use prototypes to emulate a class.

▶ Learn how a subclass inherits properties and methods from its superclass.

▶ Learn the syntax for how a child class accesses its parent class's constructor, properties, and methods.

▶ Use a `switch` statement to implement branching decisions.

▶ Use an array to store multiple data items using a common name for all of them.

▶ Learn the syntax for instantiating an array and looping through an array's elements.

▶ Use array methods to manipulate arrays.

▶ Implement an array of objects.

▶ Use an array's `sort` method to sort strings, numbers, and objects.

## CHAPTER OUTLINE

# 11.1 Introduction

You've been using objects for quite some time. The objects have come from the browser's Document Object Model (DOM). The DOM models all of the parts of a web page document as nodes in a node tree. For example, the following code fragment shows how you can use the DOM's document object and its getElementById method to retrieve the object associated with a web page element that has "street-address" for its id attribute:

```
streetAddress = document.getElementById("street-address");
```

In this chapter, you'll still use prebuilt objects that come from the DOM, but you'll also define structures for new types of objects and use those structures to create the objects. The structures you define and the objects you create will help you organize the data within a web page's JavaScript code. Using objects to organize data is known as object-oriented programming (OOP). You'll want to use OOP when there's a significant amount of data that needs to be organized. In this chapter, the web pages use more data than in prior chapters, and OOP will help make the code easier to understand.

# 11.2 Object-Oriented Programming Overview

As you can imagine, if you have a large programming task, there's great potential for creating a rat's nest of convoluted code.[1] In the 1970s, the designers of the SmallTalk programming language

---

[1] The term "rat's nest" comes from the commonly held view that rats build their nests hastily and haphazardly and use whatever materials happen to be nearby. As a programmer, you want to avoid such practices when building your programs. But don't feel like you have to avoid rats themselves. They're actually contemplative and fastidious creatures, characteristics that would serve them well in the software industry (if only their big noses didn't get in the way when typing).

addressed this convoluted-code problem by coining the term *object-oriented programming* and making it a core part of their new programming language.

The goal of the OOP paradigm is to have programs model how regular people think about a problem and its solution. When thinking about a problem, people tend to focus on the things that make up the problem. With OOP, those things are called objects. Usually, they're physical entities, but they can also be conceptual entities. As an OOP programmer, once you have identified the things you want to model, you identify their basic properties and behaviors. You group each thing's properties and behaviors together into a coherent structure called an object. In writing an OOP program, you define objects, create them, and have them interact with each other.

For example, if you're writing a program to assign courses to classrooms, you're probably going to need course objects and room objects. Course objects would contain course-name and number-of-students properties, and room objects would contain location and capacity properties. An object's behaviors refer to the activities associated with the object. For a course object, you're probably going to need a behavior that adjusts the course's number-of-students property, as students add and drop courses before the first day of class. With JavaScript, you implement an object's behaviors as methods.

One of the cornerstone features of OOP is *encapsulation*. In general, encapsulation is when something is wrapped up inside a protective covering. When applied to objects, encapsulation means that an object's data is protected by being hidden inside the object. With hidden data, the rest of the program cannot access an object's data directly; the rest of the program relies on the object's methods to access the data. *Accessing* an object's data refers either to reading the data or to modifying it. Assuming that an object's methods are well written, the methods ensure that data is accessed in an appropriate manner. By limiting access to "appropriate" access, that makes it harder to mess up a program's data, and that leads to fewer bugs. Yay! See **FIGURE 11.1**. It shows how an object's methods form the interface between the object's data and the outside world.

With objects that are built into the DOM, like the document object and a text control object, you don't have to create the objects yourself. Behind the scenes, when you load a web page, the JavaScript engine creates an object for every element on the web page (as well as for every attribute within the elements and for every text item between the element tags). But when you feel a web page's data deserves more organization than what's supplied by default by the DOM's objects, you'll want to create your own objects. To create your own objects, you first need to define an

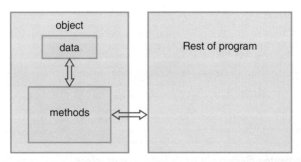

**FIGURE 11.1 Methods provide an interface between data and the rest of the program**

object's structure. More specifically, to define an object's structure, you define a class. A *class* is a description or blueprint for an object's characteristics. As you know, objects are characterized by their *members*—their properties and methods. Likewise, when you define a class, you specify the properties and methods that an object will use.

Suppose you're creating a web page that keeps track of points on a grid. To keep track of the points, you'll need to define a Point class that has *x* and *y* coordinate values for its properties. And you may need to define a color property if you want points to have different colors. For methods, you might want to define shiftX and shiftY. The shiftX and shiftY methods would translate a point along the *x* and *y* axes, respectively. You might also want to define a value method, such that the value method returns a point's value as the string "(*x*, *y*)", where *x* and *y* are replaced by numbers.

# 11.3 Classes, Constructors, Properties, `new` Operator, Methods

## Class Syntax

At a bare minimum, to implement a class, you need a class heading and a class body, and within the class body, you need a constructor and at least one method. To explain these things, we'll present a class that defines a point with `x` and `y` properties for the point's *x* and *y* coordinate positions. In **FIGURE 11.2**, note the class heading, which uses the word `class`, followed by a name that describes what the class represents. In this case, the class represents a point, so `Point` is the perfect name.

## Constructor and Property Syntax

Inside the `Point` class's body, you can see its *constructor*. A constructor is a special method that gets called when there's an attempt to create an object. The formal term for creating an object is *instantiation*. Note the constructor heading, which uses the word `constructor` followed by parentheses surrounding a comma-separated list of parameters. The parameters receive their values from a constructor call, and the parameter values can then be accessed within the constructor

```
class Point {                          ← class heading
  constructor(x, y) {                  ← constructor heading
    this.x = x;                        ← Use "this." to define x
    this.y = y;                          and y properties for the class.
  } // end constructor

  value() {                            ← A method that returns a Point object's value.
    return "(" + this.x + ", " + this.y + ")";
  } // end value
} // end class Point
```

**FIGURE 11.2 Bare-bones class definition for a `Point` class**

body. That should sound familiar because a constructor's parameters work the same as a function's parameters.

A constructor defines what happens when an object is instantiated. Typically, when you instantiate an object, you'll want the constructor to assign initial values to the newly created object's properties. Here's an example from the `Point` class's constructor:

```
this.x = x;
```

That might look a bit odd assigning x to `this.x`. The x by itself refers to the parameter named x, and `this.x` refers to the object's property named x. It's standard practice to use the same name for the parameter and its associated property, but that's not required for your code to work. In Figure 11.2's constructor definition, if you renamed the parameters to `xPosition` and `yPosition`, then the constructor's assignments should look like this:

```
this.x = xPosition;
this.y = yPosition;
```

Regardless of what you name the parameters, you'll always need to use "`this.`" when referring to an object's properties. Here we used `this.x` and `this.y` within the `Point` class's constructor to define the `Point` class's properties. Later, you'll see how we use `this.x` and `this.y` within a method to retrieve and display a `Point` object's properties.

The `this` keyword can mean different things depending on its context. In prior chapters, remember how we used `this` for event handlers in order to refer to the enclosing element? As a refresher, here's a rollover example that uses `this` within an `onmouseover` event handler:

```
<img src="../images/scrapsAtPlay.jpg"
   width="120" height="100" alt="Scraps"
   onmouseover =
      "this.src = '../images/scrapsFirstBirthday.jpg';">
```

> `this` accesses the enclosing element's object—`img` in this case

On the other hand, when you're inside a constructor or inside a method, the `this` keyword accesses the object that's associated with the constructor or method. So `this.x` accesses the instantiated object's x property.

## new **Operator**

Now that you know what a constructor is for and how you implement a constructor, let's look at how you call a constructor and create a new object. Let's start with an example. To create a `Point` object, you can do this:

```
point1 = new Point(100, 200);
```

Note how we use the `new` construct to create a new `Point` object. The `new` construct is actually an operator. Because `new` is a word instead of a symbol (like +, *, etc.), it looks weird, but it's still an operator. Whenever you use the `new` operator, you follow it with the class name for the type of object you want to create. And after the class name, you include parentheses surrounding a comma-separated list of arguments. The `new` operator calls the specified class's constructor and passes its arguments to the constructor's associated parameters. So the preceding code calls the `Point` constructor, which instantiates a `Point` object with x = 100 and y = 200. The constructor returns the instantiated object, and the returned object gets assigned into the `point1` variable.

In this example, note that we assign the returned object to the `point1` variable. By storing the object in a variable, we can access and manipulate the object later on. To manipulate an object, you'll need to define methods within the object's class. As Figure 11.1 illustrates, the methods provide the interface with the outside world. The properties are encapsulated within the object. If you attempt to access a `Point` object's x and y properties outside of the class, that violates OOP's cornerstone principle of encapsulation. So don't do it![2]

## Method Syntax

Let's now examine the `value` method in Figure 11.2's `Point` class definition, copied here for your convenience:

```
value() {
   return "(" + this.x + ", " + this.y + ")";
} // end value
```

The `value` method doesn't do much—it simply returns a `Point` object's value in the form "(x, y)." So if you instantiate a `Point` object with x and y values of 100 and 200 and later call the `value` method for that point, the method returns the value "(100, 200)." A method heading is identical to a function heading, except that you don't use the word `function` at the left. But you do specify a method name, followed by parentheses surrounding a comma-separated list of parameters. For the `value` method, no parameters are necessary, so the parentheses are empty. Within the method, notice how we access the `Point` object's x and y properties using `this.x` and `this.y`. And notice how we return a value using the `return` statement.

To call a method, you have to preface the method call with an object. That's the same as what you've been doing with method calls for DOM objects. For example, to check a form for valid input, you preface the `checkValidity` method call with a `form` object like this:

```
form.checkValidity()
```

---

[2] Many other programming languages (like SmallTalk, Java, and C++) have syntax that provides rigid enforcement of encapsulation. In other words, in those languages, you can define *private data* such that it can be accessed only from within a class's methods and it cannot be accessed from outside of the class. With JavaScript, there's no built-in syntax that can be used to enforce encapsulation. But there are work-around strategies for adding enforced encapsulation to JavaScript classes. Perhaps the most effective strategy is the one that uses the `WeakMap` object. That strategy and the others are beyond the scope of this book, but feel free to learn about them on your own by googling "JavaScript private data."

When calling a DOM-provided method like `checkValidity`, the object at the left is provided automatically by the DOM node tree. To call your homemade methods, you have to first instantiate an object and then use that object to call the method. For example:

```
point1 = new Point(100, 200);
document.getElementById("pt1").innerHTML = point1.value();
```

## 11.4 Point Tracker Web Page

In the prior section, you learned quite a bit of new OOP syntax. Let's put what you learned into practice in the context of a complete web page. The Point Tracker web page builds upon the `Point` class presented earlier. As **FIGURE 11.3** illustrates, the web page tracks the positions of where the user clicks the mouse. Initially, the web page displays nothing next to the two point labels and nothing below the **Distance apart** button. After the user clicks on the web page, the click's position displays next to the "Point 1:" label. As you can see in the figure, the position displays as an $(x, y)$ point, where $x$ and $y$ are the pixel values along the viewport's $x$ and $y$ axes. After the user clicks again, the new click's position displays next to the "Point 2:" label. Subsequent clicks cause the most recent click's position to display next to the "Point 2:" label, with the old point 2 value moving next to the "Point 1:" label. If the user clicks the **Distance apart** button, the web page calculates and displays the distance in pixels between the two displayed points. If there are no displayed points or just one displayed point, clicking the **Distance apart** button generates a warning, saying that the distance cannot be calculated.

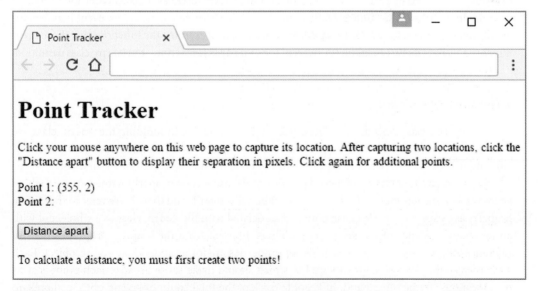

**FIGURE 11.3A** **Point Tracker web page—what happens after clicking once on the top middle part of the window and then clicking the Distance apart button**

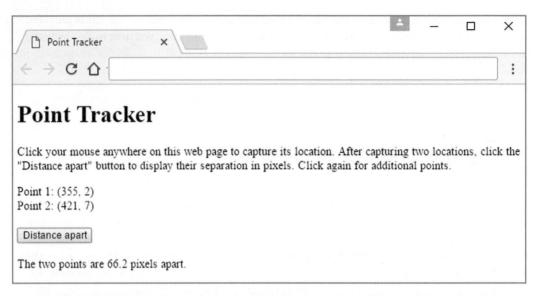

**FIGURE 11.3B Point Tracker web page—what happens after clicking at the right of the prior point and then clicking the Distance apart button**

See **FIGURE 11.4**, which shows the source code for the pointTracker.html file. Note that its script element links to an external JavaScript file. Using an external JavaScript file is appropriate because the web page requires quite a bit of JavaScript. The web page uses OOP for its Point class, and anytime you have enough going on to justify OOP, you should probably put the JavaScript in a separate file. Note the two span elements, which serve as placeholders for displaying the two points' (x, y) positions. Note the div element at the bottom, which serves as a placeholder for a message after the user clicks the **Distance apart** button. And finally, note the onclick event handlers for the html element and the **Distance apart** button. Later, we'll examine the functions that those event handlers call, but let's first focus on the heart of the web page's JavaScript—the Point class definition.

## Class Properties

Note the Point class definition in **FIGURES 11.5A** and 11.5B. In building the Point class, we started with Figure 11.2's earlier Point class definition, and then we added code to support calculating the distance between two points. In the code for that calculation, we first check to see whether there are two Point objects. Specifically, we use a class property named count, which keeps track of the number of Point objects—0 initially, then 1, and then 2. We refer to the count property as a *class property* because count is associated with the Point class as a whole, not with an individual instance of the Point class. That's different from the x and y properties that we reference with this.x and this.y. Those properties are for an individual Point object. Each Point object has its own copy of x and y, which should make sense because each point is at its own location. On the other hand, in keeping track of the total count of Point objects, there's no need to have separate count values in each Point object. If there were separate count values in each Point object, that would be a waste of memory.

```
<!DOCTYPE html>
<html lang="en"
  onclick="captureClick(event);">
<head>
<meta charset="utf-8">
<meta name="author" content="John Dean">
<title>Point Tracker</title>
<script src="pointTracker.js"></script>
</head>

<body>
<h1>Point Tracker</h1>
<p>
  Click your mouse anywhere on this web page to capture its location.
  After capturing two locations,click the "Distance apart" button to
  display their separation in pixels. Click again for additional points.
</p>
Point 1: <span id="pt1"></span>
<br>
Point 2: <span id="pt2"></span>
<br><br>
<input type="button" id="btn" value="Distance apart"
  onclick="displayDistance(event);">
<br><br>
<div id="message"></div>
</body>
</html>
```

This event handler listens for a click anywhere on the web page.

Link to external JavaScript file.

Placeholders for displaying the two points' positions.

**FIGURE 11.4 HTML code for Point Tracker web page**

The syntax for class properties is similar to the syntax for regular (object) properties. Instead of this in front of the property, it's the class name in front of the property. So in the Point class's constructor, we use Point.count to refer to the count class property. Here's the relevant Point.count code from the constructor:

```
if (Point.count == undefined) {
  Point.count = 1;
}
else if (Point.count == 1) {
  Point.count = 2;
}
```

A property is a variable, and as with all variables, if you don't initialize them, they start off with the value undefined. So in the prior code fragment, we check for count being undefined, and if that's the case, it means the constructor is being called the first time and we set the count to 1. The second time the constructor is called, we increment the count from

1 to 2. Subsequent constructor calls keep the `count` at 2, which means that there will never be more than two `Point` objects. Why only two `Point` objects? As you'll see when we look at the `captureClick` function later on, when the user clicks the mouse, that calls the constructor and instantiates a new `Point` object. When the user clicks the first and second times, the clicked positions display next to the Point1 and Point2 labels. When the user clicks a third

```
/*************************************************************
 * pointTracker.js
 * John Dean
 *
 * This file implements a Point class.
 * It stores Point objects for the locations of the two
 * most recent mouse clicks.
 *************************************************************/

class Point {
  constructor(x, y) {
    this.x = x;
    this.y = y;
    if (Point.count == undefined)  {
      Point.count = 1;
    }
    else if (Point.count == 1) {
      Point.count = 2;
    }
  } // end constructor

  //*********************************************************

  // Return the point in the format "(x, y)"

  value() {
    return "(" + this.x + ", " + this.y + ")";
  } // end value

  //*********************************************************

  // Return a count for the number of Point objects

  static getCount() {
    return (Point.count ==  undefined) ? 0 : Point.count;
  } // end getcount
```

Preface a class property with class name dot.

update `count` property's value

**FIGURE 11.5A** `Point` **class definition for Point Tracker web page**

time, a fourth time, and so on, each click produces a new point, but it replaces the oldest point, so the count remains at 2.

As mentioned earlier, to see if the constructor is being called the first time, we use if (Point. count == undefined). It would have been more elegant to initialize count to 0 and then use if (Point.count == 0) in the constructor. We could have initialized count to 0 by including Point.count = 0; below the class definition. But encapsulation says that a property should be directly accessed only from within its class, not from outside of its class, so putting the assignment below the class would violate the goal of encapsulation. Being able to initialize the count class property from within the Point class would be ideal, but JavaScript doesn't allow it.[3]

As you know, we use the term "class property" for a property that's associated with a class. So we refer to count as a class property for the Point class. It appears that ECMAScript does not have a special term for a property that's associated with a class. But to make our explanations easier, we'll continue to use the term "class property" for such properties.

## Object-Oriented Programming Coding Conventions

We haven't finished reviewing (and thoroughly enjoying) all the JavaScript code in the Point Tracker web page, but it's a good time to take a little break and point out style issues pertinent to OOP.

Above a class definition, you should provide a comment that describes the class. Normally, the class definition will be in an external file, and if that's the case, you can include the description as part of the file's prologue. If the class definition is not in an external file, then include the description as a standard comment above the class definition.

Within a class definition, include a constructor as the class's first member. Your methods go below the constructor. Above every method definition, include a line of *'s surrounded by blank lines and then a comment that describes the method. Insert a blank line below the comment. Take a look at Figures 11.5A and 11.5B and verify that we follow all these style rules for the Point class definition.

## 11.5 static Methods

In this section, we continue to work our way through the Point Tracker web page's Point class definition, with a focus on the getCount and distance methods. They're static methods, which work a bit differently than regular methods.

In the previous section, we examined the Point class's constructor. After the constructor comes the value method. It's the same value method that we looked at in Section 11.3. It returns a Point object's value in the form "$(x, y)$." Next is the getCount method....

---

[3] Personally, I think initializing class properties should be allowed. Remember Ecma International? They're the organization in charge of the ECMAScript standard, which serves as the canonical specification for JavaScript. I encourage you to write your Ecma International representatives and ask them for inclusion of class property initializations in the next version of ECMAScript. While you're at it, lobby them for rigidly enforced private data, and free Teslas for JavaScript teachers.

## `getCount` Method

As its name implies, the `getCount` method returns the `count` property (which holds the number of `Point` objects). For methods that return a property, it's standard practice to use "get" as the first word in their names. So `getCount` is properly named.

Methods that start with "get" are often trivial—they just return the property and that's it. The `getCount` method has to do some additional work because the `count` property is undefined when there are no `Point` objects, and we want to return 0 for the count when there are no `Point` objects. You can see that "additional work" in the following `getCount` method, where the `return` statement checks the `count` property for being undefined:

```
static getCount() {
  return (Point.count == undefined) ? 0 : Point.count;
} // end getCount
```

Note the `?` and `:` symbols. Together, they form the *conditional operator*. Think of the conditional operator as a compact form of an "if, else" statement that can be embedded within another statement. Here's the conditional operator's syntax:

*condition* ? *expression1* : *expression2*

If the *condition* is true, the conditional operator expression evaluates to the value of *expression1*, and it ignores *expression2*. If the condition is false, the conditional operator expression evaluates to the value of *expression2*, and it ignores *expression1*. Think of *expression1* as the true part of an "if, else" statement. Think of *expression2* as the false part of an "if, else" statement. Note that the syntax does not require parentheses around the conditional operator's condition. That's different from `if` statement and `while` loop conditions, which do require parentheses. Even though parentheses aren't required for the conditional operator's condition, feel free to add them (as we did in the `getCount` method) to help with readability.

Here's a functionally equivalent `getCount` implementation that uses an "if, else" statement instead of the conditional operator:

```
static getCount() {
  if (Point.count == undefined) {
    return 0;
  }
  else {
    return Point.count;
  }
} // end getCount
```

If you prefer this "if, else" implementation to the conditional operator implementation, that's OK. They both work. But even if you don't use conditional operators in your own code, you need to understand them when you see them in other people's code.

In the `getCount` method definition, did you notice `static` in the heading? The `static` modifier means that `getCount` is a `static` method. There are two main differences between a regular method and a `static` method:

1.  To call a regular method, you preface the method name with an object and a dot. The object is referred to as a *calling object*. For example, here's how you could display the value of the point1 object:

    ```
    alert(point1.value());
    ```

    On the other hand, to call a static method, you preface the method name with its class name and a dot. For example, here's how you could display the number of Point objects:

    ```
    alert(Point.getCount());
    ```

2.  Inside of a regular method, you can access the calling object with this, and you can access a property of the calling object by prefacing the property with this and a dot. For example, here's how you could display the x property's value within a Point class regular method:

    ```
    alert(this.x);
    ```

    On the other hand, with a static method, there is no calling object, so you cannot use the this keyword. If you attempt to do so, the method will fail.

The getCount method does not need to use the this keyword, so it's appropriate to make it a static method. Nonetheless, it would have been legal to omit static in the method heading and make getCount a regular method. So why didn't we implement getCount as a regular method? Regular methods are harder to call. With a regular method, you are required to have a calling object and preface the method call with it. If getCount were implemented as a regular method, to accommodate the no-Point-objects situation, you would need to do something like this in order to display the count:

```
var dummyPoint = new Point(null, null);
alert(dummyPoint.getCount());
```

The null values are built into the JavaScript language, and they are used to indicate the absence of a valid value. For this code to work, you'd have to modify the Point constructor so as not to increment the count property when x and y are null. This code is an example of a kludge (pronounced "klooj"). Kludgy code provides a workaround for a problem, but it's ugly and inelegant. You should try to avoid kludgy code because it tends to be hard to maintain. Moral of the story: Use static for the getCount method.

## distance Method

Next up after the getCount method is the distance method—another static method. Let's start with the code that calls the distance method:

```
distance = Point.distance(point1, point2);
```

That code comes from the displayDistance event-handler function, which we'll examine in the next section. Note that we call distance with the Point class at the left, which makes sense because distance is a static method. Note the method call's point1 and point2 arguments.

As you'd expect, they hold `Point` objects. Those `Point` objects get passed into `pt1` and `pt2` parameters in the `distance` method's heading. Here's the method's heading:

```
static distance(pt1, pt2) {
```

Take a look at the `distance` method definition in **FIGURE 11.5B**. As you can see, the method checks whether there are two defined points (i.e., both parameters hold valid `Point` objects). If yes, the method calculates the distance between the `pt1` and `pt2` `Point` objects and returns the distance between them. If there are not two defined points, the method returns the value `null` to indicate failure.

In calculating the distance between the two `Point` objects, note how we access each object's x and y properties—using the parameter names, a dot, and then the property name. For example, to find the difference in the two points' x property values, we use this code:

```
xDist = pt1.x - pt2.x;
```

After finding the x distance between the points and the y distance between the points, we use the Pythagorean Theorem to calculate the hypotenuse distance between the points.

There's no new syntax in the rest of the `distance` method, but study it for review purposes. And note that we use a local variable named `distance` within the `distance` method. As a beginning programmer, it might be confusing to use the same name, `distance`, for two things. Veteran programmers do that quite often, so try to get used to it. The rationale is that if

```
//*****************************************************

// Return the distance between the two points or null if one
// or more of the points is missing.

static distance(pt1, pt2) {
  var xDist, yDist; // distances apart in the 2 dimensions
  var distance;     // distance apart with direct connection

  if (Point.count == 2) {
    xDist = pt1.x - pt2.x;
    yDist = pt1.y - pt2.y;
    distance = Math.sqrt(xDist * xDist + yDist * yDist);
  }
  else {
    distance = null;
  }

  return distance;
} // end distance
} // end class Point
```

**FIGURE 11.5B** `Point` **class definition for Point Tracker web page**

you've got a good name, you should use it. The JavaScript engine has no problem distinguishing between the two `distance` entities because the method uses parentheses and the local variable does not.

As an alternative, we could have put the `distance` method outside of the class and made it a regular function (by using `function` in the heading instead of `static`). That would have resulted in the same functionality, so what's the benefit of using a `static` method? Readability. By putting it inside the class, someone reading the code knows that `distance` is one of the behaviors that `Point` objects support. Readability benefits again when it comes to the method call. When calling a `static` method, you're required to preface the method name with the class name. For example, `Point.distance(point1, point2)`. Having the class name in front of the method name tells someone reading the code that `distance` is associated with the `Point` class.

# 11.6 **Event Handlers**

Whew! We finally finished examining the `Point` class definition. In this section, we move on to the Point Tracker web page's event-handler functions. The Point Tracker web page's `html` element has an `onclick` attribute that calls the `captureClick` event-handler function when the user clicks anywhere on the web page. Here's the `html` element's start tag with the `onclick` attribute:

```
<html lang="en" onclick="captureClick(event);">
```

Originally, we added the `onclick` attribute to the web page's `body` element instead of to the `html` element. That works OK, but not great. We want mouse clicks to be captured anywhere on the web page's viewport. The *viewport* is the area below the browser window's address bar and within the browser window's borders. The `body` element spans the web page's content, so if the viewport is larger than the content, the body will be smaller than the viewport. In the Point Tracker web page, if you click below the message at the bottom, that's below the `body` container. To capture mouse clicks there, we had to move the `onclick` attribute to the `html` container, which spans the same area as the viewport.

Note the `event` argument in the call to the `captureClick` function. When the user interacts with a web page, the JavaScript engine generates an event object that contains information about what the user just did. For example, if the user clicks on the web page, the JavaScript engine generates a click event with information about the click's location, the DOM node that was targeted, whether the control key was down during the click, and so on. The programmer can capture an event by providing an associated event-handler attribute. Referring back to the `html` tag code shown earlier, the `html` tag provides an `onclick` event handler that captures a click event when the user clicks anywhere on the web page's viewport. To access the captured event, you simply use the word `event` in your JavaScript code. In the prior `html` tag code, you can see how we use `event` as an argument in our call to the `captureClick` event-handler function.

The JavaScript engine generates lots of events for user interactions—way too many to describe here. But to give you an idea of what's available, the JavaScript engine generates events for resizing a window, scrolling a scrollbar, and spinning a mouse wheel. To capture those events, you would use the event-handler attributes `onresize`, `onscroll`, and `onwheel`, respectively. If you're curious, feel free to peruse Mozilla's event reference at https://developer.mozilla.org/en-US/docs/Web/Events.

## `captureClick` Event-Handler Function

As mentioned earlier, the Point Tracker web page's `html` tag includes an `onclick` attribute that calls the `captureClick` function and passes a click event to it. **FIGURE 11.5C** shows the `captureClick` function definition. Note its heading, which includes an `e` parameter for the passed-in event object. Note how we use the event object's `clientX` and `clientY` properties to retrieve the mouse click's location and use that location for a newly instantiated `Point` object. Here's the relevant code:

```
point1 = new Point(e.clientX, e.clientY);
```

The `clientX` and `clientY` properties hold the mouse pointer's x and y coordinate positions. The x and y coordinates are relative to the top-left corner of the viewport, so (0, 0) indicates a top-left corner mouse click. In the assignment statement, note the `point1` variable. At the top of Figure 11.5C, above the `captureClick` function, you can see where `point1` and `point2` are declared. Because they're declared outside of the functions and methods, they're global variables. We need them to be global variables because we need their values to persist. That persistence comes in handy when the user clicks the **Distance apart** button. In calculating the distance, we need to retrieve the x and y values within `point1` and `point2`. That works because `point1` and `point2` are global variables and their values are therefore remembered.

In Figure 11.5C, try to appreciate how nicely the `captureClick` function takes advantage of the `Point` class's methods. In other words, try to appreciate the elegance of OOP. For example, the function does different things depending on how many points have been recorded, so it calls the `getCount` method to get the number of points. Here's how it checks for zero points and then for one point:

```
if (Point.getCount() == 0) {
...
else if (Point.getCount() == 1) {
...
```

Easy to understand, right? By using an object's methods (like `getCount`), there's no need to dig into an object's content, and that helps with understandability and elegance.

Another example that illustrates `captureClick`'s OOP elegance is the code for retrieving a `Point` object's value. If you want its value, there's no need to access its x and y coordinate positions—just call the `value` method like this:

```
document.getElementById("pt1").innerHTML = point1.value();
```

```
//*****************************************************

var point1, point2;  // the most recently clicked points

// This function stores a user's click location as a point.

function captureClick(e) {                    ┌─────────────────────┐
  if (Point.getCount() == 0) {                │ passed-in click event │
    point1 = new Point(e.clientX, e.clientY); └─────────────────────┘
    document.getElementById("pt1").innerHTML = point1.value();
  }
  else if (Point.getCount() == 1) {
    point2 = new Point(e.clientX, e.clientY);
    document.getElementById("pt2").innerHTML = point2.value();
  }
  else {                                  ┌──────────────────────────────┐
    point1 = point2;                      │ Retrieve mouse click's location │
    point2 = new Point(e.clientX, e.clientY);└──────────────────────────────┘
    document.getElementById("pt1").innerHTML = point1.value();
    document.getElementById("pt2").innerHTML = point2.value();
  }
} // end captureClick

//*****************************************************

// This function calculates and returns the distance between 2 points.

function displayDistance(e) {
  var distance;      // distance apart with direct connection
  var message;       // message with distance or a warning

  e.stopPropagation(); // prevent the button from creating a new point
  distance = Point.distance(point1, point2);
  if (distance == null) {
    message = "To calculate a distance, you must first create two points!";
  }
  else {
    message =
      "The two points are " + distance.toFixed(1) + " pixels apart.";
  }

  document.getElementById("message").innerHTML = message;
} // end displayDistance
```

**FIGURE 11.5C Event-handler functions for Point Tracker web page**

## `displayDistance` Event-Handler Function

The Point Tracker web page's **Distance apart** button has an `onclick` attribute that calls the `displayDistance` event-handler function. Here's the button element with the `onclick` attribute:

```
<input type="button" id="btn" value="Distance apart"
  onclick="displayDistance(event);">
```

As you can see in Figure 11.5C, the `displayDistance` function calls the `distance` method to retrieve the distance between the `point1` and `point2` points. Here's the relevant code:

```
distance = Point.distance(point1, point2);
```

Isn't that beautiful? That's the elegance of OOP shining through once again!

Remember that the `distance` method returns `null` if either of the points is undefined. Thus, after calling the `distance` method, the `displayDistance` function uses an `if` statement to check for `null` like this:

```
if (distance == null) {
  message = "To calculate a distance, you must first create two points!";
}
```

Now let's return to the button element's code:

```
<input type="button" id="btn" value="Distance apart"
  onclick="displayDistance(event);">
```

In the `onclick` event handler, note how we call `displayDistance` with an `event` argument. Also note the associated e parameter in `displayDistance`'s heading in Figure 11.5C. At the top of `displayDistance`'s body, you can see that we use the e parameter to call the `stopPropagation` method:

```
e.stopPropagation(); // prevent the button from creating a new point
```

The e parameter holds the click event generated from the user clicking the distance button. As with all event objects, the click event object has methods that can help you handle what happens when the event is fired. In this case, we call the `stopPropagation` method to stop the click event from being heard by the `html` element's `onclick` event handler. My original `displayDistance` function did not call the `stopPropagation` method. So when the user clicked the button, the click event triggered not only the button's `onclick` event handler, but also the `html` element's `onclick` event handler. That meant that every time the user clicked the button, the points would update. That behavior was somewhat unsettling, so I decided to try to stop it. Specifically, I wanted to stop the click event from triggering the `html` element's `onclick` event handler. That's when the `stopPropagation` method came to the rescue.

To fully appreciate how the stopPropagation method call solves the problem, you need to know a bit about *event bubbling*. When the JavaScript engine fires an event, the targeted DOM object is the first object to "hear" the event. If the targeted object has an event handler for that type of event, then the event handler processes the event. The JavaScript engine then passes the event up the DOM node tree to the target object's parent object, where the parent object can process the event. Normally, the event bubbles all the way up to the DOM tree's root node. In the Point Tracker web page, when the user clicks the distance button, the button object is the first object to hear the click event. We don't want the click event to bubble up to the html element, so we call the click event object's stopPropagation method, which stops the bubbling.

## 11.7 Primitive Values Versus Objects

One thing we glossed over in the Point Tracker web page's captureClick function is what happens when there are already two points and the user clicks the mouse to form another point. The point2 variable's Point object gets moved to the point1 variable, and the new point created from the mouse click gets stored in the point2 variable. Here's the code that implements that functionality:

```
point1 = point2;
point2 = new Point(e.clientX, e.clientY);
```

That code might look pretty innocuous, but there's a lot going on that deserves our attention. Remember that this code gets executed when there are already two points in existence. So the new operator creates a third point. When you first looked at that code in the captureClick method, did it strike you as odd that we're creating a third point? After assigning point2 to point1, why don't we reuse point2's object by assigning e.clientX and e.clientY to it? Then we wouldn't have to instantiate a new Point object for the point2 variable. That sounds good, but it won't work. The problem is that after the assignment statement (point1 = point2;), both variables store the same single Point object, so if you then assign e.clientX and e.clientY to point2's object, you actually assign those values to point1's object as well. To understand all that, we better take a step back.

A JavaScript variable can hold a primitive value or an object. A *primitive value* can be a number, a string, a Boolean (true or false), null, or undefined. Objects are inherently different from primitive values in that objects hold properties and methods. Another inherent difference is the way in which variables store primitive values versus objects. Variables store primitive values directly and objects indirectly. Think of a variable as a box. If the primitive value 3 gets assigned to the variable x, then 3 gets put into the x box (pardon the pun). But if a Point object gets assigned to the variable point1, then a *reference* to the object gets put into the point1 box, and that reference points to the object. You can think of an object's reference as the address of where the object is stored in memory.

So now back to the `point1 = point2;` code from the `captureClick` method. The `point2` variable holds a reference to a `Point` object and that reference gets assigned into the `point1` variable, so both `point1` and `point2` end up pointing to the same single object. For example, if `point2`'s reference holds computer memory address 23,000 (because that's where its object is stored), after the assignment, `point1` also holds 23,000 and the two variables reference the same object. The solution is to instantiate a brand-new object for `point2` to point to. After the assignment statement, you can see that the subsequent new operator creates that new object with the *x* and *y* coordinate values for the new mouse click. Yay!

# 11.8 Using `addEventListener` to Add Event Listeners

In our original Point Tracker web page implementation, the `onclick` event-handler attribute worked just fine for capturing a click on the distance button and again for capturing a click on the web page as a whole. For our improved version of the Web Tracker web page, we capture not only clicking on the web page, but also pressing the delete key on the web page. When the user presses delete, the delete key's event handler removes the most recently created point by erasing its displayed coordinates. The mouse click event and the delete key event both need to be captured, regardless of where they occur on the web page, and that means using the `html` element. We could add an `onkeydown` event-handler attribute to the `html` element to capture the user pressing the delete key, but there's a better way. You know how you're supposed to keep your CSS code separate from your HTML code to make your code more readable and satisfy the best practices police? Well, best practices also suggest keeping your JavaScript separate from your HTML code. So rather than having both an `onclick` event handler and also an `onkeydown` event handler embedded in your `html` start tag, you can bypass event-handler attributes (with accompanying JavaScript) altogether by instead using the `addEventListener` method. The `html` element is associated with the `document` object, so we call `document.addEventListener` to add a click listener, and we call `document.addEventListener` again to add a keydown listener. Here's the code:

```
document.addEventListener("click", captureClick);
document.addEventListener("keydown", removePoint);
```

In the code fragment, you can see two arguments for each `addEvenListener` method call. The first argument is the name of a predefined event built into the DOM. The first method call's first argument is `click`, which is generated every time the user clicks the mouse. The second method call's first argument is `keydown`, which is generated every time the user presses a key on the keyboard. The second argument is the name of a function that we define, and that function serves as a listener for the first argument's event firing. So in the first `addEventListener` method call, `captureClick` is a function that listens for a click event. And in the second `addEventListener` method call, `removePoint` is a function that listens for a keydown event. The `captureClick` function is part of the original Point Tracker web page. The `removePoint` function is presented in the next subsection.

There's no absolute rule about where addEventListener method calls should be positioned, but it's common to position them above the function definitions that they refer to. For the Point Tracker web page, we use an external JavaScript file with the Point class defined at the top, followed by point1 and point2 global variable declarations. For the improved Point Tracker web page, we stick the addEvenListener method calls below those point1 and point2 global variable declarations and above the function definitions.

## removePoint **Event-Handler Function**

The addEventListener("keydown", removePoint) method call specifies that the JavaScript engine passes a keydown event to the removePoint function whenever the user presses a key on the keyboard. See the removePoint function definition in **FIGURE 11.6**. In our improved version of the Point Tracker web page, we put the removePoint function below the other event-handler functions. Note the e parameter in the function's heading. The e parameter receives the keydown event, and the function uses e to check whether the pressed key is the delete key. Here's the relevant code:

```
if (e.key == "Delete") {
```

As mentioned earlier, you can find a list of events on Mozilla's events reference page at https://developer.mozilla.org/en-US/docs/Web/Events. If you search for the keydown event, you can drill down on it to find the keydown event object's properties, and one of those properties is key, which holds a string that identifies the pressed key.

After checking for the delete key, the removePoint method then checks whether there are 1 or 2 points. If there's 1 point, the method erases the first point's displayed coordinates. If

```
//**************************************************

// This function removes the most recently created point

function removePoint(e) {          ┌─ passed-in keydown event
  if (e.key == "Delete") {
    if (Point.getCount() == 1) {
      document.getElementById("pt1").innerHTML = "";
      Point.reduceCount();
    }
    else if (Point.getCount() == 2) {
      document.getElementById("pt2").innerHTML = "";
      Point.reduceCount();
    }
  } // end if key == "Delete"
} // end removePoint
```

**FIGURE 11.6** removePoint **event-handler function for improved Point Tracker web page**

```
//******************************************************

// After removing a point, call this method to reduce the count.

static reduceCount() {
  if (Point.count == 1) {
    Point.count = undefined;
  }
  else if (Point.count == 2) {
    Point.count = 1;
  }
} // end reduceCount
```

**FIGURE 11.7** `reduceCount` **method for** `Point` **class in improved Point Tracker web page**

there are 2 points, the method erases the second point's displayed coordinates. In either case, the method then calls the `Point` class's `reduceCount` method to reduce the point count. Because it's a `static` method, we call it with the class name (`Point`) at the left, like this:

```
Point.reduceCount();
```

## `reduceCount` Method

See the `reduceCount` method in **FIGURE 11.7**. In our improved version of the Point Tracker web page, we put the `reduceCount` method at the bottom of the `Point` class definition. Note how the `reduceCount` method is able to access and update the `Point.count` property directly because `reduceCount` is inside the `Point` class definition. That's different from the `removePoint` function, which calls `getCount` to access the count, because `removePoint` is outside the `Point` class definition. Hail to OOP encapsulation!

# 11.9 Using Prototypes to Emulate a Class

The `class` construct has been around a long time with other languages, but it's relatively new with JavaScript. Ecma International introduced the `class` construct with ECMAScript 6 in 2015. All of today's standard browsers support the `class` construct, except for Microsoft Internet Explorer. With Microsoft's phaseout of Internet Explorer, you should not count on IE ever supporting the `class` construct. Microsoftophiles are in the process of migrating to Edge, but it'll take a while to finish the transition. In the meantime, you should be familiar with legacy code techniques that implement the object-oriented paradigm without the `class` construct. *Legacy code* is code that is used today even though it's considered inefficient or inelegant. Why is such code still around? Because (1) developers want to support users who use old tools that can't handle the new coding techniques, and (2) developers are too busy to bother with upgrading all the old code that's out there.

To explain legacy code for classes, let's jump right into an example. See **FIGURE 11.8**, which shows a simplified version of the prior Point Tracker web page. When the user clicks the mouse, the click's position displays next to the "Point location:" label. When the user clicks again, the new click's position replaces the old click's position.

**FIGURES 11.9A** and **11.9B** show the Simplified Point Tracker web page's source code. Figure 11.9b shows the `captureClick` event-handler function and the `body` container. There's no new syntax there, so we'll focus on Figure 11.9a, which shows the code that simulates a `Point` class.

Before the `class` construct was part of JavaScript, programmers implemented the concept of a class by being creative with existing syntax. To emulate a class with legacy code, you implement a function whose name serves as a class name, and that function then serves as a constructor. In Figure 11.9A, note the `Point` function, which serves as a constructor for a `Point` class (even though there are no `class` or `constructor` keywords). We spell `Point` with an uppercase P, so it follows the standard coding convention for class names. In Figure 11.9B, note how we instantiate a `Point` object using the same technique as shown earlier—we use the `new` operator with a call to the constructor function. Note how we define properties for a `Point` object using the same technique as shown earlier—we use assignment statements with the `this` keyword inside the constructor function.

As you know, to define methods for an actual class, you put the method definitions inside the `class` construct. But with legacy code, there is no `class` construct. So what you do is define the methods as stand-alone functions and then tie those functions to the simulated class. To tie a function to the simulated class, you define a property with the same name as the function and, within the constructor, assign the function's name to the property. In Figure 11.9A, note the `value` function defined below the `Point` constructor. To tie the `value` function to the

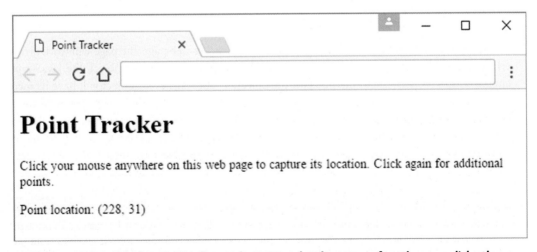

**FIGURE 11.8 Simplified Point Tracker web page—what happens after the user clicks the mouse**

```
<!DOCTYPE html>
<html lang="en" onclick="captureClick(event);">
<head>
<meta charset="utf-8">
<meta name="author" content="John Dean">
<title>Point Tracker</title>
<script>
  // This constructor creates a Point object for the location
  // of the most recent mouse click.

  function Point (x, y) {          This function serves as a constructor.
    this.x = x;
    this.y = y;
    Point.prototype.value = value;    Tie the value function to the
  } // end Point constructor            Point constructor's prototype

  // Return the point in the format "(x, y)"

  function value() {
    return "(" + this.x + ", " + this.y + ")";
  } // end value
```

**FIGURE 11.9A Simplified Point Tracker web page with prototype implementation**

simulated Point class, you could include the following assignment statement inside the Point constructor:

```
this.value = value;
```

If you use this assignment in the Simplified Point Tracker web page, the page will work properly, but it will be inefficient in terms of storage. When you instantiate an object, the JavaScript engine creates properties and methods for the object. That means every object will have its own copies of its methods. Even objects within the same class will have their own copies of their methods. That's a waste of memory because those method copies will be identical. The solution is to put an object's methods in the constructor's prototype. The constructor's *prototype*[4] holds methods that the constructor can inherit from. So when an object is created, the object gets its own set of properties, but it shares its methods with all the other objects that use the same

---

[4] Why the term "prototype" for something that holds inheritable items? In normal parlance, a prototype is a template for forming something else, and the things that are being formed inherit qualities from the template. That's like a JavaScript object inheriting members from a prototype.

```
//*****************************************************

// This function stores a user's click location as a point.

function captureClick(e) {
  var point;   // the most recently clicked point

  point = new Point(e.clientX, e.clientY);
  document.getElementById("pt").innerHTML = point.value();
} // end captureClick
</script>
</head>

<body>
<h1>Point Tracker</h1>
<p>
  Click your mouse anywhere on this web page to capture its location.
  Click again for additional points.
</p>
Point location: <span id="pt"></span>
</body>
</html>
```

Instantiate a Point object same as before.

**FIGURE 11.9B** **Simplified Point Tracker web page with prototype implementation**

constructor. Behind the scenes, objects are able to share their methods because the objects link to their constructors, and the constructors link to their shared prototype. If this is a little difficult to understand, that's OK. The bottom line is that to tie a function to a simulated class (to make it a method), within the constructor, you assign the function's name to the constructor's prototype by using the constructor's name, "prototype," and then a property name that matches the function name. For example, here's how we tie the value function to the simulated Point class for the Simplified Point Tracker web page:

```
Point.prototype.value = value;
```

Are you ready for a secret? Behind the scenes, the keywords class and construct are for the most part *syntactic sugar*. That means they don't add any new functionality to the legacy code prototype-based techniques. That's OK. The new constructs make your OOP efforts easier to code and easier to understand. In particular, to implement a method, you don't have to bother with assigning a function to your constructor's prototype. With the class and constructor constructs, methods are automatically shared by all objects of the same class, so memory is not wasted.

# 11.10 Inheritance Between Classes

## Inheritance Overview

In the Point Tracker web page, we needed only one class—a `Point` class—to organize the web page's object data. For more complicated web page logic, you might need more than one class. In this section, we introduce the concept of *inheritance* between classes, where one class is a parent of one or more other child classes. As with biological children, a child class inherits the characteristics of its parent class. With JavaScript, a child class inherits a parent class's properties and methods.

A parent class describes features that are common to all of its child classes. For example, suppose you have a web page that keeps track of a company's employee information. All employees have a name and an employee ID number, so the web page's JavaScript code implements an `Employee` parent class with `name` and `id` properties. There are two categories of employees—part time and full time. To keep things separate for payroll purposes, the JavaScript code implements a `PartTime` child class and a `FullTime` child class. The `PartTime` class defines `hourlyWage` and `hoursWorked` properties. The `FullTime` class defines a `salary` property. The two child classes calculate payments differently, so they have their own `calculatePayment` methods.

As illustrated by the relationships between the `Employee`, `PartTime`, and `FullTime` classes, a parent class is a more generic entity, whereas a child class is more specific. A child class inherits its parent class's common features, but then it adds features that are specific to the individual child class.

Programmers very often use the terms parent class and child class, but be aware that the formal terms are *superclass* and *subclass*, respectively. And speaking of formality, to depict a class inheritance relationship formally, you draw an arrow from the subclass to the superclass. Ironically, that means the arrow goes in the opposite direction from the inheritance flow. **FIGURE 11.10** shows a class diagram for the `Employee`, `PartTime`, and `FullTime` classes. Note the upward arrows that go from the `PartTime` and `FullTime` subclasses to the `Employee` superclass.

The class diagram's format comes from the *Unified Modeling Language* (UML). UML is an industry standard for modeling OOP designs. It uses diagrammatic techniques in attempting to model a wide range of programming concepts. In this book, we just barely scratch the surface of UML in terms of what it can model. If you program with more than just JavaScript, you'll probably want to learn more about UML, but for our purposes, what you see in Figure 11.10 should be good enough. In the figure, note that each class has three partitions. The top partition is for the class name, the middle partition is for the class's properties (which are called *attributes* in UML), and the bottom partition is for the class's methods (which are called *operations* in UML). Examine the properties and methods in each of the three classes and confirm that they match what we described earlier. The only new members in the class diagram are the constructors and the `PartTime` class's `addHours` method. Remember that a constructor is a special type of method, so the constructors appear in the bottom partitions. The `PartTime` class's `addHours` method enables a `PartTime` object to have work hours added to it.

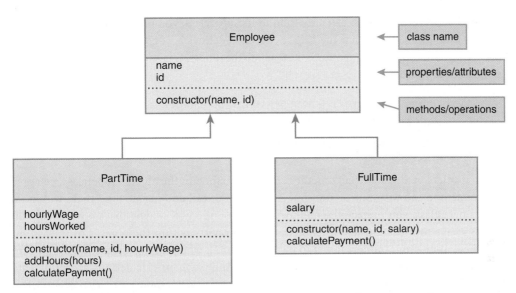

**FIGURE 11.10 Class diagram for the `Employee`, `PartTime`, and `FullTime` classes**

## Inheritance Syntax

The syntax for implementing a superclass-subclass inheritance relationship is pretty straightforward. For a superclass, there's no special syntax—just use the `class` keyword to implement a class the same way you've done it in the past. For a subclass, you need to append the keyword `extends` and then the superclass name to the end of the subclass's heading. For example, here's the heading for the `PartTime` class, which is a subclass of `Employee`:

```
class PartTime extends Employee {
```

Use `extends` to define a class as a subclass of another class.

As you know, a subclass inherits its superclass's members—its properties and methods. For a subclass method to access the properties inherited from its superclass, the syntax is easy. Just preface the property with `this` dot, which is the same way the object accesses properties defined in its own class. For example, suppose the `PartTime` class's `calculatePayment` method returns the employee's name at the left of the calculated payment value. The following code shows how to do that. Note how we access the superclass's `name` property using `this.name`:

```
return this.name + ": " + this.hoursWorked * this.hourlyWage;
```

Use `this` dot to access superclass properties.

For a subclass method to call a method in its superclass, you preface the call with `super` dot. For example, suppose that the `Employee` class defines a `getName` method. Then, as an alternative to the preceding `return` statement, the `PartTime` class's `calculatePayment` method could do this:

```
return super.getName() + ": " + this.hoursWorked * this.hourlyWage;
```

Use `super` dot to call superclass methods.

So if you're within an object's method, to call a method in the object's superclass, you preface the method call with `super` dot. But if you want to call another method that's within the object's own class, you preface the method call with `this` dot. Maybe that's obvious because you also have to use `this` dot when accessing a property within the object's own class, but many beginning programmers forget to include the `this` when calling another method within the object's own class. For example, suppose overtime payment calculations are sufficiently complicated to justify putting those calculations in a separate method, `calculateOvertime`. The `PartTime` class's `calculatePayment` method would then call `calculateOvertime` like this:

```
this.calculateOvertime();
```

Use `this` dot to call another method within the method's own class.

If you forget the `this` dot, the JavaScript engine won't be able to find the `calculate Overtime` method, and the calculation fails. If you turn on the browser's debugger, you should get an error message that helps you to identify the bug. But without a debugger, there's no error message, and the bug can be hard to identify. So remember to use `this` dot when calling another method within the method's own class!

Let's turn now to constructors. As you know, within a constructor you'll normally want to assign passed-in parameter values to the class's properties. For example, for the `PartTime` class, you'll want to do this:

```
constructor(name, id, hourlyWage) {
  this.name = name;
  this.id = id;
  this.hourlyWage = hourlyWage;
  this.hoursWorked = 0;
} // end constructor
```

But wait—because `PartTime` is a subclass, the JavaScript engine requires that you call its superclass constructor before using the `this` keyword. So the example code will generate an error and the assignments will fail. Here's the correct implementation:

```
constructor(name, id, hourlyWage) {
   super(name, id);
   this.name = name;
   this.id = id;
   this.hourlyWage = hourlyWage;
   this.hoursWorked = 0;
} // end constructor
```

Use `super` with ( )'s to call a superclass constructor.

Note how we use `super` with ( )'s to call the superclass's constructor. Try to remember that to call superclass methods, we use `super` with a dot, but to call superclass constructors, we use `super` with parentheses.

Not surprisingly, you can call a superclass constructor only if such a constructor exists. Referring back to Figure 11.10, you can see that the `Employee` class does indeed have a 2-parameter constructor that accommodates the `super(name, id);` constructor call.

If you'd like to see the code for the `Employee` class, you can find it in an end-of-chapter exercise. In that exercise, you're asked to provide the code that implements the `PartTime` class. If you'd like to see a complete web page that uses classes with an inheritance relationship, that means you're ready for the next section. Onward!

## 11.11 Pet Registry Web Page

My kids get $2 per week for their allowance, which might sound like a lot, but my older daughter Jordan thinks otherwise. To support her profligate lifestyle choices (a Spotify account, a second pair of socks, etc.), she works at a pet rescue shelter. The shelter registers animals as they arrive. To help with that process, we've put together a prototype pet registration web page.

© Robert Eastman/Shutterstock, Inc.

## Overview

**FIGURE 11.11A** and **11.11B** show how the Pet Registry web page works. The user enters a pet's name in a text control and selects the pet's type from a pull-down menu. Our prototype web page has only two types of pets to choose from—dog and hedgehog. If the user chooses dog, the web page displays a new text control for the user to enter the dog's favorite trick. When the user clicks the register button, the web page displays a confirmation message.

**FIGURE 11.11A** Pet Registry web page—what happens after the user enters a **Pet name** and clicks the **Pet type** pull-down menu's down arrow

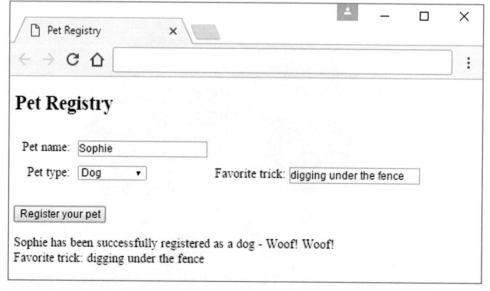

**FIGURE 11.11B** Pet Registry web page—what happens after the user selects **Dog**, enters a favorite trick, and clicks the **Register your pet** button

The Pet Registry web page stores its pet information in objects. For dogs, we define a `Dog` class, and for hedgehogs, we define a `Hedgehog` class. Because `Dog` objects and `Hedgehog` objects store some of the same type of information, we define a superclass named `Pet` to hold that common information.

See **FIGURE 11.12**, which shows a UML inheritance class hierarchy diagram for the `Pet` superclass and its two subclasses, `Dog` and `Hedgehog`. Let's begin our examination of the class diagram by describing the classes' properties. All pets have a name and a sound they make, so the `Pet` class defines `name` and `sound` properties. For a real pet registration web page, we'd store things like birth date and vaccine information and not a sound the pet makes, but we want to keep things simple. What's simpler than a hardcoded "Woof! Woof!" for a dog's `sound` property? The `Dog` class inherits the `name` and `sound` properties from its `Pet` superclass, and it adds a `trick` property that stores the dog's favorite trick (barking louder, digging under the fence, etc.). The `Hedgehog` class has no properties that are unique to it.

Continuing with our examination of Figure 11.12's class diagram, let's now briefly describe the classes' methods before looking at the code. All three classes have constructors (which are special types of methods) and they do the usual thing—they assign their passed-in parameters to the class's properties. The `Pet` class defines a `confirm` method that returns a `Pet` object's name and `sound` values. The `Dog` class adds its own `confirm` method that returns a `Dog` object's name, `sound`, and `trick` values. The `confirm` methods' returned values get embedded within the confirmation message that's displayed after the user clicks the register button.

## `style` and `body` Containers

Refer back to Figure 11.11 and note how the Pet Registry web page's pet name and pet type controls are aligned in a column, and the pet type and favorite trick controls are aligned in a row. The

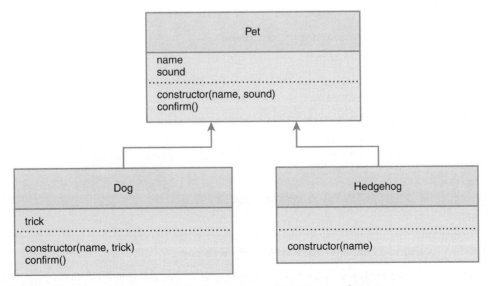

FIGURE 11.12 **Class diagram for the** `Pet`, `Dog`, **and** `Hedgehog` **classes**

web page uses a CSS table to achieve that alignment. In **FIGURE 11.13A**'s `style` container, you can see the `.table`, `.row`, and `.row > *` rules that implement the table.

   When the web page loads, we hide the favorite trick text control and its label because we want to display the trick control only if the user selects the dog option. To hide the trick control and its label, the first step is to stick them in a `div` container with `id="dog-more-info"`. Take a look at **FIGURE 11.13B**'s `body` container, and find the `div` that surrounds the trick control. And in the `style` container, find the `#dog-more-info {display: none;}` ID selector rule. As you learned in the last chapter, the `display: none` property-value pair makes the trick control `div` container invisible. Later, you'll see how we use JavaScript to make the trick control `div` container visible when the user selects dog for the pet type.

   Above the dog trick `div` container, note the comment, copied here for your convenience:

```
<!-- the following controls are dependent on pet type -->
```

The comment helps with *scalability*. If a web page is scalable, that means its content can be expanded without too much effort. Remember that the web page is a prototype with just two pet types. Presumably, when additional pet types are added, some of those pet types will need a control of their own for their unique features. The comment reminds the web developer that those new controls would go in that section of the web page.

   Note the `required` attribute for the pet name and pet type controls. Later, you'll see how we check for required input using JavaScript. The dog trick control does not have a `required` attribute because the code includes a default value of "none."

```
<!DOCTYPE html>
<html lang="en">
<head>
<meta charset="utf-8">
<meta name="author" content="John Dean">
<title>Pet Registry</title>
<style>
  .table {display: table;}
  .row {display: table-row;}
  .row > * {display: table-cell;}
  .table {border-spacing: 10px;}
  .row > :first-child {text-align: right;}
  #dog-more-info {display: none;}      ← This causes the
</style>                                  dog trick control to
<script src="petRegistry.js"></script>   be hidden initially.
</head>
```

**FIGURE 11.13A** head **container for Pet Registry web page**

```
<body>
<h2>Pet Registry</h2>
<form class="table" id="myForm">
   <div class="row">
      <label for="name">Pet name:</label>
      <input type="text" id="name" required>
   </div>
   <div class="row">
      <label for="petType">Pet type:</label>
      <select id="petType" required
        onchange="adjustForm(this.form);">
        <option value=""></option>
        <option value="dog">Dog</option>
        <option value="hedgehog">Hedgehog</option>
      </select>

      <!-- the following controls are dependent on pet type -->
      <div id="dog-more-info">
         <label for="trick">Favorite trick:</label>
         <input type="text" id="trick" value="none">
      </div>
   </div>
</form>
<br>
<input type="button" form="myForm" value="Register your pet"
   onclick="register(this.form);">
<br>
<p id="message"></p>
</body>
</html>
```

These `class` attributes indicate where the form's CSS table rules get applied.

This event handler displays or hides the dog trick control depending on what the user selects from the pull-down menu.

This event handler calls the `register` function to register the pet.

**FIGURE 11.13B** body **container for Pet Registry web page**

Note the empty p container at the bottom of the body container. It serves as a placeholder for a message generated by JavaScript when the user clicks the register button.

## Class Definitions

**FIGURE 11.14A** shows the Pet class definition. As you know, it serves as a superclass for the Dog and Hedgehog classes. To make it a superclass, we use the keyword extends in the subclasses, but there's no special superclass syntax needed in the superclass definition itself. Examine the

Pet class's constructor and note how it assigns name and sound parameters to this.name and this.sound properties. Examine the confirm method and note how it returns a confirmation message with the pet's this.name and this.sound properties. The confirmation message also includes a lowercase version of the constructor's name—"dog" for Dog and "hedgehog" for Hedgehog. We retrieve the constructor's name using this.constructor.name, and we use the retrieved name string to call the toLowerCase method.[5]

FIGURE 11.14B shows the Dog and Hedgehog class definitions. To make them subclasses, note how their headings both say extends Pet. And note how both of their constructors call the Pet superclass constructor using super with parentheses around their two arguments. The first argument is the passed-in name parameter, and the second argument is a hardcoded value for the sound property—"Woof! Woof!" for Dog objects and "snuffle, click, purr" for Hedgehog objects.

```
/**********************************************************
 * petRegistry.js
 * John Dean
 *
 * This file implements a Pet class hierarchy.
 **********************************************************/

class Pet {
  constructor(name, sound) {
    this.name = name;
    this.sound = sound;
  } // end constructor


  //*******************************************************

  // Return confirmation message data          This generates a lowercase
                                                version of the constructor's name.
  confirm() {
    return this.name + " has been successfully registered as a " +
      this.constructor.name.toLowerCase() + " - " + this.sound;
  } // end confirm
} // end class Pet
```

FIGURE 11.14A Pet **class definition for Pet Registry web page**

---

[5] Why is toLowerCase spelled with an uppercase C even though the word *lowercase* is all lowercase? Perhaps it's because of JavaScript's humble origins as a Java wannabe—Java has a toLowerCase method with an uppercase C, so we blame Java for the kerfuffle.

```
//************************************************

class Dog extends Pet {
  constructor(name, trick) {
    super(name, "Woof! Woof!");      Call the superclass constructor,
    this.trick = trick;              passing in a hardcoded "Woof! Woof!"
  } // end constructor                for the sound property.


  //************************************************

  // Return confirmation message data

  confirm() {                        Call the superclass confirm method.
    return super.confirm() +
      "<br>Favorite trick: " + this.trick;
  } // end confirm
} // end class Dog

//************************************************

class Hedgehog extends Pet {
  constructor(name) {
    super(name, "snuffle, click, purr");
  } // end constructor
} // end class Hedgehog
```

**FIGURE 11.14B** `Dog` **and** `Hedgehog` **class definitions for Pet Registry web page**

Finally, note how the `Dog` class's `confirm` method calls the `Pet` superclass `confirm` method using `super.confirm()`.

## onchange Event Handler for the Pull-Down Menu

Now that we've finished examining the class definitions, it's time to move on to the Pet Registry web page's event handlers. If you go back to Figure 11.13B, you can see that the `select` element on the pull-down menu has an `onchange` attribute that calls an `adjustForm` function. Here's the `select` element's start tag with the `onchange` attribute:

```
<select id="petType" required onchange="adjustForm(this.form);">
```

Take a look at the `adjustForm` function in **FIGURE 11.14C**. It uses `form.elements ["petType"].value` to retrieve the pull-down menu's selected value. If the selected value is "dog," we make the trick control visible so the user can enter the registered dog's favorite trick. If

```
//*************************************************

// This function reveals or hides supplemental input controls.

function adjustForm(form) {
  if (form.elements["petType"].value == "dog") {
    document.getElementById("dog-more-info").style.display = ←
      "table-cell";
  }                                    This causes the trick control to be visible.
  else {
    document.getElementById("dog-more-info").style.display = "none";
  }
} // end adjustForm                    This causes the trick control to be hidden.
```

**FIGURE 11.14C** `adjustForm` **event-handler function for Pet Registry web page**

the selected value is not "dog," then we make the trick control hidden. So, what's the mechanism for toggling the trick control between visible and hidden? The key to unraveling the mystery is to hark back to this ID selector rule, which applies to the trick control:

```
#dog-more-info {display: none;}
```

When the web page first loads, the trick control is invisible because of the `display: none` property-value pair. When the user selects the dog option from the pull-down menu, the `adjustForm` function adjusts the control's `display` property value with this code:

```
document.getElementById("dog-more-info").style.display =
  "table-cell";
```

After that code executes, the trick control's `display` property gets the value `table-cell`. Remember that `display: table-cell` is the magic CSS property-value pair that transforms an element into a table cell. So the trick control becomes visible. Voila!

When the user selects something other than the dog option from the pull-down menu, the `adjustForm` function adjusts the control's `display` property value with this code:

```
document.getElementById("dog-more-info").style.display = "none";
```

After that code executes, the trick control's `display` property gets the value `none`, which means the trick control will be hidden.

## `onclick` Event Handler for the Register Button

The register button has an `onclick` attribute that calls the `register` event-handler function. Let's examine the register function's code in **FIGURE 11.14D**. The function starts out

```
//******************************************************

// This function registers a pet.

function register(form) {
  var name;   // pet's name
  var trick;  // dog's favorite trick
  var pet;    // an object that's a subclass of Pet

  if (!form.checkValidity()) {
    document.getElementById("message").innerHTML =
      "You must enter values for all fields";
  }
  else {
    name = form.elements["name"].value;
    if (form.elements["petType"].value == "dog") {
      trick = form.elements["trick"].value;
      pet = new Dog(name, trick);
    }
    else {
      pet = new Hedgehog(name);              This method call exhibits polymorphism.
    }

    document.getElementById("message").innerHTML = pet.confirm();
  } // end else
} // end register
```

FIGURE 11.14D `register` **event-handler function for Pet Registry web page**

by calling the form's `checkValidity` method to check for valid input. As you may recall from the web page's `body` container, the pet name and pet type controls have `required` attributes. So if the pet name's text control has an empty-string value or the pet type's pull-down menu has an empty-string value, the form's `checkValidity` method returns false, indicating invalid input.

If the input is valid, the function retrieves the pet name control's value and the pet type control's value. If the pet type's selected value is "dog," we retrieve the trick control's value and then call the `Dog` constructor. If the pet type's selected value is not "dog," we call the `Hedgehog` constructor. For both constructor calls, we assign the instantiated object to a `pet` variable. After instantiating either a `Dog` or `Hedgehog` object, we use the `pet` variable to call the `confirm` method, which retrieves confirmation data about the pet. Here's the relevant code:

```
document.getElementById("message").innerHTML = pet.confirm();
```

As you may recall, there are two `confirm` methods—one defined in the `Pet` class and one defined in the `Dog` class. So how does the `pet.confirm()` method call know which `confirm` method to use? Drum roll please....

One of the cornerstones of OOP is *polymorphism*. Polymorphism is the ability for a particular method call to perform different operations at different times. It occurs when you have a variable that holds an object (more precisely, a reference to an object). The variable can refer to different types of objects during the course of a program's execution. When the variable calls the polymorphic method, the JavaScript engine determines the type of object that the variable currently holds and calls the method that's associated with that type of object. Pretty cool, eh? Polymorphism provides programs with a great deal of power and versatility. Returning to the `register` function's `pet.confirm()` method call, if `pet` contains a `Dog` object, then the `Dog` class's `confirm` method is called. If `pet` contains a `Hedgehog` object, then the `Hedgehog` class's `confirm` method is called. Wait—the `Hedghog` class does not provide a `confirm` method. No worries—remember that subclasses inherit their superclass members, so that means the `Hedgehog` class inherits the `Pet` class's `confirm` method.

The `Dog` class also inherits the `Pet` class's `confirm` method, so how does the JavaScript engine know which method to call when a `Dog` object calls the `confirm` method? The principle of locality comes to the rescue. Because the calling object is a `Dog`, it's the local `Dog` class `confirm` method that wins. As you learned earlier, if you'd like to call the superclass `confirm` method from within the `Dog` confirm method, you can do so by prefacing the `confirm` method calls with super dot.

Our Pet Registry web page is just a prototype. In registering a pet, it simply stores the pet's information in an object and then retrieves the object's information as part of a confirmation message. For a real-world registration, you'd use server-side programming to store the pet object's information in a database so you can retrieve registered pets later on for various purposes (e.g., retrieve all the dogs that can catch a Frisbee). Server-side programming is beyond the scope of this book. But after finishing this book, you are encouraged to learn about server-side programming on your own.

## 11.12 `switch` Statement

For the Pet Registry web page to be useful in the real world, you'd need to modify it to accommodate more than just two types of pets. The web page's `register` function uses an `if` statement to distinguish between two types—Dog and Hedgehog. To accommodate more pet types, you could use an `if` statement with lots of `else if` clauses. But the more elegant solution is to use a `switch` statement.

The `switch` statement works similarly to the "if, else if" form of the `if` statement in that it allows you to follow one of several paths. But a key difference between the `switch` statement and the "if, else if" statement is that the `switch` statement's determination of which path to take is based on a single value. (For an "if, else if" statement, the determination of which path to take is based on multiple conditions, with a separate condition for each path.)

```
switch (controlling-expression)
{
   case constant1:
      statement(s);
      break;
   case constant2:
      statement(s);
      break;

   .
   .
   .

   default:        ◄────── optional
      statement(s);
} // end switch
```

**FIGURE 11.15** `switch` **statement's syntax**

Having the determination based on a single value can lead to a more compact, more understandable implementation.

Study the `switch` statement's syntax in **FIGURE 11.15**. When executing a `switch` statement, control jumps to the `case` constant that matches the controlling expression's value, and the computer executes all subsequent statements up to a `break` statement. The `break` statement causes control to jump below the `switch` statement. If there are no `case` constants that match the controlling expression's value, then control jumps to the `default` label (if there is a `default` label) or below the `switch` statement (if there is no `default` label).

Usually, `break` statements are placed at the end of every `case` block. That's because you normally want to execute just one `case` block's subordinate statement(s) and then exit the `switch` statement. Forgetting to include a `break` statement is a common error. If there's no `break` at the bottom of a particular `case` block, control flows through subsequent `case` constants and executes all subordinate statements until a `break` statement is reached. If there's no `break` at the bottom of the last `case` block, control flows through to the statements in the `default` block (if there is a `default` block).

Returning to the Pet Registry web page, here's an improved version of how the register function can process the pet type pull-down menu with a `switch` statement and several additional pet types:

```
switch (form.elements["petType"].value) {
   case "dog":
      trick = form.elements["trick"].value;
      pet = new Dog(name, trick);
      break;
```

```
    case "hedgehog":
      pet = new Hedgehog(name);
      break;
    case "cat":
      hypoallergenic = form.elements["hypoallergenic"].value;
      pet = new Cat(name, hypoallergenic);
      break;
    case "southern tamandua":
      pet = new Tamandua(name);
} // end switch
```

Note that there's no `default` block. Having a `default` block is very common because it ensures that all situations are handled. But for this `switch` statement's controlling expression, we know that all situations are handled because the controlling expression is a pull-down menu, with a predefined set of options for the user to choose from.

## 11.13 **Arrays**

### Overview

Normal objects have different names for each of the object's different data items. For example, a dog object has `name`, `sound`, and `trick` properties for its different data items. Now we'll look at a special type of object that holds multiple data items and uses a common name for all of them. That special type of object is an array.

In the past, we've used the term *collection* to describe a group of items with a common name. An array is not only a special type of object; it's also a special type of collection. Remember in the last chapter how we retrieved a collection of t-shirt color radio buttons using the following code?

```
    tshirtRBs = form.elements["color"];
```

And then later, we used the `tshirtRBs` name to access individual elements within the collection. Here's an example:

```
    currentRB = tshirtRBs[i];
```

In `tshirtRBs[i]`, the `i` is an *index variable*, and it allows you to access an element within the collection. Arrays also use index variables to access individual elements.

So, what's the difference between a collection and an array? The browser engine builds collections for control groups (like radio buttons and checkboxes) automatically when it creates the DOM node tree. On the other hand, with arrays, it's up to you, the web developer, to instantiate an array before you can use it. To instantiate a class, you first have to define the class and specify the class's properties and methods. Instantiating an array is easier. You use the predefined `Array` object (that's `Array` with a capital A) with the `new` operator to instantiate an array. For example:

```
stuntGroup = new Array("Ellie", "Caiden", "Alexa",
  "Olivia");
```

That code creates an array of girls for a stunt group within my daughter Caiden's cheerleading squad. The instantiation syntax should look familiar because we've used it for instantiating objects in prior examples. But now we're using "Array" instead of a class name.

It's very common to use a `for` loop to loop through the elements of an array. For example, suppose you have a web page with the preceding `stuntGroup` assignment, and within the `body` container, you have `<div id="stunt-group"></div>`. To insert the stunt group girls' names within that `div` container, you could use this code:

```
var names = "";

for (let i=0; i<stuntGroup.length; i++) {
  names += stuntGroup[i] + "<br>";
}
document.getElementById("stunt-group").innerHTML =
  names;
```

In the `for` loop heading, note the `stuntGroup` array's `length` property. It works the same as the `length` property for radio button and checkbox collections—it returns the number of elements in the array. Note that the index variable `i` gets initialized to 0. As with collections, an array's first element is at index position 0.

Continuing with the stunt group example, suppose Caiden suffers a concussion from a fall. She has to sit out, and she gets replaced by Coach Ayers. Here's the code that models that behavior (assuming "Caiden" is stored in the `stuntGroup` array's second element):

```
stuntGroup[1] = "Coach Ayers";
```

After Caiden regains consciousness, she rejoins her teammates as a fifth member of the stunt group, with Coach Ayers continuing to help out when Caiden gets disoriented. Here's the code that models Caiden rejoining the stunt group:

```
stuntGroup[4] = "Caiden";
```

The assignment statement dynamically expands the array's size by adding a fifth element to the array at index position 4.

You've already seen how to instantiate an array with initial values for the array's elements—`new Array`(*comma-separated-list-of-initial-values*). As an alternative, you can instantiate an empty array and then later assign values into the array. For example, we could have started with an empty `stuntGroup` array and implemented an "Add cheerleader" button with an `onclick` event handler that adds a user-entered name to the array. Here's a declaration for an empty `stuntGroup` array, plus a function that could be used for an "Add cheerleader" button's event handler:

```
var stuntGroup = new Array();

function addCheerleader() {
  stuntGroup[stuntGroup.length] =
    document.getElementById("cheerleader").value;
} // end addCheerleader
```

Note how the function uses the array's `length` property as an index for the new element. Before any cheerleaders have been added, the array is empty with a length of 0. So the first time `addCheerleader` gets called, the assignment statement's left side refers to an element at index position 0. As a result of the assignment, that element becomes the first element in the array. The assignment statement's right side retrieves the contents of a text control with an `id` value of "cheerleader".

As you've seen before, JavaScript sometimes provides more than one way to accomplish the same thing. As a more elegant alternative to using `stuntGroup.length` as shown earlier, we can use the `Array` object's `push` method to add an element to the end of the array. Here's the code:

```
stuntGroup.push(document.getElementById("cheerleader").value);
```

## Methods

The `Array` object has quite a few methods, and every array you instantiate inherits those methods. Take a look at **FIGURE 11.16**. It shows a few of the more popular `Array` methods, starting with the `push` method, which you've already seen. When you call the `push`, `reverse`, `sort`, or `splice` method, the primary purpose is to modify the calling object array. That's different from when you call the `concat` or `indexOf` methods. With those methods, the purpose is to return a value, and the calling object array remains intact, unmodified.

The `reverse` method is self-explanatory. It reverses the order of the calling object array's elements.

The `sort` method can be a little tricky. If you have an array of strings, the `sort` method uses lexicographical ordering. As you might recall from Chapter 9, lexicographical ordering is pretty much the same as dictionary ordering. Here's an example:

```
stuntGroup = new Array("Ellie", "Caiden", "Alexa", "Olivia");
stuntGroup.sort();
```

<table>
<tr><td>

*array-variable*.concat (*another-array*)
    Returns a new array that is formed by concatenating the passed-in array to the end of the
    calling object array. The calling object array does not change.

</td></tr>
<tr><td>

*array-variable*.indexOf (*value*)
    Returns the index of the first element that holds the specified value. Returns -1 if
    not found.

</td></tr>
<tr><td>

*array-variable*.push (*value*)
    Creates an element with the specified value and adds that element to the end of the
    array. To add multiple elements to the end of an array, use commas to separate the
    element values. It returns the new length of the array.

</td></tr>
<tr><td>

*array-variable*.reverse ()
    Reverses the array's elements, so the first array element becomes the last, and the last
    array element becomes the first. It returns the reversed array.

</td></tr>
<tr><td>

*array-variable*.sort ()
    Sorts the array's elements, so the elements with smaller values move to the start of the
    array. It returns the sorted array.

</td></tr>
<tr><td>

*array-variable*.splice (*start, delete-count, value1, value2, ...*)
    Removes elements from the array and/or inserts elements into the array. The *start*
    parameter specifies the index position where elements are removed and/or inserted.
    The *delete-count* parameter specifies the number of elements removed. The value
    parameters specify the values for inserted elements. It returns an array of the
    deleted elements or an empty array if no elements are removed.

</td></tr>
</table>

**FIGURE 11.16 Some of the more popular Array methods—their headings and descriptions**

After this code executes, "Alexa" moves to the first position, followed by "Caiden," "Ellie," and "Olivia." Lexicographical ordering is different from dictionary ordering in that lowercase letters go after uppercase letters. As a new-age hipster, Ellie sometimes prefers lowercase *e* for the first letter in her name ("ellie"). With that spelling, the sort method would move "ellie" to the last position in the array.

By default, if you have an array of numbers, the sort method first converts the numbers to strings and then sorts using lexicographical ordering. So if you have an array that holds 4, 196, 8, and 23 initially, the array holds 196, 23, 4, and 8 after sorting. That's because the "1" character in "196" comes before the "2" character in "23," and the "2" comes before "4," which comes before "8." In the next section, you'll learn how to sort numbers in standard numerical order.

The splice method removes elements from the calling object array and/or inserts elements into the calling object array. When you call the splice method, the first argument specifies the index position where the removal and/or insertion takes place. The second argument specifies the number of elements that are to be removed from the array. If there is no second argument, then the `splice` method removes all the elements starting at the first argument's position. If the second argument is 0, that means no elements are removed. Subsequent arguments specify the values for elements that are to be inserted into the array. We'll show an example that uses the `splice` method after first describing the `concat` and `indexOf` methods.

The `concat` method returns a new array that is formed by concatenating the argument array to the end of the calling object array. Here's an example:

```
megaStuntGroup = stuntGroup1.concat(stuntGroup2);
```

After that code executes, the `megaStuntGroup` array holds all of the elements from `stuntGroup1` plus `stuntGroup2`. The `concat` method does not impact the original arrays, so `stuntGroup1` and `stuntGroup2` are unchanged.

The `indexOf` method searches for a specified value within the calling object array's elements. It returns the index of the first element that holds the value. It returns -1 if the value is not found.

To illustrate how the `indexOf` and `splice` methods work, we need another stunt group example. Let's check in on Caiden and see how she's doing with her concussion recovery. After two weeks, she's finally able to remember her name. Way to go, Caiden! With that hurdle cleared, Coach Ayers leaves the stunt group and returns to full coaching duties. The following code models Coach Ayers leaving the stunt group:

```
deletePosition = stuntGroup.indexOf("Coach Ayers");
stuntGroup.splice(deletePosition, 1);
```

Note how we use the `indexOf` method to search for Coach Ayers and then use the `splice` method to remove Coach Ayers's element.

## 11.14 Arrays of Objects

In the previous section, we kept things simple by sticking with one array, `stuntGroup`, whose elements were all strings. Be aware that JavaScript arrays are very flexible in that an array can have different types for its elements. So if you want to keep track of the cheerleaders' heights, you could use the `stuntGroup` array to store string elements for the cheerleaders' names and also number elements for the cheerleaders' heights. Although that would be legal, there's a better way to handle different types of values in an array—using an array of objects.

For an end-of-chapter exercise, you'll be asked to implement an array of cheerleader objects where each cheerleader object holds a name and height, but in this section, let's move on to a different example. Suppose your mom asks you to implement a web page for her book club. She wants book club members to use the web page to keep track of when the meetings are held and what book is associated with each meeting. To implement that functionality, you declare an array of `BookMeeting` objects, and you define a `BookMeeting` class with properties for author, book title, and meeting date. Here's the declaration for an empty array of `BookMeeting` objects:

```
var bookMtgList = new Array();
```

And here's an `addMtg` function that could be called by an "Add meeting" button's event handler to add a meeting to the `bookMtgList` array:

```
function addMtg(form) {
  var author;   // book author
  var title;    // book title
  var date;     // book club meeting date

  author = form.elements["author"].value;
  title = form.elements["title"].value;
  date = new Date(form.elements["date"].value);
  bookMtgList.push(new BookMeeting(author, title, date));
} // end addMtg
```

In the `addMtg` function, note the `BookMeeting` constructor call with the arguments `author`, `title`, and `date`. The `author` and `title` arguments come from text controls. The `date` argument comes from a date control, which was introduced in Chapter 8, but we never showed code for it. In the next section, we present the complete code for a Book Club web page, and you'll see how to implement a date control then. At the end of the `addMtg` function, note how `bookMtgList` calls the `push` method to add a new `BookMeeting` object to the end of the array.

Next is the `BookMeeting` class and its constructor. They allow you to instantiate a `BookMeeting` object. Here's the code:

```
class BookMeeting {
  constructor(author, title, date) {
    this.author = author;   // book author
    this.title = title;     // book title
    this.date = date;       // date of meeting to discuss book
  } // end constructor
} // end class BookMeeting
```

## Sorting

After adding `BookMeeting` objects to the array, you might want to sort the array. Sorting an array of strings is easy—just call `sort()` and that's it. Sorting an array of objects is a bit more work. Regardless of the type for an array's elements, all sorting algorithms perform a series of comparisons between pairs of elements. After comparing one element to another, if the first element is deemed to be less than or equal to the second element, then all is well, and nothing happens. But if the first element is deemed to be greater than the second element, then the two elements swap positions within the array. Determining whether one element is less than another element is straightforward for arrays of strings because lexicographical ordering clearly defines the < operation when two strings are compared. But for arrays of objects, it's up to the web developer (you) to define the < operation when two elements are compared.

For arrays of objects, the way you define the < operation for two elements is to implement a comparison function. The comparison function's heading must have two parameters. During the sort process, the comparison function gets called (automatically) many times. With each call, the parameters receive two elements from the array. If the function returns a negative number, then the first element is considered to be less than the second element. If the function returns a positive number, then the first element is considered to be greater than the second element. Returning a 0 means the elements have equal values.

So, was this explanation as clear as mud? Perhaps an example will help. For an array of `BookMeeting` objects, you might want to sort based on any of the three properties—author, title, or date. To sort by author, you could use this comparison function:

```
function compareAuthors(bookMtg1, bookMtg2) {
  if (bookMtg1.author < bookMtg2.author) {
    return -1;
  }
  else if (bookMtg1.author > bookMtg2.author) {
    return 1;
  }
  else {
    return 0;
  }
} // end compareAuthors
```

To sort by author, use the `author` property in the comparison function.

With that function defined, now you can sort the `bookMtgList` array by author by doing this:

```
bookMtgList.sort(compareAuthors);
```

Note how we stick the comparison function's name, `compareAuthors`, in the `sort` method call's parentheses.

The preceding sort code works OK, but to improve efficiency by reducing file size, you might want to consider a more compact alternative implementation.[6] Instead of implementing

---

[6] It says, "You might want to consider a more compact alternative implementation." That means it's optional. If this material is pushing your stress buttons, take a break and skip the compact implementation.

compareAuthors as a standalone function, you can implement it within the sort method call's parentheses like this:

```
bookMtgList.sort(
  function (a, b) {
    return (a.author < b.author) ? -1 : (a.author > b.author) ? 1 : 0;
  });
```

As you can see, by sticking the function within the sort method call's parentheses, you no longer have to provide a name for the function. When you embed a nameless function definition within another statement (in this case, a method call statement), the function definition is known as a *function expression*.

To make the sort method call more compact, in addition to using a function expression, we use short parameter names (a and b) and nested conditional operator expressions. Remember that a conditional operator expression is basically an "if, else" statement that can be embedded as a value within another statement. There are two conditional operators embedded within the return statement. The conditional operator uses left-to-right associativity, so the left conditional operator executes first. It checks the condition a.author < b.author and if true, the function returns -1. If false, the JavaScript engine executes the second conditional operator. The second conditional operator checks the condition a.author > b.author and if true, the function returns 1. If false, the function returns 0. That functionality mimics the functionality provided by the compareAuthors function, so the alternative implementations do indeed accomplish the same thing.

As you may recall, by default, if you have an array of numbers, the sort method first converts the numbers to strings and then sorts using lexicographical ordering. So if you have an array that holds 4, 196, 8, and 23 initially, the array will hold 196, 23, 4, and 8 after sorting. For a standard numerical sort, you need to provide a comparison function as an argument when you call the sort method. Here's what we're talking about:

```
var numbers = new Array(4, 196, 8, 23);
numbers.sort(
  function (a, b) {
    return (a < b) ? -1 : (a > b) ? 1 : 0;
  });
```

After this code executes, the numbers are sorted properly, and the array will hold 4, 8, 23, and 196.

## 11.15 Book Club Web Page

In this section, we present the complete code for the book club web page described earlier. See **FIGURE 11.17**. It shows what the web page looks like when it's first loaded. It also shows what the web page looks like after the user enters information for three books and clicks the **Add a new meeting** button three times. Note that the book club meetings are sorted by date. Sorting takes place each time the user adds a new book club meeting.

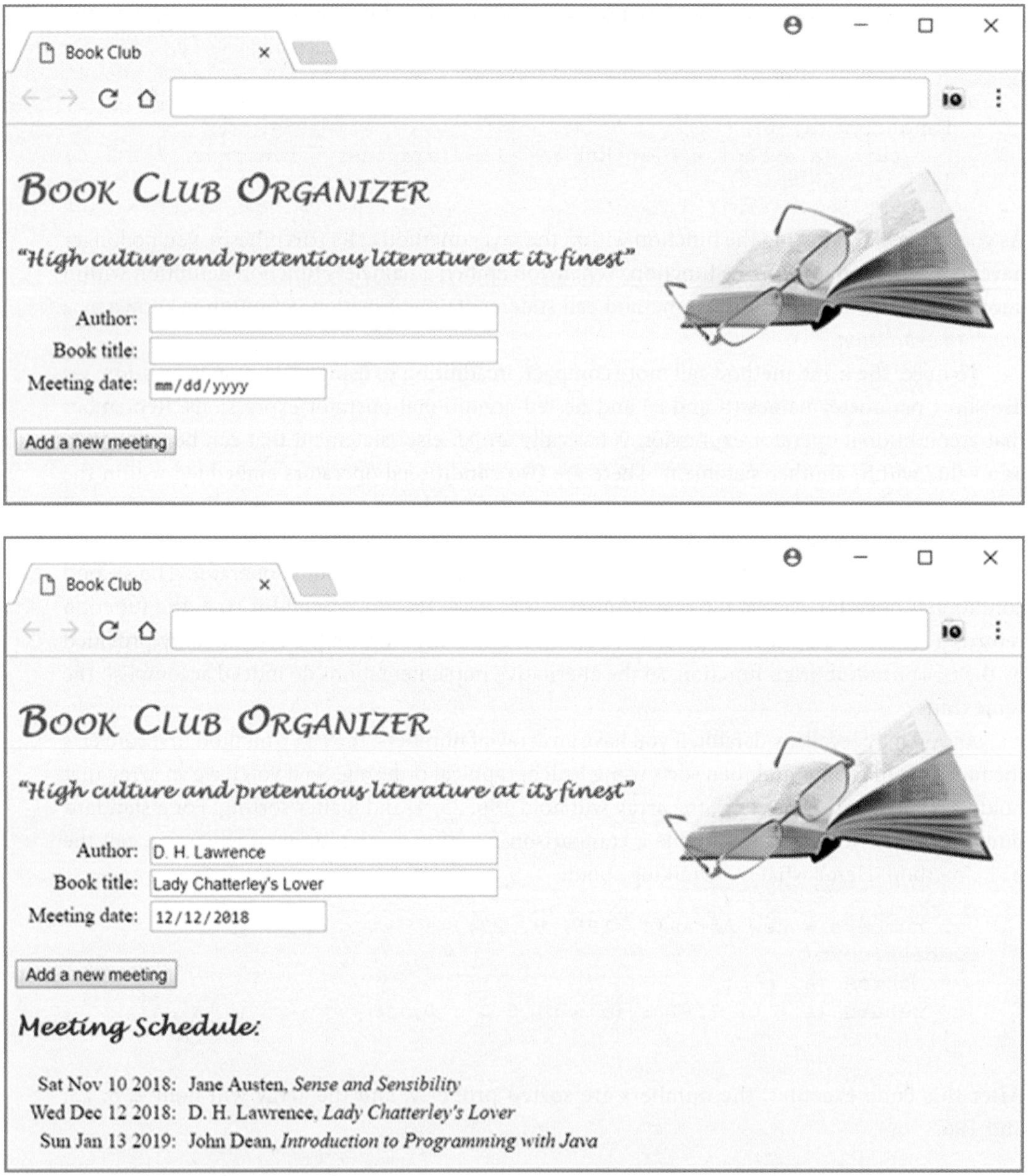

**FIGURE 11.17 Book Club web page—initial display and what happens after the user enters information and clicks the Add a new meeting button for three book club meetings**

As book club meetings are added, eventually the meeting list will grow large and unmanageable. So for a more useful web page, you'll need the ability to delete book club meetings. In an end-of-chapter exercise, you're asked to add delete buttons at the right of each book club meeting entry.

## style and body Containers

In the Book Club browser window, note the cursive olive green headings at the top. In **FIGURE 11.18A**'s style container, you can see the h1 and h4 type selector rules that implement the format for those headings. In the Book Club browser window, note how the author, book title, and meeting date prompts and controls are aligned. The web page uses a CSS table to achieve that alignment. Looking at the style container code again, you can see the .table, .row, and .row > * rules that implement the table.

Next in the style container is this body type selector rule:

```
body {display: flex; align-items: flex-start;}
```

```
<!DOCTYPE html>
<html lang="en">
<head>
<meta charset="utf-8">
<meta name="author" content="John Dean">
<title>Book Club</title>
<style>
  h1, h3, h4 {
     font-family: "Lucida Handwriting", cursive;
     color: darkolivegreen;
  }
  h1 {font-variant: small-caps;}

  .table {display: table; border-spacing: 10px 4px;}
  .row {display: table-row;}
  .row > * {display: table-cell;}
  .row > :first-child {text-align: right;}

  body {
     display: flex; align-items: flex-start;
     background-color: oldlace;
  }
  img {margin: 20px 0 0 20px;}

  #error, #mtgHeader {display: none;}
  #error {color: red: margin-bottom: 20px;}
  #mtgHeader {color: indigo;}
</style>
<script src="bookClub.js"></script>
</head>
```

This causes the web page's main content to display at the left and the book drawing to display at the right.

This causes the error message and meeting dates header to be hidden initially.

**FIGURE 11.18A head container for Book Club web page**

Do you remember what those property-value pairs do? The `display: flex` property-value pair converts the `body` container into a flexbox and causes the `body`'s child elements to conform to the size of their content (and not span the width of the web page). The `align-items: flex-start` property-value causes the flexbox container's child elements to be aligned at the top. So how does all that apply to the Book Club web page? As you'll see shortly when we examine the web page's `body` container, the `body` container has two child elements—a large `div` container for all the content shown in the left half of the browser window and an `img` element for a book drawing. Normally, the web page's heading elements (`h1`, `h3`, and `h4`) would span the entire width of the web page. The flexbox causes them to span only to the width of their content. That means the book drawing displays at the right of the headings and the other content displays below the headings. A nice look indeed!

Finally, in the `style` container, you can see several `#error` and `#mtgHeader` ID selector rules. They provide formatting for an error message and for the meeting schedule header. Here's the first such rule:

```
#error, #mtgHeader {display: none;}
```

That rule makes the error message and meeting schedule header invisible when the page first loads. As you'll see later, we use JavaScript to make the error message visible when there's invalid input. Also, we use JavaScript to make the meeting schedule header visible when the user adds the first meeting.

Take a look at the `body` container in **FIGURE 11.18B**. The `form` container's code should be pretty straightforward. Below the form, there's a `div` with an error message inside it. As we explained, we use the `#error` ID selector rule to make the error message invisible when the page first loads. Next comes the **Add a new meeting** button with an `onclick` event handler that calls an `addMtg` function. And then there's an `h3` element for a meeting schedule header. As we explained, we use the `#mtgHeader` ID selector rule to make the meeting schedule header invisible when the page first loads. Below the meeting schedule header, there's an empty `div` container that gets populated with meeting entries as the user clicks the **Add a new meeting** button. At the bottom of the `body` container, there's an `img` element for the book drawing.

## Class Definition

The Book Club web page uses an array of `BookMeeting` objects. **FIGURE 11.19A** shows the `BookMeeting` class definition followed by a declaration for `bookMtgList`, an empty array of `BookMeeting` objects. In the previous section, you saw a simplified version of the `BookMeeting` class definition. This time, the constructor is the same, but we've added a `bookMtgEntry` method to the class.

Examine the `bookMtgEntry` method and note how it returns a `div` container with two spans inside it. The `div` start tag includes `class="row"`. Consequently, the `.row` class selector

```
<body>
<div>
  <h1>Book Club Organizer</h1>
  <h4><q>High culture and pretentious literature at its finest</q></h4>
  <form class="table" id="myForm">
    <div class="row">
      <label for="author">Author:</label>
      <input type="text" id="author" size="35" required>
    </div>
    <div class="row">
      <label for="title">Book title:</label>
      <input type="text" id="title" size="35" required>
    </div>
    <div class="row">
      <label for="date">Meeting date:</label>
      <input type="date" id="date" required>
    </div>
  </form>
  <br>
  <div id="error">You must enter values for all fields.</div>
  <input type="button" form="myForm" value="Add a new meeting"
    onclick="addMtg(this.form);">
  <br>
  <h3 id="mtgHeader">Meeting Schedule:</h3>
  <div class="table" id="list"></div>
</div>
<img src="../images/bookandGlasses.png" width="280" height="153" alt="">
</body>
</html>
```

These are hidden initially.

**FIGURE 11.18B** body **container for Book Club web page**

rule gets applied to the `bookMtgEntry` method's returned `div` container, and the `div` then serves as a row in a table. And those rows form the content for a table of book meeting entries. Do you know where the table container is that surrounds the rows? If you re-examine the web page's `body` container, you can see this `div` container near the bottom:

```
<div class="table" id="list"></div>
```

With `class="table"`, the `.table` class selector rule gets applied to the `div` container. So why bother with a CSS table for the book meetings? Go back to the Book Club browser window and note that for the list of meetings at the bottom, the dates are right aligned and the authors are left aligned. That alignment is made possible by the CSS table. The alignment is subtle, but you should always strive to make your web pages look their best. After all, that alignment might be the difference between a book club member scoffing at your web page haughtily and the book club member giving you a pan of brownies next time she visits your mom's house for a book club meeting. Such are the rewards of the web developers' guild.

```
/************************************************
* bookClub.js
* John Dean
*
* This file implements a BookMeeting class, a list of
* BookMeeting objects, and a function which adds
* BookMeeting objects to the list.
************************************************/

class BookMeeting {
  constructor (author, title, date) {
    this.author = author;    // book author
    this.title = title;      // book title
    this.date = date;        // date of meeting to discuss book
  } // end constructor

  //************************************************

  // Return book meeting information as a table row

  bookMtgEntry() {
    return "<div class='row'>" +
      "<span>" + this.date.toDateString() + ":</span>" +
      "<span>" + this.author + ", <cite>" + this.title + "</cite></span>" +
      "</div>";
  } // end bookMtgEntry
} // end class BookMeeting

//************************************************

var bookMtgList = new Array() ;
```

> This generates a user-friendly string version of the `date` property.

**FIGURE 11.19A** `BookMeeting` **class definition and array declaration for Book Club web page**

Now let's examine the span elements embedded in the bookMtgEntry method's returned div container. Here's the return statement:

```
return "<div class='row'>" + "<span>" +
this.date.toDateString() + ":</span>" +
  "<span>" + this.author + ",  <cite>" + this.title + "</cite></span>" +
  "</div>";
```

The first span accesses the calling object's date property with this.date. As you'll see later when we examine how BookMeeting objects are created, a BookMeeting object's date property holds a `Date` object. In the preceding `return` statement, we use the `date` property to call the `Date` object's `toDateString` method. The `toDateString` method retrieves a user-friendly string version of the `date` property. For example, if you go back to the Book Club browser window, you can see "Sun Jan 13, 2019" for the third book meeting entry.

The second `span` displays two properties—`this.author` and `this.title`. Note how we embed `this.title` in a `cite` element to describe the title's content properly. If you go back to the Book Club browser window's list of meetings, you can see how the book titles are italicized. That's from the `cite` element.

## Event Handler for Adding a New Meeting

It's time to move on to the Book Club web page's event handler. If you refer back to the web page's `body` container, you can see that the button has an `onclick` attribute that calls an `addMtg` function. Take a look at the `addMtg` function in **FIGURE 11.19B**. It starts out by calling the form's `checkValidity` method to check for valid input. As you can see in the web page's `body` container, all three of the form's controls have `required` attributes. We use the form's `checkValidity` method to check for the user entering something in all three controls. If the form's `checkValidity` method returns false, the `addMtg` function flags the error by doing this:

```
document.getElementById("error").style.display = "block";
```

Remember the error message `div` element at the bottom of the `body` container? We use a CSS rule, `#error {display: none;}`, to make it invisible when the page first loads. This `getElementById` method call retrieves the error message `div` element, and then we use its `style` property to assign `block` to the div's `display` property. The `block` value is the default for the `div` element, and by restoring the `div` element to its default display state, the error message becomes visible.

Continuing with our examination of the `addMtg` function, if the form's `checkValidity` method returns true, the function makes the error message invisible by assigning `none` to the error message `div` element's `display` property:

```
document.getElementById("error").style.display = "none";
```

As mentioned earlier, when the page first loads, the meeting schedule header is invisible. If the form's input is valid, that means a book meeting entry will be displayed, and that entry will need to be under a meeting schedule header. Thus, the function makes the meeting schedule header visible by assigning `block` to the header element's `display` property:

```
document.getElementById("mtgHeader").style.display = "block";
```

Next up in the `addMtg` function is retrieving the three user inputs for author, book title, and meeting date. We use the `value` property for each of the three user-input controls. The `value` property returns a string, which works great for the `author` and `title` properties. But for the

```
// Add a book club meeting to the list.

function addMtg(form) {
  var author;   // book author
  var title;    // book title
  var date;     // book club meeting date

  if (!form.checkValidity()) {
    document.getElementById("error").style.display = "block";
  }
  else {
    document.getElementById("error").style.display = "none";
    document.getElementById("mtgHeader").style.display = "block";
    author = form.elements["author"].value;
    title = form.elements["title"].value;
    date = new Date(form.elements["date"].value);          Store a Date
                                                           object for the
                                                           date
                                                           property.

    bookMtgList.push(new BookMeeting(author, title, date));
    bookMtgList.sort(
      function (a, b) {
        return (a.date < b.date) ? -1 : (a.date > b.date) ? 1 : 0;
      });
    displayList();
  } // end else
} // end addMtg
```

**FIGURE 11.19B** `addMtg` **event-handler function for Book Club web page**

`date` property, we need to store a `Date` object, not a string. So we use the date control's string value as an argument for calling the `Date` constructor, like this:

```
date = new Date(form.elements["date"].value);
```

After retrieving string values for the `author` and `title` properties and a `Date` object value for the `date` property, the `addMtg` function uses those values as arguments in its call to the `BookMeeting` constructor:

```
bookMtgList.push(new BookMeeting(author, title, date));
```

You can see here that after instantiating a `BookMeeting` object, we push the object onto the end of the `bookMtgList` array.

Next, we sort the `bookMtgList` array's `BookMeeting` objects by calling the array's `sort` method:

```
bookMtgList.sort(
  function (a, b) {
    return (a.date < b.date) ? -1 : (a.date > b.date) ? 1 : 0;
});
```

That's the same `sort` method call presented in the previous section, except that this time we're sorting by date. Note how we're able to use the `<` operator to compare the `date` properties for the two passed-in array elements. `Date` objects have a built-in mechanism that allows them to be compared with the `<` operator. That's why we use `Date` objects for the `date` property instead of strings. If we used plain old strings, we'd have to do a lot of work to determine whether one date string is less than another date string (e.g., is "12/15/18" less than "03/15/19"?).

At the bottom of the `addMtg` function, we call the `displayList` function. See the `displayList` function in **FIGURE 11.19C**. It's in charge of displaying the `BookMeeting` objects in the `bookMtgList` array. Note how we use a `for` loop and the array's `length` property to loop through the array:

```
for (let i=0; i<bookMtgList.length; i++) {
  listContent += bookMtgList[i].bookMtgEntry();
}
```

In this code, note how we call the `bookMtgEntry` method to retrieve the *i*th `BookMeeting` object's information.

When a function is called by another function (as opposed to when a function is called by an event-handler attribute like `onclick`), we refer to it as a *helper function* because it's helping another function. So `displayList` is a helper function. Helper functions can make code easier to understand by breaking up large functions into smaller modules that have well-defined

```
//***********************************************

// Display the list of book club meetings.

function displayList() {
  var listContent = "";  // The contents of the list of book meetings

  for (let i=0; i<bookMtgList.length; i++) {
    listContent += bookMtgList[i].bookMtgEntry();
  }
  document.getElementById("list").innerHTML = listContent;
} // end displayList
```

**FIGURE 11.19C** `displayList` **helper function for Book Club web page**

purposes. We could have avoided implementing the `displayList` function by putting its code at the bottom of the `addMtg` function. But by using a separate `displayList` helper function, it makes the `addMtg` function smaller and easier to understand. And understandability is a key to making maintenance chores go more smoothly.

# 11.16 CASE STUDY: Downtown Properties Data Processing

In this chapter's case study, we add a Downtown Properties web page to the Lawrence Microgrid website. The new web page illustrates creation and use of arrays and objects that support user interaction with a display of real-estate property features. By "property," we mean a piece of land, not an OOP property. **FIGURE 11.20** shows a display of this web page before any user interaction other than scrolling down a bit (causing the header navigation links to scroll out of the viewport). Note the five text controls at the top—two for an address ("Address Number" and "Street Name") and three for property features ("Frontage (ft)," "Height (ft)," and "Roof Type").

Just below the text controls is a **Cancel** button that clears the text control entries. Below that are three more buttons, **Add**, **Replace**, and **Delete**. Clicking **Add** takes what is in the text controls and inserts it as a new row in the table at the bottom of the page. Clicking **Replace** replaces a particular row in the table with what is in the input boxes. Clicking **Delete** removes a particular row in the table.

Which particular row? As explained in the instructions area, the user selects a particular row in the table by clicking anywhere in that row. That click causes the values in that row to appear in the text controls at the top of the web page, and it internally saves the clicked row number. That internally saved row number determines the row to be replaced or deleted when and if the user subsequently clicks **Replace** or **Delete**. Clicking **Cancel** before clicking **Replace** or **Delete** disables the replace and delete operations until the user selects another row from the table.

**FIGURE 11.21** shows the `body` for the Downtown Properties web page. The `form` element contains the five input boxes and the four buttons. The rest is straightforward until you get to the `table` element. Notice that it contains only one row, the row of `th` elements that appears at the top of each of the five table columns. Where are the rows that contain the table's data? The table's data is not included in the HTML code. The `body` element's `onload` attribute calls the `initialize` function, which populates the table when the web page loads.

**FIGURE 11.22A** shows the code that populates the table with data. The `head` element contains two `script` elements. The first is just a one-line reference to an external JavaScript file. You'll see that later. The second is explicit, and Figure 11.22A shows the first part of it.

At the bottom of Figure 11.22A is the `initialize` function, called when the `body`'s `onload` event occurs. First it initializes the global `form` and `table` variables for use by subsequent functions. Then it calls `fillTable`, which you'll see shortly.

But before going to that, look at the big block of data assigned to the `properties` variable. The `properties` variable is an example of a *two-dimensional array*. A standard array is a list of data values. A two-dimensional array is a table of data values organized in rows and

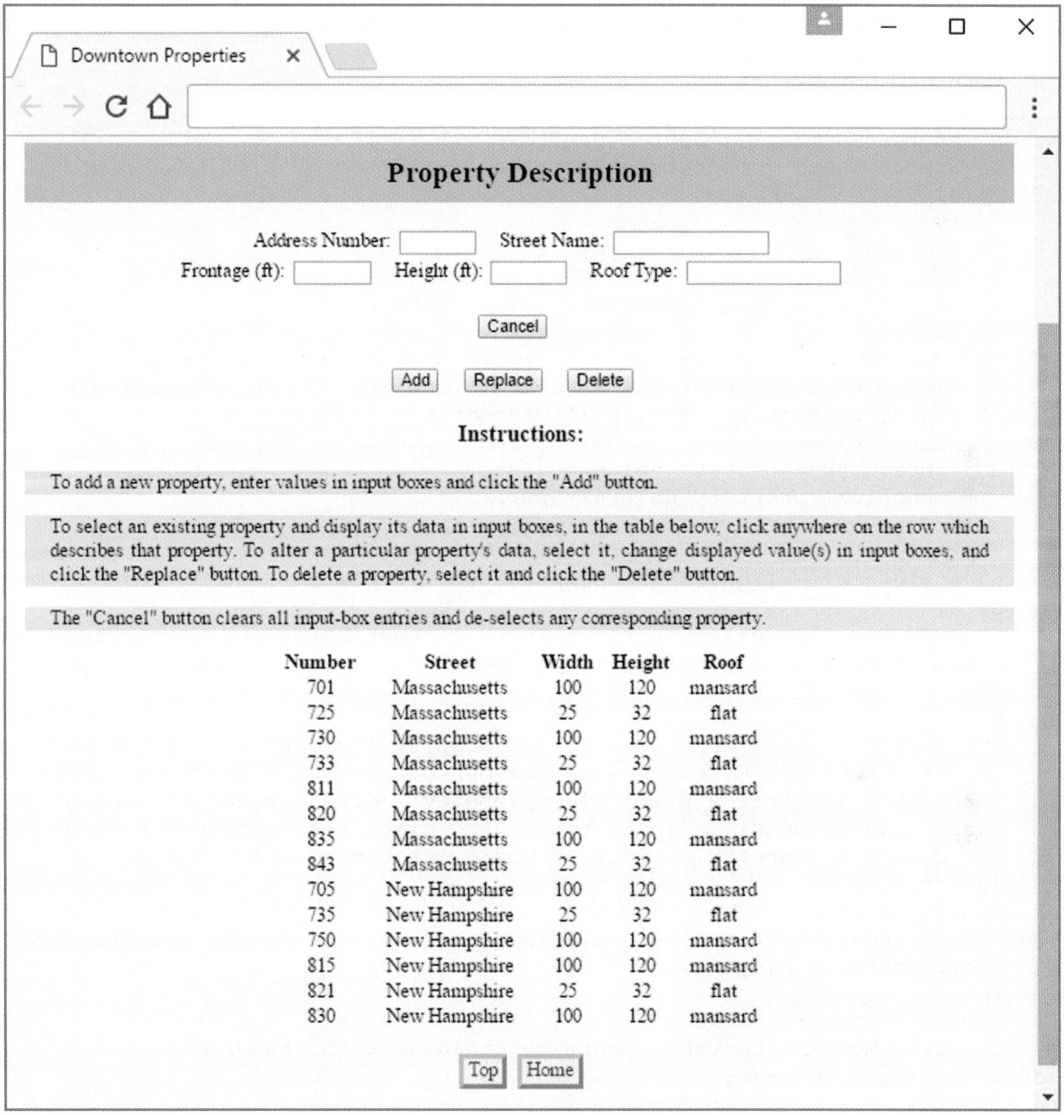

**FIGURE 11.20 Downtown Properties web page before any interaction**

columns. For the `properties` variable, each row is a real-estate property. For example, here are the `properties` variable's first two rows:

```
[750, "New Hampshire", 100, 120, "mansard"],
[811, "Massachusetts", 100, 120, "mansard"],
```

You can see that each of the two rows has five columns (for street number, street name, frontage, height, and roof type). The square brackets ( [] ) are special syntax for specifying an array's value.

```
<body onload="createHeaderFooter(), initialize()">
<h2>Property Description</h2>
<form>
  <div>
    Address Number: <input type="text" size="5">
    Street Name: <input type="text" size="15"><br>
  </div>
  <div>
    Frontage (ft): <input type="text" size="5">
    Height (ft): <input type="text" size="5">
    Roof Type: <input type="text" size="15"><br>
  </div><br>
  <div>
    <input type="button" value="Cancel" onclick="cancel()"><br><br>
    <input type="button" value="Add" onclick="add()">
    <input type="button" value="Replace" onclick="property.replace()">
    <input type="button" value="Delete"
      onclick="property.deleteProperty()">
  </div>
</form>
<h3 style="text-align:center">Instructions:</h3>
<p>
  To add a new property, enter values in input boxes and click the
  "Add" button.
</p>
<p>
  To select an existing property and display its data in input boxes,
  in the table below, click anywhere on the row which describes that
  property. To alter a particular property's data, select it, change
  displayed value(s) in input boxes, and click the "Replace" button.
  To delete a property, select it and click the "Delete" button.
</p>
<p>
  The "Cancel" button clears all input-box entries and de-selects any
  corresponding property.
</p>
<table id="descriptions">
  <tr><th>Number</th><th>Street</th><th>Width</th><th>Height</th>
    <th>Roof</th></tr>
</table>
</body>
```

**FIGURE 11.21 body container for Downtown Properties web page**

Referring back to Figure 11.22A, note that the `properties` variable's assigned value includes outer square brackets that surround the rows' inner square brackets. Those nested square brackets are how you can fill up an entire two-dimensional array.

The two-dimensional array of data at the top of the `properties.html` file facilitates maintenance. If you need to alter the properties database, it's easier to alter or add a `properties` subarray than it would be to alter or add a row in a table element. For one of those subarrays, all you need

```
<!DOCTYPE html>
<html lang="en">
<head>
  <meta charset="utf-8">
  <meta name="author" content="John Dean">
  <meta name="description" content="Chapter 11. CS Properties Web Page">
  <title>Downtown Properties</title>
  <link rel="stylesheet" href="../Library/lawrenceMicrogrid.css">
  <script src="../Library/property.js"></script>

  <script>
    var form;
    var table;
    var property = "";  // object representing one real-estate property

    // This 2D array facilitates sorting and provides data for table

    var properties = [
      // street number, street name, frontage(ft), height (ft), roof type
      [750, "New Hampshire", 100, 120, "mansard"],
      [811, "Massachusetts", 100, 120, "mansard"],
      [830, "New Hampshire", 100, 120, "mansard"],
      [735, "New Hampshire",  25,  32,    "flat"],
      [733, "Massachusetts",  25,  32,    "flat"],
      [815, "New Hampshire", 100, 120, "mansard"],
      [705, "New Hampshire", 100, 120, "mansard"],
      [843, "Massachusetts",  25,  32,    "flat"],
      [725, "Massachusetts",  25,  32,    "flat"],
      [821, "New Hampshire",  25,  32,    "flat"],
      [701, "Massachusetts", 100, 120, "mansard"],
      [730, "Massachusetts", 100, 120, "mansard"],
      [835, "Massachusetts", 100, 120, "mansard"],
      [820, "Massachusetts",  25,  32,    "flat"]
    ];

    function initialize() {
      form = document.getElementsByTagName("form")[0];
      table = document.getElementById("descriptions");
      fillTable();
    } // end initialize
```

**FIGURE 11.22A** `head` **container for Downtown Properties web page**

beyond the data itself is a pair of enclosing brackets and delimiting commas. For a table row, you would have to enclose and delimit the data with an elaborate set of opening and closing element tags.

Did you notice that the rows in the array in Figure 11.22A and rows in the table in Figure 11.20 are not in the same order? You'll see that we introduce JavaScript code that sorts the subordinate arrays in the `properties` array before copying their data into the table. How does it sort them? It sorts by the values in the rows' first cells. Then, if two rows have identical first cells, it sorts those rows by the values in their second cells. And so forth.

FIGURE 11.22B contains the three JavaScript functions that sort the addresses and fill the table with the sorted addresses. The `fillTable` function is called by the `initialize` function at the bottom of Figure 11.22A. The `fillTable` function starts by initializing a `rows` variable. Then it calls the `streetSort` function. Then it deletes all existing data rows. (Initially there are none, but this function also rebuilds the table after it has acquired data rows.) Notice that the deletion starts at the high-index end and deletes rows in reverse order. This avoids a possible empty hole and ambiguous `rows.length` values. The final `fillTable` operation steps through all of the subarrays in the `properties` array and (1) inserts a new row into the table, (2) gives the row an `onclick` event-handling attribute, and (3) populates the row with the data in the current subarray.

```javascript
// Sort properties array and re-populate table

function fillTable() {
  var rows;    // collection of rows in the table

  rows = table.getElementsByTagName("tr");
  streetSort();
  for (let j=rows.length-1; j>0; j--) {
    table.deleteRow(j);
  }
  for (let i=0; i<properties.length; i++) {
    var row;   // a new row for the table

    row = table.insertRow(rows.length);
    row.setAttribute("onclick","new Property(this)");
    for (let j=0; j<properties[0].length; j++) {
      row.insertCell(j).innerHTML = properties[i][j];
    }
  }
} // end fillTable

function streetSort() {
  for (let i=0; i<properties.length; i++) {
    properties[i] = reverseAddress(properties[i]);
  }
  properties.sort();
  for (let i=0; i<properties.length; i++) {
    properties[i] = reverseAddress(properties[i]);
  }
} // end streetSort

function reverseAddress(oneProperty) {
  var temp = oneProperty[0];

  oneProperty[0] = oneProperty[1];
  oneProperty[1] = temp;
  return oneProperty;
} // end reverseAddress
```

FIGURE 11.22B head container for Downtown Properties web page

The streetSort function steps through the subarrays in the properties array and calls the reverseAddress function to reverse the positions of the street number and street name elements in each subarray. Then it calls the standard sort function to sort the reversed-address version of the properties array. Then it reverses the positions of the street number and street name again to restore the natural address order.

The reverseAddress function performs the address reversing operation. It swaps the data in the two address components through a temp variable. This temp variable gets a copy of the first cell's data before the second cell's data overwrites that data in the first cell. Then it gives that copy to the second cell.

FIGURE 11.22C shows the remaining JavaScript code in the Downtown Properties web page's head container. The add function implements the response to a user click on the **Add** button. The add function creates a new (blank) five-cell subarray and then calls push to append it to the high-index end of the properties array. Next, it populates the cells in that new subarray with values copied from the five input boxes. Then it calls fillTable to rebuild the table. Finally, it calls the cancel function.

```
// Add another property and redisplay resorted table

function add() {
  properties.push(new Array(5));
  for (let i=0; i<5; i++) {
    properties[properties.length-1][i] = form.elements[i].value;
  }
  fillTable();        // clear, sort, and re-populate table
  cancel();
} // end add

// Clear input boxes and discard property object

function cancel() {
  for (let i=0; i<5; i++) {
    form.elements[i].value = "";
  }
  property = "";
} // end cancel
</script>
<style>
  body {text-align: center;}
  .center {display: flex; justify-content: center;}
  form {margin: 20px 0;}
  table {
    width: 400px;
    margin-top: 10px;
  }
</style>
<script src="../library/navigation.js"></script>
</head>
```

**FIGURE 11.22C head container for Downtown Properties web page**

The `cancel` function clears the text controls and resets the `property` global variable to the empty string. Resetting `property` to the empty string doesn't matter after an add operation, because the `add` function never assigns anything to `property`. However, as you'll see shortly, other operations also call the `cancel` function, and these other operations do assign something to the `property` global variable.

The replace and delete operations require user selection of a property item to be replaced or deleted; in doing that, they assign the selected item to the `property` global variable. Back in Figure 11.20, the second paragraph in the instructions area begins with the statement: "To select an existing property and display its data in input boxes, in the table below, click anywhere on the row which describes that property." Such a click selects the table row that is to be replaced or deleted and creates a record of that selection by instantiating a `Property` object.

**FIGURE 11.23** shows the `Property` class, which, of course, enables the instantiation of `Property` objects. Note the `Property` constructor. Its `row` parameter is a reference to the particular table row the user clicked. The first two statements in the constructor use the parameter to save a reference to the clicked row and the index number of that row. The `for` loop copies the data elements in the clicked table row into the corresponding input boxes at the top of the web page. The `property = this;` statement gives the `property` global variable a reference to the object being constructed.

After the constructor comes the `replace` function. It begins with a `for` loop that replaces the cells in the `properties` subarray corresponding to the table row being replaced. Notice that the row index in the `properties` array is one less than the row index in the table. That's because the table has one extra row at the beginning—the row of header elements. After this, the `replace` method calls the `fillTable` function. And finally, it calls the `cancel` function to clear the text controls and reset the `property` global variable to the empty string.

Replacing the appropriate `properties` subarray and then using `fillTable` to resort and reload the table handles cases where one of the address components needs correction. If the address never changed, one could dispense with the `fillTable` function call and directly replace the values in the original table row by adding the following statement in the `replace` function's `for` loop:

```
this.row.cells[i].innerHTML = form.elements[i].value;
```

In the `deleteProperty` function, the first statement uses the table object's `deleteRow` method to delete the selected row. The second statement uses the `properties` array's `splice` method. It removes a specified range of array elements from within the array and then splices the remaining parts of the array back together so there is no gap at the point of removal. For the two-dimensional `properties` array, the range of elements is a range of subarrays, corresponding to a range of table rows. The first argument identifies the first array element (row) to extract. As in the `replace` function, the array index is one less than the table index because the array does not contain an initial header row. The second argument indicates how many elements (rows) to extract, which, in the present application, is just one.

It's worth considering one final point. The `Property` constructor's parameter, `row`, is a copy of the argument, `this`, generated by the `onclick` event handler in the clicked table row.

```
/***************************************************************
 * property.js
 * John Dean
 *
 * An object representing one real-estate property.
 * It processes replace and delete operations for the selected
 * property within the properties table.
 ***************************************************************/

class Property {
  constructor(row) {
    this.row = row;                    // table's row element and
    this.rowIndex = row.rowIndex;      // last selected index
    for (let i=0; i<5; i++) {
      form.elements[i].value = row.childNodes[i].innerHTML;
    }
    property = this;
  } // end constructor

  //*************************************************************

  // Update arrays and displayed table

  replace() {
    for (let i=0; i<5; i++) {
      properties[this.rowIndex-1][i] = form.elements[i].value;
    }
    fillTable(); // resort and repopulate in case address changed
    cancel();
  } // end replace

  // Remove current property from properties array and from table

  deleteProperty() {
    table.deleteRow(this.rowIndex);
    properties.splice(this.rowIndex-1,1);
    cancel();
  } // end deleteProperty
} // end class Property
```

**FIGURE 11.23 External JavaScript file for the `Property` class**

Because `this` refers to the clicked table row, the `Property` constructor gets a reference to the clicked table row. But if you go back to Figure 11.21 and look for `onclick` attributes in the `table` element's HTML code, you won't find any. Where are they? They're in Figure 11.22B in the JavaScript `fillTable` function that creates the table's rows of data. Specifically, here's the magic `fillTable` code that adds an `onclick` event handler to a table row:

```
row.setAttribute("onclick", "new Property(this)");
```

# Review Questions

### 11.2 Object-Oriented Programming Overview

1. What is OOP encapsulation?

2. What are the two types of members in a JavaScript object?

3. What is a class?

### 11.3 Classes, Constructors, Properties, new Operator, Methods

4. What is a constructor and what does it do?

5. To instantiate an object, what operator should you use?

### 11.4 Point Tracker Web Page

6. How is a class property different from a regular property?

### 11.5 static Methods

7. To call a regular method, you preface the method name with an object and a dot. To call a static method, what do you preface the method name with?

8. If a method does not use the this keyword, it's a good candidate for being a static method. True or false.

9. What does a null value indicate?

### 11.6 Event Handlers

10. When the user interacts with a web page, the JavaScript engine generates an event object that contains information about what the user just did. To capture the event object, you need to add an event-handler attribute to an appropriate element. What do you need to do to access the event object?

11. What is event bubbling?

### 11.7 Primitive Values Versus Objects

12. List at least four types of primitive values.

13. When an object is assigned to a variable, the variable ends up holding a reference to the object, not the object itself. True or false.

### 11.8 Using addEventListener to Add Event Listeners

14. Why do best practices sticklers favor using addEventListener instead of event-handler attributes?

### 11.9 Using Prototypes to Emulate a Class

15. When defining your own objects with legacy code, why is it beneficial to use the object's prototype when declaring methods for the object?

### 11.10 Inheritance Between Classes

16. What does a child class inherit from its parent class?

17. What's the syntax required for a subclass method to call a method in its superclass?

### 11.11 Pet Registry Web Page

18. What does it mean if a web page is scalable?

### 11.12 `switch` Statement

19. What is a key difference between the `switch` statement and an "if, else if" statement?

20. What happens if there's no `break` at the bottom of a `switch` statement's `case` block?

### 11.13 Arrays

21. The first element in an array uses index position 1. True or false.

22. The following code attempts to declare an empty array and then add an element to the array. Does it work? Yes or no.

```
prices = new Array();
prices[0] = 22.35;
```

### 11.14 Arrays of Objects

23. What is a function expression?

### 11.15 Book Club Web Page

24. To help with sorting, strings that use the "mm/dd/yyyy" format have a built-in mechanism that allows them to be compared with the < operator. True or false.

# Exercises

1. [after Section 11.3] Describe the two ways that the `this` keyword can be used.

2. [after Section 11.4] Suppose you have a `Human` class with a class property named `avgAge`.

   a) Why is it appropriate to have `avgAge` be a class property instead of a regular property?

   b) Assume that the `avgAge` property gets assigned a value only after a `Human` object gets instantiated. Provide an `if` statement for the `Human` constructor that takes care of the avgAge property for the first instantiated `Human` object. Specifically, check for `avgAge` not having a value and if that's the case, assign the `age` parameter's value to the `avgAge` property.

3. [after Section 11.6] Improve the Point Tracker web page presented earlier by displaying a colored point whenever the user clicks the mouse. Use absolute positioning to display each point at the position at which it's clicked. So if the user clicks at position $x = 220$ and $y = 331$, then you should display a point at that location on the browser window. To implement a point, display a space character with a circular border and a colored background.

   Add a `color` property to the `Point` class. Each new point should use a different background color than its predecessor. Cycle from red, to green, to blue, and then start over with red.

4. [after Section 11.6] Improve the previous exercise's web page by enabling the user to drag the points. While dragging a point, update the point's coordinates label. Clicking on the point should not activate the click listener (in other words, it should not create a new point).

5. [after Section 11.8] Suppose you have an `iAgree` variable that holds a checkbox control object. Provide an `addEventListener` method call that adds an `onchange` event handler to the checkbox. The event handler should call a function named `agree`.

6. [after Section 11.10] Refer back to Figure 11.10, which shows a class diagram for `Employee`, `PartTime`, and `FullTime` classes. Provide the class definition for the `PartTime` class. To help you out, here's the definition for the `Employee` class:

```
class Employee {
  constructor(name, id) {
    this.name = name;
    this.id = id;
  } // end constructor
} // end class Employee
```

7. [after Section 11.12] Assume the following code is part of a working web page. What message will `console.log` display?

```
var i = 0;
var msg = "";
for (; i<3; i++) {
  switch (i + i) {
    case 0:
      msg += "uno ";
      break;
    case 1: case 2:
      msg += "dos ";
    case 3:
      msg += "tres ";
```

```
     default:
        msg += "cuatro ";
   } // end switch
} // end for
console.log("msg = " + msg);
```

8. [after Section 11.13] Declare an empty `deck` array. Use a loop to fill the array with string values that represent the 52 cards of a normal deck. The numbers go from 1 to 13 with 1 for an ace, 11 for a jack, 12 for a queen, and 13 for a king. The suits are C for clubs, D for diamonds, H for hearts, and S for spades. Here's the list of 52 values:

   1C, …, 13C, 1D, …, 13D, 1H, …, 13H, 1S, …, 13S

   To test your answer, you can stick your code in a `script` container with this line at the bottom:

   ```
   console.log("deck = " + deck);
   ```

9. [after Section 11.14] The following code implements a simple web page that creates a list of cheerleader names and sorts the names. Provide an improved version of the web page that stores each cheerleader's height in centimeters and sorts the cheerleaders by height. Among other things, you'll need to implement a `Cheerleader` class with `name` and `height` properties.

   ```
   <!DOCTYPE html>
   <html lang="en">
   <head>
   <meta charset="utf-8">
   <meta name="author" content="John Dean">
   <title>Stunt Group</title>
   <script>
     var stuntGroup = new Array();

     function addCheerleader() {
       stuntGroup.push(document.getElementById("cheerleader").value);
       stuntGroup.sort();
     } // end addCheerleader

     function displayStuntGroup() {
       var namesColumn = "";

       for (let i=0; i<stuntGroup.length; i++) {
         namesColumn += stuntGroup[i] + "<br>";
       }
       document.getElementById("stunt-group").innerHTML = namesColumn;
     } // end displayStuntGroup
   ```

```
</script>
</head>


<body>
<input type="text" id="cheerleader">
<br>
<input type="button" value="Add cheerleader"
  onclick="addCheerleader();">
<br><br>
<input type="button" value="Display stunt group"
  onclick="displayStuntGroup();">
<div id="stunt-group"></div>
</body>
</html>
```

10. [after Section 11.14] Describe what happens to the bookMtgList array if the following code executes. In your answer, you must mention the 0 return value.

```
bookMtgList.sort(function (a, b) {return 0;});
```

11. [after Section 11.15] Improve the Book Club web page presented earlier by adding a **delete** button for each book meeting. When the user clicks a book meeting's **delete** button, the book meeting should be removed from the bookMtgList array, and it should disappear from the displayed schedule.

# Project

Create a web page named `statistics.html` and an accompanying external JavaScript file named `statistics.js` that calculates the mean, variance, and standard deviation for a user-entered list of numbers. Here's what your web page should look like after it first loads and the user enters a list of numbers:

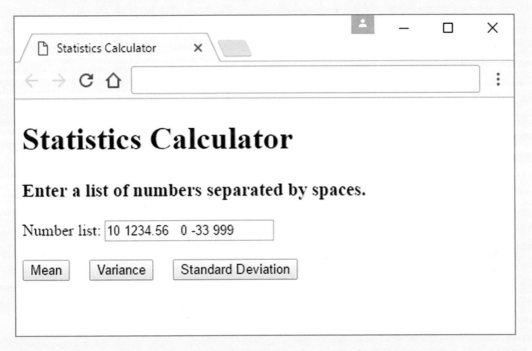

The three buttons should calculate mean, variance, and standard deviation for the user-entered list of numbers, with the result appearing below the buttons. You should perform input validation, making sure that the user enters numbers separated by one or more spaces.

To retrieve numbers from the text control, use the `split` string method as follows:

```
array-of-numbers = text-control.value.split(" ");
```

The `split` method call parses the text control's value, saves each space-separated substring as an element in an array, and returns the array.

It's up to you to display output in an aesthetically pleasing manner. If there's invalid input, display an error message below the buttons using red text. You must store the array in a `NumberList` class, and you must implement `mean`, `variance`, and `stdDeviation` methods.

# CHAPTER 12

# Canvas

## CHAPTER OBJECTIVES

- ▶ Create a canvas drawing area for a web page.
- ▶ Create and draw rectangles.
- ▶ Assign colors to a rectangle's border lines and its interior.
- ▶ Assign line width values.
- ▶ Display text on the canvas drawing area.
- ▶ Assign font and alignment values to text.
- ▶ Create and display arcs and circles, and fill their interiors.
- ▶ Draw paths by connecting line segments and arcs.

- ▶ Learn how to close subpaths.
- ▶ Implement nontrivial canvas drawings with proper coding conventions—use named constants and comments.
- ▶ Learn how to use the transformation operations—translate, rotate, and scale.
- ▶ For transformation operations, clear the canvas drawing area to prevent previously drawn shapes from leaving trails.
- ▶ Use helper functions to split up code into smaller, more manageable modules.

# CHAPTER OUTLINE

# 12.1 Introduction

Are your seat belts securely fastened? Up till now, the journey's been fun, but now it gets really fun. In this chapter, you get to experience the excitement and joy that is canvas!

Before HTML5, web programmers used tools such as applets and Flash to draw graphics objects and animate them. Although detailed explanations of applets and Flash are beyond the scope of this book, here's a brief introduction. Applets are small Java programs that embed inside web pages. Sun Microsystems developed the Java language and the applet programming model. The Oracle Corporation acquired Sun in 2010, so now Oracle is in charge of applets. Flash was a platform for making web pages with audio, video, graphics, and animation. In 2016, Flash's owner, Adobe Systems, decided to change Flash's name to Animate to distance itself from the less-than-stellar reputation associated with Flash players.

Applets and Flash were not built into browser software. So to use them, it meant end users were expected to install add-on software to their browsers. That worked, but it was an annoyance. And to make matters worse, applets and Flash were known to be security risks. In designing HTML5, the WHATWG and W3C folks addressed these problems by adding canvas to HTML. Canvas allows you to draw graphics objects (e.g., lines, rectangles, circles) and animate them, but unlike applets and Flash, canvas is built into all modern browsers, so there's no add-on software for end users to deal with.

Canvas was and is considered to be one of HTML5's most significant new features, and it has quickly gained widespread acceptance. Canvas's acceptance is illustrated by Oracle phasing out its support of applets and Adobe phasing out its support of Flash. Also, browsers no longer support applets, and browsers now turn off Flash content by default. There are other add-on tools, such as SVG, that support graphics creation and animation, but many industry practitioners think that canvas is well-positioned to be the most popular tool going forward for drawing and animating graphics objects on web pages.

# 12.2 **Canvas Syntax Basics**

To use canvas, you need (1) a `canvas` element and (2) JavaScript method calls that draw graphics objects within the `canvas` element's drawing area. Here's an example `canvas` element, which creates a 480-pixel by 250-pixel blank rectangular drawing area on a web page:

```
<body onload="rectangleExamples();">
<canvas id="canvas" width="480" height="250">
  Sorry - This page uses <code>canvas</code> and
  your browser doesn't support it.
</canvas>
</body>
```

After the web page loads, the `onload` event fires and calls the `rectangleExamples` function, which draws rectangle shapes inside the canvas drawing area. We'll examine the `rectangleExamples` function in the next section. As you might have guessed, the `canvas` element's `id` attribute allows the function to access the canvas object. Note the text that appears between the `canvas` element's tags. That's the fallback content. It gets displayed when the user's browser doesn't support the `canvas` element. If you need to support older browsers, you should include such fallback content, but because all modern browsers support canvas, we'll omit it for our upcoming examples.

Go back to the prior code fragment and verify that we use `id="canvas"` for the `canvas` element. To draw in the canvas area, the first step is for your JavaScript code to retrieve that `canvas` element's object. We do so by calling `getElementById` with "canvas" for its argument. Here's the code:

```
var canvas = document.getElementById("canvas");
```

You're not required by the browser engine to use "canvas" for the canvas element's `id` value, but "canvas" is a clear, descriptive name for the `canvas` element, so you're encouraged to use it.

After retrieving the canvas object, you can use the canvas object's `height` and `width` properties to access the `canvas` element's dimensions. But oftentimes, the only thing you'll do with the canvas object is use it as the calling object to retrieve the canvas object's *context*. The context is an object that represents the `canvas` element's drawing area. You use the context object to call methods that draw and animate graphics objects.

There are two types of canvas drawing commands—those that draw two-dimensional pictures and those that draw three-dimensional pictures. We'll keep things simple and stick with two-dimensional pictures. To create two-dimensional pictures, you retrieve the canvas's two-dimensional context like this:

```
var ctx = canvas.getContext("2d");
```

You should normally stay away from obscure abbreviations for variable names, but `ctx` is a standard abbreviation for a canvas's context, so that's what we'll use for all the upcoming canvas examples.

## 12.3 Rectangles Web Page

Take a look at the Rectangles web page in **FIGURE 12.1**. It displays four rectangles for the purpose of illustrating various drawing concepts. In examining the web page, we'll describe how to draw a rectangle and specify its position, height, width, color, and border width.

**FIGURE 12.2** shows the source code for the Rectangles web page. You can see that it includes the same `body` container that we presented in the previous section. Our primary focus will be the web page's `rectangleExamples` function, which draws the four rectangles in the canvas drawing area.

At the top of the `rectangleExamples` function, you can see that we call the `getElementById` method and then immediately call the `getContext` method. We separate the two method calls with a dot. When you concatenate two method calls with a dot, that's called *method call chaining*. Method call chaining is never required, but it can lead to compact elegant code. In the previous section, we called the `getElementById` method in a separate statement (without chaining it to the `getContext` method call), and we saved its returned canvas object in a variable. On the other hand, for the Rectangles web page, we don't bother to save the canvas object in a variable. Instead, we go with the more compact method call chaining technique.

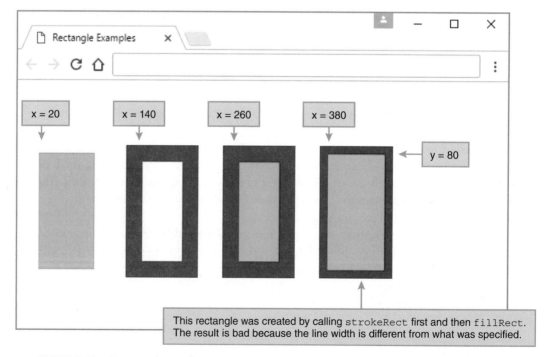

**FIGURE 12.1 Rectangles web page**

```
<!DOCTYPE html>
<html lang="en">
<head>
<meta charset="utf-8">
<meta name="author" content="John Dean">
<title>Rectangle Examples</title>
<script>
  function rectangleExamples() {
    var ctx;   // the canvas object's context
    ctx = document.getElementById("canvas").getContext("2d");
    ctx.fillStyle = "deepskyblue";
    ctx.fillRect(20, 80, 70, 140);

    ctx.lineWidth = 20;
    ctx.strokeStyle = "red";
    ctx.strokeRect(140, 80, 70, 140);

    ctx.fillRect(260, 80, 70, 140);
    ctx.strokeRect(260, 80, 70, 140);

    ctx.strokeRect(380, 80, 70, 140);
    ctx.fillRect(380, 80, 70, 140);
  } // end rectangleExamples
</script>
</head>

<body onload="rectangleExamples();">
<canvas id="canvas" width="480" height="250">
  Sorry - This page uses <code>canvas</code>, and
  your browser doesn't support it.
</canvas>
</body>
</html>
```

> Normally, it's inappropriate to call `strokeRect` first and then `fillRect`.

**FIGURE 12.2 Source code for Rectangles web page**

Go back to the Rectangles web page browser window and note that the first, third, and fourth rectangles all have blue-filled interiors. To draw a filled-in rectangle, you use the context object to call the `fillRect` method. Here's the syntax:

*context*.`fillRect`(*x*, *y*, *width*, *height*);

The *x* and *y* arguments are integers that specify the *x*, *y* coordinate position of the top-left corner of the rectangle that is to be drawn. If *x* equals 0 and *y* equals 0, then the rectangle's top-left corner will coincide with the canvas area's top-left corner. The *width* and *height* arguments are integers that specify the rectangle's width and height. For *x* and *y* position values, and width and height dimension values, JavaScript assumes units of pixels, and you do not specify units explicitly.

## Fill Color

Here's the code that draws the first rectangle in the Rectangles web page:

```
ctx.fillStyle = "deepskyblue";
ctx.fillRect(20, 80, 70, 140);
```

The `ctx` variable holds the context object for the web page's canvas drawing area. Note how we assign "deepskyblue" to the context object's `fillStyle` property. When you assign a value to the context object's `fillStyle` property, it means that subsequent shape drawing method calls will use the specified color when filling the drawn shape. So in the preceding code, when the context object calls the `fillRect` method, the JavaScript engine draws a rectangle with a fill color of deep sky blue. See the browser window and note the blue for the rectangles' fill colors. While you're at it, note the first rectangle's position and size and verify that they follow from the `fillRect` method call's 20, 80, 70, and 140 arguments. Remember that the first two arguments specify the position of the rectangle in relation to the canvas's drawing areas. With values of 20 and 80, the first rectangle's top-left corner is positioned 20 pixels to the right of the canvas area's left edge and 80 pixels down from the canvas area's top edge. The next two arguments specify the rectangle's dimensions. With values of 70 and 140, the first rectangle's width is 70 pixels and its height is 140 pixels.

The default drawing color is black. Assigning a value to the `fillStyle` property changes the fill color, and the JavaScript engine uses that new color for all future drawn shapes until the browser executes a new `fillStyle` assignment. The `fillStyle` property affects not only standard shapes like rectangles and circles, but also text characters. We'll describe how to draw text characters in a later section.

When assigning colors for canvas shapes, you can use any of the color value formats presented earlier in the CSS chapter. Here are the valid formats:

▶ color name
▶ RGB value—specifies amounts of red, green, and blue
▶ RGBA value—specifies RGB, plus the amount of opacity
▶ HSL value—specifies amounts of hue, saturation, and lightness
▶ HSLA—specifies HSL, plus the amount of opacity

For the RGB formats, the red, green, and blue values must be either (1) three integers between 0 and 255 or (2) three percentages between 0% and 100%. For the HSL formats, the hue, saturation, and lightness values must be an integer between 0 and 360 (for degrees on the hue color wheel), a percentage between 0% and 100%, and another percentage between 0% and 100%. The valid range for opacity is a number between 0.0 (fully transparent) and 1.0 (fully opaque).

## Rectangle Borders

Look again at the Rectangles web page browser window, and this time note the red borders around the second, third, and fourth rectangles. To draw a rectangle border, use the context object's `strokeRect` method. Here's its syntax:

*context*.`strokeRect(`*x, y, width, height*`)`;

The *x*, *y*, *width*, and *height* arguments work the same as with the `fillRect` method.

Here's the `strokeRect` method call for drawing the Rectangle web page's second rectangle:

```
ctx.strokeRect(140, 80, 70, 140);
```

If you go back to the browser window, you can see that the second rectangle's top-left corner is just above and to the left of the $x = 140$, $y = 80$ point specified by the `strokeRect` method call. Why isn't the rectangle's corner positioned on the $x = 140$, $y = 80$ point precisely? If the border's width was 1 pixel, then the rectangle's top-left corner would indeed be at $x = 140$, $y = 80$. But with a fat border, half of it goes on the outside of the specified rectangle's edge and half of it goes on the inside.

Here's the code that appears just above the second rectangle's `strokeRect` method call:

```
ctx.lineWidth = 20;
ctx.strokeStyle = "red";
```

In drawing a line for any shape (e.g., for a rectangle, a circle, or the border of an individual text character), the default line width is 1 pixel. To change the line width, use the `lineWidth` property. After the browser engine executes the `lineWidth` assignment statement, that line width will be used for all future line drawings until the browser engine executes a new `lineWidth` assignment. Looking at the preceding `lineWidth` assignment, you can see that subsequent lines will be drawn with a width of 20 pixels. In the Rectangles web page browser window, note the 20-pixels-wide red borders around the second and third rectangles.

The borders' red color comes from the `strokeStyle` assignment in the prior code fragment. As mentioned earlier, the default drawing color is black. To set the line color for all line drawings, assign a CSS color value to the context object's `strokeStyle` property. As with the `fillStyle` and `lineWidth` properties, after the browser executes a `strokeStyle` assignment statement, the specified line color will be used for all future line drawings until the browser executes a new `strokeStyle` assignment.

As illustrated by the Rectangle web page's second rectangle, if you call `strokeRect` and do not call `fillRect`, then nothing is drawn in the rectangle's interior, and the interior gets the same color as the fill color of the surrounding shape. If there is no surrounding shape, the interior gets the same color as the canvas background. If you want to display a rectangle's border and interior with nondefault colors, you need to call both methods: `fillRect` and `strokeRect`. Go back to the Rectangle web page's browser window and note the third rectangle, which has different colors for its border and interior. Here's the code that draws the third rectangle:

```
ctx.fillRect(260, 80, 70, 140);
ctx.strokeRect(260, 80, 70, 140);
```

If you call both methods, `fillRect` and `strokeRect`, why should you normally call `strokeRect` after `fillRect`? By calling `strokeRect` last, it draws on top of the rectangle's fill color, so `strokeRect`'s border lines display with their full widths. On the other hand, if you call `fillRect` after `strokeRect`, the inner half of the border lines gets overlaid by the fill color. Go back to the Rectangle web page's browser window and note the fourth rectangle, which is drawn by calling `fillRect` after `strokeRect`. The border lines are narrower than they should be as a result of inner overlay from the fill color.

## Using a Color Gradient to Fill a Shape

Remember when we discussed color gradients in Chapter 7? That's where you generate a continuum of two or more colors. Previously, we used color gradients to cover a web page's background. You can also apply a color gradient when drawing a shape in canvas.

Here's the syntax for retrieving a gradient object from the context object:

*context*.`createLinearGradient(`*x1, y1, x2, y2*`);`

The *x1, y1* arguments form the coordinates for the point where you can specify the first color in your gradient, and the *x2, y2* arguments form the coordinates for the point where you can specify the last color in your gradient. To specify the colors, you call the gradient object's `addColorStop` method one time for each color. Here's the syntax:

*gradient*.`addColorStop(`*offset, color*`);`

For the *color* argument, you can use any of the CSS color value formats. The *offset* argument, a number between 0 and 1, specifies where the color is positioned within the gradient's range. A 0 value indicates that the color is at the starting point formed by *x1, y1*. A 1 value indicates that the color is at the ending point formed by *x2, y2*.

For a color gradient example, let's tweak the Rectangles web page by replacing this simple `fillStyle` color assignment:

```
ctx.fillStyle = "deepskyblue";
```

With this color gradient code:

```
gradient = ctx.createLinearGradient(0, 50, 0, 250);
gradient.addColorStop(0, "green");
gradient.addColorStop(0.5, "yellow");
gradient.addColorStop(1, "blue");
ctx.fillStyle = gradient;
```

The `createLinearGradient` method call provides starting and ending points of (0, 50) and (0, 250). That specifies a straight vertical down direction for the gradient's subsequent `addColorStop` method calls. The color stops can occur anywhere between 50 and 250 pixels down from the top edge of the canvas area. Note how the `addColorStop` method calls specify green, yellow, and blue at the top, middle, and bottom of the gradient's range.

With this gradient code added, here's the resulting Rectangles web page:

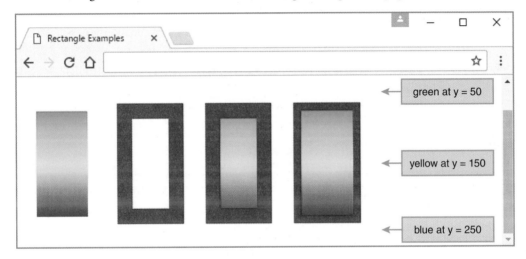

Note that a context object's gradient is global in nature in that it applies to all of the shapes drawn with the context object. For the Rectangles web page, if we add additional shapes at the right of the original shapes, they would use the same green yellow blue gradient for their interiors. If we add additional shapes below the original shapes, they would use blue for their interiors. Why? Because the colors at a gradient's starting and ending points extend all the way to the canvas area's edges. For this example, the gradient's ending point is blue, so shapes below the ending point would be blue.

## 12.4 Drawing Text with `fillText` and `strokeText`

Next up is how to draw text in the canvas drawing area. See the *1984* Quotes web page in **FIGURE 12.3**. It displays the opening and closing sentences from George Orwell's novel, *1984*.[1] For a real web page, you probably wouldn't use canvas if you just wanted to display text by itself, but we're keeping things simple for now to illustrate the concepts.

As with rectangles, when you draw text, you can draw character interiors with a fill method call or draw character borders with a stroke method call. Specifically, to draw text character interiors, use the context object's `fillText` method. Here is its syntax:

*context*.`fillText`(*text*, *x*, *y*, *max-width*);

---

[1] *1984* describes a dystopian society ruled by the privileged elite and their cult-of-personality leader, Big Brother, in which there is constant government surveillance and perpetual war.

**FIGURE 12.3** *1984* **Quotes web page**

The *text* parameter is the string that gets displayed. The *x* and *y* parameters are coordinates for the placement of the lower-left corner of the text string within the canvas drawing area. The *max-width* parameter is optional, and it specifies the maximum width of the text argument's string. If the *max-width* argument's value is less than the natural width of the string, the string does not get chopped off. Instead, the browser displays the string with a narrower font.

FIGURE 12.4 shows the code for the *1984* Quotes web page. Note the first `fillText` method call, which draws the first sentence at position *x* = 5, *y* = 30. Now go back to the browser window and verify that the sentence's lower-left corner is at that coordinate position. Note the *1984* Quotes web page's second `fillText` method call. It contains a *max-width* argument value of 350, so its string displays with a maximum width of 350 pixels. Go to the browser window and verify that the string's characters are narrow enough to accommodate the 350-pixel maximum width.

The `strokeText` method works the same as the `fillText` method except that it draws its text argument characters with borders, and it leaves the characters' interiors empty. Here is its syntax:

*context*.`strokeText`(*text, x, y, max-width*);

Note the *1984* Quotes web page's `strokeText` method call at the bottom of the `displayQuotes` event-handler function. Then go to the browser window and verify that the bottom quote's characters are drawn with borders. The `strokeText` method call contains a *max-width* argument value of 350. That's the same as for the prior `fillText` method call, but for the `strokeText` method call, the *max-width* value of 350 pixels is greater than the text argument's natural string width, so the text's string is displayed with a normal (non-narrow) font.

```
<!DOCTYPE html>
<html lang="en">
<head>
<meta charset="utf-8">
<meta name="author" content="John Dean">
<title>George Orwell's 1984</title>
<script>
  function displayQuotes() {
    var ctx;  // the canvas object's context

    ctx = document.getElementById("canvas").getContext("2d");
    ctx.font = "2em 'Times New Roman', serif";
    ctx.fillText("\"The clocks were striking thirteen.\"", 5, 30);
    ctx.textAlign = "center";
    ctx.fillText("\"The clocks were striking thirteen.\"", 300, 110, 350);
    ctx.strokeText("\"He loved Big Brother.\"", 300, 160, 350);
  } // end displayMsg
</script>
</head>

<body onload="displayQuotes();">
<canvas id="canvas" width="600" height="170">
</canvas>
</body>
</html>
```

This draws the first sentence at position x = 5, y = 30.

Center alignment around x = 300.

This redraws the first sentence with a maximum width of 350 pixels.

**FIGURE 12.4 Source code for *1984* Quotes web page**

# 12.5 **Formatting Text**

In using `fillText` and `strokeText`, there are lots of ways to customize the drawn text. Before calling either method, you can assign values to the `linewidth`, `fillStyle`, and `strokeStyle` properties. They have the same effect on text as they do on rectangles. The `lineWidth` property specifies the width in pixels of the border lines for text characters. The `fillStyle` and `strokeStyle` properties specify the color for text characters' interiors and border lines, respectively. To further customize your text drawings, you can assign values to the `font`, `textAlign`, and `textBaseline` properties. As with the context object's other formatting properties, each of these additional properties specifies the format for all subsequent drawn text until the property gets reassigned to a different value.

## `font` **Property**

Go back to the *1984* Quotes web page browser window and note that the characters are larger than normal. We expanded the font size by using the context object's `font` property. The context object's font property uses the same syntax as the CSS font property. Remember that the CSS font property is a shorthand property that subsumes all of the more granular CSS font-oriented properties? Specifically, it subsumes the font-style, font-variant, font-weight, font-size, line-height, and font-family properties. For details on each of those properties, refer back to Chapter 3.

Here's the syntax for assigning font values to the context object's font property:

*context*.font = [*font-style-value*]  [*font-variant-value*]  [*font-weight-value*]
        *font-size-value* [ / *line-height-value*]  *font-family-value* ;

As usual, the italics are the book's way of telling you that the italicized thing is a description of what goes there, so you would replace *font-style-value* with one of the font-style values, such as italic. The square brackets are the book's way of telling you that the bracketed thing is optional, so the font-style, font-variant, font-weight, and line-height values are all optional. On the other hand, the font-size and font-family values have no square brackets, so you must include them whenever you use the font property. For the property values you decide to include, they must appear in the order shown. If a line-height value is included, you must position it at the right of the font-size value, with a / separating the two values.

Here's the font property assignment from the *1984* Quotes web page:

```
ctx.font = "2em 'Times New Roman', serif";
```

In this rule, the right-hand side includes values for the two required granular font values, font-size and font-family, and no other granular font values. The 2em value means the font size will be twice as big as the default for plain text on a web page. The default value for the font property is 10px sans-serif. The 10-pixel font size is significantly smaller than the default for plain text on a web page, so you'll probably want to assign a value to the font property whenever you draw text with canvas.

As you've seen with rectangles and again with text, when you draw a shape and specify the shape's position (with *x* and *y* arguments), JavaScript assumes units of pixels, and you do not specify units explicitly. That's also the case for a shape's dimensions (with width, height, and radius arguments), if the shape has dimensions. But for text font size, JavaScript does not assume units; it's up to the programmer to provide units like you've seen with CSS (e.g., 2em for twice the current default character size or 10px for 10 pixels).

By the way, after introducing the CSS font shorthand property in Chapter 3, we haven't used it because its syntax is rather confusing. Instead, we've been using the more granular font properties (e.g., font-style, font-variant). But those granular font properties don't exist for the context object, so with canvas, you have to use the context object's font property.

## textAlign **Property**

In introducing the fillText and strokeText methods, we said that the *x* and *y* argument values specified the coordinate position of the displayed text's lower-left corner. That's the default, but you can adjust where the *x, y* point is positioned within the text. By doing that, you can adjust the text's horizontal and vertical alignment.

Let's start with horizontal alignment. Go back to the *1984* Quotes web page browser window and note that the second and third quotes are center aligned. We center aligned the text by assigning `center` to the context object's `textAlign` property. The default alignment is left alignment. If you want to specify left alignment explicitly, assign `left` or `start` to the context object's `textAlign` property. If you want to specify right alignment, assign `right` or `end` to the context object's `textAlign` property.

Here's the `textAlign` property assignment that turns on center alignment for the second and third quotes on the *1984* Quotes web page:

```
ctx.textAlign = "center";
```

Remember that once a context object's formatting property gets assigned, that assigned value remains on for all subsequent drawn text until the property gets reassigned. So in the *1984* Quotes web page, we position the center alignment code above the second quote's `fillText` method call, and the center alignment remains on for the third quote's `strokeText` method call.

After center alignment is turned on, how does the JavaScript engine know what to use as the horizontal center point for the center-aligned text? In the `fillText` and `strokeText` method calls, the *x* argument serves as an anchor point for positioning the text horizontally. So for center alignment, the *x* value will be at the center of subsequently drawn text. For left alignment, the *x* value will be at the left of subsequently drawn text, and for right alignment, the *x* value will be at the right of subsequently drawn text. The *1984* Quotes web page's second quote uses center alignment, so its `fillText` method call's *x* argument value of 300 means that the quote is centered horizontally around *x* = 300. Here's the `fillText` method call:

```
ctx.fillText("\"The clocks were striking thirteen.\"", 300, 110, 350);
```

## textBaseline Property

Remember that with `fillText` and `strokeText`, the default behavior is for the *x* and *y* argument values to specify the coordinate position of the displayed text's lower-left corner. In the previous subsection, you learned how to change the default meaning of the *x* argument. To adjust where *x* is positioned relative to the text—center, left, or right—you use the `textAlign` property. Likewise, to adjust where *y* is positioned relative to the text—bottom, middle, or top—you use the `textBaseline` property.

The `textBaseline` property allows you to adjust the position of text up or down relative to the `fillText` or `strokeText` method call's *y* argument. The up or down adjustment can be described as vertical alignment, but that description doesn't help all that much. The best way to understand what's going on is by viewing a picture of text in relation to the *y* argument for different values of the `textBaseline` property. See **FIGURE 12.5** for such a picture. The green lines show the *y* positions for each text string's baseline, so the top green line is at *y* = 40, the next green line is at *y* = 80, and so on.

In the Text Baseline Examples web page, the letters look normal (no borders), so that means we used `fillText`, not `strokeText`, to draw the text strings. As you can see from the text messages themselves, the four text strings are drawn with different `textBaseline` values— `alphabetic`, `bottom`, `middle`, and `top`. Note how the different baseline values affect how the text strings are positioned relative to their respective *y*-argument green lines.

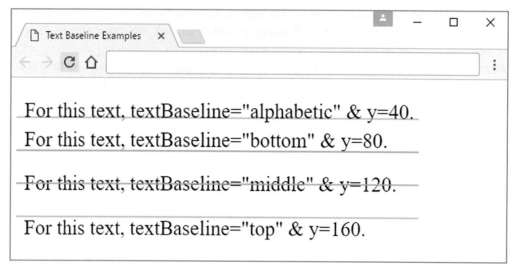

FIGURE 12.5 **Text Baseline Examples web page**

The `alphabetic` and `bottom` values are similar, but not identical. With the `alphabetic` value, the *y* value is positioned at the standard alphabetic baseline, which means at the bottom of most characters. With the bottom value, the *y* value is positioned at the bottom of the hanging characters, like a lowercase *g*.

In an end-of-chapter exercise, you're asked to provide the JavaScript function that generates the content for the Text Baseline Examples web page. We don't want to spoil your exercise fun, but here's the code for drawing the first text string:

```
ctx.textBaseline = "alphabetic";
ctx.fillText("For this text, textBaseline=\"alphabetic\" & y=40.", 10, 40);
```

The `alphabetic` value is the default for the `textBaseline` property, so we could have omitted the `textBaseline` assignment. But we prefer to keep it as a form of self-documentation. Also, it allows you to add a prior `textBaseline` assignment with a different alignment value without fear of messing up the standard alphabetic baseline alignment for the original first text string.

## 12.6 Drawing Arcs and Circles

Next up is how to draw arcs and circles in the canvas drawing area. So, what is an arc in geometry? It's any curved line that does not connect at the ends. The `arc` method creates geometrical arcs, but it's limited to creating arcs that could be part of a circle (where a circle is defined as a set of points that are equidistant from the circle's center). And unlike a geometrical arc, the `arc` method's arcs can be connected at the ends. If the ends are connected, what is the result called? A circle! So the `arc` method can create the partial or full perimeter of a circle.

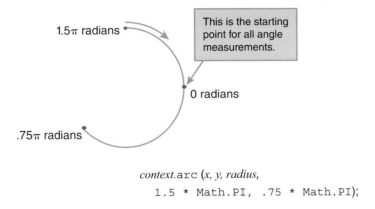

FIGURE 12.6 **How angles are determined for the context object's `arc` method**

## Creating an Arc or Circle with the `arc` Method

Here's the `arc` method's syntax:

```
context.arc(x, y, radius, start-angle, end-angle, counterclockwise);
```

The *x* and *y* arguments are coordinates for the arc's center point. The *radius* argument is the distance from the center to any point on the arc. The *start-angle* and *end-angle* arguments are the arc's starting and ending angles, in radians. **FIGURE 12.6** shows how angle values are determined for the *startangle* and *endangle* arguments. The start and end angles are measured in the clockwise direction with a value of 0 at the 3 o'clock position of the arc's circle. In the figure, note the `arc` method call with a value of 1.5 * `Math.PI` for its start-angle argument. That value represents the point at the top of the arc. Why? If you start at the 3 o'clock position (the red dot on the right side of the arc) and you go clockwise and stop at the top of the arc, that's three-fourths of the way around the circle. You might recall from grade school that there are $2\pi$ radians in a circle. Three-quarters of $2\pi$ radians is $1.5\pi$ radians.

To create a full circle, you should specify 0 and $2\pi$ for the two angles. Alternatively, you could create a circle with any pair of angles that are at least $2\pi$ apart, but 0 and $2\pi$ are standard, and sticking to standard code improves readability. If you specify angles that are the same (i.e., 0 and 0), then no arc is created.

By default, the `arc` method creates an arc by moving in the clockwise direction from the *start-angle* to the *end-angle*. If you want to go in the counterclockwise direction, specify true for the `arc` method's *counterclockwise* argument. The *counterclockwise* argument does not affect how the *start-angle* and *end-angle* arguments are specified. Positive angle values are always measured in the clockwise direction. The *counterclockwise* argument is optional. If you don't specify a value for it, or if you specify false for it, then the `arc` method creates an arc by moving in the clockwise direction.

## Displaying the Created Arc/Circle

Calling the `arc` method creates an arc or circle, but you need to do more than just create it. If used by itself, the `arc` method won't cause the created shape to display. To display it, you need to call the context object's `stroke` method, like this:

```
context.arc(x, y, radius, start-angle, end-angle, counterclockwise);
context.stroke();
```

Previously, you learned that with rectangles and text, you can draw their interiors by calling `fillRect` and `fillText`, respectively. Likewise, with arcs, you can draw their interiors by calling the context object's `fill` method. Here's an example that creates a circle, draws its interior, and then draws the circle itself:

```
ctx.strokeStyle = "darkviolet";
ctx.fillStyle = "lavender";
ctx.lineWidth = 4;
ctx.arc(80, 35, 25, 0, 2 * Math.PI);
ctx.fill();    ◄──────────  This draws the circle's interior.
ctx.stroke();
```

Here's the resulting browser window:

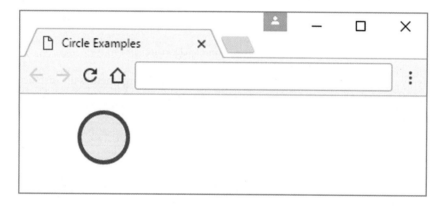

In the preceding code fragment, note how we assign values to the `strokeStyle`, `fillStyle`, and `lineWidth` properties before calling the `fill` and `stroke` methods. Those properties work the same as with rectangles and text. Note how we call `fill` before `stroke`. Why is that the norm? So the circle's border line overlays the fill color, and the line displays with its full specified width.

When the `fill` method is called for an arc that is not closed, the browser forms an invisible straight line between the arc's end points, and then it fills the newly enclosed area. For example, suppose you use the preceding code, but modify the `arc` method call, like this:

```
ctx.arc(80, 35, 25, .5 * Math.PI, 1.5 * Math.PI);
ctx.fill();
ctx.stroke();
```

With starting and ending angles of .5π and 1.5π, the arc forms only half a circle, so it's an unclosed arc. The `fill` method call connects the arc's end points and fills the interior like this:

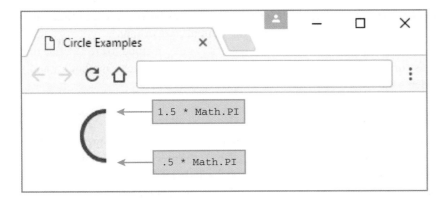

## More Complicated Curves

The arc method is the simplest way to create curves with canvas. Canvas's context object provides additional methods that let you create more complicated curves, but their details are beyond the scope of this book. If you have time, we encourage you to look up the arcTo, quadraticCurveTo, and bezierCurveTo methods. Briefly, all three methods enable you to create a curve that is tangent to two lines, thus helping you to create a smooth curve transition (a corner) between the two lines. The arcTo method generates a circular arc, which means there's a center point that is equidistant from the arc's points. The quadraticCurveTo method generates a curve that's defined by a quadratic function. The bezierCurveTo method generates a curve that's defined by a cubic function. A quadratic function is a function in which the highest-degree term is raised to the power of 2. A cubic function is a function in which the highest-degree term is raised to the power of 3. Using a cubic function can lead to a smoother-looking curve, but generating such a curve is more computationally expensive than generating a quadratic curve.

## 12.7 Drawing Lines and Paths

In the previous section, you learned how to draw curved lines with the arc method. It's also important to learn how to draw straight lines. Sometimes, you'll need to display straight lines by themselves. For more complicated drawings, you'll need to display straight lines that connect to themselves and to curved lines. In this section, you'll learn how to draw standalone lines, as well as lines that connect to other lines to form paths.

### Drawing a Line Segment

To draw a standalone line segment, you first need to move to the position where you want to start drawing the line. You do that by calling the context object's moveTo method with *x* and *y* argument values for the starting position. Here's the syntax:

```
context.moveTo(starting-x, starting-y);
```

The moveTo method moves the drawing pen. It's referred to as a *pen* because it's like lifting a pen or pencil from a piece of paper and moving it where you want to start writing.

After moving the pen, you then call the context object's lineTo method to create a line that spans from the pen's current position to the position specified by the lineTo method's *x* and *y* argument values. Here's the syntax:

```
context.lineTo(ending-x, ending-y);
```

In addition to creating a line, the lineTo method moves the pen to the line's ending position. So if you draw another line, the new line's starting position will be at the previous line's ending position.

Remember that you create arcs by calling the arc method and display arcs by calling the stroke method. It's the same with lines. After calling the lineTo method, you display the line by calling the stroke method. Note this example, which creates and displays a horizontal line that extends from the point at (50, 100) to the point at (250, 100).

```
ctx.moveTo(50, 100);
ctx.lineTo(250, 100);
ctx.stroke();
```

By default, the stroke method produces black lines with a width of 1 pixel. To modify the color, use the context object's strokeStyle property. To modify the width, use the context object's lineWidth property. That should sound familiar—the same as with rectangles and arcs.

## Drawing a Path with Straight Line Segments

Now that you know how to draw a line segment, let's connect them together to form a path. Formally, a canvas *path* is a list of points with some or all of the points connected with straight or curved lines. The first step in creating a path is to call the beginPath method. After that, you create straight and/or curved lines with the moveTo, lineTo, and arc methods. At the end, you call the stroke method to display the path.

We'll start with a simple path where the points are all connected with straight lines. Here's the syntax:

```
context.beginPath();
context.moveTo(x, y);
context.lineTo(x, y);
 .
 .
 .
context.lineTo(x, y);
context.stroke();
```

After beginPath, note the moveTo method call. As you know, the moveTo method moves the drawing pen to establish the starting position of the subsequent lineTo method's line segment. It's required before the first lineTo method call. Use it before another lineTo method call only if you'd like to have a gap in front of that lineTo's line segment. For example, here's how you can draw a dashed line with three segments:

```
ctx.strokeStyle = "red";
ctx.lineWidth = 4;
ctx.beginPath();
ctx.moveTo(40, 20);
ctx.lineTo(80, 20);
ctx.moveTo(90, 20);
ctx.lineTo(130, 20);
ctx.moveTo(140, 20);
ctx.lineTo(180, 20);
ctx.stroke();
```

And here's the resulting browser window:

In the preceding code fragment, the first thing we did was to assign red to the `strokeStyle` property and 4 to the `lineWidth` property. If you move those assignments below the call to `beginPath`, the end result will be the same. So why do we have a slight preference for positioning the assignments above the `beginPath` method call? It's a style thing. The assignments remain in effect after the path has been drawn. Having the assignments above the `beginPath` method call (i.e., outside the path) serves as a reminder to the reader that the assignments remain in effect.

## Closing a Path

In forming a path, sometimes you'll want to close the path so a line segment connects back to an earlier point in the path. You can do that with an explicit `lineTo` method call, but as a more elegant alternative, you can call the context object's `closePath` method. Specifically, the `closePath` method connects the most recently created line's end point to the most recently created subpath's starting point. But what's a subpath, you ask? A *subpath* is established automatically every time you call `beginPath` or `moveTo`. Let's put this into practice by drawing a triangle. In the following code fragment, note how we create two lines explicitly by calling `lineTo` twice. We then create the triangle's third line implicitly by calling `closePath`. In closing the path, the JavaScript engine goes back to the most recent subpath starting point, which is defined as (60, 20) by the preceding `moveTo` method call.

```
ctx.strokeStyle = "red";
ctx.lineWidth = 4;
ctx.beginPath();
ctx.moveTo(60, 20);
ctx.lineTo(40, 60);
ctx.lineTo(80, 60);
ctx.closePath();
ctx.stroke();
```

Here's the resulting browser window:

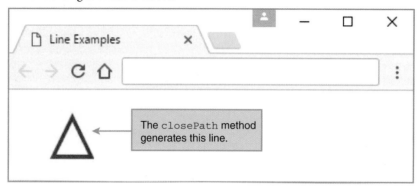

Suppose you want to add a second triangle to the web page. This code does that:

```
ctx.strokeStyle = "red";
ctx.lineWidth = 4;
ctx.beginPath();
ctx.moveTo(60, 20);
ctx.lineTo(40, 60);
ctx.lineTo(80, 60);
ctx.closePath();

ctx.moveTo(160, 20);
ctx.lineTo(140, 60);
ctx.lineTo(180, 60);
ctx.closePath();
ctx.stroke();
```

Move the pen to the second triangle.

Here's the resulting browser window:

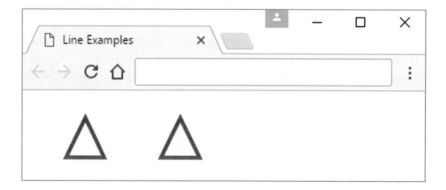

In the preceding code fragment, note how we call `moveTo` to lift the pen and move it to the second triangle's starting point. If you don't call `moveTo`, the pen won't get lifted when it moves to the second triangle, and the pen will draw an ugly connecting line between the two triangles.

## Splitting a Path

Suppose you want different colors for the two triangles. Your first inclination might be to simply assign a new color to the strokeStyle property after moving the pen. It sounds reasonable, but it won't work. If you assign red to strokeStyle at the beginning of a path and reassign it to blue later in the same path, when you call stroke at the end of the path, the JavaScript engine uses the current color value (blue) to draw the entire path. Likewise, if you assign a value to lineWidth at the beginning of a path and assign a larger value to lineWidth later in the same path, when you call stroke at the end of the path, the JavaScript engine uses the current larger width to draw the entire path.

So if you want to change the line properties for a drawing, you need to split the path into multiple paths. And for each of the resulting smaller paths, you call beginPath at the start of the path and call stroke at the end of the path. For example, the following code is the same as before, except for the three inserted lines in the middle. Note how the code calls the stroke method at the end of the first path, assigns blue to strokeStyle, and then calls beginPath at the start of the second path.

```
ctx.strokeStyle = "red";
ctx.lineWidth = 4;
ctx.beginPath();
ctx.moveTo(60, 20);
ctx.lineTo(40, 60);
ctx.lineTo(80, 60);
ctx.closePath();
ctx.stroke();

ctx.strokeStyle = "blue";        Split the path so the
ctx.beginPath();                 color can change.
ctx.moveTo(160, 20);
ctx.lineTo(140, 60);
ctx.lineTo(180, 60);
ctx.closePath();
ctx.stroke();
```

Here's the resulting browser window:

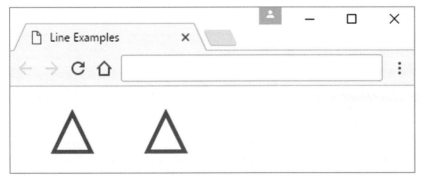

In the preceding code, what happens if you forget to call `beginPath` before creating the second triangle? When the JavaScript engine executes the first `stroke` method call (after the first `closePath` method call), the `strokeStyle` property is red, so the triangle is drawn with red lines. So far, so good. But the second `stroke` method call does something unexpected. Whenever the JavaScript engine executes a `stroke` method, it looks for the starting point of the current path and begins drawing from there. So in this example, if you don't call `beginPath` before creating the second triangle, the second `stroke` method goes all the way back to the first triangle's `beginPath` method call and draws from there. That means the first triangle gets redrawn. And this time, the current `strokeStyle` color is blue, so both triangles get drawn with blue. That's not good! So the moral of the story is, to display a line with its own line properties, remember to call `beginPath` at the beginning and call `stroke` at the end.

## 12.8 Umbrella Web Page

As stated earlier, you can form a path with straight or curved lines. In the previous section, we used only straight lines for our path examples. In this section, we use both types of lines.

### Single-Path Simple Umbrella

Let's jump right into an example. See **FIGURE 12.7**'s Simple Umbrella web page. The umbrella is very basic because for now, we're trying to keep the focus on path details and not get bogged down in presentation details.

In the figure, you can see two shapes—the semicircle for the umbrella's canopy and the vertical line for the umbrella's shaft. Because the shapes have the same line properties (color = black, width = 6 pixels), we use one path for both shapes. Take a look at **FIGURE 12.8**, which shows the web page's source code. Note how we begin the path by calling `beginPath`, and

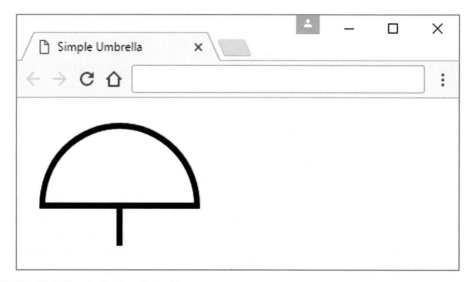

FIGURE 12.7 **Simple Umbrella web page**

```
<!DOCTYPE html>
<html lang="en">
<head>
<meta charset="utf-8">
<meta name="author" content="John Dean">
<title>Simple Umbrella</title>
<script>
  function draw() {
    var ctx;  // the canvas object's context

    ctx = document.getElementById("canvas").getContext("2d");
    ctx.lineWidth = 6;
    ctx.beginPath();
    ctx.moveTo(100, 100);
    ctx.lineTo(100, 140);

    ctx.moveTo(100, 100);
    ctx.arc(100, 100, 80, Math.PI, 2 * Math.PI);
    ctx.closePath();
    ctx.stroke();
  } // end draw
</script>
</head>

<body onload="draw();">
<canvas id="canvas" width="300" height="145">
</canvas>
</body>
</html>
```

**FIGURE 12.8 Source code for Simple Umbrella web page**

then we create the vertical line by calling moveTo and lineTo. Next, we move the pen to the bottom-left corner of the canopy by calling moveTo. Then we create the semicircle by calling the arc and closePath methods. Finally, we call the stroke method.

## Two-Path Improved Umbrella

Now that you see how easy it is to draw a simple umbrella with a single path that uses both a straight line and a curved line, let's get fancy and draw a two-toned umbrella with a shallow canopy. See the Improved Umbrella web page in **FIGURE 12.9**.

Because the improved umbrella uses different colors and line widths for its vertical line and filled arc shapes, we need separate paths for the two shapes. In **FIGURE 12.10**'s draw function, note the stroke method call at the end of the vertical line's path and the beginPath method call at the beginning of the filled arc's path. And between those method calls, you can see how we update the line and fill properties with assignments to strokeStyle, lineWidth, and fillStyle.

Refer back to the Simple Umbrella web page's source code and note the moveTo method call above the arc method call. That moveTo is necessary so the pen doesn't draw a line from the pen's previous position (at the bottom of the umbrella's shaft) to the new position (at the left of the

**FIGURE 12.9 Improved Umbrella web page**

umbrella's canopy). Now look at the Improved Umbrella web page's source code and note that there's no moveTo method call above the arc method call. Why the difference? Because the Improved Umbrella web page calls the beginPath method before calling the arc method. With the beginning of a new path, there's no attempt to connect from the pen's previous position to the upcoming shape. Instead, the pen starts anew, with its starting point dictated by the code that follows the beginPath method call. For the Improved Umbrella web page, there's an arc method call after the beginPath method call. Recall that the arc method contains *x* and *y* arguments for the arc's center point, as well as radius and starting-angle arguments. Together, those arguments dictate where the pen starts.

## Trigonometry for the Umbrella's Canopy

In the Simple Umbrella web page, we used $\pi$ and $2\pi$ for the arc method's starting and ending angles, thus forming a semicircle. Creating the semicircle was easy, but it doesn't represent the true shape of an umbrella canopy. Most umbrella canopies form circle segments that are shallower than a semicircle. So in Figure 12.10's improved umbrella code, we create the canopy shape with an arc method call that uses $1.2\pi$ and $1.8\pi$ for the starting and ending angles. That creates the desired shallow circle segment for the umbrella canopy.

We pick $1.2\pi$ and $1.8\pi$ for the arc's starting and ending angles because (1) we want angles that lead to a segment smaller than a semicircle, and (2) we want angles that are equidistant from $1.5\pi$. Why $1.5\pi$? $1.5\pi$ is the top of an arc's circle, and we want the arc's end points to be centered around the top of the arc's circle.

In Figure 12.10, after calling the arc method, we call the closePath method to connect the arc's end points, and that connecting line serves as the base of the umbrella's canopy. The trickiest part of the web page's code is finding the point on the connecting line that serves as the top of the umbrella's shaft. Finding that point requires a little trigonometry. So dust off your old high school trig book and get ready for a trip down memory lane.

```
<!DOCTYPE html>
<html lang="en">
<head>
<meta charset="utf-8">
<meta name="author" content="John Dean">
<title>Improved Umbrella</title>
<script>
  function draw() {
    var ctx;    // the canvas object's context
    var offset; // distance from circle's center to bottom of
                // umbrella's canopy

    ctx = document.getElementById("canvas").getContext("2d");
    offset = Math.sin(.2 * Math.PI) * 80;
    ctx.strokeStyle = "silver";
    ctx.lineWidth = 6;
    ctx.beginPath();
    ctx.moveTo(100, 100 - offset);      Move pen to top of
    ctx.lineTo(100, 120);               umbrella's shaft.
    ctx.stroke();

    ctx.strokeStyle = "bisque";
    ctx.lineWidth = 1;
    ctx.fillStyle = "lightseagreen";
    ctx.beginPath();
    ctx.arc(100, 100, 80, 1.2 * Math.PI, 1.8 * Math.PI);
    ctx.closePath();
    ctx.fill();          the arc's radius
    ctx.stroke();
  } // end draw
</script>
</head>

<body onload="draw();">
<canvas id="canvas" width="300" height="135">
</canvas>
</body>
</html>
```

**FIGURE 12.10 Source code for Improved Umbrella web page**

Take a look at **FIGURE 12.11**'s semicircle arc. Note how we move the arc's end points up by .2$\pi$ on both sides. That positions the compressed arc's end points at 1.2$\pi$ and 1.8$\pi$, which is what we use for the umbrella web page's `arc` method call. In connecting the compressed arc's end points, you can see a circle segment that matches the umbrella canopy's shape. The goal is to find offset, the distance from the canopy's base to the arc's center point. After finding offset, we can find the top of the umbrella's shaft with this formula:

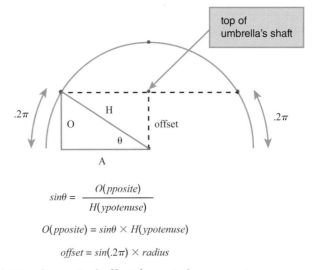

$$sin\theta = \frac{O(pposite)}{H(ypotenuse)}$$

$$O(pposite) = sin\theta \times H(ypotenuse)$$

$$offset = sin(.2\pi) \times radius$$

**FIGURE 12.11 Calculating the vertical offset for a circle segment**

Shaft's top point *y* value = Arc's center point *y* value − Offset

To find the offset, we need to examine Figure 12.11's right triangle, which you can see circumscribed within the semicircle arc. Note the triangle's θ angle, which is the amount that the semicircle arc moves up to form the left-side point for the umbrella canopy's shape. You can see that θ equals .2π radians. The right triangle has three sides labeled H, O, and A. The H side is the triangle's hypotenuse (H for hypotenuse). The O side is the side opposite from the angle θ (O for opposite). The A side is the side adjacent to the angle θ (A for adjacent). We need to find the length of the O side, because that length matches the offset's value.

Given a right triangle, if you know the angle θ and you know one of the three sides' lengths, you can find the other sides' lengths with the help of SOHCAHTOA. Does that sound familiar? I learned it as a sophomore in high school, and it's paid dividends ever since. SOHCAHTOA stands for:

sine opposite hypotenuse     cosine adjacent hypotenuse     tangent opposite adjacent

Each of the three triples helps you to remember the relationship between one of the trigonometric functions and two of the triangle's sides. Here are those relationships:

| SOH | sine opposite hypotenuse | $\sin(\theta) = \dfrac{opposite}{hypotenuse}$ |
| --- | --- | --- |
| CAH | cosine adjacent hypotenuse | $\cos(\theta) = \dfrac{adjacent}{hypotenuse}$ |
| TOA | tangent opposite adjacent | $\tan(\theta) = \dfrac{opposite}{adjacent}$ |

Looking back at the circumscribed right triangle in Figure 12.11, we need to find the length of the O side, because that length matches the offset's value. We know the length of the H side to be 80 (H is the arc's radius, and you can see 80 for the radius argument in Figure 12.10's `arc` method call). Because O and H are the sides we're interested in, which of the three equations will help us? The SOH equation uses O and H, so that's the equation we need.

We've already established that θ equals .2π radians, so here's the SOH equation with θ and hypotenuse values filled in:

$$\sin(.2\pi) = \frac{opposite}{80}$$

Solving for opposite:

$$opposite = \sin(.2\pi) \times 80$$

Remembering that offset's length equals the opposite side's length, here's the comparable JavaScript code from Figure 12.10:

```
offset = Math.sin(.2 * Math.PI) * 80;
```

There's your trigonometry refresher. Now you're ready to calculate all sorts of side lengths and angles for your future canvas arc adventures. How exciting!

## 12.9 **Face Web Page**

So far in this chapter, we've introduced constructs with one simple web page for each new construct. That helped us clarify each construct's syntax and semantics. But in the interest of keeping our focus narrow, we glossed over a few style issues. In this section, we present a web page that uses many of the constructs covered previously, and it emphasizes style issues that are important for canvas code.

See the Face Web Page in **FIGURE 12.12**. The outer black rectangle shows the canvas area's border. The border is normally invisible, but while we're building the web page, we make the border visible (with a CSS rule shown in **FIGURE 12.13**) to provide a reference for the shapes' positions within the canvas drawing area. Note the green callouts that indicate the *x* and *y* coordinate positions of those shapes relative to the canvas drawing area.

Looking at the Face web page, can you think of the methods used to generate the Hello heading, the face circle, the eyes, and the mouth? We use the `fillText` method to generate the Hello heading, the `arc` method to generate the face circle, the `strokRect` method to generate the eyes, and the `moveTo` and `lineTo` methods to generate the mouth. Take a look at the Face web page's `initialize` function in **FIGURE 12.14** and identify those method calls. Nothing tricky—this is just a sanity check.

Notice that the canvas JavaScript code is in its own external file. Normally, if you're bothering to use canvas, you'll have a significant amount of JavaScript code, and that code should go in an external file. As we've mentioned before, you should always have a prologue at the top of an external JavaScript file, and you should always have a description above each function. Verify that the Face web page's JavaScript file has those things.

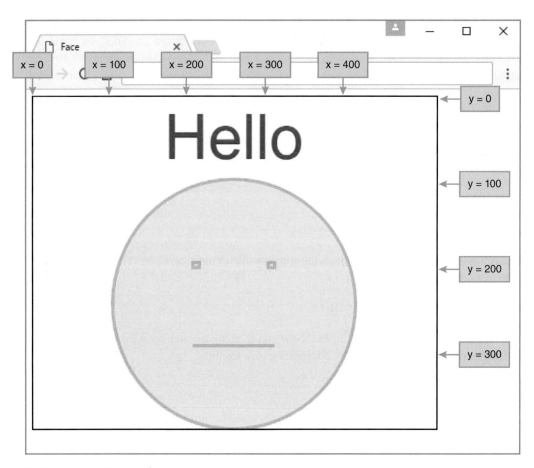

FIGURE 12.12 **Face web page**

Notice that we define named constants for the circle's center point, the circle's radius, the width of each eye, and so on. Using named constants instead of hardcoded constants means that the code is easier to understand. In particular, using named constants for shape positions and shape dimensions makes your web page drawings scalable. If you want to change a shape's position or size, it's easy. You do it in one place, using the named constants at the top of the canvas code.

Notice how we partition the code for the shapes into separate groups, and above each group, we include a comment heading. Note the comment headings for the circle, the eyes, and the mouth. And note the blank lines above the comment headings, so the heading descriptions stand out.

Note that the eyes' interiors are yellow. We could have generated that yellow fill color by calling fillRect, but it was unnecessary. Because the eyes are inside the circle, the eyes inherit their yellow fill color from the circle.

Note that we don't have separate named constants for the positions of the eyes and mouth. Instead, we position the eyes and mouth relative to the circle's center point and radius. That way, if

```
<!DOCTYPE html>
<html lang="en">
<head>
<meta charset="utf-8">
<meta name="author" content="John Dean">
<title>Face</title>
<style>
  canvas {border: this solid black;}
</style>
<script src="face.js"></script>
</head>

<body onload="initialize();">
<canvas id="canvas" width="500" height="400">
</canvas>
</body>
</html>
```

Make the drawing area's border visible.

**FIGURE 12.13 HTML file for Face web page**

we adjust the face circle's position or size later on, the eyes and mouth get adjusted automatically. For example, here's how we draw the left eye and then the right eye:

```
ctx.strokeRect(CENTER_X - RADIUS / 3,
   CENTER_Y - RADIUS / 3, EYE_WIDTH, EYE_HEIGHT);
ctx.strokeRect(CENTER_X + RADIUS / 3 - EYE_WIDTH,
   CENTER_Y - RADIUS / 3, EYE_WIDTH, EYE_HEIGHT);
```

In the preceding code, you can see that the left eye is positioned at the left of the center point by subtracting one-third of the RADIUS value from the CENTER_X value. And you can also see that the right eye is positioned at the right of the center point by adding one-third of the RADIUS value to the CENTER_X value. But after adding one-third of the RADIUS value to the CENTER_X value, we subtract the EYE_WIDTH value. Why? Because the strokeRect method call starts drawing from the rectangle's top-left corner. So to center the eyes horizontally around the face circle's center point, we need to move the right eye rectangle's starting position to the left by the width of the eye. That way, its right edge is one-third of the RADIUS value to the right of the CENTER_X value. That means the left eye rectangle's left edge and the right eye rectangle's right edge are equidistant from the circle's center point. Yay!

# 12.10 Using Canvas for Transformations

After drawing graphics objects, wouldn't it be fun to move them around? Canvas lets you do that. In this section, you'll learn how to move graphics objects in a straight line, rotate them, and scale them. You'll learn how to initiate those *transformation operations* as part of an event handler when the user

```
/****************************************************
 * face.js
 * John Dean
 *
 * This file handles drawing a face.
 ****************************************************/

// This function draws the initial face.

function initialize() {
  // x and y coordinates for the face's center point.
  const CENTER_X = 250;
  const CENTER_Y = 250;
  const RADIUS = 150;        // face's radius
  const TITLE_BASELINE = 75; // y value for title's baseline
  const EYE_WIDTH = 8;
  const EYE_HEIGHT = 6;

  var ctx;  // the canvas object's context

  ctx = document.getElementById("canvas").getContext("2d");
  ctx.fillStyle = "blue";
  ctx.textAlign = "center";
  ctx.font = "75px Arial, sans-serif";
  ctx.fillText("Hello", CENTER_X, TITLE_BASELINE);

  ctx.strokeStyle = "orange";
  ctx.fillstyle = "yellow";
  ctx.lineWidth = 4;

  // draw circle
  ctx.beginPath();
  ctx.arc(CENTER_X, CENTER_Y, RADIUS, 0, 2 * Math.PI);
  ctx.fill();
  ctx.stroke();

  // draw eyes
  ctx.strokeRect(CENTER_X - RADIUS / 3,
    CENTER_Y - RADIUS / 3, EYE_WIDTH, EYE_HEIGHT);
  ctx.strokeRect(CENTER_X + RADIUS / 3 - EYE_WIDTH,
    CENTER_Y - RADIUS / 3, EYE_WIDTH, EYE_HEIGHT);

  // draw mouth
  ctx.beginPath();
  ctx.moveTo(CENTER_X - RADIUS / 3, CENTER_Y + RADIUS / 3);
  ctx.lineTo(CENTER_X + RADIUS / 3, CENTER_Y + RADIUS / 3);
  ctx.stroke();
} // end initialize
```

> Use named constants for shape positions and dimensions.

> Include a comment above each shape.

**FIGURE 12.14 External JavaScript file for Face web page**

interacts with the web page. For example, suppose you have a web page that uses canvas to draw an airplane. You could implement a button that, when clicked, moves the airplane forward by 2 pixels and rotates the airplane's propellers by .1 radians. To make the airplane appear to fly as part of an animation sequence, you can use timer commands to execute the transformation operations repeatedly.

## Translation

As you've seen, many of the context object's methods use *x* and *y* parameters that specify the position of the shape that's being created. All of those methods' *x* and *y* values are relative to the coordinate system. By default, the coordinate system is positioned with its origin (*x* = 0, *y* = 0) at the top-left corner of the canvas rectangle. To implement movement within your canvas environment, you don't move the individual graphics objects; instead, you move the entire coordinate system. After such a move, when you redraw your graphics objects, they get redrawn from the coordinate system's new position. And that means the user sees the graphics objects displayed at a different position, which suggests to the user that those objects have moved.

So how do you move the coordinate system? You call the `translate` method, like this:

```
context.translate(x, y);
```

The `translate` method moves the origin and the coordinate system *x* pixels to the right and *y* pixels down. In the next section, we present a Moving Face web page that adds transformation operations to our previous Face web page. For now, we'll show snippets of code from that web page while explaining transformation concepts. Here's a translate method call that comes from the Moving Face web page:

```
ctx.translate(0, -(RADIUS / 3));
```

So, what happens when this code executes? Calling translate with 0 for *x* and -RADIUS/3 for *y* causes the origin to move straight up by an amount equal to one-third of the face's radius. To better understand what that means, study **FIGURE 12.15**.

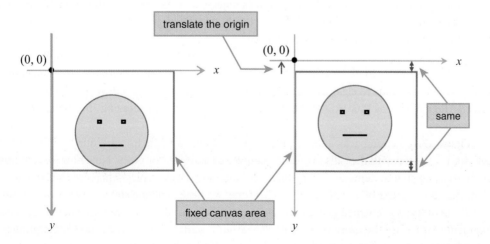

FIGURE 12.15 **Executing** `ctx.translate(0, -(RADIUS / 3));` **for Moving Face web page**

Figure 12.15's left picture shows what the canvas drawing area looks like after drawing the face initially. Its right picture shows what the canvas drawing area looks like after translating up and then redrawing the face. Even though the face on the right looks different (it's higher up in the drawing area), we're able to use the same code to draw the two faces. That means if we use `ctx.arc(CENTER_X, CENTER_Y, RADIUS, 0, 2 * Math.PI);` to draw the circle on the left, we use that same method call with the same *x* and *y* argument values to draw the circle on the right. That's because *x* and *y* position arguments are always relative to the coordinate system's origin. With the origin moving up, every drawing operation uses the raised origin as its starting point. Being able to reuse the same code makes the code easier to understand and more maintainable.

We use the term *coordinate system* to describe the *x* and *y* axes that form the reference for where *x* and *y* position values are measured. In Figure 12.15, you can see that the coordinate system moves up after executing the translate method call. The HTML standards organizations do not use the term coordinate system. Instead, they refer to the *transformation matrix*, which is similar to our coordinate system, but it includes quite a bit of complexity that might be a bit much for this book's intended audience. That said, if you're up for a challenge, look up the transformation matrix on the Internet and enjoy!

For both pictures in Figure 12.15, the circle's center point is drawn `CENTER_Y` pixels down from the coordinate system's origin. But with the origin translated up and the canvas area fixed, the user sees the face move up. Mission accomplished!

## Clearing the Canvas Drawing Area

Suppose you draw some graphics objects and then translate the coordinate system. When you perform a translate command, no redrawing takes place. You are merely telling the JavaScript engine the origin's new position so it can be used as the reference point for subsequent method calls that use *x* and *y* position arguments. So if you want the user to see your drawn graphics objects move, you not only have to call the `translate` method, you also have to re-execute the drawing operations that you used to draw the graphics objects in the first place. Oh, and one other little pesky detail: The originally drawn graphics objects don't get erased automatically. To avoid a trail of old drawings, each time you draw a newly translated graphics object, you should first delete the graphics object at its original position.

Deleting old graphics objects sounds straightforward, but, sorry, it requires quite a bit of effort. The easiest way to do it is to call the context object's `save`, `setTransform`, `clearRect`, and `restore` methods to clear the entire canvas drawing area before redrawing all the graphics objects. Take a look at **FIGURE 12.16**, which shows the code for clearing the canvas drawing area.

Figure 12.16's code packs a lot of punch, and it'll take a while to work our way through it. Let's start at the top with the calls to `getElementById` and `getContext`. Note how we call those methods in separate statements. That's different from our past examples, where we used one statement that chained the two method calls. This time, we need separate statements so we can save `getElementById`'s returned canvas object in a `canvas` variable. You can see later in the code fragment that we use the `canvas` variable for `canvas.width` and `canvas.height` arguments in a call to the `clearRect` method.

```
var canvas = document.getElementById("canvas");
var ctx = canvas.getContext("2d");
...
ctx.save();
ctx.setTransform(1, 0, 0, 1, 0, 0); // original coordinate system
ctx.clearRect(0, 0, canvas.width, canvas.height);
ctx.restore();
```

**FIGURE 12.16** **Code template for clearing entire canvas drawing area**

The clearRect method clears everything within a specified rectangular area. "Clearing" means that the rectangular area returns to the canvas element's background color, which is white by default. Here's the clearRect method's syntax:

*context*.clearRect(*top-left-x*, *top-left-y*, *width*, *height*);

The first two arguments specify the top-left corner of the rectangle area that is to be cleared. The third and fourth arguments specify the size of the rectangle area that is to be cleared. If you want to clear the entire canvas drawing area, you should specify 0, 0 for the rectangle's top-left corner arguments, and you should specify the canvas element's width and height for the rectangle's size arguments. Here's what we're talking about:

```
ctx.clearRect(0, 0, canvas.width, canvas.height);
```

As stated earlier, the goal is to clear the canvas drawing area. As with all $x$ and $y$ position arguments for context object method calls, the 0, 0 argument values are relative to the coordinate system. If the coordinate system is different from the canvas drawing area (perhaps from a prior translate method call), then executing this clearRect method call by itself won't accomplish the goal of clearing the canvas drawing area. Instead, it would clear a rectangular area whose top-left corner is positioned at the coordinate system's origin. So before calling clearRect to clear the canvas drawing area, you need to first move the coordinate system so it returns to its original position, where its origin matches the canvas drawing area's origin and its $x$ and $y$ axes match the canvas drawing area's $x$ and $y$ axes. To restore the coordinate system so it matches the canvas drawing area, you call the context object's setTransform method like this:

*context*.setTransform(1, 0, 0, 1, 0, 0);

The setTransform method's arguments are pretty confusing, and you don't really need to understand them. But in case you want a brief overview, the first and fourth arguments are for horizontal and vertical scaling. By using 1's for those arguments, the JavaScript engine undoes any scale method calls that have been used to scale up or scale down graphics objects' sizes. The other arguments are for rotations and translations. By using 0's for those arguments, the JavaScript engine undoes any translate and rotate method calls that have been used to alter the coordinate system's position. We'll describe the scale and rotate methods later on.

As an alternative to calling `setTransform` as shown earlier, you can reset the coordinate system to its original position by calling `resetTransform` like this:

```
context.resetTransform();
```

Internet Explorer does not support the `resetTransform` method, so you should stick with `setTransform` if you want to keep your IE users happy.

Normally, after you translate or rotate a shape, you'll want the next `translate` or `rotate` command to build on the previous transformation commands. You don't want to start over from the original position each time. You'll see this behavior in the upcoming Moving Face web page where the user can click translate and rotate buttons, and each button click translates or rotates the face from its current position, not from its original position. But as you know, in clearing the canvas drawing area, one of the steps has you call `setTransform` (or `resetTransform`), and that wipes out the coordinate system's current position. To restore the coordinate system to what it was before `setTransform`'s transformation, you need to call the context object's `save` method before calling `setTransform` and call the context object's `restore` method after calling `clearRect`. Go back to Figure 12.16 and see the formal code for those four method calls.

The `save` method saves the context object's current drawing state, which includes things like `lineWidth`, `strokeStyle`, the coordinate system's origin location, and the coordinate system's rotation. The `restore` method restores the context object's drawing state to a state saved by a `save` method call.

Normally, the restored drawing state comes from the most recently executed `save` method call. However, if the most recently executed `save` method call's state has already been restored (with a `restore` method call), the JavaScript engine looks for the previously executed `save` method call and restores that `save` method call's state instead. You won't normally need to rely on restoring states from `save` method calls executed before the most recently executed `save` method call, but if you do, you are taking advantage of canvas's ability to maintain a stack of drawing states for a particular context. Showing an example that uses a stack of drawing states is beyond the scope of this book, but if you're interested, see https://developer.mozilla.org/en-US/docs/Web/API/Canvas_API/Tutorial/Transformations.

## Rotation

Ready to add to your transformation tool bag? First in your tool bag was the `translate` method. Next up is the `rotate` method. The `rotate` method enables you to rotate the coordinate system around its origin by a specified angle. Here's the syntax:

```
context.rotate(clockwise-rotation-in-radians);
```

For example, this code rotates the coordinate system around the origin by one-eighth of a complete revolution in the clockwise direction:

```
ctx.rotate(Math.PI / 4);
```

Why is one-eighth of a revolution equal to π / 4? One complete revolution of a circle is 2π. And 2π * 1/8 = π / 4.

Note that π / 4 is equivalent to 45 degrees. But you cannot use 45 for the `rotate` method call's argument. Why? Because the `rotate` method assumes its passed-in parameter value is in radians, not in degrees. If you call rotate with 45 as the argument, the JavaScript engine will process 45 radians, which is wrong. Instead, we use `Math.PI / 4` when calling rotate. In that case, the JavaScript engine will process π / 4 radians, which is correct.

Rotation always takes place around the coordinate system's origin. Rotating around a different position requires some extra effort. First, you call `translate` to move the origin so it's centered at the position where you want the rotation to take place. Next, you call `rotate`. Then you call `translate` again to return the origin to its original position. For example, here's code from the Moving Face web page that rotates the face:

```
ctx.translate(CENTER_X, CENTER_Y);
ctx.rotate(Math.PI / 4);
ctx.translate(-CENTER_X, -CENTER_Y);
```

As with the `translate` command, when you perform a `rotate` command, no redrawing takes place. You are merely telling the JavaScript engine the coordinate system's new orientation so it can be used as the reference point for subsequent method calls that rely on the coordinate system. So if you want the user to see your drawn graphics objects rotate, you not only have to call the `rotate` method, you also have to re-execute the drawing operations that you used to draw the graphics objects in the first place.

## Scaling

Time for your next transformation tool—the `scale` method. By default, when you specify position and size values for context object method calls, the values are in units of pixels. So if a `lineTo` method call specifies 100 and 200 for its *x* and *y* arguments, that means the line's target is 100 pixels from the origin in the *x* direction and 200 pixels from the origin in the *y* direction.

If you want to adjust the number of pixels that position and size values represent, you can call the `scale` method like this:

```
context.scale(x-scale-factor, y-scale-factor);
```

For example, here's how you can double the number of pixels that position and size values represent:

```
ctx.scale(2, 2);
```

And here's how you can shrink the number of pixels that position and size values represent (with each value using one-third as many pixels as before):

```
ctx.scale(1/3, 1/3);
```

The `scale` method is like the other transformation methods in that after you perform a scale operation, the JavaScript engine remembers the transformation. So if you call `ctx.scale(2, 2);` twice, you end up with position and size values that use four times as many pixels as before.

When you perform a `scale` command, no redrawing takes place. You're preparing for the future. The next time there's a context object method call that uses position and/or size values, the JavaScript engine knows to use the scaled version of those values.

As part of an end-of-chapter exercise, you're asked to add a button to the Moving Face web page that, when clicked, causes the face to expand by 25%. We're making it easy for you because **FIGURE 12.17** provides the `expand` function that the button's event handler calls.

Note how the `expand` function calls the `scale` method with 1.25's for its scale-factor arguments. The 1.25's mean that the JavaScript engine will multiply all subsequent position and size values by 1.25 to come up with the number of pixels used to display shapes. That's equivalent to saying that all position and size values will be increased by 25%. After scaling takes place, the `expand` function calls `drawFace`. You'll see the code for `drawFace` in the next section. It does what you'd expect—it draws the face.

So, did you notice that we glossed over the `expand` function's first statement, the call to the `translate` function? Remember that the `scale` method adjusts not only size values (like the circle's radius and the eye rectangles' widths), but also the position values. We do want the expanded size values to create larger shapes, but we do not want the expanded position values to move the face circle away from its center position within the canvas drawing area. On the contrary, we want the face to remain where it is during the scale operation. In drawing the face, you'll use this `arc` method:

```
ctx.arc(CENTER_X, CENTER_Y, RADIUS, 0, 2 * Math.PI);
```

The scale operation will cause those `CENTER_X` and `CENTER_Y` values to use 25% more pixels. That will push the circle down and to the right. To fix the problem, we call the `translate` method to preemptively move the coordinate system's origin up and to the left. Here's the relevant code from Figure 12.17:

```
ctx.translate(-.25 * CENTER_X, -.25 * CENTER_Y);
```

For the Moving Face web page, the goal is to use the face's center point as the place where the expansion originates from. Thus, we use `CENTER_X` and `CENTER_Y` for the `translate` method's

```
function expand() {
  ctx.translate(-.25 * CENTER_X, -.25 * CENTER_Y);
  ctx.scale(1.25, 1.25);
  drawFace();
} // end expand
```

**FIGURE 12.17 expand function for Moving Face web page**

arguments, but we need to multiply those arguments by an *inverse scale factor.*[2] You calculate the inverse scale factor like this:

$$inverseScaleFactor = 1 - scaleFactor$$

In our `expand` function, we use 1.25 for the scale factor, so the inverse scale factor is –.25. Thus, in the `translate` method call shown earlier, we multiply `CENTER_X` and `CENTER_Y` by –.25.

When you perform a scale operation, the originally drawn graphics objects don't get erased automatically. That's fine if you scale up, because the new larger shapes should cover up the old shapes. But if you scale down, the new smaller shapes won't cover up the old larger shapes. So remember to clear the canvas drawing area before you draw the new scaled-down shapes. The aforementioned end-of-chapter exercise asks you to implement not only an expand button, but also a shrink button. Don't forget to clear the canvas drawing area for the shrink button's event-handler function.

# 12.11 Moving Face Web Page

As promised, in this section, we present a complete web page that applies transformation operations to the previous Face web page. This time we use black for the face's lines instead of orange. But other than that, the new page displays the face the same as before, with the face centered and upright. The new web page adds **Rotate** and **Up** buttons below the face. Clicking the **Rotate** button causes the face to rotate one-eighth of a complete revolution clockwise. Clicking the **Up** button causes the face to move up by one-third of the circle's radius, where "up" means in the direction of the face's forehead. Take a look at **FIGURE 12.18**, which shows what happens after the user clicks the **Rotate** button once and then the **Up** button once.

See **FIGURE 12.19**, which shows the HTML code for the Moving Face web page. It's pretty much the same as for the original Face web page. Examine the two button controls at the bottom, which call the `rotateClockwise` and `moveUp` event-handler functions.

## Drawing the Web Page's Initial Display

Now take a look at the web page's JavaScript code in **FIGURE 12.20A**. The named constants are the same as before. In the original Face web page, the `initialize` function contained all the JavaScript code. For this web page, `intialize` calls other functions to help perform different tasks. Specifically, `initialize` calls `drawHeading` to draw the "Hello" heading, and `draw-Face` to draw the face. In general, it's good to split up a big module (like `initialize`) into separate modules by using helper functions (like `drawHeading` and `drawFace`), so the code is easier to understand. After all, smaller chunks are easier to understand than bigger chunks. Another reason to use helper functions is that they allow you to execute the helper functions'

---

[2] Inverse scale factor is not a formal term adopted by canvas's governing bodies. But it should be.

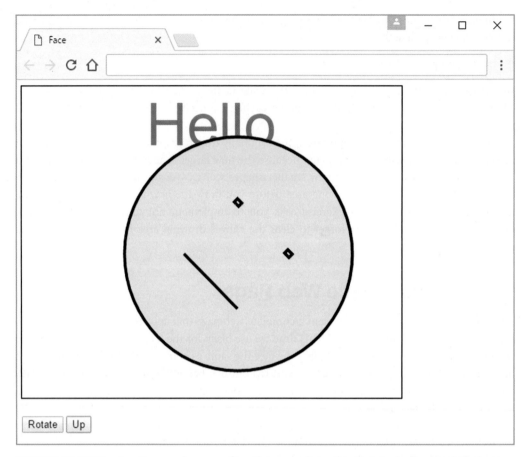

**FIGURE 12.18 Moving Face web page after the user clicks the Rotate button and Up button**

tasks from different places in your program while avoiding redundant code. We'll have more to say about that later on.

The `initialize` function takes care of certain context object properties that can be assigned once at the beginning and their values don't change when the event handlers execute. The `textAlign`, `font`, `strokeStyle`, and `lineWidth` properties fall into that category, and you should note their assignments in the `initialize` function. We could have stuck those property assignments in the helper functions, but that would have been inefficient because the helper functions get executed every time the user clicks Rotate or Up.

## Helper Functions

Let's now examine the `drawHeading` helper function in **FIGURE 12.20B**. Assigning blue to the `fillStyle` property and calling `strokeText` should look familiar because that's the

```
<!DOCTYPE html>
<html lang="en">
<head>
<meta charset="utf-8">
<meta name="author" content="John Dean">
<title>Face</title>
<style>
  canvas {border: thin solid black;}
</style>
<script src="face2.js"></script>
</head>

<body onload="initialize();">
<canvas id="canvas" width="500" height="400">
</canvas>
<br><br>
<input type="button" value="Rotate"
  onclick="rotateClockwise();">
<input type="button" value="Up"
  onclick="moveUp();">
</body>
</html>
```

canvas element's dimensions

event-handler function calls

**FIGURE 12.19 HTML file for Moving Face web page**

same code we used in the first-version Face web page. As you can verify by viewing the browser window screenshot, the Hello heading displays in the same position within the canvas drawing area, centered and at the top, even after the user clicks a button to move the face. So before we draw the heading, we call save to save the coordinate system so we can recover it later, and we call setTransform to have the coordinate system match the canvas drawing area. By transforming the coordinate system, we can then draw the heading so it's at its usual top-center position relative to the canvas drawing area. Finally, to ensure prior translations and rotations are preserved, we call restore to move the coordinate system back to its prior position.

Let's now examine the drawFace helper function in Figure 12.20B. All of its code should look familiar because it's the same as the code we used in the first-version Face web page. There's no need for the messy save, setTransform, or restore method calls as with drawHeading because we draw the face using the current position of the coordinate system. If the user clicks the Up button several times, that causes the coordinate system to move up, and we draw the face in that new position.

```
/****************************************************
 * face2.js
 * John Dean
 *
 * This file handles drawing a face and having it move.
 ****************************************************/

// x and y coordinates for the face's center point.
const CENTER_X = 250;
const CENTER_Y = 250;
const RADIUS = 150;          // face's radius
const TITLE_BASELINE = 75; // y value for title's baseline
const EYE_WIDTH = 8;
const EYE_HEIGHT = 6;

var canvas; // the canvas element
var ctx;    // the canvas object's context

//****************************************************

// This function draws the title and the initial face.

function initialize() {
  canvas = document.getElementById("canvas");
  ctx = canvas.getContext("2d");

  // for the heading:
  ctx.textAlign = "center";
  ctx.font = "75px Arial, sans-serif";

  // for the face:
  ctx.strokeStyle = "black";
  ctx.lineWidth = 4;

  drawHeading();
  drawFace();
} // end initialize
```

**FIGURE 12.20A** JavaScript file for Moving Face web page

## Event-Handler Functions

Next up are the event-handler functions. In **FIGURE 12.20C**, note the rotateClockwise function and its first three method calls—translate, rotate, and translate. In the previous section, we described how those methods take care of rotating the face around the face's center point. We also mentioned that although they rotate the coordinate system successfully, they don't redraw the face. So to draw the face, at the bottom of the rotateClockwise function, we call the drawFace helper function.

In Figure 12.20C, note how the moveUp function first clears the canvas drawing area before it redraws the Hello heading and the face. In the previous section, we described the mechanics of

```
//**************************************************

// This function draws the Hello heading.

function drawHeading() {
  ctx.save();  // enable restoration so face can be redrawn

  // reset to original coordinate system
  ctx.setTransform(1, 0, 0, 1, 0, 0);
  ctx.fillStyle = "blue";
  ctx.fillText("Hello", CENTER_X, TITLE_BASELINE);
  ctx.restore();
} // end drawHeading

//**************************************************

// This function draws the face.

function drawFace() {
  ctx.fillStyle = "yellow";

  // draw circle
  ctx.beginPath();
  ctx.arc(CENTER_X, CENTER_Y, RADIUS, 0, 2 * Math.PI);
  ctx.fill();
  ctx.stroke();

  // draw eyes
  ctx.strokeRect(CENTER_X - RADIUS / 3,
    CENTER_Y - RADIUS / 3, EYE_WIDTH, EYE_HEIGHT);
  ctx.strokeRect(CENTER_X + RADIUS / 3 - EYE_WIDTH + 1,
    CENTER_Y - RADIUS / 3, EYE_WIDTH, EYE_HEIGHT);

  // draw mouth
  ctx.beginPath();
  ctx.moveTo(CENTER_X - RADIUS / 3, CENTER_Y + RADIUS / 3);
  ctx.lineTo(CENTER_X + RADIUS / 3, CENTER_Y + RADIUS / 3);
  ctx.stroke();
} // end drawFace
```

**FIGURE 12.20B JavaScript file for Moving Face web page**

clearing the canvas drawing area. Specifically, we described how to call the save, setTransform, clearRect, and restore methods. In the moveUp function, after clearing the canvas drawing area, we then call drawHeading. Finally, we call translate and drawFace to move the face up and draw it at its new position.

Did you notice that the moveUp function clears the canvas drawing area and calls drawHeading, but the rotateClockwise function does neither of those things? Why the difference? Because when you move up, to avoid a trail, you need to delete the canvas drawing area

```
//**************************************

// This function rotates the face by 45 degrees clockwise.

function rotateClockwise() {
  ctx.translate(CENTER_X, CENTER_Y);
  ctx.rotate(Math.PI / 4);
  ctx.translate(-CENTER_X, -CENTER_Y);
  drawFace();
} // end rotateClockwise

//**************************************

// This function moves the face up by radius / 3.

function moveUp() {
  ctx.save();
  ctx.setTransform(1, 0, 0, 1, 0, 0); // original coordinate system
  ctx.clearRect(0, 0, canvas.width, canvas.height);
  ctx.restore();

  drawHeading();
  ctx.translate(0, -(RADIUS / 3));
  drawFace();
} // end moveUp
```

**FIGURE 12.20C JavaScript file for Moving Face web page**

and then redraw the deleted heading. But for rotation, there's no trail because the face stays in the same position.

## Helper Functions Can Help to Avoid Code Redundancy

The Moving Face web page calls the drawFace function from within the initialize, rotateclockWise, and moveUp functions. Suppose we did not have a drawFace helper function, and instead we put the drawFace function's code within the bodies of the initialize, rotateclockWise, and moveUp functions. That would work, but your web page would exhibit *code redundancy*. In small doses code redundancy is fine, and you sometimes can't avoid it. But in general, code redundancy is bad. With code redundancy, if you later decide to make a change (or someone else decides to make a change), you have to remember to make the change in all the places where the code appears. Thus, code redundancy makes it more difficult to fix bugs in a web page or make improvements to a web page.

## 12.12 CASE STUDY: Solar Shadowing Dynamics

In this chapter's case study, we use a canvas drawing area to show a bird's-eye view of two parallel arrays of photovoltaic solar collectors and the shadows they cast. If the arrays of collectors are close together and steeply sloped,[3] the array closest to the sun may partially shade the array behind it. Because individual cells within a panel are wired in series to maximize that panel's output voltage, and because shadowing increases series resistance, even a little shadowing substantially reduces a shaded panel's electrical output.

FIGURE 12.21 shows a typical presentation of this web page. (Header and footer navigational elements are beyond the top and bottom of the screen.) When first displayed, input boxes for Latitude, Base Spacing / Panel Height, Clearance (between the lower ends of panels and the roof below) / Panel Height, Panel Slope, Month, and Hour are filled with default values. The rectangular canvas below the inputs displays a plain light-gray background, representing a light-colored flat rooftop. The user can modify any of the default inputs. The display in Figure 12.21 assumes the user changes the Base Spacing / Panel Height input from the default 1.8 to 1.4.

When the user clicks **Install Collectors**, JavaScript writes "(North)" at the top of the canvas drawing area and draws images of two solar collector arrays. It compresses each image in the north-south direction to represent panel slope (more compression for greater slope). It adds whitening to the higher end of each sloped array to depict more sunlight reflected from these higher ends. This helps the user identify slope direction (whiter on north ends if sloped toward the south, and vice-versa).

Now, the display in Figure 12.21 assumes the user changes the Hour input from the default 12 (noon) to 14 (2 PM) and clicks **Show Behavior**. JavaScript responds by adding shadows and writing "Electrical Output: 52%" in the upper left corner of the canvas drawing area. Automatically displayed values indicate the sun's current altitude and azimuth (compass direction), and shadows show the effects of these values by running away from the sun. There are two types of shadows:

1.  Shadows on the roof below the collectors:

    If Clearance = 0, rooftop shadows connect to the collectors that cast them. But if Clearance has a positive value, shadows on the roof are disconnected from the collectors that cause them.

    Figure 12.21 illustrates this latter effect.

2.  Shadows on collectors:

    If the sun's altitude is low, the collectors themselves might be partially or totally shaded. This can happen in either of two ways:

    a.  In summer near sunrise or sunset, the sun is behind reasonably sloped collectors. For example, in the northern hemisphere reasonably sloped collectors face southward, but at sunrise the sun is north of east. This makes the collectors shade themselves.

    b.  In winter, the sun is relatively low in the sky throughout the day, and if the arrays are too steeply sloped and/or too close together, the array closer to the sun will partially shade the array behind it. Figure 12.21 illustrates this latter effect.

The development in this section uses trigonometry to determine where light goes, but it represents that light by painting its absence in the canvas drawing area.

---

[3] Panel Slope = 0 is horizontal. A positive slope tips panels toward south. A negative slope tips panels toward north (for negative latitudes).

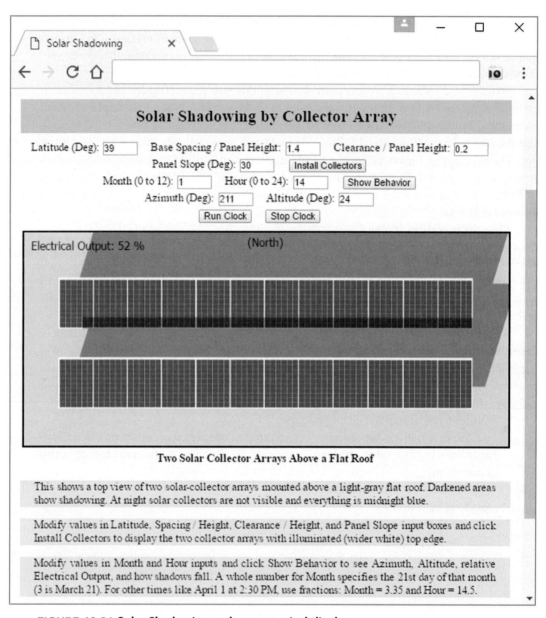

FIGURE 12.21 **Solar Shadowing web page typical display**

If the user clicks the Run Clock button, the hours value steps sequentially through the remaining hours in the current day, with a new hour value every .2-second intervals. To be able to simulate a full year in a reasonable amount of time, the program shows the hours incrementing through just one day of each month. After one day's worth of simulation (i.e., when the hours value reaches 24), the program jumps to the next month and simulates one day in that month.

When the month value reaches 12 and the hours value reaches 24, the month and hours values roll over to 1 and 0, respectively, at which point the simulation stops. At any time while the hours and months are stepping, the user can click Stop Clock to make everything freeze. At that point, the user can observe results, make input modifications, click Show Behavior, observe the new results, and so forth. At any point, the user can click Run Clock again to resume the dynamic simulation.

FIGURE 12.22A shows the first part of the `solarShadowing.html` file, which contains custom styling for the web page displayed in Figure 12.21. Common presentation details are in the `lawrenceMicrogrid.css` CSS file. All of the JavaScript code that retrieves and processes inputs and paints and repaints the canvas drawing area is in the `solarAngles.js` JavaScript file. You'll see that later.

In the HTML file's `style` element, the `canvas` rule specifies a black `border`. Without this specification, the only indication of the extent of the canvas drawing area would be the extent of its background color. The `canvas` rule's `transition` property simulates dawn and dusk by making the background color change gradually over 0.2 seconds between `lightgray` for daytime and `midnightblue` for night. Because time delays between subsequent hourly displays are also 0.2 seconds, dawn and dusk are simulated as being one hour long.[4]

FIGURE 12.22B shows the first part of the `body` element. It begins with an `img` element that is `hidden`. This little HTML element acts as a local repository for an external image. JavaScript needs a local HTML repository like this to access images.

```
<!DOCTYPE html>
<html lang="en">
<head>
<meta charset="utf-8">
<meta name="author" content="John Dean">
<title>Solar Shadowing</title>
<link rel="stylesheet" href="../library/microgrid.css">
<script src="../library/solarAngles.js"></script>
<style>
  body {text-align: center;}
  form {margin: 10px auto;}
  canvas {
    margin: -20px auto;
    border: 3px solid black;
    background-color: lightgray;
    transition: background 0.2s;
  }
</style>
<script src="../library/navigation.js"></script>
</head>
```

FIGURE 12.22A `head` **container for Solar Shadowing web page**

---

[4] Actually, the durations of the dawn and dusk transitions are shorter in the tropics and longer at high latitudes.

```
<body onload="createHeaderFooter()">
<img id="pvArray" alt= "PV" hidden src="../images/pvPanelArray.gif"/>
<h2>Solar Shadowing by Collector Array</h2>
<form>
  Latitude (Deg):
  <input id="latitude" type="text" size="3" value="39">
  Base Spacing / Panel Height:
  <input id="spacing" type="text" size="3" value="1.8">
  Clearance / Panel Height:
  <input id="clearance" type="text" size="3" value="0.2"> <br>
  Panel Slope (Deg):
  <input id="panelSlope" type="text" size="3" value="30">
  <input type="button" value="Install Collectors"
    onclick="setup(this.form)"> <br>
  Month (0 to 12):
  <input id="month" type="text" size="3" value="1">
  Hour (0 to 24):
  <input id="hour" type="text" size="3" value="12">
  <input type="button" value="Show Behavior"
    onclick="showBehavior(this.form)"> <br>
  Azimuth (Deg):    <!-- clockwise from north -->
  <input id="azimuth" type="text" size="3" readonly="readonly">
  Altitude (Deg):
  <input id="altitude" type="text" size="3" readonly="readonly"> <br>
  <input id="run" type="button" value="Run Clock"
    onclick="runClock(this.form)">
  <input id="stop" type="button" value="Stop Clock"
    onclick="stopClock(this.form)"> <br>
</form><br>

<canvas id="topView" width="700" height="300"></canvas>
```

**FIGURE 12.22B** body **container for Solar Shadowing web page**

After the `img` element comes the body's `form` element. It specifies four input text boxes, the **Install Collectors** button, two more input text boxes, and the **Show Behavior** button. The two buttons contain mouse-click event attributes that call corresponding JavaScript functions. The next two input boxes, for Azimuth and Altitude, are read-only. They display values computed by JavaScript functions. The **Run Clock** and **Stop Clock** buttons contain mouse-click event attributes that call corresponding JavaScript functions that run and stop the previously described dynamic simulation.

Figure 12.22B also shows the body's canvas element. The `canvas` element's attributes include fixed `width` and `height` specifications. The rest of the `body` is just an `h4` heading element followed by plain text in four `p` paragraph elements. By now, it should be easy for you to produce these elements, so they are not shown.

**FIGURE 12.23A** shows the first part of the external JavaScript file, `solarAngles.js`. It defines a substantial number of global variables because there are many instances where different functions need access to the same variables. These global variables appear just below the overall heading, making their commented descriptions easy to find.

```
/*************************************************************************
 * solarAngles.js
 * John Dean
 *
 * This file contains functions supporting solarShadowing.html
 *************************************************************************/

var image;                    // image of one row of PV solar collectors
var form;                     // html input form
var spacing;                  // pixel distance between array bases
var slope;                    // radians up from horizontal facing south
var canvas;                   // active display
var context;                  // nature of active display
var length = 0.5 * 160;       // 80 pixels for 160 cm panel height
var X0 = 50;                  // left side of arrays
var Y0;                       // bottom of north array
var dyP;                      // panel bottom-to-top horizontal projection
var altitude;                 // solar altitude angle above horizon
var azimuth;                  // solar azimuth angle from south
var cosIncidenceAngle;        // angle between sun and normal to panel
var timer;                    // timer controlling display dynamics

// This function is called when the Install Collectors button is clicked.

function setup(solarForm) {
  image = document.getElementById("pvArray");
  form = solarForm;
  spacing = length * parseFloat(form.elements["spacing"].value);
  slope = form.elements["panelSlope"].value * Math.PI/180;
  canvas = document.getElementById("topView");
  context = canvas.getContext("2d");
  canvas.style.backgroundColor = "lightgray";
  context.clearRect(0, 0, canvas.width, canvas.height);
  context.fillStyle = "black";
  context.font = "1em Tahoma";
  context.fillText("(North)", 324, 20);
  if (slope < 0) {           // north-facing panels
    Y0 = 0.5 * (canvas.height - spacing - length);
    dyP = + length * Math.cos(slope);  // south end higher
  }
  else {                     // south-facing panels
    Y0 = 0.5 * (canvas.height - spacing + length);
    dyP = - length * Math.cos(slope);  // north end higher
  }
  drawOneArray(Y0);
  drawOneArray(Y0 + spacing);
} // end setup
```

**FIGURE 12.23A  JavaScript file for Solar Shadowing web page**

The setup function executes when a user clicks the web page's Install Collectors button. It initializes the first five global variables and sets the canvas background color. It then clears the canvas drawing area. The clearing operation is not necessary at first, but after a change in Panel Slope, it is needed to remove previously painted panels. The setup method then writes "(North)" at the top of the canvas drawing area to orient the user.

The X0 and Y0 variables specify the location of the lower west corner of the northern panel array such that the two arrays will be equally spaced north and south of the centerline of the canvas if their slopes are zero, that is, if they are horizontal. If the panels face south—positive panelSlope—the lower end is the south end. If the panels face north—negative panelSlope—the lower end is the north end. The dyP variable is the horizontal projection of the distance from the lower end of either array to the upper end of that same array. It's the canvas's y-distance in pixels. For north-sloping (southern hemisphere) arrays, dyP is downward and positive. For south-sloping (northern hemisphere) arrays, dyP is upward and negative. The setup function ends by making a call to the subordinate drawOneArray function for each of the two panel arrays.

**FIGURE 12.23B** shows the drawOneArray function. First the function deposits a collector image that is scaled down in the y-direction to depict an overhead view of a sloped surface. Because the context.scale function scales both the image and its location, this scaling must be reversed for the y-location argument in the drawImage method call to make the deposited image's location independent of slope. Because the drawImage method specifies the location by the image's minimum-x and minimum-y (its Northwest corner), and because y0 specifies the location of the lower edge of the array and the lower edge is the southern edge when slope is

```
function drawOneArray(y0) {
  var scaleFac;     // horizontal projection of sloping surface
  var width;        // image width

  scaleFac = Math.cos(slope);
  width = image.width;
  // Scale vertically to represent top view of sloping panels
  context.scale(1.0, scaleFac);
  if (slope >= 0) {y0-= length * scaleFac;}
  context.drawImage(image, 50, y0 / scaleFac);
  context.scale(1.0, 1.0 / scaleFac);
  // Apply white line to brighten sunlit higher end
  context.strokeStyle = "white";
  context.lineWidth = 3;
  context.beginPath();
  if (slope < 0) {y0 += length * scaleFac;}
  context.moveTo(X0, y0);
  context.lineTo(X0 + width, y0);
  context.stroke();
} // end drawOneArray
```

**FIGURE 12.23B JavaScript file for Solar Shadowing web page**

positive, when `slope` is positive, `drawOneArray` must reduce y0 by the *y*-extent of the image before using it to specify the image's location.

After depositing the scaled image, `drawOneArray` draws a white line along the upper edge of this scaled image to represent sunlight reflected off the upper edge of the array. This helps the user see the direction of slope. Because the white line needs to be on the upper edge, whereas y0 (a copy of Y0) initially specifies the location of the lower edge, y0 must change. When the slope is positive and y0 is initially on the southern edge, the change made to y0 for the previous scaling operation makes y0 correct for this operation as well. But when the slope is negative and y0 is on the northern edge, y0 needs to increase by the *y*-extent of the image.

**FIGURE 12.23C** shows the third part of `solarAngles.js`. The `showBehavior` function executes when a user clicks the web page's **Show Behavior** button. Before going into details,

```
// This function is called when the Show Behavior button is clicked.

function showBehavior() {
   var degradation;                          // shadowing effect
   var output;                               // electrical output %
   var direct;                               // direct solar

   computeAngles();
   context.clearRect(0, 0, canvas.width, canvas.height);
   if (altitude > 0) {                       // daytime
     canvas.style.backgroundColor = "lightgray";
     showOneShadow(X0, Y0);                   // from north panel
     showOneShadow(X0, Y0 + spacing);         // from south panel
     drawOneArray(Y0);
     drawOneArray(Y0 + spacing);
     degradation = Math.pow(getObscuration(X0, Y0), 0.38);
     degradation += Math.pow(getObscuration(X0, Y0 + spacing), 0.38);
     form.elements["azimuth"].value = Math.round(azimuth * 180/Math.PI);
     form.elements["altitude"].value = Math.round(altitude * 180/Math.PI);
     direct = 0.86 * cosIncidenceAngle * (1.0 - 0.5 * degradation);
     // Using 1985 ASHRAE Fundamentals Guide, Chapter 27, Diffuse Solar:
     output = parseInt(100 * (direct + 0.14 * Math.sin(altitude)));
   }
   else {                                    // nighttime
     canvas.style.backgroundColor = "midnightblue";
     form.elements["azimuth"].value = "";
     form.elements["altitude"].value = "";
     output = 0;
   }
   context.fillStyle = "black";
   context.font = "1em Tahoma";
   context.fillText("Electrical Output: " + output + " %", 10, 25);
   context.fillText("(North)", 324, 20);
} // showBehavior
```

**FIGURE 12.23C JavaScript file for Solar Shadowing web page**

consider the problem it addresses: Incoming solar power has two components, one directly from the sun, and the other indirectly from the sky and reflection from surrounding surfaces. When sunlight shines straight on the faces of the solar panels, cosIncidenceAngle equals 1.0, and the direct component of incoming solar power (direct) maximizes at about 86% of the maximum total solar power. But when sunlight hits the faces of the solar panels at a glancing angle, cosIncidenceAngle is less, and the direct component of incoming solar power is less. If the solar panels are obscured from the sun, degradation further reduces the electrical output generated by light coming directly from the sun.

After declaring local variables, showBehavior calls the subordinate computeAngles function, which assigns values to the global variables, altitude, azimuth, and cosIncidenceAngle. The clearRect method call erases the canvas drawing area in preparation for new drawing.

If altitude holds a positive value, the sun is up, and it's daytime. Then the showBehavior function sets the canvas background color to light gray and calls the showOneShadow function for each solar array. Because shadow painting usually covers parts of the previously painted arrays, showBehavior calls drawOneArray again for each array to put fresh images of the collector arrays on top of the shadows they create. Then showBehavior calls getObscuration for each array and getObscuration returns the shaded fraction of that array. (Only one of the two arrays will have nonzero shading.) Then an empirical formula involving Math.pow converts the returned shaded fraction to the direct-power degradation produced by the obscuration. The getObscuration function also paints appropriate shadowing on the collector image. Next, showBehavior retrieves the global azimuth and altitude values computed previously by computeAngles and displays them in the web page's corresponding (readonly) input boxes. Then showBehavior calculates the direct component of generated electrical output using the previously computed degradation. The 0.5 multiplier accounts for the fact that degradation is the fractional degradation for just one of the two arrays.

If altitude is not positive, the sun is down, and it's night. Then the showBehavior function sets the canvas background color to midnight blue, erases anything currently in the readonly Azimuth and Altitude text boxes, and sets output to zero.

The last part of the showBehavior function writes a text description of the electrical output as a percent of maximum (rated) output in the upper-left corner of the canvas. It also rewrites the original "(North)" text at top center.

FIGURE 12.23D shows the computeAngles function. It is similar to the computeAngles function in Figure 10.22. However, this web page's global variable, slope, replaces the local panelSlope variable in Chapter 9's function. Because this chapter's HTML uses a different input format for month, it initializes the local month variable differently than Chapter 9's function did. Chapter 9's function assumed the hour was always 12 noon, but the current web page includes an explicit hour variable. The current web page includes a local hourAngle variable that expresses hour as radians relative to noon. The current web page's formula for sinAltitude includes an hourAngle term. The current web page's Math.asin conversion of sinAltitude to altitude includes a 0.999999 round-off-error-suppression factor to avoid a fatal error if round-off happens to make sinAltitude greater than unity.

```
function computeAngles() {
   var latitude;          // earth latitude
   var month;             // month number (1 = Jan, 2 = Feb, ...)
   var hour;              // hour of day
   // Using 1985 ASHRAE Fundamentals Guide, Chapter 27, Table 1, and
   // approximating earth's elliptical orbit as a circle:
   var solarDeclination; // solar altitude angle at north pole
   var hourAngle;         // angle after noon in radians
   var cosAzimuth;        // horizontal solar angle from south in radians
   // Using 1985 ASHRAE Fundamentals Guide, Chapter 27, equation (3):
   var sinAltitude;       // solar altitude in radians

   latitude = form.elements["latitude"].value * Math.PI/180;
   month = form.elements["month"].value;
   hour = form.elements["hour"].value;
   solarDeclination = (-23.45 * Math.PI/180)
      * Math.cos(month * Math.PI/6);
   hourAngle = Math.abs((hour - 12) * Math.PI/12);
   cosAzimuth = 0;
   sinAltitude =  Math.cos(hourAngle) *
      Math.cos(latitude) * Math.cos(solarDeclination)
      + Math.sin(latitude) * Math.sin(solarDeclination);
   altitude = Math.asin(sinAltitude * 0.999999);
   if (altitude > 0) {
      // Using 1985 ASHRAE Fundamentals Guide, Chapter 27, equation (4):
      cosAzimuth =
         (Math.sin(solarDeclination) - sinAltitude * Math.sin(latitude))
         / (Math.cos(altitude) * Math.cos(latitude));
      azimuth = Math.acos(cosAzimuth * 0.999999);
      azimuth = (hour <= 12) ? azimuth : 2 * Math.PI - azimuth;
      cosIncidenceAngle = sinAltitude * Math.cos(slope)
         - cosAzimuth * Math.cos(altitude) * Math.sin(slope);
      if (cosIncidenceAngle < 0) {cosIncidenceAngle = 0.0;}
   } // end if altitude > 0
} // end computeAngles
```

**FIGURE 12.23D JavaScript file for Solar Shadowing web page**

The current web page includes an explicit azimuth variable, and its Math.acos conversion of cosAzimuth to azimuth also includes a 0.999999 round-off-error-suppression factor. Because Math.acos cannot distinguish angles in the range $\pi$ radians to $2\pi$ radians from angles in the range 0 to $\pi$ radians, the current web page also includes the funny-looking *conditional assignment*:

```
azimuth = (hour <= 12) ? azimuth : 2 * Math.PI - azimuth;
```

If the hour is less than or equal to 12, azimuth equals its initial value. But if the hour is greater than 12, azimuth equals $2\pi$ minus its initial value. This conditional adjustment enables azimuth to vary through all 360 degrees. In morning, it's less than 180 degrees and in afternoon it's greater than 180 degrees.

The cosIncidenceAngle formula in Figure 12.23D is exactly the same as that in Figure 10.22, except this time both altitude and cosAzimuth vary not only with month but also with hour.

FIGURE 12.23E shows the showOneShadow function. It uses opaque paint that covers everything below it. The key question is "Where does the paint go?" To answer this question, focus on corners. The function's x0 and y0 parameters are the coordinates of the collector array's lower west corner. The xB and yB variables are the coordinates of the corresponding shadow corner. The xT and yT variables are the coordinates of the shadow corner corresponding to the array's upper west corner. The botDxS, botDyS, topDxS, and topDyS variables are the x- and y-offsets from the array's west corners to the shadow's corresponding corners. Because the other array corners are one image width to the east, the other shadow corners are also one image width to the east. The context's moveTo and lineTo method calls start at the shadow corner corresponding to the array's lower west corner and draw a clockwise path around the west, north, and east shadow sides. The fillStyle method call selects the shadow's color, and the fill method call closes the path and fills the polygon with that selected color.

FIGURE 12.23F shows the getObscuration method. Instead of drawing polygons on the roof below the collectors, it draws rectangles on the collectors themselves. Instead of using opaque

```
function showOneShadow(x0, y0) {
   var xB;          // horizontal position of bottom-left shadow corner
   var yB;          // vertical position of bottom-left shadow corner
   var xT;          // horizontal position of top-left shadow corner
   var yT;          // vertical position of top-left shadow corner
   var clearance;   // distance from roof to lower edge of panels
   var totalHeight; // distance from roof to upper edge of panels
   var botDxS;      // bottom-left horizontal shadow offset
   var botDyS;      // bottom-left vertical shadow offset
   var topDxS;      // top-left horizontal shadow offset
   var topDyS;      // top-left vertical shadow offset
   var width;       // image width (598 pixels)

   clearance = length * parseFloat(form.elements["clearance"].value);
   totalHeight = clearance + length * Math.abs(Math.sin(slope));
   botDxS = - Math.sin(azimuth) * clearance / Math.tan(altitude);
   botDyS = Math.cos(azimuth) * clearance / Math.tan(altitude);
   topDxS = - Math.sin(azimuth) * totalHeight / Math.tan(altitude);
   topDyS = Math.cos(azimuth) * totalHeight / Math.tan(altitude);
   width = image.width;
   xB = x0 + botDxS;
   yB = y0 + botDyS;
   xT = x0 + topDxS;
   yT = y0 + dyP + topDyS;
   context.beginPath();
   context.moveTo(xB, yB);
   context.lineTo(xT, yT);
   context.lineTo(xT + width, yT);
   context.lineTo(xB + width, yB);
   context.fillStyle = "gray";
   context.fill();
} // end showOneShadow
```

**FIGURE 12.23E JavaScript file for Solar Shadowing web page**

paint that covers everything below, it uses semi-transparent paint that allows some of what's below to show through. The `context`'s `globalAlpha` property is the "opacity" or pigment-to-water ratio in a water-color paintbrush. A lower value implies less pigment and allows more to show through. To use this property to simulate shadowing, it's crucial that `fillStyle` be black. Any lighter color will look like a deposition of soot or snow.

When the sun is behind the panels in early summer mornings or late summer afternoons, `getObscuration` fills a rectangle that covers all of the collector array except for the sunlit white strip at the top. The small +2 and −1 y-position adjustments move the shading slightly away from the white strip at the upper end of the image and assure coverage of the lower edge of the image.

If the collector arrays are close together, when and the sun is low in the sky in winter, there is inter-panel shading, and the array closer to the sun casts a shadow on part of the array behind it. The shade angle is the projection of the solar altitude onto a vertical north-south plane. Except at noon, it will always be steeper than the solar altitude. The extent of the shading up from the bottom of the shaded array is `shadeLength`. Given total panel length, spacing between array bases, slope angle and tangent of shade angle, one can compute `shadeLength` by equating the ratios of corresponding sides in similar triangles ( `bc/de` = `ac/ae` ) in this east-looking side view of the two arrays:

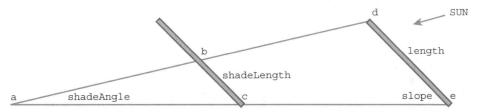

Multiplying `shadeLength` by `Math.cos(slope)` gives `projLength`, the y-direction horizontal projection of `shadeLength`. The `offset` is the value of the x-direction offset from an edge of the collector array to the edge of an off-center shadow on that array. The one-pixel adjustment to `y0` in the `if(slope>=0)` statement makes shading completely cover an otherwise disconcerting exposed sliver of image at the bottom of south-facing panels. That statement's `else` clause negates `projectLength` for north-facing panels. The next `if, else` statement paints the semi-transparent rectangular shading at the bottom of the shaded array with the unshaded `offset` on the west in the afternoon (when `Math.sin(azimuth)` is negative), or on the east in the morning.

Next, the local `obscuration` variable gets the shaded fraction of the collector array. The `context`'s `globalAlpha` is restored to unity to avoid distortions in subsequent canvas operations. Finally, the previously computed `obscuration` is returned.

**FIGURE 12.23G** shows the rest of `solarAngles.js`. The `runClock` function executes when a user clicks the web page's **Run Clock** button. It starts by initializing the global `timer` variable with a *handle*, which refers to a *handler* method. It does this by invoking a predefined `window` method called `setInterval`, whose first argument is the name of the handler method the browser is to call at the ends of successive time intervals, and whose second argument is the desired length of those time intervals in milliseconds. The handler method is usually a custom JavaScript function. In the present case, it's the `updateDisplay` function also in Figure 12.23G.

```javascript
function getObscuration(x0, y0) {
  var latitude;          // earth latitude
  var projLength;        // north-south horizontal projection
  var width;             // east-west width of panel array
  var tanShadeAngle;     // tan(shade angle)
  var shadeLength;       // upward in panel plane
  var offset;            // east-west shadow offset
  var obscuredWidth;     // east-west inter-panel shadow extent
  var obscuration = 0;   // fractional inter-panel shadowing

  latitude = form.elements["latitude"].value * Math.PI/180;
  projLength = image.height * Math.cos(slope);
  width = image.width;
  context.globalAlpha = 0.4;          // shadow opacity
  context.fillStyle = "black";

  // Sun behind panels
  if (cosIncidenceAngle <= 0) {
    // cover bottom edge but keep top edge white
    if (slope > 0) {y0 = y0 + 2 - projLength;}
    context.fillRect(x0, y0 - 1, width, projLength);
  } // end if

  // Inter-panel shading
  else if (Math.cos(azimuth) * (y0 - 0.5 * canvas.height) > 0 &&
    latitude * slope > 0) {
    tanShadeAngle = Math.tan(altitude) / Math.cos(azimuth - Math.PI);
    shadeLength = length
      - spacing / (Math.cos(slope) + Math.sin(slope) / tanShadeAngle);
    if (shadeLength < 0) {shadeLength = 0;} // no obscuration
    projLength = shadeLength * Math.cos(slope);
    offset = Math.abs(Math.tan(azimuth) *
      (spacing + projLength - length * Math.cos(slope)));
    if (slope > 0) {y0 += 1;}          // cover image bottom
    else {projLength = - projLength;}
    if (Math.sin(azimuth) < 0) {
      context.fillRect(x0 + offset, y0, width - offset, - projLength);}
    else {context.fillRect(x0, y0, width - offset, - projLength);}
    obscuration = (shadeLength * (width - offset)) / (length * width);
    if (obscuration < 0) {obscuration = 0;}
  } // end else if
  context.globalAlpha = 1.0;
  return obscuration;
} // end getObscuration
```

FIGURE 12.23F **JavaScript file for Solar Shadowing web page**

```
function runClock() {
  timer = window.setInterval(updateDisplay, 200);   // 200 ms intervals
  form.elements["run"].disabled = "disabled";
  form.elements["stop"].disabled = "";
} // end runClock

function updateDisplay() {     // after each interval
  var mo;     // month number
  var hr;     // hour number
  var nextHr; // next hour as fraction of day

  mo = parseInt(form.elements["month"].value);
  hr = parseInt(form.elements["hour"].value);
  nextHr = (hr + 1) % 24;
  if (nextHr < hr) {
    nextHr = 0;
    mo += 1;
    if (mo > 12) {
      stopClock(form);
      mo = 1;
    }
    form.elements["month"].value = mo;
  }
  form.elements["hour"].value = nextHr;
  showBehavior(form);
} // end updateDisplay

function stopClock() {
  window.clearInterval(timer);
  form.elements["stop"].disabled = "disabled";
  form.elements["run"].disabled = "";
} // end stopClock
```

**FIGURE 12.23G** **JavaScript file for Solar Shadowing web page**

The second and third statements in `runClock` alter the web page's display by disabling the **Run Clock** button and enabling the **Stop Clock** button. Disabling a button dims its text. Enabling it restores its text.

Once a click on the **Run Clock** button activates the timer, `updateDisplay` executes after each subsequent 0.2 second. It retrieves the web page's current month and hour values and increments the hour value. When the hour reaches 23, the next hour becomes 0 and the month increments. When the month and hour reach 12 and 23, the next hour and month become 1 and 0, respectively, and the `upDateDisplay` calls the `stopClock` function.

The `stopClock` function also executes if the user clicks the web page's **Stop Clock** button. This function calls the browser's prewritten `clearInterval` method to turn off the timer and stop the simulation. Then it disables the web page's **Stop Clock** button and enables the **Run Clock** button—reversing the operations performed by the previous `runClock` function.

# Review Questions

## 12.1 Introduction

1. For applets, Flash, and canvas, is each one built into modern browsers?

## 12.3 Rectangles Web Page

2. What is method call chaining?

3. Does a color gradient apply to one specified shape or to all of the shapes drawn with the context object?

## 12.4 Drawing Text with `fillText` and `strokeText`

4. If you want to display characters in a normal fashion (as you see them in this sentence), should you use `strokeText` or `fillText`?

## 12.5 Formatting Text

5. What context object property should you use to specify font size for a text string?

6. If you use the context object's `font` property, what granular font values are you required to provide?

7. What context object property is for specifying horizontal alignment for text?

## 12.6 Drawing Arcs and Circles

8. What kind of arc is created if you call the `arc` method with starting and ending angle values of 0 and $3\pi$?

9. What kind of arc is created if you call the `arc` method with starting and ending angle values of 0 and 0?

10. What happens if you call the `fill` method for an arc whose ends are not closed?

## 12.7 Drawing Lines and Paths

11. What does the `moveTo` method do?

12. What are the two methods that establish the start of a subpath?

13. What method should you call to draw a line that connects the end of the most recently drawn line segment or arc to the start of the current subpath?

14. If you want to change the line properties for a drawing, you need to split the path into multiple paths. True or false.

## 12.8 Umbrella Web Page

15. It is legal to use straight lines and curved lines together in a single path. True or false.

### 12.9 Face Web Page

16. For shape positions and shape dimensions, what are two benefits of using named constants?

### 12.10 Using Canvas for Transformations

17. What happens when you call the `translate` function?

    a)  The coordinate system's origin moves.

    b)  The drawn shapes move.

    c)  The JavaScript engine draws the current shape.

18. Typically, when clearing the canvas drawing area, what two functions should you call before calling `clearRect`? Explain the purpose of each of those function calls.

19. When you want to rotate something, why is it common to call `translate` before calling `rotate`?

### 12.11 Moving Face Web Page

20. What are two benefits of using helper functions?

## Exercises

1.  [after Section 12.3] In the Rectangles web page, suppose you want to add a 1-pixel-width black dashed border to the second rectangle that shows where the rectangle's fill border would be if there were no `strokeRect` method call. In other words, you want to display the border shown here. The following code fragment does much of the work. What single line of code should you insert above the code fragment? Hint: Look up the `setLineDash` method on the Internet and use it.

    ```
    ctx.strokeStyle = "black";
    ctx.lineWidth = 1;
    ctx.strokeRect(140, 80, 70, 140);
    ```

2.  [after Section 12.4] If you want to display text with a border and a filled interior, why should you normally call `strokeText` after `fillText`?

3.  [after Section 12.5] Assume you've got a `canvas` variable that holds the web page's canvas object and a `ctx` variable that holds the web page's context object. Given this code:

    ```
    ctx.font = "100px Arial, sans-serif";
    ctx.fillText("Bullseye", canvas.width / 2, canvas.height / 2);
    ```

What code would you need to insert above the given code in order to center the "Bullseye" string horizontally and vertically? Here's the result:

4. [after Section 12.7] Provide a JavaScript function that generates the Text Baseline Examples web page shown in Figure 12.5. For the font size, use 25 pixels. For the horizontal lines' color, use `springgreen`. For the horizontal lines' positions, use *y* values of 40, 80, 120, and 160. You may use one path or multiple paths for the four lines. Your code should be efficient—do not draw something and then redraw it later.

5. [after Section 12.8] Implement a function that draws five filled-in circles like this:

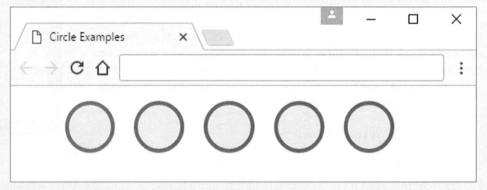

To avoid code redundancy, you must use a loop.

6. [after Section 12.8] Add code to the Umbrella web page's `draw` function in order to display a right-side curved handle like this:

Do not change the existing code. Show where your added code gets positioned within the existing code. Hint: All you need to do is add one statement.

7. [after Section 12.9] The context object's `rect` method creates a rectangle using the same four parameters as `strokeRect`—*x*, *y*, width, and height. The difference is that the `rect` method just creates the rectangle, but does not draw it. To draw it, you need to call `stroke` and/or `fill`. As with the `lineTo` and `arc` methods, if you call `rect` as part of a path, to avoid connecting the path's previous shape to the rectangle, you should call `moveTo` before calling `rect`. Rewrite the Face Web page's `initialize` function so that it uses the `rect` method instead of the `strokeRect` method. You are required to use only one path for the entire web page.

8. [after Section 12.10] Add expand and shrink buttons to the Moving Face web page. Your expand button should expand the face by the same amount as the shrink button shrinks it. So if you expand *x* times, then shrink *x* times, you should see the same face as you started with. Feel free to use the `expand` function shown in Figure 12.17, but in your solution, you must improve the style. In particular, you must use named constants for the scale factors and inverse scale factors. There's no need to submit code for the entire web page. Just submit code for the expand and shrink button elements and code for the expand and shrink event-handler functions.

9. [after Section 12.11] In the Moving Face web page, the `moveUp` function calls the `clearRect` method like this:

```
ctx.clearRect(0, 0, canvas.width, canvas.height);
```

In the web page's `body` container, you can see that the `canvas` element has width and height attributes of 500 and 400 pixels, respectively. So in the `clearRect` method call, we could have used 500 and 400 instead of `canvas.width` and `canvas.height`. Which technique is better and why?

# Project

Create a web page that displays a combination lock with 40 tick marks and number labels for every fifth number 0, 5, 10, …, 35. Provide "Nudge left" and "Nudge right" buttons that cause the combination lock's dial to turn one position left (counterclockwise) or one position right (clockwise), respectively. For details, study the sample session.

You must use an external JavaScript file. Name your files `combinationLock.html` and `combinationLock.js`.

As always, you are required to use named constants and helper functions when appropriate.

### Sample Session

After loading the web page:

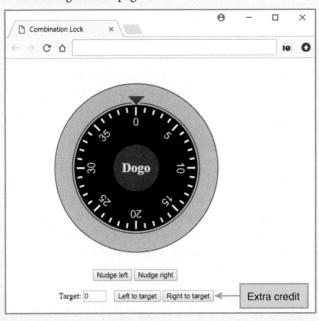

After clicking **Nudge left**:

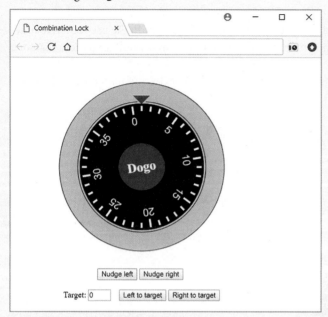

After clicking **Nudge right** 3 times:

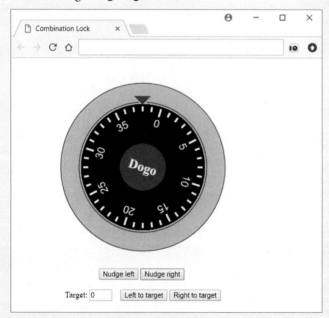

### Extra Credit

Implement a target number box that allows the user to enter a number between 0 and 39. Implement two buttons that, when clicked, cause the dial to turn left or right to the user-entered target value. When the dial turns, the turning motion must be smooth; it must not jump more than one tick at a time.

To implement the turning motion, you'll need to use the `setTimeout` method. See the Internet for `setTimeout` details.

### Sample Session

After refreshing the web page, click **Nudge right** 10 times, so the 30 is at the top:

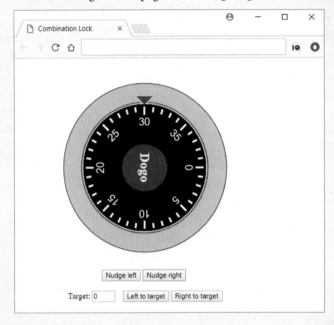

After entering 35 in the target box, and clicking **Left to target**, the dial turns 5 positions counterclockwise:

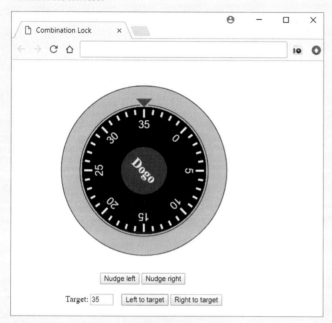

After entering 5 in the target box, and clicking **Right to target**, the dial turns 30 positions clockwise:

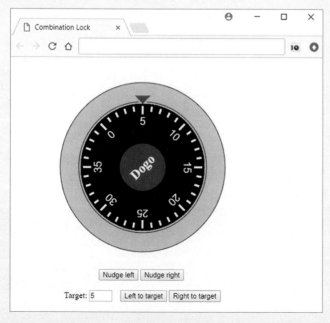

# HTML5 and CSS Coding-Style Conventions

This appendix describes HTML5 and CSS3 coding-style conventions. Most of these guidelines are widely accepted, but alternative guidelines do exist in certain areas. One way we ensure that our guidelines are followed is by going along with the 500-pound gorilla that is Google. For the most part, we match Google's HTML/CSS Style Guide document at:

https://google.github.io/styleguide/htmlcssguide.html

We attempt to present HTML coding practices that conform to the spirit of the HTML5 standard. For an overview and a short conceptual discussion of such practices, see the "Note for teachers" section in the W3C's Doctypes and Markup Styles web page at:

http://www.w3.org/community/webed/wiki/Doctypes_and_markup_styles#A_note_for_teachers

This appendix addresses only HTML coding-style issues. It does not address user-interface design issues such as layout, color aesthetics, navigability, content, and accessibility.

Jump ahead to the end of this appendix and note the sample HTML file and its associated external CSS file. You'll probably want to refer to those files while reading the upcoming coding-style conventions guidelines.

## Files

1. HTML file names should end in `.html`, not `.htm`. Using the full HTML acronym is more descriptive.

## W3C's Validation Service

1. Validate every web page and every external style sheet by using the W3C's validation services. The HTML and CSS validation services, respectively, are found here:

   http://validator.w3.org/
   http://jigsaw.w3.org/css-validator/

## Comments

1. Short comments should be written on one line. Provide a space after the `<!-`. Provide a space prior to the `--->`. For example:

   ```
   <!-- This link should be updated eventually. -->
   <a href="http://www.park.edu/compsci">Park CS Department</a>
   ```

2. Comments that require more than one line should use block-style indented text. For example:

   ```
   <!--
      The following section contains complex mathematical
      equations. Some of the equations contain errors. The point
      is to see how many visitors actually take the time to study
      the details. We'll count how many responses we get over the
      next three-month period.
   -->
   ```

## General

1. Provide end tags for all container-type elements. For example:

   ```
   <p>
      Park University, founded in 1625 by the Franciscan Monks,
      quickly became renowned for its efforts in the fields of
      alchemy and computer science.
   </p>
   ```

2. Use lowercase characters for all tags and attributes.
3. Enclose all attribute values in double quotes.

4.  Because the `name` attribute can be used to identify elements in JavaScript, and JavaScript coding conventions suggest using camel case for multiword variable names, use camel case for values for the `name` attribute.

5.  Do not use spaces around the equals sign when specifying an attribute value pair. For example:

    ```
    <meta name="author" content="John Dean">
    ```

6.  Blank lines:
    - Insert a blank line between the `head` and `body` sections.
    - Optionally, you may insert blank lines to separate two large logical chunks of code (> 8 lines each?), but do not insert a blank line unless there's a reason to do so.

7.  Indentations:
    You should use two spaces for your indentations. Do not use tabs.

8.  For void elements, HTML5 allows you to insert a blank space and slash ( /) at the left of the closing >, like this:

    ```
    <meta name="author" content="John Dean" />
    ```

    However, you should have no blank space and no slash.

## Avoid Long Lines

1.  Long lines are bad because:
    - Within an integrated development environment (IDE), it is annoying to have to scroll right in order to see the end of a line of code.
    - If you paste your code to a word processing document, line wrap occurs, which leads to visual confusion.
    - If you need to compare two files side-by-side on a computer screen, long lines make that difficult.

2.  You should split up long lines by pressing **Enter** at a natural breaking point(s). You may or may not want to indent on the continuation line—it's a bit of a gray area. If the container represents something that's supposed to look like a paragraph (e.g., `p` or `blockquote`), then do not indent. Otherwise indent. Examples will be provided in the upcoming sections.

## Top of the Web Page

1.  Include the following line at the top of your `.html` files:

    ```
    <!DOCTYPE html>
    ```

    This tells the browser to use the HTML5 version of HTML (because other versions of HTML use different forms of the doctype instruction).

The W3C and the WHATWG say that tag names, attribute names, and the doctype instruction (doctype is not considered to be an element; it's an instruction) are case insensitive. Google's Style Guide says "All code has to be lowercase" except for when it's appropriate for a value to use uppercase. Based on that, `<!DOCTYPE html>` should be `<!doctype html>`. However, the vast majority of examples on the W3C, WHATWG, and Google websites use uppercase for DOCTYPE, so that's what this document recommends. If you prefer all lowercase for the doctype instruction, you may use it if your boss or teacher approves.

# head Container

The following items should be included in the order shown.

1. To avoid content being interpreted incorrectly, provide this `charset meta` element:

   ```
   <meta charset="utf-8">
   ```

2. Provide an `author` meta element. For example:

   ```
   <meta name="author" content="John Dean">
   ```

3. As an option, to help search engines find your pages, you may also want to provide `description` and `keywords` meta elements. For example:

   ```
   <meta name="description"
     content="This web page presents Dean family highlights.">
   <meta name="keywords" content="Dean family">
   ```

   In the first `meta` element, note the indentation for the continuation line.

4. Provide a meaningful `title` element on each page. For example:

   ```
   <title>Dean Family</title>
   ```

5. For external CSS files, use the `link` element. For example:

   ```
   <link rel="stylesheet" href="style.css">
   ```

# body Container

1. Blank lines
   - Insert a blank line between the head container and the body container.
   - Optionally, insert a blank line between large (≥ 5 lines?) block elements, where a *block element* is an element that expands to fill the width of its container.
   - Do not insert blank lines between short, related heading elements. In the following example, h1 and h2 are short and related so there is no blank line separator. On the other hand, the heading elements can be separated from the p element with a blank line.

```
<h1>Our Furry Friend</h1>
<h2>The Common House Rat</h2>

<p>
   Doesn't every child dream of having his/her very own pet rat?
   With the "One Child, One Rat" program, that dream can become a
   reality.
</p>
```

2. Indentations:

- Use indentations for (1) block elements whose code is too long for one line, and (2) continuation code for phrasing elements whose code is too long for one line.
- Block elements:
  - In the following code, the text is indented inside the p block element because it's too long to fit on one line. When the start and end tags appear on lines by themselves aligned in the same column, and the contained code is indented, that is called *block notation*.

```
<p>
   <q>Parkville's pristine white sandy beaches along the
   Missouri River attract vacationers from the world over.</q>
   -Parkville Mayor, Angie Klein. After sun-worshipping all day,
   relax and enjoy Parkville's <em>scintillating</em> nightlife.
   Pirate Grounds is always a big hit with the singles!
</p>
```

  - Optionally, use block notation for short block elements that are inside other block elements. Thus, in the following example, it's OK to put the h1 block element on a line by itself and indent it. The strong element should not use block notation because it is not a block element.

```
<header class="exotic">
   <h1>Paradise in Parkville!</h1>
</header>
<p>Welcome to Parkville - <strong>Party Town</strong>, USA.</p>
```

- Continuation code for phrasing elements whose code is too long for one line:
  - If a phrasing element cannot fit on one line, you should insert newlines at logical breaking points. In the following examples, the a element cannot fit on one line so newline insertions are required. In the "bad" example, newlines are inserted after href= and onclick=. Those are poor breaking points because the href and onclick assignments are split. In the "good" example, newlines are inserted after website and after the a start tag. Those are good breaking points because they help prevent the href and onclick assignments from being split.

**Bad:**
```
<p>
   For additional information on our ICS
   program, check out this website - <a href=
   "http://www.park.edu/csis" onclick=
   "return confirm('Are you sure?');">
   http://www.park.edu/csis</a>
</p>
```

**Good:**
```
<p>
   For additional information on our ICS program,
   check out this website -
   <a href="http://www.park.edu/csis"
   onclick="return confirm('Are you sure?');">
   http://www.park.edu/csis</a>
</p>
```

- Note that the a element's continuation lines are aligned with the a element's first line; that is, they are not indented. That's because the a element is within a p container. If the a element were in a container (like nav) that was not supposed to look like a paragraph, then you should indent like this:

```
<a href="http://www.park.edu/csis"
   onclick="return confirm('Are you sure?');">
```

3. Lists:

- Normally, you should nest ol, ul, dl, and li elements as follows:

```
<ol>
  <li>
    Morning
    <ul>
      <li>Wake up</li>
      <li>Go to school</li>
    </ul>
  </li>
  <li>
    Afternoon
    <ul>
      <li>Kick back and relax.</li>
      <li>
        Lecture period - not much prepared so allow students to
        ask questions and surf the Internet for cool web pages.
      </li>
      <li>Go home and watch TV.</li>
    </ul>
  </li>
  <li>Evening</li>
</ol>
```

- As shown in the preceding example, when embedding a list inside a list, the outer list's end tag must be placed below the embedded list.

4. Tables:

   - Normally, you should nest `table`, `thead`, `tbody`, and `tr` elements as follows:

```
<table>
  <caption>Dumb table</caption>
  <thead>
    <tr>
      <th>A</th>
      <th>B</th>
    </tr>
  </thead>
  <tbody>
    <tr>
      <td>one</td>
      <td>two</td>
    </tr>
    <tr>
      <td>three</td>
      <td>four</td>
    </tr>
  </tbody>
</table>
```

   - As an alternative to the indentation shown in the preceding example, if all the code in a `tr` container can fit on one line, then it's acceptable to put the entire `tr` container code on one line.

5. Images and colors:

   - Include `width` and `height` attributes for all `img` elements.
   - Include the `alt` attribute for all `img` elements. Use `alt=""` for decorative images (A *decorative image* is an image that doesn't add any information to the page and isn't mentioned by the page's content).
   - Do not use animated GIFs, or use them sparingly.

6. Character references:

   - In the interest of readability, if there's a choice, use regular characters and not character references. Here's when it's appropriate to use a character reference:
     - Use a character reference to display a character that's not on the keyboard.
     - Use a character reference to display a character that would normally have a special meaning in HTML:

       `<, >, &`

       double quote (`"`), single quote (`'`), but only when they are inside an attribute value string

- Use an ` ` character reference if you need to:

  Display a blank space without allowing a line break (to ensure that a group of words will be displayed on the same line).

  Display multiple blank spaces without allowing whitespace collapsing.

- Character references fall into two categories—named character references and numeric character references. Named character references use the format `&`*name*`;`. Numeric character references use the format `&#`*unicode-value*`;`. Some symbols are represented by both a named character reference and a numeric character reference. For example, the less than symbol is represented by `&lt;` and by `&#60;`. If a symbol is represented by both types of character references, you should use the named character reference version because named character references are more understandable. Some symbols are represented only by a numeric character reference and not a named character reference. Because numeric character references are rather cryptic, you should provide a comment whenever you use a numeric character reference for the first time in a web page.

7. Miscellaneous not-quite-as-important guidelines:

   These guidelines are useful, but if your web page is small or you're in a hurry, don't worry if you fail to follow these rules:

   - *Plain text* refers to characters that are not part of a tag. In other words, plain text is not a tag type, a tag attribute, or a tag attribute's value.

   - Plain text should not be positioned immediately within the `html` container, the `head` container, or the `body` container. Plain text should appear only within container elements that are within the `body` element. This style rule leads to page content that is defined more accurately. And that makes it possible for CSS and JavaScript to manipulate the page content more effectively.

   - Phrasing elements should not be positioned immediately inside the `body` container. Normally, they should be positioned within a block element other than the `body` container.

   - Do not specify precise sizes for text font. Instead, use header tags (`h1`, `h2`, etc.) or use style sheets with `font-size` values such as `small`, `large`, `smaller`, `larger`, `125%`, etc.

# Keep Content and Presentation Separate

1. Use HTML elements for content and CSS for presentation.
2. Since the `b`, `i`, and `u` elements implement presentational semantics, do not use them. Instead, use other elements that properly describe the text or use the following CSS property-value pairs:

   ```
   font-weight: bold
   font-style: italic
   text-decoration: underline
   ```

# Cascading Style Sheets

1. In a `style` element and also in a `link` element to an external style sheet, do not include a `type` attribute with a value of `"text/css"`. Instead, you should rely on the browser engine supplying `"text/css"` as the default. Here are two separate examples that show the right way to do it:

   ```
   <style>
      ...
   </style>

   <link rel="stylesheet" href="style.css">
   ```

2. Comments:
   - You should supply comments within your CSS code for any rules that are nonintuitive.
   - If the comment is short, insert it at the right of the rule that the comment applies to.
   - If the comment is long, insert it immediately above the rule(s) that the comment applies to. To give the comment more prominence, insert a blank line above the comment.
   - For external CSS files, you should provide your name as a comment at the top. For example:

     ```
     /* John Dean */
     ```

3. Surround logical groups of rules with blank lines.
4. Short rules:
   - If you have just one property-value pair, or you have just a few property-value pairs and none of the values are `font-family` lists, then you may put them on one line, with a space following each interior semicolon, like this:

     ```
     .opening-statement {font-style: italic; color: blue;}
     .closing-statement {font-family: "Times New Roman", Times, serif;}
     ```

   - With one-line rules, insert a blank space before the opening brace. There should be no blank space at the right of the opening brace and at the left of the closing brace.
5. Long rules:
   - If you have a rule with a long heading and/or lots of property-value pairs, use block notation. For example:

     ```
     body {
        background-color: white;
        color: black;
        a:visited: green;
        a:link: red;
        font-family: "Arial Black", Helvetica, sans-serif;
     }
     ```

   - With block notation, place the opening brace on the same line as the selector, separated from the selector by one space.

6. Provide a blank space after a CSS property's colon. There should be no blank space before the colon.
7. For a font family list, provide a space after each comma.
8. Use hyphens to separate multiword `class` values and multiword `id` values (blank spaces are not allowed within a `class` value or within an `id` value).
9. Provide a semicolon after the last property-value pair.
   Although CSS standards allow you to omit the semicolon after the last property-value pair, you should include it. That way, if another rule is added later on, there will be less likelihood of accidentally forgetting the semicolon to separate the prior property-value pair from the new one.
10. Unless there's a special reason, do not use the `blink` value for the `text-decoration` property.
11. Only use a type selector if you're sure that type selector's rule should always be applied to all instances of that element type. For example, the following rule would be appropriate if you (or your company's webmaster) have determined that all figure captions should use 12-point font:

    ```
    figcaption {font-size: 12pt;}
    ```

    However, `div` is supposed to be generic, and it would be inappropriate to use the following rule to force `div` to always be a layout table:

    ```
    div {display: table;}
    ```

12. Google's Style Guide says if you have a zero value for a CSS property, you should omit the unit in order to make the code more compact. You should follow that rule with one exception. The CSS validation service confirms that for color percentage values, you must include the % unit even when the value is 0%.

## Sample HTML File

```
<!DOCTYPE html>
<html lang="en">
<head>
<meta charset="utf-8">
<meta name="author" content="John Dean">
<meta name="description"
  content="This web page presents Dean family highlights.">
<meta name="keywords" content="Dean family">
<title>Dean Family</title>
<link rel="stylesheet" href="style.css">
</head>
```

```html
<body>
<nav>
  <a href="index.html">HOME</a>
  <a href="travels.html">TRAVELS</a>
  <span class="current-tab">FAMILY</span>
  <a href="school.html"
    onmouseover="alert('Be careful. If you click, you\'ll' +
      ' be taken to the kids\' school cafeteria.');">
    SCHOOL</a>
</nav>
<h1>Dean Family</h1>
<p>
  As usual, not much has happened this year. We just forge
  ahead with the usual mundane, ho-hum stuff. Let's see ...
  divorced, open-heart surgery, tornado destroyed my house, etc.
</p>
<img class="right" src="images/family.gif"
  width="300" height="200" alt="family picture">
<p>
  Caiden made her middle school cheer team. Jordan made her high school
  tennis team. The squirrels are stealing the tomatoes.
</p>
<p>
  Eventually, we'd like to add a family tree to this web page.
  If anyone in the family is interested in working on that project,
  <em>please</em> feel free to get started by evaluating these family
  tree tools:
</p>
<ul>
  <li>
    Family Search Personal Ancestral File (PAF), available from
    <a href="https://www.familysearch.org">Family Search</a>.
  </li>
  <li>
    GedHTree, available from
    <a href="http://www.gedhtree.com/">http://www.gedhtree.com</a>.
  </li>
</ul>
<address>
  Send comments &amp; questions to johndean@yahoo.com.
</address>
<p class="date">Updated October 18, 2018</p>
</body>
</html>
```

# External CSS File (style.css)

```css
/* John Dean */

body {background-color: white; color: black;}
nav {text-align: center;}

/* Apply special formatting to the links at the top. */
nav a, .current-tab {
  color: white;
  font-family: Arial, Helvetica, sans-serif;
}
nav a {background-color: #666666;}
nav a:hover {background-color: blue;}
.current-tab {background-color: green;}

h1 {text-align: center;}
hr {
  background-color: red;
  height: 1px; /* hr color works only if height is specified */
}

.date {
  color:red;
  font-family: "Trebuchet MS", Helvetica, sans-serif;
  font-size: smaller;
}
```

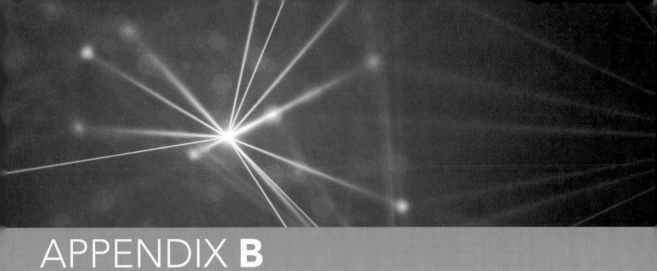

# APPENDIX B

# JavaScript Coding-Style Conventions

This appendix describes JavaScript coding-style conventions. Most of these guidelines are widely accepted, but alternative guidelines do exist in certain areas. We pattern our JavaScript coding-style conventions on Google's JavaScript coding-style conventions. For the most part, we match Google's JavaScript Style Guide document at:

https://google.github.io/styleguide/jsguide.html

We attempt to present JavaScript coding practices that conform to the spirit of a W3C wiki on JavaScript best practices at:

https://www.w3.org/wiki/JavaScript_best_practices

Jump ahead to the end of this appendix, and note the sample JavaScript file. You'll probably want to refer to that file while reading the upcoming coding-style conventions guidelines.

## JavaScript Code Placement

1. JavaScript function and class definitions should be positioned at the bottom of the web page's `head` container or in an external JavaScript file.
2. Normally, function and class definitions should be placed in an external file if they are large, need to be shared by multiple web pages, or contain proprietary code.

## `script` Element

1. When you use a `script` element, omit the `script` element's `type` attribute (and rely on the default being JavaScript). For example:

```
<script>
  alert("This is a test.");
</script>
```

## Prologue for an External JavaScript File

1. You should provide the following prologue section at the top of every one of your external JavaScript files:

```
/ * * * * * * * * * * * * * * * * * * * * * * * * * * * * * * * * * * * * * * * * * * *
 * your-filename
 * your-name
 *
 * file-description
 * * * * * * * * * * * * * * * * * * * * * * * * * * * * * * * * * * * * * * * * * * * /
```

2. You should provide a blank line below the prologue section.

## Avoid Long Lines

1. Long lines are bad because:

   - Within an integrated development environment (IDE), it is annoying to have to scroll right in order to see the end of a line of code.
   - If you paste your code to a word processing document, line wrap occurs, which leads to visual confusion.
   - If you need to compare two files side-by-side on a computer screen, long lines make that difficult.

2. Google's style guide says to avoid lines with more than 80 characters (including blank spaces).
3. You should split up long lines by pressing enter at a natural breaking point(s) and indenting on the continuation line(s).

# Delimiter Comments

1. Enter the following line of stars between function, method, and constructor definitions.

   ```
   //***********************************************************
   ```

   The preceding line should be surrounded by blank lines.
2. Insert a blank line between logical sections of your code. For example, you should insert a blank line between the end of one loop and the beginning of another loop (unless the loops are small and intimately related).

# Text Comments

1. Comments should be used for code that might be confusing to someone reading your program for the first time. You should assume that the reader understands JavaScript syntax.
2. Do not use comment code that is obvious. For example, this comment is unnecessary (and therefore exhibits poor style):

   ```
   for (let i=0; i<10; i++)    // for loop heading
   ```

3. Write your programs with clear, self-documenting code in order to reduce the need for comments. For example, use mnemonic (descriptive) identifier names.
4. Always include a single space between the `//` and the comment text.
5. The format of a comment is determined by its length.

   - Comments that occupy more than one line are block comments, and they can use either of these formats:

     ```
     // This block comment format uses //'s.
     // Note the space after the //. That's a style thing.

     /* This block comment format is for longer comments. It uses
     slash asterisk and asterisk slash. Note the space after the
     slash asterisk and the space before the asterisk slash. Note
     the indentation for the lines after the first line. */
     ```

   - If a comment resides on a line by itself, it should be positioned above the line of code that it describes. The `//` should be indented the same as the described line of code. Provide a blank line above the comment line. For example, note the following:

     ```
     // Test for an MSIE x.x browser
     if (/MSIE (\d+\.\d+);/.test(navigator.userAgent)) {
     ```

   - Many comments are small enough such that they can be placed at the right of the code that they describe. When such comments are on adjacent lines, they should start in the same column, if possible.

6. Provide an "end …" comment for each closing brace that is a significant number of lines (five or more?) down from its matching opening brace. For example:

```
function getSum(table, rows, cols) {
  for (let row=0; row<rows; row++) {
    for (let col=0; col<cols; col++) {
      sum += table[row][ col];
    }
  } // end for row

  return sum;
} // end getSum
```

# Variable Declarations

1. Normally, you should declare only one variable per line. For example:

```
var avgScore;      // average score on the test
var numOfStudents; // number of students in the class
```

Exception: If several variables are intimately related, it is acceptable to declare them together on one line. For example:

```
var x, y, z;  // coordinates for a point
```

2. Normally, you should provide a comment for each variable declaration line. Exception: You do not have to provide a comment for names that are obvious (e.g., studentId) or standard (e.g., i for a for loop index variable, ch for a character variable).
3. You should declare all your variables with var. Exception: If you want block scope for a variable (as with a for loop index variable), declare it with let.
4. For JavaScript code that's not inside a function, place the code above the function definitions.

# Braces That Surround One Statement

1. For if, else, for, while, and do constructs that have one statement enclosed in the construct, you should use a compound statement (a compound statement is a brace-enclosed series of zero or more statements). For example:

```
for (; num>=2; num--) {
  factorial *= num;
}
```

2. Exception to the preceding rule: If your teacher or manager allows it, you may omit the braces, like this:

```
for (; num>=2; num--)
    factorial *= num;
```

# Placement of Braces

1. Place an opening brace on the same line as the previous code, separated from the previous code by a single space. Place a closing brace on a line by itself such that the brace is aligned with the beginning of the line that contains the opening brace. For do loops, put the `while` condition on the same line as the closing brace.
2. Examples:

```
if (...) {
    statements
}
else if (...) {
    statements
}
else {
    statements
}

for/while (...) {
    statements
}

switch (...) {
    case ... :
        statements
        break;
    case ... :
        statements
        break;
        ...
    default:
        statements
}

do {
    statements
} while (...);

int doIt() {
    statements
}
```

# Alignment and Indentation

1.  Align all code that is logically at the same level. See the prior brace placement section for examples of proper alignment.
2.  Indent all code that is logically inside other code. See the prior brace placement section for examples of proper indentation.
3.  For all indentations, use an indentation width of two spaces.
4.  For nested logic code, use nested indentation. For example:

```
for (...) {
  while (...) {
    statements
  }
}
```

5.  For a statement that is too long to fit on one line, write it on multiple lines such that the continuation lines are indented appropriately. If the long statement is followed by a single statement that is logically inside the long statement, you must use curly braces to enclose the single statement.
    To indent the continuation lines, use either of these two techniques:
    *   Indent to a column position such that similar entities are aligned. In the following example, the entities that are aligned are the three function calls:

    ```
    while (bucklingTest(expectedLoad, testWidth, length) &&
           compressionTest(expectedLoad, testWidth) &&
           snappingTest(recommendedWidth, length)) {
      numOfSafeBeams++;
    }
    ```

    *   Indent the same number of spaces as all other indents. For example:

    ```
    while (bucklingTest(expectedLoad, testWidth, length) &&
      compressionTest(expectedLoad, testWidth) &&
      snappingTest(recommendedWidth, length)) {
      numOfSafeBeams++;
    }
    ```

# Multiple Statements on One Line

1.  Normally, you should put each statement on a separate line.
    Exception: If you have statements that are intimately related and very short, it is acceptable (but not required) to put them together on one line. For example:

    ```
    a++; b++; c++;
    ```

2.  For assignment statements that are intimately related and use the same assigned value, you may combine them into one assignment statement, like this:

```
x = y = z = 0;
```

# Spaces Within a Line of Code

1.  Never include a space at the left of a semicolon.
2.  Parentheses:
    - Never enter a space on the inside of and adjacent to enclosing parentheses.
    - If the entity at the left of a left parenthesis is an operator or a construct keyword (`if`, `switch`, etc.), then precede the parenthesis with a space.
    - If the entity at the left of a left parenthesis is a function, method, or constructor name, then do not precede the parenthesis with a space.

    For example:

```
if ((a == 10) && (b == 10)) {
   printIt(x);
}
```

3.  Operators:
    - Normally, you should surround an operator with spaces. For example:

```
if (response == "avg") {
   y = (a + b) / 2;
}
```

    - Complex expressions—within an inner component of a complex expression, do not surround the inner component's operators with spaces. Two common occurrences of complex expressions are conditional expressions and `for` loop headings. See the following examples.
    - Dot operator—no spaces at its left or right.
    - Comma operator—no space at its left.
    - Unary operators—no space between the unary operator and its associated operand.

    For example:

```
if (reverseIt) {
   x = (x<0 ? -x : x);
}
while (list1.row != list2.row) {
   statements
}

for (let i=0,j=0; i<=bigI; i++,j++) {
   statements
}
```

# Operators

1. Use increment and decrement operators instead of their equivalent longer forms. For example:

   | Do not use | Use this |
   |---|---|
   | x = x + 1 | x++ or ++x (depending on the context) |
   | x = x - 1 | x-- or --x (depending on the context) |

2. Use compound assignment operators instead of their equivalent longer forms. For example:

   | Do not use | Use this |
   |---|---|
   | x = x + 5 | x += 5 |
   | x = x * y | x *= y |

3. Google's JavaScript Style Guide uses == and != in its examples and does not mention === or !==. So normally you should use == and !=. But if you need to compare values without performing a type conversion for different types, you should use === and !== instead of == and !=.

# Naming Conventions

1. Use mnemonic identifiers.
2. For constants, use all uppercase letters. If there are multiple words, use underscores to separate the words. For example:

   ```
   const SECONDS_IN_DAY = 86400;
   const ARRAY_SIZE = 20;
   ```

3. For all identifiers other than constants and class names, use camel case. Camel case means lowercase for all letters, except if there are multiple words in the identifier, then use uppercase for the first letter of all words that follow the first word. For example:

   ```
   var numOfStudents;    // number of students in the class
   var studentId;        // a student's school ID
   var htmlTagName;      // an HTML tag, like body or p
   ```

4. For class names, use *Pascal case*. Pascal case means use uppercase for the first letter of each word and use lowercase for all other letters. For example:

   ```
   class SalesPerson {
       ...
   }
   ```

# Functions

1. Above each function definition, provide a commented description and blank line.

2. Between function definitions, above the commented descriptions, provide a line of *'s surrounded by blank lines, like this:

```
//*********************************************************

// This method prompts the user to enter a move, validates the
// entry, and then assigns that move to the board. It checks
// whether that move is a winning move. It receives board
// (an array for tic-tac-toe) and player (the current player,
// 'X' or 'O').

function handleMove(board, player) {
```

3. Position local variable declarations immediately below the heading for the function.

# Classes

1. Above a class definition, you should provide a comment that describes the class. If the class is defined in an external file, the comment can be part of the file's prologue.
2. Provide a constructor definition as the first member within a class.
3. Below the constructor definition and below every method definition except the last one, provide a line of *'s surrounded by blank lines.
4. Above each method definition, include a commented description and blank line.
5. To further the goal of encapsulation, do not attempt to directly access an object's properties outside of the object's class. If you need to retrieve and update an object's property from outside of the object's class, you should use a method.
6. Optionally, you may want to follow Google's style guide when it comes to naming an object's properties. Google says to name all object properties with a trailing underscore. In the following example, note this.x_ and this.y_:

```
class Point {
  constructor(x, y) {
    this.x_ = x;
    this.y_ = y;
  } // end constructor

//*********************************************************

  // Return the point in the format "(x, y)"

  value() {
    return "(" + this.x_ + ", " + this.y_ + ")";
  } // end value
} // end class Point
```

7. Optionally, you may want to follow Google's style guide when it comes to using JSDoc to document the parts of your OOP code. Google says to use JSDoc tags to annotate your classes, constructors, properties, and methods.

# Sample JavaScript File

Assume that there is an HTML file with the following code in its head container:

```
<script src="compoundInterest.js"></script>
```

That script element refers to a JavaScript file, and here is that file:

```
/*******************************************************
* compoundInterest.js
* John Dean
*
* This file contains a function that supports the
* compound interest web page.
*******************************************************/

// This function generates a compound interest table.

function generateTable(form) {
  var amount;     // accumulated value for each new year
  var rate;       // interest rate
  var years;      // years for principal to grow
  var interest;   // interest earned each year
  var table;      // compound interest table
  var year = 1;   // the year being calculated

  amount = form.elements["deposit"].valueAsNumber;
  rate = form.elements["rate"].valueAsNumber;
  years = form.elements["years"].valueAsNumber;

  table =
    "<table>" +
    "<tr><th>Year</th><th>Starting Value</th>" +
    "<th>Interest Earned</th><th>Ending Value</th></tr>";

  while (year <= years) {
    table += "<tr>";
    table += "<td>" + year + "</td>";
    table += "<td>$" + amount.toFixed(2) + "</td>";
    interest = amount * rate / 100;
    table += "<td>$" + interest.toFixed(2) + "</td>";
    amount += interest;
    table += "<td>$" + amount.toFixed(2) + "</td>";
    table += "</tr>";
    year++;
  } // end while

  table += "</table>";
  document.getElementById("result").innerHTML = table;
} // end generateTable
```

# Review Question Solutions

## Chapter 1

1. A web server is a computer system that enables users to access web pages stored on the web server's computer. The term "web server" can refer to the web-page-accessing software that runs on the computer, or it can refer to the computer itself.

2. Two features of a web authoring tool are intellisense and WYSIWYG.

3. The term used to describe code that is freely available to view and edit is "open source."

4. HTTP stands for hypertext transfer protocol.

5. URL stands for Uniform Resource Locator.

6. `h6` is the HTML element that generates the smallest heading.

7. Syntax refers to the words, grammar, and punctuation that make up a language.

8. The `title` element (a) provides documentation for someone trying to maintain your web page and (b) helps web search engines find your web page.

9. For the `meta` element, the `name` attribute specifies the `meta` element's type, and the `content` attribute specifies the `meta` element's value.

10. The value utf-8 stands for UCS transformation format—8-bit.

   or

   universal character set transformation format—8-bit

   or

   Unicode transformation format—8-bit

11. That CSS rule causes all p elements (paragraphs) to be right-aligned.

12. Tim Berners-Lee designed the HTTP protocol.

13. Tim Berners-Lee founded the W3C.

14. Users disliked XHTML 1.1 because if a web page's code did not fully comply with the standard, the browser would display an error message and not attempt to display the web page's normal content.

15. False

# Chapter 2

1. False

2. Dave Raggett developed the original HTML Tidy tool.

3. A browser engine is the software in the browser that's in charge of reading the HTML code and rendering it on a web page.

4. Documentation is a description of a program.

5. Specify five categories that are completely inside the flow category: interactive, phrasing, embedded, heading, and sectioning

6. A block element spans the width of its container, so for a given row, there will be only one block element.

7. The typical default display properties for a `blockquote` element are block element and margins on all four sides.

8. Whitespace collapsing characters—blank, newline, and tab characters.

9. Presentation refers to the appearance and format of a displayed element.

10. A q element is for quoted text that is rendered within the flow of surrounding text. The `blockquote` element spans the width of its container.

11. False

12. `wbr` stands for "word break."

13. False

# Chapter 3

1. The universal selector uses the asterisk, *. It matches every element in a web page's collection of elements.

2. type selector

3. True

4. They are called class selectors because their purpose is to select elements that have a particular value for a `class` attribute.

5. The symbol used for an ID selector is the #.

6. The word "Cascading" in "Cascading Style Sheets" refers to the list of different places where CSS rules can be defined. To handle the possibility of conflicting rules at different places, the browser will check for CSS rules that match the element, starting the search at the top of the list above and continuing the search down the list, as necessary.

7. A global attribute is an attribute that can be used with any element.

8. `<link rel="stylesheet" href="`*name-of-style-sheet-file*`">`

9. Each integer value must be between 0 and 255, with 0 providing the least intensity and 255 providing the most.

10. With an opacity value of .5, the word gets 50% opacity for both its `color` property and its `background-color` property.

11.  HSL stands for hue, saturation, and lightness.

12.  `font-variant: small-caps;`

13.  Different browsers support different fonts. By having a list of font values, with a generic font value at the end, you enable different browsers to each display an appropriate font.

14.  `text-decoration: underline;`

15.  For the `border-width` property to work (i.e., to make the border visible), you need to use the `border-style` property in conjunction with it.

16.  The `border` shorthand property can be used to specify a border's width, style, and color in that order.

17.  The `border-radius` property allows you to specify how much curvature you want at each of the four corners of an element.

# Chapter 4

1.  `li` element

2.  `list-style-type: none;`

3.  descendant

4.  `lower-roman`

5.  The `start` attribute causes list item labels to start at a specified position.

6.  False. It must be inside the `figure` element, immediately above the `figure` end tag.

7.  `alt`

8.  One or more sections in an `article` container.

9.  links

10. If you apply the background color to the individual heading elements, you'll get a narrow white background in the margin areas between them.

11. CSS inheritance is when a CSS property value flows down from a parent element to one or more of its child elements.

12. If a parent element and its child element have two different CSS rules with the same property specified, then the child element's property-value pair (and <u>not</u> the parent element's property-value pair) gets applied to the child element. Formally, we say that the child element's property-value pair overrides the inherited property-value pair.

# Chapter 5

1. (a) `<tr>`    (b) `<td>`    (c) `<th>`

2. CSS rule that gives tables a single-line border and single-line row and column separation:

```
table, th, td {
  border: thin solid;
  border-collapse: collapse;
}
```

3. CSS rule that pads the text in table header and data cells:

```
th, td {padding: 5px;}
```

4. CSS pseudo-class selector that selects every other row starting with the third:

```
tr:nth-of-type(2n+3)
```

5. The `thead` and `tbody` elements help distinguish the labels over table columns (`thead`) from data in table columns (`tbody`).

6. The `body {display: flex; justify-content: center;}` rule tells the browser to center all the elements in the `body` container horizontally within the browser window's borders.

7. Here is the display generated by the code with `rowspan` and `colspan` attributes:

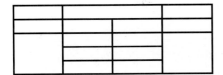

8.  A screen reader is software that figures out what the user's screen is displaying and sends a text description of it to a speech synthesizer. The speech synthesizer then reads the text aloud.

9.  HTML elements and corresponding CSS property-value pairs:
    a) `table`          `display: table`
    b) `caption`        `display: table-caption`
    c) `tr`             `display: table-row`
    d) `td`             `display: table-cell`

10. The `div` element is good for implementing table and row components because, except for automatically generating a new line at the end, it's generic. That means it doesn't add any formatting features of its own.

11. To apply `display: table-cell` to an embedded-content element like `img`, `audio`, or `video`, put that element inside a `span` element and apply `display: table-cell` to the `span` element.

12. To apply absolute positioning to an element, add a CSS rule for the element with `position: absolute;` in the rule.

13. With absolute positioning, the `top` and `left` properties indicate the position of the target element's top-left corner relative to the element's containing block. Typically, an element's containing block resolves to the web page's `body` element. However, you can use the `position: relative` property-value pair to designate an element as a containing block for absolute positioned elements inside of it.

14. The CSS properties that establish offsets from container sides to corresponding component sides are `top`, `right`, `bottom`, and `left`.

15. With relative positioning, the `top` and `left` properties indicate the position of the target element's top-left corner relative to the element's normal flow within its surrounding content.

16. True

# Chapter 6

1.  `href`

2.  A home page is the default first page a user sees when the user visits a website.

3. ".." tells the browser to go from a directory to the directory's parent directory.

4. User interface design (UID) refers to the mechanisms by which end users can use a website. For web pages, the mechanisms are things like text, color, pictures, buttons, text boxes, and progress bars. User experience design is the feeling produced by those UID elements.

5. For nontrivial websites, the most popular navigation organizational structure is the mixed structure.

6. A placeholder link has no `href` attribute and it links to nowhere. The idea is that it will be replaced later on with an active link.

7. If you have `table-cell` elements that are not surrounded by a `table-row` element, the browser engine generates an anonymous (hidden) `table-row` element around those `table-cell` elements.

8. Blue for an unvisited link. Purple for a visited link.

9. `a:hover`

10. `target="_blank"`

11. True

12. With bitmap image files, an image is comprised of a group of pixels. Within a bitmap image file, every pixel gets mapped to a particular color value, and each color value is a sequence of bits. For a browser to display a bitmap image, it simply displays each pixel's mapped color. This reliance on mapping color bit values to pixels is the basis for the name "bitmap image."

13. A color palette is the entire set of colors used in a particular image file.

14. JPG

15. MNG

16. End users who are visually impaired will often use screen readers, and screen readers attempt to render `img` elements by reading aloud the `alt` attribute's value.

17. Including the `img` element's `width` and `height` attributes improves download speed.

18. The browser engine uses the image's formulas to redraw the image while accommodating the grid's new rectangular grid of pixels.

19. SVG files tend to be smaller, and that leads to faster web page downloads.

20. For SVG images, an advantage of using an `svg` element as opposed to an `img` element is that with an `svg` element, the SVG code is embedded within the HTML code, and that means you can use JavaScript to dynamically manipulate any of the elements in the SVG code.

21. Responsive web design is the practice of writing code that dynamically generates web pages that conform to different screen sizes and viewing orientations (portrait or landscape).

# Chapter 7

1. False

2. True

3. You should use a shortcut icon with small square dimensions to prevent the browser from having to resize the icon, which can lead to degradation.

4. A browsing context is an area within a web page that can display an embedded web document, where a web document is something with a URL; that is, a web page or a stored image.

5. A thumbnail is a small image that serves as a representative for a larger version of that same image.

6. A rollover is when an image file changes because the user moves the mouse over the image.

7. The `background-position` property specifies the $x$ and $y$ coordinates for where the image file content's top-left corner gets positioned in relation to the background image's element.

8. With HTML5, no audio plug-in is necessary. Browsers that support HTML5 have built-in audio players.

9. If an `audio` element includes `preload="auto"`, the browser takes that as a suggestion to download the audio file when the page loads initially.

10. False

11. The browser fills the entire viewport by displaying multiple copies of the image using a tiled layout.

12. `@font-face`

13. The two recommended file formats for web fonts are WOFF and WOFF 2.0.

14. In defining a web font, it's good to use multiple versions of the web font file, with a different format for each file, because different browsers support different file formats.

15. The `poster` attribute specifies an image file that serves as a placeholder for display while the video is not playing.

16. For a `video` element, the purpose of specifying `preload="none"` is:
    To avoid using too much bandwidth.
    or
    When you're unsure as to whether your users will want to view the video.

17. To center a flexbox element's content vertically, use the `align-items: center` property-value pair.

18. The default direction for positioning a linear gradient's colors is top to bottom.

# Chapter 8

1. LiveScript

2. The standard for the interactive programming languages embedded in all of today's popular browsers

3. The button's label

4. An event handler is code that specifies what's supposed to happen when an event occurs, such as a mouse click.

5. A word that is part of the JavaScript language. Examples: `function`, `var`

6. A property is an attribute of an object.

7. True

8. element, text, attribute

9. `document`

10. The `size` attribute specifies the text control's width, whereas the `maxlength` attribute specifies the maximum number of characters that can be entered in the box.

11. An attribute that is by itself. It has no = and no value.

12. The `this` keyword refers to the object that contains the JavaScript in which `this` appears.

13. The string concatenation operator, +

14. Use `/* ... */` for long comments that span more than one line.

15. A local variable's scope is the function body for the function in which the variable is declared.

16. `onmouseover, onmouseout`

17. JavaScript is unable to access a user's computer in terms of the computer's files and what's in the computer's memory. JavaScript can send requests to web servers only in a constrained (and safe) manner.

18. For web pages that use JavaScript, it's good practice to use the `noscript` element to display a warning message on browsers that have JavaScript disabled.

# Chapter 9

1. The `location` property retrieves an object that stores information about the current web page's URL

2. The `window` object's `navigator` property retrieves an object that stores information about the current browser.

3. The more common way to get information from a user is with a control on a browser window.

4. True

5. A block statement is zero or more statements surrounded by braces.

6. Significant differences between the `confirm` method and the `prompt` method:
   The `confirm` method asks a yes/no question, whereas the `prompt` method asks the user to enter something.
   The `confirm` method returns a Boolean value, whereas the `prompt` method returns a string.
   The `prompt` method has a second parameter, which holds the prompt message.

7. The empty string is two quotes with nothing in between (`""`), which indicates that the string has no characters.

8. If a user sees a `prompt` dialog and clicks **Cancel** or clicks the close-out **X** button, the `prompt` method returns a `null` value.

9. To display a double quote within an `alert` dialog message, use the escape sequence `\"`.

10. `\n` is an escape sequence for the newline character.

11. For string objects, `length` is a property.

12. The `Math.ceil` method returns the smallest whole number that is greater than or equal to the given number.

13. The `Math.floor` method returns the largest whole number that is less than or equal to the given number.

14. The `:first-child` pseudo-class matches elements that are the first child of another element.

15. For a number control, the `required` attribute indicates that the user must enter a value.

16. For a number control, the `min` and `max` attributes determine the range for the number control's spinner.

17. The `input:valid:focus` selector matches the currently selected input element if it has valid input.

18. These operators have right-to-left associativity:

    not operator (!)

    exponentiation operator (**)

    assignment operators (+=, -=, ...)

19. Expression evaluations:

    a) `x + num / 2 % 2 ⇒`
       `3.0 + 9 / 2 % 2 ⇒`
       `3.0 + 4.5 % 2 ⇒`
       `3.0 + .5 ⇒`
       `3.5`

    b) `x >= 4 || y < 7 && num != 3 ** 2 ⇒`
       `3.0 >= 4 || 6.2 < 7 && 9 != 3 ** 2 ⇒`
       `3.0 >= 4 || 6.2 < 7 && 9 != 9 ⇒`
       `false || true && false ⇒`
       `false || false ⇒`
       `false`

20. If you use a form object to call the `checkValidity` method, it returns true if all of the form's controls hold valid input and false otherwise.

# Chapter 10

1. Infinite loop

2. Normally, redundant code is bad because if you need to fix or enhance the code, you have to do it in more than one place, and that takes more time, and you might forget.

3. The file extension for an external JavaScript file is `.js`.

4. A prologue's asterisk box should contain the filename, the programmer's name, a blank line, and a description of what the file's code is for.

5. To load Chrome's debugger, press ctrl+shift+j.

6. Use a do loop when you're sure that the loop body should be executed at least one time.

7. A Boolean variable can hold true or false.

8. To access the first radio button in a radio button collection named `years`, use `years[0]`.

9. If you have a radio button group with none of the radio buttons selected, the radio button collection's `value` property returns the empty string.

10. A radio button object's `defaultChecked` property returns true or false, for whether the radio button was preselected.

11. If you'd like to form a collection of checkboxes, include a `name` attribute with the same value.

12. Here's what's legal:
    `class` attribute value: spaces are not allowed
    `id` attribute value: spaces are not allowed
    `name` attribute value: spaces are allowed
    `value` attribute value: spaces are allowed

13. The three components in a standard `for` loop's heading are the initialization, condition, and update components.

14. You should use a standard `for` loop if you know the exact number of loop iterations before the loop begins.

15. The JavaScript property associated with the HTML class attribute is `className`.

16. The JavaScript property associated with the HTML style attribute is `style`.

17. With `visibility: hidden`, the browser provides layout space for the element, whereas with `display: none`, no space is provided.

18. The element with a `z-index` value of 0 displays in front of the other element.

19. Persistence refers to how long a variable's value survives before it's wiped out.

20. If the function is called a second time, a global variable's previous value will be remembered.

21. Here's how you can clear a `recommendation` text area's box:

    ```
    recommendation.value = "";
    ```

22. The Chesnut Hall bass player lives in the dorm's basement.

23. If a list box object's `selectedIndex` property is -1, that means no options are selected.

# Chapter 11

1. OOP encapsulation means that an object's data are protected by being "hidden" inside the object. Methods form the interface between an object's hidden data and the outside world.

2. A JavaScript object's members are properties and methods.

3. A class is a description or blueprint for an object's characteristics.

4. A constructor is a special method that gets called when there's an attempt to create an object. It defines what happens when an object is instantiated.

5. To instantiate an object, use the `new` operator.

6. A class property is associated with a class as a whole, not with an individual instance of the class.

7. To call a `static` method, you preface the method name with the class name and a dot.

8. True

9. A `null` value indicates the absence of a valid value.

10. In an event handler, to access the event object, you need to use the word `event` in your JavaScript code.

11. When the JavaScript engine fires an event for a DOM object, that DOM object is the first object to be given an opportunity to process the event. The JavaScript engine then passes (bubbles) the event up the DOM node tree, stopping at each node for possible processing.

12. Primitive values: number, string, Boolean (true or false), `null`, undefined

13. True

14. In the interest of readability, it's good to keep your JavaScript separate from your HTML code.

15. Without prototypes, every object would have its own copies of its methods. That would be a waste of memory for objects within the same class because the method copies would be identical.

16. A child class inherits properties and methods from its parent class.

17. For a subclass method to call a method in its superclass, you preface the call with `super` dot.

18. If a web page is scalable, that means its content can be expanded without too much effort.

19. A key difference between the `switch` statement and the "if, else if" statement is that the `switch` statement's determination of which path to take is based on a single value.

20. If there's no `break` at the bottom of a `case` block, control flows through subsequent `case` constants and executes all subordinate statements until a `break` statement is reached or the end of the `switch` statement is reached.

21. False

22. Yes

23. A function expression is a nameless function definition embedded within another statement.

24. False. To sort date strings, first you have to convert the strings to `Date` objects, and then the < operator can compare date values properly.

# Chapter 12

1. Applets and Flash are not built in. Canvas is built in.

2. Method call chaining is when you concatenate two method calls with a dot.

3. Color gradients are global, and they apply to all the shapes drawn with the context object.

4. To display characters in a normal fashion, use `fillText`, not `strokeText`.

5. `font` property

6. `font-size` and `font-family`

7. `textAlign`

8. If you call the `arc` method with starting and ending angle values of 0 and 3π, that creates a full circle.

9. If you call the `arc` method with starting and ending angle values of 0 and 0, that creates no arc at all.

10. When you call the `fill` method for an arc that is not closed, the browser forms an invisible straight line between the arc's end points, and then it fills the newly enclosed area.

11. The `moveTo` method moves the drawing pen.

12. A subpath is established automatically every time you call `beginPath` or `moveTo`.

13. `closePath`

14. True

15. True

16. Using named constants can lead to code that's easier to understand. Using named constants makes your web page drawings scalable.

17. When you call the `translate` function, the coordinate system's origin moves.

18. Before calling `clearRect`, you should:
    First call the `save` function to save the context object's current drawing state.
    Then call the `setTransform` function to move the coordinate system so its origin and rotation match the canvas drawing area.

19. Very often, you'll want to call `translate` before calling `rotate` so you can rotate around something different from the coordinate system's origin.

20. Benefits of using helper functions:
    They enable you to split up a big module into smaller modules, so the code is easier to understand. They enable you to execute the helper functions' tasks from different places in your program while avoiding redundant code.

# INDEX